LE MORTE D'ARTHUR

SIR THOMAS MALORY'S BOOK OF KING
ARTHUR AND OF HIS NOBLE KNIGHTS
OF THE ROUND TABLE

SENATE

Le Morte D'Arthur

First published in 1889 by Macmillan & Co, London

This edition published in 1998 by Senate,
an imprint of Tiger Books International plc,
26A York Street, Twickenham,
Middlesex TW1 3LJ, United Kingdom.

Cover design © Tiger Books International 1998

1 3 5 7 9 10 8 6 4 2

ISBN 1 85958 532 9

Printed and bound in the UK by
Cox & Wyman, Reading, England

CONTENTS.

INTRODUCTION.

INTRODUCTION.

§ 1. THE ORIGIN AND MATTER OF THE BOOK.

WE owe this our English Epic of Morte Arthur to Sir Thomas Malory, and to William Caxton the first English printer. Caxton's Preface shows (what indeed would have been certain from his appeal to the 'Knights of England' at the end of 'The Order of Chivalry') that however strongly he, 'William Caxton, simple person,' may have been urged to undertake the work by 'divers gentlemen of this realm of England,' he was not less moved by his own love and reverence for 'the noble acts of chivalry,' and his deep sense of his duty and responsibility in printing what he believed would be for the instruction and profit of his readers, 'of whatever estate or degree.' But to Sir Thomas Malory he gives all the honour of having provided him with the copy which he printed. I retain the more usual spelling of Sir Thomas Malory's name, though it is also written Malorye and Maleore. The last indeed is the form in the words with which he himself concludes his work; but as Caxton printed, and therefore knew, this no less than the other forms, and as even so late as the time of Marvell and Pym men of education did not keep to one way of writing their own names, we cannot infer that one is more correct than the others, though probably we may that Malory most nearly represents the pronunciation to us. Malory was an old Yorkshire name in Leland's time[1], and is mentioned in the next century in Burton's 'Description of Leicestershire[2];' but we have nothing but the name to connect Sir Thomas Malory with these families. Leland indeed, according to the 'Biographia Britannica,' says he was a Welchman[3]. From his own words we learn that he was a knight, and from his adding that he was 'a servant of Jesu both day and night,' as well as from the general tone of the book, it has been inferred that he was a priest. And he tells us that he ended his book in the ninth year of Edward the Fourth, or about fifteen years before Caxton

[1] 'There be 2 Lordshipps lyenge not very far from *Ripon* . . . . *Malory* hath *Hutton Coniers.* Thes Lands cam to their Aunciters by two Dowghtars, Heirs Generall of that *Coniers. Malory* hath another Place caullyd *Highe Studly,* a litle from *Fontaines.*' Leland's Itinerary, viii. 2. p. 55. Hearne, 1712.

[2] 'In Kirby-Malory those [arms and pedigree] of the Malorys.' 'In Swinford arms and pedigrees of the Malorys.' Burton's Description of Leicestershire, 1622, Fol. Quoted by Oldys, The British Librarian, pp. 293, 297.

[3] Biographia Britannica, art. 'Caxton;' but no reference is given by which to verify the quotation.

finished printing it. It has been usual to assume that, because Caxton says that Sir Thomas Malory took his work 'out of certain books of French and reduced it into English,' he was a mere compiler and translator. But the book itself shows that he was its author—its 'maker,' as he would have called it. Notwithstanding his occasionally inartificial manner of connecting the materials drawn from the old romances—'in Welch many, and also in French, and some in English'—there is an epic unity and harmony, and a beginning, middle, and end, which, if they have come by chance and not of design, have come by that chance which only befalls an Homeric or a Shakspeare-like man. If we compare the first part of Malory's work with the old prose romance[1] which supplied the materials for it, we see at once how he has converted that prose into poetry, giving life and beauty to the coarse clods of earth, and transmuting by his art the legends which he yet faithfully preserves. For the long and repulsive narrative of Merlin's origin he substitutes a slight allusion to it; without disguising what he probably believed to be at least an half historical record of Arthur's birth, he gives a grace and dignity to the story by the charms of his mother's character, the finer touches of which are wanting in the original: and so through the whole of this part of the story. The plan of the book is properly epic. While the glory of Arthur as the head of the kingdoms no less than of the chivalry of Christendom is only in its early dawn, Merlin warns him that the seeds of death will spring up in all this fair promise through the sin of himself and of his queen. Still the fame and the honour of the king and his knights of the Round Table continually into new and brighter forms, which seem above the reach of any adverse fate, till the coming of the Sancgreal, into the quest of which all the knights enter with that self-reliance which had become them so well in the field of worldly chivalry, but which would be of no avail now. They are now to be tried by other tests than those by which they had been proved as 'earthly knights and lovers,' tests which even Launcelot, Ector de Maris, Gawaine, and the other chiefest of the fellowship could not stand. The quest is achieved by the holy knights alone : two depart from this life to a higher, while Sir Bors, not quite spotless, yet forgiven and sanctified, the link between the earthly and the spiritual worlds, returns to aid in restoring the glory of the feasts and tournaments at Camelot and Westminster. But the curse is at work: the severance between good and evil which had been declared through the Sancgreal cannot be closed again ; and the tragic end comes on, in spite of the efforts—touching from their very weakness—of Arthur and Launcelot to avert the woe, the one by vainly trying to resist temptation, the other by refusing to believe evil of his dearest friend. The black clouds open for a moment as the sun goes down ; and we see Arthur in the barge which bears him to the Holy

[1] Merlin, or the Early History of King Arthur, edited by Henry B. Wheatley, for the Early English Text Society, 1865-8. This is a translation, contemporary with Malory's work, from the French which he doubtless used.

Isle; Guenever, the nun of Almesbury, living in fasting, prayers, and alms-deeds; and Launcelot with his fellowship, once knights but now hermit-priests, 'doing bodily all manner of service.'

Nor are the marks of harmony and unity less plain in the several characters than in the events of the story. Arthur is a true knight, sharing the characteristics of his nobler knights, yet he differs from them all in showing also that he is, and feels himself to be, a king; as when—with an imperiousness which reminds us of Froissart's story of Edward III refusing to listen to Sir Walter Manny's remonstrances on behalf of the burgesses of Calais—he tells Sir Launcelot that he 'takes no force whom he grieves,' or insists on his entering the lists against a tired knight whom he is not willing to see victorious over the whole field; or as when he sadly regrets that he cannot do battle for his wife, though he believes her innocent, but must be a rightful judge according to the laws. There are many others of the Round Table who are 'very perfect gentle knights,' yet we feel that Launcelot stands distinct among them all in the pre-eminence of his knightliness, notwithstanding his one great sin. Thus, to take one of many instances, who but Launcelot would have borne the taunts and the violence of Gawaine with his humble patience and ever-renewed efforts for a reconciliation, when he was leaving the realm, and when he was besieged in Joyous Gard. Modern critics of great name agree in censuring Sir Thomas Malory for departing from the old authorities who represented Gawaine as the very counterpart of Launcelot in knightly character: but I rather see a proof of Malory's art in giving us a new Gawaine with a strongly individual character of his own. Gawaine's regard for his mother's honour, his passion for Ettard, and his affection for his brothers, are savage impulses driving him to unknightly and unworthy deeds, yet he is far from being represented as a mere villain. If Malory depicts him thirsting to revenge upon Launcelot the unintentional killing of Gaheris and Gareth, he depicts also his long previous affection for Launcelot and his opposition to the hostility of his other brother, Mordred, against him; his devotion to his uncle Arthur; his hearty repentance towards Launcelot at the last; and his entreaty that he would 'see his tomb, and pray some prayer more or less for his soul.' Nor must we forget that it was by the prayer of those ladies for whom Gawaine had 'done battle in a rightwise quarrel,' that his ghost was permitted to give Arthur a last warning. Distinct again from the character of this fierce knight is that of the Saracen Palamides, whose unquestionable courage and skill in deeds of chivalry also want—though in another way than Gawaine's—the gentleness, the meekness, and the delicate sense of honour of the Christian knight. Sir Dinadan again, who can give and take hard knocks if need be, though he has no great bodily strength, and who is always bantering the good knights who know and esteem him with his humorous protests against love and arms, is a distinctly drawn character. So is Merlin; so are many others whose names I might recite. The dignity of queen Guenever towards her husband and her court is not less marked than her guilty passion

for Launcelot, and the unreasoning jealousy it excites in her. The wife-like simplicity of Igraine, the self-surrender beyond all limit, though from different
impulses, of the two Elaines, the pertness of the damsel Linet, and the piety
and self-sacrifice of Sir Percivale's sister, will occur to the reader among the
distinctive characteristics of the different ladies and damsels who live and move,
each in her own proper form, in the story. Sir Thomas Malory, as we know, found
many of these men and women already existing in the old romances as he represents them to us; but we may believe that those earlier books were to him
something of what the pages of Plutarch and Holinshed were to Shakspeare.

In the Introduction to Southey's edition of Morte Arthur the student will find
an account of the principal early prose romances in which sources of Sir Thomas
Malory's book have been found, and the English translation of one of these has
been mentioned above; while the volumes of Ellis, Sir Walter Scott's ' Sir Tristrem,'
and the publications of the Early English Text and the Camden Societies, and of
Mr. Furnivall, supply specimens of the metrical romances of the like kind. But as
they are only attractive to the antiquarian student, who requires the originals and
not abstracts, I shall say no more of them here.

Nor shall I attempt to illustrate Malory's book by the ancient historical or
legendary accounts of the British King Arthur. The most recent critics are disposed to prefer Gibbon's belief to Milton's scepticism as to the actual existence
of Arthur : but of the history and the geography of the book before us we can only
say that they are something

> ' Apart from place, withholding time,
> But flattering the golden prime '

of the great hero of English romance. We cannot bring within any limits of
history the events which here succeed each other, when the Lords and Commons
of England, after the death of King Uther at St. Alban's, assembled at the
greatest church of London, guided by the joint policy of the magician Merlin and
the Christian bishop of Canterbury, and elected Arthur to the throne; when
Arthur made Carlion, or Camelot, or both, his head-quarters in a war against
Cornwall, Wales, and the North, in which he was victorious by help of the
king of France ; when he met the demand for tribute by the Roman emperor
Lucius with a counter-claim to the empire for himself as the real representative of
Constantine, held a parliament at York to make the necessary arrangements,
crossed the sea from Sandwich to Barflete in Flanders, met the united forces of
the Romans and Saracens in Burgundy, slew the emperor in a great battle,
together with his allies, the sowdan of Syria, the king of Egypt, and the king of
Ethiopia, sent their bodies to the Senate and Podestà of Rome as the only tribute
he would pay, and then followed over the mountains through Lombardy and
Tuscany to Rome, where he was crowned emperor by the Pope, ' sojourned there
a time, established all his lands from Rome unto France, and gave lands and realms
unto his servants and knights,' and so returned home to England, where he

seems thenceforth to have devoted himself wholly to his duties as the head of Christian knighthood.

There is indeed one point of the legendary history on which the reader may wish me to give some explanation :—What was the Sancgreal ? Graal or greal (derived from *crater*) in the Romance language[1] signifies a drinking-vessel, a dish, or a tureen: and according to the romances of Le S. Graal, Lancelot du Lac, Perceforest, and Morte Arthur, the Sancgreal, or Holy Graal, was the dish which held the paschal lamb of the Last Supper. Joseph of Arimathéa having gone into the house where the Supper had been eaten, took away the dish, and in it received the blood from the wounds of Jesus ; and this dish, 'with part of the blood of our Lord,' he brought with him into England, and with it converted many heathens ; and it was kept in a tower expressly built for it at Corbenicy.   The romance of Merlin says that 'this vessel was brought to this said knight [Joseph of Arimathea] by our Lord Jesu Christ while he was in prison xl. winter, him to comfort,' but does not mention its earlier history.   And notwithstanding the authority of Perceforest that the Sancgreal was preserved in England, it may still be seen in the cathedral of Genoa, there called Sacro Catino, with the same tradition as to its original uses as is given above. It was brought from Cæsarea in 1101, and is an hexagonal dish, of two palms width, long supposed to be of real emerald, which it resembles in colour and brilliancy.

The geography of Arthur's Roman war is very coherent ; but that of the rest of the book it is often impossible to harmonise. The scene opens within a night's ride of the castle of Tintagil, the ruins of which may still be seen in Cornwall. Thence we pass to St. Alban's, to London, and to Carlion. This last is, no doubt, Caerleon-upon-Usk ; but it seems through this, as in other romances, to be inter-changeable in the author's mind with Carlisle, or (as written in its Anglo-Norman form) Cardoile, which latter in the History of Merlin is said to be in Wales, while elsewhere Wales and Cumberland are confounded in like manner. So of Camelot, where Arthur chiefly held his court, Caxton in his Preface speaks as though it were in Wales, probably meaning Caerleon, where the Roman amphitheatre is still called Arthur's Round Table.   Malory himself, though at page 49 he seems to connect Camelot with Avelion, or Glastonbury, yet farther on, page 63, says that Camelot is Winchester, where, too, there is a Round Table, mentioned by Caxton, and still to be seen,—an oaken board with the knights' names on it. And yet at the time these authorities wrote Camelot itself existed in Somersetshire with its proper name, and with all the remains of an important town and fortress, and, doubtless, the traditions of Arthur which Leland found there, and which in great part at least remain to this day.   Leland calls it Camallate or Camalat, 'sometime a famous town or castle, upon a very torre or hill, wonderfully

---

[1] Roquefort, Glossaire de Langue Romane, art. 'Graal :' where are also given the original passages from the first three romances named in the text.

enstrengthened of nature[1].'   Four ditches and as many walls surrounded a central
space of about thirty acres where foundations and remains of walls might be seen,
and whence Roman pavements, urns, coins, and other relics have been found up
to the present time. I find it called the Castle of Camellek in maps of the dates
of 1575 and 1610, and in that of the 1727 edition of Camden's Magna Britannica,
the text of which says 'the inhabitants call it King Arthur's Palace.' But soon
after that date a learned antiquarian[2] writes that the name had been superseded by
that of Cadbury Castle, which trilingual appellation may seem to indicate
the Roman, British, and Saxon possessors by whom it was probably held in suc-
cession. The neighbouring villages which, according to Leland, bore 'the name
of Camalat with an addition, as Queen-Camel,' still exist as Queen-Camel, or East
Camel, and West Camel, and near by runs the river Camel, crossed by Arthur's
Bridge. Arthur's Well still springs from the hill-side, and if Arthur's Hunting
Causeway in the field below, Arthur's Round Table and Arthur's Palace within
the camp, cannot still, as of old, be pointed out to the visitor, the peasant girl
will still tell him that within that charmed circle they who look may see through
golden gates a king sitting in the midst of his court. Drayton describes the river
Ivel in Somersetshire as

> 'The nearest neighbouring flood to Arthur's ancient seat,
> Which made the Britaines name thro' all the world so great.
> Like Camelot what place was ever yet renown'd?
> Where, as at Caerleon, oft he kept the Table Round,
> Most famous for the sports at Pentecost so long,
> From whence all knightly deeds and brave atchievements sprong[3].'

Glastonbury—founded by Joseph of Arimathea, and his burial-place, though his
body was vainly sought in Edward III's reign—still claims to possess the coffin of
Arthur. It is said that Henry II found the bodies of Arthur and Guenever there,
and that Guenever had yellow hair. Their skulls were afterwards taken for relics
by Edward Longshanks and Eleanor.

Almesbury, where Guenever died a nun, is a town in Wiltshire, seven and a half
miles from Salisbury, where may still be seen the ruins of its celebrated abbey.
The name was originally Ambrosebury, then Ambresbury, and lastly Amesbury, as
it is now spelt.

Joyous Gard, Launcelot's favourite castle, is sometimes identified with Berwick.
Malory tells us that 'some men say it was Anwick, and some men say it was Bamborow.' Bamborow, or Bamborough, is in Northumberland, sixteen miles south-
east of Berwick. The castle, founded in the middle of the sixth century, which is
the supposed time of Arthur's reign, stands on a high rock projecting into the
North Sea. It now contains a granary, hospital, and other endowments made
for the poor in 1715 by Lord Crewe, bishop of Durham. Did he think of his

---

[1] Itinerary, ii. pp. 38, 39 ; Hearne, 1711.
[2] Somersetshire Illustrated, by John Strachey, MS. 1736.   [3] Polyolbion, 3rd Song.

predecessor Launcelot, and his doles of ' flesh, fish, wine and ale, and twelve pence to any man and woman, come who would ? '

The names of some other places in this book are given in the Glossary.

Lastly, the perplexed question of the morality of the book demands our notice. If it does not deserve the unqualified denunciation of the learned Ascham, it cannot be denied that Morte Arthur exhibits a picture of a society far lower than our own in morals, and depicts it with far less repugnance to its evil elements, on the part either of the author or his personages, than any good man would now feel. Still—with the exception of stories like those of the birth of Arthur and Galahad, which show not only another state of manners from our own, but also a really different standard of morals from any which we should now hold up—the writer does for the most part endeavour, though often in but an imperfect and confused manner, to distinguish between vice and virtue, and honestly to reprobate the former; and thus shows that his object is to recognise and support the nobler elements of the social state in which he lived, and to carry them towards new triumphs over the evil. And even where, as in the story of Tristram, there is palliation rather than reprobation of what Sir Walter Scott justly calls ' the extreme ingratitude and profligacy of the hero,' still the fact that such palliation, by representing King Mark as the most worthless of men, was thought necessary in the later, though not in the earlier, romance on the same subject, shows an upward progress in morals; while a real effort to distinguish virtue from vice is to be seen in the story of Launcelot, with his sincere though weak struggles against temptation, and his final penitence under the punishment of the woes which his guilt has brought on all dear to him as well as to himself. Or if we look at the picture which Chaucer's works give us of the co-existence in one mind—and that perhaps the noblest of its age—of the most virtuous Christian refinement and the most brutish animal coarseness, and then see how in the pages of Malory, inferior as we must hold him to be to Chaucer, the brutish vice has dwindled to half its former size, and is far more clearly seen to be vice, while the virtue, if not more elevated in itself, is more avowedly triumphant over the evil, we find the same upward progress. And I cannot doubt that it was helped on by this book, and that notwithstanding Ascham's condemnation of Morte Arthur, Caxton was right in believing that he was serving God and his countrymen by printing it; and that he justly estimated its probable effect when he says, ' Herein may be seen noble chivalry, courtesy, humanity, friendliness, hardiness, love, friendship, cowardice, murder, hate, virtue, sin. Do after the good, and leave the evil, and it shall bring you to good fame and renommée. . . . All is written for our doctrine, and for to beware that we fall not to vice nor sin, but to exercise and follow virtue, by which we may come and attain to good fame and renomme in this life, and after this short and transitory life to come unto everlasting bliss in heaven; the which He grant us that reigneth in heaven, the blessed Trinity. Amen.'

§ 2. THE TEXT, AND ITS SEVERAL EDITIONS.

THE first edition of Le Morte Darthur was printed by Caxton at West-minster in 1485, as he tells us in the colophon. Two copies only are known: they are folio, black-letter, with wide margin, and among the finest speci-mens of Caxton's printing. One is in the library of the Earl of Jersey at Osterley; and the other in that of Earl Spencer at Althorp. The Osterley copy, which has the autograph 'Oxford' on the first leaf, was sold with the Harleian Library to Osborne the bookseller, and apparently bought of him for £5 5s. by Bryan Fairfax, who sold his library to Mr. Child, maternal ancestor of the Earl of Jersey[1]. It is perfect, except that it has no title-page, though, as the Proheme or Preface begins at the top of the recto of signature ij (not 'a ij' as Dibdin says), I infer that a title did exist on the leaf j, thus shown to be wanting. The Althorp copy, which was bought at Mr. Lloyd's sale in 1816 for £320, had eleven leaves deficient; but these were supplied by Mr. Whittaker in fac-simile from the Osterley copy with remark-able skill[2], though on collation with the original I have found some oversights.

The two next editions of Morte Arthur were printed by Wynkyn de Worde, the chief workman and successor of Caxton, in 1498 and 1529. Only one copy of each is known. That of 1498 is in the Althorp Library: it wants the Title and part of the Table of Contents, but contains the Preface, which is a reprint of that of Caxton, though it here follows instead of preceding the Table of Contents. This edition, which has numerous woodcuts, is not an exact reprint of Caxton's; there are differences of spelling and occasionally of a word; and the passage in the last chapter but one, beginning 'Oh ye mighty and pompous lords,' and ending with 'turn again to my matter,' which is not in Caxton's edition, appears here, as in all later editions[3]. The edition of 1529 is in the British Museum, and wants the Title, Preface, and part of the Table of Contents.

In 1557 the book was reprinted by William Copland, with the title of 'The story of the most noble and worthy kynge Arthur, the whiche was one of the worthyes chrysten, and also of his noble and valiaūte knyghtes of the rounde

---

[1] Dibdin's Typographical Antiquities, 1810, vol. i. pp. 242, 254.

[2] Dibdin's Supplement to the Biblio-theca Spenceriana, vol. ii. p. 213; or Ædes Althorpianæ, vol. vi. p. 213. I would here express my thanks to Earl Spencer for send-ing to the British Museum for my use his Caxton, and his unique copy of Wynkyn de Worde's first edition of Morte Arthur, as also for favouring me with details of information respecting the former; and to the Earl of Jersey for permitting me to examine his Caxton at Osterley.

[3] As the passage is worth preserving I have given it at the end of the volume, Note A, p. 488.

Table. Newly imprynted and corrected mcccclvij. ¶ Imprynted at London by
Wyllyam Copland.' And on the title-page, above the last line, is a woodcut of
St. George and the Dragon, of which that on the title-page of Southey's edition is
a bad copy. A copy of this edition is in the British Museum, with a note that this
is the only one with a title which the annotator has seen.

There is a folio edition by Thomas East, without date, in the British Museum;
and there is said to be a quarto edition, also without date.

The next, and last black-letter, edition is that of 1634, which has been reprinted
by Mr. Wright, and which contains the woodcut of the Round Table with Arthur
in the middle and his knights around, a copy of which is familiar to many of us in
one of the small editions of 1816. From the fact of an omission in this edition
which exactly corresponds with a complete leaf in East's folio, Mr. Wright concludes that the one was printed from the other. Each succeeding edition departs
more than the previous one from the original of Caxton; but if we compare
this of 1634 with Caxton's, we find the variations almost infinite. Besides re-
modelling the preface, dividing the book into three parts, and modernising the
spelling and many of the words, there are a number of more or less considerable
variations and additions, of which Mr. Wright has given some of the more important in his notes, but which I estimate at above twenty thousand in the
whole; and which have plainly arisen in the minor instances from the printer reading a sentence and then printing it from recollection, without farther reference to
his ' copy,' but in the others from a desire to improve the original simplicity by
what the editor calls ' a more eloquent and ornated style and phrase.'

No new edition seems to have been published till 1816, when two independent
editions appeared, one in two, and the other in three 24mo. volumes. Both are
modernised for popular use, and are probably the volumes through which most of
us made our first acquaintance with King Arthur and his knights; but neither
has any merit as to its editing.

In 1817 Messrs. Longmans & Co. published an edition in two volumes quarto,
with an introduction and notes by Southey, who says, ' The present edition is a
reprint with scrupulous exactness from the first edition by Caxton, in Earl
Spencer's library[1].' As it appears from a note[2] that he had nothing to do with
the superintendence of the press, which was undertaken by Mr. Upcott, he was
probably unaware that eleven leaves were, as I have mentioned above, then
wanting in the copy from which this reprint was made. These had not then
been restored in fac-simile; for Earl Spencer's copy contains a note, signed by
Messrs. Longmans and dated 1816, which gives a list of the pages then wanting;
and, in fact, the substitutes for them which actually appear in Southey's edition
differ widely from the restored, or the original, text. Thus in chapter xii. of the
last book, besides the interpolation of the long passage ' O ye myghty and

---

[1] Vol. i. p. xxviii.   [2] Ibid. p. lviii.

pompous lordes,' &c., which is not in Caxton, there are in the first eleven lines thirty-five variations of spelling and punctuation, besides the introduction of the words ' but continually mourned un—' and ' needfully as nature required,' which are not in Caxton, and the change of Caxton's ' on the tombe of kyng Arthur & quene Guenever' into ' on kynge Arthur's & quene Gwenever's tombe.' And thus throughout the pages in question—seventeen in number [1]—the spelling constantly, and words and even sentences occasionally, differ from the real text of Caxton [2].

When at page 113 of volume i. the editor introduces the words ' certayne cause ' to complete the sense, he is careful to call attention, in a foot-note, to the fact that these words are not in the original, but taken from ' the second edition,' by which I presume he means that of 1498. But when he subsequently supplies seventeen pages which were also not in his original, he gives no hint of the fact; and his reti-cence has been so successful that for fifty years the interpolations have passed as genuine among learned critics, who have quoted from them passages wholly spurious as Caxton's genuine text. It was only last year that, in collating Earl Spencer's copy with the edition of Southey, I discovered that these passages—to which my attention was directed by Messrs. Longmans' note above mentioned— did not correspond with Caxton's text, as represented by Whittaker's restorations : and on afterwards collating them with the Osterley text itself I found the like result. It remained to trace them to their real sources. This has not been so easy as might be supposed, for though it was evident that Mr. Upcott must have had recourse to one or other of the existing editions, the interpolated passages in fact agree exactly with none of them. But a careful collation of the last four chapters of the book (which include more than half the interpolations, and may be taken as a fair speci-men of the whole) with the old texts, leaves no doubt that, with the exception of ·the first thirty-six lines of chapter x, they were taken, like the two words mentioned above, from the first edition of Wynkyn de Worde, but with the spelling occa-sionally altered, and here and there a small word put in, left out, or changed. These alterations throw an ingenious disguise over the whole ; but if we penetrate through this we find that in these four chapters there are only thirteen words differing from those in Wynkyn de Worde's first edition, and these unimportant ; while in his second edition, and in those of Copland, and East, the variations from Mr. Upcott's text of the same chapters are respectively fifty-seven, fifty-six, and fifty in number, and many of them important in kind : and if we go to the edition of 1634 we find the differences still greater, except as to those thirty-six lines, which are supplied from this edition, as they were wanting in the other copy. But the colo-phon, or concluding paragraph of the book, Mr. Upcott could not take from any of

---

[1] The pages are vol. i. p. 167, line 18, to p. 169, line 17; p. 275, third line from bottom, to p. 279, line 5 from bottom; vol. ii. p. 202, line 13, to p. 204, line 14; p. 446, line 5, to end of 455.

[2] An account of these interpolations was given by me in the Athenæum of Sept. 7 and Dec. 10, 1867, and Feb. 10, 1868.

the editions which followed that of Caxton; for though Wynkyn de Worde might, and in fact did, supply at least one or two of the first words, the latter part of his colophon relates to his own edition, and departs widely from that of Caxton, while those in the later editions are still more unlike; and yet Mr. Upcott's colophon is a tolerable, though not an exact, representation of that of Caxton. But his other materials can be ascertained beyond a doubt. They are, the colophon as given by Ames, and repeated by Dibdin in a modernised and otherwise inexact form[1], and that which first appeared in the Catalogue of the Harleian Library[2], and was thence copied in the article on Caxton in the Biographia Britannica, and also in Herbert's Additions to Ames. The colophons of Ames and of the Harleian Catalogue have important variations from each other and from that of Caxton; and as Mr. Upcott adopts some portions of each which are not found either in the other, or in Caxton, we see the manner in which the paragraph in question was compounded. Each stone of the ingeniously fitted mosaic may be referred to the place from which it was taken. We cannot indeed choose positively between Ames and Dibdin, or among the Harleian Catalogue, the Biographia, and Herbert; but as the two paragraphs which are required in addition to that of Wynkyn de Worde are both found in Herbert's Ames, it seems most probable that Mr. Upcott had recourse to that work, though another combination would have served the purpose equally well. That the interpolated passages are not taken from the Osterley Caxton itself, even in the roughest and most careless manner, is quite evident[3].

Lastly, in 1858 Mr. Wright published an edition reprinted from that of 1634, with an introduction and notes of considerable interest.

The Early English Text Society promise us a reprint of the original Caxton which shall be free from the faults of that of Southey, which meanwhile is, except in the interpolated passages, a very faithful representation of that original for the purposes of the antiquarian and philologist; and whatever like interest there may be in the edition of 1634 is available in the reprint of Mr. Wright. But neither is readable with pleasure by any but the student, and the two modernised editions are out of print. What is wanted, therefore, is an edition for ordinary readers, and especially for boys, from whom the chief demand for this book will always come; and such an edition the present professes to be. It is a reprint of the original Caxton with the spelling modernised, and those few words which are unintelligibly obsolete replaced by others which, though not necessarily unknown to Caxton, are still in use, yet with all old forms retained which do not interfere with this requirement of being readable. For when, as indeed is oftenest the case, the context makes even an obsolete phrase probably, if not precisely, known,

---

[1] Typographical Antiquities, by Ames and Herbert, 1785, vol. i. p. 61; Ibid. enlarged by Dibdin, 1810, vol. i. p. 253. The 'Additions' are at the end of vol. iii. of Herbert's edition.

[2] Catalogus Bibl. Harleianæ, 1744, vol. iii. no. 372.

[3] See Note B at the end of the volume, p. 488.

I have left it in the text, and given its meaning in the Glossary, in which I have chiefly followed Roquefort, Halliwell, and Wright. In the Glossary I have also added a few geographical notes for those readers who may care for them. And for the like reason—of making the book readable—such phrases or passages as are not in accordance with modern manners have been also omitted or replaced by others which either actually occur or might have occurred in Caxton's text elsewhere. I say manners, not morals, because I do not profess to have remedied the moral defects of the book which I have already spoken of. Mr. Tennyson has shown us how we may deal best with this matter for modern uses, in so far as Sir Thomas Malory has himself failed to treat it rightly; and I do not believe that when we have excluded what is offensive to modern manners there will be found anything practically injurious to the morals of English boys, for whom I have chiefly undertaken this work, while there is much of moral worth which I know not where they can learn so well as from the ideals of magnanimity, courage, courtesy, reverence for women, gentleness, self-sacrifice, chastity, and other manly virtues, exhibited in these pages.

The omissions, not many, were essential to the publication of the book at all for popular reading; but if any one blames the other departures from the exact form of the original, I would ask him to judge from the specimens of the old type and spelling which I have given at the end of each book, and of the volume, whether a literal and verbal reproduction of the whole would not be simply unreadable except by students of old English. And if some departure from the original was necessary, it was reasonable to carry it so far as, though no farther than, my purpose required. And, subject to these conditions, the present volume is in fact a more accurate reproduction of Caxton's text than any other except that of Southey. I have, indeed, made use of Southey's text for this edition, having satisfied myself by collation with the Althorp and Osterley Caxtons that it is an accurate reprint excepting as to the passages above mentioned; and these have been taken by me, in like manner, from the only existing original.

There is no title-page, as I have already mentioned, to the Osterley or the Althorp Caxton, that which is given by several bibliographers being only an extract, not very critically selected, from Caxton's preface. But it is evident from Caxton's colophon that the real title or name of the book was LE MORTE DARTHUR, and he explains that it was so 'entitled' notwithstanding it treated of Arthur's birth, life, and acts as well as death, and also of the adventures of his knights of the Round Table. And the concluding words of Malory, 'Here is the end of the death of Arthur,' taken with their context, point to the same title. It was indeed before Malory's time, and has been ever since, the traditional title of this story. We have Mort Artus and Morte Arthure in the earlier times; Ascham, in Henry VIII's reign, calls this book La Morte d'Arthure; Tyrwhitt, Mort d'Arthur; and Walter Scott and Southey, Morte Arthur, which last probably many of us are familiar with as the old name which we heard from our own fathers.

§ 3. An Essay on Chivalry.

St. Augustine replied to the enquiry, What is time? by saying, 'I know when you do not ask me:' and a like answer suggests itself to us if we try to find an adequate reply to the question, What is Chivalry? For chivalry is one of those words, like love, duty, patriotism, loyalty, which make us feel their meaning, and the reality of what they mean, though their ideal and comprehensive character hinders us from readily putting it into the forms of a definition. When the alchemist in the Eastern tale compounds, with all the resources of his art, the universal solvent before the expectant eyes of his pupil, the pupil, seeing the mysterious fluid lie quietly in the crucible, exclaims, with not unreasonable doubt, 'O Sage, be not deceived: how can that which dissolves all things be itself contained in a ladle?' And how shall chivalry, sparkling and flashing everywhere as it runs through that great complicated tissue of human life which we call modern civilisation,—how shall chivalry, the humaniser of society, be brought within the limits of a definition?

Chivalry, indeed, exists for us in spirit rather than in outward and visible form. It no longer comes to us with the outward symbols of war-horse, and armour, and noble birth, and strength of arm, and high-flown protestations of love and gallantry; yet we never fail to know and feel its presence, silent and unobtrusive as it now is: we recognise the lady and the gentleman not less surely now than they did in old times; and we acknowledge their rights and their power over us now no less than then. And if the spirit of chivalry does live among us still, we may read its past history by its present light, and say in Spenser's words,—

> 'By infusion sweete
> Of thine own spirit which doth in me survive,
> I follow still the footing of thy feete,
> That with thy meaning so I may the rather meete.'

Let us then look back to those times when chivalry had an outward, visible form, and was embodied in its own proper institutions, with orders, and statutes, and courts of its own jurisdiction, and rituals, and customs, like those of other great social institutions and members of the body politic.

The deluge of the Teutonic nations which broke up the old Roman civilisation threatened for some centuries to overwhelm Europe with mere barbarism. We know now that the germs of a far higher and better civilisation were everywhere ready to open into life as soon as the fury of that deluge had spent itself; but for a long period the evil seemed mightier than the good. From time to time the clear head, the noble heart and conscience, and the strong arm of an Alfred, a Charlemagne, or an Otho, might bring a temporary calm and order into the storm; but when the personal influences of such great men were withdrawn, society relapsed again and again into ever new anarchy, and war—at once the effect and the cause of anarchy—savage, cruel war became the business of all men throughout Europe. The selfish, the rapacious, and the unscrupulous fought for power, and plunder, and love of fighting; and while violence could only be resisted by violence, and each man had to defend himself, his family, and his possessions as best he could, with no effectual aid from law and government, there was a constant tendency to increasing barbarism and brutish, or worse than brutish, instead of human, existence.

But man differs from the brutes in this, that while he can fall lower than they, he can also rise higher, and that even the passions and the impulses which he has in common with them may be subdued, and refined, and modified, till they become the servants and instruments of his human life, and the means by which all that is properly spiritual in his being may be reflected and symbolised upon this earth in outward, visible form. The nobler races of men—the historical races, as they have been called—constantly show this aptitude for contending with these downward tendencies of our nature, and for advancing, through the conquest of them, to new and higher life.

And so it was in the Middle Ages. The Church was, no doubt, the great civiliser of the nations: still, whatever aid the State derived from the Church, it then, no less than now, had a position and processes of its own, by which it did its own work of civilisation too. And its first great work for controlling the universal anarchy of which I have spoken was the extension and firm establishment of that half-patriarchal, half-military organisation which we call the Feudal System. Every man who was not rich and powerful enough to be a lord became—willingly or unwillingly—a vassal; and all men, from the king downwards, were bound to each other for reciprocal service and protection—a service and protection partly military, but partly patriarchal, since they were rendered not by men strangers to each other except for what Mr. Carlyle calls ' the nexus of cash payment,' but united by ties of family, and neighbourhood, and clanship, and by the interests and sympathies that grow out of these. But the protector of his own vassals easily became the invader of the rights and ravages of the possessions of his neighbour and his vassals; and so the old evils of anarchy and violence grew afresh out of the remedy which had been devised to meet them. The ' monarchies sank into impotence; petty, lawless tyrants trampled all social order under foot,' says a recent historian of this period, ' and all attempts after scientific instruction and artistic pleasures were as effectually crushed by this state of general insecurity as the external well-being and material life of the people. This was a dark and stormy period for Europe, merciless, arbitrary, and violent. It is a sign of the prevailing feeling of misery and hopelessness that, when the first thousand years of our æra were drawing to their close, the people in every country in Europe

looked with certainty for the destruction of the world. Some squandered their
wealth in riotous living, others bestowed it for the good of their souls on churches
and convents; weeping multitudes lay day and night around the altars; some
looked forward with dread, but most with secret hope, towards the burning of
the earth and the falling in of heaven. Their actual condition was so miserable
that the idea of destruction was relief, spite of all its horrors[1].'

The palliatives with which men tried to meet the evils of the times indicate
the greatness of the evils, but also the moral feeling which was the promise of
better things. Such was the so-called 'Peace of the King,' by which private wars
were not to be entered on till forty days after the committal of the alleged crime
which was to be avenged; and the 'Truce of God,' by which all these acts of
private hostility were suspended from Thursday to Monday in each week. And at
the Council of Cleremont, held by Urban II in November, 1095, a severe censure
was pronounced against the licence of private war; the Truce of God was confirmed; women and priests were placed under the safeguard of the Church; and
a protection of three years was extended to husbandmen and merchants, the de-
fenceless victims of military rapine. We are reminded of the law of Moses, which
provided Cities of Refuge for the man who accidentally and without malice killed
his neighbour, but who could not look for protection from the vengeance of the
family of the slain man except within those special safeguards. In each case there
is the same unreasoning rage of the half-civilised man brought face to face with
the demands of religion and civil law: and each is obliged to yield something to
the other till the better cause has had time to prepare and strengthen itself for
a more complete triumph.

Chivalry, then, was the offspring of the same spirit which dictated the Peace of
the King, the Truce of God, and the decrees of the Council of Cleremont. Chivalry
has another name—Knighthood—and the two are wanted to express all that we
mean by either[2]. The chevalier was the soldier who rode the war-horse: he whose
birth entitled him, and whose wealth gave him the means, to ride at the head of
his vassals and retainers to the war: all ideas of lordship, and mastery, and outward dignity and power, are here embodied before us. But this 'chevalier,' this
'ritter,' or rider of the war-horse, was also to be a 'knecht,' or servant: 'He that
will be chief among you, let him be your servant.' The knight was to obey, no
less than to command; he was to exert his strength and power, not for selfish ends,
but in the service of others; and especially in the service of the poor, the weak, and
the oppressed, who could not help or defend themselves. It was, indeed, no new
discovery in the world, that such are the duties of him who possesses power, and
above all the power of the sword; and they who have tried to trace the origin

[1] Von Sybel's History of the Crusades, English Translation, p. 11.
[2] For this distinction I am indebted to my friend the Rev. F. D. Maurice, whose genius lights up every subject it approaches.

of chivalry to some particular place and time have had to go to the Germans of Tacitus, to the Crusaders, to the Saracens, to the Romans, the Greeks, the Trojans, the Hebrews, only to come to the conclusion that chivalry belongs in its spirit to man as man; though the form in which that spirit was clothed in Europe in the Middle Ages has an individuality of which some of the sources may be ascertained, and though from that time forward its power has been established, and extended, in a manner, and with a greatness unknown to the ancients.

In those days society was essentially military. In this our own time the main offices, interests, and occupations of the great body politic are non-military, and the army is but a small portion of the nation, specially trained for a minor, though indispensable, function therein. Peace, for its own sake, and for the sake of the objects which can only be obtained by the arts and with the opportunities of peace, is the end and aim of every civilised nation now; and war is only an occasional means to secure that end. But in the Middle Ages war was, or seemed to be, the chief end of life to the greater part of every nation, and especially to all who possessed rank, and wealth, and power, and were in fact the leaders of the nation. And therefore chivalry, the spirit which was to humanise those warriors, needed to be warlike too, and thus to sympathise with those to whom it addressed itself.

Much, too, of its special form it no doubt owed to that wonderful race of heroes, the Normans. The romantic love of adventure; the religious and the martial enthusiasm; the desire to revenge injuries, and to win wealth and power; the delight in arms and horses, in the luxury of dress, and in the exercises of hunting and hawking; the eloquence and sagacity in council; the patience with which when need was they could endure the inclemency of every climate, and the toil and abstinence of a military life; and the gentleness, the affability and the gallantry, which were the characteristics of the Norman race; these must have been more or less impressed on men's minds wherever the Norman sway or influence extended, from England to Sicily, and must have reproduced something of themselves in the social habits and manners of the times. When we read the description of William of the Iron Arm, the first Norman count of Apulia, so strong, so brave, so affable, so generous, and so sage above other men—a lion in battle, a lamb in society, and an angel in council—we are reminded of the heroes of chivalry in the days of its greatest refinement, the Black Prince, Sir John Chandos, and Sir Walter of Manny, as they still live in the pages of Froissart; or their counterparts in romance, King Arthur, Sir Launcelot, Amadis of Gaul, or Palmerin of England.

The Normans, the latest of the Teutonic races who descended, full of wild life, from their mountains and forests, upon the comparatively civilised plains of Europe, may have brought a newer and fresher feeling for those old manners and customs which Tacitus describes as characterising the Germans of his time, and which are with so much probability connected with the chivalry of the Middle Ages. In ancient Germany, and in Scandinavia, it was the custom for each youth, when he was of an age to bear arms, to be presented with a sword, a shield, and a lance, by his father, or some near relation, in an assembly of the chiefs of the nation; and from that time he became a member of the commonwealth, and ranked as a citizen. He then entered the train of some chief, of whom he and his brother youths became the followers and companions, forming one brotherhood, though not without ranks and degrees, while a generous spirit of equality ran through all.

In ancient Germany, too, women were held in a peculiar reverence, beyond what was known in the other—and otherwise more civilized—nations of antiquity; and the presence of women in the hour of battle with their husbands, brothers, and fathers, was regarded by those warriors as an incentive to courage, and a pledge of victory, which (as they boasted) their Roman foes were unable to appeal to for themselves. And this old Teutonic reverence for women conspired with the new Christian reverence for the Virgin Mary as the type and representative at once of her sex and of the Church, to supply the purer and nobler elements of the gallantry which forms so large a part, not only of the romance, but of the actual history, of chivalry.

But Christianity exercised not only an indirect, but also a direct and avowed action upon the forms of chivalry, as they attained to their full proportions. Knighthood was certainly a feature and distinction of society before the days of Charlemagne, who in permitting the governor of Friesland to make knights by girding them with a sword, and giving them a blow, adds, 'as is the custom.' But no ritual of the Church as yet consecrated that custom. Charlemagne girt the sword on his son Louis the Good without religious ceremonies; and a century later the Saxon king of England, Edward the Elder, clothed Athelstan in a soldier's dress of scarlet, and girded him with a girdle ornamented with precious stones and a sword with sheath of gold, but without religious rites. But in the next century, in the reign of Edward the Confessor, we read that Hereward, a noble Anglo-Saxon youth, was knighted by the Abbot of Peterborough, with confession, absolution, and prayer that he might be a true knight. And this the historian describes as the custom of the English, as indeed it was, or soon became, that of all Europe; the Normans resisting the innovation longest, but at last adopting it with their wonted ardour. The candidate for knighthood confessed his sins on the eve of his consecration (for such it now was), and passed the night in prayer and fasting in the church: the godfathers, the bath, the white garment, and the tonsure (sometimes limited indeed to a single lock) were the symbols of the new and holy state of life to which he was now called: next morning he heard mass, offered his sword on the altar, where it was blessed by the priest; and he was created a knight—either by the priest of highest rank present, or by some knight, who, in virtue of his knighthood, was qualified to confer the sacred office he had himself received—in the name of God, of St. George, and of St. Michael the Archangel. He swore, and received the holy communion in confirmation of his oath, to fulfil the duties of his profession; to speak the truth; to maintain the right; to protect women, the poor, and the distressed; to practise courtesy; to pursue the infidels; to despise the allurements of ease and safety, and to maintain his honour in every perilous adventure. And the Council of Cleremont, of which I have already spoken—as if in order to give the sanction of the Church in a still more formal and comprehensive manner to the whole system of chivalry—decreed that every person of noble birth, on attaining the age of twelve years, should take a solemn oath before the bishop of his diocese to defend to the uttermost the oppressed, the widow, and the orphans; that women of noble birth, both married and single, should enjoy his especial care; and that nothing should be wanting in him to render travelling safe, and to destroy tyranny.

Thus, as has been justly observed, all the humanities of chivalry were sanctioned by legal and ecclesiastical power: it was intended that they should be spread over the whole face of Christendom, in order to check the barbarism and ferocity of the times. While the form of chivalry was martial, its objects became to a great extent religious and social: from a mere military array chivalry obtained the name of the Order, the Holy Order, and a character of seriousness and solemnity was given to it; and it was accounted an honourable office above all offices, orders, and acts of the world, except the order of priesthood.

The education for knighthood usually began at a still earlier age than that mentioned in the Canons of Cleremont. The castles of the princes and nobles were the schools of those days, at least for the youth of their own class. Every feudal lord had his court, to which he drew the sons and daughters of the poorer gentry of his domains; and if he were a knight distinguished for his merits, his castle was also frequented by the children of men of equal rank and reputation with himself: for the prudent and careful father would often have some brother in arms whom he thought better fitted than himself to educate his children in the accomplishments and duties of his station. So, long after, Ben Jonson, looking back on those old times, and picturing them in their ideal aspect, says, that then

> ' Goodness gave the greatness,
> And greatness worship: every house became
> An academy of honour.'

And that this method of education

> ' By a line
> Of institution from our ancestors,
> Hath been deriv'd down to us, and receiv'd
> In a succession, for the noblest way
> Of breeding up our youth in letters, arms,
> Fair mien, discourses, civil exercises,
> And all the blazon of a gentleman.
> Where can he learn to vault, to ride, to fence,
> To move his body gracefuller, to speak
> His language purer, or to tune his mind
> Or manners more to the harmony of nature,
> Than in these nurseries of nobility ?'

The boy of gentle birth, when he thus began his education, was called by the names of Childe, or Damoiseau, or Valet, said to be a contraction of Vassalet or little Vassal; and also Page, though this last name was originally appropriated to the youths of inferior rank. He usually entered the castle which was to be his school about the age of seven or eight. He was to learn modesty, obedience, and address in arms and horsemanship, and was duly exercised in the use of his weapons, beginning with such as were suited to his strength. He was instructed how to guide a horse with grace and dexterity, how to use the bow and the sword, and how to manage the lance,—an art which was taught him by making him ride against a wooden figure, which, if not struck in true knightly fashion, was so contrived as to turn round and give the awkward cavalier a blow with its wooden sword. He attended his lord in the chase, and learnt all its arts; he attended him also in many offices which we should now call menial, but which were then held to be the proper symbols of modesty and obedience for the youth of highest birth and rank. Thus the Black Prince was held to show the highest respect to the French king, his prisoner, by personal attendance on him. In the words of Froissart: 'The same day of the battle, at night, the prince made a supper in his lodging to the French king, and to the most part of the great lords that were prisoners . . . . and always the prince served before the king as humbly as he could, and would not sit at the king's board for any desire that the king could make; but he said he was not sufficient to sit at the table with so great a prince as the king was.'

And not the least important of the youth's duties were those towards the ladies of the house in which he lived. He was to wait on them rather as attending a sort of superior beings to whom adoration and obsequious service were due, than as ministering to the convenience of human creatures like himself. The most modest demeanour, the most profound respect, were to be observed in the presence of these fair idols. And as not only the youths, but the maidens—the damoiselles no less than the damoiseaux—were sent to the courts of the barons and their ladies for education, it would often happen that this veneration in which the boy was so early trained towards the ladies of maturer years, would find an object in some young maiden whose more suitable age might lead him, as he grew up, from mere boyish regard to that passionate and abiding devotion which was the duty of every true knight to his lady, and by the strength of which he held that all his power for good was to be maintained. Here is a description of the beginning of the loves of Amadis and Oriana, which is as charming as it is simple; and which, though we find it in the pages of a romance, we cannot doubt is a picture of actual life and manners. 'Oriana,' says the old book, 'was about ten years old, the fairest creature that ever was seen; wherefore she was called the one " without a peer". . . . The child of the sea (that is, Amadis) was now twelve years old, but in stature and size he seemed fifteen, and he served the queen; but, now that Oriana was there, the queen gave her the child of the sea, that he should serve her, and Oriana said that " it pleased her;" and that word which she said, the child kept in his heart, so that he never lost it from his memory, and in all his life he was never weary of serving her, and his heart was surrendered to her; and this love lasted as long as they lasted, for as well as he loved her did she also love him. But the child of the sea, who knew nothing of her love, thought himself presumptuous to have placed his thoughts on her, and dared not speak to her; and she, who loved him in her heart, was careful not to speak more with him than with another; but their eyes delighted to reveal to the heart what was the thing on earth that they loved best. And now the time came that he thought he could take arms if he were knighted; and this he greatly desired, thinking that he would do such things that, if he lived, his mistress should esteem him.'

Such was the beginning of the loves of Amadis and Oriana, so famous in romance, and so generally held by knights and ladies to be a model for themselves. Constancy, such as that of Amadis, was a virtue of the true lover which those times of long inevitable separations and absences demanded in forms hardly known in our days; and in proportion was it insisted upon, and held in honour. So Spenser says:

> 'Young knight whatever, that dost arms profess,
> And through long labours huntest after fame,
> Beware of fraud, beware of fickleness,
> In choice and change of thy dear loved dame;
> Lest thou of her believe too lightly blame,
> And rash misweening do thy heart remove;
> For unto knight there is no greater shame,
> Than lightness and inconstancy in love.'

The peerless Amadis passed with more than ordinary rapidity to the rank of knighthood. The youth more usually remained an esquire—the next step to that of page—till he was twenty. He attended the knight to whose person he was attached, dressed and undressed him, trained his horses, kept his arms bright and burnished, and did the honours of the household to the strangers who visited it; so that Spenser takes the squire as the type of such courtesy. Here is Chaucer's description of the squire:

> 'With him there was his son, a youngé squire,
> A lover and a lusty bachelor,
> With lockés curl'd as they were laid in press;
> Of twenty years of age he was, I guess.
> Of his stature he was of even length,
> And wonderly deliver, and great of strength;
> And he had been some time in chevachie (military expeditions),
> In Flanders, in Artois, and Picardie,
> And borne him well, as of so little space,
> In hope to standen in his lady's grace.
> Embroider'd was he, as it were a mead
> All full of freshé flowers, white and red;
> Singing he was, or fluting, all the day;
> He was as fresh as is the month of May;

> Short was his gown, with sleevés long and wide:
> Well could he sit on horse, and fairé ride;
> He couldé songés make, and well indite,
> Just, and eke dance, and well pourtray and write:
> So hot he lovéd, that by nightertale
> He slept no more than doth the nightingale.
> Courteous he was; lowly and serviceable;
> And carv'd before his father at the table.'

I have already spoken of the religious rites with which the esquire was admitted into the order of knighthood, and of the solemn and noble engagements into which he then entered. He had next to 'win his spurs,' as it was called; a phrase happily illustrated in the story of Edward III and the Black Prince, which Froissart thus relates :—

'This battle between Broy and Cressy, this Saturday, was right cruel and fell, and many a feat of arms done that came not to my knowledge. . . . In the morning, the day of the battle, certain Frenchmen and Almagnes perforce opened the archers of the prince's battle, [*division* as we should now say,] and came and fought with the men of arms, hand to hand. Then the second battle of the Englishmen came to succour the prince's battle, the which was time, for they had as then much ado. And they with the prince sent a messenger to the king, who was on a little windmill hill : then the knight said to the king, "Sir, the earl of Warwick, and the earl of Oxford, Sir Reynold Cobham, and other, such as lie about the prince your son, are fiercely fought withal, and are sore handled, wherefore they desire you that you and your battle will come and aid them, for if the Frenchmen increase, as they doubt they will, your son and they shall have much ado." Then the king said, "Is my son dead, or hurt, or on the earth felled?" "No, sir," quoth the knight, "but he is hardly matched, wherefore he hath need of your aid." "Well," said the king, "return to him, and to them that sent you hither, and say to them, that they send no more to me for any adventure that falleth, as long as my son is alive: and also say to them, that they suffer him this day to win his spurs; for, if God be pleased, I will this day's work be his, and the honour thereof, and to them that be about him." Then the knight returned again to them, and showed the king's words, the which greatly encouraged them, and repented in that they had sent to the king as they did.' Brave knights, to be 'greatly encouraged' by such stern though manly words. We are reminded of the not less brave and knightly demeanour of Sir Colin Halket and his men at Waterloo, when the Duke of Wellington rode up and asked how they were, and the general replied that two-thirds of the brigade were down, and the remainder so exhausted that the relief of fresh troops, for however short a time, was most desirable. But when the duke said that no relief was possible, that all depended on *them*, the answer which the officer made for himself and his men was, 'Enough, my lord, we stand here till the last man falls.'

Thenceforth the knight's career depended, he would not have said on himself, but on God and his lady: and if we may judge by the ordinary language of the romances, his lady was often the object of actual adoration, little differing from that he would have addressed to the saints in the hour of danger or of triumph. Philosophic divines teach us that although the worship of the saints may become in practice a gross and degrading superstition, it has in it an element of true, and in itself ennobling, faith in ideals of humanity more or less perfectly revealed in human form : and so while we smile at the fictions of extravagant fancy in which the mediæval knight was wont to clothe his love, and his professions of love, for his mistress, we cannot reasonably doubt that in the main, and for that time of youthful imaginations rather than of sober reasonings, the knight was right. When I think of what society was, and what it would still be, without the humanizing influences of womanhood and ladyhood, and what it is by means of these, I say that the tree may be judged by its fruits, and that it is from a right noble stock, rightly and wisely cultivated in the main, in those old days, that we are still gathering such noble fruits. Much evil there was along with the good; and, what is worse, much confusion between good and evil. I need not tell the reader of chivalry romances, or of Mr. Tennyson's glorious reproductions of some of their incidents in modern form of thought as well as language, how painfully this confusion defaces many of the fairest characters and most interesting tales of chivalry, while the historical records of the times in which those romances were written and read, show that the actual state of morals and manners exhibited the like confusions of good and evil, in the ideals as well as in the conduct of life. But, as I have already observed, we see, at least in the romance before us, the good contending with, and mastering the evil, and this not least in the end of the story of the guilty loves of Guenever and Launcelot, the knight whose fame in romance perhaps surpasses that of Amadis, though even mediæval morality was obliged to censure the constancy of Launcelot's love, while it might unhesitatingly extol that of Amadis.

Mr. Tennyson has, I may assume, made every one familiar with the retirement of queen Guenever to the nunnery of Almesbury, and with the death of Arthur; and I venture for the completion of this sketch to show, though from the present volume, how the old story which the poet chiefly follows relates the death and draws the character of Launcelot. Launcelot, when he heard of those events, went to Almesbury, and after taking leave of the queen, resolved to follow her example; and became a hermit and penitent, taking up his abode in a forest where was an hermitage and a chapel that stood between two cliffs; and there he served God day and night with prayers and fastings. Thus he, and other knights who followed his example, ' endured great penance six years, and then Sir Launcelot took the habit of priesthood, and a twelvemonth he sang mass.' At the end of that time a vision directed him to take the body of queen Guenever, now dead at Almesbury, and bury her with king Arthur at Glastonbury. Then the story goes on :—' And when she was put in the earth Sir Launcelot swooned and lay long still, while the hermit came out and awaked him, and said, Ye be to blame, for ye displease God with such manner of sorrow making. Truly, said Sir Launcelot, I trust I do not displease God, for He knoweth mine intent, for my sorrow was not, nor is not, for any rejoicing of sin, but my sorrow may never have end. For when I remember of her beauty, and of her noblesse, that was both with her king and with her; so when I saw his corpse and her corpse so lie together, truly mine heart would not serve to sustain my careful body. Also when I remember me how by my default, and mine orgule, and my pride, that they were both laid full low, that were peerless that ever was living of christian people, wit ye well, said Sir Launcelot, this remembered, of their kindness and mine unkindness, sank so to my heart, that all my natural strength failed me, so that I might not sustain myself.' The story goes on to say that there he wasted away, praying night and day at the tomb of the king and queen. He died, and was taken to his own castle of Joyous Gard to be buried. 'And right thus as they were at their service there came Sir Ector de Maris, that had seven year sought all England, Scotland, and Wales, seeking his brother Sir Launcelot. And when Sir Ector heard such noise and light in the quire of Joyous Gard he alight, and put his horse from him, and came into the quire, and there he saw men sing and weep. And all they knew Sir Ector, but he knew not them. Then went Sir Bors unto Sir Ector, and told him how there lay his brother Sir Launcelot dead. And then Sir Ector threw his shield, sword, and helm from him; and when he beheld Sir Launcelot's visage he fell down in a swoon; and when he awaked it were hard for any tongue to tell the doleful complaints that he made for his brother. Ah, Launcelot, he said, thou were head of all Christian knights! And now, I dare say, said Sir Ector, thou Sir Launcelot, there thou liest, that thou were never matched of earthly knight's hands; and thou were the courtiest knight that ever bare shield; and thou were the truest friend to thy lover that ever bestrode horse; and thou were the truest lover, of a sinful man, that ever loved woman; and thou were the kindest man that ever strake with sword; and thou were the goodliest person ever came among press of knights; and thou was the meekest man and the gentlest that ever ate in hall among ladies; and thou were the sternest knight to thy mortal foe that ever put spear in the rest.'

Let me compare with this Chaucer's description of the knight of his times :—

> 'A knight there was, and that a worthy[1] man,
> That from the timé that he first began
> To riden out, he loved chivalry,
> Truth and honóur, freedom and courtesy.
> Full worthy was he in his lordés war,
> And thereto had he ridden, no man farre,
> As well in Christendom as in Heatheness,
> And ever honoured for his worthiness.
> At Alisandre he was when it was won :
> Full often-time he had the board begun

[1] Valiant.

> Aboven allé natións in Prusse :[1]
> In Lethowe had he reyséd[2], and in Russe,
> No Christian man so oft, of his degree :
> In Gernade at the siege eke had he be
> Of Algesir, and ridden in Belmarie ;
> At Leyés was he, and at Satalie,
> When they were won; and in the Greaté Sea
> At many a noble army had he be.
> At mortal battles had he been fifteen,
> And foughten for our faith at Tramissene
> In listés thriés, and aye slain his foe.
> This ilké worthy knight had been also
> Sometimé with the lord of Palathie
> Against another heathen in Turkey ;
> And evermore he had a sovereign prize[3],
> And though that he was worthy he was wise,
> And of his port as meek as is a maid.
> He never yet no villainy ne said
> In all his life unto no manner wight :
> He was a very perfect, gentle knight.'

In an age when all men, not of the clergy, were divided between the two classes of freemen or gentlemen, and serfs or villains, and the villains were in habits and in human culture little better than the domestic animals of which they shared the labours, the knight almost inevitably belonged to the class of free, or gentle, birth. Still, in theory always, and to a great extent in practice, it was not his birth, but his personal merit, which qualified him for knighthood. The personal merit would oftener exist, and still oftener come to light, where it had the advantages and aids of education and general social culture. But if it was recognised in the villain, or man of no rights of birth, he might be, and often was, knighted, and was thereby immediately enfranchised, and accounted a gentleman, in law no less than in name. Thus Froissart tells us of Sir Robert Sale, the governor of Norwich, that ' he was no gentleman born, but he had the grace to be reputed sage and valiant in arms, and for his valiantness King Edward made him knight.' He was governor during the popular insurrection of which Wat Tyler and Jack Straw were the London leaders ; and he was invited to put himself at the head of one of the risings by men who urged upon him—' Sir Robert, ye are a knight and a man greatly beloved in this country, and renowned a valiant man; and though ye be thus, yet we know you well : ye be no gentleman born, but son to a villain, such as we be : therefore come you with us, and be our master, and we shall make you so great a lord that one quarter of England shall be under your obeisance.' He refused, and they killed him. The same king also knighted a man-at-arms, who had originally been a tailor, and who greatly distinguished himself under the name of Sir John Hacond,

---

[1] Having gone to find adventures in Prussia with the Teutonic knights who carried on war with the still Pagan Lithuania, he had been often placed at the head of the table above the like adventurers from other nations, in compliment to his especial merit.

[2] Ridden in arms.

[3] Praise.

or Hawkwood. And the courtly as well as knightly Chaucer, who must more or less have reflected the feeling of the royal and noble personages among whom he lived, goes farther, and asserts that not only does virtue make the gentleman, but also baseness of mind the villain or churl :—

> ' But understand in thine intent,
> That this is not mine intendement,
> To clepen no wight in no age
> Only gentle for his lineage ;
> But whoso that is virtuous,
> And in his port nought outrageous,
> Though he be not gentle born,
> Thou may'st well see this in soth,
> That he is gentle because he doth
> As longeth to a gentleman ;
> Of them none other deem I can :
> For certainly, withouten drede,
> A churl is deemed by his deed,
> Of high or low, as you may see,
> Or of what kindred that he be.'

Akin to this recognition of gentleness of mind and manners, as that which made a gentleman, was the sense of brotherhood among knights and gentlemen, which led them to trust in each other's honour, even when they were fighting under the banners of hostile kings. The chronicles are full of the instances of such consideration of the English and French knights for each other in the wars between the two nations ; and it is not without probability that to these and suchlike manifestations of the spirit of chivalry have been traced the courtesy and humanity which characterise modern warfare in a degree unknown to the ancients.

Much indeed of barbarism and cruelty there was in the usages of war in the best times of chivalry, even of the knights among themselves, and still more when they came, with passions infuriated by resistance, upon the people of lower rank than themselves. Edward III of England, and the knights whom he gathered round him, are held alike by contemporary historians and romance writers, and by those of modern times, to have best exhibited the characteristics of chivalry in its day of greatest refinement as well as splendour ; yet no one can read the chronicles of even the admiring Froissart without seeing how much savage passion and cruelty was often mingled with their better dispositions : though we do see also that the cruelty was not because, but in spite of, their chivalry. Froissart laments bitterly the iniquity of the massacre by the Black Prince of the people of Limoges, men, women, and children, more than three thousand. And when Edward III, before him, intended, as would seem, to have treated the town of Calais in like manner, not only did the French knights who had offered to surrender declare that they would ' endure as much pain as knights ever did, rather than the poorest lad in the town should have any more evil than the greatest of us all '—showing that they made no selfish distinction between the noble and the villain—but the English

knights, headed by Sir Walter of Manny, that flower of knighthood, protested to
the utmost against their king's purpose. And when he had yielded so far to their
urgency as to say that he would be content with the lives of the six chief burgesses,
Sir Walter of Manny again remonstrated, saying, 'Ah, noble king, for God's sake
refrain your courage: ye have the name of sovereign noblesse; therefore now do
not a thing that should blemish your renown, nor to give cause to some to speak
of you villainy [to charge you with conduct unworthy of a knight and gentleman];
every man will say it is a great cruelty to put to death such honest persons, who by
their own wills put themselves into your grace to save their company. Then the
king wryed away from him, and commanded to send for the hangman, and said,
"They of Calais had caused many of my men to be slain, wherefore these shall die
in likewise." '

It needed a stronger influence than that of Sir Walter of Manny to save their
lives: and this brings me to speak of the LADY of the mediæval times; the LADY,
who was the counterpart of the KNIGHT, and without whom he could never have
existed. Here, indeed, I meet a difficulty which reminds me of what Coleridge
says of the female characters of Shakspeare, that their truth to nature, and therefore
their beauty, consists in the absence of strongly marked features. It is impossible
to read the poems, romances, or chronicles of the mediæval times, without feeling
all through how important a part the lady plays everywhere; and yet it is far from
easy to draw her from her retirement and bring distinctly before ourselves what she
did, and get a picture of her as definite as we can do of the knight. Still I must
try to trace the outlines of such a picture of one lady:—Philippa, queen of
Edward III, whom Froissart calls 'the most gentle queen, most liberal, and most
courteous that ever was queen in her days;' and who was the very type and representative of the lady, in the highest and best sense, in an age in which the
ladies—such as the princess Blanche, the good queen Ann, the countess of Salisbury, Jane de Montfort, and the wife of Charles de Blois —were renowned for their
gentle or their heroic characters.

When Isabel, queen of Edward II, visited Hainault with her son, afterwards
Edward III, we are told that William, earl of Hainault, 'had four fair daughters,
Margaret, Philippa, Jane, and Isabell: among whom the young Edward set most
his love and company on Philippa; and also the young lady in all honour was
more conversant with him than any of her sisters.' Queen Isabel had come to ask
for aid against her enemies, and Froissart gives an account of the discussion between the earl and his council, who objected on prudential grounds to interfering
with the quarrels of the English, and the earl's brother, Sir John Hainault, who
maintained that 'all knights ought to aid to their powers all ladies and damsels
chased out of their own countries, being without counsel or comfort.' The earl
finally yielded, saying, 'My fair brother, God forbid that your good purpose should
be broken or let. Therefore, in the name of God, I give you leave; and kissed him,
straining him by the hand in sign of great love.' The whole passage is too long

to quote, but thus much gives a lively picture of the temper of the home and court in which the young Philippa was brought up.

Her marriage with Edward, then only fifteen years old, was agreed on, and sanctioned by the Pope. I am sorry to say that the chronicler gives no account of the lady's bridal outfit[1], except in the general terms, that 'there was devised and purveyed for their apparel, and for all things honourable that belonged to such a lady, who should be queen of England.' They were married, and she arrived in England and was crowned, 'with great justs, tourneys, dancing, carolling, and great feasts, the which endured the space of three weeks.' And then 'this young queen Philippa abode still in England, with small company of any persons of her own country, saving one who was named Walter of Manny, who was her carver, and after did so many great prowesses in divers places, that it were hard to make mention of them.' If we couple this statement, that she retained hardly any of her own people, with that which Froissart makes in reviewing her whole life, that 'she loved always her own nation where she was born,' we have pleasing thoughts suggested of the cheerful acceptance of new duties in a foreign land by the young wife; while, if I had space to describe in detail the noble life of Sir Walter of Manny, the reader would agree with me that his habitual presence in the English court must have done much to make both Edward and the Black Prince, as well as the rest of the princes and nobles, what they were, as knights and gentlemen.

The next glimpse we get of the queen is when she appears, accompanied with three hundred ladies and damsels 'of noble lineage, and apparelled accordingly, at the yearly feast at Windsor, in honour of the order and brotherhood of the Knights of the Blue Garter, there established on St. George's day.' Again, when the king of Scots had advanced to Newcastle, while king Edward lay before Calais, we see the queen arriving to meet the English army, and going from division to division, 'desiring them to do their devoir'—duty was then, as now, the English soldier's word—'to defend the honour of her lord the king of England, and, in the name of God, every man to be of good heart and courage; promising them that to her power she would remember them as well or better as though her lord the king were there personally. Then the queen departed from them, recommending them to God and St. George.' She does not seem, like some of the ladies of that generation, to have considered the field to be her place while the battle was going on; but after it was won she returned, and with her council made all necessary arrangements and plans. Shortly after she joined her husband while he lay before Calais, 'bringing many ladies and damsels with her, as well to accompany her, as to see their husbands, fathers, brethren, and other friends that lay at siege there before Calais, and had done a long time.' And I think we may attribute it as well

---

[1] It appears from Morte Arthur, p. 474, that London was the proper place to go to, 'to buy all manner of things that longed unto a wedding.'

to the general humanising influence of all those ladies, as to the personal persuasion of Philippa, that Calais did not suffer the same horrors of war as did Limoges at the hands of the Black Prince. To what I have already quoted from Froissart as to this story, I must now add what he tells us of Philippa, after Edward had refused to hear Sir Walter of Manny. 'Then the queen kneeled down, and sore weeping, said, " Ah, gentle sir, sith I passed the sea in great peril, I have desired nothing of you; therefore now I humbly require you, in the honour of the Son of the Virgin Mary, and for the love of me, that ye will take mercy of these six burgesses." The king beheld the queen, and stood still in a study a space, and then said, " Ah dame, I would ye had been as now in some other place; ye make such request to me that I cannot deny you; wherefore I give them to you, to do your pleasure with them." '

And lastly, as a counterpart to the picture I have already given you of the death of the knight of romance, here is the account of the death of her who was the lady of the brightest day of historical chivalry :—

'In the mean season there fell in England a heavy case and a common : howbeit it was right piteous for the king, his children, and all his realm; for the good queen of England—that so many good deeds had done in her time, and so many knights succoured, and ladies and damosels comforted, and had so largely departed of her goods to her people, and naturally loved always the nation of Haynault, the country where she was born—she fell sick in the castle of Windsor, the which sickness continued on her so long, that there was no remedy but death; and the good lady, when she knew that there was no remedy but death, she desired to speak with the king her husband, and when he was before her, she put out of her bed her right hand, and took the king by his right hand, who was right sorrowful at his heart. Then she said, " Sir, we have in peace, joy, and great prosperity, used all our time together : sir, now I pray you at our departing, that ye will grant me three desires." The king, right sorrowfully weeping, said, " Madam, desire what ye will, I grant it." The three requests of the dying woman were—that the king should pay all that she owed to any man; that he should fulfil all the promises she had made to the churches where she had " had her devotion," and that " it might please him to take none other sepulture, whensoever it should please God to call him out of this transitory life, but beside her in Westminster." The king, all weeping, said, " Madam, I grant all your desire." Then the good lady and queen made on her the sign of the cross, and commended the king her husband to God, and her youngest son Thomas, who was there beside her; and anon after she yielded up the spirit, which I believe surely the holy angels received with great joy up to heaven; for in all her life she did neither in thought nor deed thing to lose her soul, as far as any creature could know. Thus the good queen of England died in the year of our Lord 1369, in the vigil of our Lady, in the midst of August.'

We have all pictured to ourselves, again and again, how the lady sat in her bower with her embroidery and her missal or romance, and saw from her lattice window her knight going from the castle with lance and pennon, hoping to meet his foe: how the minstrel recited in the castle hall the feats of arms of this or that hero in some distant battle-field; and how the matron or the maiden heard those feats, and thought with silent joy that it was her lord, her husband, or her lover, whose deeds were thus winning the praises of the troubadour, and the applause of the listening knights and squires. We have all seen in imagination the tournament, with the pomp and splendour of its mimic contests: contests which surpassed the Olympic and Corinthian games of classic antiquity, not only in their gorgeous show, but still more in the presence of the ladies, noble in birth, and fame, and beauty; whose scarf, or glove, the combatants wore as the token of that favour which was their highest incentive to distinguish themselves; and from whose hands the conqueror received the prize of skill and bravery; while the honourably vanquished might be sure that he would have the hardly less welcome lot of being cared for by the same ladies, who never shrank from this their acknowledged and well fulfilled duty of tending the wounded knight.

Perhaps too we have listened in fancy to the proceedings of the so-called Courts or Parliaments of Love, in which the ladies were wont to hear questions of gallantry gravely argued on both sides by poets pleading in verse, and then to give their judgments according to the logical and metaphysical rules which the schoolmen applied to theological enquiries. But I can now but remind my reader that such things were; and must hasten forward, leaving ungathered flowers that would make many a wreath and nosegay.

The golden age of chivalry was the period from about the middle of the eleventh to the end of the fourteenth century. We may say, with Gibbon, that the Crusades were at once a cause and an effect of chivalry. In the Crusades the spirit of knighthood, with all its characteristic features, actuated vast bodies of men of every rank and nation, and found a foe believed by all Christendom to be to it what the individual robber and plunderer was to the knight errant who went forth in his own country to defend or rescue the widow and orphan and their possessions, or the traveller along the road which passed the castle of some powerful though unworthy baron. The chivalry at home was kept alive, and raised to its highest energy, both in man and woman, by the chivalry in the Holy Land. It is in this period that the chief institutions of chivalry took their rise, or reached their full form; while their ruder features were gradually softened with the increasing refinement of the times, till they presented that aspect with which we find them in the days of Edward III and the Black Prince, as drawn by Froissart or Chaucer, or in the romances which were then written or remodelled out of older materials, and which show that even in the estimation of other nations the English court then afforded the pattern of knighthood for Christendom.

Thenceforward the outward forms of chivalry began to decay; very gradually indeed, and not without apparent resuscitations from time to time. But no real revival was possible; for the immortal spirit was seeking new habitations for itself,

more fitted to the new world which was succeeding to that of the Middle Ages.
And perhaps Cervantes, by helping to tear up with his merciless satire the last
remnants of an honest faith in the old forms of chivalry, did as real, though we
cannot say as genial, a service to the cause of chivalry itself, as Spenser did in
endeavouring to preserve its spirit by transferring it to the region of allegory.
The last expiring token of the old spirit in the old forms which I have found, is in
the records of the Knights of Malta—the Knights Hospitallers of St. John of Jerusalem—when the news of the great earthquake in Sicily, in 1783, arrived at Malta.
Then those poor feeble-minded sybarites remembered for a moment their manhood
and their knighthood, and their vows as Hospitallers: they manned their galleys,
and, with food and clothing and medicines, and the consolations of their faith, were
speedily seen, in their half-military, half-priestly garb—the armour covered by the
black robe with the white cross—at the bedsides of the wounded and the dying, as
they lay amid the still tottering ruins of their devastated houses. In a very few
years, in that same generation, the Order had passed away for ever: but it is
pleasant to him who stands in the palace of the Grand Masters among the trophies
of their former greatness, or treads the aisles of the cathedral of St. John, where
every step is upon the emblazoned gravestone of a knight, to think of this, and not
of any less worthy deed, as their last act.

> ' The knight's bones are dust,
> And his good sword rust :
> His soul is with the saints, I trust :'—

but he has left to us an imperishable and a rich inheritance, won for us by him. To
him we owe our MANNERS—all that world of existence implied in the names LADY
and GENTLEMAN. Through the Middle Ages it was ' Our Lady,' the Virgin mother,
who embodied and represented to all men and women, from the prince to the peasant, their ideals of womanhood and ladyhood. In modern times St. Paul has been
held to be the model of a gentleman; in whose acts and writings are found all the
principles, maxims, and spirit of a character entirely chivalrous, in the amplest
sense of the term : while one of our old dramatists has ventured, in words of
touching tenderness and reverence, to point to a yet higher realisation of that
ideal ;—

> ' The best of men
> That e'er wore earth about him, was a sufferer,
> A soft, meek, patient, humble, tranquil spirit ;
> The first true gentleman that ever breathed.'

And it was the transference of these Christian ethics into the practice of common,
daily, worldly life, in rude, half-barbarous times, which we owe to the knights and
ladies of the Middle Ages ; a transference effected slowly, and with much mixture
of evil with the good : nor is the work nearly completed yet ; but the worth of
it can hardly be overrated.

There is not indeed all, but there is much truth in the old motto, 'Manners makyth man.' Manners, like laws, create a region and atmosphere of virtue within which all good more easily lives and grows, and evil finds it harder to maintain itself. How large a portion of the small, spontaneous kindnesses of hourly life, in which, after all, so much of our happiness consists, are not only unknown, but impossible, where habitual, unaffected politeness is wanting.

But manners are good, not only as affording a fairer field for the exercise of the higher virtues, but good in themselves. They are a real part of the beauty and grace of our human life. Courtesy, and self-possession, and deference and respect for others; modesty and gentleness towards all men, and recognition in all of the true gold of humanity, whether it bear the guinea stamp or no; love of truth and honour; and not only readiness, but eagerness to help the weak, and defend their cause against the strong; and all these irradiated and glorified, as often as may be, by that sentiment which

> ' Gives to every power a double power,
> Above their functions and their offices ;'—

these are the things which make the lady and the gentleman.

And if it should seem as though the chivalry of our own times is reduced to something less noble than that of old, when men risked life, and things dearer than life, in defending the weak and attacking the oppressor in his strongholds—when the hardness of the actual fight against evil-doers was not exaggerated in the romances which pictured the knights contending with dragons and enchanters and giants—we must remember that our nineteenth century world is yet far from cleared of the monstrous powers of evil, which still oppress and devour the weak; and that a battle, not really less resolute, nor, if need be, less desperate, than those of old, is still carried on by those who, under the modest guise of common life, are fighting in the true spirit of chivalry—uniting the most adventurous enthusiasm with the most patient endurance, and both with the gentlest service of the poor, the weak, and the oppressed; and, what is most worthy of admiration, the service of the morally poor, and weak, and oppressed, who, but for such deliverers, must remain in a house of bondage darker than can be built or barred by earthly hands.

But whether we are content with the chivalry of manners, or aspire to a place in the brotherhood of the chivalry of action, our principles, our maxims, and our examples have come down to us as an inheritance from the past :—an inheritance common to all who care to claim it; and won for us by the old knights, fighting in the name of God and of their ladies[1].

---

[1] My principal authorities—whose words as well as facts I have frequently availed myself of—are Mills's History of Chivalry, which alone almost exhausts the subject; Gibbon's Decline and Fall; Godwin's Life of Chaucer; Scott's Essay on Chivalry; Lord Berners's Froissart; and Southey's Amadis of Gaul.

THE BOOK OF

KING ARTHUR

AND OF HIS NOBLE

KNIGHTS OF THE ROUND TABLE.

PREFACE OF WILLIAM CAXTON.

AFTER that I had accomplished and finished divers histories, as well of contemplation as of other historial and worldly acts of great conquerors and princes, and also certain books of ensamples and doctrine, many noble and divers gentlemen of this realm of England came and demanded me many and ofttimes, wherefore that I have not do made and imprint the noble history of the Saint Greal, and of the most renowned Christian king, first and chief of the three best Christian, and worthy, king Arthur, which ought most to be remembered amongst us Englishmen tofore all other Christian kings; for it is notoriously known through the universal world, that there be nine worthy and the best that ever were, that is to wit, three Paynims, three Jews, and three Christian men. As for the Paynims, they were tofore the Incarnation of Christ, which were named, the first Hector of Troy, of whom the history is comen both in ballad and in prose, the second Alexander the Great, and the third Julius Cæsar, Emperor of Rome, of whom the histories be well known and had. And as for the three Jews, which also were tofore the incarnation of our Lord, of whom the first was duke Joshua which brought the children of Israel into the land of behest, the second David king of Jerusalem, and the third Judas Machabeus. Of these three the Bible rehearseth all their noble histories and acts. And since the said incarnation have been three noble Christian men, stalled and admitted through the universal world into the number of the nine best and worthy. Of whom was first the noble Arthur, whose noble acts I purpose to write in this present book here following. The second was Charlemain, or Charles the Great, of whom the history is had in many places, both in French and in English. And the third and last was Godfrey of Boloine, of whose acts and life I made a book unto the excellent prince and king of noble memory, king Edward the Fourth. The said noble gentlemen instantly required me to imprint the history of the said noble king and conqueror king Arthur, and of his knights, with the history of the Saint Greal, and of the death and ending of the said Arthur; affirming that I ought rather to imprint his acts and noble feats, than of Godfrey of Boloine, or any of the other eight, considering that he was a man born within this realm, and king and emperor of the same: and that there be in French divers and many noble volumes of his acts, and also of his knights. To whom I answered that divers men hold opinion that there was no such Arthur, and that all such books as been made of him, be but feigned and fables, because that some chronicles make of him no mention, nor remember him nothing, nor of his knights. Whereto they answered, and one in special said, that in him that should say or think that there was never such a king called Arthur, might well be aretted great folly and blindness. For he said that there were many evidences of the contrary. First ye may see his sepulchre in the monastery of Glastingbury. And also in Policronicon, in the fifth book the sixth chapter, and in the seventh book the twenty-third chapter, where his body was buried, and after found, and translated into the said monastery. Ye shall see also in the history of Bochas in his book *De Casu Principum* part of his noble acts, and also of his fall. Also Galfridus, in his British book recounteth his life: and in divers places of England many remembrances be yet of him, and shall remain perpetually, and also of his knights. First in the abbey of Westminster, at St. Edward's shrine, remaineth the print of his seal in red wax closed in beryl, in which is written, *Patricius Arthurus Britannie, Gallie, Germanie, Dacie, Imperator*. Item in the castle of Dover ye may see Gawaine's scull, and Cradok's mantle: at Winchester the Round Table: in other places Launcelot's sword and many other things. Then all these things considered, there can no man reasonably gainsay but that there was a king of this land named Arthur. For in all places, Christian and heathen, he is reputed and taken for one of the nine worthy, and the first of the three Christian men. And also, he is more spoken of beyond the sea, more books made of his noble acts, than there be in England, as well in Dutch, Italian, Spanish, and Greekish, as in French. And yet of record remain in witness of him in Wales, in the town of Camelot, the great stones and the marvellous works of iron lying under the ground, and royal vaults, which divers now living have seen. Wherefore it is a marvel why he is no more renowned in his own country, save only it accordeth to the Word of God, which saith that no man is accepted for a prophet in his own country. Then all these things aforesaid alleged, I could not well deny but that there was such a noble king named Arthur, and reputed one of the nine worthy, and first and chief of the Christian men. And many noble volumes be made of him and of his noble knights in French, which I have seen and read beyond the sea, which be not had in our maternal tongue. But in Welsh be many and also in French, and some in English but no where nigh all. Wherefore, such as have late been drawn out briefly into English I have after the simple conning that God hath sent to me, under the favour and correction of all noble lords and gentlemen, enprised to imprint a book of the noble histories of the said king Arthur, and of certain of his knights, after a copy unto me delivered, which copy Sir Thomas Malorye did take out of certain books of French, and reduced it into English. And I, according to my copy, have down set it in print, to the intent that noble men may see and learn the noble acts of chivalry, the gentle and virtuous deeds that some knights used in those days, by which they came to honour, and how they that were vicious were punished and oft put to shame and rebuke; humbly beseeching all noble lords and ladies, with all other estates of what estate or degree they been of, that shall see and read in this said book and work, that they take the good and honest acts in their remembrance, and to follow the same. Wherein they shall find many joyous and pleasant histories, and noble and renowned acts of humanity, gentleness, and chivalry. For herein may be seen noble chivalry, courtesy, humanity, friendliness, hardiness, love, friendship, cowardice, murder, hate, virtue, and sin. Do after the good and leave the evil, and it shall bring you to good fame and renommee. And for to pass the time this book shall be pleasant to read in, but for to give faith and belief that all is true that is contained herein, ye be at your liberty: but all is written for our doctrine, and for to beware that we fall not to vice nor sin, but to exercise and follow virtue, by the which we may come and attain to good fame and renown in this life, and after this short and transitory life to come unto everlasting bliss in heaven; the which He grant us that reigneth in heaven, the blessed Trinity. Amen.

Then to proceed forth in this said book, the which I direct unto all noble princes, lords and ladies, gentlemen or gentlewomen, that desire to read or hear read of the noble and joyous history of the great conqueror and excellent king, King Arthur, sometime king of this noble realm, then called Britain; I, William Caxton, simple person, present this book following, which I have enprised to imprint: and treateth of the noble acts, feats of arms of chivalry, prowess, hardiness, humanity, love, courtesy, and very gentleness, with many wonderful histories and adventures. And for to understand briefly the content of this volume, I have divided it into XXI Books, and every book chaptered, as hereafter shall by God's grace follow. The First Book shall treat how Uther Pendragon gat the noble conqueror king Arthur, and containeth xxviii chapters. The Second Book treateth of Balin the noble knight, and containeth xix chapters. The Third Book treateth of the marriage of king Arthur to queen Guenever, with other matters, and containeth xv chapters. The Fourth Book, how Merlin was assotted, and of war made to king Arthur, and containeth xxix chapters. The Fifth Book treateth of the conquest of Lucius the emperor, and containeth xii chapters. The Sixth Book treateth of Sir Launcelot and Sir Lionel, and marvellous adventures, and containeth xviii chapters. The Seventh Book treateth of a noble knight called Sir Gareth, and named by Sir Kay Beaumains, and containeth xxxvi chapters. The Eighth Book treateth of the birth of Sir Tristram the noble knight, and of his acts, and containeth xli chapters. The Ninth Book treateth of a knight named by Sir Kay Le Cote male taille, and also of Sir Tristram, and containeth xliv chapters. The Tenth Book treateth of Sir Tristram, and other marvellous adventures, and containeth lxxxviii chapters. The Eleventh Book treateth of Sir Launcelot and Sir Galahad, and containeth xiv chapters. The Twelfth Book treateth of Sir Launcelot and his madness, and containeth xiv chapters. The Thirteenth Book treateth how Galahad came first to king Arthur's court, and the quest how the Sangreal was begun, and containeth xx chapters. The Fourteenth Book treateth of the quest of the Sangreal, and containeth x chapters. The Fifteenth Book treateth of Sir Launcelot, and containeth vi chapters. The Sixteenth Book treateth of Sir Bors and Sir Lionel his brother, and containeth xvii chapters. The Seventeenth Book treateth of the Sangreal, and containeth xxiii chapters. The Eighteenth Book treateth of Sir Launcelot and the queen, and containeth xxv chapters. The Nineteenth Book treateth of queen Guenever and Launcelot, and containeth xiii chapters. The Twentieth Book treateth of the piteous death of Arthur, and containeth xxii chapters. The Twenty-first Book treateth of his last departing, and how Sir Launcelot came to revenge his death, and containeth xiii chapters. The sum is twenty-one books, which contain the sum of five hundred and seven chapters, as more plainly shall follow hereafter.

The Table or Rubrysshe

of the

Content of Chapters.

Shortly of the First Book of King Arthur.

The Second Book.

𝕳ere follow the 𝕮hapters of the 𝕿hird 𝕭ook.

𝕳ere follow the 𝕮hapters of the 𝕱ourth 𝕭ook.

Of the Fifth Book the Chapters follow.

8 · CONTENTS.

Here follow the Chapters of the Sixth Book.

Here follow the Chapters of the Seventh Book.

Here follow the Chapters of the Eighth Book.

Here follow the Chapters of the Ninth Book.

Here follow the Chapters of the Tenth Book.

Here follow the Chapters of the Eleventh Book.

Here follow the Chapters of the Twelfth Book.

Here follow the Chapters of the Thirteenth Book.

Here follow the Chapters of the Fourteenth Book.

Here follow the Chapters of the Seventeenth Book.

Here follow the Chapters of the Eighteenth Book.

Here follow the Chapters of the Nineteenth Book.

Here followeth the Book of the Piteous History which is of the Morte or Death of king Arthur, and the Chapters of the Twentieth Book.

Here follow the Chapters of the Twenty=first Book.

𝔈𝔵𝔭𝔩𝔦𝔠𝔦𝔱 𝔱𝔥𝔢 𝔗𝔞𝔟𝔩𝔢.

THE BOOK OF

KING ARTHUR

AND OF HIS NOBLE

KNIGHTS OF THE ROUND TABLE.

𝕿𝖍𝖊 𝕱𝖎𝖗𝖘𝖙 𝕭𝖔𝖔𝖐 𝖔𝖋 𝕶𝖎𝖓𝖌 𝕬𝖗𝖙𝖍𝖚𝖗.

CHAP. I.

First how Uther Pendragon sent for the duke of Cornwall and Igraine his wife, and of their departing suddenly again.

IT befell in the days of Uther Pendragon, when he was king of all England, and so reigned, that there was a mighty duke in Cornwall that held war against him long time. And the duke was named the duke of Tintagil. And so by means king Uther sent for this duke, charging him to bring his wife with him, for she was called a fair lady, and a passing wise, and her name was called Igraine. So when the duke and his wife were come unto the king, by the means of great lords they were accorded both: the king liked and loved this lady well, and he made them great cheer out of measure, and desired to have had her love. But she was a passing good woman, and would not assent unto the king. And then she told the duke her husband, and said, I suppose that we were sent for that I should be dishonoured, wherefore, husband, I counsel you that we depart from hence suddenly, that we may ride all night to our own castle. And in like wise as she said so they departed, that neither the king nor none of his council were ware of their departing. All so soon as king Uther knew of their departing so suddenly, he was wonderly wroth. Then he called to him his privy council, and told them of the sudden departing of the duke and his wife. Then they advised the king to send for the duke and his wife by a great charge: and if he will not come at your summons, then may ye do your best; then have ye cause to make mighty war upon him. So that was done, and the messengers had their answers, and that was this, shortly, that neither he nor his wife would not come at him. Then was the king wonderly wroth. And then the king sent him plain word again, and bade him be ready and stuff him and garnish him, for within forty days he would fetch him out of the biggest castle that he hath. When the duke had this warning, anon he went and furnished and garnished two strong castles of his, of the which the one hight Tintagil and the other castle hight Terrabil. So his wife, dame Igraine, he put in the castle of Tintagil, and himself he put in the castle of Terrabil, the which had many issues and posterns out. Then in all haste came Uther with a great host, and laid a siege about the castle of Terrabil. And there he pight many pavilions, and there was great war made on both parties, and much people slain. Then for pure anger and for great love of fair Igraine the king Uther fell sick. So came to the king Uther Sir Ulfius, a noble knight, and asked the king why he was sick. I shall tell thee, said the king; I am sick for anger and for love of fair Igraine, that I may not be whole. Well, my lord, said Sir Ulfius, I shall seek Merlin, and he shall do you remedy that your heart shall be pleased. So Ulfius departed, and by adventure he met Merlin in a beggar's array, and there Merlin asked Ulfius whom he sought? and he said he had little ado to tell him. Well, said Merlin, I know whom thou seekest, for thou seekest Merlin; therefore seek no further, for I am he, and if king Uther will well reward me, and be sworn unto me to fulfil my desire, that shall be his honour and profit more than mine, for I shall cause him to have all his desire. All this will I undertake, said Ulfius, that there shall be nothing reasonable but thou shalt have thy desire. Well, said Merlin, he shall have his intent and desire. And therefore, said Merlin, ride on your way, for I will not be long behind.

CHAP. II.

How Uther Pendragon made war on the duke of Cornwall, and how by the means of Merlin he made the duchess his queen.

THEN Ulfius was glad, and rode on more than a pace till that he came to Uther Pendragon, and told him he had met with Merlin. Where is he? said the king. Sir, said Ulfius, he will not dwell long. Therewithal Ulfius was ware where Merlin stood at the porch of the pavilion's door. And then Merlin was bound to come to the king. When king Uther saw him he said he was welcome. Sir, said Merlin, I know all your heart every deal; so ye will be sworn unto me, as ye be a true king anointed, to fulfil my desire, ye shall have your desire. Then the king was sworn upon the four Evangelists. Sir, said Merlin, this is my desire: after ye shall win Igraine ye shall have a child by her, and when that is born that it shall be delivered to me for to nourish there as I will have it; for it shall be your worship and the child's avail, as mickle as the child is worth. I will well, said the king, as thou wilt have it. Now make you ready, said Merlin: this night shall you see Igraine in the castle of Tintagil, and ye shall be like the duke her husband, Ulfius shall be like Sir Brastias, a knight of the duke's, and I will be like a knight that hight Sir Jordanus, a knight of the duke's. But wait ye make not many questions with her nor with her men, but say you are diseased, and so hie you to bed, and rise not on the morn till I come to you, for the castle of Tintagil is but ten mile hence. So this was done as they had devised. But the duke of Tintagil espied how the king rode from the siege of Terrabil, and therefore that night he issued out of the castle at a postern, for to have distressed the king's host. And so, through his own issue, the duke himself was slain or ever the king came at the castle of Tintagil. So after the death of the duke king Uther came to the castle, more than three hours after his death; and there he found Igraine. And or day came Merlin came to the king and bade him make him ready, and so he kissed the lady Igraine and departed in all haste. But when the lady heard tell of the duke her husband, and by all record he was dead or ever king Uther came to her, then she marvelled who that might be that came to her in likeness of her lord; so she mourned privily and held her peace. Then all the barons by one assent prayed the king of accord between the lady Igraine and him. The king gave them leave, for fain would he have been accorded with her. So the king put all the trust in Ulfius to entreat between them; so, by the entreat, at the last the king and she met together. Now will we do well, said Ulfius: our king is a lusty knight and wifeless, and my lady

Igraine is a passing fair lady; it were great joy unto us all and it might please the king to make her his queen. Unto that they were all well accorded, and moved it to the king: and anon, like a lusty knight, he assented thereto with good will, and so in all haste they were married in a morning with great mirth and joy.

And king Lot of Lothian and of Orkney then wedded Margawse that was Gawaine's mother: and king Nentres of the land of Garlot wedded Elaine. All this was done at the request of king Uther. And the third sister, Morgan le Fay, was put to school in a nunnery: and there she learned so much that she was a great clerk of nigromancy. And after she was wedded to king Uriens of the land of Gore, that was Sir Ewaine's le Blanchemains father.

CHAP. III.

Of the birth of king Arthur, and of his nouriture; and of the death of king Uther Pendragon; and how Arthur was chosen king; and of wonders and marvels of a sword that was taken out of a stone by the said Arthur.

THEN the time came that the queen Igraine should bear a child. So it fell within half a year, as king Uther was with his queen, he asked her, by the faith she owed unto him, whose was the child that should be born: then was she sore abashed to give answer. Dismay you not, said the king, but tell me the truth, and I shall love you the better, by the faith of my body. Sir, said she, I shall tell you the truth. The same night that my lord was dead, the hour of his death, as his knights record, there came into my castle of Tintagil a man like my lord in speech and countenance, and two knights with him in likeness of his two knights Brastias and Jordans, and so I welcomed him as I ought to welcome my lord: and thus, as I shall answer unto God, this child was begotten. That is truth, said the king, as you say, for it was I myself that came

in the likeness, and therefore dismay you not, for I am father to the child. And there he told her all the cause how it was by Merlin's counsel. Then the Queen made great joy when she knew who was the father of her child. Soon came Merlin unto the king and said, Sir, ye must purvey you for the nourishing of your child. As thou wilt, said the king, be it. Well, said Merlin, I know a lord of yours in this land, that is a passing true man and a faithful, and he shall have the nourishing of your child, and his name is Sir Ector, and he is a lord of fair livelihood in many parts in England and Wales. And this lord, Sir Ector, let him be sent for, for to come and speak with you, and desire him yourself, as he loveth you, that he will put his own child to nourishing to another woman, and that his wife nourish yours. And when the child is born let it be delivered unto me at yonder privy postern unchristened. So like as Merlin devised it was done. And when Sir Ector was come he made affiance to the king for to nourish the child like as the king desired; and there the king granted Sir Ector great rewards. Then when the lady was delivered, the king commanded two knights and two ladies to take the child bound in a cloth of gold, and that ye deliver him to what poor man ye meet at the postern gate of the castle. So the child was delivered unto Merlin, and so he bare it forth unto Sir Ector, and made an holy man to christen him, and named him Arthur: and so Sir Ector's wife nourished him with her own breast.

Then within two years king Uther fell sick of a great malady. And in the meanwhile his enemies usurped upon him, and did a great battle upon his men, and slew many of his people. Sir, said Merlin, ye may not lie so as ye do, for ye must to the field, though ye ride on an horse-litter; for ye shall never have the better of your enemies but if your person be there, and then shall ye have the victory. So it was done as Merlin had devised, and they carried the king forth in a horse-litter with a great host towards his enemies. And at St. Albans there met with the king a great host of the North. And that day Sir Ulfius and Sir Brastias did great deeds of arms, and king Uther's men overcame the Northern battle, and slew many people, and put the remnant to flight. And then the king returned unto London, and made great joy of his victory. And then he fell passing sore sick, so that three days and three nights he was speechless ; wherefore all the barons made great sorrow, and asked Merlin what counsel were best. There is none other remedy, said Merlin, but God will have his will. But look ye all barons be before king Uther to-morn, and God and I shall make him to speak. So on the morn all the barons with Merlin came tofore the king : then Merlin said aloud unto king Uther, Sir, shall your son Arthur be king after your days, of this realm, with all the appurtenance ? Then Uther Pendragon turned him and said in hearing of them all, I give him God's blessing and mine, and bid him pray for my soul, and righteously and worshipfully that he claim the crown upon forfeiture of my blessing. And therewith he yielded up the ghost. And then was he interred as longed to a king. Wherefore the queen, fair Igraine, made great sorrow and all the barons. Then stood the realm in great jeopardy long while, for every lord that was mighty of men made him strong, and many wend to have been king. Then Merlin went to the archbishop of Canterbury, and counselled him for to send for all the lords of the realm, and all the gentlemen of arms, that they should to London come by Christmas upon pain of cursing : and for this cause—that Jesus, that was born on that night, that he would of his great mercy shew some miracle, as he was come to be king of mankind, for to shew some miracle who should be rightwise king of this realm. So the archbishop by the advice of Merlin sent for all the lords and gentlemen of arms, that they should come by Christ-

mas even unto London. And many of them made them clean of their life, that their prayer might be the more acceptable unto God. So in the greatest church of London (whether it were Paul's or not, the French book maketh no mention) all the estates were long or day in the church for to pray. And when matins and the first mass was done, there was seen in the churchyard against the high altar a great stone four square, like unto a marble stone, and in the midst thereof was like an anvil of steel a foot on high, and therein stack a fair sword naked by the point, and letters there were written in gold about the sword that said thus : Whoso pulleth out this sword of this stone and anvil is rightwise king born of all England. Then the people marvelled, and told it to the archbishop. I command, said the archbishop, that ye keep you within your church, and pray unto God still; that no man touch the sword till the high mass be all done. So when all masses were done all the lords went to behold the stone and the sword. And when they saw the scripture, some assayed—such as would have been king. But none might stir the sword nor move it. He is not here, said the archbishop, that shall achieve the sword, but doubt not God will make him known. But this is my counsel, said the archbishop, that we let purvey ten knights, men of good fame, and they to keep this sword. So it was ordained, and then there was made a cry, that every man should assay that would, for to win the sword. And upon New Year's Day the barons let make a justs and a tournament, that all knights that would just or tourney there might play: and all this was ordained for to keep the lords together and the commons, for the archbishop trusted that God would make him known that should win the sword. So upon New Year's Day when the service was done the barons rode to the field, some to just, and some to tourney; and so it happed that Sir Ector, that had great livelihood about London, rode unto the justs, and with him rode

Sir Kay his son and young Arthur that was his nourished brother, and Sir Kay was made knight at Allhallowmas afore. So as they rode to the justs-ward Sir Kay had lost his sword, for he had left it at his father's lodging, and so he prayed young Arthur to ride for his sword. I will well, said Arthur, and rode fast after the sword; and when he came home the lady and all were out to see the justing. Then was Arthur wroth, and said to himself, I will ride to the churchyard and take the sword with me that sticketh in the stone, for my brother Sir Kay shall not be without a sword this day. So when he came to the churchyard Sir Arthur alighted, and tied his horse to the stile, and so he went to the tent, and found no knights there, for they were at the justing; and so he handled the sword by the handles, and lightly and fiercely pulled it out of the stone, and took his horse and rode his way till he came to his brother Sir Kay, and delivered him the sword. And as soon as Sir Kay saw the sword he wist well it was the sword of the stone, and so he rode to his father Sir Ector, and said: Sir, lo here is the sword of the stone; wherefore I must be king of this land. When Sir Ector beheld the sword he returned again and came to the church, and there they alighted all three and went into the church, and anon he made Sir Kay to swear upon a book how he came to that sword. Sir, said Sir Kay, by my brother Arthur, for he brought it to me. How gat ye this sword? said Sir Ector to Arthur. Sir, I will tell you: when I came home for my brother's sword, I found nobody at home to deliver me his sword, and so I thought my brother Sir Kay should not be swordless, and so I came hither eagerly and pulled it out of the stone without any pain. Found ye any knights about this sword? said Sir Ector. Nay, said Arthur. Now, said Sir Ector to Arthur, I understand ye must be king of this land. Wherefore I, said Arthur, and for what cause? Sir, said Ector, for God will have it so: for there should

never man have drawn out this sword but he that shall be rightwise king of this land. Now let me see whether ye can put the sword there as it was, and pull it out again. That is no mastery, said Arthur: and so he put it into the stone. Therewith Sir Ector assayed to pull out the sword and failed.

CHAP. IV.

How king Arthur pulled out the sword divers times.

Now assay, said Sir Ector to Sir Kay. And anon he pulled at the sword with all his might, but it would not be. Now shall ye assay, said Sir Ector to Arthur. I will well, said Arthur, and pulled it out easily. And therewithal Sir Ector kneeled down to the earth, and Sir Kay. Alas, said Arthur, mine own dear father and brother, why kneel ye to me. Nay, nay, my lord Arthur, it is not so: I was never your father nor of your blood, but I wote well ye are of an higher blood than I wend ye were. And then Sir Ector told him all, how he was betaken him for to nourish him, and by whose commandment, and by Merlin's deliverance. Then Arthur made great dole when he understood that Sir Ector was not his father. Sir, said Ector unto Arthur, will ye be my good and gracious lord when ye are king? Else were I to blame, said Arthur, for ye are the man in the world that I am most beholding to, and my good lady and mother your wife, that as well as her own hath fostered me and kept. And if ever it be God's will that I be king, as ye say, ye shall desire of me what I may do, and I shall not fail you: God forbid I should fail you. Sir, said Sir Ector, I will ask no more of you but that you will make my son, your foster-brother Sir Kay, seneschal of all your lands. That shall be done, said Arthur, and more by the faith of my body, that never man shall have that office but he while he and I live. Therewithal they went unto the archbishop, and told him how the sword was achieved, and by

whom. And on Twelfth Day all the
barons came thither, and to assay to
take the sword who that would assay.
But there afore them all there might
none take it out but Arthur, wherefore
there were many lords wroth, and said
it was great shame unto them all and
the realm, to be over governed with a
boy of no high blood born. And so
they fell out at that time that it was
put off till Candlemas, and then all the
barons should meet there again. But
always the ten knights were ordained
to watch the sword day and night, and
so they set a pavilion over the stone
and the sword, and five always watched.
So at Candlemas many more great lords
came thither for to have won the sword,
but there might none prevail. And
right as Arthur did at Christmas he did
at Candlemas, and pulled out the sword
easily, whereof the barons were sore
aggrieved, and put it off in delay till the
high feast of Easter. And as Arthur
sped afore, so did he at Easter: yet
there were some of the great lords had
indignation that Arthur should be their
king, and put it off in a delay till the
feast of Pentecost. Then the archbishop of Canterbury by Merlin's providence let purvey then of the best
knights that they might get, and such
knights as king Uther Pendragon loved
best and most trusted in his days, and
such knights were put about Arthur, as
Sir Baudwin of Britain, Sir Kay, Sir
Ulfius, Sir Brastias. All these, with
many other, were always about Arthur,
day and night, till the feast of Pentecost.

CHAP. V.

*How King Arthur was crowned, and how
be made officers.*

AND at the feast of Pentecost all
manner of men assayed to pull at the
sword that would assay, but none
might prevail but Arthur; and he pulled
it out afore all the lords and commons
that were there, wherefore all the commons cried at once, We will have
Arthur unto our king; we will put him

no more in delay, for we all see that it
is God's will that he shall be our king,
and who that holdeth against it we will
slay him. And therewithal they kneeled
down all at once, both rich and poor,
and cried Arthur mercy, because they
had delayed him so long. And Arthur
forgave them, and took the sword between both his hands, and offered it upon the altar where the archbishop was,
and so was he made knight of the best
man that was there. And so anon was
the coronation made, and there was he
sworn unto his lords and the commons
for to be a true king, to stand with true
justice from thenceforth the days of this
life. Also then he made all lords that
held of the crown to come in, and to do
service as they ought to do. And many
complaints were made unto Sir Arthur
of great wrongs that were done since
the death of king Uther, of many lands
that were bereaved lords, knights,
ladies, and gentlemen. Wherefore king
Arthur made the lands to be given again
unto them that owned them. When
this was done that the king had stablished all the countries about London,
then he let make Sir Kay seneschal of
England; and Sir Baudwin of Britain
was made constable; and Sir Ulfius was
made chamberlain; and Sir 'Brastias
was made warden to wait upon the
north from Trent forwards, for it was
that time for the most part the king's
enemies. But within few years after,
Arthur won all the north, Scotland,
and all that were under their obeisance.
Also Wales, a part of it held against
Arthur, but he overcame them all as
he did the remnant through the noble
prowess of himself and his knights of
the Round Table.

CHAP. VI.

*How king Arthur held in Wales at a
Pentecost a great feast, and what kings
and lords came to his feast.*

THEN the king removed into Wales,
and let cry a great feast, that it should
be holden at Pentecost, after the incoro-
nation of him at the city of Carlion.

Unto the feast came king Lot of Lothian and of Orkney with five hundred knights with him. Also there came to the feast king Uriens of Gore with four hundred knights with him. Also there came to that feast king Nentres of Garloth with seven hundred knights with him. Also there came to the feast the king of Scotland with six hundred knights with him, and he was but a young man. Also there came to the feast a king that was called the king with the hundred knights, but he and his men was passing well beseen at all points. Also there came the king of Carados with five hundred knights. And king Arthur was glad of their coming, for he wend that all the kings and knights had come for great love, and for to have done him worship at his feast, wherefore the king made great joy, and sent the kings and knights great presents. But the kings would none receive, but rebuked the messengers shamefully, and said they had no joy to receive no gifts of a beardless boy that was come of low blood, and sent him word they would have none of his gifts, but that they were come to give him gifts with hard swords betwixt the neck and the shoulders: and therefore they came thither, so they told to the messengers plainly, for it was great shame to all them to see such a boy to have a rule of so noble a realm as this land was. With this answer the messengers departed, and told to king Arthur this answer. Wherefore, by the advice of his barons, he took him to a strong tower with five hundred good men with him : and all the kings aforesaid in a manner laid a siege tofore him, but king Arthur was well victualled. And within fifteen days there came Merlin among them into the city of Carlion. Then all the kings were passing glad of Merlin, and asked him, For what cause is that boy Arthur made your king? Sirs, said Merlin, I shall tell you the cause. For he is king Uther Pendragon's son, born in wedlock of Igraine, the duke's wife of Tintagil. After the death of the duke thirteen days king Uther Pendragon wedded fair Igraine. And

who saith nay, he shall be king, and overcome all his enemies ; and, or he die, he shall be long king of all England, and have under his obeisance Wales, Ireland, and Scotland, and more realms than I will now rehearse. Some of the kings had marvel of Merlin's words, and deemed well that it should be as he said: and some of them laughed him to scorn, as king Lot : and more other called him a witch. But then were they accorded with Merlin that king Arthur should come out and speak with the kings, and to come safe and go safe, such assurance was there made. So Merlin went unto king Arthur and told him how he had done, and bade him fear not, but come out boldly and speak with them, and spare them not, but answer them as their king and chieftain, for ye shall overcome them all whether they will or nill.

CHAP. VII.

Of the first war that king Arthur had, and how he won the field.

THEN king Arthur came out of his tower, and had under his gown a jesseraunt of double mail, and there went with him the archbishop of Canterbury, and Sir Baudwin of Britain, and Sir Kay, and Sir Brastias ; these were the men of most worship that were with him. And when they were met there was no meekness, but stout words on both sides: but always king Arthur answered them, and said that he would make them to bow and he lived. Wherefore they departed with wrath, and king Arthur bade keep them well, and they bade the king keep him well. So the king returned him to the tower again, and armed him and all his knights. What will ye do? said Merlin to the kings ; ye were better for to stint, for ye shall not here prevail though ye were ten so many. Be we well advised to be afraid of a dream-reader? said king Lot. With that Merlin vanished away, and came to king Arthur, and bade him set on them fiercely; and in the meanwhile there were three hundred good men of the best that were with the kings that went straight unto king Arthur, and that comforted him greatly. Sir, said Merlin to Arthur, fight not with the sword that ye had by miracle, till that ye see ye go unto the worse; then draw it out and do your best. So forthwithal king Arthur set upon them in their lodging. And Sir Baudwin, Sir Kay, and Sir Brastias slew on the right hand and on the left hand that it was marvellous; and always king Arthur on horseback laid on with a sword, and did marvellous deeds of arms, that many of the kings had great joy of his deeds and hardiness. Then king Lot brake out on the back side, and the king with the hundred knights, and king Carados, and set on Arthur fiercely behind him. With that Sir Arthur turned with his knights and smote behind and before, and ever Sir Arthur was in the foremost press till his horse was slain underneath him. And therewith king Lot smote down king Arthur. With that his four knights received him, and set him on horseback. Then he drew his sword Excalibur, but it was so bright in his enemies' eyes, that it gave light like thirty torches. And therewith he put them on back, and slew much people. And then the commons of Carlion arose with clubs and staves, and slew many knights; but all the kings held them together with their knights that were left alive, and so fled and departed. And Merlin came unto Arthur, and counselled him to follow them no farther.

CHAP. VIII.

How Merlin counselled king Arthur to send for king Ban and king Bors, and of their counsel taken for the war.

So after the feast and tourney king Arthur drew him unto London, and so by the counsel of Merlin the king let call his barons to council. For Merlin had told the king that the six kings that made war upon him would in all haste be awroke on him and on his lands. Wherefore the king asked counsel at them all. They could no counsel give, but said they were big enough. Ye say well, said Arthur; I thank you for your good courage; but will ye all that love me speak with Merlin: ye know well that he hath done much for me, and he knoweth many things, and when he is afore you I would that ye prayed him heartily of his best advice. All the barons said they would pray him and desire him. So Merlin was sent for, and fair desired of all the barons to give them best counsel. I shall say you, said Merlin, I warn you all, your enemies are passing strong for you, and they are good men of arms as be on live, and by this time they have gotten to them four kings more, and a mighty duke; and unless that our king have more chivalry with him than he may make within the bounds of his own realm, and he fight with them in battle he shall be overcome and slain. What were best to do in this cause? said all the barons. I shall tell you, said Merlin, mine advice: There are two brethren beyond the sea, and they be kings both, and marvellous good men of their hands; and that one hight king Ban of Benwick, and that other hight king Bors of Gaul, that is France. And on these two kings warreth a mighty man of men, the king Claudas, and striveth with them for a castle; and great war is betwixt them: but this Claudas is so mighty of goods, whereof he getteth good knights, that he putteth these two kings the most part to the worse. Wherefore this is my counsel, that our king and sovereign lord send unto the kings Ban and Bors by two trusty knights with letters well devised, that if they will come and see king Arthur and his court, and so help him in his wars, that he will be sworn unto them to help them in their wars against king Claudas. Now what say ye unto this counsel? said Merlin. This is well counselled, said the king and all the barons. Right so in all haste there were ordained to go two knights on the message unto the two kings. So were there made letters in the pleasant wise according unto king Arthur's desire. Ulfius and Brastias were made the messengers, and rode forth well horsed and well armed, and as the guise was that time, and so passed the sea and rode toward the city of Benwick. And there besides were eight knights who espied them, and at a straight passage they met with Ulfius and Brastias, and would have taken them prisoners. So they prayed them that they might pass, for they were messengers unto king Ban and Bors sent from king Arthur. Therefore, said the eight knights, ye shall die, or be prisoners, for we be knights of king Claudas. And therewith two of them dressed their spears, and Ulfius and Brastias dressed their spears, and ran together with great might, and Claudas's knights brake their spears, and theirs to-held, and bare the two knights out of their saddles to the earth, and so left them lying, and rode their ways. And the other six knights rode afore to a passage to meet with them again, and so Ulfius and Brastias smote other two down, and so passed on their ways. And at the fourth passage there met two for two, and both were laid to the earth: so there was none of the eight knights but he was sore hurt or bruised. And when they came to Benwick it fortuned there were both kings Ban and Bors. And when it was told the kings that there were come messengers, there were sent to them two knights of worship, the one hight Lionses, lord of the country of Payarne, and Sir Phariance a worshipful knight. Anon they asked from whence they came, and they said from king Arthur king of England: so they took them in their arms, and made great joy each of other. But anon as the two kings wist they were messengers of Arthur's, there was made no tarrying, but forthwith they spake with the knights and welcomed them in the faithfullest wise, and said they were most welcome unto them before all the kings living. And therewith they kissed the letters and delivered them; and when Ban and Bors understood the letters, then were they more welcome than they were before. And after the haste of the letters they gave them this answer, that they would fulfil the desire of king Arthur's writing, and let Ulfius and Brastias tarry there as long as they would, they should have such cheer as might be made them in those marches. Then Ulfius and Brastias told the king of the adventure at their passages of the eight knights. Ha, ha, said Ban and Bors, they were my good friends. I would I had wist of them, they should not have escaped so. So Ulfius and Brastias had good cheer and great gifts as much as they might bear away, and had their answer by mouth and by writing, that those two kings would come unto Arthur in all the haste that they might.

So the two knights rode on afore, and passed the sea, and came to their lord and told him how they had sped, whereof king Arthur was passing glad. At what time suppose ye the two kings will be here? Sir, said they, afore Allhallowmas. Then the king let purvey for a great feast, and let cry a great justs. And by Allhallowmas the two kings were come over the sea with three hundred knights well arrayed both for the peace and for the war. And king Arthur met with them ten mile out of London, and there was great joy as could be thought or made. And on Allhallowmas at the great feast sat in the hall the three kings, and Sir Kay the seneschal served in the hall, and Sir Lucas the butler, that was duke Corneus's son, and Sir Griflet that was the son of Cardol, these three knights had the rule of all the service that served the kings. And anon as they had washed and risen, all knights that would just made them ready. By then they were ready on horseback there were seven hundred knights. And Arthur, Ban, and Bors, with the archbishop of Canterbury, and Sir Ector, Kay's father, they were in a place covered with cloth of gold, like an hall, with ladies and gentlewomen, for to behold who did best, and thereon to give judgment.

CHAP. IX.

*Of a great tourney made by king Arthur
and the two kings Ban and Bors, and
how they went over the Sea.*

AND king Arthur and the two kings let part the seven hundred knights in two parties. And there were three hundred knights of the realm of Benwick and of Gaul turned on the other side. Then they dressed their shields, and began to couch their spears many good knights. So Griflet was the first that met with a knight, one Ladinas, and they met so eagerly that all men had wonder; and they so fought that their shields fell to pieces, and horse and man fell to the earth, and both the French knight and the English knight lay so long, that all men wend they had been dead. When Lucas the butler saw Griflet so lie, he horsed him again anon, and they two did marvellous deeds of arms with many bachelors. Also Sir Kay came out of an embushment with five knights with him, and they six smote other six down. But Sir Kay did that day marvellous deeds of arms, that there was none did so well as he that day. Then there came Ladinas and Grastian, two knights of France, and did passing well, that all men praised them. Then came there Sir Placidas, a good knight, and met with Sir Kay and smote him down, horse and man, wherefore Sir Griflet was wroth, and met with Sir Placidas so hard that horse and man fell to the earth. But when the five knights wist that Sir Kay had a fall they were wroth out of wit, and therewith each of them five bare down a knight. When king Arthur and the two kings saw them begin to wax wroth on both parts, they leapt on small hackneys, and let cry that all men should depart unto their lodging. And so they went home and unarmed them, and so to even-song and supper. And after the three kings went into a garden, and gave the prize unto Sir Kay, and to Lucas the butler, and unto Sir Griflet. And then they went unto council, and with them Gwenbaus, the brother unto Sir Ban and Bors, a wise clerk, and thither went Ulfius, and Brastias, and Merlin. And after they had been in council they went unto bed. And on the morn they heard mass, and to dinner, and so to their council, and made many arguments what were best to do. At the last they were concluded, that Merlin should go with a token of king Ban, (and that was a ring,) unto his men and king Bors's : and Gracian and Placidas should go again and keep their castles and their countries, as king Ban of Benwick and king Bors of Gaul had ordained them ; and so they passed the sea and came to Benwick. And when the people saw king Ban's ring, and Gracian and Placidas, they were glad, and asked how the kings fared, and made great joy of their welfare and according. And according unto the sovereign lords' desire, the men of war made them ready in all haste possible, so that they were fifteen thousand on horse and foot, and they had great plenty of victual with them by Merlin's provision. But Gracian and Placidas were left to furnish and garnish the castles for dread of king Claudas. Right so Merlin passed the sea, well victualled both by water and by land. And when he came to the sea he sent home the footmen again, and took no more with him but ten thousand men on horseback, the most part men of arms, and so shipped and passed the sea into England, and landed at Dover : and through the wit of Merlin he led the host northward, the priviest way that could be thought, unto the forest of Bedegraine, and there in a valley he lodged them secretly.

Then rode Merlin unto king Arthur and the two kings and told them how he had sped, whereof they had great marvel, that man on earth might speed so soon, and go and come. So Merlin told them ten thousand were in the forest of Bedegraine, well armed at all points. Then was there no more to say, but to horseback went all the host as Arthur had afore purveyed. So with twenty thousand he passed by night and day. But there was made such an ordinance afore by Merlin, that there should no man of war ride nor go in no country on this side Trent water, but if he had a token from king Arthur, where through the king's enemies durst not ride, as they did tofore, to espy.

CHAP. X.

How eleven kings gathered a great host against king Arthur.

AND so within a little space the three kings came unto the castle of Bedegraine, and found there a passing fair fellowship and well beseen, whereof they had great joy, and victual they wanted none.

This was the cause of the northern host: that they were reared for the despite and rebuke that the six kings had at Carlion. And those six kings by their means gat unto them five other kings, and thus they began to gather their people, and how they sware that for weal nor woe they should not leave each other till they had destroyed Arthur. And then they made an oath. The first that began the oath was the duke of Cambenet, that he would bring with him five thousand men of arms, the which were ready on horseback. Then sware king Brandegoris of Stranggore that he would bring five thousand men of arms on horseback. Then sware king Clariance of Northumberland that he would bring three thousand men of arms. Then sware the king of the hundred knights, that was a passing good man and a young, that he would bring four thousand men on horseback. Then there sware king Lot, a passing good knight and Sir Gawaine's father, that he would bring five thousand men of arms on horseback. Also there sware king Urience, that was Sir Uwaine's father, of the land of Gore, and he would bring six thousand men of arms on horseback. Also there sware king Idres of Cornwall, that he would bring

five thousand men of arms on horseback. Also there swore king Cradelmas to bring five thousand men of arms on horseback. Also there swore king Agwisance of Ireland, to bring five thousand men of arms on horseback. Also there swore king Nentres to bring five thousand men of arms on horseback. Also there swore king Carados to bring five thousand men of arms on horseback. So their whole host was of clean men of arms on horseback fifty thousand; and afoot ten thousand of good mens' bodies. Then were they soon ready and mounted upon horse, and sent forth their fore-riders: for these eleven kings in their way laid siege unto the castle of Bedegraine; and so they departed and drew toward Arthur, and left few to abide at the siege, for the castle of Bedegraine was holden of king Arthur, and the men that were therein were Arthur's.

CHAP XI.

Of a dream of the king with the hundred knights.

So by Merlin's advice there were sent fore-riders to skim the country, and they met with the fore-riders of the north, and made them to tell which way the host came, and then they told it to Arthur, and by king Ban and Bors's counsel they let burn and destroy all the country afore them where they should ride.

The king with the hundred knights dreamed a wonder dream two nights afore the battle, that there blew a great wind, and blew down their castles and their towns, and after that came a water and bare it all away. All that heard of the dream said it was a token of great battle. Then, by counsel of Merlin, when they wist which way the eleven kings would ride and lodge that night, at midnight they set upon them, as they were in their pavilions. But the scout-watch by their host cried, Lords! at arms! for here be your enemies at your hand!

CHAP. XII.

How the eleven kings with their host fought against Arthur and his host, and many great feats of the war.

THEN king Arthur and king Ban and king Bors, with their good and trusty knights, set on them so fiercely that they made them overthrow their pavilions on their heads; but the eleven kings by manly prowess of arms took a fair field. But there was slain that morrow tide ten thousand good men's bodies. And so they had afore them a strong passage, yet were they fifty thousand of hardy men. Then it drew toward day. Now shall ye do by mine advice, said Merlin unto the three kings: I would that king Ban and king Bors with their fellowship of ten thousand men were put in a wood here beside in an embushment, and keep them privy, and that they be laid or the light of the day come, and that they stir nor till ye and your knights have fought with them long: and when it is daylight dress your battle even afore them and the passage, that they may see all your host, for then they will be the more hardy when they see you but about twenty thousand, and be the gladder to suffer you and your host to come over the passage. All the three kings and the whole barons said that Merlin said passingly well, and it was done anon as Merlin had devised. So on the morn, when either host saw other, the host of the north was well comforted. Then to Ulfius and Brastias were delivered three thousand men of arms, and they set on them fiercely in the passage, and slew on the right hand and on the left hand, that it was wonder to tell. When that the eleven knights saw that there was so few a fellowship did such deeds of arms, they were ashamed, and set on them again fiercely, and there was Sir Ulfius's horse slain under him, but he did marvellously well on foot. But the duke Eustace of Cambenet, and king Clariance of Northumberland, were alway grievous on Sir Ulfius. When Brastias saw his fellow fared so withal, he smote the duke with a spear, that horse and man fell down. That saw king Clariance, and returned to Brastias, and either smote other so that horse and man went to the earth, and so they lay long astonied, and their horses' knees brast to the hard bone. Then came Sir Kay the seneschal with six fellows with him, and did passing well. With that came the eleven kings, and there was Griflet put to the earth, horse and man, and Lucas the butler, horse and man, by king Brandegoris and king Idres and king Agwisance. Then waxed the meddle passing hard on both parties. When Sir Kay saw Griflet on foot he rode on king Nentres and smote him down, and led his horse to Sir Griflet and horsed him again. Also Sir Kay with the same spear smote down king Lot, and hurt him passing sore. That saw the king with the hundred knights, and ran unto Sir Kay and smote him down and took his horse, and gave him to king Lot, whereof he said gramercy. When Sir Griflet saw Sir Kay and Lucas the butler on foot, he took a sharp spear great and square and rode to Pinel, a good man of arms, and smote horse and man down, and then he took his horse and gave him unto Sir Kay. When king Lot saw king Nentres on foot he ran unto Melot de la Roche and smote him down horse and man, and gave king Nentres the horse and horsed him again. Also the king of the hundred knights saw king Idres on foot; then he ran unto Gwimiart de Bloi, and smote him down horse and man, and gave king Idres the horse and horsed him again; and king Lot smote down Clariance de la Forest Savage, and gave the horse unto duke Eustace. And so when they had horsed the kings again they drew them all eleven kings together, and said they would be revenged of the damage they had taken that day. The meanwhile came in Sir Ector with an eager countenance, and found Ulfius and Brastias on foot in great peril of death, that were foul bruised under the horse feet. Then king Arthur as a lion ran unto king Cradelment of North Wales, and smote him through the left side, that the horse and the king fell down; and then he took the horse by the rein and led him unto Ulfius, and said, Have this horse, mine old friend, for great need hast thou of horse. Gramercy, said Ulfius. Then Sir Arthur did so marvellously in arms that all men had wonder. When the king with the hundred knights saw king Cradelment on foot he ran unto Sir Ector, that was well horsed, Sir Kay's father, and smote horse and man down, and gave the horse unto the king and horsed him again. And when king Arthur saw the king ride on Sir Ector's horse he was wroth, and with his sword he smote the king on the helm, that a quarter of the helm and shield fell down, and the sword carved down unto the horse's neck, and so the king and the horse fell down to the ground. Then Sir Kay came to Sir Morganore, seneschal with the king of the hundred knights, and smote him down horse and man, and led the horse unto his father Sir Ector: then Sir Ector ran unto a knight, hight Lardans, and smote horse and man down, and led the horse unto Sir Brastias that great need had of an horse, and was greatly bruised. When Brastias beheld Lucas the butler, that lay like a dead man under the horse feet, and ever Sir Griflet did marvellously for to rescue him, and there were always fourteen knights on Sir Lucas, then Brastias smote one of them on the helm that it went to the teeth, and he rode to another and smote him that the arm flew into the field. Then he went to the third, and smote him on the shoulder that shoulder and arm flew in the field. And when Griflet saw rescues he smote a knight on the temples, that head and helm went to the earth, and Griflet took the horse of that knight and led him unto Sir Lucas, and bad him mount upon the horse and revenge his hurts. For Brastias had slain a knight tofore, and horsed Griflet.

CHAP. XIII.

Yet of the same battle.

THEN Lucas saw king Agwisance, that late had slain Moris de la Roche, and Lucas ran to him with a short spear that was great, that he gave him such a fall that the horse fell down to the earth. Also Lucas found there on foot Bloias de la Flandres and Sir Gwinas, two hardy knights, and in that woodness that Lucas was in he slew two bachelors, and horsed them again. Then waxed the battle passing hard on both parties, but Arthur was glad that his knights were horsed again, and then they fought together that the noise and sound rang by the water and the wood. Wherefore king Ban and king Bors made them ready and dressed their shields and harness, and they were so courageous that many knights shook and trembled for eagerness. All this while Lucas, and Gwinas, and Briant, and Bellias of Flanders, held strong meddle against six kings, that was king Lot, king Nentres, king Brandegoris, king Idres, king Uriens, and king Agwisance. So with the help of Sir Kay and of Sir Griflet they held these six kings hard, that unneth they had any power to defend them. But when Sir Arthur saw the battle would not be ended by no manner he fared wood as a lion, and steered his horse here and there, on the right hand and on the left hand, that he stinted not till he had slain twenty knights. Also he wounded king Lot sore on the shoulder, and made him to leave that ground, for Sir Kay and Griflet did with king Arthur there great deeds of arms. Then Ulfius, Brastias, and Sir Ector, encountered against the duke Eustace, and king Cradelment, and king Cradelmas, and king Clariance of Northumberland, and king Carados, and against the king with the hundred knights. So these knights encountered with these kings that they made them to avoid the ground. Then king Lot made great dole for his damages and his fellows, and said unto the eleven kings, But if ye will do as I devise we shall be slain and destroyed : let me have the king with the hundred knights, and king Agwisance, and king Idres, and the duke of Cambenet, and we five kings will have fifteen thousand men of arms with us, and we will go apart while ye six kings hold the meddle with twelve thousand, and when we see that ye have foughten with them long then will we come on fiercely, and else shall we never match them, said king Lot, but by this mean. So they departed as they here devised, and six kings made their party strong against Arthur, and made great war long. In the meanwhile brake the embushment of king Ban and Bors, and Lionses and Phariance had the advant guard, and they two knights met with king Idres and his fellowship, and there began a great meddle of breaking of spears and smiting of swords with slaying of men and horses, and king Idres was near at discomfiture.

That saw Agwisance the king, and put Lionses and Phariance in point of death : for the duke of Cambenet came on withal with a great fellowship, so these two knights were in great danger of their lives that they were fain to return, but always they rescued themselves and their fellowship marvellously. When king Bors saw those knights put aback it grieved him sore ; then he came on so fast that his fellowship seemed as black as Inde. When king Lot had espied king Bors he knew him well ; then he said, O defend us from death and horrible maims, for I see well we be in great peril of death ; for I see yonder a king, one of the most worshipfulest men, and one of the best knights of the world, is inclined unto his fellowship. What is he? said the king with the hundred knights. It is, said king Lot, king Bors of Gaul ; I marvel how they came into this country without witting of us all. It was by Merlin's advice, said the knight. As for him, said king Carados, I will encounter with king Bors, if ye will rescue me when need is. Go on, said they all, we

will do all that we may. Then king Carados and his host rode on a soft pace till that they came as nigh king Bors as a bow draught : then either battle let their horses run as fast as they might. And Bleoberis that was god-son unto king Bors he bare his chief standard, that was a passing good knight. Now shall we see, said king Bors, how these northern Britons can bear their arms. And king Bors encountered with a knight, and smote him throughout with a spear that he fell dead unto the earth, and after drew his sword and did marvellous deeds of arms, that all parties had great wonder thereof ; and his knights failed not but did their part, and king Carados was smitten to the earth. With that came the king with the hundred knights and rescued king Carados mightily by force of arms, for he was a passing good knight of a king, and but a young man.

CHAP. XIV.
Yet more of the same battle.

By then came into field king Ban as fierce as a lion, with bands of green and thereupon gold. Ha, ha, said king Lot, we must be discomfited, for yonder I see the most valiant knight of the world, and the man of the most renown : for such two brethren as is king Ban and king Bors are not living, wherefore we must needs void or die ; and but if we avoid manly and wisely there is but death. When king Ban came into the battle, he came in so fiercely that the strokes resounded again from the wood and the water ; wherefore king Lot wept for pity and dole that he saw so many good knights take their end. But through the great force of king Ban they made both the northern battles that were parted to hurtle together for great dread, and the three kings with their knights slew on ever, that it was pity to behold that multitude of the people that fled. But king Lot and the king of the hundred knights and king Morganore gathered the people together passing knightly, and did great prowess of arms, and held the battle all that day like hard. When the king of the hundred knights beheld the great damage that king Ban did, he thrust unto him with his horse, and smote him on high upon the helm a great stroke, and astonied him sore. Then king Ban was wroth with him, and followed on him fiercely: the other saw that, and cast up his shield and spurred his horse forward, but the stroke of king Ban fell down and carved a cantel of the shield, and the sword slid down by the hauberk behind his back, and cut through the trapping of steel, and the horse even in two pieces, that the sword felt the earth. Then the king of the hundred knights voided the horse lightly, and with his sword he broched the horse of king Ban through and through. With that king Ban voided lightly from the dead horse, and then king Ban smote at the other so eagerly and smote him on the helm, that he fell to the earth. Also in that ire he felled king Morganore, and there was great slaughter of good knights and much people. By then came into the press king Arthur, and found king Ban standing among dead men and dead horses, fighting on foot as a wood lion, that there came none nigh him as far as he might reach with his sword but that he caught a grievous buffet; whereof king Arthur had great pity. And Arthur was so bloody that by his shield there might no man know him, for all was blood and brains on his sword. And as Arthur looked by him he saw a knight that was passing well horsed, and therewith Sir Arthur ran to him and smote him on the helm that his sword went unto his teeth, and the knight sank down to the earth dead, and anon Arthur took the horse by the rein and led him unto king Ban, and said, Fair brother have this horse, for ye have great need thereof, and me repenteth sore of your great damage. It shall be soon revenged, said king Ban, for I trust mine use is not such but some of them may sore repent this. I will well, said Arthur, for I see your deeds full actual; nevertheless, I might

not come at you at that time. But when king Ban was mounted on horseback, then there began new battle the which was sore and hard, and passing great slaughter. And so through great force king Arthur, and king Ban, and king Bors made their knights a little to withdraw them. But always the eleven kings with their chivalry never turned back, and so withdrew them to a little wood, and so over a little river, and there they rested them, for on the night they might have no rest in the field. And then the eleven kings and knights put them on a heap all together, as men adread and out of all comfort. But there was no man might pass them, they held them so hard together, both behind and before, that king Arthur had marvel of their deeds of arms, and was passing wroth. Ah, Sir Arthur, said king Ban and king Bors, blame them not, for they do as good men ought to do. For by my faith, said king Ban, they are the best fighting men and knights of most prowess that ever I saw or heard speak of, and those eleven kings are men of great worship, and if they were belonging unto you there were no king under the heaven had such eleven knights, and of such worship. I may not love them, said Arthur, they would destroy me. That wot we well, said king Ban and king Bors, for they are your mortal enemies, and that hath been proved aforehand, and this day they have done their part, and that is great pity of their wilfulness.

Then all the eleven kings drew them together, and then said king Lot: Lords, ye must other ways than ye do, or else the great loss is behind: ye may see what people we have lost, and what good men we lose, because we wait always upon these footmen, and ever in saving of one of the footmen we lose ten horsemen for him; therefore this is mine advice, let us put our footmen from us, for it is near night, for the noble Arthur will not tarry on the footmen, for they may save themselves, the wood is near hand. And when we horsemen be together, look every each of you kings let make such ordinance that none break upon pain of death. And who that seeth any man dress him to flee, lightly that he be slain, for it is better that we slay a coward than through a coward all we to be slain. How say ye? said king Lot, answer me, all ye kings. It is well said, quoth king Nentres; so said the king of the hundred knights; the same said the king Carados, and king Uriens; so did king Idres, and king Brandegoris; and so did king Cradelmas, and the duke of Cambenet; the same said king Clariance, and king Agwisance;—and sware they would never fail other, neither for life nor for death. And whoso that fled, but did as they did, should be slain. Then they amended their harness, and righted their shields, and took new spears and set them on their thighs, and stood still as it had been a plump of wood.

CHAP. XV.

Yet more of the said battle, and how it was ended by Merlin.

WHEN Sir Arthur and King Ban and Bors beheld them and all their knights, they praised them much for their noble cheer of chivalry, for the hardiest fighters that ever they heard or saw. With that there dressed them a forty noble knights, and said unto the three kings they would break their battle: these were their names: Lionses, Phariance, Ulfius, Brastias, Ector, Kay, Lucas the butler, Griflet la Fise de Dieu, Mariet de la Roche, Guynas de Bloy, Briant de la Forest Savage, Bellaus, Morians of the Castle of Maidens, Flannedrius of the Castle of Ladies, Annecians that was king Bors's godson, a noble knight, Ladinas de la Rouse, Emerause, Caulas, and Graciens le Castlein, one Bloise de la Case, and Sir Colgrevaunce de Gorre. All these knights rode on afore with spears on their thighs, and spurred their horses mightily as the horses might run. And the eleven kings with part of their knights rushed with their horses as fast as they might with their spears, and

there they did on both parties marvellous deeds of arms. So came into the thick of the press Arthur, Ban, and Bors, and slew down right on both hands, that their horses went in blood up to the fetlocks. But ever the eleven kings and their host were ever in the visage of Arthur. Wherefore Ban and Bors had great marvel, considering the great slaughter that there was, but at the last they were driven aback over a little river. With that came Merlin on a great black horse, and said unto Arthur: Thou hast never done: hast thou not done enough? of three-score thousand this day hast thou left on live but fifteen thousand, and it is time to say Ho! For God is wroth with thee that thou wilt never have done, for yonder eleven kings at this time will not be overthrown, but and thou tarry on them any longer thy fortune will turn and they shall increase. And therefore withdraw you unto your lodging, and rest you as soon as ye may, and reward your good knights with gold and with silver, for they have well deserved it; there may no riches be too dear for them, for of so few men as ye have there were never men did more of prowess than they have done to day, for ye have matched this day with the best fighters of the world. That is truth, said king Ban and Bors. Also said Merlin, withdraw you where ye list, for this three year I dare undertake they shall not dare you; and by then ye shall hear new tidings. And then Merlin said unto Arthur: These eleven kings have more on hand than they are ware of, for the Saracens are landed in their countries, more than forty thousand that burn and slay, and have laid siege at the castle Wandesborow, and made great destruction; therefore dread you not this three year. Also Sir, all the goods that be gotten at this battle let it be searched: and when ye have it in your hands let it be given freely unto these two kings, Ban and Bors, that they may reward their knights withal; and that shall cause strangers to be of better will to do you service at need. Also ye be able to reward your own knights of your own goods whensoever it liketh you. It is well said, quoth Arthur, and as thou hast devised so shall it be done. When it was delivered to Ban and Bors, they gave the goods as freely to their knights as it was given them.

Then Merlin took his leave of Arthur and of the two kings, for to go and see his master Bleise that dwelt in Northumberland, and so he departed and came to his master, that was passing glad of his coming. And there he told how Arthur and the two kings had sped at the great battle, and how it was ended, and told the names of every king and knight of worship that was there. And so Bleise wrote the battle, word by word, as Merlin told him, how it began, and by whom, and in likewise how it was ended, and who had the worse. All the battles that were done in Arthur's days Merlin did his master Bleise do write. Also, he did do write all the battles that every worthy knight did of Arthur's court. After this Merlin departed from his master and came to king Arthur, that was in the castle of Bedegraine, that was one of the castles that stood in the forest of Sherwood. And Merlin was so disguised that king Arthur knew him not, for he was all befurred in black sheepskins, and a great pair of boots, and a bow and arrows, in a russet gown, and brought wild geese in his hand, and it was on the morn after Candlemas Day, but king Arthur knew him not. Sir, said Merlin unto the king, will ye give me a gift? Wherefore said king Arthur should I give thee a gift, churl? Sir, said Merlin, ye were better to give me a gift that is not in your hand, than to lose great riches; for here, in the same place where the great battle was, is great treasure hid in the earth. Who told thee so, churl? said Arthur. Merlin told me so, said he. Then Ulfius and Brastias knew him well enough, and smiled. Sir, said these two knights, it is Merlin that so speaketh unto you. Then king Arthur was greatly abashed, and had marvel of Merlin, and

so had king Ban and king Bors, and so they had great disport at him.

So, in the mean while, there came a damsel which was an earl's daughter, and his name was Sanam, and her name was Lionors, a passing fair damsel, and so she came thither for to do homage, as other lords did after the great battle. And king Arthur set his love greatly upon her, and so did she upon him, and she bare a child and his name was Borre, that was after a good knight, and of the Table Round. Then there came word that the king Rience of North Wales made great war upon king Leodegrance of Cameliard, for the which thing Arthur was wroth, for he loved him well and hated king Rience, for he was always against him. So by ordinance of the three kings that was sent home to Benwick, all they would depart for dread of king Claudas; Phariance, and Antemes, and Gratian, and Lionses of Payarne, with the leaders of those that should keep the kings' lands.

CHAP. XVI.

How king Arthur, king Ban, and king Bors rescued king Leodegrance, and other incidents.

AND then king Arthur and king Ban and king Bors departed with their fellowship, a twenty thousand, and came within six days into the country of Cameliard, and there rescued king Leodegrance and slew there much people of king Rience unto the number of ten thousand men, and put him to flight. And then had these three kings great cheer of king Leodegrance that thanked them of their great goodness, that they would revenge him of his enemies. And there had Arthur the first sight of Guenever, the king's daughter of Cameliard, and ever after he loved her. After they were wedded, as it telleth in the book. So, briefly to make an end, they took their leave to go into their own countries, for king Claudas did great destruction on their lands. Then said Arthur, I will go with you. Nay, said the kings, ye shall not at this time, for ye have much to do yet in these lands, therefore we will depart, and with the great goods that we have gotten in these lands by your gifts, we shall wage good knights, and withstand the king Claudas's malice, for, by the grace of God, and we have need we will send to you for your succour; and if ye have need, send for us, and we will not tarry, by the faith of our bodies. It shall not, said Merlin, need that these two kings come again in the way of war: but I know well king Arthur may not be long from you, for within a year or two ye shall have great need, and then shall he revenge you on your enemies, as ye have done on his. For these eleven kings shall die all in a day, by the great might and prowess of arms of two valiant knights (as it telleth after) their names being Balin le Savage, and Balan his brother, which be marvellous good knights as be any living.

Now turn we to the eleven kings, that returned unto a city that hight Sorhaute, the which city was within king Uriens, and there they refreshed them as well as they might, and made leeches search their wounds, and sorrowed greatly for the death of their people. With that there came a messager and told how there was come into their lands people that were lawless as well as Saracens a forty thousand, and have burnt and slain all the people that they may come by without mercy and have laid siege on the castle of Wandesborow. Alas! said the eleven kings, here is sorrow on sorrow, and if we had not warred against Arthur as we had done, he would soon revenge us: as for king Leodegrance, he loveth king Arthur better than us, and as for king Rience he hath enough to do with king Leodegrance, for he hath laid siege unto him. So they consented together to keep all the marches of Cornwall, of Wales, and of the North. So first they put king Idres in the city of Nauntes in Britain with four thousand men of arms, to watch both the water and the land. Also they put in the city of Windesan king Nentres of Garlot with four thousand knights, to watch

both on water and on land. Also they had of other men of war more than eight thousand, for to fortify all the fortresses in the marches of Cornwall. Also they put more knights in all the marches of Wales and Scotland with many good men of arms. And so they kept them together the space of three years, and ever allied them with mighty kings, and dukes, and lords. And to them fell king Rience of North Wales, the which was a mighty man of men, and Nero that was a mighty man of men. And all this while they furnished them and garnished them of good men of arms and victual, and of all manner of habiliment that pretendeth to the war, to avenge them for the battle of Bedegraine, as it telleth in the book of adventures following.

CHAP. XVII.

How king Arthur rode to Carlion, and of his dream, and how he saw the questing beast.

THEN after the departing of king Ban and of king Bors king Arthur rode unto Carlion. And thither came to him Lot's wife of Orkney, in manner of a messenger, but she was sent thither to espy the court of king Arthur; and she came richly beseen with her four sons, Gawaine, Gaheris, Agravaine, and Gareth, with many other knights and ladies, and she was a passing fair lady; wherefore the king cast great love unto her, and they were agreed, and she was his sister, on the mother side Igraine. So there she rested her a month, and at the last departed. Then the king dreamed a marvellous dream whereof he was sore adread. But all this time king Arthur knew not that king Lot's wife was his sister. Thus was the dream of Arthur. Him thought that there was come into this land griffons and serpents, and him thought they burnt and slew all the people in the land, and then him thought he fought with them, and they did him passing great harm and wounded him full sore, but at the last he slew them. When the king awaked he was passing heavy of his dream, and so to put it out of thoughts he made him ready with many knights to ride on hunting. As soon as he was in the forest the king saw a great hart afore him. This hart will I chase, said king Arthur, and so he spurred the horse and rode after long, and so by fine force oft he was like to have smitten the hart, till the king had chased the hart so long that his horse had lost his breath, and fell down dead. Then a yeoman fetched the king another horse. So the king saw the hart embushed and his horse dead; he sat him down by a fountain, and there he fell in great thoughts; and as he sat so him thought he heard a noise of hounds, to the sum of thirty. And with that the king saw coming toward him the strangest beast that ever he saw or heard of; so the beast went to the well and drank, and the noise was in the beast's belly like unto the questing of thirty couple hounds; but all the while the beast drank there was no noise in the beast's belly, and therewith the beast departed with a great noise, whereof the king had great marvel. And so he was in great thought, and therewith he fell on sleep. Right so there came a knight afoot unto Arthur, and said, Knight, full of thought and sleepy, tell me if thou sawest a strange beast pass this way. Such one saw I, said king Arthur, that is past two miles: what would you with the beast? said Arthur. Sir, I have followed that beast long time, and have killed my horse; so would I had another to follow my quest. Right so came one with the king's horse, and when the knight saw the horse he prayed the king to give him the horse, For I have followed this quest this twelvemonth, and either I shall achieve him or bleed of the best blood of my body. Pellinore that time king followed the questing beast, and after his death Sir Palomides followed it.

CHAP. XVIII.

How king Pellinore took Arthur's horse and followed the questing beast, and how Merlin met with Arthur.

SIR knight, said the king, leave that quest and suffer me to have it, and I will follow it another twelve month. Ah fool, said the knight unto Arthur, it is in vain thy desire, for it shall never be achieved but by me, or my next kin. Therewith he stert unto the king's horse, and mounted into the saddle, and said, Gramercy, this horse is mine own. Well, said the king, thou mayest take my horse by force, but and I might prove thee whether thou wert better on horseback or I. Well, said the knight, seek me here when thou wilt, and here nigh this well thou shalt find me; and so passed on his way. Then the king sat in a study, and bad his men fetch his horse as fast as ever they might. Right so came by him Merlin like a child of fourteen year of age, and saluted the king, and asked him why he was so pensive? I may well be pensive, said the king, for I have seen the marvellest sight that ever I saw. That know I well, said Merlin, as well as thyself, and of all thy thoughts; but thou art but a fool to take thought, for it will not amend thee. Also I know what thou art, and who was thy father, and of whom thou wert born; king Uther Pendragon was thy father, and had thee of Igraine. That is false, said king Arthur; how shouldest thou know it? for thou art not so old of years to know my father. Yes, said Merlin, I know it better than ye or any man living. I will not believe thee, said Arthur, and was wroth with the child. So departed Merlin; and came again in the likeness of an old man of fourscore years of age, whereof the king was right glad, for he seemed to be right wise.

Then said the old man, Why are ye so sad? I may well be heavy, said Arthur, for many things. Also here was a child, and told me many things that me seemeth he should not know, for he was not of age to know my father. Yes, said the old man, the child told you truth, and more would he have told you and ye would have suffered him. But ye have done a thing late that God is displeased with you, and your sister shall have a child that shall destroy you and all the knights of your realm. What are ye, said Arthur, that tell me these tidings? I am Merlin, and I was he in the child's likeness. Ah, said king Arthur, ye are a marvellous man, but I marvel much of thy words that I must die in battle. Marvel not, said Merlin, for it is God's will your body to be punished for your foul deeds. But I may well be sorry, said Merlin, for I shall die a shameful death, to be put in the earth quick, and ye shall die a worshipful death. And as they talked this, came one with the king's horse, and so the king mounted on his horse and Merlin on another, and so rode unto Carlion. And anon the king asked Ector and Ulfius how he was born. And they told him that Uther Pendragon was his father, and queen Igraine his mother: then he said to Merlin, I will that my mother be sent for, that I may speak with her, and if she say so herself, then will I believe it. In all haste the queen was sent for, and she came and brought with her Morgan le Fay her daughter, that was as fair a lady as any might be. And the king welcomed Igraine in the best manner.

CHAP. XIX.

How Ulfius appeached queen Igraine, Arthur's mother, of treason: and how a knight came and desired to have the death of his master revenged.

RIGHT so came Ulfius and said openly, that the king and all might hear that were feasted that day, Ye are the falsest lady of the world, and the most traitress unto the king's person. Beware, said Arthur, what thou sayest; thou speakest a great word. I am well ware, said Sir Ulfius, what I speak, and here is my glove to prove it upon any man that will say the contrary, that this queen Igraine is causer of your great damage, and of your great war. For, and she would have uttered it in the life of king Uther Pendragon of the birth of you, ye had never had half the

mortal wars that ye have had: for the most part of your barons of your realm knew never whose son ye were, nor of whom ye were born. And she that bear you should have made it known openly in excusing of her worship and yours, and in likewise to all the realm; wherefore I prove her false to God and to you and to all your realm, and who will say the contrary I will prove it upon his body.

Then spake Igraine and said, I am a woman, and I may not fight, but rather than I should be dishonoured there would some good man take my quarrel. More she said, Merlin knoweth well, and ye Sir Ulfius, how king Uther came to me in the castle of Tintagel, in the likeness of my lord that was dead three hours tofore. And after my lord was dead king Uther wedded me, and by his commandment when the child was born it was delivered unto Merlin, and nourished by him, and so I saw the child never after, nor wot not what is his name, for I knew him never yet. And there Ulfius said to the queen, Merlin is more to blame than ye. Well I wot, said the queen, that I bare a child by my lord king Uther, but I wot not where he is become. Then Merlin took the king by the hand, saying, This is your mother. And therewith Sir Ector bare witness how he nourished him by Uther's commandment. And, therewith king Arthur took his mother queen Igraine in his arms and kissed her and either wept upon other. And then the king let make a feast that lasted eight days. Then on a day there came into the court a squire on horseback, leading a knight before him wounded to the death, and told him how there was a knight in the forest had reared up a pavilion by a well, and hath slain my master, a good knight, his name was Miles; wherefore I beseech you that my master may be buried, and that some knight may revenge my master's death. Then the noise was great of that knight's death in the court, and every man said his advice: then came Griflet that was but a squire, and he was but young, of the age of king Arthur; so he besought the king for all his service that he had done him to give him the order of knighthood.

CHAP. XX.

How Griflet was made knight, and justed with a knight.

THOU art full young and tender of age, said Arthur, for to take so high an order on thee. Sir, said Griflet, I beseech you make me knight. Sir, said Merlin, it were great pity to lose Griflet, for he will be a passing good man when he is of age, abiding with you the term of his life. And if he adventure his body with yonder knight at the fountain it is in great peril if ever he come again, for he is one of the best knights of the world, and the strongest man of arms. Well, said king Arthur. So at the desire of Griflet the king made him knight. Now, said Arthur unto Sir Griflet, since I have made you knight, thou must give me a gift. What ye will, said Griflet. Thou shalt promise me by the faith of thy body, when thou hast justed with the knight at the fountain, whether it fall ye be on foot or on horseback, that right so ye shall come again unto me without making any more debate. I will promise you, said Griflet, as you desire. Then took Griflet his horse in great haste, and dressed his shield, and took a spear in his hand, and so he rode a great wallop till he came to the fountain, and thereby he saw a rich pavilion, and thereby under a cloth stood a fair horse well saddled and bridled, and on a tree a shield of divers colours, and a great spear. Then Griflet smote on the shield with the butt of his spear that the shield fell down to the ground. With that the knight came out of the pavilion and said, Fair knight, why smote ye down my shield? For I will just with you, said Griflet. It is better ye do not, said the knight, for ye are but young, and late made knight, and your might is nothing to mine. As for

that, said Griflet, I will just with you. That is me loth, said the knight, but since I must needs I will dress me thereto: of whence be ye? said the knight. Sir, I am of Arthur's court. So the two knights ran together, that Griflet's spear all to-shivered, and therewithal he smote Griflet through the shield and the left side, and brake the spear, that the truncheon stack in his body, that horse and knight fell down.

CHAP. XXI.

How twelve knights came from Rome and asked truage for this land of Arthur, and how Arthur fought with a knight.

WHEN the knight saw him lie so on the ground he alighted, and was passing heavy, for he wend he had slain him, and then he unlaced his helm and gat him wind, and so with the truncheon he set him on his horse and gat him wind, and so betook him to God, and said he had a mighty heart, and if he might live he would prove a passing good knight. And so Sir Griflet rode to the court, where great dole was made for him. But through good leeches he was healed and saved.

Right so came into the court twelve knights, and were aged men, and they came from the emperor of Rome, and they asked of Arthur truage for this realm, other else the emperor would destroy him and his land. Well, said king Arthur, ye are messagers, therefore may ye say what ye will, other else ye should die therefore. But this is mine answer; I owe the emperor no truage, nor none will I hold him; but on a fair field I shall give him my truage, that shall be with a sharp spear or else with a sharp sword, and that shall not be long, by my father's soul, Uther Pendragon. And therewith the messagers departed passingly wroth, and king Arthur as wroth, for in evil time came they then, for the king was passingly wroth for the hurt of Sir Griflet. And so he commanded a privyman of his chamber, that or it be day his best horse and armour, with all that belongeth unto his person, be without the city or to-morrow day. Right so, or to-morrow day, he met with his man and his horse, and so mounted up, and dressed his shield, and took his spear, and bade his chamberlain tarry there till he came again.

And so Arthur rode a soft pace till it was day, and then was he aware of three churls chasing Merlin, and would have slain him. Then the king rode unto them and bade them, Flee churls! Then were they afeard when they saw a knight, and fled. O Merlin, said Arthur, here haddest thou been slain for all thy crafts, had I not been. Nay, said Merlin, not so, for I could save myself an I would, and thou art more near thy death than I am, for thou goest to the death-ward, and God be not thy friend. So as they went thus talking they came to the fountain, and the rich pavilion there by it. Then king Arthur was ware where sat a knight armed in a chair. Sir knight, said Arthur, for what cause abidest thou here, that there may no knight ride this way but if he just with thee, said the king: I rede thee leave that custom, said Arthur. This custom, said the knight, have I used and will use maugre who saith nay; and who is grieved with my custom let him amend it that will. I will amend it, said Arthur. I shall defend thee, said the knight. Anon he took his horse, and dressed his shield, and took a spear, and they met so hard either in other's shields that they all to-shivered their spears. Therewith Arthur anon pulled out his sword. Nay, not so, said the knight, it is fairer that we twain run more together with sharp spears. I will well, said Arthur, and I had any more spears. I have enow, said the knight. So there came a squire, and brought two good spears, and Arthur chose one and he another, so they spurred their horses, and came together with all their mights, that either brake their spears to their hands.. Then Arthur set hand on his sword. Nay, said the knight, ye shall do better; ye

are a passing good juster as ever I met withal, and once for the love of the high order of knighthood let us just once again. I assent me, said Arthur. Anon there were brought two great spears, and every knight gat a spear, and therewith they ran together that Arthur's spear all to-shivered. But the other knight hit him so hard in midst of the shield that horse and man fell to the earth, and therewith Arthur was eager, and pulled out his sword, and said, I will assay thee, Sir knight, on foot, for I have lost the honour on horseback. I will be on horseback, said the knight. Then was Arthur wroth, and dressed his shield towards him with his sword drawn. When the knight saw that, he alight, for him thought no worship to have a knight at such avail, he to be on horseback, and he on foot, and so he alight and dressed his shield unto Arthur. And there began a strong battle with many great strokes, and so hewed with their swords that the cantels flew in the fields, and much blood they bled both, that all the place there as they fought was over-bled with blood, and thus they fought long, and rested them, and then they went to the battle again, and so hurtled together like two rams that either fell to the earth. So at the last they smote together, that both their swords met even together. But the sword of the knight smote king Arthur's sword in two pieces, wherefore he was heavy. Then said the knight unto Arthur, Thou art in my danger whether me list to save thee or slay thee, and but thou yield thee as overcome and recreant thou shalt die. As for death, said king Arthur, welcome be it when it cometh; but to yield me unto thee as recreant I had lever die than to be so shamed. And therewithal the king leapt unto Pellinore, and took him by the middle, and threw him down, and rased off his helmet. When the knight felt that he was adread, for he was a passing big man of might, and anon he brought Arthur under him, and rased off his helm, and would have smitten off his head.

CHAP. XXII.

How Merlin saved Arthur's life, and threw an enchantment upon king Pellinore, and made him to sleep.

THEREWITHAL came Merlin, and said, Knight, hold thy hand, for and thou slay that knight thou puttest this realm in the greatest damage that ever was realm: for this knight is a man of more worship than thou wotest of. Why, who is he? said the knight. It is king Arthur. Then would he have slain him for dread of his wrath, and heaved up his sword, and therewith Merlin cast an enchantment to the knight, that he fell to the earth in a great sleep. Then Merlin took up king Arthur, and rode forth on the knight's horse. Alas, said Arthur, what hast thou done, Merlin? hast thou slain this good knight by thy crafts? There lived not so worshipful a knight as he was; I had lever than the stint of my land a year that he were onlive. Care ye not, said Merlin, for he is wholer than ye, for he is but on sleep, and will awake within three hours. I told you, said Merlin, what a knight he was; here had ye be slain had I not been. Also there liveth not a bigger knight than he is one, and he shall hereafter do you right good service, and his name is Pellinore, and he shall have two sons that shall be passing good men; save one, they shall have no fellow of prowess and of good living; and their names shall be Percivale of Wales and Lamerake of Wales: and he shall tell you the name of your sister's son that shall be the destruction of all this realm.

CHAP. XXIII.

How Arthur by the mean of Merlin gat Excalibur his sword of the Lady of the lake.

RIGHT so the king and he departed, and went until an hermit that was a good man and a great leach. So the hermit searched all his wounds and gave him good salves; so the king was

there three days, and then were his wounds well amended that he might ride and go, and so departed. And as they rode, Arthur said, I have no sword. No force, said Merlin, hereby is a sword that shall be yours and I may. So they rode till they came to a lake, the which was a fair water and broad, and in the midst of the lake Arthur was ware of an arm clothed in white samite, that held a fair sword in that hand. Lo, said Merlin, yonder is that sword that I spake of. With that they saw a damsel going upon the lake: What damsel is that? said Arthur. That is the Lady of the lake, said Merlin; and within that lake is a rock, and therein is as fair a place as any on earth, and richly beseen, and this damsel will come to you anon, and then speak ye fair to her that she will give you that sword. Anon withal came the damsel unto Arthur and saluted him, and he her again. Damsel, said Arthur, what sword is that, that yonder the arm holdeth above the water? I would it were mine, for I have no sword. Sir Arthur king, said the damsel, that sword is mine, and if ye will give me a gift when I ask it you, ye shall have it. By my faith, said Arthur, I will give you what gift ye will ask. Well, said the damsel, go ye into yonder barge and row yourself to the sword, and take it and the scabbard with you, and I will ask my gift when I see my time. So Sir Arthur and Merlin alight, and tied their horses to two trees, and so they went into the ship, and when they came to the sword that the hand held, Sir Arthur took it up by the handles, and took it with him. And the arm and the hand went under the water; and so they came unto the land and rode forth. And then Sir Arthur saw a rich pavilion: What signifieth yonder pavilion? It is the knight's pavilion, said Merlin, that ye fought with last, Sir Pellinore, but he is out, he is not there; he hath ado with a knight of yours, that hight Egglame, and they have fought together, but at the last Egglame fled, and else he had been dead, and he hath chased him even to Carlion, and we shall meet with him anon in the high way. That is well said, said Arthur, now have I a sword, now will I wage battle with him and be avenged on him. Sir, ye shall not so, said Merlin, for the knight is weary of fighting and chasing, so that ye shall have no worship to have ado with him; also he will not lightly be matched of one knight living; and therefore it is my counsel, let him pass, for he shall do you good wage service in short time, and his sons after his days. Also ye shall see that day in short space, ye shall be right glad to give him your sister to wed. When I see him, I will do as ye advise me, said Arthur. Then Sir Arthur looked on the sword, and liked it passing well. Whether liketh you better, said Merlin, the sword or the scabbard? Me liketh better the sword, said Arthur. Ye are more unwise, said Merlin, for the scabbard is worth ten of the sword, for while ye have the scabbard upon you ye shall never lose no blood, be ye never so sore wounded, therefore keep well the scabbard always with you. So they rode unto Carlion, and by the way they met with Sir Pellinore; but Merlin had done such a craft that Pellinore saw not Arthur, and he passed by without any words. I marvel, said Arthur, that the knight would not speak. Sir, said Merlin, he saw you not, for and he had seen you ye had not lightly departed. So they came unto Carlion, whereof his knights were passing glad. And when they heard of his adventures they marvelled that he would jeopard his person so alone. But all men of worship said it was merry to be under such a chieftain that would put his person in adventure as other poor knights did.

CHAP. XXIV.

How tidings came to Arthur that king Ryons had overcome eleven kings, and how he desired Arthur's beard to trim his mantle.

THIS meanwhile came a messenger from king Ryons of North Wales, and king he was of all Ireland, and of many Isles. And this was his message, greeting well king Arthur in this manner wise, saying that king Ryons had discomfited and overcome eleven kings, and every each of them did him homage, and that was this —they gave him their beards clean flayed off, as much as there was; wherefore the messager came for king Arthur's beard. For king Ryons had trimmed a mantle with kings' beards, and there lacked one place of the mantle, wherefore he sent for his beard, or else he would enter into his lands, and burn and slay, and never leave till he have the head and the beard. Well, said Arthur, thou hast said thy message, the which is the most villainous and lewdest message that ever man heard sent unto a king: also thou mayest see my beard is full young yet to make a trimming of it. But tell thou thy king this: I owe him none homage, nor none of mine elders; but or it be long he shall do me homage on both his knees, or else he shall lose his head, by the faith of my body, for this is the most shamefulest message that ever I heard speak of. I see well thy king met never yet with worshipful man, but tell him I will have his head without he do me homage. Then the messager departed. Now is there any here, said Arthur, that knoweth king Ryons? Then answered a knight that hight Naram, Sir, I know the king well; he is a passing good man of his body as few be living, and a passing proud man; and, Sir, doubt ye not he will make war on you with a mighty puissance. Well, said Arthur, I shall ordain for him in short time.

CHAP. XXV.

How all the children were sent for that were born on May-day, and how Mordred was saved.

THEN king Arthur let send for all the children born on May-day of lords and ladies, for Merlin told king Arthur that he that should destroy him should be born on May-day, wherefore he sent for them all upon pain of death. And so there were found many lords' sons, and all were sent unto the king, and so was Mordred sent by king Lot's wife, and all were put in a ship to the sea, and some were four weeks old, and some less. And so by fortune the ship drove unto a castle, and was all to-riven, and destroyed the most part, save that Mordred was cast up, and a good man found him, and nourished him till he was fourteen year old, and then he brought him to the court, as it rehearseth afterward toward the end of the Death of Arthur. So many lords and barons of this realm were displeased, for their children were so lost, and many put the blame on Merlin more than on Arthur; so what for dread and for love they held their peace. But when the messenger came to king Ryons then was he wood out of measure, and purveyed him for a great host, as it rehearseth after in the book of Balin le Savage that followeth next after, how by adventure Balin gat the sword.

Explicit liber primus.   Incipit liber secundus.

Book the Second.

CHAP. I.

Of a damsel which came girt with a sword for to find a man of such virtue to draw it out of the scabbard.

AFTER the death of Uther Pendragon reigned Arthur his son, the which had great war in his days for to get all England into his hand. For there were many kings within the realm of England, and in Wales, Scotland, and Cornwall. So it befel on a time when king Arthur was at London, there came a knight and told the king tidings how that the king Ryons of North Wales had reared a great number of people, and were entered into the land, and burnt and slew the king's true liege people. If this be true, said Arthur, it were great shame unto mine estate but that he were mightily withstood. It is truth, said the knight, for I saw the host myself. Well, said the king, let make a cry, that all the lords, knights, and gentlemen of arms, should draw unto a castle, called Camelot in those days, and there the king would let make a council general, and a great justs.

So when the king was come thither with all his baronage, and lodged as they seemed best, there was come a damsel the which was sent on message from the great lady Lile of Avelion. And when she came before king Arthur, she told from whom she came, and how she was sent on message unto him for these causes. Then she let her mantle fall that was richly furred; and then was she girt with a noble sword, whereof the king had marvel, and said, Damsel, for what cause are ye girt with that sword? it beseemeth you not. Now shall I tell you, said the damsel: this sword that I am girt withal doth me great sorrow and cumberance, for I may not be delivered of this sword but by a knight, but he must be a passing good man of his hands and of his deeds, and without villainy or treachery, and without treason. And if I may find such a knight that hath all these virtues, he may draw out this sword out of the sheath. For I have been at king Ryons'; it was told me there were passing good knights, and he and all his knights have assayed it, and none can speed. This is a great marvel, said Arthur; if this be sooth, I will myself assay to draw out the sword, not presuming upon myself that I am the best knight, but that

I will begin to draw at your sword in giving example to all the barons,· that they shall assay every one after other when I have assayed it. Then Arthur took the sword by the sheath and by the girdle, and pulled at it eagerly, but the sword would not out. Sir, said the damsel, ye need not to pull half so hard, for he that shall pull it out, shall do it with little might. Ye say well, said Arthur: now assay ye, all my barons, but beware ye be not defiled with shame, treachery, nor guile. Then it will not avail, said the damsel, for he must be a clean knight without villainy, and of a gentle stock of father side and mother side. Most of all the barons of the Round Table that were there at that time assayed all by row, but there might none speed; wherefore the damsel made great sorrow out of measure, and said, Alas! I wend in this court had been the best knights, without treachery or treason. By my faith, saith Arthur, here are good knights as I deem any been in the world, but their grace is not to help you, wherefore I am displeased.

CHAP. II.

How Balin, arrayed like a poor knight, pulled out the sword, which afterward was cause of his death.

THEN fell it so that time there was a poor knight with king Arthur, that had been prisoner with him half a year and more, for slaying of a knight the which was cousin unto king Arthur. The name of this knight was called Balin, and by good means of the barons he was delivered out of prison, for he was a good man named of his body, and he was born in Northumberland. And so he went privily into the court, and saw this adventure, whereof it raised his heart, and he would assay it as other knights did, but for he was poor and poorly arrayed he put him not far in press; but in his heart he was fully assured to do as well, if his grace happed him, as any knight that there was. And as the damsel took her leave of Arthur and of all the barons, so de-

parting, this knight Balin called unto her and said, Damsel, I pray you of your courtesy suffer me as well to assay as these lords; though that I be so poorly clothed, in mine heart me seemeth I am fully assured as some of these other, and me seemeth in my heart to speed right well. The damsel beheld the poor knight, and saw he was a likely man, but for of his poor arrayment she thought he should be of no worship without villainy or treachery. And then she said unto the knight, Sir, it needeth not to put me to more pain or labour, for it seemeth not you to speed there as other have failed. Ah, fair damsel, said Balin, worthiness and good qualities and good deeds are not all only in arrayment, but manhood and worship is hid within man's person, and many a worshipful knight is not known unto all people, and therefore worship and hardiness is not in arrayment. Ye say sooth, said the damsel, therefore ye shall assay to do what ye may. Then Balin took the sword by the girdle and sheath and drew it out easily, and when he looked on the sword it pleased him much. Then had the king and all the barons great marvel that Balin had done that adventure, and many knights had great despite of Balin. Certes, said the damsel, this is a passing good knight, and the best that ever I found, and most of worship without treason, treachery, or villainy, and many marvels shall he do. Now, gentle and courteous knight, give me the sword again. Nay, said Balin, for this sword will I keep, but it be taken from me by force. Well, said the damsel, ye are not wise to keep the sword from me, for ye shall slay with the sword the best friend that ye have, and the man that ye most love in the world, and the sword shall be your destruction. I shall take the adventure, said Balin, that God will ordain me, but the sword ye shall not have at this time, by the faith of my body. Ye shall repent it within short time, said the damsel, for I would have the sword more for your avail than for mine, for I am passing heavy for your sake; for ye will not believe that sword shall be your destruction, and that is great pity. With that the damsel departed, making great sorrow.

Anon after Balin sent for his horse and his armour, and so would depart from the court, and took his leave of king Arthur. Nay, said the king, I suppose ye will not depart so lightly from this fellowship. I suppose that ye are displeased that I have shewed you unkindness; blame me the less, for I was misinformed against you, but I wend you had not been such a knight as ye are of worship and prowess, and if ye will abide in this court among my fellowship, I shall so advance you as ye shall be pleased. God thank your highness, said Balin, for your bounty and highness may no man praise half to the value; but at this time I must needs depart, beseeching you alway of your good grace. Truly, said the king, I am right wroth for your departing: I pray you, fair knight, that ye tarry not long, and ye shall be right welcome to me and to my barons, and I shall amend all amiss that I have done against you. God thank your great lordship, said Balin, and therewith made him ready to depart. Then the most part of the knights of the Round Table said that Balin did not this adventure all only by might, but by witchcraft.

CHAP. III.

How the Lady of the lake demanded the knight's head that had won the sword, or the maiden's head.

THE meanwhile that this knight was making him ready to depart, there came into the court a lady that hight the Lady of the lake. And she came on horseback, richly beseen, and saluted king Arthur; and there asked him a gift that he promised her when she gave him the sword. That is sooth, said Arthur, a gift I promised you, but I have forgotten the name of my sword that ye gave me. The name of it, said the lady, is Excalibur, that is as much to say as Cut-steel. Ye say well, said the king, ask what ye will and ye shall

have it, and it lie in my power to give it. Well, said the lady, I ask the head of the knight that hath won the sword, or else the damsel's head that brought it; I take no force though I have both their heads, for he slew my brother, a good knight and a true, and that gentlewoman was causer of my father's death. Truly, said king Arthur, I may not grant neither of their heads with my worship, therefore ask what ye will else, and I shall fulfil your desire. I will ask none other thing, said the lady. When Balin was ready to depart he saw the Lady of the lake that by her means had slain Balin's mother, and he had sought her three years, and when it was told him that she asked his head of king Arthur he went to her straight and said, Evil be you found, ye would have my head and therefore ye shall lose yours. And with his sword lightly he smote off her head before king Arthur. Alas! for shame, said Arthur, why have you done so? ye have shamed me and all my court, for this was a lady that I was beholden to, and hither she came under my safe conduct; I shall never forgive you that trespass. Sir, said Balin, me forthinketh of your displeasure, for this same lady was the untruest lady living, and by enchantment and sorcery she hath been the destroyer of many good knights, and she was causer that my mother was burnt through her falsehood and treachery. What cause so ever ye had, said Arthur, ye should have forborne her in my presence; therefore, think not the contrary, ye shall repent it, for such another despite had I never in my court: therefore withdraw you out of my court in all haste that ye may. Then Balin took up the head of the lady, and bare it with him to his hostry, and there he met with his squire, that was sorry he had displeased king Arthur, and so they rode forth out of the town. Now, said Balin, we must part; take thou this head and bear it to my friends, and tell them how I have sped, and tell my friends in Northumberland that my most foe is dead. Also tell them how I am out of prison, and also what adventure befel me at the getting of this sword. Alas, said the squire, ye are greatly to blame for to displease king Arthur. As for that, said Balin, I will hie me in all the haste that I may, to meet with king Ryons and destroy him, or else to die therefore; and if it may hap me to win him, then will king Arthur be my good and gracious lord. Where shall I meet with you? said the squire. In king Arthur's court, said Balin. So his squire and he departed at that time. Then king Arthur and all the court made great dole, and had shame of the death of the Lady of the lake. Then the king buried her richly.

CHAP. IV.

How Merlin told the adventure of this damsel.

At that time there was a knight the which was the king's son of Ireland, and his name was Lanceor, the which was an orgulous knight, and counted himself one of the best of the court, and he had great despite at Balin for the achieving of the sword, that any should be accounted more hardy, or of more prowess; and he asked king Arthur if he would give him leave to ride after Balin, and to revenge the despite that he had done. Do your best, said Arthur, I am right wroth with Balin, I would he were quit of the despite that he hath done to me and to my court. Then this Lanceor went to his hostry to make him ready. In the meanwhile came Merlin unto the court of king Arthur, and there was told him the adventure of the sword, and the death of the Lady of the lake. Now shall I say you, said Merlin, this same damsel that here standeth, that brought the sword unto your court, I shall tell you the cause of her coming, — she was the falsest damsel that liveth. Say not so, said they. She hath a brother, a passing good knight of prowess and a full true man, and this damsel loved another knight that held her to paramour, and this good knight her brother met with the knight that held her to paramour,

and slew him by force of his hands. When this false damsel understood this she went to the lady Lile of Avelion, and besought her of help, to be avenged on her own brother. And so this lady Lile of Avelion took her this sword, that she brought with her, and told there should no man pull it out of the sheath but if he be one of the best knights of this realm, and he should be hardy and full of prowess, and with that sword he should slay her brother. This was the cause that the damsel came into this court. I know it as well as ye. Would she had not come into this court, but she came never in fellowship of worship to do good, but alway great harm. And that knight that hath achieved the sword shall be destroyed by that sword, for the which will be great damage, for there liveth not a knight of more prowess than he is, and he shall do unto you, my lord Arthur, great honour and kindness, and it is great pity he shall not endure but a while, for of his strength and hardiness I know not his match living.

CHAP. V.

How Balin was pursued by Sir Lanceor, knight of Ireland, and how he justed and slew him.

So the knight of Ireland armed him at all points, and dressed his shield on his shoulder, and mounted upon horseback, and took his spear in his hand, and rode after a great pace as much as his horse might go, and within a little space on a mountain he had a sight of Balin, and with a loud voice he cried, Abide knight, for ye shall abide whether ye will or nill, and the shield that is tofore you shall not help. When Balin heard the noise he turned his horse fiercely, and said, Fair knight what will ye with me, will ye just with me? Yea, said the Irish knight, therefore come I after you. Peradventure, said Balin, it had been better to have holden you at home, for many a man weneth to put his enemy to a rebuke, and oft it falleth to himself. Of what court be ye sent from? said Balin. I am come from the court of king Arthur, said the knight of Ireland, that come hither for to revenge the despite ye did this day to king Arthur and to his court. Well, said Balin, I see well I must have ado with you, that me forthinketh for to grieve king Arthur, or any of his court; and your quarrel is full simple, said Balin, unto me, for the lady that is dead did me great damage, and else would I have been loth as any knight that liveth for to slay a lady. Make you ready, said the knight Lanceor, and dress you unto me, for that one shall abide in the field. Then they took their spears, and came together as much as their horses might drive, and the Irish knight smote Balin on the shield, that all went shivers of his spear, and Balin hit him through the shield, and the hauberk perished, and so pierced through his body and the horse croup, and anon turned his horse fiercely and drew out his sword, and wist not that he had slain him, and then he saw him lie as a dead corpse.

CHAP. VI.

How a damsel, which was love to Lanceor, slew herself for love; and how Balin met with his brother Balan.

THEN he looked by him, and was ware of a damsel that came riding full fast as the horse might ride, on a fair palfrey. And when she espied that Lanceor was slain she made sorrow out of measure, and said, O Balin, two bodies thou hast slain and one heart, and two hearts in one body, and two souls thou hast lost. And therewith she took the sword from her love that lay dead, and fell to the ground in a swoon. And when she arose she made great dole out of measure, the which sorrow grieved Balin passingly sore, and he went unto her for to have taken the sword out of her hand, but she held it so fast he might not take it out of her hand unless he should have hurt her, and suddenly she set the pommel to the ground, and rove herself through the body. When Balin espied her deeds, he

was passing heavy in his heart, and ashamed that so fair a damsel had destroyed herself for the love of his death. Alas, said Balin, me repenteth sore the death of this knight for the love of this damsel, for there was much true love betwixt them both. And for sorrow he might no longer hold him, but turned his horse and looked towards a great forest, and there he was ware, by the arms, of his brother Balan. And when they were met they put off their helms and kissed together, and wept for joy and pity. Then Balan said, I little wend to have met with you at this sudden adventure; I am right glad of your deliverance out of your dolorous prisonment, for a man told me in the castle of Four Stones that ye were delivered, and that man had seen you in the court of king Arthur, and therefore I came hither into this country, for here I supposed to find you. Anon the knight Balin told his brother of his adventure of the sword, and of the death of the Lady of the lake, and how king Arthur was displeased with him: Wherefore he sent this knight after me that lieth here dead; and the death of this damsel grieveth me sore. So doth it me, said Balan, but ye must take the adventure that God will ordain you. Truly, said Balin, I am right heavy that my lord Arthur is displeased with me, for he is the most worshipful knight that reigneth now on earth, and his love I will get or else I will put my life in adventure; for the king Ryons lieth at a siege at the castle Terrabil, and thither will we draw in all haste, to prove our worship and prowess upon him. I will well, said Balan, that we do, and we will help each other as brethren ought to do.

CHAP. VII.

How a dwarf reproved Balin for the death of Lanceor, and how king Mark of Cornwall found them, and made a tomb over them.

Now go we hence, said Balin, and well be we met. The meanwhile as they talked there came a dwarf from the city of Camelot on horseback, as much as he might, and found the dead bodies, wherefore he made great dole, and pulled out his hair for sorrow, and said, Which of you knights have done this deed? Whereby askest thou it, said Balan. For I would wit it, said the dwarf. It was I, said Balin, that slew this knight in my defence, for hither came he to chase me, and either I must slay him or he me; and this damsel slew herself for his love, which repenteth me, and for her sake I shall owe all women the better love. Alas, said the dwarf, thou hast done great damage unto thyself, for this knight that is here dead was one of the most valiantest men that lived, and trust well, Balin, the kin of this knight will chase you through the world till they have slain you. As for that, said Balin, I fear not greatly, but I am right heavy that I have displeased my lord king Arthur for the death of this knight. So as they talked together there came a king of Cornwall riding, the which hight king Mark. And when he saw these two bodies dead, and understood how they were dead by the two knights above said, then made the king great sorrow for the true love that was betwixt them, and said, I will not depart till I have on this earth made a tomb. And there he pight his pavilions, and sought through all the country to find a tomb, and in a church they found one was fair and rich, and then the king let put them both in the earth, and put the tomb upon them, and wrote the names of them both on the tomb:—How here lieth Lanceor the king's son of Ireland that at his own request was slain by the hands of Balin, and how his lady Colombe slew herself with her love's sword for dole and sorrow.

CHAP. VIII.

How Merlin prophesied that two the best knights of the world should fight there, which were Sir Lancelot and Sir Tristram.

THE meanwhile as this was adoing, in came Merlin to king Mark, and seeing all his doing said, Here shall be in this same place the greatest battle betwixt two knights that was or ever shall be, and the truest lovers, and yet none of them shall slay other. And there Merlin wrote their names upon the tomb with letters of gold that should fight in that place, whose names were Launcelot de Lake, and Tristram. Thou art a marvellous man, said king Mark unto Merlin, that speakest of such marvels, thou art a rude man and an unlikely to tell of such deeds; what is thy name? said king Mark. At this time, said Merlin, I will not tell, but at that time when Sir Tristram is taken with his sovereign lady, then ye shall hear and know my name, and at that time ye shall hear tidings that shall not please you. Then said Merlin to Balin, Thou hast done thyself great hurt, because thou savedst not this lady that slew herself, that might have saved her and thou wouldest. By the faith of my body, said Balin, I might not save her, for she slew herself suddenly. Me repenteth, said Merlin, because of the death of that lady thou shalt strike a stroke the most dolorous that ever man struck, except the stroke of our Lord, for thou shalt hurt the truest knight and the man of most worship that now liveth, and through that stroke three kingdoms shall be in great poverty, misery, and wretchedness, twelve year, and the knight shall not be whole of that wound many years. Then Merlin took his leave of Balin. And Balin said, If I wist it were sooth that ye say, I should do such a perilous deed as that I would slay myself to make thee a liar. Therewith Merlin vanished away suddenly. And then Balin and his brother took their leave of king Mark. First, said the king, tell me your name. Sir, said Balan, ye may see he beareth two swords, thereby ye may call him the knight with the two swords. And so departed king Mark unto Camelot to king Arthur, and Balin took the way to king Ryons: and as they rode together they met with Merlin disguised, but they knew him not. Whither ride you? said Merlin. We have little to do, said the two knights, to tell thee: But what is thy name? said Balin. At this time, said Merlin, I will not tell it thee. It is evil seen, said the two knights, that thou art a true man that thou wilt not tell thy name. As for that, said Merlin, be it as it be may, I can tell you wherefore ye ride this way, for to meet king Ryons, but it will not avail you without ye have my counsel. Ah, said Balin, ye are Merlin: we will be ruled by your counsel. Come on, said Merlin, ye shall have great worship, and look that ye do knightly, for ye shall have great need. As for that, said Balin, dread you not, we will do what we may.

CHAP. IX.

How Balin and his brother by the counsel of Merlin took king Ryons, and brought him to king Arthur.

THEN Merlin lodged them in a wood among leaves beside the highway, and took off the bridles of their horses and put them to grass, and laid them down to rest them till it was nigh midnight. Then Merlin bad them rise and make them ready, for the king was nigh them, that was stolen away from his host with a threescore horses of his best knights, and twenty of them rode tofore, to warn the lady De Vance that the king was coming. Which is the king? said Balin. Abide, said Merlin, here in a straight way ye shall meet with him; and therewith he shewed Balin and his brother where he rode. Anon Balin and his brother met with the king, and smote him down, and wounded him fiercely, and laid him to the ground, and there they slew on the right hand and the left hand, and slew more than forty of his men; and the remnant fled. Then went they again to king Ryons, and would have slain him had he not yielded him unto their grace. Then said he thus: Knights full of prowess, slay me not, for by my life ye may win, and by my death ye shall win nothing. Then said these two knights, Ye say sooth and truth;

and so laid him on an horse-litter. With that Merlin was vanished, and came to king Arthur, aforehand, and told him how his most enemy was taken and discomfited. By whom? said king Arthur. By two knights, said Merlin, that would please your lordship, and to-morrow ye shall know what knights they are. Anon after came the knight with the two swords, and Balan his brother, and brought with them king Ryons of North Wales, and there delivered him to the porters, and charged them with him; and so they two returned again in the dawning of the day. King Arthur came then to king Ryons and said, Sir king ye are welcome: by what adventure come ye hither? Sir, said king Ryons, I came hither by an hard adventure. Who won you? said king Arthur. Sir, said the king, the knight with the two swords and his brother, which are two marvellous knights of prowess. I know them not, said Arthur, but much I am beholden to them. Ah, said Merlin, I shall tell you, it is Balin that achieved the sword, and his brother Balan, a good knight, there liveth not a better of prowess and of worthiness; and it shall be the greatest dole of him that ever I knew of knight, for he shall not long endure. Alas, said king Arthur, that is great pity, for I am much beholden unto him, and I have ill deserved it unto him for his kindness. Nay, said Merlin, he shall do much more for you, and that shall ye know in haste. But, Sir, are ye purveyed? said Merlin; for to-morn the host of Nero, king Ryons's brother, will set on you or noon with a great host, and therefore make you ready, for I will depart from you.

CHAP. X.

How king Arthur had a battle against Nero and king Lot of Orkney, and how king Lot was deceived by Merlin, and how twelve kings were slain.

THEN king Arthur made ready his host in ten battles, and Nero was ready in the field afore the castle

Terrabil with a great host, for he had ten battles, with many more people than Arthur had. Then Nero had the vaward with the most party of his people: and Merlin came to king Lot of the Isle of Orkney, and held him with a tale of prophecy till Nero and his people were destroyed. And there Sir Kay the seneschal did passingly well, that the days of his life the worship went never from him. And Sir Hervis de Revel did marvellous deeds with king Arthur, and king Arthur slew that day twenty knights and maimed forty. At that time came in the knight with the two swords, and his brother Balan, but they two did so marvellously that the king and all the knights marvelled of them, and all they that beheld them said they were sent from heaven as angels, or devils from hell: and king Arthur said himself they were the best knights that ever he saw, for they gave such strokes that all men had wonder of them. In the meanwhile came one to king Lot, and told him while he tarried there Nero was destroyed and slain with all his people. Alas, said king Lot, I am ashamed, for by my default there is many a worshipful man slain, for and we had been together there had been none host under the heaven that had been able for to have matched with us: this deceiver with his prophecy hath mocked me. All that did Merlin, for he knew well that if king Lot had been with his body there at the first battle, king Arthur had been slain and all his people destroyed. And well Merlin knew that one of the kings should be dead that day; and loth was Merlin that any of them both should be slain, but of the twain he had lever king Lot had been slain than king Arthur.

Now what is best to do? said king Lot of Orkney, whether is me better to treat with king Arthur or to fight, for the greater part of our people are slain and destroyed. Sir, said a knight, set on Arthur, for they are weary and for-foughten, and we be fresh. As for me, said king Lot, I would that every knight would do his part as I would do mine.

And then they advanced banners and smote together, and all to-shivered their spears; and Arthur's knights, with the help of the knight with the two swords and his brother Balan, put king Lot and his host to the worse. But alway king Lot held him in the foremost front, and did marvellous deeds of arms, for all his host was borne up by his hands, for he abode all knights. Alas, he might not endure, the which was great pity, that so worthy a knight as he was should be overmatched, that of late time afore had been a knight of king Arthur's, and wedded the sister of king Arthur, and for the wrong king Arthur did him therefore king Lot held against Arthur. So there was a knight that was called the knight with the strange beast, and at that time his right name was called Pellinore, the which was a good man of prowess, and he smote a mighty stroke at king Lot as he fought with all his enemies, and he failed of his stroke, and he smote the horse's neck, that he fell to the ground with king Lot; and therewith anon Sir Pellinore smote him a great stroke through the helm and head unto the brows. And then all the host of Orkney fled for the death of king Lot; and there were slain many mothers' sons. But king Pellinore bare the blame of the death of king Lot, wherefore Sir Gawaine revenged the death of his father the tenth year after he was made knight, and slew king Pellinore with his own hands. Also there were slain at that battle twelve kings on the side of king Lot with Nero, and all were buried in the church of Saint Stephen's, in Camelot; and the remnant of knights and of other were buried in a great rock.

CHAP. XI.

Of the interment of twelve kings, and of the prophecy of Merlin, and how Balin should give the dolorous stroke.

So at the interment came king Lot's wife Morgause, with her four sons, Gawaine, Agravaine, Gaheris, and Gareth. Also there came thither king

Uriens, Sir Ewaine's father, and Morgan le Fay his wife, that was king Arthur's sister. All these came to the interment. But of all these twelve kings king Arthur let make the tomb of king Lot passing richly, and made his tomb by his own; and then king Arthur let make twelve images of laton and copper, and over-gilt it with gold, in the sign of twelve kings, and each one of them held a taper of wax that burnt day and night: and king Arthur was made in sign of a figure standing above them with a sword drawn in his hand: and all the twelve figures had countenance like unto men that were overcome. All this made Merlin by his subtil craft; and there he told the king, When I am dead these tapers shall burn no longer; and soon after the adventures of the Sangreal shall come among you and be achieved. Also he told Arthur how Balin the worshipful knight shall give the dolorous stroke, whereof shall fall great vengeance. O where is Balin, and Balan, and Pellinore? said king Arthur. As for Pellinore, said Merlin, he will meet with you soon: and as for Balin, he will not be long from you: but the other brother will depart; ye shall see him no more. By my faith, said Arthur, they are two marvellous knights, and namely Balin passeth of prowess of any knight that ever I found, for much beholden am I unto him; would that he would abide with me. Sir, said Merlin, look ye keep well the scabbard of Excalibur, for ye shall lose no blood while ye have the scabbard upon you, though ye have as many wounds upon you as ye may have. So after, for great trust Arthur betook the scabbard to Morgan le Fay his sister, and she loved another knight better than her husband king Uriens or king Arthur, and she would have had Arthur her brother slain, and therefore she let make another scabbard like it by enchantment, and gave the scabbard of Excalibur to her love. And the knight's name was called Accolon, that after had near slain king Arthur. After this Merlin told unto king Arthur of the

prophecy that there should be a great battle beside Salisbury, and that Mordred his sister's son should be against him. Also he told him that Basdemegus was his cousin, and germain unto king Uriens.

CHAP. XII.

How a sorrowful knight came tofore king Arthur, and how Balin fetched him, and how that knight was slain by a knight invisible.

WITHIN a day or two king Arthur was somewhat sick, and he let pitch his pavilion in a meadow, and there he laid him down on a pallet to sleep, but he might have no rest. Right so he heard a great noise of an horse, and therewith the king looked out at the porch of the pavilion, and saw a knight coming even by him making great dole. Abide, fair sir, said Arthur, and tell me wherefore thou makest this sorrow? Ye may little amend me, said the knight, and so passed forth to the castle of Meliot. Anon after there came Balin, and when he saw king Arthur he alight off his horse, and came to the king on foot, and saluted him. By my head, said Arthur, ye be welcome. Sir, right now came riding this way a knight making great mourn, for what cause I cannot tell, wherefore I would desire of you of your courtesy and of your gentleness to fetch again that knight either by force or else by his good-will. I will do more for your lordship than that, said Balin: and so he rode more than a pace, and found the knight with a damsel in a forest, and said, Sir knight, ye must come with me unto king Arthur, for to tell him of your sorrow. That will I not, said the knight, for it will scathe me greatly, and do you none avail. Sir, said Balin, I pray you make you ready, for ye must go with me, or else I must fight with you and bring you by force, and that were me loth to do. Will ye be my warrant, said the knight, and I go with you? Yea, said Balin, or else I will die therefore. And so he made him ready to go with Balin, and left the damsel still. And as they were even afore king Arthur's pavilion there came one invisible, and smote this knight that went with Balin throughout the body with a spear. Alas, said the knight, I am slain under your conduct, with a knight called Garlon : therefore take my horse, that is better than your's, and ride to the damsel, and follow the quest that I was in as she will lead you, and revenge my death when ye may. That shall I do, said Balin, and that I make a vow unto knighthood. And so he departed from this knight with great sorrow. So king Arthur let bury this knight richly, and made a mention on his tomb how there was slain Herlews le Berbeus, and by whom the treachery was done,—the knight Garlon. But ever the damsel bare the truncheon of the spear with her that Sir Herlews was slain withal.

CHAP. XIII.

How Balin and the damsel met with a knight which was in likewise slain, and how the damsel bled for the custom of a castle.

So Balin and the damsel rode into a forest, and there met with a knight that had been on hunting, and that knight asked Balin for what cause he made so great sorrow. Me list not to tell you, said Balin. Now, said the knight, and I were armed as ye be I would fight with you. That should little need, said Balin ; I am not afeard to tell you ; and told him all the cause, how it was. Ah, said the knight, is this all : here I ensure you by the faith of my body never to depart from you while my life lasteth. And so they went to the hostry and armed them, and so rode forth with Balin. And as they came by an hermitage even by a church-yard, there came the knight Garlon invisible, and smote this knight, Perin de Mountbeliard, through the body with a spear. Alas, said the knight, I am slain by this traitor knight that rideth invisible. Alas, said Balin, it is not the first despite that he hath done me. And there the hermit and Balin buried

the knight under a rich stone, and a tomb royal. And on the morn they found letters of gold written, how Sir Gawaine shall revenge his father's death, king Lot, on the king Pellinore. Anon after this Balin and the damsel rode till they came to a castle, and there Balin alighted, and he and the damsel wend to go into the castle. And anon as Balin came within the castle gate the portcullis fell down at his back, and there fell many men about the damsel, and would have slain her. When Balin saw that, he was sore grieved, for he might not help the damsel. And then he went up into the tower, and lept over the walls into the ditch, and hurt him not ; and anon he pulled out his sword, and would have foughten with them. And they all said nay, they would not fight with him, for they did nothing but the old custom of the castle, and told him how their lady was sick, and had lain many years, and she might not be whole, but if she had a dish of silver full of blood of a maid and a king's daughter ; and therefore the custom of this castle is that there shall no damsel pass this way, but that she shall bleed of her blood in a silver dish full. Well, said Balin, she shall bleed as much as she may bleed, but I will not lose the life of her while my life lasteth. And so Balin made her to bleed by her good-will, but her blood helped not the lady. And so he and she rested there all night, and had there right good cheer, and on the morn they passed on their ways. And as it telleth after in the Sangreal, that Sir Percivale's sister helped that lady with her blood, whereof she died.

CHAP. XIV.

How Balin met with that knight named Garlon at a feast, and there he slew him, to have his blood to heal therewith the son of his host.

THEN they rode three or four days and never met with adventure, and by hap they were lodged with a gentleman that was a rich man and well at ease.

And as they sat at their supper, Balin heard one complain grievously by him in a chair. What is this noise? said Balin. Forsooth, said his host, I will tell you. I was but late at a justing, and there I justed with a knight that is brother unto king Pellam, and twice smote I him down; and then he promised to quit me on my best friend, and so he wounded my son, that cannot be whole till I have of that knight's blood, and he rideth alway invisible, but I know not his name. Ah, said Balin, I know that knight, his name is Garlon, he hath slain two knights of mine in the same manner, therefore I had rather meet with that knight than all the gold in this realm, for the despite he hath done me. Well, said his host, I shall tell you, king Pellam of Listeneise hath made cry in all this country a great feast that shall be within these twenty days, and no knight may come there but if he bring his wife with him, or his love; and that knight, your enemy and mine, ye shall see that day. Then I promise you, said Balin, part of his blood to heal your son withal. We will be forward to-morrow, said his host. So on the morn they rode all three toward Pellam, and they had fifteen days' journey or they came thither; and that same day began the great feast. And so they alight and stabled their horses, and went into the castle; but Balin's host might not be let in because he had no lady. Then Balin was well received, and brought unto a chamber and unarmed him, and they brought him robes to his pleasure, and would have had Balin leave his sword behind him. Nay, said Balin, that do I not, for it is the custom of my country a knight alway to keep his weapon with him, and that custom will I keep, or else I will depart as I came. Then they gave him leave to wear his sword, and so he went unto the castle, and was set among knights of worship, and his lady afore him. Soon Balin asked a knight, Is there not a knight in this court whose name is Garlon? Yonder he goeth, said a knight, he with the black face; he

is the marvellest knight that is now living, for he destroyeth many good knights, for he goeth invisible. Ah, well, said Balin, is that he? Then Balin advised him long:—If I slay him here I shall not escape, and if I leave him now peradventure I shall never meet with him again at such a good time, and much harm he will do and he live. Therewith this Garlon espied that this Balin beheld him, and then he came and smote Balin on the face with the back of his hand, and said, Knight, why beholdest thou me so? for shame, therefore, eat thy meat, and do that thou came for. Thou sayest sooth, said Balin, this is not the first despite that thou hast done me, and therefore I will do that I came for; and rose up fiercely, and clave his head to the shoulders. Give me the truncheon, said Balin to his lady, wherewith he slew your knight. Anon she gave it him, for alway she bare the truncheon with her; and therewith Balin smote him through the body, and said openly, With that truncheon thou hast slain a good knight, and now it sticketh in thy body. And then Balin called to him his host, saying, Now may ye fetch blood enough to heal your son withal.

CHAP. XV.

How Balin fought with king Pellam, and how his sword brake, and how he gat a spear wherewith he smote the dolorous stroke.

ANON all the knights arose from the table for to set on Balin. And king Pellam himself arose up fiercely, and said, Knight, hast thou slain my brother? thou shalt die therefore or thou depart. Well, said Balin, do it yourself. Yes, said king Pellam, there shall no man have ado with thee but myself, for the love of my brother. Then king Pellam caught in his hand a grim weapon and smote eagerly at Balin, but Balin put the sword betwixt his head and the stroke, and therewith his sword burst in sunder. And when Balin was weaponless he ran into a chamber for to seek some weapon, and so from chamber to chamber, and no weapon he could find, and alway king Pellam after him. And at the last he entered into a chamber that was marvellously well dight and richly, and a bed arrayed with cloth of gold, the richest that might be thought, and one lying therein, and thereby stood a table of clean gold, with four pillars of silver that bare up the table, and upon the table stood a marvellous spear, strangely wrought. And when Balin saw that spear he gat it in his hand, and turned him to king Pellam, and smote him passingly sore with that spear, that king Pellam fell down in a swoon, and therewith the castle roof and walls brake and fell to the earth, and Balin fell down so that he might not stir foot nor hand. And so the most part of the castle that was fallen down through that dolorous stroke lay upon Pellam and Balin three days.

CHAP. XVI.

How Balin was delivered by Merlin, and saved a knight that would have slain himself for love.

THEN Merlin came thither and took up Balin, and gat him a good horse, for his was dead, and bade him ride out of that country. I would have my damsel, said Balin. Lo, said Merlin, where she lieth dead. And king Pellam lay so many years sore wounded, and might never be whole, till Galahad, the haut prince, healed him in the quest of the Sangreal; for in that place was part of the blood of our Lord Jesus Christ, that Joseph of Arimathea brought into this land, and there himself lay in that rich bed. And that was the same spear that Longius smote our Lord to the heart; and king Pellam was nigh of Joseph's kin, and that was the most worshipful man that lived in those days, and great pity it was of his hurt, for that stroke turned to great dole, trouble, and grief.

Then departed Balin from Merlin, and said, In this world we meet never no more. So he rode forth through the fair countries and cities, and found the people dead, slain on every side. And all that were alive cried, O Balin, thou hast caused great damage in these countries; for the dolorous stroke thou gavest unto king Pellam three countries are destroyed, and doubt not but the vengeance will fall on thee at the last. When Balin was past those countries he was passing glad. So he rode eight days or he met with adventure. And at the last he came into a fair forest in a valley, and was ware of a tower, and there beside he saw a great horse of war tied to a tree, and there beside sat a fair knight on the ground and made great mourning; and he was a likely man and a well made. Balin said, God save you, why be ye so heavy? tell me, and I will amend it and I may to my power. Sir knight, said he again, thou doest me great grief, for I was in merry thoughts, and now thou puttest me to more pain. Balin went a little from him, and looked on his horse; then heard Balin him say thus: Ah, fair lady, why have ye broken my promise, for thou promisedst me to meet me here by noon, and I may curse thee that ever ye gave me this sword, for with this sword I slay myself,—and pulled it out; and therewith Balin start unto him, and took him by the hand. Let go my hand, said the knight, or else I shall slay thee. That shall not need, said Balin, for I shall promise you my help to get you your lady, and ye will tell me where she is. What is your name? said the knight. My name is Balin le Savage. Ah, sir, I know you well enough; ye are the knight with the two swords, and the man of most prowess of your hands living. What is your name? said Balin. My name is Garnish of the Mount, a poor man's son, but by my prowess and hardiness a duke hath made me knight, and gave me lands; his name is duke Hermel, and his daughter is she that I love, and she me as I deemed. How far is she hence? said Balin. But six mile, said the knight. Now ride we hence, said these two knights. So they rode more than a pace till they came to a fair castle, well walled and ditched. I will into the castle, said Balin, and look if she be there. So he went in, and searched from chamber to chamber, and found her bed, but she was not there; then Balin looked into a fair little garden, and under a laurel tree he saw her lie upon a quilt of green samite, and a knight with her, and under their heads grass and herbs. When Balin saw her with the foulest knight that ever he saw, and she a fair lady, then Balin went through all the chambers again, and told the knight how he found her, as she had slept fast, and so brought him in the place where she lay fast sleeping.

CHAP. XVII.

How that knight slew his love and a knight with her, and after how he slew himself with his own sword, and how Balin rode toward a castle where he lost his life.

AND when Garnish beheld her so lying, for pure sorrow his mouth and nose burst out on bleeding, and with his sword he smote off both their heads, and then he made sorrow out of measure and said, Oh Balin, much sorrow hast thou brought unto me, for hadst thou not shewn me that sight I should have passed my sorrow. Forsooth, said Balin, I did it to this intent that it should better thy courage, and that ye might see and know her falsehood, and to cause you to leave love of such a lady: truly I did none other but as I would ye did to me. Alas! said Garnish, now is my sorrow double that I may not endure: now have I slain that I most loved in all my life. And therewith suddenly he rove himself on his own sword unto the hilts. When Balin saw that, he dressed him thenceward, lest folks would say he had slain them, and so he rode forth, and within three days he came by a cross, and thereon were letters of gold written that said, It is not for any knight alone to ride toward this castle. Then saw he an old hoar gentleman coming toward him that said, Balin le Savage, thou passest thy bounds to come this way, therefore turn again and it will avail thee. And he vanished away anon; and so he heard an horn blow as it had been the death of a beast. That blast, said Balin, is blown for me, for I am the prize, yet am I not dead. Anon withal he saw an hundred ladies and many knights, that welcomed him with fair semblance, and made him passing good cheer unto his sight, and led him into the castle, and there was dancing and minstrelsy, and all manner of joy. Then the chief lady of the castle said, Knight with the two swords, ye must have ado with a knight hereby that keepeth an island, for there may no man pass this way but he must just or he pass. That is an unhappy custom, said Balin, that a knight may not pass this way but if he just. Ye shall not have ado but with one knight, said the lady. Well, said Balin, since I shall, thereto am I ready, but travelling men are oft weary, and their horses also; but though my horse be weary my heart is not weary. I would be fain there my death should be. Sir, said a knight to Balin, me thinketh your shield is not good, I will lend you a bigger: therefore I pray you: and so he took the shield that was unknown and left his own, and so rode unto the island, and put him and his horse in a great boat, and when he came on the other side he met with a damsel, and she said, O knight Balin, why have ye left your own shield? alas! ye have put your self in great danger, for by your shield ye should have been known: it is great pity of you as ever was of knight, for of thy prowess and hardiness thou hast no fellow living. Me repenteth, said Balin, that ever I came within this country, but I may not turn now again for shame, and what adventure shall fall to me, be it life or death, I will take the adventure that shall come to me. And then he looked on his armour, and understood he was well armed, and therewith blessed him, and mounted upon his horse.

CHAP. XVIII.

*How Balin met with his brother Balan, and
how each of them slew other unknown, till
they were wounded to death.*

THEN afore him he saw come riding
out of a castle a knight, and his horse
trapped all red, and himself in the same
colour. When this knight in the red
beheld Balin, him thought it should be
his brother Balin because of his two
swords, but because he knew not his
shield, he deemed it was not he. And
so they aventred their spears, and
came marvellously fast together, and
they smote each other in the shields, but
their spears and their course were so big
that it bare down horse and man, that
they lay both in a swoon. But Balin
was bruised sore with the fall of his
horse, for he was weary of travel. And
Balan was the first that rose on foot
and drew his sword, and went toward
Balin, and he arose and went against
him, but Balan smote Balin first, and
he put up his shield, and smote him
through the shield and cleft his helm.
Then Balin smote him again with that
unhappy sword, and well nigh had
felled his brother Balan, and so they
fought there together till their breaths
failed. Then Balin looked up to the
castle, and saw the towers stand full of
ladies. So they went to battle again,
and wounded each other dolefully, and
then they breathed oft-times, and so
went unto battle, that all the place
there as they fought was blood red.
And at that time there was none of
them both but they had either smitten
other seven great wounds, so that the
least of them might have been the death
of the mightiest giant in this world.
Then they went to battle again so marvellously that doubt it was to hear of
that battle for the great bloodshedding,
and their hauberks unnailed, that naked
they were on every side. At the last
Balan, the younger brother, withdrew
him a little and laid him down. Then
said Balin le Savage, What knight art
thou? for or now I found never no

knight that matched me. My name is,
said he, Balan, brother to the good
knight Balin. Alas! said Balin, that
ever I should see this day. And therewith he fell backward in a swoon.
Then Balan went on all four feet and
hands, and put off the helm of his
brother, and might not know him by
the visage it was so full hewen and
bled; but when he awoke he said, O
Balan, my brother, thou hast slain me
and I thee, wherefore all the wide world
shall speak of us both. Alas! said
Balan, that ever I saw this day, that
through mishap I might not know you,
for I espied well your two swords, but
because ye had another shield I deemed
you had been another knight. Alas!
said Balin, all that made an unhappy
knight in the castle, for he caused me to
leave mine own shield to our both's
destruction, and if I might live I would
destroy that castle for ill customs. That
were well done, said Balan, for I had
never grace to depart from them since
that I came hither, for here it happed me
to slay a knight that kept this island, and
since might I never depart, and no more
should ye brother, and ye might have
slain me as ye have, and escaped yourself with the life. Right so came the
lady of the tower with four knights and
six ladies and six yeomen unto them,
and there she heard how they made
their moan either to other, and said,
We came both out of one womb, and so
shall we lye both in one pit. So Balan
prayed the lady of her gentleness, for
his true service that she would bury
them both in that same place there the
battle was done. And she granted
them with weeping it should be done
richly in the best manner. Now will ye
send for a priest, that we may receive our
sacrament and receive the blessed body
of our Lord Jesus Christ. Yea, said
the lady, it shall be done. And so she
sent for a priest and gave them their
rites. Now, said Balin, when we are
buried in one tomb, and the mention
made over us how two brethren slew
each other, there will never good knight
nor good man see our tomb but they

will pray for our souls. And so all the ladies and gentlewomen wept for pity. Then, anon Balan died, but Balin died not till the midnight after, and so were they buried both, and the lady let make a mention of Balan how he was there slain by his brother's hands, but she knew not Balin's name.

CHAP. XIX.

How Merlin buried them both in one tomb, and of Balin's sword.

IN the morn came Merlin and let write Balin's name upon the tomb, with letters of gold, That here lieth Balin le Savage, that was the knight with the two swords, and he that smote the dolorous stroke. Also Merlin let make there a bed, that there should never man lye therein but he went out of his wit, yet Launcelot de Lake fordid that bed through his nobleness. And anon after Balin was dead, Merlin took his sword and took off the pommel, and set on another pommel. So Merlin bad a knight that stood afore him to handle that sword, and he assayed, and he might not handle it. Then Merlin laughed. Why laugh ye? said the knight. This is the cause, said Merlin: there shall never man handle this sword but the best knight of the world, and that shall be Sir Launcelot, or else Galahad his son, and Launcelot with this sword shall slay the man that in the world he loved best, that shall be Sir Gawaine. All this he let write in the pommel of the sword. Then Merlin let make a bridge of iron and of steel into that island, and it was but half a foot broad, and there shall never man pass that bridge, nor have hardiness to go over, but if he were a passing good man and a good knight without treachery or villainy. Also the scabbard of Balin's sword Merlin left it on this side the island that Galahad should find it. Also Merlin let make by his subtilty that Balin's sword was put in a marble stone standing upright as great as a millstone, and the stone hoved always above the water, and did many years, and so by adventure it swam down the stream to the city of Camelot, that is in English Winchester. And that same day Galahad the haut prince came with king Arthur, and so Galahad brought with him the scabbard, and achieved the sword that was there in the marble stone hoving upon the water. And on Whitsunday he achieved the sword, as it is rehearsed in the book of the Sangreal. Soon after this was done Merlin came to king Arthur and told him of the dolorous stroke that Balin gave to king Pellam, and how Balin and Balan fought together the most marvellous battle that ever was heard of, and how they were buried both in one tomb. Alas! said king Arthur, this is the greatest pity that ever I heard tell of two knights, for in the world I know not such two knights. Thus endeth the tale of Balin and Balan, two brethren born in Northumberland, good knights.

𝔖equitur iii liber.

The Third Book.

CHAP. I.

How king Arthur took a wife, and wedded Guenever daughter to Leodegrance, king of the land of Cameliard, with whom he had the Round Table.

In the beginning of Arthur, after he was chosen king by adventure and by grace,—for the most part of the barons knew not that he was Uther Pendragon's son, but as Merlin made it openly known,—many kings and lords made great war against him for that cause; but well Arthur overcame them all; for the most part of the days of his life he was ruled much by the counsel of Merlin. So it fell on a time king Arthur said unto Merlin, My barons will let me have no rest, but needs I must take a wife, and I will none take but by thy counsel and by thine advice. It is well done, said Merlin, that ye take a wife, for a man of your bounty and nobleness should not be without a wife. Now is there any that ye love more than another? Yea, said king Arthur, I love Guenever, the daughter of king Leodegrance, of the land of Cameliard, which Leodegrance holdeth in his house the Table Round, that ye told he had of my father, Uther. And this damsel is the most valiant and fairest lady that I know living, or yet that ever I could find. Sir, said Merlin, as of her beauty and fairness she is one of the fairest on live. But and ye loved her not so well as ye do, I could find you a damsel of beauty and of goodness that should like you and please you, and your heart were not set; but there as a man's heart is set, he will be loth to return. That is truth, said king Arthur. But Merlin warned the king covertly that Guenever was not wholesome for him to take to wife, for he warned him that Launcelot should love her, and she

him again; and so he turned his tale to the adventures of the Sangreal. Then Merlin desired of the king to have men with him that should enquire of Guenever, and so the king granted him. And Merlin went forth to king Leodegrance of Cameliard, and told him of the desire of the king that he would have unto his wife Guenever his daughter. That is to me, said king Leodegrance, the best tidings that ever I heard, that so worthy a king of prowess and noblesse will wed my daughter. And as for my lands I will give him wist I it might please him, but he hath lands enough, him needeth none, but I shall send him a gift shall please him much more, for I shall give him the Table Round, the which Uther Pendragon gave me, and when it is full complete there is an hundred knights and fifty. And as for an hundred good knights I have myself, but I lack fifty, for so many have been slain in my days. And so king Leodegrance delivered his daughter Guenever unto Merlin, and the Table Round, with the hundred knights, and so they rode freshly, with great royalty, what by water and what by land, till that they came nigh unto London.

CHAP. II.

How the knights of the Round Table were ordained, and their sieges blessed by the bishop of Canterbury.

When king Arthur heard of the coming of Guenever and the hundred knights with the Table Round, then king Arthur made great joy for their coming, and that rich present, and said openly, This fair lady is passing welcome unto me, for I have loved her long, and therefore there is nothing so lief to me. And these knights with the Round Table please me more than right great riches. And in all haste the king let ordain for the marriage and the coronation in the most honourablest wise that could be devised. Now Merlin, said king Arthur, go thou and espy me in all this land fifty knights which be of most prowess and worship. Within short time Merlin had found such knights that should fulfil twenty and eight knights, but no more he could find. Then the bishop of Canterbury was fetched, and he blessed the sieges with great royalty and devotion, and there set the eight and twenty knights in their sieges. And when this was done Merlin said, Fair sirs, ye must all arise and come to king Arthur for to do him homage; he will have the better will to maintain you. And so they arose and did their homage. And when they were gone Merlin found in every siege letters of gold that told the knights' names that had sitten therein. But two sieges were void. And so anon came young Gawaine, and asked the king a gift. Ask, said the king, and I shall grant it you. Sir, I ask that ye will make me knight that same day ye shall wed fair Guenever. I will do it with a good will, said king Arthur, and do unto you all the worship that I may, for I must by reason you are my nephew, my sister's son.

CHAP. III.

How a poor man riding upon a lean mare desired king Arthur to make his son knight.

FORTHWITHAL there came a poor man into the court, and brought with him a fair young man of eighteen year of age, riding upon a lean mare. And the poor man asked all men that he met, Where shall I find king Arthur? Yonder he is, said the knights, wilt thou anything with him? Yea, said the poor man, therefore I came hither. Anon as he came before the king, he saluted him and said: O king Arthur, the flower of all knights and kings, I beseech Jesu save thee: Sir, it was told me that at this time of your marriage ye would give any man the gift that he would ask out, except that were unreasonable. That

is truth, said the king, such cries I let make, and that will I hold, so it impair not my realm nor mine estate. Ye say well and graciously, said the poor man: Sir, I ask nothing else but that ye will make my son here a knight. It is a great thing that thou askest of me: what is thy name? said the king to the poor man. Sir, my name is Aries the cowherd. Whether cometh this of thee or of thy son? said the king. Nay Sir, said Aries, this desire cometh of my son and not of me. For I shall tell you I have thirteen sons, and all they will fall to what labour I put them to, and will be right glad to do labour, but this child will do no labour for me, for anything that my wife or I may do, but always he will be shooting or casting darts, and glad for·to see battles, and to behold knights; and always day and night he desireth of me to be made a knight. What is thy name? said the king unto the young man. Sir, my name is Tor. The king beheld him fast, and saw he was passingly well visaged and passingly well made of his years. Well, said king Arthur to Aries the cowherd, fetch all thy sons afore me that I may see them. And so the poor man did, and all were shapen much like the poor man: but Tor was not like none of them all in shape nor in countenance, for he was much more than any of them. Now, said king Arthur unto the cowherd, where is the sword that he shall be made knight withal? It is here, said Tor. Take it out of the sheath, said the king, and require me to make you a knight. Then Tor alight off his mare, and pulled out his sword, kneeling, and requiring the king that he would make him knight, and that he might be a knight of the Table Round. As for a knight I will make you; and therewith smote him in the neck with the sword, saying, Be ye a good knight, and so I pray to God so ye may be, and if ye be of prowess and of worthiness ye shall be a knight of the Table Round. Now Merlin, said Arthur, say whether this Tor shall be a good knight or no. Yea, sir, he ought to be a good knight, for he is come of as good a man as any is on live, and of king's blood. How so, sir? said the king. I shall tell you, said Merlin: this poor man, Aries the cowherd, is not his father, he is nothing like to him, for king Pellinore is his father. I suppose nay, said the cowherd. Fetch thy wife afore me, said Merlin, and she shall not say nay. Anon, the wife was fetched, which was a fair house-wife, and there she answered Merlin full womanly. And there she told the king and Merlin that when she was a maid, and went to milk kine, There met with me a stern knight, and half by force he held me, and after that time was born my son Tor, and he took away from me my greyhound that I had that time with me, and said that he would keep the greyhound for my love. Ah, said the cowherd, I wend not this, but I may believe it well, for he had never no taches of me. Sir, said Tor to Merlin, dishonour not my mother. Sir, said Merlin, it is more for your worship than hurt, for your father is a good man and a king, and he may right well advance you and your mother, for ye were begotten or ever she was wedded. That is truth, said the wife. It is the less grief to me, said the cowherd.

CHAP. IV.

How Sir Tor was known for son of king Pellinore, and how Gawaine was made knight.

So on the morn king Pellinore came to the court of king Arthur, which had great joy of him, and told him of Tor, how he was his son, and how he had made him knight at the request of the cowherd. When king Pellinore beheld Tor he pleased him much. So the king made Gawaine knight, but Tor was the first he made at the feast. What is the cause, said king Arthur, that there be two places void in the sieges? Sir, said Merlin, there shall no man sit in those places but they that shall be of most worship. But in the Siege Perilous there shall no man sit therein but one, and if there be any so hardy to do it he shall be destroyed, and he that shall sit

there shall have no fellow. And therewith Merlin took king Pellinore by the hand, and in the one hand next the two sieges and the Siege Perilous he said, in open audience, This is your place, and best ye are worthy to sit therein of any that is here. Thereat sat Sir Gawaine in great envy, and told Gaheris his brother, Yonder knight is put to great worship, the which grieveth me sore, for he slew our father king Lot, therefore I will slay him, said Gawaine, with a sword that was sent me that is passing trenchant. Ye shall not so, said Gaheris, at this time; for at this time I am but a squire, and when I am made knight I will be avenged on him; and therefore brother it is best ye suffer till another time, that we may have him out of the court, for and we did so we should trouble this high feast. I will well, said Gawaine, as ye will.

CHAP. V.

How at the feast of the wedding of king Arthur to Guenever, a white hart came into the hall, and thirty couple hounds, and how a brachet pinched the hart, which was taken away.

THEN was the high feast made ready, and the king was wedded at Camelot unto Dame Guenever in the church of Saint Stephen's, with great solemnity. And as every man was set after his degree, Merlin went to all the knights of the Round Table, and bad them sit still, that none of them remove, For ye shall see a strange and a marvellous adventure. Right so as they sat there came running in a white hart into the hall, and a white brachet next him, and thirty couple of black running hounds came after with a great cry, and the hart went about the Table Round. As he went by other boards, the white brachet bit him by the haunch and pulled out a piece, where through the hart lept a great leap and overthrew a knight that sat at the board side, and therewith the knight arose and took up the brachet, and so went forth out of the hall, and took his horse and rode his way with the brachet.

Right so anon came in a lady on a white palfrey, and cried aloud to king Arthur, Sir, suffer me not to have this despite, for the brachet was mine that the knight led away. I may not do therewith, said the king. With this there came a knight riding all armed on a great horse, and took the lady away with him with force, and ever she cried and made great dole. When she was gone the king was glad, for she made such a noise. Nay, said Merlin, ye may not leave these adventures so lightly, for these adventures must be brought again or else it would be disworship to you and to your feast. I will, said the king, that all be done by your advice. Then, said Merlin, let call Sir Gawaine, for he must bring again the white hart. Also, sir, ye must let call Sir Tor, for he must bring again the brachet and the knight, or else slay him. Also let call king Pellinore, for he must bring again the lady and the knight, or else slay him. And these three knights shall do marvellous adventures or they come again. Then were they called all three as it rehearseth afore, and every each of them took his charge, and armed them surely. But Sir Gawaine had the first request, and therefore we will begin at him.

CHAP. VI.

How Sir Gawaine rode for to fetch again the hart, and how two brethren fought each against other for the hart.

Sir Gawaine rode more than a pace, and Gaheris his brother rode with him instead of a squire, to do him service. So as they rode they saw two knights fight on horseback passing sore, so Sir Gawaine and his brother rode betwixt them, and asked them for what cause they fought so. The one knight answered and said : We fight for a simple matter, for we two be two brethren, born and begotten of one man and of one woman. Alas! said Sir Gawaine, why do ye so? Sir, said the elder, there came a white hart this way this day, and many hounds chased him, and a white brachet was alway next him,

and we understood it was adventure made for the high feast of king Arthur, and therefore I would have gone after to have won me worship; and here my younger brother said he would go after the hart, for he was a better knight than I ; and for this cause we fell at debate, and so we thought to prove which of us both was better knight. This is a simple cause, said Sir Gawaine; strange men ye should debate withal, and not brother with brother; therefore but if ye will do by my counsel I will have ado with you—that is, ye shall yield you unto me, and that ye go unto king Arthur and yield you unto his grace. Sir knight, said the two brethren, we are for-foughten, and much blood have we lost through our wilfulness, and therefore we would be loth to have ado with you. Then do as I will have you, said Sir Gawaine. We will agree to fulfil your will ; but by whom shall we say that we be thither sent ? Ye may say, by the knight that followeth the quest of the hart that was white. Now what is your name ? said Sir Gawaine. Sorlouse of the Forest, said the elder. And my name is, said the younger, Brian of the Forest. And so they departed and went to the king's court, and Sir Gawaine on his quest. And as Gawaine followed the hart by the cry of the hounds, even afore him there was a great river, and the hart swam over ; and as Sir Gawaine would follow after there stood a knight over the other side, and said, Sir knight, come not over after this hart, but if thou wilt just with me. I will not fail as for that, said Sir Gawaine, to follow the quest that I am in, and so made his horse to swim over the water, and anon they gat their spears and ran together full hard, but Sir Gawaine smote him off his horse, and then he turned his horse and bad him yield him. Nay, said the knight, not so, though thou have the better of me on horseback : I pray thee, valiant knight, alight afoot, and match we together with swords. What is your name? said Sir Gawaine. Allardin of the Isles, said the other. Then either dressed their shields and smote together, but Sir Gawaine smote him so hard through the helm that it went to the brains, and the knight fell down dead. Ah! said Gaheris, that was a mighty stroke of a young knight.

CHAP. VII.

How the hart was chased into a castle, and there slain, and how Gawaine slew a lady.

THEN Gawaine and Gaheris rode more than a pace after the white hart, and let slip at the hart three couple of greyhounds, and so they chased the hart into a castle, and in the chief place of the castle they slew the hart: Sir Gawaine and Gaheris followed after. Right so there came a knight out of a chamber with a sword drawn in his hand and slew two of the greyhounds, even in the sight of Sir Gawaine, and the remnant he chased them with his sword out of the castle. And when he came again, he said, O my white hart, me repenteth that thou art dead, for my sovereign lady gave thee to me, and evil have I kept thee, and thy death shall be dear bought and I live. And anon he went into his chamber and armed him, and came out fiercely, and there met he with Sir Gawaine. Why have ye slain my hounds, said Sir Gawaine, for they did but their kind, and lever I had ye had wroken your anger upon me than upon a dumb beast. Thou sayst truth, said the knight, I have avenged me on thy hounds, and so I will on thee or thou go. Then Sir Gawaine alight afoot, and dressed his shield, and they stroke together mightily, and clave their shields, and stoned their helms, and brake their hauberks that the blood ran down to their feet. At the last Sir Gawaine smote the knight so hard that he fell to the earth; and then he cried mercy and yielded him, and besought him as he was a knight and gentleman to save his life. Thou shalt die, said Sir Gawaine, for slaying of my hounds. I will make amends, said the knight, unto my power. Sir Gawaine would no mercy have, but unlaced his

helm to have striken off his head; right so came his lady out of a chamber and fell over him, and so he smote off her head by misadventure. Alas! said Gaheris, that is foul and shamefully done; that shame shall never from you. Also, ye should give mercy unto them that ask mercy; for a knight without mercy is without worship. Sir Gawaine was so astonied at the death of this fair lady that he wist not what he did, and said unto the knight, Arise, I will give thee mercy. Nay, nay, said the knight, I care for no mercy now, for thou hast slain my love and my lady that I loved best of all earthly things. Me repenteth it, said Sir Gawaine, for I thought to strike unto thee. But now thou shalt go unto king Arthur, and tell him of thine adventures, and how thou art overcome by the knight that went in the quest of the white hart. I take no force, said the knight, whether I live or die. But so for dread of death he swore to go unto king Arthur: and he made him to bear one greyhound before him on his horse, and another behind him. What is your name, said Sir Gawaine, or we part? My name is, said the knight, Ablamor of the Marsh. So he departed toward Camelot.

CHAP. VIII.

How four knights fought against Sir Gawaine and Gaheris, and how they were overcome, and their lives saved at the request of four ladies.

AND Sir Gawaine went into the castle, and made him ready to lie there all night, and would have unarmed him. What will ye do? said Gaheris, will ye unarm you in this country? ye may think ye have many enemies here. They had not sooner said that word but there came four knights well armed, and assailed Sir Gawaine hard, and said unto him, Thou new made knight, thou hast shamed thy knighthood, for a knight without mercy is dishonoured. Also thou hast slain a fair lady to thy great shame to the world's end, and doubt thou not thou shalt have great need of mercy or thou depart from us. And therewith one of them smote Sir Gawaine a great stroke, that nigh he fell to the earth, and Gaheris smote him again sore, and so they were on the one side and on the other, that Sir Gawaine and Gaheris were in jeopardy of their lives; and one with a bow, an archer, smote Sir Gawaine through the arm that it grieved him wonderly sore. And as they should have been slain, there came four ladies and besought the knights of grace for Sir Gawaine. And goodly at the request of the ladies they gave Sir Gawaine and Gaheris their lives, and made them to yield them as prisoners. Then Gawaine and Gaheris made great dole. Alas! said Sir Gawaine, mine arm grieveth me sore, I am like to be maimed; and so made his complaint piteously. Early on the morrow there came to Sir Gawaine one of the four ladies that had heard all his complaint, and said, Sir knight, what cheer? Not good, said he. It is your own default, said the lady, for ye have done a passing foul deed in the slaying of the lady, the which will be great villainly unto you. But be ye not of king Arthur's kin? said the lady. Yes, truly, said Sir Gawaine. What is your name? said the lady, ye must tell it me or ye pass. My name is Gawaine, the king Lot of Orkney's son, and my mother is king Arthur's sister. Ah, then are ye nephew unto king Arthur, said the lady, and I shall so speak for you that ye shall have conduct to go to king Arthur for his love. And so she departed and told the four knights how their prisoner was king Arthur's nephew, and his name is Sir Gawaine, king Lot's son of Orkney. And they gave him the hart's head, because it was in his quest. Then anon they delivered Sir Gawaine under this promise, that he should bare the dead lady with him in this manner: the head of her was hanged about his neck, and the whole body of her lay before him on his horse mane. Right so rode he forth unto Camelot. And anon as he was come, Merlin desired of king Arthur that Sir Gawaine should be

sworn to tell of all his adventures, and how he slew the lady, and how he would give no mercy unto the knight, where through the lady was slain. Then the king and the queen were greatly displeased with Sir Gawaine for the slaying of the lady. And there by ordinance of the queen there was set a quest of ladies on Sir Gawaine, and they judged him for ever while he lived to be with all ladies, and to fight for their quarrels; and that ever he should be courteous, and never to refuse mercy to him that asketh mercy. Thus was Gawaine sworn upon the four Evangelists that he should never be against lady nor gentlewoman, but if he fought for a lady and his adversary fought for another. And thus endeth the adventure of Sir Gawaine, that he did at the marriage of king Arthur. Amen.

CHAP. IX.

How Sir Tor rode after the knight with the brachet, and of his adventure by the way.

WHEN Sir Tor was ready he mounted upon his horse's back, and rode after the knight with the brachet. So as he rode he met with a dwarf suddenly that smote his horse on the head with a staff, that he went backward his spear's length. Why dost thou so? said Sir Tor. For thou shalt not pass this way, but if thou just with yonder knights of the pavilions. Then was Sir Tor ware where two pavilions were, and great spears stood out, and two shields hung on trees by the pavilions. I may not tarry, said Sir Tor, for I am in a quest that I must needs follow. Thou shalt not pass, said the dwarf; and therewithal he blew his horn. Then there came one armed on horseback, and dressed his shield, and came fast toward Tor, and he dressed him against him, and so ran together that Sir Tor bare him from his horse. And anon the knight yielded him to his mercy: But, sir, I have a fellow in yonder pavilion that will have ado with you anon. He shall be welcome, said Sir Tor. Then was he ware of another knight coming with great force, and each of them dressed to other that marvel it was to see: but the knight smote Sir Tor a great stroke in the midst of the shield that his spear all to-shivered, and Sir Tor smote him through the shield so low that it went through the side of the knight, but the stroke slew him not. And therewith Sir Tor alight and smote him on the helm a great stroke, and therewith the knight yielded him, and besought him of mercy. I will well, said Sir Tor; but thou and thy fellow must go unto king Arthur, and yield you prisoners unto him. By whom shall we say are we thither sent? Ye shall say by the knight that went in the quest of the knight that went with the brachet. Now what be your two names? said Sir Tor. My name is, said the one, Sir Felot of Langduk. And my name is, said the other, Sir Petipase of Winchelsea. Now go ye forth, said Sir Tor, and God speed you and me. Then came the dwarf and said unto Sir Tor: I pray you give me a gift. I will well, said Sir Tor: ask. I ask no more, said the dwarf, but that ye will suffer me to do you service, for I will serve no more recreant knights. Take an horse, said Sir Tor, and ride on with me. I wot ye ride after the knight with the white brachet, and I shall bring you where he is, said the dwarf. And so they rode throughout a forest, and at the last they were ware of two pavilions even by a priory, with two shields, and the one shield was renewed with white, and the other shield was red.

CHAP. X.

How Sir Tor found the brachet with a lady, and how a knight assailed him for the said brachet.

THEREWITH Sir Tor alighted and gave the dwarf his glaive, and so came to the white pavilion, and saw three damsels lie in it on one pallet sleeping. And so he went to the other pavilion, and there he found a lady lying sleeping therein. But there was the white brachet, that

bayed at her fast, and therewith the lady awoke and went out of the pavilion, and all her damsels. But anon as Sir Tor espied the white brachet he took her by force, and took her to the dwarf. What, will ye so, said the lady, take my brachet from me? Yea, said Sir Tor, this brachet have I sought from king Arthur's court hither. Well, said the lady, knight, ye shall not go far with her but that ye shall be met, and grieved. I shall abide what adventure that cometh, by the grace of God, and so mounted upon his horse and passed on his way toward Camelot; but it was so near night he might not pass but little farther. Know ye any lodging? said Tor. I know none, said the dwarf, but here beside is an hermitage, and there ye must take lodging as ye find. And within awhile they came to the hermitage and took lodging; and was there grass, oats, and bread, for their horses; soon it was sped, and full hard was their supper; but there they rested them all the night till on the morn, and heard a mass devoutly, and took their leave of the hermit, and Sir Tor prayed the hermit to pray for him. He said he would, and betook him to God: and so he mounted on horseback, and rode towards Camelot a long while. With that they heard a knight call loud that came after them, and he said, Knight, abide and yield my brachet that thou tookest from my lady. Sir Tor returned again and beheld him how he was a seemly knight and well horsed, and well armed at all points; then Sir Tor dressed his shield, and took his spear in his hands, and the other came fiercely upon him and smote both horse and man to the earth. Anon they arose lightly and drew their swords as eagerly as lions, and put their shields afore them, and smote through the shields, and the cantels fell off of both parts. Also they hewed their helms, that the hot blood ran out, and the thick mails of their hauberks they carved and rove in sunder, that the hot blood ran to the earth, and both they had many wounds and were passing weary. But Sir Tor espied that the other knight fainted, and then he sued fast upon him, and doubled his strokes, and made him go to the earth on the one side. Then Sir Tor bad him yield him. That will I not, said Abelleus, while my life lasteth and the soul is within my body, unless that thou wilt give me the brachet. That will I not do, said Sir Tor, for it was my quest to bring again thy brachet, thee, or both.

CHAP. XI.

How Sir Tor overcame the knight, and how he lost his head at the request of a lady.

WITH that came a damsel riding on a palfrey as fast as she might drive and cried with a loud voice unto Sir Tor. What will ye with me? said Sir Tor. I beseech thee, said the damsel, for king Arthur's love, give me a gift; I require thee, gentle knight, as thou art a gentleman. Now, said Sir Tor, ask a gift, and I will give it you. Gramercy, said the damsel, Now, I ask the head of the false knight Abelleus, for he is the most outrageous knight that liveth, and the greatest murderer. I am loth, said Sir Tor, of that gift I have given you; let him make amends in that he hath trespassed unto you. Now, said the damsel, he may not, for he slew mine own brother afore mine own eyes, that was a better knight than he, and he had had grace; and I kneeled half an hour afore him in the mire for to save my brother's life, that had done him no damage, but fought with him by adventure of arms, and so for all that I could do he struck off his head; wherefore, I require thee, as thou art a true knight, to give me my gift, or else I shall shame thee in all the court of king Arthur; for he is the falsest knight living, and a great destroyer of good knights. Then when Abelleus heard this, he was more afeard, and yielded him and asked mercy. I may not now, said Sir Tor, but if I should be found false of my promise, for while I would have taken you to mercy ye would none

ask, but if ye had the brachet again that was my quest. And therewith he took off his helm, and he arose and fled, and Sir Tor after him, and smote off his head quite. Now, sir, said the damsel, it is near night; I pray you come and lodge with me here at my place, it is here fast by. I will well, said Sir Tor; for his horse and he had fared evil since they departed from Camelot, and so he rode with her, and had passing good cheer with her; and she had a passing fair old knight to her husband that made him passing good cheer, and well eased both his horse and him. And on the morn he heard his mass, and brake his fast, and took his leave of the knight and of the lady, that besought him to tell them his name. Truly, he said, my name is Sir Tor, that late was made knight, and this was the first quest of arms that ever I did, to bring again that this knight Abelleus took away from king Arthur's court. O fair knight, said the lady and her husband, and ye come here in our marches, come and see our poor lodging, and it shall be always at your commandment. So Sir Tor departed, and came to Camelot on the third day by noon. And the king and the queen and all the court was passing fain of his coming, and made great joy that he was come again; for he went from the court with little succour, but as king Pellinore his father gave him an old courser, and king Arthur gave him armour and a sword, and else had he none other succour, but rode so forth himself alone. And then the king and the queen by Merlin's advice made him to swear to tell of his adventures, and so he told and made proofs of his deeds as it is afore rehearsed, wherefore the king and the queen made great joy. Nay, nay, said Merlin, these be but jests to that he shall do; he shall prove a noble knight of prowess, as good as any is living, and gentle and courteous, and of good parts, and passing true of his promise, and never shall outrage. Where through Merlin's words king Arthur gave him an earldom of lands that fell unto him. And here endeth the quest of Sir Tor, king Pellinore's son.

CHAP. XII.

How king Pellinore rode after the lady and the knight that led her away, and how a lady desired help of him, and how he fought with two knights for that lady, of whom he slew the one at the first stroke.

THEN king Pellinore armed him and mounted upon his horse, and rode more than a pace after the lady that the knight led away. And as he rode in a forest, he saw in a valley a damsel sit by a well, and a wounded knight in her arms, and Pellinore saluted her. And when she was ware of him, she cried over loud, Help me knight, for Christ's sake, king Pellinore! And he would not tarry he was so eager in his quest, and ever she cried an hundred times after help. When she saw he would not abide, she prayed unto God to send him as much need of help as she had, and that he might feel it or he died. So as the book telleth, the knight died that there was wounded, wherefore the lady for pure sorrow slew herself with his sword. As king Pellinore rode in that valley he met with a poor man, a labourer: Sawest thou not, said Pellinore, a knight riding and leading away a lady? Yea, said the poor man, I saw that knight, and the lady that made great dole. And yonder beneath in a valley there shall ye see two pavilions, and one of the knights of the pavilions challenged that lady of that knight, and said she was his cousin near, wherefore he should lead her no farther. And so they waged battle in that quarrel; the one said he would have her by force, and the other said he would have the rule of her because he was her kinsman, and would lead her to her kin. For this quarrel I left them fighting, and if ye will ride a pace ye shall find them fighting, and the lady was beleft with the two squires in the pavilions. I thank thee, said king Pellinore. Then he rode a wallop till that he had a sight of the two pavilions, and the two knights fighting. Anon he rode unto the pavilions, and saw the lady that was his quest, and said, Fair lady, ye must go with me unto the court of king Arthur. Sir knight, said the two squires that were with her, yonder are two knights that fight for this lady, go thither and depart them, and be agreed with them, and then ye may have her at your pleasure. Ye say well, said king Pellinore. And anon he rode betwixt them, and departed them, and asked them the cause why that they fought. Sir knight, said the one, I shall tell you. This lady is my kinswoman nigh, mine aunt's daughter, and when I heard her complain that she was with him maugre her head, I waged battle to fight with him. Sir knight, said the other, whose name was Hontzlake of Wentland, and this lady I gat by my prowess of arms this day at Arthur's court. That is untruly said, said king Pellinore, for ye came in suddenly there as we were at the high feast, and took away this lady or any man might him ready, and therefore it was my quest for to bring her again and you both, or else the one of us to abide in the field; therefore the lady shall go with me, or I will die for it, for I have promised it king Arthur. And therefore fight ye no more, for none of you shall have no part of her at this time, and if ye list to fight for her, fight with me, and I will defend her. Well, said the knights, make you ready, and we shall assail you with all our power. And as king Pellinore would have put his horse from them, Sir Hontzlake rove his horse through with a sword, and said: Now art thou on foot as well we are. When king Pellinore espied that his horse was slain, lightly he leapt from his horse and pulled out his sword, and put his shield afore him, and said: Knight, keep well thy head, for thou shalt have a buffet for the slaying of my horse. So king Pellinore gave him such a stroke upon the helm that he clave the head down to the chin, that he fell to the earth dead.

CHAP. XIII.

How king Pellinore gat the lady and brought her to Camelot to the court of king Arthur.

AND then he turned him to the other knight that was sore wounded. But when he saw the other's buffet he would not fight, but kneeled down and said, Take my cousin, the lady, with you at your request, and I require you, as ye be a true knight, put her to no shame nor villainy. What, said king Pellinore, will ye not fight for her? No, sir, said the knight, I will not fight with such a knight of prowess as ye be. Well, said Pellinore, ye say well, I promise you she shall have no villainy by me, as I am true knight; but now me lacketh an horse, said Pellinore, but I will have Hontzlake's horse. Ye shall not need, said the knight, for I shall give you such a horse as shall please you, so that ye will lodge with me, for it is near night. I will well, said king Pellinore, abide with you all night. And there he had with him right good cheer, and fared of the best with passing good wine, and had merry rest that night. And on the morrow he heard a mass, and dined: and then was brought him a fair bay courser, and king Pellinore's saddle set upon him. Now, what shall I call you? said the knight, inasmuch as ye have my cousin at your desire of your quest. Sir, I shall tell you; my name is king Pellinore, of the Isles, and knight of the Table Round. Now I am glad, said the knight, that such a noble man shall have the rule of my cousin. What is now your name? said Pellinore, I pray you tell me. Sir, my name is Sir Meliot of Logurs, and this lady my cousin, hight Nimue, and the knight that was in the other pavilion is my sworn brother, a passing good knight, and his name is Brian of the Isles, and he is full loth to do wrong, and full loth to fight with any man, but if he be sore sought on, so that for shame he may not leave it. It is marvel, said Pellinore, that he will not have ado with me. Sir, he will not have ado with no man but if it be at his request. Bring him to the court, said Pellinore, one of these days. Sir, we will come together. And ye shall be welcome, said king Pellinore, to the court of king Arthur, and greatly allowed for your coming. And so he departed with the lady, and brought her to Camelot. So as they rode in a valley it was full of stones, and there the lady's horse stumbled and threw her down, wherewith her arm was sore bruised, and near she swooned for pain. Alas! sir, said the lady, mine arm is out of joint, where through I must needs rest me. Ye shall well, said king Pellinore. And so he alighted under a fair tree where was fair grass, and he put his horse thereto, and so laid him under the tree and slept till it was nigh night. And when he awoke he would have ridden. Sir, said the lady, it is so dark that ye may as well ride backward as forward. So they abode still and made there their lodging. Then Sir Pellinore put off his armour; then a little afore midnight they heard the trotting of an horse. Be ye still, said king Pellinore, for we shall hear of some adventure.

CHAP. XIV.

How on the way king Pellinore heard two knights, as he lay by night in a valley, and of other adventures.

AND therewith he armed him. So right even afore him there met two knights, the one came from Camelot and the other from the north, and either saluted other. What tidings at Camelot? said the one. By my head, said the other, there have I been, and espied the court of king Arthur, and there is such a fellowship they may never be broken, and well nigh all the world holdeth with Arthur, for there is the flower of chivalry. Now for this cause I am riding into the north to tell our chieftains of the fellowship that is withholden with king Arthur. As for that, said the other knight, I have brought a remedy with me, that is the greatest poison that ever ye heard speak of, and to Camelot will I with it, for we have a friend right nigh king Arthur, and well cherished, that shall poison king Arthur, for so he hath promised our chieftains, and received great gifts for to do it. Beware, said the other knight, of Merlin, for he knoweth all things by the devil's craft. Therefore will I not let it, said the knight. And so they departed in sunder. Anon after Pellinore made him ready, and his lady, and rode toward Camelot. And as they came by the well there as the wounded knight was and the lady, there he found the knight, and the lady eaten with lions or wild beasts all save the head, wherefore he made great sorrow, and wept passing sore, and said: Alas, her life might I have saved, but I was so fierce in my quest therefore I would not abide. Wherefore make ye such dole, said the lady. I wot not, said Pellinore, but my heart mourneth sore for the death of her, for she was a passing fair lady and a young. Now will ye do by mine advice, said the lady, take this knight and let him be buried in an hermitage, and then take the lady's head and bear it with you unto Arthur. So king Pellinore took this dead knight on his shoulders and brought him to the hermitage, and charged the hermit with the corpse, that service should be done for the soul; and take his harness for your pain. It shall be done, said the hermit, as I will answer unto God.

CHAP. XV.

How when king Pellinore was come to Camelot he was sworn upon a book to tell truth of his quest.

AND therewith they departed and came there as the head of the lady lay with a fair yellow hair, that grieved king Pellinore passingly sore when he looked on it, for much he cast his heart on the visage. And so by noon they came to Camelot. And the king and the queen were passing fain of his coming to the court. And there he was made to swear upon the four Evangelists to tell the truth of his quest from the one to the other. Ah, Sir Pellinore, said queen Guenever, ye were greatly to blame that ye saved not this lady's life. Madam, said Pellinore, ye were greatly to blame and ye would not save your own life and ye might; but saving your pleasure, I was so furious in my quest that I would not abide, and that repenteth me, and shall the days of my life. Truly, said Merlin, ye ought sore to repent it, for the lady was your own daughter, and that knight that was dead was her love, and should have wedded her, and he was a right good knight of a young man, and would have proved a good man, and to this court was he coming, and his name was Sir Miles of the lands, and a knight came behind him and slew him with a spear, and his name is Loraine le Savage, a false knight and a coward; and she for great sorrow and dole slew herself with his sword, and her name was Eleine. And because ye would not abide and help her, ye shall see your best friend fail you when ye be in the greatest distress that ever ye were or shall be. And that penance God hath ordained you for that deed, that he that ye shall most trust to of any man alive, he shall leave you there as ye shall be slain. Me forthinketh, said king Pellinore, that this shall betide, but God may well fordo destiny.

Thus when the quest was done of the white hart, the which followed Sir Gawaine; and the quest of the brachet followed of Sir Tor, Pellinore's son; and the quest of the lady that the knight took away, the which king Pellinore at that time followed; then the king stablished all his knights, and them that were of lands not rich he gave them lands, and charged them never to do outrage, nor murder, and always to flee treason. Also, by no mean to be cruel, but to give mercy unto him that asketh mercy, upon pain of forfeiture of their worship and lordship of king Arthur for evermore; and alway to do ladies, damsels, and gentlewomen succour upon pain of death. Also, that no man take no battles in a wrongful quarrel for no law, nor for world's goods. Unto this were all the knights sworn of the Table Round, both old and young. And every year were they sworn at the high feast of Pentecost.

𝔈𝔵𝔭𝔩𝔦𝔠𝔦𝔱 𝔱𝔥𝔢 𝔴𝔢𝔡𝔡𝔶𝔫𝔤𝔢 𝔬𝔣 𝔨𝔶𝔫𝔤𝔢 𝔄𝔯𝔱𝔥𝔲𝔯.
𝔖𝔢𝔮𝔲𝔦𝔱𝔲𝔯 𝔮𝔲𝔞𝔯𝔱𝔲𝔰 𝔩𝔦𝔟𝔢𝔯.

𝔗𝔥𝔢 𝔉𝔬𝔲𝔯𝔱𝔥 𝔅𝔬𝔬𝔨.

CHAP. I.

How Merlin was assotted and doted on one of the ladies of the lake, and how he was shut in a rock under a stone, and there died.

So after these quests of Sir Gawaine, Sir Tor, and king Pellinore, it fell so that Merlin fell in a dotage on the damsel that king Pellinore brought to court, and she was one of the damsels of the lake, that hight Nimue. But Merlin would let her have no rest, but always he would be with her. And ever she made Merlin good cheer till she had learned of him all manner thing that she desired; and he was assotted upon her that he might not be from her. So on a time he told king Arthur that he should not dure long, but for all his crafts he should be put in the earth quick, and so he told the king many things that should befall, but always he warned the king to keep well his sword and the scabbard, for he told him how the sword and the scabbard should be stolen by a woman from him that he most trusted. Also he told king Arthur that he should miss him : —Yet had ye lever than all your lands to have me again. Ah, said the king, since ye know of your adventure, purvey for it, and put away by your crafts that misadventure. Nay, said Merlin, it will not be. So he departed from the king. And within awhile the damsel of the lake departed, and Merlin went with her evermore wheresoever she went. And oft times Merlin would have had her privily away by his subtle crafts : then she made him to swear that he should never do none enchantment upon her if he would have his will. And so he sware : so she and Merlin went over the sea unto the land of Benwick, where as king Ban was king that had great war against king Claudas, and there Merlin spake with king Ban's wife, a fair lady and a good, and her name was Elaine, and there he saw young Launcelot. There the queen made great sorrow for the mortal war that king Claudas made on her lord and on her lands. Take none heaviness, said Merlin, for this same child within this twenty year shall revenge you on king Claudas, that all christendom shall speak of it : and this same child shall be the man of most worship of the world, and his first name is Galahad, that know I well, said Merlin, and since ye have confirmed him, Launcelot. That is truth, said the queen, his first name was Galahad. O, Merlin, said the queen, shall I live to see my son such a man of prowess? Yea, lady, on my peril ye shall see it, and live many winters after. And so, soon after the lady and Merlin departed ; and by the way Merlin shewed her many wonders, and came into Cornwall. And always Merlin lay about the lady to have her love, and she was ever passing weary of him, and fain would have been delivered of him, for she was afeard of him because he was a devil's son, and she could not put him away by no means.

And so on a time it happed that Merlin shewed to her in a rock whereas was a great wonder, and wrought by enchantment, that went under a great stone. So by her subtle working, she made Merlin to go under that stone to let her wit of the marvels there, but she wrought so there for him that he came never out for all the craft that he could do. And so she departed and left Merlin.

CHAP. II.

How five kings came into this land to war against king Arthur, and what counsel Arthur had against them.

AND as king Arthur rode to Camelot, and held there a great feast with mirth and joy, so soon after he returned unto Cardoile, and there came unto Arthur new tidings that the king of Denmark, and the king of Ireland that was his brother, and the king of the Vale, and the king of Soleise, and the king of the Isle of Longtainse, all these five kings with a great host were entered into the land of king Arthur, and burnt and slew clean afore them both cities and castles, that it was pity to hear. Alas, said Arthur, yet had I never rest one month since I was crowned king of this land. Now shall I never rest till I meet with those kings in a fair field, that I make mine avow; for my true liege people shall not be destroyed in my default, go with me who will, and abide who that will. Then the king let write unto king Pellinore, and prayed him in all haste to make him ready with such people as he might lightliest rear, and hie him after in all haste. All the barons were privily wroth that the king would depart so suddenly : but the king by no mean would abide, but made writing unto them that were not there, and bad them hie after him, such as were not at that time in the court. Then the king came to queen Guenever, and said, Lady, make you ready, for ye shall go with me, for I may not long miss you, ye shall cause me to be the more hardy, what adventure so befall me : I will not wit my lady to be in no jeopardy. Sir, said she, I am at your commandment, and shall be ready what time so ye be

ready. So on the morn the king and the queen departed with such fellowship as they had, and came into the north into a forest beside Humber, and there lodged them. When the word and tiding came to the five kings above said, that king Arthur was beside Humber in a forest, there was a knight, brother unto one of the five kings, that gave them this counsel: Ye know well that Sir Arthur hath the flower of chivalry of the world with him, as it is proved by the great battle he did with the eleven kings; and therefore hie unto him night and day till that we be nigh him, for the longer he tarrieth the bigger he is, and we ever the weaker; and he is so courageous of himself, that he is come to the field with little people, and therefore let us set upon him or day, and we shall slay down of his knights there shall none escape.

CHAP. III.

How king Arthur had ado with them and overthrew them, and slew the five kings, and made the remnant to flee.

UNTO this counsel these five kings assented, and so they passed forth with their host through North Wales, and came upon Arthur by night, and set upon his host as the king and his knights were in their pavilions. King Arthur was unarmed, and had laid him to rest with his queen Guenever. Sir, said Sir Kay, it is not good we be unarmed : we shall have no need, said Sir Gawaine and Sir Griflet, that lay in a little pavilion by the king. With that they heard a great noise, and many cried treason, treason ! Alas, said king Arthur, we are betrayed ! Unto arms, fellows ! then he cried. So they were armed anon at all points. Then came there a wounded knight unto the king, and said, Sir, save yourself and my lady the queen, for our host is destroyed, and much people of ours slain. So anon the king and the queen and the three knights took their horses, and rode toward Humber to pass over it, and the water was so rough that they were afeard to pass over. Now may ye choose, said king Arthur, whether ye will abide and take the adventure on this side, for and ye be taken they will slay you. It were me lever, said the queen, to die in the water than to fall in your enemies' hands, and there be slain. And as they stood so talking, Sir Kay saw the five kings coming on horseback by themselves alone, with their spears in their hands even toward them. Lo, said Sir Kay, yonder be the five kings, let us go to them and match them. That were folly, said Sir Gawaine, for we are but four and they be five. That is truth, said Sir Griflet. No force, said Sir Kay, I will undertake for two of them, and then may ye three undertake for the other three. And therewithal Sir Kay let his horse run as fast as he might, and struck one of them through the shield and the body a fathom, that the king fell to the earth stark dead. That saw Sir Gawaine and ran unto another king so hard that he smote him through the body. And therewithal king Arthur ran to another, and smote him through the body with a spear, that he fell to the earth dead. Then Sir Griflet ran unto the fourth king, and gave him such a fall that his neck brake. Anon Sir Kay ran unto the fifth king, and smote him so hard on the helm that the stroke clave the helm and the head to the earth. That was well stricken, said king Arthur, and worshipfully hast thou holden thy promise, therefore I shall honour thee while that I live. And therewithal they set the queen in a barge into Humber, but always queen Guenever praised Sir Kay for his deeds, and said, What lady that ye love, and she love you not again, she were greatly to blame; and among ladies, said the queen, I shall bear your noble fame, for ye spake a great word, and fulfilled it worshipfully. And therewith the queen departed. Then the king and the three knights rode into the forest, for there they supposed to hear of them that were escaped; and there king Arthur found the most part of his people, and told them all how the five kings were dead.—

And therefore let us hold us together till it be day, and when their host have espied that their chieftains be slain, they will make such dole that they shall no more help themselves. And right so as the king said, so it was; for when they found the five kings dead, they made such dole that they fell from their horses. Therewithal came king Arthur but with a few people, and slew on the left hand and on the right hand, that well nigh there escaped no man, but all were slain to the number of thirty thousand. And when the battle was all ended, the king kneeled down and thanked God meekly. And then he sent for the queen, and soon she was come, and she made great joy of the overcoming of that battle.

CHAP. IV.

How the battle was finished or king Pellinore came, and how king Arthur founded an abbey where the battle was.

THEREWITHAL came one to king Arthur, and told him that king Pellinore was within three mile with a great host; and he said, Go unto him, and let him understand how we have sped. So within awhile king Pellinore came with a great host, and saluted the people and the king: and there was great joy made on every side. Then the king let search how much people of his party there was slain: and there were found but little past two hundred men slain, and eight knights of the Table Round in their pavilions. Then the king let rear and devise in the same place there as the battle was done a fair abbey, and endowed it with great livelihood, and let call it the Abbey of La Beale Adventure. But when some of them came into their countries whereof the five kings were kings, and told them how they were slain, there was made great dole. And when all king Arthur's enemies, as the king of North Wales, and the kings of the North, wist of the battle they were passing heavy. And so the king returned to Camelot in haste. And when he was come to Camelot he called king

Pellinore unto him, and said, Ye understand well, that we have lost eight knights of the best of the Table Round, and by your advice we will choose eight again of the best we may find in this court. Sir, said Pellinore, I shall counsel you after my conceit the best; there are in your court full noble knights both of old and young, and therefore by mine advice ye shall choose half of the old and half of the young. Which be the old? said king Arthur. Sir, said king Pellinore, me seemeth that king Uriens that hath wedded your sister Morgan le Fay, and the king of the Lake, and Sir Hervise de Revel, a noble knight, and Sir Galagars the fourth. This is well devised, said king Arthur, and right so shall it be. Now, which are the four young knights? said Arthur. Sir, said Pellinore, the first is Sir Gawaine your nephew, that is as good a knight of his time as any is in this land; and the second, as me seemeth, is Sir Griflet le Fise de Dieu, that is a good knight, and full desirous in arms, and who may see him live he shall prove a good knight; and the third as me seemeth is well to be one of the knights of the Round Table, Sir Kay the seneschal, for many times he hath done full worshipfully, and now at your last battle he did full honourably for to undertake to slay two kings. By my head, said king Arthur, he is best worthy to be a knight of the Round Table of any that ye have rehearsed, and he had done no more prowess in his life days.

CHAP. V.

How Sir Tor was made knight of the Round Table, and how Bagdemagus was displeased.

Now, said king Pellinore, I shall put to you two knights, and ye shall choose which is most worthy, that is Sir Bagdemagus, and Sir Tor, my son. But because Sir Tor is my son I may not praise him, but else, and he were not my son, I durst say that of his age there is not in this land a better knight then he is, nor of better conditions, and loth to do any wrong, and loth to take any

wrong. By my head, said Arthur, he is a passing good knight, as any ye spake of this day, that wot I well, said the king, for I have seen him proved, but he saith little, and he doth much more, for I know none in all this court, and he were as well born on his mother's side as he is on your side, that is like him of prowess and of might; and therefore I will have him at this time, and leave Sir Bagdemagus till another time. So when they were so chosen by the assent of all the barons, so were there found in their sieges every knight's names that here are rehearsed. And so were they set in their sieges, whereof Sir Bagdemagus was wonderly wroth, that Sir Tor was advanced afore him, and therefore suddenly he departed from the court, and took his squire with him, and rode long in a forest till they came to a cross, and there alight and said his prayers devoutly. The meanwhile his squire found written upon the cross, that Bagdemagus should never return unto the court again till he had won a knight's body of the Round Table, body for body. Lo, sir, said his squire, here I find writing of you, therefore I counsel you return again to the court. That shall I never, said Bagdemagus, till men speak of me great worship, and that I be worthy to be a knight of the Round Table. And so he rode forth. And there by the way he found a branch of an holy herb that was the sign of the Sangreal, and no knight found such tokens but he were a good liver. So as Sir Bagdemagus rode to see many adventures, it happed him to come to the rock there as the lady of the lake had put Merlin under a stone, and there he heard him make great dole; whereof Sir Bagdemagus would have holpen him, and went unto the great stone, and it was so heavy that an hundred men might not lift it up. When Merlin wist he was there, he bad leave his labour, for all was in vain, for he might never be holpen but by her that put him there. And so Sir Bagdemagus departed, and did many adventures, and proved after a full good knight, and came again to the court, and was made knight of the Round Table. So on the morn there fell new tidings and other adventures.

CHAP. VI.

How king Arthur, king Uriens, and Sir Accolon of Gaul chased an hart, and of their marvellous adventures.

THEN it befel that Arthur and many of his knights rode on hunting into a great forest, and it happed king Arthur, king Uriens, and Sir Accolon of Gaul followed a great hart, for they three were well horsed, and so they chased so fast that within awhile they three were then ten mile from their fellowship. And at the last they chased so sore that they slew their horses underneath them. Then were they all three on foot, and ever they saw the hart afore them passing weary and enbushed. What will ye do? said king Arthur, we are hard bested. Let us go on foot, said king Uriens, till we may meet with some lodging. Then were they ware of the hart that lay on a great water bank, and a brachet biting on his throat, and more other hounds came after. Then king Arthur blew the prise and dight the hart. Then the king looked about the world, and saw afore him in a great water a little ship, all apparelled with silk down to the water, and the ship came right unto them, and landed on the sands. Then Arthur went to the bank and looked in, and saw none earthly creature therein. Sirs, said the king, come thence, and let us see what is in this ship. So they went in all three, and found it richly behanged with cloth of silk. By then it was dark night, and there suddenly were about them an hundred torches set upon all the sides of the ship boards, and it gave great light; and therewithal there came out twelve fair damsels and saluted king Arthur on their knees, and called him by his name, and said he was right welcome, and such cheer as they had he should have of the best. The king thanked them fair. Therewithal they led the king and his two fellows into a fair chamber, and there was a cloth laid richly beseen of all that longed unto a table, and there were they served of all wines and meats that they could think; of that the king had great marvel, for he fared never better in his life as for one supper. And so when they had supped at their leisure, king Arthur was led into a chamber, a richer beseen chamber saw he never none; and so was king Uriens served, and led into such another chamber; and Sir Accolon was led into the third chamber, passing richly and well beseen: and so were they laid in their beds easily. And anon they fell on sleep, and slept marvellously sore all that night. And on the morrow king Uriens was in Camelot with his wife, Morgan le Fay. And when he awoke he had great marvel how he came there, for on the even afore he was two days' journey from Camelot. And when king Arthur awoke he found himself in a dark prison, hearing about him many complaints of woful knights.

CHAP. VII.

How Arthur took upon him to fight to be delivered out of prison, and also for to deliver twenty knights that were in prison.

WHAT are ye that so complain? said king Arthur. We be here twenty knights prisoners, said they, and some of us have lain here seven year, and some more and some less. For what cause? said Arthur. We shall tell you, said the knights; This lord of this castle his name is Sir Damas, and he is the falsest knight that liveth, and full of treason, and a very coward as any liveth, and he hath a younger brother, a good knight of prowess, his name is Sir Ontzlake, and this traitor Damas, the elder brother, will give him no part of his livelihood but as Sir Ontzlake keepeth through prowess of his hands, and so he keepeth from him a full fair manor and a rich, and therein Sir Ontzlake dwelleth worshipfully and is well beloved of all people. And this Sir Damas our master is as evil beloved, for he is without mercy, and he is a coward, and great war hath been betwixt them both, but Ontzlake hath ever the better, and ever he proffereth Sir Damas to fight for the livelihood, body for body; but if he will not do it to find a knight to fight for him. Unto that Sir Damas hath granted to find a knight, but he is so evil beloved and hated, that there is never a knight will fight for him. And when Damas saw this, that there was never a knight would fight for him, he hath daily lain await with many knights with him and taken all the knights in this country to see and espy their adventures: he hath taken them by force and brought them to his prison. And so he took us severally as we rode on our adventures, and many good knights have died in this prison for hunger, to the number of eighteen knights: and if any of us all that here is or hath been, would have fought with his brother Ontzlake he would have delivered us, but for because this Damas is so false and so full of treason, we would never fight for him to die for it. And we be so lean with hunger that hardly we may stand on our feet. God deliver you for his mercy, said Arthur. Anon therewithal there came a damsel unto Arthur, and asked him, What cheer? I cannot say, said he. Sir, said she, and ye will fight for my lord, ye shall be delivered out of prison, and else ye escape never with life. Now, said Arthur, that is hard, yet had I lever to fight with a knight than to die in prison: with this, said Arthur, that I may be delivered and all these prisoners I will do the battle. Yes, said the damsel. I am ready, said Arthur, and I had horse and armour. Ye shall lack none, said the damsel. Me seemeth, damsel, that I should have seen you in the court of Arthur. Nay, said the damsel, I came never there, I am the lord's daughter of this castle. Yet was she false, for she was one of the damsels of Morgan le Fay. Anon she went unto Sir Damas, and told him how he would do battle for him, and so he

sent for Arthur. And when he came he was well coloured, and well made of his limbs, that all knights that saw him said it were pity that such a knight should die in prison. So Sir Damas and he were agreed that he should fight for him upon this covenant, that all other knights should be delivered; and unto that was Sir Damas sworn unto Arthur, and also to do the battle to the uttermost. And with that all the twenty knights were brought out of the dark prison into the hall and delivered. And so they all abode to see the battle.

CHAP. VIII.

How Accolon found himself by a well, and he took upon him to do battle against Arthur.

Now turn we unto Accolon of Gaul, that when he awoke he found himself by a deep well side, within half a foot, in great peril of death. And there came out of that fountain a pipe of silver, and out of that pipe ran water all on high in a stone of marble. When Sir Accolon saw this he blessed him and said: Jesu save my lord king Arthur, and king Uriens, for these damsels in this ship have betrayed us. They were devils and no women, and if I may escape this misadventure, I shall destroy all where I may find these false damsels that use enchantments.

Right with that there came a dwarf with a great mouth and a flat nose, and saluted Sir Accolon, and said how he came from queen Morgan le Fay; and she greeteth you well, and biddeth you be of strong heart, for ye shall fight to morn with a knight at the hour of prime, and therefore she hath sent you here Excalibur Arthur's sword, and the scabbard, and she biddeth you as ye love her, that ye do the battle to the uttermost without any mercy, like as ye had promised her when ye spake together in private: and what damsel that bringeth her the knight's head that ye shall fight withal, she will make her a queen. Now I understand you well, said Accolon: I shall hold that I have promised her, now I have the sword: when saw ye my lady queen Morgan le Fay? Right late, said the dwarf. Then Accolon took him in his arms, and said, Recommend me unto my lady queen, and tell her all shall be done that I have promised her, and else I will die for it. Now I suppose, said Accolon, she hath made all these crafts and enchantments for this battle. Ye may well believe it, said the dwarf. Right so there came a knight and a lady with six squires, and saluted Sir Accolon and prayed him for to arise, and come and rest him at his manor. And so Accolon mounted upon a void horse, and went with the knight unto a fair manor by a priory, and there he had passing good cheer. Then Sir Damas sent unto his brother Sir Ontzlake, and bade make him ready by to morn at the hour of prime, and to be in the field to fight with a good knight, for he had found a good knight that was ready to do battle at all points. When this word came unto Sir Ontzlake he was passing heavy, for he was wounded a little tofore through both his thighs with a spear, and made great dole: but as he was wounded he would have taken the battle on hand. So it happed at that time, by the means of Morgan le Fay, Accolon was with Sir Ontzlake lodged; and when he heard of that battle, and how Ontzlake was wounded, he said he would fight for him, because Morgan le Fay had sent him Excalibur and the sheath for to fight with the knight on the morn; this was the cause Sir Accolon took the battle on hand. Then Sir Ontzlake was passing glad, and thanked Sir Accolon with all his heart that he would do so much for him. And therewithal Sir Ontzlake sent word unto his brother Sir Damas that he had a knight that for him should be ready in the field by the hour of prime. So on the morn Sir Arthur was armed and well horsed, and asked Sir Damas, When shall we to the field? Sir, said Sir Damas, ye shall hear mass; and so Arthur heard a mass. And when mass was done there came a squire on a great horse, and asked Sir

Damas if his knight were ready, for our knight is ready in the field. Then Sir Arthur mounted upon horseback, and there were all the knights and commons of that country; and so by all advices there were chosen twelve good men of the country for to wait upon the two knights. And right as Arthur was upon horseback there came a damsel from Morgan le Fay, and brought unto Sir Arthur a sword like unto Excalibur, and the scabbard, and said unto Arthur, Morgan le Fay sendeth you here your sword for great love. And he thanked her, and wend it had been so, but she was false, for the sword and the scabbard was counterfeit, and brittle, and false.

CHAP. IX.
Of the battle between king Arthur and Accolon.

AND then they dressed them on both parts of the field, and let their horses run so fast that either smote other in the midst of the shield with their spears' head, that both horse and man went to the earth; and then they started up both, and pulled out their swords. The mean while that they were thus at the battle, came the damsel of the lake into the field, that put Merlin under the stone, and she came thither for love of king Arthur, for she knew how Morgan le Fay had so ordained that king Arthur should have been slain that day, and therefore she came to save his life. And so they went eagerly to the battle, and gave many great strokes. But alway king Arthur's sword bit not like Accolon's sword, but for the most part every stroke that Accolon gave wounded he sore Arthur, that it was marvel he stood; and alway his blood fell from him fast. When Arthur beheld the ground so sore be-bled he was dismayed, and then he deemed treason, that his sword was changed; for his sword bit not steel as it was wont to do, therefore he dread him sore to be dead, for ever him seemed that the sword in Accolon's hand was Excalibur, for at every stroke that Sir Accolon struck he drew blood on Arthur. Now knight, said Accolon unto Arthur, keep thee well from me : but Arthur answered not again, and gave him such a buffet on the helm that he made him to stoop, nigh falling down to the. earth. Then Sir Accolon withdrew him a little, and came on with Excalibur on high, and smote Sir Arthur such a buffet that he fell nigh to the earth. Then were they wroth both, and gave each other many sore strokes, but always Sir Arthur lost so much blood that it was marvel he stood on his feet, but he was so full of knighthood that knightly he endured the pain. And Sir Accolon lost not a deal of blood, therefore he waxed passing light, and Sir Arthur was passing feeble, and wend verily to have died; but for all that he made countenance as though he might endure, and held Accolon as short as he might. But Accolon was so bold because of Excalibur that he waxed passing hardy. But all men that beheld him said they never saw knight fight so well as Arthur did, considering the blood that he bled. So was all the people sorry for him, but the two brethren would not accord; then always they fought together as fierce knights, and Sir Arthur withdrew him a little for to rest him, and Sir Accolon called him to battle, and said, It is no time for me to suffer thee to rest. And therewith he came fiercely upon Arthur, and Sir Arthur was wroth for the blood that he had lost, and smote Accolon on high upon the helm so mightily that he made him nigh to fall to the earth; and therewith Arthur's sword brast at the cross, and fell in the grass among the blood, and the pommel and the sure handles he held in his hands. When Sir Arthur saw that, he was in great fear to die, but always he held up his shield, and lost no ground, nor bated no cheer.

CHAP. X.

How king Arthur's sword that he fought with brake, and how he recovered of Accolon his own sword Excalibur, and overcame his enemy.

THEN Sir Accolon began with words of treason, and said, Knight, thou art overcome, and mayest not endure, and also thou art weaponless, and thou hast lost much of thy blood, and I am full loth to slay thee, therefore yield thee to me as recreant. Nay, said Sir Arthur, I may not so, for I have promised to do the battle to the uttermost by the faith of my body while me lasteth the life, and therefore I had lever to die with honour than to live with shame; and if it were possible for me to die an hundred times I had lever to die so oft than yield me to thee; for though I lack weapon I shall lack no worship, and if thou slay me weaponless that shall be thy shame. Well, said Accolon, as for the shame I will not spare: now keep thee from me, for thou art but a dead man. And therewith Accolon gave him such a stroke that he fell nigh to the earth, and would have had Arthur to have cried him mercy. But Sir Arthur pressed unto Accolon with his shield, and gave him with the pommel in his hand such a buffet that he went three strides aback. When the damsel of the lake beheld Arthur, how full of prowess his body was, and the false treason that was wrought for him to have had him slain, she had great pity that so good a knight and such a man of worship should be destroyed. And at the next stroke Sir Accolon struck him such a stroke, that by the damsel's enchantment the sword Excalibur fell out of Accolon's hand to the earth; and therewithal Sir Arthur lightly leapt to it, and got it in his hand, and forthwithal he knew that it was his sword Excalibur, and said, Thou hast been from me all too long, and much damage hast thou done me. And therewith he espied the scabbard hanging by his side, and suddenly he start to him, and pulled the scabbard from him, and anon threw it from him as far as he might throw it. O knight, said Arthur, this day hast thou done me great damage with this sword; now are ye come unto your death, for I shall not warrant you but ye shall as well be rewarded with this sword or ever we depart, as thou hast rewarded me, for much pain have ye made me to endure, and much blood have I lost. And therewith Sir Arthur rushed on him with all his might and pulled him to the earth, and then rushed off his helm, and gave him such a buffet on the head that the blood came out at his ears, his nose, and his mouth. Now will I slay thee, said Arthur. Slay me ye may well, said Accolon, and it please you, for ye are the best knight that ever I found, and I see well that God is with you: but for I promised to do this battle to the uttermost, said Accolon, and never to be recreant while I lived, therefore shall I never yield me with my mouth, but God do with my body what he will. Then Sir Arthur remembered him, and thought he should have seen this knight. Now tell me, said Arthur, or I will slay thee, of what country art thou, and of what court? Sir knight, said Sir Accolon, I am of the court of king Arthur, and my name is Accolon of Gaul. Then was Arthur more dismayed than he was beforehand; for then he remembered him of his sister Morgan le Fay, and of the enchantment of the ship. O Sir knight, said he, I pray you tell me who gave you this sword, and by whom ye had it.

CHAP. XI.

How Accolon confessed the treason of Morgan le Fay, king Arthur's sister, and how she would have done slay him.

THEN Sir Accolon bethought him, and said, Woe worth this sword, for by it have I gotten my death. It may well be, said the king. Now Sir, said Sir Accolon, I will tell you: This sword hath been in my keeping the most part of this twelvemonth, and Morgan le Fay, king Uriens' wife, sent it me yesterday by a dwarf, to this intent that I should slay king Arthur her brother. For ye shall understand king Arthur is the man in the world that she most hateth, because he is most of worship and of prowess of any of her blood.

Also, she loveth me out of measure as paramour, and I her again. And if she might bring about to slay Arthur by her crafts, she would slay her husband king Uriens lightly, and then had she me devised to be king in this land, and so to reign, and she to be my queen; but that is now done, said Sir Accolon, for I am sure of my death. Well, said king Arthur, I feel by you ye would have been king in this land. It had been great damage for to have destroyed your lord, said Arthur. It is truth, said Sir Accolon, but now I have told you truth, wherefore I pray you tell me of whence ye are, and of what court? O Accolon, said king Arthur, now I let thee wit that I am king Arthur to whom thou hast done great damage. When Accolon heard that he cried aloud, Fair sweet lord, have mercy on me, for I knew you not. O Sir Accolon, said king Arthur, mercy shalt thou have, because I feel by thy words at this time thou knewest not my person. But I understand well by thy words that thou hast agreed to the death of my person, and therefore thou art a traitor; but I blame thee the less, for my sister Morgan le Fay by her false crafts made thee to agree and consent to her false lusts, but I shall be sore avenged upon her and I live, that all Christendom shall speak of it. God knoweth I have honoured her and worshipped her more than all my kin, and more have I trusted her than mine own wife, and all my kin after. Then Sir Arthur called the keepers of the field, and said, Sirs, come hither, for here are we two knights that have fought unto a great damage unto us both, and like each one of us to have slain other, if it had happed so; and had any of us known other, here had been no battle, nor stroke stricken. Then all aloud cried Sir Accolon unto all the knights and men that were then there gathered together, and said to them in this manner: O lords, this noble knight that I have fought withal, the which me sore repenteth, is the most man of prowess, of manhood, and of worship in the world, for it is himself king Arthur, our alther liege lord, and with mishap and with misadventure have I done this battle with the king and lord that I am holden withal.

CHAP. XII.

How Arthur accorded the two brethren, and delivered the twenty knights, and how Sir Accolon died.

THEN all the people fell down on their knees, and cried king Arthur mercy. Mercy shall ye have, said Arthur: here may ye see what adventures befall oft time of errant knights, how that I have fought with a knight of mine own unto my great damage and his both. But sirs, because I am sore hurt, and he both, and I had great need of a little rest, ye shall understand the opinion betwixt you two brethren: As to thee, Sir Damas, for whom I have been champion, and won the field of this knight, yet will I judge because ye Sir Damas are called an orgulous knight, and full of villainy, and not worth of prowess of your deeds, therefore I will that ye give unto your brother all the whole manor with the appurtenance, under this form, that Sir Ontzlake hold the manor of you, and yearly to give you a palfrey to ride upon, for that will become you better to ride on than upon a courser. Also I charge thee, Sir Damas, upon pain of death, that thou never distress no knights errant that ride on their adventure. And also that thou restore these twenty knights that thou hast long kept prisoners of all their harness that they be content for, and if any of them come to my court and complain of thee, by my head thou shalt die therefore. Also, Sir Ontzlake, as to you, because ye are named a good knight, and full of prowess, and true and gentle in all your deeds, this shall be your charge: I will give you that in all goodly haste ye come unto me and my court, and ye shall be a knight of mine, and if your deeds be thereafter I shall so

prefer you, by the grace of God, that ye shall in short time be in ease for to live as worshipfully as your brother Sir Damas.—God thank your largeness of your goodness and of your bounty, and I shall be from henceforth at all times at your commandment: for, Sir, said Sir Ontzlake, I was hurt but late with an adventurous knight through both my thighs, which grieved me sore, and else had I done this battle with you. Would, said Arthur, it had been so, for then had not I been hurt as I am. I shall tell you the cause why: for I had not been hurt as I am had not it been mine own sword that was stolen from me by treason; and this battle was ordained aforehand to have slain me, and so it was brought to the purpose by false treason, and by false enchantment. Alas, said Sir Ontzlake, that is great pity, that ever so noble a man as ye are of your deeds and prowess, that any man or woman might find in their hearts to work any treason against you. I shall reward them, said Arthur, in short time by the grace of God. Now tell me, said Arthur, how far am I from Camelot? Sir, ye are two days' journey therefrom. I would fain be at some place of worship, said Sir Arthur, that I might rest me. Sir, said Sir Ontzlake, hereby is a rich abbey of your elders' foundation, of Nuns, but three mile hence. So the king took his leave of all the people, and mounted upon horseback, and Sir Accolon with him. And when they were come to the abbey, he let fetch leeches and search his wounds and Accolon's both, but Sir Accolon died within four days, for he had bled so much blood that he might not live, but king Arthur was well recovered. So when Accolon was dead he let send him on an horse-bier with six knights unto Camelot, and said, Bear him to my sister Morgan le Fay, and say that I send her him to a present, and tell her that I have my sword Excalibur, and the scabbard. So they departed with the body.

CHAP. XIII.

How Morgan would have slain Sir Uriens her husband, and how Sir Uwaine her son saved him.

THE mean while Morgan le Fay had wend king Arthur had been dead. So on a day she espied king Uriens lay in his bed sleeping, then she called unto her a maiden of her counsel, and said: Go fetch me my lord's sword, for I saw never better time to slay him than now. O Madam, said the damsel, and ye slay my lord, ye can never escape. Care not you, said Morgan le Fay, for now I see my time in the which it is best to do it, and therefore hie thee fast, and fetch me the sword. Then the damsel departed, and found Sir Uwaine sleeping upon a bed in another chamber, so she went unto Sir Uwaine, and awaked him, and bad him, Arise, and wait on my lady your mother, for she will slay the king your father sleeping in his bed, for I go to fetch his sword. Well, said Sir Uwaine, go on your way, and let me deal. Anon the damsel brought Morgan the sword with quaking hands, and she lightly took the sword, and pulled it out, and went boldly unto the bed-side, and awaited how and where she might slay him best. And as she lift up the sword to smite, Sir Uwaine lept unto his mother, and caught her by the hand, and said, Ah, fiend, what wilt thou do? And thou wert not my mother, with this sword I should smite off thy head. Ah, said Sir Uwaine, men say that Merlin was begotten of a devil, but I may say an earthly devil bare me. Oh fair son Uwaine, have mercy upon me; I was tempted with a devil, wherefore I cry thee mercy; I will never more do so; and save my worship and discover me not. On this covenant, said Sir Uwaine, I will forgive it you, so ye will never be about to do such deeds. Nay, son, said she, and that I make you assurance.

CHAP. XIV.

How queen Morgan le Fay made great sorrow for the death of Accolon, and how she stole away the scabbard from Arthur.

THEN came tidings unto Morgan le Fay that Accolon was dead, and his body brought unto the church, and how king Arthur had his sword again. But when queen Morgan wist that Accolon was dead she was so sorrowful that near her heart to burst. But because she would not it were known, outward she kept her countenance, and made no semblance of sorrow. But well she wist, and she abode till her brother Arthur came thither, there should no gold go for her life.

Then she went unto queen Guenever, and asked her leave to ride into the country. Ye may abide, said queen Guenever, till your brother the king come home. I may not, said Morgan le Fay, for I have such hasty tidings that I may not tarry. Well, said Guenever, ye may depart when ye will. So early on the morn, or it was day, she took her horse and rode all that day, and most part of the night, and on the morn by noon she came to the same abbey of nuns, whereas lay king Arthur, and she, knowing he was there, asked where he was: and they answered how he had laid him in his bed to sleep, for he had had but little rest these three nights. Well, said she, I charge you that none of you awake him till I do. And then she alight off her horse, and thought for to steal away Excalibur his sword, and so she went straight unto his chamber, and no man durst disobey her commandment, and there she found Arthur asleep in his bed, and Excalibur in his right hand naked. When she saw that, she was passing heavy that she might not come by the sword without she had awaked him, and then she wist well she had been dead. Then she took the scabbard, and went her way on horseback. When the king awoke and missed his scabbard, he was wroth, and he asked who had been there, and they said his sister queen Morgan had been there, and had put the scabbard under her mantle, and was gone. Alas, said Arthur, falsely have ye watched me. Sir, said they all, we durst not disobey your sister's commandment. Ah, said the king, let fetch the best horse that may be found, and bid Sir Ontzlake arm him in all haste, and take another good horse and ride with me. So anon the king and Ontzlake were well armed, and rode after this lady; and so they came by a cross, and found a cowherd, and they asked the poor man if there came any lady late riding that way. Sir, said this poor man, right late came a lady riding with a forty horses, and to yonder forest she rode. Then they spurred their horses and followed fast, and within awhile Arthur had a sight of Morgan le Fay; then he chased as fast as he might. When she espied him following her, she rode a greater pace through the forest till she came to a plain. And when she saw she might not escape, she rode unto a lake thereby, and said, Whatsoever becometh of me, my brother shall not have this scabbard. And then she let throw the scabbard in the deepest of the water, so it sank, for it was heavy of gold and precious stones. Then she rode into a valley where many great stones were, and when she saw that she must be overtaken, she shaped herself, horse and man, by enchantment, unto a great marble stone. Anon withal came Sir Arthur and Sir Ontzlake, whereas the king might not know his sister and her men, and one knight from another. Ah, said the king, here may ye see the vengeance of God, and now am I sorry that this misadventure is befallen. And then he looked for the scabbard, but it would not be found. So he returned to the abbey there he came from. So when Arthur was gone she turned all into the likeness as she and they were before, and said, Sirs, now may we go where we will.

CHAP. XV.

How Morgan le Fay saved a knight that should have been drowned, and how king Arthur returned home again.

THEN said Morgan, Saw ye Arthur my brother? Yea, said her knights, right well, and that ye should have found and we might have stirred from one stead, for by his warlike countenance he would have caused us to have fled. I believe you, said Morgan. Anon after as she rode she met a knight leading another knight on his horse before him, bound hand and foot blindfold, to have drowned him in a fountain. When she saw this knight so bound, she asked him, What will ye do with that knight? Lady, said he, I will drown him. For what cause? she asked. For I found him with my wife, and she shall have the same death anon. That were pity, said Morgan le Fay: now what say ye, knight, is it truth that he saith of you? she said to the knight that should be drowned. Nay truly, madam, he saith not right of me. Of whence be ye? said Morgan le Fay, and of what country? I am of the court of king Arthur, and my name is Manassen, cousin unto Accolon of Gaul. Ye say well, said she, and for the love of him ye shall be delivered, and ye shall have your adversary in the same case ye be in. So Manassen was loosed and the other knight bound. And anon Manassen unarmed him, and armed himself in his harness, and so mounted on horseback, and the knight afore him, and so threw him into the fountain and drowned him. And then he rode unto Morgan again, and asked her if she would anything unto king Arthur. Tell him that I rescued thee not for the love of him but for the love of Accolon, and tell him I fear him not while I can make me and them that be with me in likeness of stones; and let him wit I can do much more when I see my time. And so she departed into the country of Gore, and there was she richly received, and made her castles and towns passing strong, for always she drad much king Arthur. When the king had well rested him at the abbey he rode unto Camelot, and found his queen and his barons right glad of his coming. And when they heard of his strange adventures as is afore rehearsed, they all had marvel of the falsehood of Morgan le Fay: many knights wished her burnt. Then came Manassen to the court and told the king of his adventure. Well, said the king, she is a kind sister, I shall so be avenged on her and I live, that all christendom shall speak of it. So on the morn there came a damsel from Morgan to the king, and she brought with her the richest mantle that ever was seen in that court, for it was set as full of precious stones as one might stand by another, and there were the richest stones that ever the king saw. And the damsel said, Your sister sendeth you this mantle, and desireth that ye should take this gift of her, and in what thing she hath offended you she will amend it at your own pleasure. When the king beheld this mantle it pleased him much, but he said but little.

CHAP. XVI.

How the damsel of the lake saved king Arthur from a mantle which should have burnt him.

With that came the damsel of the lake unto the king, and said, Sir, I must speak with you in private. Say on, said the king, what ye will. Sir, said the damsel, put not on you this mantle till ye have seen more, and in no wise let it not come on you, nor on no knight of yours, till ye command the bringer thereof to put it upon her. Well, said king Arthur, it shall be done as ye counsel me. And then he said unto the damsel that came from his sister, Damsel, this mantle that ye have brought me I will see it upon you. Sir, said she, it will not beseem me to wear a king's garment. By my head, said Arthur, ye shall wear it or it come on my back, or any man's that here is. And so the king made it to be put upon her, and forthwithal she fell down dead, and never more spake word after, and burnt to coals. Then was the king wonderly wroth, more than he was toforehand, and said unto king Uriens, My sister your wife is alway about to betray me, and well I wot either ye, or my nephew your son, is of counsel with her to have me

destroyed; but as for you, said the king to king Uriens, I deem not greatly that ye be of her counsel, for Accolon confessed to me by his own mouth, that she would have destroyed you as well as me, therefore I hold you excused; but as for your son Sir Uwaine, I hold him suspected, therefore I charge you put him out of my court. So Sir Uwaine was discharged. And when Sir Gawaine wist that, he made him ready to go with him, and said: Who so banisheth my cousin german shall banish me. So they two departed and rode into a great forest. And so they came to an abbey of monks, and there were well lodged. But when the king wist that Sir Gawaine was departed from the court there was made great sorrow among all the estates. Now, said Gaheris, Gawaine's brother, we have lost two good knights for the love of one. So on the morn they heard their masses in the abbey, and so they rode forth till they came to a great forest; then was Sir Gawaine ware in a valley by a turret, of twelve fair damsels, and two knights armed on great horses, and the damsels went to and fro by a tree. And then was Sir Gawaine ware how there hung a white shield on that tree, and ever as the damsels came by it they spit upon it, and some threw mire upon the shield.

CHAP. XVII.

How Sir Gawaine and Sir Uwaine met with twelve fair damsels, and how they complained on Sir Marhaus.

Then Sir Gawaine and Sir Uwaine went and saluted them, and asked why they did that despite to the shield. Sirs, said the damsels, we shall tell you. There is a knight in this country that owneth this white shield, and he is a passing good man of his hands, but he hateth all ladies and gentlewomen, and therefore we do all this despite to the shield. I shall say you, said Sir Gawaine, it beseemeth evil a good knight to despise all ladies and gentlewomen, and peradventure though he hate you he hath some cause, and peradventure he loveth in some other places ladies and gentlewomen, and to be loved again, and he be such a man of prowess as ye speak of. Now what is his name? Sir, said they, his name is Marhaus, the king's son of Ireland. I know him well, said Sir Uwaine, he is a passing good knight as any is on live, for I saw him once proved at a justs where many knights were gathered, and that time there might no man withstand him. Ah! said Sir Gawaine, damsels, methinketh ye are to blame, for it is to suppose he that hung that shield there he will not be long therefrom, and then may those knights match him on horseback, and that is more your worship than thus; for I will abide no longer to see a knight's shield dishonoured. And therewith Sir Uwaine and Gawaine departed a little from them, and then were they ware where Sir Marhaus came riding on a great horse straight towards them. And when the twelve damsels saw Sir Marhaus they fled into the turret as they were wild, so that some of them fell by the way. Then the one of the knights of the tower dressed his shield, and said on high, Sir Marhaus, defend thee. And so they ran together that the knight brake his spear on Marhaus, and Sir Marhaus smote him so hard that he brake his neck and the horse's back. That saw the other knight of the turret, and dressed him toward Marhaus, and they met so eagerly together that the knight of the turret was soon smitten down, horse and man, stark dead.

CHAP. XVIII.

How Sir Marhaus justed with Sir Gawaine and Sir Uwaine, and overthrew them both.

AND then Sir Marhaus rode unto his shield, and saw how it was defouled, and said, Of this despite I am a part avenged, but for her love that gave me this white shield I shall wear thee, and hang mine where thou wast: and so he hanged it about his neck. Then he rode straight unto Sir Gawaine and to Sir Uwaine, and asked them what they did

there. They answered him that they came from king Arthur's court for to see adventures. Well, said Marhaus, here am I ready, an adventurous knight that will fulfil any adventure that ye will desire. And so departed from them to fetch his range. Let him go, said Sir Uwaine unto Sir Gawaine, for he is a passing good knight as any is living: I would not by my will that any of us were matched with him. Nay, said Sir Gawaine, not so; it were shame to us were he not assayed, were he never so good a knight. Well, said Sir Uwaine, I will assay him afore you, for I am more weaker than ye, and if he smite me down then may ye revenge me. So these two knights came together with great random, that Sir Uwaine smote Sir Marhaus that his spear brast in pieces on the shield, and Sir Marhaus smote him so sore that horse and man he bare to the earth, and hurt Sir Uwaine on the left side. Then Sir Marhaus turned his horse and rode toward Gawaine with his spear. And when Sir Gawaine saw that, he dressed his shield, and they aventred their spears, and they came together with all the might of their horses, that either knight smote other so hard in the midst of their shields, but Sir Gawaine's spear brake, but Sir Marhaus's spear held; and therewith Sir Gawaine and his horse rushed down to the earth. And lightly Sir Gawaine rose upon his feet, and pulled out his sword, and dressed him toward Sir Marhaus on foot. And Sir Marhaus saw that, and pulled out his sword, and began to come to Sir Gawaine on horseback. Sir knight, said Sir Gawaine, alight on foot, or else I will slay thy horse. Gramercy, said Sir Marhaus, of your gentleness, ye teach me courtesy, for it is not for one knight to be on foot and the other on horseback. And therewith Sir Marhaus set his spear against a tree and alighted, and tied his horse to a tree, and dressed his shield, and either came unto other eagerly, and smote together with their swords that their shields flew in cantels, and they bruised their helms and their hauberks, and wounded either other. But Sir Ga-waine, fro it passed nine of the clock waxed ever stronger and stronger, till it came to the hour of noon, and thrice his might was increased. All this espied Sir Marhaus, and had great wonder how his might increased, and so they wounded other passing sore. And then when it was past noon, and when it drew toward even-song, Sir Gawaine's strength feebled and waxed passing faint, that unnethes he might dure any longer, and Sir Marhaus was then bigger and bigger. Sir knight, said Sir Marhaus, I have well felt that ye are a passing good knight, and a marvellous man of might as ever I felt any, while it lasteth, and our quarrels are not great, and therefore it were pity to do you hurt, for I feel ye are passing feeble. Ah, said Sir Gawaine, gentle knight, ye say the word that I should say. And therewith they took off their helms and either kissed other, and there they swore together either to love other as brethren. And Sir Marhaus prayed Sir Gawaine to lodge with him that night. And so they took their horses and rode toward Sir Marhaus's house. And as they rode by the way, Sir knight, said Sir Gawaine, I have marvel that so valiant a man as ye be love no ladies nor damsels. Sir, said Sir Marhaus, they name me wrongfully those that give me that name, but well I wot it be the damsels of the turret that so name me, and other such as they be. Now shall I tell you for what cause I hate them. For they be sorceresses and enchanters many of them, and be a knight never so good of his body and full of prowess as man may be, they will make him a stark coward to have the better of him, and this is the principal cause that I hate them ; and to all good ladies and gentlewomen I owe my service as a knight ought to do. As the book rehearseth in French, there were many knights that overmatched Sir Gawaine, for all the thrice-might that he had: Sir Launcelot de Lake, Sir Tristram, Sir Bors de Ganis, Sir Percivale, Sir Pelleas, and Sir Marhaus, these six knights had the better of Sir

Gawaine. Then within a little while they came to Sir Marhaus's place, which was in a little priory, and there they alight, and ladies and damsels unarmed them, and hastily looked to their hurts, for they were all three hurt. And so they had all three good lodging with Sir Marhaus, and good cheer : for when he wist that they were king Arthur's sister's sons, he made them all the cheer that lay in his power. And so they sojourned there a seven nights, and were well eased of their wounds, and at the last departed. Now, said Sir Marhaus, we will not part so lightly, for I will bring you through the forest : and rode day by day well a seven days or they found any adventure. At the last they came into a great forest, that was named the country and forest of Arroy, and the country of strange adventures. In this country, said Sir Marhaus, came never knight since it was christened, but he found strange adventures. And so they rode and came into a deep valley full of stones, and thereby they saw a fair stream of water ; above thereby was the head of the stream, a fair fountain, and three damsels sitting thereby. And then they rode to them, and either saluted other, and the eldest had a garland of gold about her head, and she was threescore winter of age or more, and her hair was white under the garland. The second damsel was of thirty winter of age, with a circlet of gold about her head. The third damsel was but fifteen year of age, and a garland of flowers about her head. When these knights had so beheld them, they asked them the cause why they sat at that fountain. We be here, said the damsels, for this cause, if we may see any errant knights, to teach them unto strange adventures, and ye be three knights that seek adventures, and we be three damsels, and therefore each one of you must choose one of us. And when ye have done so we will lead you unto three high ways, and there each of you shall choose a way, and his damsel with him. And this day twelvemonth ye must meet here again, and God send you your lives, and thereto ye must plight your troth. This is well said, said Sir Marhaus.

CHAP. XIX.

How Sir Marhaus, Sir Gawaine, and Sir Uwaine met three damsels, and each of them took one.

Now shall every each of us choose a damsel. I shall tell you, said Sir Uwaine: I am the youngest and most weakest of you both, therefore I will have the eldest damsel, for she hath seen much and can help me best when I have need, for I have most need of help of you both. Now, said Sir Marhaus, I will have the damsel of thirty winter age, for she fallest best to me. Well, said Sir Gawaine, I thank you, for ye have left me the youngest and the fairest, and she is most liefest to me. Then every damsel took her knight by the reins of his bridle, and brought them to the three ways, and there was their oath made to meet at the fountain that day twelvemonth and they were living, and so they kissed and departed, and every each knight set his lady behind him. And Sir Uwaine took the way that lay west, and Sir Marhaus took the way that lay south, and Sir Gawaine took the way that lay north.

Now will we begin at Sir Gawaine that held that way till he came unto a fair manor, where dwelled an old knight and a good householder, and there Sir Gawaine asked the knight if he knew any adventures in that country. I shall shew you some to-morn, said the old knight, and that marvellous. So on the morn they rode into the forest of adventures till they came to a lawn, and thereby they found a cross, and as they stood and hoved there came by them the fairest knight and the seemliest man that ever they saw, making the greatest dole that ever man made. And then he was ware of Sir Gawaine, and saluted him, and prayed God to send him much worship. As to that, said Sir Gawaine, Gramercy! Also, I pray to God that he send you honour and worship. Ah, said the knight, I may lay that aside, for sorrow and shame cometh to me after worship.

CHAP. XX.

How a knight and a dwarf strove for a lady.

AND therewith he passed unto the one side of the lawn. And on the other side Sir Gawaine saw ten knights that hoved still, and made them ready with their shields and spears against that one knight that came by Sir Gawaine. Then this one knight aventred a great spear, and one of the ten knights encountered with him, but this woful knight smote him so hard that he fell over his horse tail. So this same dolorous knight served them all, that at the least way he smote down horse and man, and all he did with one spear. And so when they were all ten on foot they went to that one knight, and he stood stone still, and suffered them to pull him down off his horse, and bound him hand and foot, and tied him under the horse belly, and so led him with them. Oh, said Sir Gawaine, this is a doleful sight, to see the yonder knight so to be entreated, and it seemeth by the knight that he suffereth them to bind him so, for he maketh no resistance. No, said his host, that is truth, for and he would they all were too weak so to do him. Sir, said the damsel unto Sir Gawaine, me seemeth it were your worship to help that dolorous knight, for me thinketh he is one of the best knights that ever I saw. I would do for him, said Sir Gawaine, but it seemeth that he will have no help. Then said the damsel, me seemeth ye have no lust to help him. Thus as they talked they saw a knight on that other side of the lawn, all armed save the head. And on the other side there came a dwarf on horseback all armed save the head, with a great mouth and a short nose. And when the dwarf came nigh he said, Where is the lady should meet us here? and therewithal she came forth out of the wood. And then they began to strive for the lady; for the knight said he would have her, and the dwarf said he would have her. Will we do well? said the dwarf; yonder is a knight at the cross, let us put it both upon him, and as he deemeth so shall it be. I will well, said the knight; and so they went all three unto Sir Gawaine, and told him wherefore they strove. Well sirs, said he, will ye put the matter into my hand? Yea, they said both. Now, damsel, said Sir Gawaine, ye shall stand betwixt them both, and whether ye list better to go to, he shall have you. And when she was set between them both she left the knight and went to the dwarf. And the dwarf took her and went his way singing, and the knight went his way with great mourning. Then came there two knights all armed, and cried on high, Sir Gawaine, knight of king Arthur, make thee ready in all haste and just with me. So they ran together that either fell down. And then on foot they drew their swords and did full actually. In the meanwhile the other knight went to the damsel and asked her why she abode with that knight, and if ye would abide with me, I will be your faithful knight. And with you will I be, said the damsel, for with Sir Gawaine I may not find in mine heart to be with him: for now here was one knight discomfited ten knights, and at the last he was cowardly led away; and therefore let us two go our way whilst they fight. And Sir Gawaine fought with that other knight long, but at the last they accorded both. And then the knight prayed Sir Gawaine to lodge with him that night. So as Sir Gawaine went with this knight he asked him, What knight is he in this country that smote down the ten knights? For when he had done so manfully, he suffered them to bind him hand and foot, and so led him away. Ah! said the knight, that is the best knight I trow in the world, and the most man of prowess, and he hath been served so as he was even more than ten times, and his name hight Sir Pelleas, and he loveth a great lady in this country, and her name is Ettard. And so when he loved her there

was cried in this country a great justs three days: and all the knights of this country were there and gentlewomen; and who that proved him the best knight should have a passing good sword and a circlet of gold, and the circlet the knight should give it to the fairest lady that was at the justs. And this knight, Sir Pelleas, was the best knight that was there, and there were five hundred knights, but there was never man that ever Sir Pelleas met withal, but he struck him down, or else from his horse. And every day of three days he struck down twenty knights, therefore they gave him the prize. And forthwithal he went there as the lady Ettard was, and gave her the circlet, and said openly she was the fairest lady that there was, and that would he prove upon any knight that would say nay.

CHAP. XXI.

How king Pelleas suffered himself to be taken prisoner because he would have a sight of his lady, and how Sir Gawaine promised him for to get to him the love of his lady.

AND so he chose her for his sovereign lady, and never to love other but her. But she was so proud that she had scorn of him, and said she would never love him, though he would die for her. Wherefore all ladies and gentlewomen had scorn of her that she was so proud, for there were fairer than she, and there was none that was there but and Sir Pelleas would have proffered them love, they would have loved him for his noble prowess. And so this knight promised the lady Ettard to follow her into this country, and never to leave her till she loved him. And thus he is here the most part nigh her, and lodged by a priory, and every week she sendeth knights to fight with him. And when he hath put them to the worse, then will he suffer them wilfully to take him prisoner, because he would have a sight of this lady. And alway she doth him great despite, for sometimes she maketh her knights to tie him to his horse tail, and some to bind him under the horse belly. Thus in the most shamefullest wise that she can think he is brought to her. And all she doth it for to cause him to leave this country, and to leave his loving. But all this cannot make him to leave, for and he would have fought on foot he might have had the better of the ten knights as well on foot as on horseback. Alas! said Sir Gawaine, it is great pity of him, and after this night I will seek him to-morrow in this forest, to do him all the help that I can. So on the morn Sir Gawaine took his leave of his host Sir Carados, and rode into the forest. And at the last he met with Sir Pelleas making great moan out of measure, so each of them saluted other, and asked him why he made such sorrow. And as it is above rehearsed, Sir Pelleas told Sir Gawaine: But alway I suffer her knights to fare so with me as ye saw yesterday, in trust at the last to win her love, for she knoweth well all her knights should not lightly win me and me list to fight with them to the uttermost. Wherefore I loved her not so sore I had lever die an hundred times, and I might die so oft, rather than I would suffer that despite; but I trust she will have pity upon me at the last, for love causeth many a good knight to suffer to have his intent, but, alas! I am unfortunate. And therewith he made so great dole and sorrow that unnethe he might hold him on horseback. Now, said Sir Gawaine, leave your mourning, and I shall promise you by the faith of my body, to do all that lieth in my power to get you the love of your lady, and thereto I will plight you my troth. Ah, said Sir Pelleas, of what court are ye? tell me, I pray you, my good friend. And then Sir Gawaine said, I am of the court of king Arthur, and his sister's son, and king Lot of Orkney was my father, and my name is Sir Gawaine. And then he said, My name is Sir Pelleas, born in the Isles, and of many isles I am lord, and never have I loved lady nor damsel till now in an unhappy time; and Sir

knight, since ye are so nigh cousin unto king Arthur, and a king's son, therefore betray me not but help me, for I may never come by her but by some good knight, for she is in a strong castle here fast by within this four mile, and over all this country she is lady of. And so I may never come to her presence but as I suffer her knights to take me, and but if I did so that I might have a sight of her, I had been dead long or this time, and yet fair word had I never of her, but when I am brought tofore her she rebuketh me in the foulest manner. And then they take my horse and harness, and put me out of the gates, and she will not suffer me to eat nor drink, and always I offer me to be her prisoner, but that she will not suffer me, for I would desire no more what pains soever I had, so that I might have a sight of her daily. Well, said Sir Gawaine, all this shall I amend, and ye will do as I shall devise. I will have your horse and your armour, and so will I ride to her castle, and tell her that I have slain you, and so shall I come within her to cause her to cherish me, and then shall I do my true part that ye shall not fail to have the love of her.

CHAP. XXII.

How Sir Gawaine came to the lady Ettard, and how Sir Pelleas found them sleeping.

AND therewith Sir Gawaine plight his troth unto Sir Pelleas to be true and faithful unto him. So each one plight their troth to other, and so they changed horses and harness, and Sir Gawaine departed and came to the castle whereas stood the pavilions of this lady without the gate. And as soon as Ettard had espied Sir Gawaine she fled in toward the castle. Sir Gawaine spake on high, and bad her abide, for he was not Sir Pelleas: I am another knight that hath slain Sir Pelleas. Do off your helm, said the lady Ettard, that I may see your visage. And so when she saw that it was not Sir Pelleas she made him alight, and led him unto her castle, and asked him faithfully whether he had slain Sir Pelleas. And he said her yea, and told her his name was Sir Gawaine of the court of king Arthur, and his sister's son. Truly, said she, that is great pity, for he was a passing good knight of his body, but of all men on live I hated him most, for I could never be quit of him. And for ye have slain him I shall be your lady, and to do anything that may please you. So she made Sir Gawaine good cheer. Then Sir Gawaine said that he loved a lady, and by no mean she would love him. She is to blame, said Ettard, and she will not love you, for ye that be so well born a man, and such a man of prowess, there is no lady in the world too good for you. Will ye, said Sir Gawaine, promise me to do all that ye may, by the faith of your body, to get me the love of my lady? Yea, sir, said she, and that I promise you by the faith of my body. Now, said Sir Gawaine, it is yourself that I love so well, therefore I pray you hold your promise. I may not choose, said the lady Ettard, but if I should be forsworn. And so she granted him to fulfil all his desire.

So it was then in the month of May that she and Sir Gawaine went out of the castle and supped in a pavilion, and in another pavilion she laid her damsels, and in the third pavilion she laid part of her knights, for then she had no dread of Sir Pelleas. And there Sir Gawaine abode with her in that pavilion two days and two nights. And on the third day in the morning early Sir Pelleas armed him, for he had never slept since Sir Gawaine departed from him. For Sir Gawaine had promised him, by the faith of his body, to come to him unto his pavilion by that priory within the space of a day and a night. Then Sir Pelleas mounted upon horseback, and came to the pavilions that stood without the castle, and found in the first pavilion three knights in three beds, and three squires lying at their feet. Then went he to the second pavilion and found four gentlewomen lying in four beds. And then he went to the third pavilion and found Sir Gawaine with his lady Ettard, and when he saw that his heart

well nigh burst for sorrow, and said: Alas! that ever a knight should be found so false. And then he took his horse, and might not abide no longer for pure sorrow. And when he had ridden nigh half a mile, he turned again and thought to slay them both: and when he saw them both sleeping fast, unnethe he might hold him on horseback for sorrow, and said thus to himself, Though this knight be never so false I will never slay him sleeping; for I will never destroy the high order of knighthood. And therewith he departed again. And or he had ridden half a mile he returned again, and thought then to slay them both, making the greatest sorrow that ever man made. And when he came to the pavilions he tied his horse to a tree, and pulled out his sword naked in his hand, and went to them there as they lay, and yet he thought it were shame to slay them sleeping, and laid the naked sword overthwart both their throats, and so took his horse and rode his way. And when Sir Pelleas came to his pavilions he told his knights and his squires how he had sped, and said thus to them: For your true and good service ye have done me I shall give you all my goods, for I will go unto my bed, and never arise until I am dead. And when that I am dead I charge you that ye take the heart out of my body and bear it her betwixt two silver dishes, and tell her how I saw her with the false knight Sir Gawaine. Right so Sir Pelleas unarmed himself and went unto his bed, making marvellous dole and sorrow.

Then Sir Gawaine and Ettard awoke out of their sleep, and found the naked sword overthwart their throats. Then she knew well it was Sir Pelleas' sword. Alas! said she to Sir Gawaine, ye have betrayed me and Sir Pelleas both, for ye told me ye had slain him, and now I know well it is not so, he is on live. And if Sir Pelleas had been as uncourteous to you as ye have been to him, ye had been a dead knight: but ye have deceived me and betrayed me falsely, that all ladies and damsels may beware by you and me. And therewith Sir Gawaine made him ready and went into the forest. So it happed then that the damsel of the lake Nimue met with a knight of Sir Pelleas, that went on his foot in the forest making. great dole, and she asked him the cause. And so the woful knight told her how that his master and lord was betrayed through a knight and a lady, and how he will never arise out of his bed till he be dead. Bring me to him, said she, anon, and I will warrant his life, he shall not die for love, and she that hath caused him so to love she shall be in as evil plight as he is or it be long, for it is no joy of such a proud lady that will have no mercy of such a valiant knight. Anon that knight brought her unto him. And when she saw him lie in his bed, she thought she saw never so likely a knight : and therewith she threw an enchantment upon him, and he fell on sleep. And therewhile she rode unto the lady Ettard, and charged no man to awake him till she came again. So within two hours she brought the lady Ettard thither, and both ladies found him on sleep. Lo, said the damsel of the lake, ye ought to be ashamed for to murder such a knight. And therewith she threw such an enchantment upon her that she loved him sore, that well nigh she was out of her mind. Alas! said the lady Ettard, how is it befallen unto me that I love now him that I have most hated of any men alive. That is the righteous judgment of God, said the damsel. And then anon Sir Pelleas awaked, and looked upon Ettard. And when he saw her he knew her, and then he hated her more than any woman alive, and said : Away traitress, come never in my sight. And when she heard him say so, she wept and made great sorrow out of measure.

CHAP. XXIII.

How Sir Pelleas loved no more Ettard by means of the damsel of the lake, whom he loved ever after.

Sir knight Pelleas, said the damsel of the lake, take your horse and come forth with me out of this country, and ye shall love a lady that shall love you. I will well, said Sir Pelleas, for this lady Ettard hath done me great despite and shame. And there he told her the beginning and ending, and how he had purposed never to have arisen till that he had been dead,—and now I hate her as much as ever I loved her. Thank me, said the damsel of the lake. Anon Sir Pelleas armed him, and took his horse, and commanded his men to bring after his pavilions and his stuff where the damsel of the lake would assign. So the lady Ettard died for sorrow, and the damsel of the lake rejoiced Sir Pelleas, and loved together during their life days.

CHAP. XXIV.

How Sir Marhaus rode with the damsel, and how he came to the duke of the South Marches.

Now turn we unto Sir Marhaus that rode with the damsel of thirty winter of age southward. And so they came into a deep forest, and by fortune they were nighted, and rode long in a deep way, and at the last they came into a courtelage, and there they asked harbour. But the man of the courtelage would not lodge them for no treaty that they could treat. But thus much the good man said : And ye will take the adventure of your lodging, I shall bring you there ye shall be lodged. What adventure is that that I shall have for my lodging? said Sir Marhaus. Ye shall wit when ye come there, said the good man. Sir, what adventure so it be bring me thither, I pray thee, said Sir Marhaus, for I am weary, my damsel and my horse. So the good man went and opened the gate, and within an hour he brought him unto a fair castle. And then the poor man called the porter, and anon he was let into the castle, and so told the lord how he brought him a knight errant and a damsel that would be lodged with him. Let him in, said the lord, it may happen he shall repent that they took their lodging here.

So Sir Marhaus was let in with torch light, and there was a goodly sight of young men that welcomed him. And then his horse was led into the stable, and he and the damsel were brought into the hall, and there stood a mighty duke, and many goodly men about him. Then this lord asked him what he hight, and from whence he came, and with whom he dwelt. Sir, said he, I am a knight of king Arthur's, and knight of the Table Round, and my name is Sir Marhaus, and born I am in Ireland. And then said the duke to him, That me sore repenteth: the cause is this: for I love not thy lord, nor none of thy fellows of the Table Round, and therefore ease thyself this night as well as thou mayest, for as to-morn I and my six sons shall match with you. Is there no remedy but that I must have ado with you and your six sons at once? said Sir Marhaus. No, said the duke, for this cause I made mine avow, for Sir Gawaine slew my seven sons in a recounter, therefore I made mine avow that there should never knight of king Arthur's court lodge with me, or come there as I might have ado with him, but that I would have a revenging of my sons' death. What is your name? said Sir Marhaus; I require you tell me, and it please you. Wit ye well that I am the duke of South Marches. Ah, said Sir Marhaus, I have heard say that ye have been a long time a great foe unto my lord Arthur and to his knights. That shall ye feel to-morn, said the duke. Shall I have ado with you? said Sir Marhaus. Yea, said the duke, thereof shalt thou not choose, and therefore take you to your chamber, and ye shall have all that to you belongeth. So Sir Marhaus departed, and was led to a chamber, and his damsel was led unto her chamber. And on the morn the duke sent unto Sir Marhaus, and bad make him ready. And so Sir Marhaus arose and armed him, and then there was a mass sung afore him, and he brake his fast, and so mounted on horseback in the court of the castle, there they should do the battle. So there was the duke already on horseback, clean armed, and his six sons by him, and every each had a spear in his hand, and so they encountered, where as the duke and his two sons brake their spears upon him, but Sir Marhaus held up his spear and touched none of them.

CHAP. XXV.

How Sir Marhaus fought with the duke and his six sons, and made them to yield them.

THEN came the four sons by couples, and two of them brake their spears, and so did the other two. And all this while Sir Marhaus touched them not. Then Sir Marhaus ran to the duke, and smote him with his spear that horse and man fell to the earth. And so he served his sons. And then Sir Marhaus alight down, and bad the duke yield him or else he would slay him. And then some of his sons recovered, and would have set upon Sir Marhaus. Then Sir Marhaus said to the duke, Cease thy sons, or else I will do the uttermost to you all. When the duke saw he might not escape the death, he cried to his sons, and charged them to yield them to Sir Marhaus. And they kneeled all down and put the pommels of their swords to the knight, and so he received them. And then they holp up their father, and so by their common assent promised unto Sir Marhaus never to be foes unto king Arthur, and thereupon at Whitsuntide after, to come he and his sons, and put them in the king's grace. Then Sir Marhaus departed, and within two days his damsel brought him where as was a great tournament that the lady de Vawse had cried. And who that did best should have a rich circlet of gold worth a thousand besaunts. And there Sir Marhaus did so nobly that he was renowned, and had some time down forty knights, and so the circlet of gold was rewarded him. Then he departed from thence with great worship. And so within seven nights the damsel brought him to an earl's place, his name was the earl Fergus, that after was Sir Tristram's knight. And this earl was but a young man, and late come into his lands, and there was a giant fast by him that hight Taulurd, and he had another brother in Cornwall that hight Taulas, that Sir Tristram slew when he was out of his mind. So this earl made his complaint unto Sir Marhaus, that there was a giant by him that destroyed all his lands, and how he durst nowhere ride nor go for him. Sir, said the knight, whether useth he to fight on horseback or on foot? Nay, said the earl, there may no horse bear him. Well, said Sir Marhaus, then will I fight with him on foot. So on the morn Sir Marhaus prayed the earl that one of his men might bring him whereas the giant was, and so he was, for he saw him sit under a tree of holly, and many clubs of iron and gisarms about him. So this knight dressed him to the giant, putting his shield afore him, and the giant took an iron club in his hand, and at the first stroke he clave Sir Marhaus's shield in two pieces. And there he was in great peril, for the giant was a wily fighter, but at the last Sir Marhaus smote off his right arm above the elbow. Then the giant fled, and the knight after him, and so he drove him into a water, but the giant was so high that he might not wade after him. And then Sir Marhaus made the earl Fergus's man to fetch him stones, and with those stones the knight gave the giant many sore knocks, till at the last he made him fall down into the water, and so was he there dead. Then Sir Marhaus went unto the giant's castle, and there he delivered twenty-four ladies and twelve knights out of the giant's prison, and there he had great riches without number, so that the days of his life he was never poor man. Then he returned to the earl Fergus, the which thanked him greatly and would have given him half his lands, but he would none take. So Sir Marhaus dwelled with the earl nigh half a year, for he was sore bruised with the giant, and at the last he took his leave. And as he rode by the way, he met with Sir Gawaine and Sir Uwaine,

and so by adventure he met with four knights of king Arthur's court, the first was Sir Sagramore le Desirous, Sir Osanna, Sir Dodinas le Savage, and Sir Felot of Listinoise; and there Sir Marhaus with one spear smote down these four knights, and hurt them sore. So he departed to meet at his day afore set.

CHAP. XXVII.

How Sir Uwaine rode with the damsel of threescore years of age, and how he got the prize at tourneying.

Now turn we unto Sir Uwaine, that rode westward with his damsel of threescore winter of age, and she brought him there as was a tournament nigh the march of Wales. And at that tournament Sir Uwaine smote down thirty knights, therefore was given him the prize, and that was a gerfalcon and a white steed trapped with cloth of gold. So then Sir Uwaine did many strange adventures by the means of the old damsel, and so she brought him unto a lady that was called the lady of the Rock, the which was much courteous. So there were in the country two knights that were brethren, and they were called two perilous knights, the one hight Sir Edward of the Red Castle, and the other hight Sir Hue of the Red Castle. And these two brethren had disherited the lady of the Rock of a barony of lands by their extortion. And as this knight was lodged with this lady, she made her complaint to him of these two knights. Madam, said Sir Uwaine, they are to blame, for they do against the high order of knighthood and the oath that they made; and if it like you I will speak with them, because I am a knight of king Arthur's, and I will entreat them with fairness; and if they will not, I shall do battle with them, and in the defence of your right. Gramercy! said the lady, and there as I may not acquit you, God shall. So on the morn the two knights were sent for, that they should come hither to speak with the lady of the Rock. And wit ye well they failed not, for they came with an hundred horse. But when this lady saw them in this manner so big, she would not suffer Sir Uwaine to go out to them upon no surety nor for no fair language, but she made him speak with them over a tower. But finally these two brethren would not be entreated, and answered that they would keep that they had. Well, said Sir Uwaine, then will I fight with one of you, and prove that ye do this lady wrong. That will we not, said they, for and we do battle we two will fight with one knight at once, and therefore if ye will fight so we will be ready at what hour ye will assign. And if ye win us in battle the lady shall have her lands again. Ye say well, said Sir Uwaine, therefore make you ready, so that ye be here tomorn in the defence of the lady's right.

CHAP. XXVIII.

How Sir Uwaine fought with two knights, and overcame them.

So was there agreement made on both parties, that no treason should be wrought on neither party. So then the knights departed and made them ready. And that night Sir Uwaine had great cheer. And on the morn he arose early and heard mass, and brake his fast, and so he rode unto the plain without the gates, where hoved the two brethren abiding him. So they rode together passing sore, that Sir Edward and Sir Hue brake their spears upon Sir Uwaine. And Sir Uwaine smote Sir Edward that he fell over his horse, and yet his spear brast not. And then he spurred his horse and came upon Sir Hue, and overthrew him ; but they soon recovered and dressed their shields and drew their swords, and bad Sir Uwaine alight and do his battle to the uttermost. Then Sir Uwaine avoided his horse suddenly, and put his shield afore him and drew his sword, and so they dressed together, and either gave other such strokes, and there these two brethren wounded Sir Uwaine

passing grievously, that the lady of the Rock wend he should have died. And thus they fought together five hours as men enraged out of reason. And at the last Sir Uwaine smote Sir Edward upon the helm such a stroke that his sword carved unto his collarbone, and then Sir Hue abated his courage. But Sir Uwaine pressed fast to have slain him. That saw Sir Hue : he kneeled down and yielded him to Sir Uwaine. And he of his gentleness received his sword, and took him by the hand and went into the castle together. Then the lady of the Rock was passing glad, and the other brother made great sorrow for his brother's death. Then the lady was restored of all her lands, and Sir Hue was commanded to be at the court of king Arthur at the next feast of Pentecost. So Sir Uwaine dwelt with the lady nigh half a year, for it was long or he might be whole of his great hurts. And so when it drew nigh the term-day that Sir Gawaine, Sir Marhaus, and Sir Uwaine should meet at the cross way, then every knight drew him thither to hold his promise that they had made. And Sir Marhaus and Sir Uwaine brought their damsels with them, but Sir Gawaine had lost his damsel, as it is afore rehearsed.

CHAP. XXIX.

How at the year's end all three knights with their three damsels met at the fountain.

Right so at the twelvemonth's end they met all three knights at the fountain, and their damsels. But the damsel that Sir Gawaine had could say but little worship of him. So they departed from the damsels and rode through a great forest, and there they met with a messager that came from king Arthur, that had sought them well nigh a twelvemonth throughout all England, Wales, and Scotland, and charged if ever he might find Sir Gawaine and Sir Uwaine, to bring them to the court again. And then were they all glad. And so prayed they Sir

Marhaus to ride with them to the king's court. And so within twelve days they came to Camelot; and the king was passing glad of their coming, and so was all the court. Then the king made them to swear upon a book to tell him all their adventures that had befallen them that twelvemonth, and so they did. And there was Sir Marhaus well known; for there were knights that he had matched aforetime, and he was named one of the best knights living. Against the feast of Pentecost came the damsel of the lake, and brought with her Sir Pelleas. And at that high feast there was great justing of knights, and of all the knights that were at that justs Sir Pelleas had the prize, and Sir Marhaus was named the next; but Sir Pelleas was so strong that there might but few knights sit him a buffet with a spear. And at that next feast Sir Pelleas and Sir Marhaus were made knights of the Table Round, for there were two sieges void, for two knights were slain that twelvemonth; and great joy had king Arthur of Sir Pelleas and of Sir Marhaus. But Pelleas loved never after Sir Gawaine, but as he spared him for the love of king Arthur. But ofttimes at justs and tournaments Sir Pelleas quit Sir Gawaine, for so it rehearseth in the book of French. So Sir Tristram many days after fought with Sir Marhaus in an island, and there they did a great battle, but at the last Sir Tristram slew him. So Sir Tristram was wounded that hardly he might recover, and lay at a nunnery half a year. And Sir Pelleas was a worshipful knight, and was one of the four that achieved the Sangreal. And the damsel of the lake made by her means that never he had ado with Sir Launcelot de Lake, for where Sir Launcelot was at any justs or any tournament she would not suffer him to be there that day, but if it were on the side of Sir Launcelot.

𝔈𝔵𝔭𝔩𝔦𝔠𝔦𝔱 𝔩𝔦𝔟𝔢𝔯 𝔮𝔲𝔞𝔯𝔱𝔲𝔰.   𝔍𝔫𝔠𝔦𝔭𝔦𝔱 𝔩𝔦𝔟𝔢𝔯 𝔮𝔲𝔦𝔫𝔱𝔲𝔰.

𝔗𝔥𝔢 𝔉𝔦𝔣𝔱𝔥 𝔅𝔬𝔬𝔨.

CHAP. I.

How twelve aged ambassadors of Rome came to king Arthur to demand truage for Britain.

WHEN king Arthur had after long war rested, and held a royal feast and Table Round with his allies of kings, princes, and noble knights all of the Round Table, there came into his hall, he sitting in his throne royal, twelve ancient men, bearing each of them a branch of olive in token that they came as ambassadors and messagers from the emperor Lucius, which was called at that time Dictator or Procuror of the Public Weal of Rome. Which said messagers, after their entering and coming into the presence of king Arthur, did to him their obeisance in making to him reverence, and said to him in this wise: The high and mighty emperor Lucius sendeth to the king of Britain greeting, commanding thee to acknowledge him for thy lord, and to send him the truage due of this realm unto the empire, which thy father and other tofore thy predecessors have paid as is of record, and thou as rebel not knowing him as thy sovereign, withholdest and retainest contrary to the statutes and decrees made by the noble and worthy Julius Cesar, conqueror of this realm, and first emperor of Rome. And if thou refuse his demand and commandment, know thou for certain that he shall make strong war against thee, thy realms and lands, and shall chastise thee and thy subjects, that it shall be ensample perpetual unto all kings and princes for to deny their truage unto that noble empire which domineth upon the universal world. Then when they had shewed the effect of their message, the king commanded them to withdraw them, and said he should take advice of council, and give to them an answer. Then some of the young knights hearing this their message would have run on them to have slain them, saying that it was a rebuke unto all the knights there being present to suffer them to say so to the king. And anon the king commanded that none of them upon pain of death to missay them, nor do them any harm, and commanded a knight to bring them to their lodging, and see that they have all that is necessary and requisite for them with the best cheer, and that no dainty be spared, for the Romans be great lords, and though their message please me not, nor my court, yet I must remember mine honour. After this the king let call all his lords and knights of the Round Table to council upon this matter, and desired them to say their advice. Then Sir Cador of Cornwall spake first, and said, Sir, this message liketh me well, for we have many days rested us and have been idle, and now I hope ye shall make sharp war on the Romans, where I doubt not we shall get honour. I believe well, said Arthur, that this matter pleaseth thee well, but these answers may not be answered, for the demand grieveth me sore; for truly I will never pay no truage to Rome, wherefore I pray you to counsel me. I have understood that Belinus and Brenius, kings of Britain, have had the empire in their hands many days, and also Constantine the son of queen Heleine, which is an open evidence that we owe no tribute to Rome, but of right we that be descended of them have right to claim the title of the empire.

CHAP. II.
How the kings and lords promised to king Arthur aid and help against the Romans.

THEN answered king Anguish of Scotland, Sir, ye ought of right to be above all other kings, for unto you is none like nor pareil in all Christendom, of knighthood ne of dignity, and I counsel you never to obey the Romans, for when they reigned on us they distressed our elders, and put this land to great extortions and tallages, wherefore I make here mine avow to avenge me on them; and for to strengthen your quarrel I shall furnish twenty thousand good men of war, and wage them on my costs, which shall await on you with myself, when it shall please you. And the king of Little Britain granted him to the same thirty thousand; wherefore king Arthur thanked them. And then every man agreed to make war, and to aid after their power; that is to wit, the lord of West Wales promised to bring thirty thousand men, and Sir Uwaine, Sir Ider his son, with their cousins, promised to bring thirty thousand. Then Sir Launcelot with all other promised in likewise every man a great multitude. And when king Arthur understood their courages and good wills he thanked them heartily, and after let call the ambassadors to hear their answer. And in presence of all his lords and knights he said to them in this wise: I will that ye return unto your lord and Procuror of the Common Weal for the Romans, and say to him, Of his demand and commandment I set nothing, and that I know of no truage, ne tribute, that I owe to him, ne to none earthly prince, Christian ne heathen; but I pretend to have and occupy the sovereignty of the empire, wherein I am entitled by the right of my predecessors, sometime kings of this land; and say to him that I am deliberated, and fully concluded, to go with mine army with strength and power unto Rome by the grace of God to take possession in the empire, and subdue them that be rebel. Wherefore I command him, and all them of Rome, that incontinent they make to me their homage, and to acknowledge me for their emperor and governor, upon pain that shall ensue. And then he commanded his treasurer to give them great and large gifts, and to pay all their expenses, and assigned Sir Cador to convey them out of the land. And so they took their leave and departed, and took their shipping at Sandwich, and passed forth by Flanders, Almain, the mountains, and all Italy, until they came unto Lucius. And after the reverence made, they made relation of their answer, like as ye tofore have heard. When the emperor Lucius had well understood their credence, he was sore moved as he had been all enraged, and said: I had supposed that Arthur would have obeyed to my commandment, and have served you himself, as him well beseemed or any other king to do. O sir, said one of the senators, let be such vain words, for we let you wit that I and my fellows were full sore afeard to behold his countenance; I fear me ye have made a rod for yourself, for he intendeth to be lord of this empire, which sore is to be doubted if he come, for he is all another man than ye ween, and holdeth the most noble court of the world; all other kings ne princes may not compare unto his noble maintenance. On new year's day we saw him in his estate, which was the royalest that ever we saw, for he was served at his table with nine kings and the noblest fellowship of other princes, lords, and knights, that be in the world, and every knight approved and like a lord, and holdeth Table Round: and in his person the most manly man that liveth, and is like to conquer all the world, for unto his courage it is too little: wherefore I advise you to keep well your marches and straits in the mountains; for certainly he is a lord to be doubted. Well, said Lucius, before Easter I suppose to pass the mountains and so forth into France, and there bereave him his lands with Genoese and other mighty warriors of Tuscany and Lombardy. And I shall send for them

all that be subjects and allied to the empire of Rome to come to mine aid. And forthwith sent old wise knights unto these countries following: first, to Ambage and Arrage, to Alisandrie, to Inde, to Hermonie where as the river of Euphrates runneth into Asia, to Affrike, and Europe the large, to Ertaine and Elamie, to Arabie, Egypt, and to Damaske, to Damiete and Cayer, to Capadoce, to Tarce, Turkey, Pounce, and Pampoille, to Surrie, and Galacie. And all these were subject to Rome, and many more, as Greece, Cyprus, Macedone, Calabre, Cateland, Portingale, with many thousands of Spaniards. Thus all these kings, dukes, and admirals assembled about Rome with sixteen kings at once, with great multitude of people. When the emperor understood their coming, he made ready his Romans and all the people between him and Flanders. Also he had gotten with him fifty giants which had been born of fiends; and they were ordained to guard his person, and to break the front of the battle of king Arthur.

And thus he departed from Rome, and came down the mountains for to destroy the lands that king Arthur had conquered, and came to Cologne, and besieged a castle thereby, and won it soon, and stuffed it with two hundred Saracens or infidels, and after destroyed many fair countries which Arthur had won of king Claudas. And thus Lucius came with all his host which were spread out threescore mile in breadth, and commanded them to meet with him in Burgoyne, for he purposed to destroy the realm of Little Britain.

CHAP. III.

How king Arthur held a parliament at York, and how he ordained how the realm should be governed in his absence.

Now leave we of Lucius the emperor, and speak we of king Arthur, that commanded all them of his retinue to be ready at the utas of Hilary for to hold a parliament at York. And at that parliament was concluded to arrest all the navy of the land, and to be ready within fifteen days at Sandwich; and there he shewed to his army how he purposed to conquer the empire which he ought to have of right. And there he ordained two governors of this realm, that is to say, Sir Bawdwin of Britain, for to counsel to the best, and Sir Constantine, son to Sir Cador of Cornwall, which after the death of Arthur was king of this realm. And in the presence of all his lords he resigned the rule of the realm and Guenever his queen unto them, wherefore Sir Launcelot was wroth, for he left Sir Tristram with king Mark for the love of Beale Isould. Then the queen Guenever made great sorrow for the departing of her lord and other, and swooned in such wise that the ladies bare her into her chamber. Thus the king with his great army departed, leaving the queen and realm in the governance of Sir Bawdwin and Constantine. And when he was on his horse he said with an high voice, If I die in this journey, I will that Sir Constantine be mine heir and king crowned of this realm as next of my blood. And after departed and entered into the sea at Sandwich with all his army, with a great multitude of ships, galleys, cogges, and dromons, sailing on the sea.

CHAP. IV.

How king Arthur being shipped and lying in his cabin had a marvellous dream, and of the exposition thereof.

AND as the king lay in his cabin in the ship, he fell in a slumbering, and dreamed a marvellous dream: him seemed that a dreadful dragon did drown much of his people, and he came flying out of the west, and his head was enamelled with azure, and his shoulders shone as gold, his belly like mails of a marvellous hue, his tail full of tatters, his feet full of fine sable, and his claws like fine gold; and an hideous flame of fire flew out of his mouth, like as the land and water had flamed all of fire.

After him seemed there came out of the orient a grimly boar all black in a cloud, and his paws as big as a post; he was rugged looking roughly, he was the foulest beast that ever man saw, he roared and romed so hideously that it were marvel to hear. Then the dreadful dragon advanced him, and came in the wind like a falcon, giving great strokes on the boar, and the boar hit him again with his grisly tusks that his breast was all bloody, and that the hot blood made all the sea red of his blood. Then the dragon flew away all on an height, and came down with such a swough, and smote the boar on the ridge, which was ten foot large from the head to the tail, and smote the boar all to powder, both flesh and bones, that it flittered all abroad on the sea. And therewith the king awoke anon and was sore abashed of this dream; and sent anon for a wise philosopher, commanding to tell him the signification of his dream. Sir, said the philosopher, the dragon that thou dreamedst of betokeneth thine own person that sailest here, and the colour of his wings be thy realms that thou hast won, and his tail which is all to-tattered signifieth the noble knights of the Round Table. And the boar that the dragon slew coming from the clouds, betokeneth some tyrant that tormenteth the people, or else thou art like to fight with some giant thyself, being horrible and abominable, whose peer ye saw never in your days; wherefore of this dreadful dream doubt thee nothing, but as a conqueror come forth thyself. Then after this soon they had sight of land, and sailed till they arrived at Barflete in Flanders, and when they were there he found many of his great lords ready as they had been commanded to await upon him.

CHAP. V.

How a man of the country told to him of a marvellous giant, and how he fought and conquered him.

THEN came to him an husbandman of the country, and told him how there was in the country of Constantine, beside Britany, a great tyrant which had slain, murdered, and devoured much people of the country, and had been sustained seven year with the children of the commons of that land, insomuch, that all the children be all slain and destroyed, and now late he hath taken the duchess of Britany as she rode with her train, and hath led her to his lodging which is in a mountain, for to keep her to her life's end; and many people followed her, more than five hundred, but all they might not rescue her, but they left her shrieking and crying lamentably, wherefore I suppose that he hath slain her. She was wife unto thy cousin Sir Howell, whom we call full nigh of thy blood. Now as thou art a rightful king have pity on this lady, and revenge us all as thou art a noble conqueror. Alas! said king Arthur, this is a great mischief, I had lever than the best realm that I have that I had been a furlong way tofore him, for to have rescued that lady. Now fellow, said king Arthur, canst thou bring me there as this giant haunteth? Yea, Sir, said the good man, lo yonder where as thou seest those two great fires, there thou shalt find him, and more treasure than I suppose is in all France. When the king had understood this piteous case he returned into his tent.

Then he called unto him Sir Kay and Sir Bedivere, and commanded them secretly to make ready horse and harness for himself and them twain, for after even-song he would ride on pilgrimage with them two only unto Saint Michael's mount. And then anon he made him ready and armed him at all points, and took his horse and his shield. And so they three departed thence, and rode forth as fast as ever they might till that they came unto the foot of that mount. And there they alighted, and the king commanded them to tarry there, for he would himself go up into that mount. And so he ascended up into that hill till he came to a great fire, and there he found a careful widow wringing her hands and making great

sorrow, sitting by a grave new made. And then king Arthur saluted her, and demanded of her wherefore she made such lamentation: to whom she answered and said, Sir knight, speak soft, for yonder is a devil: if he hear thee speak he will come and destroy thee; I hold thee unhappy; what dost thou here in this mountain? for if ye were such fifty as ye be, ye were not able to make resistance against this devil: here lieth a duchess dead, the which was the fairest of all the world, wife to Sir Howell duke of Britany; he hath murdered her. Dame, said the king, I come from the noble conqueror king Arthur, for to treat with that tyrant for his liege people. Fie upon such treaties, said the widow, he setteth not by the king, nor by no man else. But and if thou have brought Arthur's wife, dame Guenever, he shall be gladder than thou hadst given to him half France. Beware, approach him not too nigh, for he hath vanquished fifteen kings, and hath made him a coat full of precious stones, embroidered with their beards, which they sent him to have his love for salvation of their people at this last Christmas. And if thou wilt, speak with him at yonder great fire at supper. Well, said Arthur, I will accomplish my message for all your fearful words; and went forth by the crest of that hill, and saw where he sat at supper gnawing on a limb of a man, baking his broad limbs by the fire, and three fair damsels turning three spits, whereon were broached twelve young children late born, like young birds. When king Arthur beheld that piteous sight he had great compassion on them so that his heart bled for sorrow, and hailed him saying in this wise: He that all the world wieldeth, give thee short life and shameful death, and the devil have thy soul! Why hast thou murdered these young innocent children, and murdered this duchess? Therefore arise and dress thee, thou glutton; for this day shalt thou die of my hand. Then the glutton anon start up and took a great club in his hand, and smote at the king that his coronal fell to the earth. And the king hit him again that he carved his belly that his entrails fell down to the ground. Then the giant threw away his club, and caught the king in his arms that he crushed his ribs. Then the three maidens kneeled down and called to Christ for help and comfort of Arthur. And then Arthur weltered and wrung that he was other while under and another time above. And so weltering and wallowing they rolled down the hill till they came to the sea mark, and ever as they so weltered Arthur smote him with his dagger, and it fortuned they came to the place where as the two knights were and kept Arthur's horse. Then when they saw the king fast in the giant's arms they came and loosed him. And then the king commanded Sir Kay to smite off the giant's head, and to set it upon a truncheon of a spear and bear it to Sir Howell, and tell him that his enemy was slain, and after let this head be bound to a barbican that all the people may see and behold it ; and go ye two up to the mountain and fetch me my shield, my sword, and the club of iron. And as for the treasure take ye it, for ye shall find there goods out of number. So I have the kirtle and the club I desire no more. This was the fiercest giant that ever I met with, save one in the mount of Arabe which I overcame, but this was greater and fiercer. Then the knights fetched the club and the kirtle, and some of the treasure they took to themselves, and returned again to the host. And anon this was known through all the country, wherefore the people came and thanked the king. And he said again, Give the thanks to God, and part the goods among you. And after that, king Arthur said and commanded his cousin Howell that he should ordain for a church to be builded on the same hill, in the worship of Saint Michael. And on the morn the king removed with his great battle and came into Champayne, and in a valley, and there they pight their tents. And the king being set at his dinner, there came in two messagers, of whom the one was mar-

shal of France, and said to the king that the emperor was entered into France and had destroyed a great part, and was in Burgoyne, and had destroyed and made great slaughter of people, and burnt towns and boroughs ; wherefore, if thou come not hastily, they must yield up their bodies and goods.

CHAP. VI.

How king Arthur sent Sir Gawaine and others to Lucius, and how they were assailed and escaped with worship.

THEN the king did do call Sir Gawaine, Sir Bors, Sir Lionel, and Sir Bedivere, and commanded them to go straight to Sir Lucius, and say ye to him that hastily he remove out of my land. And if he will not, bid him make him ready to battle, and not distress the poor people. Then anon these noble knights dressed them to horseback. And when they came to the green wood, they saw many pavilions set in a meadow, of silk of divers colours, beside a river, and the emperor's pavilion was in the middle with an eagle displayed above. To the which tent our knights rode toward, and ordained Sir Gawaine and Sir Bors to do the message, and left in a bushment Sir Lionel and Sir Bedivere. And then Sir Gawaine and Sir Bors did their message, and commanded Lucius in Arthur's name to avoid his land, or shortly to address him to battle. To whom Lucius answered and said : Ye shall return to your lord and say ye to him, that I shall subdue him and all his lands. Then Sir Gawaine was wroth, and said, I had lever than all France fight against thee. And so had I, said Sir Bors, lever than all Britany or Burgoyne. Then a knight named Sir Gainus, high cousin to the emperor, said, Lo, how these Britons be full of pride and boast, and they brag as though they bare up all the world. Then Sir Gawaine was sore grieved with these words, and pulled out his sword and smote off his head. And therewith turned their horses and rode over waters and through woods till they came to their bushment where as

Sir Lionel and Sir Bedivere were hoving. The Romans followed fast after on horseback and on foot over a champaign unto a wood; then Sir Bors turned his horse and saw a knight come fast on, whom he smote through the body with a spear, that he fell dead down to the earth. Then came Caliburn, one of the strongest of Pavie, and smote down many of Arthur's knights. And when Sir Bors saw him do so much harm, he addressed toward him, and smote him through the breast, that he fell down dead to the earth. Then Sir Feldenak thought to revenge the death of Gainus upon Sir Gawaine, but Sir Gawaine was ware thereof, and smote him on the head, which stroke stinted not till it came to his breast. And then he returned and came to his fellows in the bushment. And there was a recounter, for the bushment brake on the Romans, and slew and hewed down the Romans, and forced the Romans to flee and return; whom the noble knights chased unto their tents. Then the Romans gathered more people, and also footmen came on, and there was a new battle, and so much people that Sir Bors and Sir Berel were taken. But when Sir Gawaine saw that, he took with him Sir Idrus the good knight, and said he would never see king Arthur but if he rescued them, and pulled out Galatine his good sword, and followed them that led those two knights away, and he smote him that led Sir Bors, and took Sir Bors from him, and delivered him unto his fellows. And Sir Idrus in like wise rescued Sir Berel. Then began the battle to be great, that our knights were in great jeopardy, wherefore Sir Gawaine sent to king Arthur for succour, and that he hie him, for I am sore wounded, and that our prisoners may pay good out of number. And the messenger came to the king, and told him his message. And anon the king did do assemble his army, but anon or he departed the prisoners were come, and Sir Gawaine and his fellows gat the field and put the Romans to flight, and after returned and came with their fellowship in such wise

that no man of worship was lost of them, save that Sir Gawaine was sore hurt. Then the king did do ransack his wounds, and comforted him. And thus was the beginning of the first day's fighting of the Britons and Romans. And there were slain of the Romans more than ten thousand, and great joy and mirth was made that night in the host of king Arthur. And on the morn he sent all the prisoners into Paris, under the guard of Sir Launcelot, with many knights, and of Sir Cador.

CHAP. VII.

How Lucius sent certain spies in a bushment for to have taken his knights being prisoners, and how they were letted.

Now turn we to the emperor of Rome which espied that these prisoners should be sent to Paris, and anon he sent to lie in a bushment certain knights and princes with sixty thousand men for to rescue his knights and lords that were prisoners. And so on the morn as Sir Launcelot and Sir Cador, chieftains and governors of all them that conveyed the prisoners, as they should pass through a wood, Sir Launcelot sent certain knights to espy if any were in the woods to let them. And when the said knights came into the wood, anon they espied and saw the great enbushment, and returned and told Sir Launcelot that there lay in await for them threescore thousand Romans. And then Sir Launcelot with such knights as he had, and men of war to the number of ten thousand, put them in array, and met with them, and fought with them manly, and slew and cut to pieces many of the Romans, and slew many knights and admirals of the party of the Romans and Saracens: there was slain the king of Lyly and three great lords, Alakuke, Herawd, and Heringdale. But Sir Launcelot fought so nobly that no man might endure a stroke of his hand, but where he came he shewed his prowess and might, for he slew down right on every side. And the Romans and Saracens fled from him as the sheep from the wolf or from the lion, and put them all that abode alive to flight. And so long they fought that tidings came to king Arthur, and anon he made him ready and came to the battle, and saw his knights how they had vanquished the battle: he embraced them knight by knight in his arms, and said: Ye be worthy to bear all your honour and worship, there was never king save myself that had so noble knights. Sir, said Cador, there was none of us failed other, but of the prowess and manhood of Sir Launcelot were more than wonder to tell, and also of his cousins which did this day many noble feats of war. And also Sir Cador told who of his knights were slain, as Sir Berel and other Sir Moris and Sir Maurel, two good knights. Then the king wept, and dried his eyes with a kerchief and said, Your courage had near hand destroyed you, for though ye had returned again ye had lost no worship; for I call it folly, knights to abide when they be over-matched. Nay, said Sir Launcelot and the other, for once shamed may never be recovered.

CHAP. VIII.

How a senator told to Lucius of their discomfiture, and also of the great battle between Arthur and Lucius.

Now leave we king Arthur and his noble knights which had won the field, and had brought their prisoners to Paris, and speak we of a senator which escaped from the battle, and came to Lucius the emperor, and said to him, Sir emperor, I advise thee to withdraw thee: what doest thou here? thou shalt win nothing in these marches but great strokes out of all measure. For this day one of Arthur's knights was worth in the battle an hundred of ours. Fie on thee, said Lucius, thou speakest cowardly, for thy words grieve me more than all the loss that I had this day. And anon he sent forth a king, which hight Sir Leomie, with a great army, and bad him hie him fast

tofore, and he would follow hastily after. King Arthur was warned privily, and sent his people to Sessoyne, and took up the towns and castles from the Romans. Then the king commanded Sir Cador to take the rereward, and to take with him certain knights of the Round Table,—and Sir Launcelot, Sir Bors, Sir Kay, Sir Marrok, with Sir Marhaus, shall await on our person. Thus king Arthur distributed his host in divers parts, to the end that his enemies should not escape. When the emperor was entered into the vale of Sessoyne, he might see where king Arthur was embattled and his banner displayed: and he was beset round about with his enemies, that needs he must fight or yield him, for he might not flee, but said openly unto the Romans, Sirs, I admonish you that this day ye fight and acquit you as men, and remember how Rome domineth, and is chief and head over all the earth and universal world, and suffer not these Britons this day to abide against us. And therewith he did command his trumpets blow the bloody sounds, in such wise that the ground trembled and shook. Then the battles approached, and shove and shouted on both sides, and great strokes were smitten on both sides, many men overthrown, hurt, and slain; and great valiances, prowesses, and feats of war were that day shewed, which were over long to recount the noble feats of every man, for they should contain a whole volume. But in especial king Arthur rode in the battle, exhorting his knights to do well, and himself did as nobly with his hands as was possible a man to do; he drew out Excalibur his sword, and awaited ever where as the Romans were thickest and most grieved his people; and anon he addressed him on that part, and hewed and slew down right, and rescued his people, and he slew a great giant named Galapas, which was a man of an huge quantity and height, he shorted him and smote off both his legs by the knees, saying, Now art thou better of a size to deal with than thou were; and after smote off his head. There Sir Gawaine fought nobly, and slew three admirals in that battle. And so did all the knights of the Round Table. Thus the battle between king Arthur and Lucius the emperor endured long. Lucius had on his side many Saracens which were slain. And thus the battle was great, and oftsides that one party was at a vantage, and anon at a disadvantage, which endured so long till at the last king Arthur espied where Lucius the emperor fought and did wonder with his own hands. And anon he rode to him, and either smote other fiercely: and at the last Lucius smote Arthur thwart the visage, and gave him a large wound. And when king Arthur felt himself hurt anon he smote him again with Excalibur, that it cleft his head from the summit of his head, and stinted not till it came to his breast. And then the emperor fell down dead, and there ended his life. And when it was known that the emperor was slain, anon all the Romans with all their host put them to flight; and king Arthur with all his knights followed the chase, and slew down right all them that they might attain. And thus was the victory given to king Arthur, and the triumph. And there were slain on the part of Lucius more than an hundred thousand. And after, king Arthur did do ransack the dead bodies, and did do bury them that were slain of his retinue, every man according to the state and degree that he was of. And them that were hurt he let the surgeons do search their hurts and wounds, and commanded to spare no salves nor medicines till they were whole.

Then the king rode straight to the place where the emperor Lucius lay dead, and with him he found slain the Sowdan of Surrey, the king of Egypt and the king of Ethiope, which were two noble kings, with seventeen other kings of divers regions, and also sixty senators of Rome, all noble men, whom the noble king Arthur did do balm and gum with many good gums aromatic, and after did do cere them in sixty fold of cered cloth of Sendal, and laid them in chests of lead, because they should not chafe nor savour; and upon all these bodies their shields with their arms and banners were set, to the end they should be known of what country they were. And after, he found three senators that were onlive, to whom he said, For to save your lives I will that ye take these dead bodies, and carry them with you unto great Rome, and present them to the Potestate on my behalf, shewing him my letters, and tell them that I in my person shall hastily be at Rome. And I suppose the Romans shall be ware how they shall demand any tribute of me. And I command you to say when ye shall come to Rome to the Potestate, and all the Council and Senate, that I send to them these dead bodies for the tribute that they have demanded. And if they be not content with these, I shall pay more at my coming, for other tribute owe I none, nor none other will I pay. And me thinketh this sufficeth for Britain, Ireland, and all Almaine, with Germany. And furthermore I charge you to say to them that I command them upon pain of their heads never to demand tribute ne tax of me ne of my lands.

Then with this charge and commandment the three senators aforesaid departed with all the said dead bodies lying, the body of Lucius in a car covered with the arms of the empire all alone, and after alway two bodies of kings in a chariot, and then the bodies of the senators after them, and so went toward Rome, and shewed their legation and message to the Potestate and Senate, recounting the battle done in France, and how the field was lost, and much people and innumerable slain. Wherefore they advised them in no wise to move no more war against that noble conqueror, Arthur; — for his might and prowess is most to be doubted, seeing the noble kings, and great multitude of knights of the Round Table, to whom none earthly prince may compare.

CHAP. IX.

How Arthur, after he had achieved the battle against the Romans, entered into Almaine, and so into Italy.

Now turn we unto king Arthur and his noble knights, which, after the great battle achieved against the Romans, entered into Loraine, Brabant, and Flanders, and thence returned into high Almaine, and so over the mountains into Lombardy, and after into Tuscany, wherein was a city which in no wise would yield themselves nor obey, wherefore king Arthur besieged it, and lay long about it, and gave many assaults to the city. And they within defended them valiantly. Then, on a time, the king called Sir Florence, a knight, and said to him they lacked victual, and not far from hence be great forests and great woods, wherein be many of mine enemies with much cattle: I will that thou make thee ready, and go thither in foraging, and take with thee Sir Gawaine my nephew, Sir Wisshard, Sir Clegis, Sir Cleremond, and the captain of Cardiff, with other, and bring with you all the beasts that ye there can get. And anon these knights made them ready, and rode over holts and hills, through forests and woods, till they came into a fair meadow full of fair flowers and grass. And there they rested them and their horses all that night. And in the springing of the day in the next morn Sir Gawaine took his horse and stole away from his fellows to seek some adventures. And anon he was ware of a man armed, walking his horse easily by a wood's side, and his shield laced to his shoulder, sitting on a strong courser, without any man saving a page bearing a mighty spear. The knight bare in his shield three griffons of gold in sable carbuncle the chief of silver. When Sir Gawaine espied this gay knight he fewtred his spear, and rode straight to him, and demanded him from whence that he was. That other answered and said he was of Tuscany, and demanded of Sir Gawaine, What profferest thou proud knight so boldly? Here gettest thou no prey: thou mayest prove what thou wilt, for thou shalt be my prisoner or thou depart. Then said Gawaine, Thou vauntest thee greatly, and speakest proud words; I counsel thee for all thy boast that thou make thee ready, and take thy gear to thee, tofore greater grief fall to thee.

CHAP. X.

Of a battle done by Gawaine against a Saracen, which after was yielden and became Christian.

THEN they took their spears, and ran each at other with all the might they had, and smote each other through their shields into their shoulders, wherefore anon they pulled out their swords, and smote great strokes, that the fire sprang out of their helms. Then Sir Gawaine was all abashed, and with Galatine, his good sword, he smote through shield and thick hauberk made of thick mails, and all to-rushed and brake the precious stones, and made him a large wound, that men might see both liver and lung. Then groaned that knight, and addressed him to Sir Gawaine, and with an awk stroke gave him a great wound, and cut a vein, which grieved Sir Gawaine sore, and he bled sore. Then the knight said to Sir Gawaine, Bind thy wound or thy bleeding change, for thou be-bleedest all thy horse and thy fair arms; for all the barbers of Britain can not stanch thy blood; for whosoever is hurt with this blade, he shall never be stanched of bleeding. Then answered Gawaine, It grieveth me but little; thy great words shall not fear me nor lessen my courage, but thou shalt suffer teen and sorrow or we depart: but tell me in haste who may stanch my bleeding? That may I do, said the knight, if I will, and so I will if thou wilt succour and aid me, that I may be christened and believe on God, and thereof I require thee of thy manhood, and it shall be great merit for thy soul. I grant, said Gawaine, so God help me, to accomplish all thy desire: but first tell me what thou soughtest here thus alone, and of what land and liegiance thou art. Sir, he said, my name is Priamus, and a great prince is my father, and he hath been rebel unto Rome, and over ridden many of their lands. My father is lineally descended of Alexander and of Hector by right line. And duke Joshua and Maccabæus were of our lineage. I am right inheritor of Alexandria and Africa, and all the out isles, yet will I believe on thy Lord that thou believest on; and for thy labour I shall give thee treasure enough. I was so elate and haughty in my heart, that I thought no man my peer, nor to me semblable. I was sent into this war with seven-score knights, and now I have encountered with thee which hast given to me of fighting my fill; wherefore sir knight I pray thee to tell me what thou art? I am no knight, said Gawaine, I have been brought up in the guard-robe with the noble king Arthur many years, for to take heed to his armour and his other array, and to point his paltocks that belong to himself. At Yule last he made me yeoman, and gave to me horse and harness and an hundred pound in money: and if fortune be my friend I doubt not but to be well advanced and holpen by my liege lord. Ah, said Priamus, if his knaves be so keen and fierce, his knights be passing good. Now, for the king's love of heaven, whether thou be a knave or a knight, tell thou me thy name. By heaven, said Sir Gawaine, now will I say thee sooth: my name is Sir Gawaine, and known I am in his court and in his chamber, and one of the knights of the Round Table: he dubbed me a duke with his own hand. Therefore grudge not if this grace is to me fortuned; it is the goodness of God that lent to me my strength. Now am I better pleased, said Priamus, than if thou hadst given me all the province, and Paris the rich. I had lever to have been torn with wild horses, than any varlet had won such praise, or any page or pricker should have had prize on me. But now, sir knight, I warn thee that hereby is a duke of Loraine with all his army, and the noblest men of Dolphine, and lords of Lombardy, with the garrison of Godard, and Saracens of Southland, that numbered sixty thousand of good men of arms; wherefore, but if we hie us hence, it will harm us both, for we be sore hurt, never like to recover. But take heed to my page that he no horn blow, for if he do, there be hoving here fast by an hundred good knights, awaiting on my person, and if they take thee there shall no ransom of gold ne silver acquit thee. Then Sir Gawaine rode over a water for to save him, and the knight followed him, and so rode forth till they came to his fellows which were in the meadow, where they had been all the night. Anon as Sir Wisshard was ware of Sir Gawaine and saw that he was hurt, he ran to him sorrowfully weeping, and demanded of him who had so hurt him. And Gawaine told how he had fought with that man, and each of them had hurt other, and how he had salves to heal them; but I can tell you other tidings, that soon we shall have ado with many enemies. Then Sir Priamus and Sir Gawaine alighted, and let their horses graze in the meadow, and unarmed them, and then the blood ran freshly from their wounds. And Priamus took from his page a phial full of the four waters that came out of Paradise, and with certain balm anointed their wounds, and washed them with that water, and within an hour after they were both as whole as ever they were. And then with a trumpet were they all assembled to council, and there Priamus told unto them what lords and knights had sworn to rescue him, and that without fail they should be assailed with many thousands, wherefore he counselled them to withdraw them. Then Sir Gawaine said, it were great shame to them to avoid without any strokes; wherefore I advise to take our arms, and to make us ready to meet with these Saracens and misbelieving men, and with the help of God we shall overthrow them, and have a fair day on them. And Sir

Florence shall abide still in this field to keep the post as a noble knight, and we shall not forsake yonder fellows. Now, said Priamus, cease your words, for I warn you ye shall find in yonder woods many perilous knights: they will put forth beasts to call you on: they be out of number, and ye are not past seven hundred, which be over few to fight with so many. Nevertheless, said Sir Gawaine, we shall once encounter them and see what they can do, and the best shall have the victory.

CHAP. XI.

How the Saracens came out of a wood for to rescue their beasts, and of a great battle.

Then Sir Florence called to him Sir Floridas with an hundred knights, and drove forth the herd of beasts. Then followed him seven hundred men of arms, and Sir Ferant of Spain on a fair steed came springing out of the woods, and came to Sir Florence, and asked him why he fled. Then Sir Florence took his spear, and rode against him, and smote him in the forehead and brake his neck bone. Then all the other were moved, and thought to avenge the death of Sir Ferant, and smote in among them, and there was great fight, and many slain and laid down to ground, and Sir Florence with his hundred knights always kept the post, and fought manly. Then when Priamus the good knight perceived the great fight, he went to Sir Gawaine and bad him that he should go and succour his fellowship, which were sore bested with their enemies. Sir, grieve you not, said Sir Gawaine, for their honour shall be theirs: I shall not once move my horse to themward but if I see more than there be, for they be strong enough to match them. And with that he saw an earl called Sir Ethelwold and the duke of Dutchmen come leaping out of a wood, with many thousands, and Priamus's knights, and came straight unto the battle. Then Sir Gawaine comforted his knights, and bad them not be

abashed, for all shall be ours. Then they began to gallop, and met with their enemies: there were men slain and overthrown on every side. Then thrust in among them the knights of the Table Round, and smote down to the earth all them that withstood them, insomuch that they made them to recoil and flee. Truly, said Sir Gawaine, this gladdeth my heart, for now be they less in number by twenty thousand. Then entered into the battle Jubance a giant, and fought and slew downright, and distressed many of our knights, among whom was slain Sir Gherard, a knight of Wales. Then our knights took heart to them, and slew many Saracens. And then came in Sir Priamus with his pennon, and rode with the knights of the Round Table, and fought so manfully that many of their enemies lost their lives. And there Sir Priamus slew the Marquis of Moises land. And Sir Gawaine with his fellows so quit them that they had the field, but in that fight was Sir Chestelaine, a child and ward of Sir Gawaine, slain, wherefore was much sorrow made, and his death was soon avenged. Thus was the battle ended, and many lords of Lombardy and Saracens left dead in the field.

Then Sir Florence and Sir Gawaine harboured surely their people, and took great plenty of cattle, of gold and silver and great treasure and riches, and returned unto king Arthur, which lay still at the siege. And when they came to the king they presented their prisoners, and recounted their adventures, and how they had vanquished their enemies.

CHAP. XII.

How Sir Gawaine returned to king Arthur with his prisoners, and how the king won a city, and how he was crowned emperor.

Now thanked be God, said the noble king Arthur. But what manner man is he that standeth by himself? he seemeth no prisoner. Sir, said Gawaine, this is a good man of arms; he hath matched me, but he is yielden unto God and to me for to become Christian: had not he been we should never have returned, wherefore I pray you that he may be baptized, for their liveth not a nobler man nor better knight of his hands. Then the king let him anon be christened, and did do call him his first name Priamus, and made him a duke and knight of the Table Round. And then anon the king let do cry assault to the city, and there was rearing of ladders, breaking of walls, and the ditch filled, that men with little pain might enter into the city. Then came out a duchess, and Clarisin the countess, with many ladies and damsels, and kneeling before king Arthur required him for the love of God to receive the city and not to take it by assault, for then should many guiltless be slain. Then the king availed his visor with a meek and noble countenance, and said, Madam, there shall none of my subjects misdo you nor your maidens, nor to none that to you belong, but the duke shall abide my judgment. Then anon the king commanded to leave the assault; and anon the duke's eldest son brought out the keys, and kneeling, delivered them to the king, and besought him of grace: and the king seized the town by assent of his lords, and took the duke and sent him to Dover, there for to abide prisoner the term of his life, and assigned certain rents for the dower of the duchess and for her children. Then he made lords to rule those lands, and laws, as a lord ought to do in his own country. And after he took his journey toward Rome, and sent Sir Floris and Sir Floridas tofore with five hundred men of arms, and they came to the city of Urbine, and laid there a bushment as them seemed most best for them, and rode tofore the town, where anon issued out much people and skirmished with the fore riders. Then brake out the bushment, and won the bridge, and after the town, and set upon the walls the king's banner. Then came the king upon a hill, and saw the city and his banner on the walls, by the which he knew that the city was won. And anon he sent and commanded that none of his liege

men should misuse no lady, wife, nor maid: and when he came into the city he passed to the castle, and comforted them that were in sorrow, and ordained there a captain, a knight of his own country. And when they of Milan heard that the same city was won, they sent to king Arthur great sums of money, and besought him as their lord to have pity on them, promising to be his subjects for ever, and yield to him homage and fealty for the lands of Pleasance and Pavia, Petersaint, and the port of Tremble, and to give him yearly a million of gold all his lifetime. Then he rideth into Tuscany, and winneth towns and castles, and wasted all in his way that to him will not obey, and so to Spolute and Viterbe: and from thence he rode into the vale of Vicecount among the vines. And from thence he sent to the senators to wit whether they would know him for their lord. But soon after on a Saturday came unto king Arthur all the senators that were left on live, and the noblest cardinals that then dwelled in Rome, and prayed him of peace, and proffered him full large, and besought him as governor to give licence for six weeks, for to assemble together all the Romans, and then to crown him emperor with crism, as it belongeth to so high a state. I assent, said the king, like as ye have devised, and at Christmas there to be crowned, and to hold my Round Table with my knights as me liketh. And then the senators made things ready for his enthronization. And at the day appointed, as the romance telleth, he came into Rome, and was crowned emperor by the Pope's hand with all the royalty that could be made, and sojourned there a time, and established all his lands from Rome unto France, and gave lands and realms unto his servants and knights, to every each after his desert, in such wise that none complained, rich nor poor. And he gave to Sir Priamus the duchy of Loraine; and he thanked him, and said that he would serve him the days of his life: and after made dukes and earls, and made every man rich. Then after this all his knights and lords and all the great men of estate assembled them afore him, and said : Blessed be God, your war is finished, and your conquest achieved, insomuch that we know none so great nor mighty that dare make war against you : wherefore we beseech you to return homeward and give us licence to go home to our wives, from whom we have been long, and to rest us, for your journey is finished with honour and worship. Then said the king, Ye say truth, and for to tempt God it is no wisdom, and therefore make you ready and return we into England. Then was there trussing of harness and baggage, and great carriage. And after licence given, he returned and commanded that no man in pain of death should rob nor take victual, nor other thing by the way, but that he should pay therefore. And thus he came over the sea, and landed at Sandwich, against whom queen Guenever his wife came and met him : and he was nobly received of all his commons in every city and burgh, and great gifts presented to him at his home coming, to welcome him with.

Thus endeth the fyfthe booke of the conqueste that kynge Arthur hadde ageynste Lucius the Emperoure of Rome, and here foloweth the syxth book, which is of syr Launcelot du lake.

The Sixth Book.

CHAP. I.

How Sir Launcelot and Sir Lionel departed from the court for to seek adventures, and how Sir Lionel left him sleeping, and was taken.

Soon after that king Arthur was come from Rome into England, then all the knights of the Table Round resorted unto the king, and made many justs and tournaments ; and some there were that were but knights which increased so in arms and worship that they passed all their fellows in prowess and noble deeds, and that was well proved on many. But in especial it was proved on Sir Launcelot du Lake ; for in all tournaments and justs and deeds of arms, both for life and death, he passed all other knights, and at no time he was never overcome but if it were by treason or enchantment. So Sir Launcelot increased so marvellously in worship and honour ; therefore he is the first knight that the French book maketh mention of after king Arthur came from Rome. Wherefore queen Guenever had him in great favour above all other knights, and in certain he loved the queen again above all other ladies and damsels all his life, and for her he did many deeds of arms, and saved her from the fire through his noble chivalry. Thus Sir Launcelot rested him long with play and game. And then he thought himself to prove himself in strange adventures : then he bad his nephew Sir Lionel for to make him ready, for we two will seek adventures. So they mounted on their horses, armed at all rights, and rode into a deep forest, and so into a deep plain. And then the weather was hot about noon, and Sir Launcelot had great lust to sleep. Then Sir Lionel espied a great apple tree that stood by an hedge, and said, Brother, yonder is a fair shadow, there may we rest us and our horses. It is well said, fair brother, said Sir Launcelot, for this seven year I was not so sleepy as I am now. And so they there alighted, and tied their horses unto sundry trees, and so Sir Launcelot laid him down under an apple tree, and his helm he laid under his head. And Sir Lionel waked while he slept. So Sir Launcelot was asleep passing fast. And in the meanwhile there came three knights riding, as fast fleeing as ever they might ride. And there followed them three but one knight. And when Sir Lionel saw him, him thought he saw never so great a knight nor so well faring a man, neither so well apparelled unto all rights. So within a while this strong knight had overtaken one of these knights, and there he smote him to the cold earth that he lay still. And then he rode unto the second knight, and smote him so that man and horse fell down. And then straight to the third knight he rode, and he smote him behind his horse tail a spear's length. And then he alight down, and reined his horse on the bridle, and bound all the three knights fast with the reins of their own bridles. When Sir Lionel saw him do thus, he thought to assay him, and made him ready, and stilly and privily he took his horse, and thought not for to awake Sir Launcelot. And when he was mounted upon his horse he overtook this strong knight and bad him turn: and the other smote Sir Lionel so hard that horse and man he bare to the earth, and so he alight down and bound him fast, and threw him overthwart his own horse, and so he served them all four, and rode with them away to his own castle. And when he came there, he made unarm them, and beat them with thorns all naked, and after put them in a deep prison where there were many more knights that made great dolour.

CHAP. II.

How Sir Ector followed for to seek Sir Launcelot, and how he was taken by Sir Turquine.

WHEN Sir Ector de Maris wist that Sir Launcelot was past out of the court to seek adventures he was wroth with himself, and made him ready to seek Sir Launcelot, and as he had ridden long in a great forest, he met with a man that was like a forester. Fair fellow, said Sir Ector, knowest thou in this country any adventures that be here nigh hand? Sir, said the forester, this country know I well, and hereby within this mile is a strong manor, and well dyked, and by that manor, on the left hand, there is a fair ford for horses to drink of, and over that ford there groweth a fair tree, and thereon hangeth many fair shields that wielded sometime good knights: and at the hole of the tree hangeth a bason of copper and laton, and strike upon that bason with the butt of thy spear thrice, and soon after thou shalt hear new tidings, and else hast thou the fairest grace that many a year had ever knight that passed through this forest. Gramercy, said Sir Ector, and departed and came to the tree, and saw many fair shields, and among them he saw his brother's shield, Sir Lionel, and many more that he knew that were his fellows of the Round Table, the which grieved his heart, and he promised to revenge his brother. Then anon Sir Ector beat on the bason as he were wood, and then he gave his horse drink at the ford: and there came a knight behind him and bad him come out of the water and make him ready; and Sir Ector anon turned him shortly, and in fewter cast his spear, and smote the other knight a great buffet that his horse turned twice about. This was well done, said the strong knight, and knightly thou hast stricken me: and therewith he rushed his horse on Sir Ector and caught him under his right arm, and bare him clean out of the saddle, and rode with him away into his own hall, and threw him down in the midst of the floor. The name of this knight was Sir Turquine. Then he said unto Sir Ector, For thou hast done this day more unto me than any knight did these twelve years, now will I grant thee thy life, so thou wilt be sworn to be my prisoner all thy life days. Nay, said Sir Ector, that will I never promise thee, but that I will do mine advantage. That me repenteth, said Sir Turquine. And then he made to unarm him, and beat him with thorns all naked, and after put him down in a deep dungeon, where he knew many of his fellows. But when Sir Ector saw Sir Lionel, then made he great sorrow. Alas, brother, said Sir Ector, where is my brother Sir Launcelot? Fair brother, I left him on sleep when that I from him went, under an apple tree, and what is become of him I cannot tell you. Alas, said the knights, but Sir Launcelot help us we may never be delivered, for we know now no knight that is able to match our master Turquine.

CHAP. III.

How four queens found Sir Launcelot sleeping, and how by enchantment he was taken and led into a castle.

Now leave we these knights prisoners, and speak we of Sir Launcelot du Lake that lieth under the apple tree sleeping. Even about the noon there came by him four queens of great estate ; and, for the heat of the sun should not annoy them, there rode four knights about them and bare a cloth of green silk on four spears, betwixt them and the sun, and the queens rode on four white mules.

Thus as they rode they heard by them a great horse grimly neigh, and then were they ware of a sleeping knight that lay all armed under an apple tree ; anon as these queens looked on his face they knew that it was Sir Launcelot. Then they began for to strive for that knight ; every one said she would have him to her love. We shall not strive, said Morgan le Fay, that was king Arthur's sister ; I shall put an enchantment upon him that he shall not awake in six hours, and then I will lead him away unto my castle, and when he is surely within my hold I shall take the enchantment from him, and then let him choose which of us he will have for his love. So this enchantment was cast upon Sir Launcelot, and then they laid him upon his shield, and bare him so on horseback betwixt two knights, and brought

him unto the castle Chariot, and there they laid him in a chamber cold, and at night they sent unto him a fair damsel with his supper ready dight. By that the enchantment was past, and when she came she saluted him, and asked him what cheer ? I cannot say, fair damsel, said Sir Launcelot, for I wot not how I came into this castle but it be by an enchantment. Sir, said she, ye must make good cheer, and if ye be such a knight as is said ye be, I shall tell you more tomorn by prime of the day. Gramercy, fair damsel, said Sir Launcelot, of your good will I require you. And so she departed. And there he lay all that night without comfort of any body.

And on the morn early came these four queens, passingly well beseen, all they bidding him good morn, and he them again. Sir knight, the four queens said, thou must understand thou art our prisoner, and we here know thee well, that thou art Sir Launcelot du Lake, king Ban's son. And truly we understand your worthiness that thou art the noblest knight living ; and, as we know well, there can no lady have thy love but one, and that is queen Guenever, and now thou shalt lose her for ever, and she thee, and therefore thee behoveth now to choose one of us four. I am the queen Morgan le Fay, queen of the land of Gore, and here is the queen of Northgalis, and the queen of Eastland, and the queen of the OutIsles ; now choose ye one of us which thou wilt have to thy love, for thou mayst not choose or else in this prison to die. This is an hard case, said Sir Launcelot, that either I must die or else choose one of you, yet had I lever to die in this prison with worship, than to have one of you to my love maugre my head. And therefore ye be answered, for I will have none of you, for ye be false enchantresses. And as for my lady dame Guenever, were I at my liberty as I was, I would prove it on you or upon yours, that she is the truest lady unto her lord living. Well, said the queens, is this your answer, that you will refuse us? Yea, on my life, said Sir Launcelot, refused ye be of me. So they departed and left him there alone that made great sorrow.

CHAP. IV.

How Sir Launcelot was delivered by the mean of a damsel.

RIGHT so at the noon came the damsel unto him with his dinner, and asked him what cheer? Truly, fair damsel, said Sir Launcelot, in my life days never so ill. Sir, she said, that me repenteth, but and ye will be ruled by me I shall help you out of this distress, and ye shall have no shame nor villainy, so that ye hold me a promise. Fair damsel I will grant you, and sore I am of these queens sorceresses afeard, for they have destroyed many a good knight. Sir, said she, that is sooth, and for the renown and bounty they hear of you they would have your love, and, sir, they say your name is Sir Launcelot du Lake, the flower of knights, and they be passing wroth with you that ye have refused them. But sir, and ye would promise me for to help my father on Tuesday next coming, that hath made a tournament betwixt him and the king of Northgalis, (for the last Tuesday past my father lost the field through three knights of king Arthur's court,) and if ye will be there upon Tuesday next coming and help my father, tomorn ere prime, by the grace of God, I shall deliver you clean. Fair maiden, said Sir Launcelot, tell me what is your father's name, and then shall I give you an answer. Sir knight, she said, my father is king Bagdemagus, that was foul rebuked at the last tournament. I know your father well, said Sir Launcelot, for a noble king, and a good knight, and by the faith of my body, ye shall have my body ready to do your father and you service at that day. Sir, she said, gramercy, and tomorn await ye be ready betimes, and I shall be she that shall deliver you, and take you your armour and your horse, shield and spear: and hereby, within

this ten mile, is an abbey of white monks, there I pray you that ye me abide, and thither shall I bring my father unto you. All this shall be done, said Sir Launcelot, as I am true knight. And so she departed, and came on the morn early, and found him ready. Then she brought him out of twelve locks, and brought him unto his armour, and when he was armed clean, she brought him until his own horse, and lightly he saddled him, and took a great spear in his hand, and so rode forth, and said, Fair damsel I shall not fail you by the grace of God. And so he rode into a great forest all that day, and never could find no high way, and so the night fell on him, and then was he ware in a valley of a pavilion of red sendal. By my faith, said Sir Launcelot, in that pavilion will I lodge all this night. And so there he alight down, and tied his horse to the pavilion, and there he un-'armed him, and there he found a bed, and laid him therein and he fell on sleep heavily.

CHAP. V.

How a knight found Sir Launcelot lying in his bed, and how Sir Launcelot fought with the knight.

THEN within an hour there came the knight to whom belonged the pavilion, and so he laid him down beside Sir Launcelot. And when Sir Launcelot felt him, he started out of the bed lightly, and the other knight after him, and either of them gat their swords in their hands, and out at the pavilion door went the knight of the pavilion, and Sir Launcelot followed him, and there, by a little slake, Sir Launcelot wounded him sore nigh unto the death. And then he yielded him unto Sir Launcelot, and so he granted him, so that he would tell him why he came into the bed. Sir, said the knight, the pavilion is mine own, and there this night would I have slept, and now I am likely to die of this wound. That me repenteth, said Sir Launcelot, of your hurt; but I was adread of treason, for I was late beguiled; and therefore come on your way into your pavilion, and take your rest, and as I suppose I shall stanch your blood. So they went both into the pavilion, and anon Sir Launcelot stanched his blood.

Therewithal came the knight's lady, which was a passing fair lady. And when she espied that her lord Belleus was so sore wounded, she cried out on Sir Launcelot, and made great dole out of measure. Peace my lady and my love, said Belleus, for this knight is a good man, and a knight adventurous; and there he told her all the cause how he was wounded; and when that I yielded me unto him, he left me goodly and hath stanched my blood. Sir, said the lady, I require thee tell me what knight ye be, and what is your name? Fair lady, said he, my name is Sir Launcelot du Lake. So me thought ever by your speech, said the lady, for I have seen you oft or this, and I know you better than ye ween. But now and ye would promise me of your courtesy, for the harms that ye have done to me and to my lord Belleus, that when he cometh unto Arthur's court for to cause him to be made knight of the Round Table, for he is a passing good man of arms, and a mighty lord of lands of many out isles. Fair lady, said Sir Launcelot, let him come unto the court the next high feast, and look that ye come with him, and I shall do my power, and ye prove you doughty of your hands, that ye shall have your desire. So thus within awhile as they thus talked, the night passed, and the day shone, and then Sir Launcelot armed him, and took his horse, and they taught him to the abbey, and thither he rode within the space of two hours.

CHAP. VI.

How Sir Launcelot was received of king Bagdemagus's daughter, and he made his complaint to her father.

AND soon as Sir Launcelot came within the abbey yard the daughter of king Bagdemagus heard a great horse go on the pavement. And she then arose and went unto a window, and there she saw Sir Launcelot, and anon she made men fast to take his horse from him and let lead him into a stable, and himself was led into a fair chamber, and unarmed him, and the lady sent him a long gown, and anon she came herself. And then she made Launcelot passing good cheer, and she said he was the knight in the world was most welcome to her. Then in all haste she sent for her father Bagdemagus that was within twelve mile of that abbey, and afore even he came with a fair fellowship of knights with him. And when the king was alight off his horse he went straight unto Sir Launcelot's chamber, and there he found his daughter, and then the king embraced Sir Launcelot in his arms, and either made other good cheer. Anon Sir Launcelot made his complaint unto the king how he was betrayed, and how his brother Sir Lionel was departed from him he wist not where, and how his daughter had delivered him out of prison,—therefore while I live I shall do her service and all her kindred. Then am I sure of your help, said the king, on Tuesday next coming. Yea, sir, said Sir Launcelot, I shall not fail you, for so I have promised my lady your daughter. But sir, what knights been they of my lord Arthur's, that were with the king of Northgalis? And the king said it was Sir Mador de la Porte, and Sir Mordred, and Sir Gahalatine, that all for-fared my knights, for against them three I nor my knights might bear no strength. Sir, said Sir Launcelot, as I hear say that the tournament shall be within this three mile of this abbey, ye shall send unto me three knights of yours such as ye trust, and look that the three knights have all white shields, and I also, and no painture on the shields, and we four will come out of a little wood in the midst of both parties, and we shall fall in the front of our enemies and grieve them that we may; and thus shall I not be known what knight I am. So they took their rest that night, and this was on the Sunday. And so the king departed, and sent unto Sir Launcelot three knights, with the four white shields.

And on the Tuesday they lodged them in a little leaved wood beside there the tournament should be. And there were scaffolds and holes that lords and ladies might behold and to give the prize. Then came into the field the king of Northgalis with eightscore helms. And then the three knights of Arthur stood by themselves. Then came into the field king Bagdemagus with fourscore of helms. And then they fewtred their spears, and came together with a great dash, and there were slain of knights, at the first recounter, twelve of king Bagdemagus's party, and six of the king of Northgalis' party, and king Bagdemagus's party was far set aback.

CHAP. VII.

How Sir Launcelot behaved him in a tournament, and how he met with Sir Turquine leading away Sir Gaheris.

With that came Sir Launcelot du Lake, and he thrust in with his spear in the thickest of the press, and there he smote down with one spear five knights, and of four of them he brake their backs. And in that throng he smote down the king of Northgalis, and brake his thigh in that fall. All this doing of Sir Launcelot saw the three knights of Arthur. Yonder is a shrewd guest, said Sir Mador de la Porte, therefore have here once at him. So they encountered, and Sir Launcelot bare him down horse and man, so that his shoulder went out of joint. Now befalleth it to me to just, said Mordred, for Sir Mador hath a sore fall. Sir Launcelot was ware of him, and gat a great spear in his hand, and met him, and Sir Mordred brake a spear upon him, and Sir Launcelot gave him such a buffet that the bow of his saddle brake, and so he flew over his horse tail, that his helm went into the earth a foot and more, that nigh his neck was broken, and there he lay long in a swoon. Then came in Sir Gahalatine with a spear, and Launcelot against him, with all their strength that

they might drive, that both their spears to-brast even to their hands, and then they flung out with their swords, and gave many a grim stroke. Then was Sir Launcelot wroth out of measure, and then he smote Sir Gahalatine on the helm, that his nose burst out on blood, and ears and mouth both, and therewith his head hung low. And therewith his horse ran away with him, and he fell down to the earth.

Anon therewithal Sir Launcelot gat a great spear in his hand, and, or ever that great spear brake, he bare down to the earth sixteen knights, some horse and man, and some the man and not the horse, and there was none but that he hit surely he bare none arms that day. And then he gat another great spear, and smote down twelve knights, and the most part of them never throve after. And then the knights of the king of Northgalis would just no more, and there the prize was given unto king Bagdemagus. So either party departed unto his own place, and Sir Launcelot rode forth with king Bagdemagus unto his castle, and there he had passing good cheer both with the king and with his daughter, and they proffered him great gifts. And on the morn he took his leave, and told king Bagdemagus that he would go and seek his brother Sir Lionel, that went from him when that he slept. So he took his horse, and betaught them all to God. And there he said unto the king's daughter, If ye have need any time of my service, I pray you let me have knowledge, and I shall not fail you, as I am true knight.

And so Sir Launcelot departed, and by adventure he came into the same forest where he was taken sleeping. And in the midst of an highway he met a damsel riding on a white palfrey, and there either saluted other. Fair damsel, said Sir Launcelot, know ye in this country any adventures? Sir knight, said that damsel, here are adventures near hand, and thou durst prove them. Why should I not prove adventures? said Sir Launcelot; for that cause came

I hither. Well, said she, thou seemest well to be a good knight, and if thou dare meet with a good knight, I shall bring thee where is the best knight and the mightiest that ever thou found, so thou wilt tell me what is thy name, and what knight thou art. Damsel, as for to tell thee my name, I take no great force: truly, my name is Sir Launcelot du Lake. Sir, thou beseemest well, here be adventures by that fall for thee, for hereby dwelleth a knight that will not be overmatched for no man that I know, unless ye overmatch him, and his name is Sir Turquine. And, as I understand, he hath in his prison of Arthur's court good knights threescore and four that he hath won with his own hands. But when ye have done that day's work ye shall promise me as ye are a true knight for to go with me, and to help me and other damsels that are distressed daily with a false knight. All your intent, damsel, and desire I will fulfil, so ye will bring me unto this knight. Now, fair knight, come on your way. And so she brought him unto the ford, and unto the tree where hung the basin. So Sir Launcelot let his horse drink, and then he beat on the basin with the butt of his spear so hard with all his might till the bottom fell out, and long he did so, but he saw nothing. Then he rode endlong the gates of that manor nigh half an hour. And then was he ware of a great knight that drove an horse afore him, and overthwart the horse there lay an armed knight bound. And ever as they came near and near, Sir Launcelot thought he should know him; then Sir Launcelot was ware that it was Sir Gaheris, Gawaine's brother, a knight of the Table Round. Now fair damsel, said Sir Launcelot, I see yonder cometh a knight fast bound that is a fellow of mine, and brother he is unto Sir Gawaine. And at the first beginning I promise you, by the leave of God, to rescue that knight; and unless his master sit better in the saddle I shall deliver all the prisoners that he hath out of danger, for I am sure that he hath two brethren of mine prisoners

with him. By that time that either had seen other they gripped their spears unto them. Now fair knight, said Sir Launcelot, put that wounded knight off the horse, and let him rest awhile, and let us two prove our strengths. For as it is informed me, thou doest and hast done great despite and shame unto knights of the Round Table, and therefore now defend thee. And thou be of the Table Round, said Turquine, I defy thee and all thy fellowship. That is over much said, said Sir Launcelot.

CHAP. VIII.

How Sir Launcelot and Sir Turquine fought together.

AND then they put their spears in the rests, and came together with their horses as fast as they might run, and either smote other in the midst of their shields, that both their horses' backs brast under them, and the knights were both astonied, and as soon as they might avoid their horses they took their shields afore them, and drew out their swords, and came together eagerly, and either gave other many strong strokes, for there might neither shields nor harness hold their strokes. And so within awhile they had both grimly wounds, and bled passing grievously. Thus they fared two hours or more, trasing and rasing either other where they might hit any bare place. Then at the last they were breathless both, and stood leaning on their swords. Now fellow, said Sir Turquine, hold thy hand awhile, and tell me what I shall ask thee. Say on. Then Turquine said, Thou art the biggest man that ever I met withal, and the best breathed, and like one knight that I hate above all other knights; so be it that thou be not he I will lightly accord with thee, and for thy love I will deliver all the prisoners that I have, that is threescore and four, so thou wilt tell me thy name. And thou and I we will be fellows together, and never to fail the while that I live. It is well said, said Sir Launcelot, but sithen it is so that I may have thy friendship, what knight is he that thou so hatest above all other? Faithfully, said Sir Turquine, his name is Sir Launcelot du Lake, for he slew my brother Sir Carados at the dolorous tower, that was one of the best knights on live; and therefore him I except of knights, for may I once meet with him the one of us shall make an end of other, I make mine avow. And for Sir Launcelot's sake I have slain an hundred good knights, and as many I have maimed all utterly that they might never after help themselves, and many have died in prison, and yet I have threescore and four, and all shall be delivered, so thou wilt tell me thy name, so it be that thou be not Sir Launcelot.

Now see I well, said Sir Launcelot, that such a man I might be that I might have peace; and such a man I might be that there should be war mortal betwixt us: and now sir knight, at thy request I will that thou wit and know that I am Launcelot du Lake, king Ban's son of Benwick, and very knight of the Table Round. And now I defy thee, do thy best. Ah, said Turquine, Launcelot, thou art unto me most welcome that ever was knight, for we shall never part till the one of us be dead. Then they hurtled together as two wild bulls, rashing and lashing with their shields and swords that sometimes they fell both over their noses. Thus they fought still two hours and more, and never would have rest, and Sir Turquine gave Sir Launcelot many wounds that all the ground there as they fought was all bespeckled with blood.

CHAP. IX.

How Sir Turquine was slain, and how Sir Launcelot bade Sir Gaheris deliver all the prisoners.

THEN at the last Sir Turquine waxed faint, and gave somewhat aback, and bare his shield low for weariness. That espied Sir Launcelot and lept upon him fiercely and got him by the beaver of his helmet, and plucked him down on his knees, and anon he rased off his helm, and smote his neck in sunder. And when Sir Launcelot had done this he went unto the damsel and said, Damsel, I am ready to go with you where ye will have me, but I have no horse. Fair sir, said she, take this wounded knight's horse, and send him into this manor, and command him to deliver all the prisoners. So Sir Launcelot went unto Gaheris, and prayed him not to be aggrieved for to lend him his horse. Nay, fair lord, said Sir Gaheris, I will that ye take my horse at your own commandment, for ye have both saved me and my horse, and this day I say ye are the best knight in the world, for ye have slain this day in my sight the mightiest man and the best knight, except you, that ever I saw; and sir, said Sir Gaheris, I pray you tell me your name? Sir, my name is Sir Launcelot du Lake, that ought to help you of right for king Arthur's sake, and in especial for my lord Sir Gawaine's sake, your own dear brother; and when that ye come within yonder manor I am sure ye shall find there many knights of the Round Table, for I have seen many of their shields that I know on yonder tree. There is Kay's shield, and Sir Brandel's shield, and Sir Marhaus' shield, and Sir Galind's shield, and Sir Brian Listonoise's shield, and Sir Aliduke's shield, with many more that I am not now advised of, and also my two brethren's shields, Sir Ector de Maris and Sir Lionel; wherefore I pray you greet them all from me, and say that I bid them take there such stuff as they find, and that in any wise my brethren go unto the court and abide me there till that I come, for by the feast of Pentecost I cast me to be there, for at this time I must ride with this damsel for to save my promise. And so he departed from Gaheris, and Sir Gaheris went into the manor, and there he found a yeoman porter keeping there many keys. Anon withal Sir Gaheris threw the porter unto the ground, and took the keys from him, and hastily he opened the prison door, and there he let out all the prisoners, and every man loosed other of their bonds. And when they saw Sir Gaheris, all they thanked him, for they wend that he was wounded. Not so, said Gaheris, it was Launcelot that slew him worshipfully with his own hands, I saw it with mine own eyes. And he greeteth you all well, and prayeth you to haste you to the court, and as unto Sir Lionel and Ector de Maris, he prayeth you to abide him at the court. That shall we not do, said his brethren, we will find him and we may live. So shall I, said Sir Kay, find him or I come at the court, as I am true knight. Then all those knights sought the house where as the armour was, and then they armed them, and every knight found his own horse, and all that belonged unto him. And when ever this was done, there came a forester with four horses laden with fat venison. Anon Sir Kay said, Here is good meat for us for one meal, for we had not many a day no good repast. And so that venison was roasted, baked, and sodden, and so after supper some abode there all that night, but Sir Lionel and Ector de Maris and Sir Kay rode after Sir Launcelot to find him if they might.

CHAP. X.

How Sir Launcelot rode with the damsel and slew a knight that distressed all ladies, and also a villain that kept a bridge.

Now turn we unto Sir Launcelot that rode with the damsel in a fair high way. Sir, said the damsel, here by this way haunteth a knight that distresseth all ladies and gentlewomen, and at the least he robbeth them or ill-useth them. What, said Sir Launcelot, is he a thief and a knight, and a ravisher of women? He doth shame unto the order of knighthood and contrary to his oath, it is pity that he liveth. But fair damsel ye shall ride on afore yourself, and I will keep myself in covert, and if

that he trouble you or distress you, I shall be your rescue, and learn him to be ruled as a knight. So the maid rode on by the way a soft ambling pace. And within awhile came out that knight on horseback out of the wood, and his page with him, and there he put the damsel from her horse, and then she cried. With that came Launcelot as fast as he might, till he came to that knight, saying, Oh thou false knight and traitor unto knighthood, who did learn thee to distress ladies and gentlewomen? When the knight saw Sir Launcelot thus rebuking him, he answered not, but drew his sword and rode unto Sir Launcelot. And Sir Launcelot threw his spear from him, and drew out his sword, and strake him such a buffet on the helmet that he clave his head and neck unto the throat. Now hast thou thy payment that long thou hast deserved. That is truth, said the damsel, for like as Turquine watched to destroy knights, so did this knight attend to destroy and distress ladies, damsels, and gentlewomen, and his name was Sir Peris de Forest Savage. Now damsel, said Sir Launcelot, will ye any more service of me? Nay sir, she said, at this time; but Almighty Jesu preserve you wheresoever ye ride or go, for the courtiest knight thou art and meekest unto all ladies and gentlewomen that now liveth. But one thing, sir knight, me thinketh ye lack, ye that are a knight wifeless, that ye will not love some maiden or gentlewoman, for I could never hear say that ever ye loved any of no manner degree, and that is great pity; but it is noised that ye love queen Guenever, and that she hath ordained by enchantment that ye shall never love none other but her, nor none other damsel nor lady shall rejoice you; wherefore many in this land, of high estate and low, make great sorrow. Fair damsel, said Sir Launcelot, I may not warn people to speak of me what it pleaseth them: but for to be a wedded man I think it not, for then I must couch with her, and leave arms and tournaments, battles and adventures. And as for to say for to take my pleasance with paramours, that will I refuse in principal for dread of God. For knights that be adulterous, or wanton, shall not be happy nor fortunate unto the wars, for either they shall be overcome with a simpler knight than they be themselves, or else they shall by mishap and their cursedness slay better men than they be themselves; and who that so useth shall be unhappy, and all thing is unhappy that is about them. And so Sir Launcelot and she departed.

And then he rode in a deep forest two days and more, and had strait lodging. So on the third day he rode over a long bridge, and there start upon him suddenly a passing foul churl, and he smote his horse on the nose that he turned about, and asked him why he rode over that bridge without his licence. Why should I not ride this way? said Sir Launcelot, I may not ride beside. Thou shalt not choose, said the churl, and lashed at him with a great club shod with iron. Then Sir Launcelot drew his sword, and put the stroke aback, and clave his head unto the breast. At the end of the bridge was a fair village, and all the people men and women cried on Sir Launcelot, and said, A worse deed diddest thou never for thyself, for thou hast slain the chief porter of our castle. Sir Launcelot let them say what they would, and straight he went into the castle; and when he came into the castle he alight, and tied his horse to a ring on the wall; and there he saw a fair green court, and thither he dressed himself, for there him thought was a fair place to fight in. So he looked about, and saw much people in doors and windows, that said, Fair knight thou art unhappy.

CHAP. XI.

How Sir Launcelot slew two giants, and made a castle free.

ANON withal came there upon him two great giants, well armed all save the heads, with two horrible clubs in their hands. Sir Launcelot put his shield afore him, and put the stroke away of the one giant, and with his sword he clave his head asunder. When his fellow saw that, he ran away as he were wood, for fear of the horrible strokes, and Sir Launcelot after him with all his might, and smote him on the shoulder, and clave him to the middle. Then Sir Launcelot went into the hall, and there came afore him threescore ladies and damsels, and all kneeled unto him, and thanked God and him of their deliverance. For, sir, said they, the most part of us have been here this seven year their prisoners, and we have worked all manner of silk works for our meat, and we are all great gentlewomen born, and blessed be the time, knight, that ever thou wert born; for thou hast done the most worship that ever did knight in the world, that will we bear record, and we all pray you to tell us your name, that we may tell our friends who delivered us out of prison. Fair damsels, he said, my name is Sir Launcelot du Lake. Ah, sir, said they all, well mayest thou be he, for else save yourself, as we deemed, there might never knight have the better of these two giants, for many fair knights have assayed it, and here have ended, and many times have we wished after you, and these two giants dread never knight but you. Now may ye say, said Sir Launcelot, unto your friends, how and who hath delivered you, and greet them all from me, and if that I come in any of your marches, shew me such cheer as ye have cause; and what treasure that there is in this castle I give it you for a reward for your grievance: and the lord that is the owner of this castle I would that he received it as is right. Fair sir, said they, the name of this castle is Tintagil, and a duke owned it some time that had wedded fair Igraine, and after wedded her Uther Pendragon and gat on her Arthur. Well, said Sir Launcelot, I understand to whom this castle belongeth. And so he departed from them and betaught them unto God. And then he mounted upon his horse, and rode into many strange and wild countries and through many waters and valleys, and evil was he lodged. And at the last by fortune him happened against a night to come to a fair courtelage, and therein he found an old gentlewoman that lodged him with a good will, and there he had good cheer for him and his horse. And when time was, his host brought him into a fair garret over the gate to his bed. There Sir Launcelot unarmed him, and set his harness by him, and went to bed, and anon he fell on sleep. So soon after there came one on horseback, and knocked at the gate in great haste. And when Sir Launcelot heard this he arose up, and looked out at the window, and saw by the moon-light three knights came riding after that one man, and all three lashed on him at once with swords, and that one knight turned on them knightly again and defended him. Truly, said Sir Launcelot, yonder one knight shall I help, for it were shame for me to see three knights on one, and if he be slain I am partner of his death. And therewith he took his harness and went out at a window by a sheet down to the four knights, and then Sir Launcelot said on high, Turn you knights unto me, and leave your fighting with that knight. And then they all three left Sir Kay, and turned unto Sir Launcelot, and there began great battle, for they alight all three, and strake many great strokes at Sir Launcelot, and assailed him on every side. Then Sir Kay dressed him for to have holpen Sir Launcelot. Nay, sir, said he, I will none of your help, therefore as ye will have my help let me alone with them. Sir Kay for the pleasure of the knight suffered him for to do his will, and so stood aside. And then anon within six strokes Sir Launcelot had stricken them to the earth.

And then they all three cried, Sir knight, we yield us unto you as man of might matchless. As to that, said Sir Launcelot, I will not take your yielding unto me, but so that ye yield you unto Sir Kay the seneschal, on that covenant I will save your lives and else not. Fair knight, said they, that were we loth to do; for as for Sir Kay we chased him hither, and had overcome him had not ye been; therefore to yield us unto him it were no reason. Well, as to that, said Sir Launcelot, advise you well, for ye may choose whether ye will die or live, for and ye be yielden it shall be unto Sir Kay. Fair knight, then they said, in saving our lives we will do as thou commandest us. Then shall ye, said Sir Launcelot, on Whitsunday next coming go unto the court of king Arthur, and there shall ye yield you unto queen Guenever, and put you all three in her grace and mercy, and say that Sir Kay sent you thither to be her prisoners. Sir, they said, it shall done by the faith of our bodies, and we be living. And there they swore, every knight upon his sword. And so Sir Launcelot suffered them so to depart. And then Sir Launcelot knocked at the gate with the pommel of his sword, and with that came his host, and in they entered, Sir Kay and he. Sir, said his host, I wend ye had been in your bed. So I was, said Sir Launcelot, but I arose and lept out at my window for to help an old fellow of mine. And so when they came nigh the light Sir Kay knew well that it was Sir Launcelot, and therewith he kneeled down and thanked him of all his kindness that he hath holpen him twice from the death. Sir, he said, I have done nothing but that I ought to do, and ye are welcome, and here shall ye repose you and take your rest. So when Sir Kay was unarmed he asked after meat, so there was meat fetched him, and he ate strongly. And when he had supped they went to their beds, and were lodged together in one bed. On the morn Sir Launcelot arose early, and left Sir Kay sleeping: and Sir Launcelot took Sir Kay's armour and his shield and armed him: and so he went to the stable and took his horse, and took his leave of his host, and so he departed. Then soon after arose Sir Kay and missed Sir Launcelot: and then he espied that he had his armour and his horse. Now by my faith I know well that he will grieve some of the court of king Arthur: for on him knights will be bold, and deem that it is I, and that will beguile them: and because of his armour and shield I am sure I shall ride in peace. And then soon after departed Sir Kay, and thanked his host.

CHAP. XII.

How Sir Launcelot rode disguised in Sir Kay's harness, and how he smote down a knight.

Now turn we unto Sir Launcelot that had ridden long in a great forest, and at the last he came into a low country full of fair rivers and meadows. And afore him he saw a long bridge, and three pavilions stood thereon of silk and sandal of divers hue. And without the pavilions hung three white shields on truncheons of spears, and great long spears stood upright by the pavilions, and at every pavilion's door stood three fresh squires, and so Sir Launcelot passed by them, and spake no word. When he was past the three knights said that it was the proud Kay, he weeneth no knight so good as he, and the contrary is ofttime proved. By my faith, said one of the knights, his name was Sir Gaunter, I will ride after him and assay him for all his pride, and ye may behold how that I speed. So this knight, Sir Gaunter, armed him, and hung his shield upon his shoulder and mounted upon a great horse, and gat his spear in his hand, and galloped after Sir Launcelot. And when he came nigh him, he cried, Abide thou proud knight Sir Kay, for thou shalt not pass quit. So Sir Launcelot turned him, and either fewtred their spears, and came together with all their mights, and Sir Gaunter's spear brake, but Sir Launcelot smote him down, horse and man. And when Sir Gaunter was at the earth his brethren said each one to other, Yonder knight is not Sir Kay, for he is bigger than he. I dare lay my head, said Sir Gilmere, yonder knight hath slain Sir Kay and hath taken his horse

and harness. Whether it be so or no, said Sir Raynold the third brother, let us now go mount upon our horses and rescue our brother Sir Gaunter upon pain of death. We all shall have work enough to match that knight, for ever me seemeth by his person it is Sir Launcelot, or Sir Tristam, or Sir Pelleas the good knight. Then anon they took their horses and overtook Sir Launcelot, and Sir Gilmere put forth his spear and ran to Sir Launcelot and Sir Launcelot smote him down that he lay in a swoon. Sir knight, said Sir Raynold, thou art a strong man, and, as I suppose, thou hast slain my two brethren, for the which riseth my heart sore against thee; and if I might with my worship I would not have ado with thee, but needs I must take part as they do; and therefore knight, he said, keep thyself. And so they hurtled together with all their mights, and all to-shivered both their spears. And then they drew their swords and lashed together eagerly. Anon therewith arose Sir Gaunter, and came unto his brother Sir Gilmere, and bad him arise and help we our brother Sir Raynold, that yonder marvellously matcheth yonder good knight. Therewithal they lept on their horses, and hurtled unto Sir Launcelot. And when he saw them come, he smote a sore stroke unto Sir Raynold, that he fell off his horse to the ground, and then he struck to the other two brethren, and at two strokes he strake them down to the earth. With that Sir Raynold began to start up with his head all bloody, and came straight unto Sir Launcelot. Now let be, said Sir Launcelot, I was not far from thee when thou wert made knight, Sir Raynold, and also I know thou art a good knight, and loth I were to slay thee. Gramercy, said Sir Raynold, as for your goodness; and I dare say as for me and my brethren, we will not be loth to yield us unto you, with that we knew your name; for well we know ye are not Sir Kay. As for that be it as it may, for ye shall yield you unto dame Guenever, and look that ye be with her on Whitsunday, and yield you unto her as prisoners, and say that Sir Kay sent you unto her. Then they swore it should be done. And so passed forth Sir Launcelot, and each one of the brethren helped each other as well as they might.

CHAP. XIII.

How Sir Launcelot justed against four knights of the Round Table, and overthrew them.

So Sir Launcelot rode into a deep forest, and there by in a slade he saw four knights hoving under an oak, and they were of Arthur's court; one was Sagramour le Desirous, and Sir Ector de Maris, and Sir Gawaine, and Sir Uwaine. Anon as these four knights had espied Sir Launcelot they wend by his arms it had been Sir Kay. Now by my faith, said Sir Sagramour, I will prove Sir Kay's might, and gat his spear in his hand, and came toward Sir Launcelot. Therewith Sir Launcelot was ware, and knew him well, and fewtred his spear against him, and smote Sir Sagramour so sore that horse and man fell both to the earth. Lo, my fellows, said Sir Ector, yonder ye may see what a buffet he hath; that knight is much bigger than ever was Sir Kay. Now shall ye see what I may do to him. So Sir Ector gat his spear in his hand and galloped toward Sir Launcelot, and Sir Launcelot smote him through the shield and shoulder that horse and man went to the earth, and ever his spear held. By my faith, said Sir Uwaine, yonder is a strong knight, and I am sure he hath slain Sir Kay; and I see by his great strength it will be hard to match him. And therewithal Sir Uwaine gat his spear in his hand and rode toward Sir Launcelot, and Sir Launcelot knew him well, and so he met him on the plain and gave him such a buffet that he was astonied, that long he wist not where he was. Now see I well, said Sir Gawaine, I must encounter with that knight. Then he dressed his shield and gat a good spear in his hand, and Sir Launcelot knew

him well, and then they let run their horses with all their mights, and either knight smote other in midst of the shield. But Sir Gawaine's spear to-brast, and Sir Launcelot charged so sore upon him that his horse reversed up so down. And much sorrow had Sir Gawaine to avoid his horse, and so Sir Launcelot passed on a pace, and smiled, and said, God give him joy that this spear made, for there came never a better in my hand. Then the four knights went each one to other, and comforted each other. What say ye by this gest? said Sir Gawaine, that one spear hath felled us four. We command him unto the devil, they said all, for he is a man of great might. Ye may well say it, said Sir Gawaine, that he is a man of might, for I dare lay my head it is Sir Launcelot, I know it by his riding. Let him go, said Sir Gawaine, for when we come to the court then shall we wit. And then had they much sorrow to get their horses again.

CHAP. XIV.

How Sir Launcelot followed a brachet into a castle where he found a dead knight, and how he after was required of a damsel to heal her brother.

Now leave we there and speak of Sir Launcelot that rode a great while in a deep forest, where he saw a black brachet, seeking in manner as it had been in the track of an hurt deer, and therewith he rode after the brachet, and he saw lie on the ground a large track of blood. And then Sir Launcelot rode after. And ever the brachet looked behind her, and so she went through a great marsh, and ever Sir Launcelot followed. And then was he ware of an old manor, and thither ran the brachet, and so over the bridge. So Sir Launcelot rode over that bridge that was old and feeble; and when he came in midst of a great hall, there he saw lie a dead knight that was a seemly man, and that brachet licked his wounds. And therewithal came out a lady weeping and wringing her hands, and she said, Oh knight, too much sorrow hast thou brought me. Why say ye so? said Sir Launcelot, I did never this knight no harm, for hither by track of blood this brachet brought me; and therefore fair lady be not displeased with me, for I am full sore aggrieved of your grievance. Truly sir, she said, I trow it be not ye that have slain my husband, for he that did that deed is sore wounded, and he is never likely to recover, that shall I ensure him. What was your husband's name? said Sir Launcelot. Sir, said she, his name was called Sir Gilbert, one of the best knights of the world, and he that hath slain him I know not his name. Now God send you better comfort, said Sir Launcelot. And so he departed and went into the forest again, and there he met with a damsel, the which knew him well, and she said aloud, Well be ye found, my lord; and now I require thee on thy knighthood help my brother that is sore wounded, and never stinteth bleeding, for this day fought he with Sir Gilbert and slew him in plain battle, and there was my brother sore wounded, and there is a lady a sorceress that dwelleth in a castle here beside, and this day she told me my brother's wounds should never be whole till I could find a knight that would go into the chapel perilous, and there he should find a sword and a bloody cloth that the wounded knight was lapped in, and a piece of that cloth and sword should heal my brother's wounds, so that his wounds were searched with the sword and the cloth. This is a marvellous thing, said Sir Launcelot, but what is your brother's name? Sir, said she, his name is Sir Meliot de Logres. That me repenteth, said Sir Launcelot, for he is a fellow of the Table Round, and to his help I will do my power. Then, sir, said she, follow even this high way, and it will bring you unto the chapel perilous, and there I shall abide till God send you here again, and but you speed I know no knight living that may achieve that adventure.

CHAP. XV.

How Sir Launcelot came into the chapel perilous, and gat there of a dead corpse a piece of the cloth and a sword.

RIGHT so Sir Launcelot departed, and when he came unto the chapel perilous he alight down, and tied his horse to a little gate. And as soon as he was within the churchyard he saw on the front of the chapel many fair rich shields turned up so down, and many of the shields Sir Launcelot had seen knights bear beforehand. With that he saw by him stand there a thirty great knights, more by a yard than any man that ever he had seen, and all those grinned and gnashed at Sir Launcelot. And when he saw their countenance he dread him sore, and so put his shield afore him, and took his sword in his hand ready unto battle; and they were all armed in black harness, ready with their shields and their swords drawn. And when Sir Launcelot would have gone throughout them, they scattered on every side of him, and gave him the way, and therewith he waxed all bold and entered into the chapel, and then he saw no light but a dim lamp burning, and then was he ware of a corpse covered with a cloth of silk. Then Sir Launcelot stooped down and cut a piece away of that cloth, and then it fared under him as the earth had quaked a little; there withal he feared. And then he saw a fair sword lie by the dead knight, and that he gat in his hand and hied him out of the chapel. Anon as ever he was in the chapel-yard all the knights spake to him with a grimly voice, and said, Knight, Sir Launcelot, lay that sword from thee, or else thou shalt die. Whether I live or die, said Sir Launcelot, will no great word get it again, therefore fight for it and ye list. Then right so he passed throughout them, and beyond the chapel-yard there met him a fair damsel, and said, Sir Launcelot, leave that sword behind thee, or thou wilt die for it. I leave it not, said Sir Launcelot, for no entreaties. No, said she, and thou didst leave that sword queen Guenever should ye never see. Then were I a fool and I would leave this sword, said Sir Launcelot. Now gentle knight, said the damsel, I require thee to kiss me but once. Nay, said Sir Launcelot, that God me forbid. Well sir, said she, and thou haddest kissed me thy life days had been done, but now alas, she said, I have lost all my labour, for I ordained this chapel for thy sake, and for Sir Gawaine. And once I had Sir Gawaine within my power, and at that time he fought with that knight that lieth there dead in yonder chapel, Sir Gilbert, and at that time he smote off the left hand of Sir Gilbert. And Sir Launcelot now I tell thee, I have loved thee this seven year, but there may no woman have thy love but queen Guenever. But since I may not rejoice thee to have thy body alive, I had kept no more joy in this world but to have thy body dead. Then would I have balmed it and preserved it, and so have kept it my life days, and daily I should have kissed thee in despite of queen Guenever. Ye say well, said Sir Launcelot, God preserve me from your subtil crafts. And therewithal he took his horse and so departed from her. And as the book saith, when Sir Launcelot was departed she took such sorrow that she died within a fourteen night, and her name was Hellawes the sorceress, lady of the castle Nigramous. Anon Sir Launcelot met with the damsel, Sir Meliot's sister. And when she saw him she clapped her hands and wept for joy, and then they rode unto a castle thereby, where Sir Meliot lay. And anon as Sir Launcelot saw him he knew him, but he was pale as the earth for bleeding. When Sir Meliot saw Sir Launcelot, he kneeled upon his knees and cried on high: O lord Sir Launcelot help me! Anon Sir Launcelot leapt unto him, and touched his wounds with Sir Gilbert's sword, and then he wiped his wounds with a part of the bloody cloth that Sir Gilbert was wrapped in, and anon a wholer man in his life was he never. And then there was great joy between them, and they made Sir Launcelot all the cheer that they might, and so on the morn Sir Launcelot took his leave, and bad Sir Meliot hie him to the court of my lord Arthur, for it draweth nigh to the feast of Pentecost, and there, by the grace of God, ye shall find me. And therewith they departed.

CHAP. XVI.

How Sir Launcelot at the request of a lady recovered a falcon, by which he was deceived.

AND so Sir Launcelot rode through many strange countries, over marshes and valleys, till by fortune he came to a fair castle, and as he passed beyond the castle him thought he heard two bells ring. And then was he ware of a falcon came flying over his head toward an high elm, and long lines about her feet, and as she flew unto the elm to take her perch, the lines overcast about a bough. And when she would have taken her flight she hung by the legs fast, and Sir Launcelot saw how she hung, and beheld the fair falcon perigot, and he was sorry for her. The meanwhile came a lady out of the castle, and cried on high, O Launcelot, Launcelot, as thou art flower of all knights help me to get my hawk, for and my hawk be lost my lord will destroy me; for I kept the hawk and she slipt from me, and if my lord my husband wit it, he is so hasty that he will slay me. What is your lord's name? said Sir Launcelot. Sir, she said, his name is Sir Phelot, a knight that longeth unto the king of Northgalis. Well, fair lady, since that ye know my name, and require me of knighthood to help you, I will do what I may to get your hawk, and yet truly I am an ill climber, and the tree is passing high, and few boughs to help me withal. And therewith Sir Launcelot alight, and tied his horse to the same tree, and prayed the lady to unarm him. And so when he was unarmed, he put off all his clothes unto his shirt and breeches, and with might and force he climbed up to the falcon, and tied the lines to a great rotten branch, and threw the hawk down and it withal. Anon the lady gat the hawk in her hand, and therewithal came out Sir Phelot out of the groves suddenly, that was her husband, all armed, and with his naked sword in his hand, and said, O knight, Launcelot, now have I found thee as I would : and stood at the bole of the tree to slay him. Ah lady, said Sir Launcelot, why have ye betrayed me? She hath done, said Sir Phelot, but as I commanded her, and therefore there is none other boot but thine hour is come that thou must die. That were shame unto thee, said Sir Launcelot, thou an armed knight to slay a naked man by treason. Thou gettest none other grace, said Sir Phelot, and therefore help thyself and thou canst. Truly, said Sir Launcelot, that shall be thy shame, but since thou wilt do none other, take mine harness with thee, and hang my sword upon a bough that I may get it, and then do thy best to slay me and thou canst. Nay, nay, said Sir Phelot, for I know thee better than thou weenest, therefore thou gettest no weapon and I may keep you therefro. Alas, said Sir Launcelot, that ever knight should die weaponless. And therewith he awaited above him and under him, and over his head he saw a rounspik, a big bough leafless, and therewith he brake it off by the body ; and then he came lower, and awaited how his own horse stood, and suddenly he lept on the farther side of the horse from the knight. And then Sir Phelot lashed at him eagerly, weening to have slain him ; but Sir Launcelot put away the stroke with the rounspik, and therewith he smote him on the one side of the head, that he fell down in a swoon to the ground. So then Sir Launcelot took his sword out of his hand, and struck his neck from the body. Then cried the lady, Alas, why hast thou slain my husband? I am not causer, said Sir Launcelot, for with false-hood ye would have had slain me with treason, and now it is fallen on you

both. And then she swooned as though she would die. And therewithal Sir Launcelot gat all his armour as well as he might, and put it upon him, for dread of more resort, for he dread that the knight's castle was so nigh. And so soon as he might he took his horse and departed, and thanked God that he had escaped that adventure.

CHAP. XVII.

How Sir Launcelot overtook a knight which chased his wife to have slain her, and how he said to him.

So Sir Launcelot rode many wild ways, throughout marshes and many wild ways. And as he rode in a valley he saw a knight chasing a lady with a naked sword to have slain her. And by fortune, as this knight should have slain this lady, she cried on Sir Launcelot and prayed him to rescue her. When Sir Launcelot saw that mischief he took his horse and rode between them, saying, Knight, fie for shame, why wilt thou slay this lady? thou dost shame unto thee and all knights. What hast thou to do betwixt me and my wife? said the knight ; I will slay her, maugre thy head. That shall ye not, said Sir Launcelot, for rather we two will have ado together. Sir Launcelot, said the knight, thou doest not thy part, for this lady hath betrayed me. It is not so, said the lady, truly he saith wrong on me, and because I love and cherish my cousin german, he is jealous betwixt him and me, and as I shall answer to God, there was never sin betwixt us. But, sir, said the lady, as thou art called the worshipfullest knight of the world, I require thee of true knighthood keep me and save me, for whatsoever ye say he will slay me, for he is without mercy. Have ye no doubt, said Launcelot, it shall not lie in his power. Sir, said the knight, in your sight I will be ruled as ye will have me. And so Sir Launcelot rode on the one side and she on the other : he had not ridden but a while but the knight bad Sir Launcelot turn him and look behind him and said,

Sir, yonder come men of arms after us riding. And so Sir Launcelot turned him, and thought no treason. And therewith was the knight and the lady on one side, and suddenly he swapped off his lady's head. And when Sir Launcelot had espied him what he had done, he said, and called him, Traitor thou hast shamed me for ever. And suddenly Sir Launcelot alight off his horse, and pulled out his sword to slay him. And therewithal he fell flat to the earth, and gripped Sir Launcelot by the thighs, and cried mercy. Fie on thee, said Sir Launcelot, thou shameful knight, thou mayest have no mercy, and therefore arise and fight with me. Nay, said the knight, I will never arise till ye grant me mercy. Now will I proffer thee fair, said Launcelot: I will unarm me unto my shirt, and will have nothing upon me but my shirt, and my sword in my hand, and if thou canst slay me quit be thou for ever. Nay, sir, said Pedivere, that will I never. Well, said Sir Launcelot, take this lady and the head, and bear it upon thee, and here shalt thou swear upon my sword to bear it alway upon thy back, and never to rest till thou come to queen Guenever. Sir, said he, that will I do, by the faith of my body. Now, said Launcelot, tell me what is your name. Sir, my name is Pedivere. In a shameful hour wert thou born, said Launcelot. So Pedivere departed with the dead lady and the head, and found the queen with king Arthur at Winchester, and there he told all the truth. Sir knight, said the queen, this is an horrible deed and a shameful, and a great rebuke unto Sir Launcelot: but notwithstanding his worship is not known in divers countries. But this shall I give you in penance: make ye as good skift as ye can, ye shall bear this lady with you on horseback unto the Pope of Rome, and of him receive your penance for your foul deeds, and ye shall never rest one night there as ye do another, and if ye go to any bed the dead body shall lie with you. This oath there he made, and so departed,

and as it telleth in the French book, when he came to Rome the Pope bad him go again to queen Guenever, and in Rome was his lady buried by the Pope's commandment. And after this Sir Pedivere fell to great goodness, and was an holy man and an hermit.

CHAP. XVIII.

How Sir Launcelot came to king Arthur's court, and how there were recounted all his noble feats and acts.

Now turn me unto Sir Launcelot du Lake, that came home two days afore the feast of Pentecost. And the king and all the court were passing fain of his coming. And when Sir Gawaine, Sir Uwaine, Sir Sagramour, Sir Ector de Maris, saw Sir Launcelot in Kay's armour, then they wist well it was he that smote them down all with one spear. Then there was laughing and smiling among them. And ever now and now came all the knights home that Sir Turquine had prisoners, and they all honoured and worshipped Sir Launcelot. When Sir Gaheris heard them speak, he said, I saw all the battle from the beginning to the ending, and there he told king Arthur all how it was, and how Sir Turquine was the strongest knight that ever he saw except Sir Launcelot: there were many knights bear him record, nigh three-score. Then Sir Kay told the ·king how Sir Launcelot had rescued him when he should have been slain, and how he made the knights yield them to me, and not to him. And there they were, all three, and bare record. And by my faith, said Sir Kay, because Sir Launcelot took my harness and left me his I rode in good peace, and no man would have ado with me. Anon therewithal came the three knights that fought with Sir Launcelot at the long bridge, and there they yielded them unto Sir Kay, and Sir Kay forsook them and said he fought never with them: But I shall ease your hearts, said Sir Kay, yonder is Sir Launcelot that overcame you. When they wist that, they were glad. And then Sir Meliot de Logres came home, and told king Arthur how Sir Launcelot had saved him from the death. And all his deeds were known, how four queens, sorceresses, had him in prison, and how he was delivered by king Bagdemagus's daughter. Also there were told all the great deeds of arms that Sir Launcelot did betwixt the two kings, that is to say, the king of Northgalis and king Bagdemagus. All the truth Sir Gahalantine did tell, and Sir Mador de la Porte, and Sir Mordred, for they were at that same tournament. Then came in the lady that knew Sir Launcelot when that he wounded Sir Belleus at the pavilion. And there, at the request of Sir Launcelot, Sir Belleus was made knight of the Round Table.

And so at that time Sir Launcelot had the greatest name of any knight of the world, and most he was honoured of high and low.

Explicit the noble tale of syr Launcelot du lake, whiche is the bi. book. Here foloweth the tale of syr Gareth of Orkeney, that was called Beaumayns by syr kay, and is the sebenth book.

The Sebenth Book.

CHAP. I.

How Beaumains came to king Arthur's court and demanded three petitions of king Arthur.

WHEN Arthur held his Round Table most fully, it fortuned that he commanded that the high feast of Pentecost should be holden at a city and a castle, the which in those days was called Kink-Kenadon, upon the sands that marched nigh Wales. So ever the king had a custom that at the feast of Pentecost, in especial afore other feasts in the year, he would not go that day to meat until he had heard or seen of a great marvel. And for that custom all manner of strange adventures came before Arthur as at that feast before all other feasts. And so Sir Gawaine, a little tofore noon of the day of Pentecost, espied at a window three men upon horseback, and a dwarf on foot. And so the three men alight and the dwarf kept their horses, and one of the three men was higher than the other twain by a foot and a half. Then Sir Gawaine went unto the king and said, Sir, go to your meat, for here at the hand come strange adventures. So Arthur went unto his meat with many other kings. And there were all the knights of the Round Table, save those that were prisoners or slain at a recounter. Then at the high feast evermore they should be fulfilled the whole number of an hundred and fifty, for then was the Round Table fully complished. Right so came into the hall two men well beseen and richly, and upon their shoulders there leaned the goodliest young man and the fairest that ever they all saw, and he was large and long and broad in the shoulders, and well visaged, and the fairest and the largest handed that ever man saw, but he fared as though he might not go nor bear himself, but if he leaned upon their shoulders. Anon as Arthur saw him there was made peace and room, and right so they went with him unto the high dais, without saying of any words. Then this much young man pulled him aback, and easily stretched up straight, saying, King Arthur, God you bless, and all your fair fellowship, and in especial the fellowship of the Table Round. And for this cause I am come hither, to pray you and require you to give me three gifts, and they shall not be unreasonably asked, but that ye may worshipfully and honourably grant them me, and to you no great hurt nor loss. And the first done and gift I will ask now, and the other two gifts I will ask this day twelvemonth wheresoever ye hold your high feast. Now ask, said Arthur, and ye shall have your asking. Now sir, this is my petition for this feast, that ye will give me meat and drink sufficiently for this twelvemonth, and at that day I will ask mine other two gifts. My fair son, said Arthur, ask better, I counsel thee, for this is but a simple asking, for my heart giveth me to thee greatly that thou art come of men of worship, and greatly my conceit faileth me but thou shalt prove a man of right great worship. Sir, said he, thereof be as it may, I have asked that I will ask. Well, said the king, ye shall have meat and drink enough, that I never defended that none, neither my friend nor my foe. But what is thy name I would wit? I cannot tell you, said he. That is marvel, said the king, that thou knowest not thy name, and thou art the goodliest young man that ever I saw. Then the king betook him to Sir Kay, the steward, and charged him that he should give him of all manner of meats and drinks of the best, and also that he had all manner of finding as though he were a lord's son. That shall little need, said Sir Kay, to do such cost upon him; for I dare undertake he is a villain born, and never will make man, for and he had come of gentlemen he would have asked of you horse and armour, but such as he is, so he asketh. And since he hath no name, I shall give him a name that shall be Beaumains, that is Fair-hands, and into the kitchen I shall bring him, and there he shall have fat browis every day, that he shall be as fat by the twelvemonth's end as a pork hog. Right so the two men departed, and beleft him to Sir Kay, that scorned him and mocked him.

CHAP. II.

How Sir Launcelot and Sir Gawaine were wroth because Sir Kay mocked Beaumains, and of a damsel which desired a knight for to fight for a lady.

THEREAT was Sir Gawaine wroth, and in especial Sir Launcelot bad Sir Kay leave his mocking, for I dare lay my head he shall prove a man of great worship. Let be, said Sir Kay, it may not be, by no reason, for as he is so hath he asked. Beware, said Sir Launcelot, so ye gave the good knight Brewnor, Sir Dinadan's brother, a name, and ye called him La Cote Male Taile, and that turned you to anger afterward. As for that, said Sir Kay, this shall never prove none such; for Sir Brewnor desired ever worship, and this desireth bread and drink, and broth; upon pain of my life he was fostered up in some abbey, and, howsoever it was, they failed meat and drink, and so hither he is come for his sustenance. And so Sir Kay bad get him a place and sit down to meat, so Beaumains went to the hall door, and set him down among boys and lads, and there he eat sadly. And then Sir Launcelot after meat bad him come to his chamber, and there he should have meat and drink enough. And so did Sir Gawaine: but he refused them all; he would do none other but as Sir Kay commanded him, for no proffer. But as touching Sir Gawaine, he had reason to proffer him lodging, meat, and drink, for that proffer came of his blood, for he was nearer kin to him than he wist. But that as Sir Launcelot did was of his great gentleness and courtesy. So thus he was put into the kitchen, and lay nightly as the boys of the kitchen did. And so he endured all that twelvemonth, and never displeased man nor child, but always he was meek and mild. But ever when that he saw any justing of knights, that would he see and he might. And ever Sir Launcelot would give him gold to spend, and clothes, and so did Sir Gawaine. And where were any masteries done thereat would he be, and there might none cast bar nor stone to him by two yards. Then would Sir Kay say, How liketh you my boy of the kitchen? So it passed on till the feast of Whitsuntide. And at that time the king held it at Carlion in the most royalest wise that might be, like as he did yearly.

But the king would no meat eat upon the Whitsunday until he heard some adventures. Then came there a squire to the king and said, Sir, ye may go to your meat, for here cometh a damsel with some strange adventures. Then was the king glad, and set him down. Right so there came a damsel into the hall, and saluted the king, and prayed him of succour. For whom, said the king, what is the adventure? Sir, she said, I have a lady of great worship and renown, and she is besieged with a tyrant, so that she may not out of her castle. And because here are called the noblest knights of the world, I come to you to pray you of succour. What highteth your lady, and where dwelleth she? and who is he, and what is his name, that hath besieged her? Sir king, she said, as for my lady's name that shall not ye know for me as at this time, but I let you wit she is a lady of great worship, and of great lands. And as for the tyrant that besiegeth her and destroyeth her lands, he is called the red knight of the red lawns. I know him not, said the king. Sir, said Sir Gawaine, I know him well, for he is one of the perilousest knights of the world: men say that he hath seven men's strength, and from him I escaped once full hard with my life. Fair damsel, said the king, there be knights here would do their power to rescue your lady, but because ye will not tell her name, nor where she dwelleth, therefore none of my knights that be here now shall go with you by my will. Then must I speak further, said the damsel.

CHAP. III.

How Beaumains desired the battle, and how it was granted to him, and how he desired to be made knight of Sir Launcelot.

WITH these words came before the king Beaumains, while the damsel was there, and thus he said: Sir king, God thank you, I have been these twelvemonth in your kitchen, and have had my full sustenance, and now I will ask my two gifts that be behind. Ask upon my peril, said the king. Sir, this shall be my two gifts. First, that ye will grant me to have this adventure of the damsel, for it belongeth unto me. Thou shalt have it, said the king, I grant it thee. Then, sir, this is the other gift, that ye shall bid Launcelot du Lake make me knight, for of him I will be made knight, and else of none. And when I am past, I pray you let him ride after me, and make me knight when I require him. All this shall be done, said the king. Fie on thee, said the damsel, shall I have none but one that is your kitchen page. Then was she wroth, and took her horse and departed.

And with that there came one to Beaumains, and told him that his horse and armour was come for him, and there was the dwarf come with all thing that him needed in the richest manner. Thereat all the court had much marvel from whence came all that gear. So when he was armed there was none but few so goodly a man as he was. And right so he came into the hall and took his leave of king Arthur and Sir Gawaine and Sir Launcelot, and prayed that he would hie after him. And so departed and rode after the damsel.

CHAP. IV.

How Beaumains departed, and how he gat of Sir Kay a spear and a shield, and how he justed and fought with Sir Launcelot.

BUT there went many after to behold how well he was horsed and trapped in cloth of gold, but he had neither shield nor spear. Then Sir Kay said all openly in the hall, I will ride after my boy in the kitchen, to wit whether he will know me for his better. Said Sir Launcelot and Sir Gawaine, Yet abide at home. So Sir Kay made him ready and took his horse and his spear and rode after him. And right as Beaumains overtook the damsel, right so came Sir Kay, and said, Beaumains, what sir know ye not me? Then he turned his horse and knew it was Sir Kay, that had done him all the despite as ye have heard afore. Yea, said Beaumains, I know you for an ungentle knight of the court, and therefore beware of me. Therewith Sir Kay put his spear in the rest, and ran straight upon him, and Beaumains came as fast upon him with his sword in his hand; and so he put away his spear with his sword, and with a foin thrust him through the side, that Sir Kay fell down as he had been dead, and he alight down and took Sir Kay's shield and his spear, and start upon his own horse and rode his way. All that saw Sir Launcelot, and so did the damsel. And then he bad his dwarf start upon Sir Kay's horse, and so he did. By that Sir Launcelot was come. Then he proffered Sir Launcelot to just, and either made them ready, and came together so fiercely that either bare down other to the earth, and sore were they bruised. Then Sir Launcelot arose and helped him from his horse. And then Beaumains threw his shield from him, and proffered to fight with Sir Launcelot on foot, and so they rushed together like boars, tracing, racing, and foining, to the mountenance of an hour, and Sir Launcelot felt him so big that he marvelled of his strength, for he fought more like a giant than a knight, and that his fighting was durable and passing perilous. For Sir Launcelot had so much ado with him that he dread himself to be shamed, and said, Beaumains, fight not so sore, your quarrel and mine is not so great but we may leave off. Truly, that is truth, said Beaumains, but it doth me good to feel your might, and yet, my lord, I shewed not the utterance.

CHAP. V.

How Beaumains told to Sir Launcelot his name, and how he was dubbed knight of Sir Launcelot, and after overtook the damsel.

WELL, said Sir Launcelot, for I promise you by the faith of my body I had as much to do as I might to save myself from you unshamed, and therefore have ye no doubt of none earthly knight. Hope ye so that I may any while stand a proved knight? said Beaumains. Yea, said Launcelot, do ye as ye have done, and I shall be your warrant. Then, I pray you, said Beaumains, give me the order of knighthood. Then must ye tell me your name, said Launcelot, and of what kin ye be born. Sir, so that ye will not discover me I shall, said Beaumains. Nay, said Sir Launcelot, and that I promise you by the faith of my body, until it be openly known. Then, Sir, he said, my name is Gareth, and brother unto Sir Gawaine, of father and mother. Ah! Sir, said Launcelot, I am more gladder of you than I was, for ever me thought ye should be of great blood, and that ye came not to the court neither for meat nor for drink. And then Sir Launcelot gave him the order of knighthood. And then Sir Gareth prayed him for to depart, and let him go. So Sir Launcelot departed from him and came to Sir Kay, and made him to be borne home upon his shield, and so he was healed hard with the life, and all men scorned Sir Kay, and in especial Sir Gawaine and Sir Launcelot said it was not his part to rebuke no young man, for full little knew he of what birth he is come, and for what cause he came to this court. And so we leave off Sir Kay and turn we unto Beaumains. When he had overtaken the damsel anon she said, What doest thou here? thou stinkest all of the kitchen, thy clothes be foul of the grease and tallow that thou gainedst in king Arthur's kitchen; weenest thou, said she, that I allow thee for yonder knight that thou killedst? Nay truly, for thou slewest him unhappily and cowardly, therefore turn again foul kitchen page. I know thee well, for Sir Kay named thee Beaumains; what art thou but a lubber and a turner of spits, and a ladle washer? Damsel, said Beaumains, say to me what ye will, I will not go from you whatsoever ye say, for I have undertaken to king Arthur for to achieve your adventure, and so shall I finish it to the end, or I shall die therefore. Fie on thee, kitchen knave, wilt thou finish mine adventure? thou shalt anon be met withall, that thou wouldest not for all the broth that ever thou suppedst once look him in the face. I shall assay, said Beaumains. So thus as they rode in the wood, there came a man flying all that ever he might. Whither wilt thou? said Beaumains. O lord, he said, help me, for hereby in a slade are six thieves, that have taken my lord and bound him, so I am afeard lest they will slay him. Bring me thither, said Sir Beaumains. And so they rode together until they came there as was the knight bound, and then he rode unto them and struck one unto the death, and then another, and at the third stroke he slew the third thief: and then the other three fled. And he rode after them, and he overtook them, and then those three thieves turned again and assailed Beaumains hard, but at the last he slew them, and returned and unbound the knight. And the knight thanked him, and prayed him to ride with him to his castle there a little beside, and he should worshipfully reward him for his good deeds. Sir, said Beaumains, I will no reward have, I was this day made knight of noble Sir Launcelot, and therefore I will no reward have, but God reward me. And also I must follow this damsel. And when he came nigh her, she bad him ride from her, for thou smellest all of the kitchen; weenest thou that I have joy of thee? for all this deed thou hast done, is but mishapped thee; but thou shalt see a sight that shall make thee turn again, and that lightly. Then the same knight which was rescued of the thieves rode after that damsel, and prayed her to lodge

with him all that night. And because it was near night the damsel rode with him to his castle, and there they had great cheer. And at supper the knight set Sir Beaumains afore the damsel. Fie, fie, said she, sir knight, ye are uncourteous to set a kitchen page afore me, him beseemeth better to stick a swine than to sit afore a damsel of high parentage. Then the knight was ashamed at her words, and took him up and set him at a side board, and set himself afore him. And so all that night they had good cheer and merry rest.

CHAP. VI.

How Sir Beaumains fought and slew two knights at a passage.

AND on the morn the damsel and he took their leave and thanked the knight, and so departed, and rode on their way until they came to a great forest. And there was a great river and but one passage, and there were ready two knights on the further side, to let them the passage. What sayest thou, said the damsel, wilt thou match yonder knights, or turn again? Nay, said Sir Beaumains, I will not turn again and they were six more. And therewithal he rushed into the water, and in the midst of the water either brake their spears upon other to their hands, and then they drew their swords and smote eagerly at other. And at the last Sir Beaumains smote the other upon the helm that his head stonied, and therewithal he fell down in the water, and there was he drowned. And then he spurred his horse upon the land, where the other knight fell upon him and brake his spear, and so they drew their swords and fought long together. At the last Sir Beaumains clave his helm and his head down to the shoulders: and so he rode unto the damsel, and bade her ride forth on her way. Alas, she said, that ever a kitchen page should have that fortune to destroy such two doughty knights; thou weenest thou hast done doughtily; that is not so, for the first knight his horse stumbled, and there he was drowned in the water, and never it was by thy force nor by thy might. And the last knight by mishap thou camest behind him and mishappily thou slewest him. Damsel, said Beaumains, ye may say what ye will, but with whomsoever I have ado withall I trust to God to serve him or he depart, and therefore I reck not what ye say, so that I may win your lady. Fie, fie, foul kitchen knave, thou shalt see knights that shall abate thy boast. Fair damsel, give me goodly language, and then my care is past, for what knights soever they be I care not, nor I doubt them not. Also, said she, I say it for thine avail, yet mayest thou turn again with thy worship, for and thou follow me thou art but slain, for I see all that ever thou dost is but by misadventure, and not by prowess of thy hands. Well, damsel, ye may say what ye will, but wheresoever ye go I will follow you. So this Beaumains rode with that lady till even-song time, and ever she chid him, and would not rest. And then they came to a black lawn, and there was a black hawthorn, and thereon hung a black banner, and on the other side there hung a black shield, and by it stood a black spear great and long, and a great black horse covered with silk, and a black stone fast by.

CHAP. VII.

How Sir Beaumains fought with the knight of the black lawns, and fought with him till he fell down and died.

THERE sat a knight all armed in black harness, and his name was the knight of the black lawn. Then the damsel, when she saw that knight, she bade him flee down the valley, for his horse was not saddled. Gramercy, said Beaumains, for always ye would have me a coward. With that the black knight, when she came nigh him, spake and said, Damsel, have ye brought this knight of king Arthur to be your champion? Nay, fair knight, said she, this is but a kitchen knave, that was fed in king Arthur's kitchen for alms. Why cometh he, said

the knight, in such array? it is shame that he beareth you company. Sir, I cannot be delivered of him, said she, for with me he rideth maugre mine head; would that ye should put him from me, or else to slay him and ye may, for he is an unhappy knave, and unhappily he hath done this day; through mishap I saw him slay two knights at the passage of the water, and other deeds he did before right marvellous, and through unhappiness. That marvelleth me, said the black knight, that any man that is of worship will have ado with him. They know him not, said the damsel, and because he rideth with me they think he is some man of worship born. That may be, said the black knight, how be it as ye say that he be no man of worship, he is a full likely person, and full like to be a strong man; but thus much shall I grant you, said the black knight, I shall put him down upon one foot, and his horse and his harness he shall leave with me, for it were shame to me to do him any more harm. When Sir Beaumains heard him say thus, he said, Sir knight, thou art full liberal of my horse and my harness, I let thee wit it cost thee nought, and whether it liketh thee or not this lawn will I pass, maugre thine head, and horse nor harness gettest thou none of me, but if thou win them with thy hands; and therefore let see what thou canst do. Sayest thou that, said the black knight, now yield thy lady from thee, for it beseemeth never a kitchen page to ride with such a lady. Thou liest, said Beaumains, I am a gentleman born, and of more high lineage than thou, and that will I prove on thy body. Then in great wrath they departed with their horses, and came together as it had been the thunder; and the black knight's spear brake, and Beaumains thrust him through both his sides, and therewith his spear brake, and the truncheon left still in his side. But nevertheless the black knight drew his sword and smote many eager strokes and of great might, and hurt Beaumains full sore. But at the last the black knight within an hour and a half he fell down off his horse in a swoon, and there he died. And then Beaumains saw him so well horsed and armed, then he alight down, and armed him in his armour, and so took his horse, and rode after the damsel. When she saw him come nigh, she said, Away, kitchen knave, out of the wind, for the smell of thy foul clothes grieveth me. Alas, she said, that ever such a knave as thou art should by mishap slay so good a knight as thou hast done, but all this is thine unhappiness. But hereby is one shall pay thee all thy payment, and therefore yet I counsel thee, flee. It may happen me, said Beaumains, to be beaten or slain, but I warn you, fair damsel, I will not flee away nor leave your company for all that ye can say, for ever ye say that they will kill me or beat me, but how soever it happeneth I escape, and they lie on the ground. And therefore it were as good for you to hold you still, thus all day rebuking me, for away will I not till I see the uttermost of this journey, or else I will be slain or truly beaten; therefore ride on your way, for follow you I will whatsoever happen.

CHAP. VIII.

How the brother of the knight that was slain met with Beaumains, and fought with Beaumains till he was yielden.

THUS as they rode together, they saw a knight come driving by them all in green, both his horse and his harness; and when he came nigh the damsel he asked her, Is that my brother the black knight that ye have brought with you? Nay, nay, said she, this unhappy kitchen knave hath slain your brother through unhappiness. Alas, said the green knight, that is great pity that so noble a knight as he was should so unhappily be slain, and namely of a knave's hand, as ye say that he is. Ah! traitor, said the green knight, thou shalt die for slaying of my brother, he was a full noble knight, and his name was Sir Percard. I defy thee, said Beaumains, for I let thee wit I slew him knightly, and not shamefully. Therewithall the

green knight rode unto an horn that was green, and he hung upon a thorn, and there he blew three deadly notes, and there came two damsels and armed him lightly. And then took he a great horse, and a green shield and a green spear. And then they ran together with all their mights, and brake their spears unto their hands. And then they drew their swords, and gave many sad strokes, and either of them wounded other full ill. And at the last at an overthwart Beaumains' horse struck the green knight's horse upon the side, he fell to the earth. And then the green knight avoided his horse lightly, and dressed him upon foot. That saw Beaumains, and therewithal he alight, and they rushed together like two mighty champions a long while, and sore they bled both. With that came the damsel and said, My lord the green knight, why for shame stand ye so long fighting with the kitchen knave? Alas, it is shame that ever ye were made knight, to see such a lad match such a knight, as the weed overgrew the corn. Therewith the green knight was ashamed, and therewithal he gave a great stroke of might, and clave his shield through. When Beaumains saw his shield cloven asunder he was a little ashamed of that stroke, and of her language; and then he gave him such a buffet upon the helm that he fell on his knees: and so suddenly Beaumains pulled him upon the ground groveling. And then the green knight cried him mercy, and yielded him unto Sir Beaumains, and prayed him to slay him not. All is in vain, said Beaumains, for thou shalt die, but if this damsel that came with me pray me to save thy life. And therewithal he unlaced his helm, like as he would slay him. Fie upon thee, false kitchen page, I will never pray thee to save his life, for I never will be so much in thy danger. Then shall he die, said Beaumains. Not so hardy thou foul knave, said the damsel, that thou slay him. Alas, said the green knight, suffer me not to die, for a fair word may save me. Fair knight, said the green knight, save my life, and I will forgive thee the death of my brother, and for ever to become thy man, and thirty knights that hold of me for ever shall do you service. In the devil's name, said the damsel, that such a foul kitchen knave should have thee and thirty knights' service. Sir knight, said Beaumains, all this availeth thee not, but if my damsel speak with me for thy life. And therewithal he made a semblant to slay him. Let be, said the damsel, thou foul knave, slay him not, for and thou do thou shall repent it. Damsel, said Beaumains, your charge is to me a pleasure, and at your commandment his life shall be saved, and else not. Then he said, Sir knight with the green arms, I release thee quit at this damsel's request, for I will not make her wroth; I will fulfill all that she chargeth me. And then the green knight kneeled down, and did him homage with his sword. Then said the damsel, Me repenteth, green knight, of your damage, and of your brother's death the black knight, for of your help I had great need, for I dread me sore to pass this forest. Nay, dread you not, said the green knight, for ye shall lodge with me this night, and to morn I shall help you through this forest. So they took their horses and rode to his manor, which was fast there beside.

CHAP. IX.

How the damsel ever rebuked Sir Beaumains, and would not suffer him to sit at her table, but called him kitchen boy.

AND ever she rebuked Beaumains, and would not suffer him to sit at her table, but as the green knight took him and sat him at a side table. Marvel me thinketh, said the green knight to the damsel, why ye rebuke this noble knight as ye do, for I warn you, damsel, he is a full noble knight, and I know no knight is able to match him, therefore ye do great wrong to rebuke him, for he shall do you right good service, for whatsoever he maketh himself ye shall prove at the end that he is come of a noble blood, and of king's lineage. Fie, fie,

said the damsel, it is shame for you to say of him such worship. Truly, said the green knight, it were shame for me to say of him any disworship, for he hath proved himself a better knight than I am, yet have I met with many knights in my days, and never or this time have I found no knight his match. And so that night they went unto rest, and all that night the green knight commanded thirty knights privily to watch Beaumains, for to keep him from all treason. And so on the morn they all arose, and heard their mass and brake their fast, and then they took their horses and rode on their way, and the green knight conveyed them through the forest, and there the green knight said, My lord Beaumains, I and these thirty knights shall be alway at your summons, both early and late, at your calling, and where that ever ye will send us. It is well said, said Beaumains; when that I call upon you ye must yield you unto king Arthur and all your knights. If that ye so command us, we shall be ready at all times, said the green knight. Fie, fie upon thee, said the damsel, that any good knights should be obedient unto a kitchen knave. So then departed the green knight and the damsel. And then she said unto Beaumains, Why followest thou me thou kitchen boy, cast away thy shield and thy spear and flee away, yet I counsel thee betimes or thou shall say right soon, Alas! For were thou as wight as ever was Wade, or Launcelot, Tristram, or the good knight Sir Lamorake, thou shalt not pass a pass here, that is called the pass perilous. Damsel, said Beaumains, who is afeard let him flee, for it were shame to turn again since I have ridden so long with you. Well, said the damsel, ye shall soon, whether ye will or not.

CHAP. X.

How the third brother, called the red knight, justed and fought against Beaumains, and how Beaumains overcame him.

So within a while they saw a tower as white as any snow, well matchcold all about, and double diked. And over the tower-gate there hung a fifty shields of divers colours; and under that tower there was a fair meadow. And therein were many knights and squires to behold scaffolds and pavilions, for there upon the morn should be a great tournament; and the lord of the tower was in his castle, and looked out at a window, and saw a damsel, a dwarf, and a knight armed at all points. By my faith, said the lord, with that knight will I just, for I see that he is a knight errant. And so he armed him, and horsed him hastily. And when he was on horseback with his shield and his spear, it was all red, both his horse and his harness, and all that to him belonged. And when that he came nigh him he wend it had been his brother the black knight. And then he cried aloud, Brother what do ye in these marches? Nay, nay, said the damsel, it is not he; this is but a kitchen knave, that was brought up for alms in king Arthur's court. Nevertheless, said the red knight, I will speak with him or he depart. Ah, said the damsel, this knave hath killed thy brother, and Sir Kay named him Beaumains, and this horse and harness was thy brother's the black knight. Also I saw thy brother the green knight overcome of his hands. Now may ye be revenged upon him, for I may never be quit of him.

With this either knight departed in sunder, and they came together with all their might, and either of their horses fell to the earth, and they avoided their horses, and put their shields afore them, and drew their swords, and either gave other sad strokes, now here, now there, racing, tracing, foining, and hurling like two boars, the space of two hours. And then she cried on high to the red knight, Alas, thou noble red knight, think what worship hath followed thee, let never a kitchen knave endure thee so long as he doth. Then the red knight waxed wroth, and doubled his strokes, and hurt Beaumains wonderly sore, that the blood ran down to the ground, that it was wonder to see that strong

battle. Yet at the last Sir Beaumains strake him to the earth, and as he would have slain the red knight he cried mercy, saying, Noble knight slay me not, and I shall yield me to thee with fifty knights with me that be at my commandment. And I forgive thee all the despite that thou hast done to me, and the death of my brother the black knight. All this availeth not, said Sir Beaumains, but if my damsel pray me to save thy life. And therewith he made semblant to strike off his head. Let be, thou Beaumains, slay him not, for he is a noble knight, and not so hardy upon thine head but thou save him. Then Beaumains bad the red knight stand up, and thank the damsel now of thy life. Then the red knight prayed him to see his castle, and to be there all night. So the damsel then granted him, and there they had merry cheer. But always the damsel spake many foul words unto Beaumains, whereof the red knight had great marvel, and all that night the red knight made threescore knights to watch Beaumains, that he should have no shame nor villainy. And upon the morn they heard mass, and dined, and the red knight came before Beaumains with his threescore knights, and there he proffered him his homage and fealty at all times, he and his knights to do him service. I thank you, said Beaumains, but this ye shall grant me when I call upon you, to come afore my lord king Arthur and yield you unto him to be his knights. Sir, said the red knight, I will be ready and my fellowship at your summons. So Sir Beaumains departed and the damsel, and ever she rode chiding him in the foullest manner.

CHAP. XI.

How Sir Beaumains suffered great rebukes of the damsel, and he suffered it patiently.

DAMSEL, said Beaumains, ye are uncourteous so to rebuke me as ye do, for me seemeth I have done you good service, and ever ye threaten me I shall be beaten with knights that we meet, but ever for all your boast they lie in the dust or in the mire, and therefore I pray you rebuke me no more : and when ye see me beaten or yielden as recreant, then may ye bid me go from you shamefully, but first I let you wit I will not depart from you, for I were worse than a fool and I would depart from you all the while that I win worship. Well, said she, right soon there shall meet a knight shall pay thee all thy wages, for he is the most man of worship of the world, except king Arthur. I will well, said Beaumains; the more he is of worship the more shall be my worship to have ado with him. Then anon they were ware where was before them a city rich and fair. And betwixt them and the city a mile and a half, there was a fair meadow that seemed new mown, and therein were many pavilions fair to behold. Lo, said the damsel, yonder is a lord that owneth yonder city, and his custom is when the weather is fair to lie in this meadow to just and tourney; and ever there be about him five hundred knights and gentlemen of arms, and there be all manner of games that any gentleman can devise. That goodly lord, said Beaumains, would I fain see. Thou shalt see him time enough, said the damsel. And so as she rode near she espied the pavilion where he was. Lo, said she, seest thou yonder pavilion, that is all of the colour of Inde, and all manner of thing that there is about, men and women, and horses trapped, shields and spears, all of the colour of Inde, and his name is Sir Persant of Inde, the most lordliest knight that ever thou lookedest on. It may well be, said Beaumains, but be he never so stout a knight, in this field I shall abide till that I see him under his shield. Ah fool, said she, thou were better flee betimes. Why, said Beaumains, and he be such a knight as ye make him, he will not set upon me with all his men, or with his five hundred knights. For and there come no more but one at once, I shall him not fail whilst my

life lasteth. Fie, fie, said the damsel, that ever such a dirty knave should blow such a boast. Damsel, he said, ye are to blame so to rebuke me, for I had lever do five battles than so to be rebuked ; let him come, and then let him do his worst. Sir, she said, I marvel what thou art, and of what kin thou art come : boldly thou speakest, and boldly thou hast done, that have I seen : therefore I pray thee save thyself and thou mayest, for thy horse and thou have had great travail, and I dread we dwell over long from the siege, for it is but hence seven mile, and all perilous passages we are past, save all only this passage, and here I dread me sore lest ye shall catch some hurt, therefore I would ye were hence, that ye were not bruised nor hurt with this strong knight. But I let you wit this Sir Persant of Inde is nothing of might nor strength unto the knight that laid the siege about my lady. As for that, said Sir Beaumains, be it as it may; for since I am come so nigh this knight I will prove his might or I depart from him, and else I shall be shamed and I now withdraw me from him. And therefore, damsel, have ye no doubt by the grace of God I shall so deal with this knight, that within two hours after noon I shall deliver him, and then shall we come to the siege by day light. Oh mercy, marvel have I, said the damsel, what manner a man ye be, for it may never be otherwise but that ye be come of a noble blood, for so foul and shamefully did never woman rule a knight as I have done you, and ever courteously ye have suffered me, and that came never but of a gentle blood.

Damsel, said Beaumains, a knight may little do that may not suffer a damsel ; for whatsoever ye said unto me I took none heed to your words, for the more ye said the more ye angered me, and my wrath I wreaked upon them that I had ado withal. And therefore all the missaying that ye missayed me furthered me in my battle, and caused me to think to shew and prove myself at the end what I was ; for peradventure though I had meat in king Arthur's kitchen, yet I might have had meat enough in other places; but all that I did it for to prove and to assay my friends, and that shall be known another day, and whether that I be a gentleman born or none, I let you wit, fair damsel, I have done you gentleman's service, and peradventure better service yet will I do or I depart from you. Alas, she said, fair Beaumains, forgive me all that I have missaid or done against thee. With all my heart, said he, I forgive it you, for ye did nothing but as ye should do, for all your evil words pleased me; and damsel, said Beaumains, since it liketh you to say thus fair to me, wit ye well it gladdeth mine heart greatly, and now me seemeth there is no knight living but I am able enough for him.

CHAP. XII.

How Sir Beaumains fought with Sir Persant of Inde, and made him to be yielden.

WITH this Sir Persant of Inde had espied them as they hoved in the field, and knightly he sent to them whether he came in war or in peace. Say to thy lord, said Beaumains, I take no force, but whether as him list himself. So the messenger went again unto Sir Persant, and told him all his answer. Well, then will I have ado with him to the utterance. And so he purveyed him and rode against him. And Beaumains saw him and made him ready, and there they met with all that ever their horses might run, and brake their spears either in three pieces, and their horses rushed so together that both their horses fell dead to the earth, and lightly they avoided their horses, and put their shields afore them, and drew their swords, and gave many great strokes, that sometime they hurtled together that they fell groveling on the ground. Thus they fought two hours and more, that their shields and their hauberks were all forhewn, and in many places they were wounded. So at the last Sir Beaumains smote him through the side of the body, and then

he drew him back here and there, and knightly maintained his battle long time. And at the last, though him loth were, Beaumains smote Sir Persant above upon the helm that he fell groveling to the earth, and then he lept upon him overthwart, and unlaced his helm to have slain him. Then Sir Persant yielded him and asked him mercy. With that came the damsel, and prayed to save his life. I will well, for it were pity that this noble knight should die. Gramercy, said Persant, gentle knight and damsel; for certainly now I wot well it was ye that slew my brother the black knight, at the black thorn; he was a full noble knight, his name was Sir Percard. Also, I am sure that ye are he that won mine other brother the green knight, his name was Sir Pertolepe. Also, ye won my brother the red knight Sir Perimones. And now since ye have won these, this shall I do for to please you; ye shall have homage and fealty of me, and an hundred knights, to be always at your commandment, to go and ride where ye will command us. And so they went unto Sir Persant's pavilion, and drank the wine and eat spices. And afterward Sir Persant made him to rest upon a bed until supper time, and after supper to bed again. And so we leave him there till on the morn.

CHAP. XIII.

Of the goodly communication between Sir Persant and Beaumains, and how he told him that his name was Sir Gareth.

AND so on the morn the damsel and Sir Beaumains heard mass and brake their fast, and so took their leave. Fair damsel, said Persant, whitherward are ye away leading this knight? Sir, she said, this knight is going to the siege that besiegeth my sister in the castle dangerous. Ah, ah, said Persant, that is the knight of the red lawn, the which is the most perilous knight that I know now living, and a man that is without mercy, and men say that he hath seven men's strength. God save you, said he to Beaumains, from that knight, for he doth great wrong to that lady, and that is great pity, for she is one of the fairest ladies of the world, and me seemeth that your damsel is her sister. Is not your name Linet ? said he. Yea, sir, said she, and my lady my sister's name is dame Liones. Now shall I tell you, said Sir Persant, this red knight of the red lawn hath lain long at the siege, well nigh this two years, and many times he might have had her and he had would, but he prolongeth the time to this intent for to have Sir Launcelot du Lake to do battle with him, or Sir Tristram, or Sir Lamorak de Galis, or Sir Gawaine: and this is his tarrying so long at the siege. Now, said the damsel Linet, I require you that ye will make this gentleman knight, or ever he fight with the red knight. I will with all my heart, said Sir Persant, and it please him to take the order of knighthood of so simple a man as I am. Sir, said Beaumains, I thank you for your good will, for I am better sped, for certainly the noble knight Sir Launcelot made me knight. Ah, said Persant, of a more renowned knight might ye not be made knight. For of all knights he may be called chief of knighthood: and so all the world saith that betwixt three knights is parted clearly knighthood, that is Launcelot du Lake, Sir Tristram de Liones, and Sir Lamorak de Galis: these bear now the renown. There be many other knights, as Sir Pala-mides the Saracen, and Sir Sasere his brother ; also Sir Bleoberis, and Sir Blamore de Ganis his brother ; also Sir Bors de Ganis, and Sir Ector de Maris, and Sir Percivale de Galis ; these and many more be noble knights, but there be none that pass the three above said ; therefore God speed you well, said Sir Persant, for and ye may match the red knight ye shall be called the fourth of the world. Sir, said Beaumains, I would fain be of good fame and of knighthood. And I let you wit I came of good men, for I dare say my father was a noble man, and so that ye will keep it in close,

and this damsel, I will tell you of what kin I am. We will not discover you, said they both, till ye command us, by the faith we owe unto God. Truly then, said he, my name is Gareth of Orkney, and king Lot was my father, and my mother is king Arthur's sister ; her name is dame Morgawse, and Sir Gawaine is my brother, and Sir Agra-vaine, and Sir Gaheris, and I am the youngest of them all. And yet wot not king Arthur nor Sir Gawaine what I am.

CHAP. XIV.

How the lady that was besieged had word from her sister how she had brought a knight to fight for her, and what battles he had achieved.

So the book saith that the lady that was besieged had word of her sister's coming by the dwarf, and a knight with her, and how he had passed all the perilous passages. What manner a man is he? said the lady. He is a noble knight, truly, madam, said the dwarf, and but a young man, but he is as likely a man as ever ye saw any. What is he, said the lady, and of what kin is he come, and of whom was he made knight? Madam, said the dwarf, he is the king's son of Orkney, but his name I will not tell you as at this time; but wit ye well, of Sir Launcelot was he made knight, for of none other would he be made knight, and Sir Kay named him Beaumains. How escaped he, said the lady, from the brethren of Persant ? Madam, he said, as a noble knight should. First, he slew two brethren at a passage of a water. Ah! said she, they were good knights, but they were murderers, the one hight Gherard de Breusse, and that other knight hight Sir Arnold de Breusse. Then, madam, he recountered with the black knight, and slew him in plain battle, and so he took his horse and his armour and fought with the green knight, and wan him in plain battle, and in likewise he served the red knight, and after in the same wise he served the blue knight, and wan him in plain battle. Then, said the lady, he hath overcome Sir Persant of Inde, one of the noblest knights of the world. And the dwarf said, He hath won all the four brethren, and slain the black knight. And yet he did more tofore: he overthrew Sir Kay, and left him nigh dead upon the ground; also he did a great battle with Sir Launcelot, and there they departed on even hands: and then Sir Launcelot made him knight. Dwarf, said the lady, I am glad of these tidings, therefore go thou in an hermitage of mine here by, and there shalt thou bear with thee of my wine in two flaggons of silver, they are of two gallons, and also two cast of bread, with fat venison baked, and dainty fowls; and a cup of gold here I deliver thee, that is rich and precious, and bear all this to mine hermitage, and put it in the hermit's hands. And then go thou unto my sister and greet her well, and command me unto that gentle knight, and pray him to eat and to drink, and make him strong; and say ye him I thank him of his courtesy. and goodness, that he would take upon him such labour for me that never did him bounty nor courtesy. Also pray him that he be of good heart and good courage, for he shall meet with a full noble knight, but he is neither of bounty, courtesy, nor gentleness, for he attendeth unto no thing but to murder, and that is the cause I cannot praise him nor love him. So this dwarf departed and came to Sir Persant, where he found the damsel Linet and Sir Beaumains, and there he told them all as ye have heard, and then they took their leave; but Sir Persant took an ambling hackney and conveyed them on their ways and then beleft them to God. And so within a little while they came to that hermitage, and there they drank the wine, and eat the venison and the fowls baken.

And so when they had repasted them well, the dwarf returned again with his vessel unto the castle again, and there met with him the red knight of the red lawns, and asked him from whence that he came, and where he

had been. Sir, said the dwarf, I have been with my lady's sister of this castle, and she hath been at king Arthur's court, and brought a knight with her. Then I account her travail but lost. For though she had brought with her Sir Launcelot, Sir Tristram, Sir Lamorak, or Sir Gawaine, I would think myself good enough for them all. It may well be, said the dwarf, but this knight hath passed all the perilous passages, and hath slain the black knight, and other two more, and won the green knight, the red knight, and the blue knight. Then is he one of these four that I have afore rehearsed. He is none of those, said the dwarf, but he is a king's son. What is his name? said the red knight of the red lawn. That will I not tell you, said the dwarf, but Sir Kay upon scorn named him Beaumains. I care not, said the knight, what knight soever he be, for I shall soon deliver him; and if I ever match him he shall have a shameful death, as many other have had. That were pity, said the dwarf, and it is marvel that ye make such shameful war upon noble knights.

CHAP. XV.

How the damsel and Beaumains came to the siege, and came to a sycamore tree, and there Beaumains blew a horn, and then the knight of the red lawns came to fight with him.

Now leave we the knight and the dwarf, and speak we of Beaumains, that all night lay in the hermitage, and upon the morn he and the damsel Linet heard their mass, and brake their fast. And then they took their horses and rode throughout a fair forest, and then they came to a plain, and saw where were many pavilions and tents, and a fair castle, and there was much smoke and great noise. And when they came near the siege Sir Beaumains espied upon great trees, as he rode, how there hung full goodly armed knights by the neck, and their shields about their necks with their swords, and gilt spurs upon their heels, and so there hung nigh a forty knights shamefully with full rich arms. Then Sir Beaumains abated his countenance, and said, What meaneth this? Fair Sir, said the damsel, abate not your cheer for all this sight, for ye must encourage yourself, or else ye be all shent, for all these knights came hither to this siege to rescue my sister dame Liones, and when the red knight of the red lawn had overcome them he put them to this shameful death, without mercy and pity. And in the same wise he will serve you but if ye quit you better. Now Jesu defend me, said Sir Beaumains, from such a villainous death and disgrace of arms, for rather than I should so be farewithal, I would rather be slain manly in plain battle. So were ye better, said the damsel; for trust not in him is no courtesy, but all goeth to the death or shameful murder; and that is pity, for he is a full likely man, well made of body, and a full noble knight of prowess, and a lord of great lands and possessions. Truly, said Beaumains, he may well be a good knight, but he useth shameful customs, and it is marvel that he endureth so long, that none of the noble knights of my lord Arthur have not dealt with him. And then they rode to the dikes, and saw them double diked with full warlike walls, and there were lodged many great lords nigh the walls, and there was great noise of minstrelsy, and the sea betid upon the one side of the walls, where were many ships and mariners' noise, with 'hale and how.' And also, there was fast by a sycamore tree, and there hung a horn, the greatest that ever they saw, of an elephant's bone, and this knight of the red lawn had hanged it up there, that if there came any errant knight he must blow that horn, and then will he make him ready, and come to him to do battle. But Sir, I pray you, said the damsel Linet, blow ye not the horn till it be high noon, for now it is about prime, and now encreaseth his might, that, as men say, he hath seven men's strength. Ah, fie for shame, fair damsel, say ye never so more to me, for, and he were as good a knight as

ever was, I shall never fail him in his most might, for either I will win worship worshipfully, or die knightly in the field. And therewith he spurred his horse straight to the sycamore tree, and blew so the horn eagerly that all the siege and the castle rang thereof. And then there lept out knights out of their tents and pavilions, and they within the castle looked over the walls and out at windows. Then the red knight of the red lawns armed him hastily, and two barons set on his spurs upon his heels, and all was blood-red, his armour, spear, and shield. And an earl buckled his helm upon his head, and then they brought him a red spear and a red steed, and so he rode into a little vale under the castle, that all that were in the castle and at the siege might behold the battle.

CHAP. XVI.

How the two knights met together, and of their talking, and how they began their battle.

Sir, said the damsel Linet unto Sir Beaumains, look ye be glad and light, for yonder is your deadly enemy, and at yonder window is my lady my sister, dame Liones. Where? said Beaumains. Yonder, said the damsel, and pointed with her finger. That is truth, said Beaumains. She beseemeth afar the fairest lady that ever I looked upon, and truly, he said, I ask no better quarrel than now for to do battle, for truly she shall be my lady, and for her I will fight. And ever he looked up to the window with glad countenance. And the lady Liones made courtesy to him down to the earth, with holding up both their hands. With that the red knight of the red lawns called to Sir Beaumains, Leave, sir knight, thy looking, and behold me, I counsel thee, for I warn thee well she is my lady, and for her I have done many strong battles. If thou have so done, said Beaumains, me seemeth it was but waste labour, for she loveth none of thy fellowship, and thou to love that loveth not thee, is but great folly.

For and I understood that she were not glad of my coming I would be advised or I did battle for her. But I understand by the besieging of this castle, she may forbear thy fellowship. And therefore wit thou well, thou red knight of the red lawns, I love her, and will rescue her, or else to die. Sayest thou that, said the red knight, me seemeth thou ought of reason to beware by yonder knights that thou sawest hang upon yonder trees. Fie for shame, said Beaumains, that ever thou shouldest say or do so evil, for in that thou shamest thyself and knighthood, and thou mayest be sure there will no lady love thee that knoweth thy wicked customs. And now thou weenest that the sight of these hanged knights should fear me. Nay truly, not so, that shameful sight causeth me to have courage and hardiness against thee, more than I would have had against thee and thou were a well-ruled knight. Make thee ready, said the red knight of the red lawns, and talk no longer with me. Then Sir Beaumains bad the damsel go from him, and then they put their spears in their rests, and came together with all their might that they had both, and either smote other in the midst of their shields, that the breastplates, horse-girths, and cruppers brast, and fell to the earth both, and the reins of their bridles in their hands, and so they lay a great while sore astonied; and all they that were in the castle and in the siege wend their necks had been broken, and then many a stranger and other said the strange knight was a big man and a noble juster, for or now we saw never no knight match the red knight of the red lawns: thus they said, both within the castle and without. Then lightly they avoided their horses, and put their shields afore them, and drew their swords, and ran together like two fierce lions, and either gave other such buffets upon their helms that they reeled backward both two strides, and then they recovered both, and hewed great pieces of their harness and their shields, that a great part fell into the fields.

CHAP. XVII.

How after long fighting Beaumains overcame the knight and would have slain him, but at the request of the lords he saved his life, and made him to yield him to the lady.

AND then thus they fought till it was past noon and never would stint till at last they lacked wind both, and then they stood wagging and scattering, panting, blowing and bleeding, that all that beheld them for the most part wept for pity. So when they had rested them a while they went to battle again, tracing, racing, foining, as two boars. And at sometime they took their run as it had been two rams, and hurtled together that sometime they fell groveling to the earth: and at sometime they were so amazed that either took other's sword in stead of his own.

Thus they endured till even-song time, that there was none that beheld them might know whether was like to win the battle; and their armour was so far hewn that men might see their naked sides, and in other places they were naked, but ever the naked places they did defend. And the red knight was a wily knight of war, and his wily fighting taught Sir Beaumains to be wise; but he abought it full sore ere he did espy his fighting. And thus by assent of them both, they granted either other to rest; and so they set them down upon two mole-hills there beside the fighting place, and either of them unlaced his helm and took the cold wind, for either of their pages was fast by them, to come when they called to unlace their harness and to set them on again at their commandment. And then when Sir Beaumains' helm was off he looked by to the window, and there he saw the fair lady dame Liones; and she made him such countenance that his heart waxed light and jolly; and therewith he bade the red knight of the red lawns make him ready, and let us do the battle to the utterance. I will well, said the knight. And then they laced up their helms, and their pages avoided, and they stept together and fought freshly. But the red knight of the red lawns awaited him, and at an overthwart smote him within the hand, that his sword fell out of his hand: and yet he gave him another buffet on the helm that he fell groveling to the earth, and the red knight fell over him for to hold him down. Then cried the maiden Linet on high, O Sir Beaumains, where is thy courage become! Alas, my lady my sister beholdeth thee, and she sobbeth and weepeth, that maketh mine heart heavy. When Sir Beaumains heard her say so, he started up with a great might and gat him upon his feet, and lightly he lept to his sword and griped it in his hand, and doubled his pace unto the red knight, and there they fought a new battle together. But Sir Beaumains then doubled his strokes, and smote so thick that he smote the sword out of his hand, and then he smote him upon the helm that he fell to the earth, and Sir Beaumains fell upon him, and unlaced his helm to have slain him; and then he yielded him and asked mercy, and said with a loud voice, O noble knight I yield me to thy mercy. Then Sir Beaumains bethought him upon the knights that he had made to be hanged shamefully, and then he said, I may not with my worship save thy life, for the shameful deaths thou hast caused many full good knights to die. Sir, said the red knight of the red lawns, hold your hand and ye shall know the causes why I put them to so shameful a death. Say on, said Sir Beaumains. Sir, I loved once a lady, a fair damsel, and she had her brother slain, and she said it was Sir Launcelot du Lake, or else Sir Gawaine, and she prayed me as that I loved her heartily that I would make her a promise by the faith of my knighthood, for to labour daily in arms until I met with one of them, and all that I might overcome I should put them unto a villainous death; and this is the cause that I have put all these knights to death, and so I ensured her to do all the villainy unto king Arthur's knights, and that I should take

vengeance upon all these knights. And, Sir, now I will thee tell that every day my strength encreaseth till noon, and all this time have I seven men's strength.

CHAP. XVIII.

How the knight yielded him, and how Beaumains made him to go unto king Arthur's court, and to cry Sir Launcelot mercy.

THEN came there many earls, and barons, and noble knights, and prayed that knight to save his life, and take him to your prisoner: and all they fell upon their knees and prayed him of mercy, and that he would save his life, and, Sir, they all said, it were fairer of him to take homage and fealty, and let him hold his lands of you, than for to slay him: by his death ye shall have none advantage, and his misdeeds that be done may not be undone; and therefore he shall make amends to all parties, and we all will become your men, and do you homage and fealty. Fair lords, said Beaumains, wit you well I am full loth to slay this knight, nevertheless he hath done passing ill and shamefully. But insomuch all that he did was at a lady's request I blame him the less, and so for your sake I will release him, that he shall have his life upon this covenant, that he go within the castle and yield him there to the lady, and if she will forgive and quit him, I will well; with this that he make her amends of all the trespass he hath done against her and her lands. And also, when that is done, that ye go unto the court of king Arthur, and there that ye ask Sir Launcelot mercy, and Sir Gawaine, for the evil will ye have had against them. Sir, said the red knight of the red lawns, all this will I do as ye command, and certain assurance and sureties ye shall have. And so then when the assurance was made, he made his homage and fealty, and all those earls and barons with him. And then the maiden Linet came to Sir Beaumains and unarmed him, and searched his wounds, and stinted his blood, and in likewise she did to the red knight of the red lawns. And there they sojourned ten days in their tents, and the red knight made his lords and servants to do all the pleasure that they might unto Sir Beaumains. And so within a while the red knight of the red lawns went unto the castle and put him in the lady Liones' grace, and so she received him upon sufficient surety; so all her hurts were well restored of all that she could complain. And then he departed unto the court of king Arthur, and there openly the red knight of the red lawns put him in the mercy of Sir Launcelot and Sir Gawaine, and there he told openly how he was overcome and by whom, and also he told all the battles from the beginning unto the ending. Mercy, said king Arthur and Sir Gawaine, we marvel much of what blood he is come, for he is a noble knight. Have ye no marvel, said Sir Launcelot, for ye shall right well wit that he is come of a full noble blood, and as for his might and hardiness there be but few now living that is so mighty as he is, and so noble of prowess. It seemeth by you, said king Arthur, that ye know his name, and from whence he is come, and of what blood he is. I suppose I do so, said Launcelot, or else I would not have given him the order of knighthood; but he gave me such charge at that time that I should never discover him until he required me, or else it be known openly by some other.

CHAP. XIX.

How Beaumains came to the lady, and when he came to the castle the gates were closed against him, and of the words that the lady said to him.

Now turn we unto Sir Beaumains, that desired of Linet that he might see her sister his lady. Sir, said she, I would fain ye saw her. Then Sir Beaumains all armed him, and took his horse and his spear, and rode straight unto the castle. And when he came to the gate he found there many men armed, and pulled up the drawbridge and drew the port close. Then marvelled he why

they would not suffer him to enter. And then he looked up to the window; and there he saw the fair Liones, that said on high, Go thy way, Sir Beaumains, for as yet thou shalt not have wholly my love, unto the time that thou be called one of the number of the worthy knights. And therefore go labour in worship this twelvemonth, and then thou shalt hear new tidings. Alas, fair lady, said Beaumains, I have not deserved that ye should shew me this strangeness, and I had wend that I should have right good cheer with you, and unto my power I have deserved thank, and well I am sure I have bought your love with part of the best blood within my body. Fair courteous knight, said dame Liones, be not displeased nor over hasty; for wit ye well your great travail nor good love shall not be lost, for I consider your great travail and labour, your bounty and your goodness, as me ought to do. And therefore go on your way, and look that ye be of good comfort, for all shall be for your worship and for the best, and perdy a twelvemonth will soon be done, and trust me, fair knight, I shall be true to you, and never to betray you, but to my death I shall love you and none other. And therewithal she turned her from the window; and Sir Beaumains rode away ward from the castle, making great dole, and so he rode here and there, and wist not where he rode, till it was dark night. And then it happened him to come to a poor man's house, and there he was harboured all that night. But Sir Beaumains had no rest, but wallowed and writhed for the love of the lady of the castle. And so upon the morrow he took his horse, and rode until underne, and then he came to a broad water, and thereby was a great lodge, and there he alight to sleep, and laid his head upon the shield, and betook his horse to the dwarf, and commanded him to watch all night. Now turn we to the lady of the same castle that thought much upon Beaumains, and then she called unto her Sir Gringamore her brother, and prayed him in all manner, as he loved her heartily, that he would ride after Sir Beaumains, and ever have ye wait upon him till ye may find him sleeping, for I am sure in his heaviness he will alight down in some place and lay him down to sleep : and therefore have ye your wait upon him, and in the priviest manner ye can, take his dwarf, and go ye your way with him as fast as ever ye may or Sir Beaumains awake. For my sister Linet telleth me that he can tell of what kindred he is come, and what is his right name. And the mean while I and my sister will ride unto your castle to await when ye bring with you the dwarf. And then when ye have brought him unto your castle I will have him in examination myself : unto the time I know what is his right name and of what kindred he is come, shall I never be merry at my heart. Sister, said Sir Gringamore, all this shall be done after your intent. And so he rode all the other day and the night till that he found Sir Beaumains lying by a water, and his head upon his shield, for to sleep. And then when he saw Sir Beaumains fast on sleep, he came stilly stalking behind the dwarf, and plucked him fast under his arm, and so he rode away with him as fast as ever he might unto his own castle. And this Sir Gringamore's arms were all black, and that to him belonged. But ever as he rode with the dwarf toward his castle, he cried unto his lord and prayed him of help. And therewith awoke Sir Beaumains, and up he lept lightly, and saw where Sir Gringamore rode his way with the dwarf, and so Sir Gringamore rode out of his sight.

CHAP. XX.

How Sir Beaumains rode after to rescue his dwarf, and came into the castle where he was.

THEN Sir Beaumains put on his helm anon, and buckled his shield, and took his horse and rode after him all that ever he might ride, through marshes and fields and great dales, that many times his horse and he plunged over the head in deep mires, for he knew not the way, but took the gainest way in that fury, that many times he was like to perish. And at the last him happened to come to a fair green way, and there he met with a poor man of the country whom he saluted, and asked him whether he met not with a knight upon a black horse and all black harness, and a little dwarf sitting behind him with heavy cheer. Sir, said this poor man, here by me came Sir Gringamore the knight, with such a dwarf mourning as ye say, and therefore I counsel you not follow him, for he is one of the most perilous knights of the world, and his castle is here nigh hand but two mile, therefore we advise you ride not after Sir Gringamore, but if ye owe him good will.

So leave we Sir Beaumains riding toward the castle, and speak we of Sir Gringamore and the dwarf. Anon as the dwarf was come to the castle, dame Liones and dame Linet her sister, asked the dwarf where was his master born, and of what lineage he was come? And but if thou tell me, said dame Liones, thou shalt never escape this castle, but ever here to be prisoner. As for that, said the dwarf, I fear not greatly to tell his name, and of what kin he is come. Wit ye well he is a king's son, and his mother is sister to king Arthur, and he is brother to the good knight Sir Gawaine, and his name is Sir Gareth of Orkney. And now I have told you his right name, I pray you, fair lady, let me go to my lord again, for he will never out of this country until that he have me again. And if he be angry he will do much harm or that he be stint, and work you wrack in this country. As for that threatening, said Sir Gringamore, be it as it be may, we will go to dinner. And so they washed and went to meat, and made them merry and well at ease, and because the lady Liones of the castle was there they made great joy. Truly madam, said Linet unto her sister, well may he be a king's son, for he hath many good taches on him, for he is courteous and mild, and the most suffering man that ever I met withall. For I dare say there was never gentlewoman reviled man in so foul manner as I have rebuked him; and at all times he gave me goodly and meek answers again. And as they sat thus talking, there came Sir Gareth in at the gate with an angry countenance, and his sword drawn in his hand, and cried aloud that all the castle might hear it, saying, Thou traitor Sir Gringamore, deliver me my dwarf again, or by the faith that I owe to the order of knighthood, I shall do thee all the harm that I can. Then Sir Gringamore looked out at a window and said, Sir Gareth of Orkney, leave thy boasting words, for thou gettest not thy dwarf again. Thou coward knight, said Sir Gareth, bring him with thee, and come and do battle with me, and win him and take him. So will I do, said Sir Gringamore, and me list, but for all thy great words thou gettest him not. Ah! fair brother, said dame Liones, I would he had his dwarf again, for I would he were not wroth, for now he hath told me all my desire I keep no more of the dwarf. And also, brother, he hath done much for me, and delivered me from the red knight of the red lawns, and therefore, brother, I owe him my service afore all knights living. And wit ye well that I love him before all other, and full fain I would speak with him. But in no wise I would that he wist what I were, but that I were another strange lady. Well, said Sir Gringamore, since I know now your will, I will obey now unto him. And right therewithall he went down unto Sir Gareth, and said, Sir, I cry you mercy, and all that I have misdone I will amend it at your will. And therefore I pray you and take such cheer as I can make you in this castle. Shall I have my dwarf? said Sir Gareth. Yea, sir, and all the pleasure that I can make you; for as soon as your dwarf told me what ye were, and of what blood ye are come, and what noble deeds ye have done in these marches, then I repented of my deeds. And then Sir Gareth alight,

and there came his dwarf and took his horse. O my fellow, said Sir Gareth, I have had many adventures for thy sake. And so Sir Gringamore took him by the hand, and led him into the hall where his own wife was.

CHAP. XXI.

How Sir Gareth, otherwise called Beaumains, came to the presence of his lady, and how they took acquaintance, and of their love.

AND then came forth dame Liones arrayed like a princess, and there she made him passing good cheer, and he her again. And they had goodly language and lovely countenance together. And Sir Gareth thought many times, Would that the lady of the castle perilous were so fair as she was. There were all manner of games and plays of dancing and singing. And ever the more Sir Gareth beheld that lady, the more he loved her, and so he burned in love that he was past himself in his reason. And forth toward night they went unto supper, and Sir Gareth might not eat for his love was so hot, that he wist not where he was. All these looks espied Sir Gringamore, and then after supper he called his sister dame Liones unto a chamber and said, Fair sister, I have well espied your countenance between you and this knight, and I will, sister, that ye wit he is a full noble knight, and if ye can make him to abide here I will do to him all the pleasure that I can, for and ye were better than ye are, ye were well bestowed upon him. Fair brother, said dame Liones, I understand well that the knight is good, and come he is of a noble house. Notwithstanding I will assay him better, how be it I am most beholding to him of any earthly man; for he hath had great labour for my love, and passed many a dangerous passage. Right so Sir Gringamore went unto Sir Gareth and said, Sir, make ye good cheer, for ye shall have none other cause, for this lady my sister is yours at all times, her worship saved, for wit ye well she loveth you as well as ye do her, and better if better may be. And I wist that, said Sir Gareth, there lived not a gladder man than I would be. Upon my worship, said Sir Gringamore, trust unto my promise; and as long as it liketh you ye shall sojourn with me, and this lady shall be with us daily and nightly to make you all the cheer that she can. I will well, said Sir Gareth, for I have promised to be nigh this country this twelvemonth. And well I am sure king Arthur and other noble knights will find me where that I am within this twelvemonth. For I shall be sought and found, if that I be on live. And then the noble knight Sir Gareth went unto the dame Liones, which he then much loved, and kissed her many times, and either made great joy of other. And there she promised him her love, certainly to love him and none other the days of her life. Then this lady, dame Liones, by the assent of her brother, told Sir Gareth all the truth what she was, and how she was the same lady that he did battle for, and how she was lady of the castle perilous. And there she told him how she caused her brother to take away his dwarf.

CHAP. XXII.

How, at night, came an armed knight and fought with Sir Gareth, and he, sore hurt in the thigh, smote off the knight's head.

For this cause, to know the certainty what was your name, and of what kin ye were come. And then she let fetch before him Linet the damsel, which had ridden with him many dreary ways. Then was Sir Gareth more gladder than he was tofore. And then they troth plight each other to love, and never to fail while their life lasted. And at after supper was made clean avoidance, that every lord and lady should go unto his rest. But Sir Gareth said plainly that he would go no further than the hall, for in such places, he said, was convenient for an errant knight to take his rest in. And so there were ordained great couches, and thereon feather beds,

and there laid him down to sleep. And within awhile he looked afore him and perceived and saw come an armed knight, with many lights about him. And this knight had a long battle-axe in his hand, and made grim countenance to smite him. When Sir Gareth saw him come in that wise, he lept out of his bed, and gat in his hand his sword, and lept straight toward that knight. And when the knight saw Sir Gareth come so fiercely upon him, he smote him with a thrust through the thick of the thigh, that the wound was a shaftmon broad, and had cut a-two many veins and sinews. And therewithal Sir Gareth smote him upon the helm such a buffet that he fell groveling, and then he lept over him, and unlaced his helm, and smote off his head from the body. And then he bled so fast that he might not stand, but so he laid him down upon his bed, and there he swooned, and lay as he had been dead. Then dame Liones found him, and cried aloud, that her brother Sir Gringamore heard and came down. And when he saw Sir Gareth so shamefully wounded, he was sore displeased, and said, I am shamed that this noble knight is thus honoured. Sister, said Sir Gringamore, How may this be that ye be here, and this noble knight wounded? Brother, said dame Liones, I cannot tell you, for it was not done by me, nor by mine assent. For he is my lord, and I am his, and he must be my husband, therefore, brother, I will that ye wit I shame me not to be with him, nor to do him all the pleasure that I can. Sister, said Sir Gringamore, and I will that ye wit it, and Sir Gareth both, that it was never done by me nor by mine assent that this unhappy deed was done. And there they stanched his bleeding as well as they might. And great sorrow made Sir Gringamore and dame Liones. And forthwithal came dame Linet and took up the head in the sight of them all, and anointed it with an ointment there as it was smitten off, and in the same wise she did to the other part there as the head stuck, and then she set it together, and it stuck as fast as ever it did. And the knight arose lightly up, and the damsel Linet put him in her chamber. All this saw Sir Gringamore and dame Liones, and so did Sir Gareth, and well he espied that it was the damsel Linet that rode with him through the perilous passages. Ah well, damsel, said Sir Gareth, I wend ye would not have done as ye have done. My lord Gareth, said the damsel Linet, all that I have done I will avow, and all that I have done shall be for your honour and worship, and to us all. And so within a while, Sir Gareth was nigh whole, and waxed light and jocund, and sang, danced, and gamed. And at night, because he was wounded afore, he laid his armour and his sword nigh his bed side.

CHAP. XXIII.

How the said knight came again the next night, and was beheaded again. And how at the feast of Pentecost all the knights that Sir Gareth had overcome came and yielded them to king Arthur.

RIGHT as soon as Sir Gareth was in his bed he espied an armed knight coming toward the bed, and therewith he leaped lightly out, and they hurtled together with great ire and malice all about the hall, and there was great light as it had been the number of twenty torches both before and behind, so that Sir Gareth strained him so that his old wound burst out again bleeding, but he was hot and courageous, and took no keep, but with his great force he struck down that knight, and voided his helm and struck off his head. Then he hewed the head in an hundred pieces. And when he had done so, he took up all those pieces and threw them out at a window into the ditches of the castle; and by this done he was so faint that scarcely he might stand for bleeding. And then he fell in a deadly swoon in the floor. And then dame Liones found him, and cried so that Sir Gringamore heard. And when he came and found Sir Gareth in that plight, he made great sorrow, and there he awaked Sir

Gareth, and gave him a drink that relieved him wonderly well, but the sorrow that dame Liones made there may no tongue tell, for she so fared with herself as she would have died. Right so came this damsel Linet before them all, and she had fetched all the gobbets of the head that Sir Gareth had thrown out at a window, and there she anointed them as she had done tofore, and set them together again. Well, damsel Linet, said Sir Gareth, I have not deserved all this despite that ye do unto me. Sir knight, she said, I have nothing done but I will avow, and all that I have done shall be to your worship and to us all. And then was Sir Gareth stanched of his bleeding. But the leeches said that there was no man that bare the life should heal him throughout of his wound, but if they healed him that caused that stroke by enchantment.

So leave we Sir Gareth there with Sir Gringamore and his sisters, and turn we unto king Arthur, that at the next feast of Pentecost held his feast, and there came the green knight with fifty knights, and yielded them all unto king Arthur. And so there came the red knight, his brother, and yielded him to king Arthur, and threescore knights with him. Also there came the blue knight, brother to them, with an hundred knights, and yielded them unto king Arthur. And the green knight's name was Pertolepe, and the red knight's name was Perimones, and the blue knight's name was Sir Persant of Inde. These three brethren told king Arthur how they were overcome by a knight that a damsel had with her, and called him Beaumains. By my faith, said the king, I marvel what knight he is, and of what lineage he is come; he was with me a twelvemonth, and poorly and shamefully he was fostered, and Sir Kay in scorn named him Beaumains. So right as the king stood so talking with these three brethren there came Sir Launcelot du Lake, and told the king that there was come a goodly lord with six hundred knights with him. Then the king went out of Carlion, for there was the feast, and there came to him this lord, and saluted the king in a goodly manner. What ye? said king Arthur, and what is your errand? Sir, he said, my name is the red knight of the red lawns, but my name is Sir Ironside, and, sir, wit ye well here I am sent to you of a knight that is called Beaumains, for he won me in plain battle, hand for hand, and so did never no knight but he that ever had the better of me this thirty winter, the which commanded to yield me to you at your will. Ye are welcome, said the king, for ye have been long a great foe to me and to my court, and now I trust I shall so entreat you that ye shall be my friend. Sir, both I and these six hundred knights shall always be at your summons to do you service as may lie in our powers. Truly, said king Arthur, I am much beholding unto that knight that· hath so put his body in devoir to worship me and my court. And as to thee, Ironside, that art called the red knight of the red lawns, thou art called a perilous knight. And if thou wilt hold of me I shall worship thee and make thee knight of the Table Round: but then thou must be no more a murderer. Sir, as to that I have promised unto Sir Beaumains never more to use such customs, for all the shameful customs that I used I did at the request of a lady that I loved; and therefore I must go unto Sir Launcelot, and unto Sir Gawaine, and ask them forgiveness of the evil will I had unto them, for all that I put to death was all only for the love of Sir Launcelot and Sir Gawaine. They be here now, said the king, afore thee, now may ye say to them what ye will. And then he kneeled down unto Sir Launcelot and to Sir Gawaine, and prayed them of forgiveness of his enmity that ever he had against them.

CHAP. XXIV.
How king Arthur pardoned them, and demanded of them where Sir Gareth was.

THEN goodly they said all at once, God forgive you, and we do, and pray you that ye will tell us where we may find Sir Beaumains. Fair lords, said Sir Ironside, I cannot tell you, for it is full hard to find him, for all such young knights as he is one, when they be in their adventures be never abiding in one place. But to say the worship that the red knight of the red lawns and Sir Persant and his brothers said of Beaumains it was marvel to hear. Well, my fair lords, said king Arthur, wit you well I shall do you honour for the love of Sir Beaumains, and as soon as ever I meet with him I shall make you all upon one day knights of the Table Round. And as to thee, Sir Persant of Inde, thou hast ever been called a full noble knight, and so have ever been thy three brethren called. But I marvel, said the king, that I hear not of the black knight your brother, he was a full noble knight. Sir, said Pertolepe the green knight, Sir Beaumains slew him in a recounter with his spear, his name was Sir Percard. That was great pity, said the king, and so said many knights. For these four brethren were full well known in the court of king Arthur for noble knights, for long time they had holden war against the knights of the Table Round. Then said Pertolepe the green knight unto the king: At a passage of the water of Mortaise there encountered Sir Beaumains with two brethren that ever for the most part kept that passage, and they were two deadly knights, and there he slew the eldest brother in the water, and smote him upon the head such a buffet that he fell down in the water and there he was drowned, and his name was Gherard le Breusse: and after he slew the other brother upon the land, and his name was Sir Arnold le Breusse.

CHAP. XXV.
How the queen of Orkney came to this feast of Pentecost, and Sir Gawaine and his brethren came to ask her blessing.

So then the king and they went to meat, and were served in the best manner. And as they sat at the meat, there came in the queen of Orkney, with ladies and knights a great number. And then Sir Gawaine, Sir Agravaine and Gaheris arose and went to her, and saluted her upon their knees and asked her blessing: for in fifteen year they had not seen her. Then she spake on high to her brother king Arthur: Where have ye done my young son Sir Gareth. He was here amongst us a twelve-month, and ye made a kitchen knave of him, the which is shame to you all. Alas, where have ye done my dear son that was my joy and bliss? Oh dear mother, said Sir Gawaine, I knew him not. Nor I, said the king, that now me repenteth, but thanked be God he is proved a worshipful knight as any is now living of his years, and I shall never be glad till I may find him. Ah brother, said the queen unto king Arthur, and to Sir Gawaine, and to all her sons, ye did yourself great shame when ye amongst you kept my son Gareth in the kitchen and fed him like a poor hog. Fair sister, said king Arthur, ye shall right well wit I knew him not, nor no more did Sir Gawaine nor his brethren. But since it is so that he is thus gone from us all, we must shape a remedy to find him. Also, sister, me seemeth ye might have done me to wit of his coming, and then, and I had not done well to him, ye might have blamed me. For when he came to this court he came leaning upon two men's shoul-ders, as though he might not have gone. And then he asked me three gifts, and one he asked the same day, that was that I would give him meat enough that twelvemonth. And the other two gifts he asked that day a twelvemonth, and that was that he might have the adven-ture of the damsel Linet, and the third was that Sir Launcelot should make him knight when he desired him. And so I granted him all his desire, and many in this court marvelled that he desired his sustenance for a twelvemonth, and thereby we deemed many of us that he was not come of a noble house. Sir, said the queen of Orkney unto king Arthur her brother, wit you well that I

sent him unto you right well armed and horsed, and worshipfully beseen of his body; and gold and silver plenty to spend. It may be, said the king, but thereof saw we none, save that same day as he departed from us, knights told me that there came a dwarf hither suddenly, and brought him armour and a good horse, full well and richly be-seen, and thereat we had all marvel from whence that riches came, that we deemed all that he was come of men of worship. Brother, said the queen, all that ye say I believe, for ever since he was grown he was marvellously witted: and ever he was faithful and true of his promise. But I marvel, said she, that Sir Kay did mock him and scorn him, and gave him that name Beaumains: yet Sir Kay, said the queen, named him more righteously than he wend; for I dare say, and he be on live, he is as fair an handed man and well disposed as any is living. Sister, said Arthur, let this language be still, and by the grace of God he shall be found and he be within these seven realms; and let all this pass, and be merry, for he is proved to be a man of worship, and that is my joy.

CHAP. XXVI.

How king Arthur sent for the lady Liones, and how she let cry a tourney at her castle, where as came many knights.

THEN said Sir Gawaine and his brethren unto Arthur, Sir, and ye will give us leave we will go and seek our brother. Nay, said Sir Launcelot, that shall ye not need, and so said Sir Baudwin of Britain: for as by our ad-vice the king shall send unto dame Liones a messenger, and pray her that she will come to the court in all the haste that she may, and doubt ye not she will come, and then she may give you best counsel where ye shall find him. This is well said of you, said the king. So then goodly letters were made, and the messenger sent forth, that night and day he went till he came unto the castle perilous. And then the lady dame Liones was sent for there as she was with Sir Gringamore her brother and Sir Gareth. And when she understood this message, she bad him ride on his way unto king Arthur, and she would come after in all goodly haste. Then when she came to Sir Gringamore and to Sir Gareth, she told them all how king Arthur had sent for her. That is because of me, said Sir Gareth. Now advise me, said dame Liones, what shall I say, and in what manner I shall rule me. My lady and my love. said Sir Gareth, I pray you in no manner of wise be ye aknown where I am, but well I wot my mother is there and all my brethren, and they will take upon them to seek me; and I wot well that they do. But this, madam, I would ye said and advised the king, when he questioneth with you of me: then may ye say, this is your advice, that, and it like his good grace, ye will do make a cry against the feast of the Assumption of our Lady, that what knight there proveth him best, he shall weld you and all your land. And if so be that he be a wedded man, that his wife shall have the degree and a coronal of gold, beset with stones of virtue to the value of a thousand pound, and a white jerfalcon.

So dame Liones departed and came to king Arthur, where she was nobly received, and there she was sore questioned of the king, and of the queen of Orkney. And she answered, where Sir Gareth was she could not tell. But thus much she said unto Arthur; Sir, I will let cry a tournament, that shall be done before my castle at the Assumption of our Lady, and the cry shall be this, that you my lord Arthur shall be there and your knights, and I will purvey that my knights shall be against yours: and then I am sure ye shall hear of Sir Gareth. This is well advised, said king Arthur: and so she departed. And the king and she made great provision for that tournament. When dame Liones was come to the Isle of Avilion, that was the same isle there as her brother Sir Gringamore dwelt, then she told him all how

she had done, and what promise she had made to king Arthur. Alas, said Sir Gareth, I have been so wounded by mishap sithen I came into this castle, that I shall not be able to do at that tournament like a knight, for I was never thoroughly whole since I was hurt. Be ye of good cheer, said the damsel Linet, for I undertake within these fifteen days for to make you whole, and as lusty as ever ye were. And then she laid an ointment and a salve to him as it pleased her, that he was never so fresh nor so lusty. Then said the damsel Linet: Send you unto Sir Persant of Inde, and summon him and his knights to be here with you as they have promised. Also, that ye send unto Sir Ironside, that is the red knight of the red lawns, and charge him that he be ready with you with his whole sum of knights, and then shall ye be able to match with king Arthur and his knights. So this was done, and all knights were sent for unto the castle perilous. And then the red knight answered and said unto dame Liones, and to Sir Gareth, Madam, and my lord Sir Gareth, ye shall understand that I have been at the court of king Arthur, and Sir Persant of Inde and his brethren, and there we have done our homage as ye commanded us. Also, Sir Ironside said, I have taken upon me with Sir Persant of Inde and his brethren to hold party against my lord Sir Launcelot and the knights of that court. And this have I done for the love of my lady dame Liones, and you my lord Sir Gareth. Ye have well done, said Sir Gareth. But wit you well ye shall be full sore matched with the most noble knights of the world, therefore we must purvey us of good knights, where we may get them. That is well said, said Sir Persant, and worshipfully. And so the cry was made in England, Wales, and Scotland, Ireland, and Cornwall, and in all the out isles, and in Britany, and in many countries; that at the feast of the Assumption of our Lady next coming, men should come to the castle perilous, beside the Isle of

Avilion, and there all the knights that there came should have the choice whether them list to be on the one party with the knights of the castle, or on the other party with king Arthur. And two months was to the day that the tournament should be. And so there came many good knights that were at large, and held them for the most part against king Arthur and his knights of the Round Table, and came on the side of them of the castle. For Sir Epinogrus was the first, and he was the king's son of Northumberland, and Sir Palamides the Saracen was another, and Sir Safere his brother, and Sir Sagwarides his brother, but they were christened, and Sir Malegrine another, and Sir Brian de les Isles, a noble knight, and Sir Grummore Gummursum, a good knight of Scotland, and Sir Carados of the dolorous tower, a noble knight, and Sir Turquin his brother, and Sir Arnold and Sir Gauter, two brethren, good knights of Cornwall: there came Sir Tristram de Liones, and with him Sir Dinadan the seneschal and Sir Sadok; but this Sir Tristram was not at that time knight of the Table Round, but he was one of the best knights of the world. And so all these noble knights accompanied them with the lady of the castle, and with the red knight of the red lawns, but as for Sir Gareth, he would not take upon him more but as other mean knights.

CHAP. XXVII.

How king Arthur went to the tournament with his knights, and how the lady received him worshipfully, and how the knights encountered.

AND then there came with king Arthur Sir Gawaine, Agravaine and Gaheris, his brethren. And then his nephews Sir Uwaine le Blanchemains, and Sir Aglovale, Sir Tor, Sir Percivale de Galis, and Sir Lamorak de Galis. Then came Sir Launcelot du Lake with his brethren, nephews, and cousins, as Sir Lionel, Sir Ector de Maris, Sir Bors de Ganis, and Sir Galihodin, Sir Galihud,

and many more of Sir Launcelot's blood; and Sir Dinadan, Sir La Cote Male Taile his brother, a good knight, and Sir Sagramore, a good knight; and all the most part of the Round Table. Also there came with king Arthur these knights, the king of Ireland, king Agwisaunce, and the king of Scotland, king Carados, and king Uriens of the land of Gore, and king Bagdemagus, and his son Sir Meliaganus, and Sir Galahault the noble prince. All these kings, princes, earls, barons, and other noble knights, as Sir Brandiles, Sir Uwaine les Avoutres, and Sir Kay, Sir Bedivere, Sir Meliot de Logris, Sir Petipase of Winchelsea, Sir Godelake. All these came with king Arthur, and many more that cannot be rehearsed.

Now leave we of these kings and knights, and let us speak of the great array that was made within the castle and about the castle for both parties. The lady dame Liones ordained great array upon her part for her noble knights, for all manner of lodging and victual that came by land and by water, that there lacked nothing for her party, nor for the other, but there was plenty to be had for gold and silver for king Arthur and his knights. And then there came the harbingers from king Arthur, for to harbour him and his kings, dukes, earls, barons, and knights. And then Sir Gareth prayed dame Liones, and the red knight of the red lawns, and Sir Persant and his brother, and Sir Gringamore, that in no wise there should none of them tell his name, and make no more of him than of the least knight that there was; for he said, I will not be known of neither more nor less, neither at the beginning neither at the ending.

Then dame Liones said unto Sir Gareth, Sir, I will lend you a ring, but I would pray you as ye love me heartily let me have it again when the tournament is done, for that ring increaseth my beauty much more than it is of itself. And the virtue of my ring is that that is green it will turn to red, and that is red it will turn in likeness to green, and that is blue it will turn to likeness of white, and that is white it will turn in likeness to blue, and so it will do of all manner of colours. Also, who that beareth my ring shall lose no blood, and for great love I will give you this ring. Gramercy, said Sir Gareth, mine own lady, for this ring is passing meet for me, for it will turn all manner of likeness that I am in, and that shall cause me that I shall not be known. Then Sir Gringamore gave Sir Gareth a bay courser that was a passing good horse : also he gave him good armour and sure, and a noble sword that some time Sir Gringamore's father won upon an heathen tyrant. And so thus every knight made him ready to that tournament. And king Arthur was come two days tofore the Assumption of our Lady. And there was all manner of royalty of all minstrelsy that might be found. Also there came queen Guenever, and the queen of Orkney, Sir Gareth's mother. And upon the Assumption day, when mass and matins was done, there were heralds with trumpets commanded to blow to the field. And so there came out Sir Epinogrus, the king's son of Northumberland, from the castle, and there encountered with him Sir Sagramore le Desirous, and either of them brake their spears to their hands. And then came in Sir Palamides out of the castle, and there encountered with him Gawaine, and either of them smote other so hard that both the good knights and their horses fell to the earth. And then knights of either party rescued their knights. And then came in Sir Safere and Sir Sagwarides, brethren unto Sir Palamides, and there encountered Sir Agravaine with Sir Safere, and Sir Gaheris encountered with Sir Sagwarides. So Sir Safere smote down Agravaine, Sir Gawaine's brother, and Sir Segwarides, Sir Safere's brother, smote down Sir Gaheris. And Sir Malgrine, a knight of the castle, encountered with Sir Uwaine le Blanchemains, and there Sir Uwaine gave Sir Malgrine a fall, that he had almost broken his neck.

CHAP. XXVIII.

How the knights bare them in battle.

THEN Sir Brian de les Isles, and Grummore Grummorsum, knights of the castle, encountered with Sir Aglovale and Sir Tor, and Sir Tor smote down Sir Grummore Grummorsum to the earth. Then came in Sir Carados of the dolorous tower, and Sir Turquine, knights of the castle, and there encountered with them Sir Percivale de Galis and Sir Lamorak de Galis, that were two brethren, and there encountered Sir Percivale with Sir Carados, and either brake their spears unto their hands, and then Sir Turquine with Sir Lamorak, and either of them smote down other, horse and all, to the earth, and either parties rescued other and horsed them again. And Sir Arnold, and Sir Gauter, knights of the castle, encountered with Sir Brandiles and Sir Kay, and these four knights encountered mightily, and brake their spears to their hands. Then came in Sir Tristram, and Sir Saduk, and Sir Dinas, knights of the castle, and there encountered Sir Tristram with Sir Bedivere, and there Sir Bedivere was smitten to the earth, both horse and man : and Sir Saduk encountered with Sir Petipase, and there Sir Saduk was overthrown. And there Uwaine les Avoutres smote down Sir Dinas the seneschal. Then came in Sir Persant of Inde, a knight of the castle, and there encountered with him Sir Launcelot du Lake, and there he smote Sir Persant, horse and man, to the earth. Then came Sir Pertolope from the castle, and there encountered with him Sir Lionel, and there Sir Pertolope the green knight smote down Sir Lionel, brother to Sir Launcelot. All this was marked by noble heralds, who bare him best, and their names. And then came into the field Sir Perimones the red knight, Sir Persant's brother, that was a knight of the castle, and he encountered with Sir Ector de Maris, and either smote other so hard that both their horses and they fell to the earth. And then came in the red knight of the red lawns, and Sir Gareth, from the castle, and there encountered with them Sir Bors de Ganis and Sir Bleoberis, and there the red knight and Sir Bors smote other so hard that their spears brast, and their horses fell groveling to the earth. Then Sir Bleoberis brake his spear upon Sir Gareth, but of that stroke Sir Bleoberis fell to the earth. When Sir Galihodin saw that, he bad Sir Gareth keep him, and Sir Gareth smote him to the earth. Then Sir Galihud gat a spear to avenge his brother, and in the same wise Sir Gareth served him, and Sir Dinadan and his brother La Cote Male Taile, and Sir Sagramor le Desirous, and Sir Dodinas le Savage; all these he bare down with one spear. When king Agwisance of Ireland saw Sir Gareth fare so he marvelled what he might be, that one time seemed green, and another time, at his again coming, he seemed blue. And thus at every course that he rode to and fro he changed his colour, so that there might neither king nor knight have ready cognisance of him. Then Sir Agwisance the king of Ireland encountered with Sir Gareth, and there Sir Gareth smote him from his horse, saddle and all. And then came king Carados of Scotland, and Sir Gareth smote him down, horse and man. And in the same wise he served king Uriens of the land of Gore. And then there came in Sir Bagdemagus, and Sir Gareth smote him down horse and man to the earth. And Bagdemagus's son Meliganus brake a spear upon Sir Gareth mightily and knightly. And then Sir Galahault the noble prince cried on high, Knight with the many colours, well hast thou justed; now make thee ready that I may just with thee. Sir Gareth heard him, and he gat a great spear, and so they encountered together, and there the prince brake his spear: but Sir Gareth smote him upon the left side of the helm, that he reeled here and there, and he had fallen down had not his men recovered him. Truly, said king Arthur, that knight with the many colours is a good knight. Wherefore the king called unto him Sir Launcelot, and prayed him to encounter with that knight. Sir, said Launcelot, I may well find in my heart for to forbear him as at this time, for he hath had travail enough this day, and when a good knight doth so well upon some day, it is no good knight's part to let him of his worship, and, namely, when he seeth a knight hath done so great labour: for peradventure, said Sir Launcelot, his quarrel is here this day, and peradventure he is best beloved with this lady of all that be here, for I see well he paineth himself and enforceth him to do great deeds, and therefore, said Sir Launcelot, as for me, this day he shall have the honour; though it lay in my power to put him from it, I would not.

CHAP. XXIX.

Yet of the said Tournament.

THEN when this was done, there was drawing of swords; and then there began a sore tournament. And there did Sir Lamorak marvellous deeds of arms, and betwixt Sir Lamorak and Sir Ironside, that was the red knight of the red lawns, there was a strong battle, and betwixt Sir Palamides and Bleoberis was a strong battle; and Sir Gawaine and Sir Tristram met, and there Sir Gawaine had the worst, for he pulled Sir Gawaine from his horse, and there he was long upon foot and defouled. Then came in Sir Launcelot, and he smote Sir Turquine, and he him, and then came Sir Carados his brother, and both at once they assailed him, and he, as the most noblest knight of the world, worshipfully fought with them both, that all men wondered of the nobleness of Sir Launcelot. And then came in Sir Gareth and knew that it was Sir Launcelot that fought with those two perilous knights. And then Sir Gareth came with his good horse and hurtled them in sunder, and no stroke would he smite to Sir Launcelot. That espied Sir Launcelot, and deemed it should be the good knight Sir Gareth; and then Sir Gareth rode here and there, and smote on the right hand and on the left hand, that all the folk might well espy where that he rode. And by fortune he met with his brother Sir Gawaine, and there he put Sir Gawaine to the worse, for he put off his helm; and so he served five or six knights of the Round Table, that all men said he put him in the most pain, and best he did his devoir. For when Sir Tristram beheld him how he first justed and after fought so well with a sword, then he rode unto Sir Ironside and to Sir Persant of Inde, and asked them by their faith, What manner a knight is yonder knight that seemeth in so many divers colours; truly, me seemeth, said Tristram, that he putteth himself in great pain, for he never ceaseth. Wot ye not what he is? said Sir Ironside. No, said Sir Tristram. Then shall ye know that this is he that loveth the lady of the castle, and she him again; and this is he that won me when I besieged the lady of this castle, and this is he that won Sir Persant of Inde and his three brethren. What is his name, said Sir Tristram, and of what blood is he come? He was called in the court of king Arthur Beaumains, but his name is Sir Gareth of Orkney, brother to Sir Gawaine. By my head, said Sir Tristram, he is a good knight, and a big man of arms, and if he be young he shall prove a full noble knight. He is but a child, they all said; and of Sir Launcelot he was made knight. Therefore he is mickle the better, said Tristram. And then Sir Tristram, Sir Ironside, Sir Persant, and his brother, rode together for to help Sir Gareth, and then there were given many strong strokes. And then Sir Gareth rode out on the one side to amend his helm. And then said his dwarf, Take me your ring, that ye lose it not while that ye drink. And so when he had drunk, he gat on his helm, and eagerly took his horse and rode into the field, and left his ring with his dwarf, and the dwarf was glad the ring was from him, for then he wist well he should be known. And then when Sir Gareth was in the field, all folks saw him well and

plainly that he was in yellow colours, and there he rashed off helms, and pulled down knights, that king Arthur had marvel what knight he was, for the king saw by his hair that it was the same knight.

CHAP. XXX.

How Sir Gareth was espied by the heralds, and how he escaped out of the field.

BUT before he was in so many colours, and now he is but in one colour, that is yellow : now go, said king Arthur unto divers heralds, and ride about him, and espy what manner knight he is, for I have asked of many knights this day that be upon his party, and all say they know him not. And so an herald rode nigh Gareth as he could, and there he saw written about his helm in gold, This helm is Sir Gareth's of Orkney. Then the herald cried as he were wood, and many heralds with him, This is Sir Gareth of Orkney, in the yellow arms, that all kings and knights of Arthur's beheld him and awaited, and then they pressed all to behold him: and ever the heralds cried, This is Sir Gareth of Orkney, king Lot's son. And when Sir Gareth espied that he was discovered, then he doubled his strokes, and smote down Sir Sagramore, and his brother Sir Gawaine. O brother, said Sir Gawaine, I wend ye would not have stricken me. So when he heard him say so, he thrang here and there, and so with great pain he gat out of the press, and there he met with his dwarf. O boy, said Sir Gareth, thou hast beguiled me foul this day that thou kept my ring. Give it me anon again, that I may hide my body withal; and so he took it him. And then they all wist not where he was become; and Sir Gawaine had in manner espied where Sir Gareth rode, and then he rode after with all his might. That espied Sir Gareth, and rode lightly into the forest, that Sir Gawaine wist not where he was become. And when Sir Gareth wist that Sir Gawaine was past, he asked the dwarf of best counsel. Sir, said the dwarf, me seemeth it were best, now that ye are

escaped from spying, that ye send my
lady dame Liones her ring. It is well
advised, said Sir Gareth; now have it
here, and bear it to her, and say that I
recommend me unto her good grace,
and say her I will come when I may,
and I pray her to be true and faithful
to me, as I will be to her. Sir, said the
dwarf, it shall be done as ye command :
and so he rode his way, and did his
errand unto the lady. Then she said,
Where is my knight Sir Gareth? Madam, said the dwarf, he bad me say that
he would not be long from you. And
so lightly the dwarf came again unto
Sir Gareth, that would fain have had
a lodging, for he had need to be reposed. And then fell there a thunder
and a rain, as heaven and earth should
go together. And Sir Gareth was not
a little weary, for of all that day he had
but little rest, neither his horse nor he.
So this Sir Gareth rode so long in that
forest until the night came. And ever
it lightened and thundered, as it had
been wood. At the last by fortune he
came to a castle, and there he heard the
waits upon the walls.

CHAP. XXXI.

*How Sir Gareth came to a castle where he
was well lodged, and how he justed with
a knight and he slew him.*

THEN Sir Gareth rode unto the barbican of the castle, and prayed the
porter fair to let him into the castle.
The porter answered ungoodly again,
and said, Thou gettest no lodging here.
Fair sir, say not so, for I am a knight
of king Arthur's, and pray the lord or
the lady of this castle to give me harbour for the love of king Arthur. Then
the porter went unto the duchess, and
told her how there was a knight of king
Arthur's would have harbour. Let him
in, said the duchess, for I will see that
knight, and for king Arthur's sake he
shall not be harbourless. Then she went
up into a tower over the gate, with great
torch light. When Sir Gareth saw that
torch light, he cried on high, Whether
thou be lord or lady, giant or champion,

I take no force, so that I may have harbour this night, and if it be so that I
must needs fight, spare me not to morn
when I have rested me, for both I and
my horse be weary. Sir knight, said
the lady, thou speakest knightly and
boldly, but wit thou well that the lord
of this castle loveth not king Arthur,
nor none of his court, for my lord hath
ever been against him, and therefore
thou were better not to come within
this castle. For and thou come in this
night, thou must come in under such
form, that wheresoever thou meet my
lord, by lane, or by street, thou must
yield thee to him as prisoner. Madam,
said Sir Gareth, what is your lord, and
what is his name? Sir, my lord's name
is the duke de la Rowse. Well, madam,
said Sir Gareth, I shall promise you in
what place I meet your lord, I shall yield
me unto him and to his good grace,
with that I understand he will do me no
harm : and if I understand that he will,
will I release myself and I can with my
spear and with my sword. Ye say well,
said the duchess, and then she let the
draw-bridge down. And so he rode
into the hall, and there he alight, and
his horse was led into a stable, and in
the hall he unarmed him and said,
Madam, I will not out of this hall this
night; and when it is day-light let see
who will have ado with me, he shall
find me ready. Then was he set unto
supper, and had many good dishes.
Then Sir Gareth list well to eat, and
knightly he ate his meat, and eagerly;
there was many a fair lady by him, and
some of them said they never saw a
goodlier man, nor so well of eating.
Then they made him passing good
cheer. And shortly when he had supped, his bed was made there; so he
rested him all night. And on the morn
he heard mass, and broke his fast, and
took his leave at the duchess, and at
them all, and thanked her goodly of
her lodging, and of his good cheer.
And then she asked him his name.
Madam, said he, truly, my name is
Gareth of Orkney, and some men call
me Beaumains. Then knew she well it

was the same knight that fought for dame Liones. So Sir Gareth departed, and rode up into a mountain, and there met him a knight, his name was Sir Bendelaine, and said to Sir Gareth, Thou shalt not pass this way, for either thou shalt just with me, or be my prisoner. Then will I just, said Sir Gareth. And so they let their horses run, and there Sir Gareth smote him throughout the body, and Sir Bendelaine rode forth to his castle there beside, and there died. So Sir Gareth would have rested him, and he came riding to Bendelaine's castle. Then his knights and his servants espied that it was he that had slain their lord. Then they armed twenty good men, and came out and assailed Sir Gareth, and so he had no spear, but his sword, and put his shield afore him, and there they brake their spears upon him, and they assailed him passingly sore. But ever Sir Gareth defended him as a knight.

CHAP. XXXII.

How Sir Gareth fought with a knight that held within his castle thirty ladies, and how he slew him.

So when they saw that they might not overcome him, they rode from him and took their counsel to slay his horse, and so they came in upon Sir Gareth, and with spears they slew his horse, and then they assailed him hard. But when he was on foot there was none that he fought but he gave him such a buffet that he did never recover. So he slew them by one and one till they were but four, and there they fled, and Sir Gareth took a good horse that was one of theirs, and rode his way. Then he rode a great pace till that he came to a castle, and there he heard much mourning of ladies and gentlewomen. So there came by him a page: What noise is this, said Sir Gareth, that I hear within this castle? Sir knight, said the page, here be within this castle thirty ladies, and all they be widows, for here is a knight that waiteth daily upon this castle, and his name is the brown knight

without pity, and he is the most perilous knight that now liveth. And, therefore, sir, said the page, I rede you flee. Nay, said Sir Gareth, I will not flee, though thou be afeard of him. And then the page saw where came the brown knight. Lo, said the page, yonder he cometh. Let me deal with him, said Sir Gareth. And when either of other had a sight, they let their horses run, and the brown knight brake his spear, and Sir Gareth smote him throughout the body, that he overthrew him to the ground stark dead. So Sir Gareth rode into the castle, and prayed the ladies that he might repose him. Alas, said the ladies, ye may not be lodged here. Make him good cheer, said the page, for this knight hath slain your enemy. Then they all made him good cheer as lay in their power. But wit ye well they made him good cheer, for they might none otherwise do, for they were but poor. And so on the morn he went to mass, and there he saw the thirty ladies kneel, and lay groveling upon divers tombs, making great dole and sorrow. Then Sir Gareth wist well that in the tombs lay their lords. Fair ladies, said Sir Gareth, ye must at the next feast of Pentecost be at the court of king Arthur, and say that I Sir Gareth sent you thither. We shall do this, said the ladies. So he departed, and by fortune he came to a mountain, and there he found a goodly knight that bad him, Abide Sir knight, and just with me. What are ye? said Sir Gareth. My name is, said he, the duke de la Rowse. Ah! Sir, ye are the same knight that I lodged once in your castle, and there I made promise unto your lady that I should yield me unto you. Ah! said the duke, art thou that proud knight that proffered to fight with my knights? therefore make thee ready, for I will have ado with thee. So they let their horses run, and there Sir Gareth smote the duke down from his horse. But the duke lightly avoided his horse, and dressed his shield, and drew his sword, and bad Sir Gareth alight and fight with him. So he did alight, and they did great battle together more than an hour, and either hurt other full sore. At the last Sir Gareth gat the duke to the earth, and would have slain him, and then he yielded him to him. Then must ye go, said Sir Gareth, unto Sir Arthur my lord at the next feast, and say that I Sir Gareth of Orkney sent you unto him. It shall be done, said the duke, and I will do to you homage and fealty with an hundred knights with me, and all the days of my life to do you service where ye will command me.

CHAP. XXXIII.

How Sir Gawaine and Sir Gareth fought each against other, and how they knew each other by the damsel Linet.

So the duke departed, and Sir Gareth stood there alone, and there he saw an armed knight coming toward him. Then Sir Gareth took the duke's shield and mounted upon horseback, and so without bidding they ran together as it had been the thunder. And there that knight hurt Sir Gareth under the side with his spear. And then they alight and drew their swords, and gave great strokes, that the blood trailed to the ground. And so they fought two hours. At the last there came the damsel Linet, that some men call the damsel Savage, and she came riding upon an ambling mule, and there she cried all on high, Sir Gawaine, Sir Gawaine, leave thy fighting with thy brother Sir Gareth. And when he heard her say so he threw away his shield and his sword, and ran to Sir Gareth and took him in his arms, and then kneeled down and asked him mercy. What are ye, said Sir Gareth, that right now were so strong and so mighty, and now so suddenly yield you to me? O Gareth, I am your brother Sir Gawaine, that for your sake have had great sorrow and labour. Then Sir Gareth unlaced his helm, and kneeled down to him and asked him mercy. Then they rose both, and embraced either other in their arms, and wept a great while or they might speak, and either of them gave other the prize of the battle. And there were many kind

words between them. Alas, my fair brother, said Sir Gawaine, perdy I ought of right to worship you and ye were not my brother, for ye have worshipped king Arthur and all his court, for ye have sent him more worshipful knights this twelvemonth than six the best of the Round Table have done, except Sir Launcelot. Then came the damsel Savage, that was the lady Linet that rode with Sir Gareth so long, and there she did stanch Sir Gareth's wounds and Sir Gawaine's. Now what will ye do? said the damsel Savage; me seemeth it were well done that Arthur had tidings of you both, for your horses are so bruised that they may not bear. Now, fair damsel, said Sir Gawaine, I pray you ride unto my lord, mine uncle king Arthur, and tell him what adventure is to me betid here, and I suppose he will not tarry long. Then she took her mule, and lightly she came to king Arthur that was but two miles thence, and when she had told him the tidings, the king bad get him a palfrey. And when he was upon his back he bad the lords and ladies come after who that would: and there was saddling and bridling of queens' horses, and princes' horses, and well was him that soonest might be ready. So when the king came there as they were, he saw Sir Gawaine and Sir Gareth sit upon a little hill side, and then the king avoided his horse. And when he came nigh Sir Gareth he would have spoken but he might not, and therewith he sank down in a swoon for gladness. And so they start unto their uncle, and required him of his good grace to be of good comfort. Wit ye well the king made great joy, and many a piteous complaint he made unto Sir Gareth, and ever he wept as he had been a child. With that came his mother the queen of Orkney, dame Morgause, and when she saw Sir Gareth readily in the visage, she might not weep, but suddenly fell down in a swoon, and lay there a great while like as she had been dead. And then Sir Gareth recomforted his mother in such a wise that she recovered, and made good cheer. Then the king commanded that all manner of knights that were under his obeisance should make their lodging right there for the love of his nephews. And so it was done, and all manner of purveyance purveyed that there lacked nothing that might be gotten of tame nor wild for gold or silver. And then by the means of the damsel Savage Sir Gawaine and Sir Gareth were healed of their wounds, and there they sojourned eight days. Then said king Arthur unto the damsel Savage, I marvel that your sister dame Liones cometh not here to me, and in especial that she cometh not to visit her knight, my nephew Sir Gareth, that hath had so much travail for her love. My lord, said the damsel Linet, ye must of your good grace hold her excused, for she knoweth not that my lord Sir Gareth is here. Go then for her, said king Arthur, that we may be appointed what is best to be done, according unto the pleasure of my nephew. Sir, said the damsel, that shall be done, and so she rode unto her sister. And as lightly as she might she made her ready, and she came on the morn with her brother Sir Gringamore, and with her forty knights. And so when she was come, she had all the cheer that might be done, both of the king and of many other kings and queens.

CHAP. XXXIV.

How Sir Gareth acknowledged that they loved each other to king Arthur, and of the appointment of their wedding.

AND among all these ladies she was named the fairest and peerless. Then when Sir Gareth saw her, there was many a goodly look and goodly words, that all men of worship had joy to behold them. Then came king Arthur and many other kings, and dame Guenever and the queen of Orkney. And there the king asked his nephew Sir Gareth whether he would have that lady to his wife? My lord, wit you well that I love her above all ladies living. Now, fair lady, said king Arthur, what say ye?

Most noble king, said dame Liones, wit you well that my lord Sir Gareth is to me more lever to have and hold as my husband, than any king or prince that is christened, and if I may not have him I promise you I will never have none. For, my lord Arthur, said dame Liones, wit ye well he is my first love, and he shall be the last: and if ye will suffer him to have his will and free choice, I dare say he will have me. That is truth, said Sir Gareth, and I have not you and hold not you as my wife, there shall never lady nor gentlewoman rejoice me. What nephew, said the king, is the wind in that door! for wit ye well I would not for the stint of my crown to be causer to withdraw your hearts, and wit ye well ye cannot love so well but I shall rather increase it than distress it. And also ye shall have my love and my lordship in the uttermost wise that may lie in my power. And in the same wise said Sir Gareth's mother. Then was there made a provision for the day of marriage, and by the king's advice it was provided that it should be at Michaelmas following, at Kinkenadon by the sea-side, for there is a plentiful country. And so it was cried in all the places through the realm. And then Sir Gareth sent his summons unto all these knights and ladies that he had won in battle tofore, that they should be at his day of marriage at Kinkenadon by the sands. And then dame Liones and the damsel Linet, with Sir Gringamore, rode to their castle, and a goodly and a rich ring she gave to Sir Gareth, and he gave her another. And king Arthur gave her a rich bee of gold, and so she departed. And king Arthur and his fellowship rode toward Kinkenadon, and Sir Gareth brought his lady on the way, and so came to the king again and rode with him. Oh the great cheer that Sir Launcelot made of Sir Gareth and he of him: for there was never no knight that Sir Gareth loved so well as he did Sir Launcelot, and ever for the most part he would be in Sir Launcelot's company: for after Sir Gareth had espied Sir Gawaine's conditions, he withdrew himself from his brother Sir Gawaine's fellowship, for he was vengeable, and where he hated he would be avenged with murder, and that hated Sir Gareth.

CHAP. XXXV.

Of the great royalty, and what officers were made at the feast of the wedding, and of the justs at the feast.

So it drew fast to Michaelmas, and thither came dame Liones the lady of the castle perilous and her sister dame Linet, with Sir Gringamore their brother with them : for he had the conduct of these ladies. And there they were lodged at the devise of king Arthur. And upon Michaelmas-day the bishop of Canterbury made the wedding betwixt Sir Gareth and the lady Liones with great solemnity. And king Arthur made Gaheris to wed the damsel Savage, that was dame Linet ; and king Arthur made Sir Agravaine to wed dame Liones' niece, a fair lady, her name was dame Laurel. And so when this solemnization was done, then there came in the green knight Sir Pertolope with thirty knights, and there he did homage and fealty unto Sir Gareth, and these knights to hold of him for evermore. Also Sir Pertolope said, I pray you that at this feast I may be your chamberlain. With a good will, said Sir Gareth, sith it liketh you to take so simple an office. Then came in the red knight with threescore knights with him, and did to Sir Gareth homage and fealty, and all those knights to hold of him for evermore, and then this Sir Perimones prayed Sir Gareth to grant him to be his chief butler at that high feast. I will well, said Sir Gareth, that ye have this office and it were better. Then came in Sir Persant of Inde with an hundred knights with him, and there he did homage and fealty unto Sir Gareth, and all his knights should do him service, and hold their lands of him for ever ; and there he prayed Sir Gareth to make him his sewer chief at the feast. I will well, said Sir Gareth, that ye have it and it were better. Then came in the

duke de la Rowse with an hundred knights with him, and there he did homage and fealty unto Sir Gareth, and so to hold their lands of him for ever ; and he required Sir Gareth that he might serve him of the wine that day at the feast. I will well, said Sir Gareth, and it were better. Then came in the red knight of the red lawns, that was Sir Ironside, and he brought with him three hundred knights, and there he did homage and fealty, and all these knights to hold their lands of him for ever, and then he asked Sir Gareth to be his carver. I will well, said Sir Gareth, and it please you. Then came into the court thirty ladies, and all they seemed widows, and those thirty ladies brought with them many fair gentlewomen ; and all they kneeled down at once unto king Arthur and to Sir Gareth, and there all those ladies told the king how Sir Gareth had delivered them from the dolorous tower, and slew the brown knight without pity ; and therefore we and our heirs for evermore will do homage unto Sir Gareth of Orkney. So then the kings and queens, princes, earls and barons, and many bold knights went unto meat, and well may ye wit that there was all manner of meat plenteously, all manner revels and games, with all manner of minstrelsy that was used in those days. Also there was great justs three days. But the king would not suffer Sir Gareth to just because of his new bride : for as the French book saith that dame Liones desired the king that none that were wedded should just at that feast. So the first day there justed Sir Lamorak de Galis, for he overthrew thirty knights and did passing marvellously deeds of arms. And then king Arthur made Sir Persant of Inde and his two brethren knights of the Round Table, to their lives' end, and gave them great lands. Also the second day there justed Tristram best, and he overthrew forty knights, and did there marvellous deeds of arms. And there king Arthur made Ironside, that was the red knight of the red lawns, a knight of the Table

Round unto his life's end, and gave him great lands. The third day there justed Sir Launcelot du Lake, and he overthrew fifty knights and did many marvellous deeds of arms, that all men wondered on him. And there king Arthur made the duke de la Rowse a knight of the Round Table to his life's end, and gave him great lands to spend.

But when these justs were done, Sir Lamorak and Sir Tristram departed suddenly and would not be known, for the which king Arthur and all the court were sore displeased. And so they held the court forty days with great solemnity. And this Sir Gareth was a noble knight, and a well ruled, and fair languaged.

𝕿𝖍𝖚𝖘 𝖊𝖓𝖉𝖊𝖙𝖍 𝖙𝖍𝖎𝖘 𝖙𝖆𝖑𝖊 𝖔𝖋 𝖘𝖞𝖗 𝕲𝖆𝖗𝖊𝖙𝖍 𝖔𝖋 𝕺𝖗𝖐𝖊𝖓𝖊𝖞 𝖙𝖍𝖆𝖙 𝖜𝖊𝖉𝖉𝖊𝖉 𝖉𝖆𝖒𝖊 𝕷𝖞𝖔𝖓𝖊𝖘 𝖔𝖋 𝖙𝖍𝖊 𝖈𝖆𝖘𝖙𝖊𝖑 𝖕𝖊𝖗𝖞𝖑𝖑𝖔𝖚𝖘. 𝕬𝖓𝖉 𝖆𝖑𝖘𝖔 𝖘𝖞𝖗 𝕲𝖆𝖍𝖊𝖗𝖎𝖘 𝖜𝖊𝖉𝖉𝖊𝖉 𝖍𝖊𝖗 𝖘𝖞𝖘𝖙𝖊𝖗 𝖉𝖆𝖒𝖊 𝕷𝖞𝖓𝖊𝖙, 𝖙𝖍𝖆𝖙 𝖜𝖆𝖘 𝖈𝖆𝖑𝖑𝖊𝖉 𝖙𝖍𝖊 𝖉𝖆𝖒𝖔𝖞𝖘𝖊𝖑 𝖘𝖆𝖚𝖊𝖆𝖌𝖊. 𝕬𝖓𝖉 𝖘𝖞𝖗 𝕬𝖌𝖗𝖆𝖚𝖆𝖞𝖓𝖊 𝖜𝖊𝖉𝖉𝖊𝖉 𝖉𝖆𝖒𝖊 𝕷𝖆𝖚𝖗𝖊𝖑 𝖆 𝖋𝖆𝖞𝖗 𝖑𝖆𝖉𝖞, 𝖆𝖓𝖉 𝖌𝖗𝖊𝖙𝖊 𝖆𝖓𝖉 𝖒𝖞𝖌𝖍𝖙𝖞 𝖑𝖆𝖓𝖉𝖊𝖘 𝖜𝖎𝖙𝖍 𝖌𝖗𝖊𝖙𝖊 𝖗𝖞𝖈𝖍𝖊𝖘𝖘𝖊 𝖌𝖆𝖋𝖊 𝖜𝖎𝖙𝖍 𝖙𝖍𝖊𝖒 𝖐𝖞𝖓𝖌 𝕬𝖗𝖙𝖍𝖚𝖗, 𝖙𝖍𝖆𝖙 𝖗𝖞𝖆𝖑𝖑𝖞 𝖙𝖍𝖊𝖞 𝖒𝖞𝖌𝖍𝖙 𝖑𝖞𝖚𝖊 𝖙𝖞𝖑 𝖙𝖍𝖊𝖎𝖗 𝖑𝖞𝖚𝖊𝖘 𝖊𝖓𝖉𝖊.

𝕳𝖊𝖗𝖊 𝖋𝖔𝖑𝖔𝖜𝖊𝖙𝖍 𝖙𝖍𝖊 𝖇𝖎𝖎𝖎. 𝖇𝖔𝖔𝖐 𝖙𝖍𝖊 𝖜𝖍𝖎𝖈𝖍 𝖎𝖘 𝖙𝖍𝖊 𝖋𝖎𝖗𝖘𝖙 𝖇𝖔𝖔𝖐 𝖔𝖋 𝕾𝖎𝖗 𝕿𝖗𝖎𝖘𝖙𝖗𝖆𝖒 𝖉𝖊 𝕷𝖞𝖔𝖓𝖊𝖘, & 𝖜𝖍𝖔 𝖜𝖆𝖘 𝖍𝖎𝖘 𝖋𝖆𝖉𝖊𝖗 & 𝖍𝖎𝖘 𝖒𝖔𝖉𝖊𝖗, & 𝖍𝖔𝖚 𝖍𝖊 𝖜𝖆𝖘 𝖇𝖔𝖗𝖓𝖊 𝖆𝖓𝖉 𝖋𝖔𝖘𝖙𝖊𝖗𝖞𝖉. 𝕬𝖓𝖉 𝖍𝖔𝖜 𝖍𝖊 𝖜𝖆𝖘 𝖒𝖆𝖉𝖊 𝖐𝖓𝖞𝖌𝖍𝖙𝖊.

𝕿𝖍𝖊 𝕰𝖎𝖌𝖍𝖙𝖍 𝕭𝖔𝖔𝖐.

CHAP. I.

How Sir Tristram de Liones was born, and how his mother died at his birth, wherefore she named him Tristram.

It was a king that hight Meliodas, and he was lord and king of the country of Liones, and this king Meliodas was a likely knight as any was that time living. And by fortune he wedded king Mark's sister of Cornwall; and she was called Elizabeth, that was called both good and fair. And at that time king Arthur reigned, and he was whole king of England, Wales, and Scotland, and of many other realms: howbeit there were many kings that were lords of many countries, but all they held their lands of king Arthur. For in Wales were two kings, and in the north were many kings; and in Cornwall and in the west were two kings; also in Ire-

land were two or three kings; and all were under the obeisance of king Arthur. So was the king of France, and the king of Britany, and all the lordships unto Rome. And the wife of this king Meliodas was a full meek lady, and well she loved her lord, and he her again, and the time came that she should bear a child, so there was great joy betwixt them. Then was there a lady in that country that had loved king Meliodas long, and by no mean she never could get his love, therefore she let ordain upon a day, as king Meliodas rode on hunting, for he was a great chaser, and there by an enchantment she made him chase an hart by himself alone till that he came to an old castle, and there anon he was taken prisoner by the lady that him loved. When Elizabeth king Meliodas missed, her lord, she was nigh out of her wit, and she took a gentlewoman with her, and ran into the forest to seek her lord.

And when she was far in the forest she might no farther, for she began to travail fast of her child. And she had many grimly throws, and her gentlewoman holp her all that she might, and so by miracle of our Lady of heaven she was delivered with great pains. But she had taken such cold for the default of help that deep draughts of death took her, that needs she must die and depart out of this world, there was none other boot. And when this queen Elizabeth saw that there was none other boot, then she made great dole, and said unto her gentlewoman, When ye see my lord king Meliodas recommend me unto him, and tell him what pains I endure here for his love, and how I must die here for his sake, for default of good help, and let him wit that I am full sorry to depart out of this world from him, therefore pray him to be friend to my soul. Now let me see my little child for whom I have had all this sorrow. And when she saw him she said thus: Ah my little son, thou hast murdered thy mother, and therefore I suppose, thou that art a murderer so young, thou art full likely to be a manly man in thine age. And because I shall die of the birth of thee, I charge thee, gentlewoman, that thou beseech my lord king Meliodas, that when he is christened let call him Tristram, that is as much to say as a sorrowful birth. And therewith this queen gave up the ghost and died. Then the gentlewoman laid her under the shadow of a great tree, and then she lapped the child as well as she might for cold. Right so there came the barons, following after the queen, and when they saw that she was dead, and understood none other but the king was destroyed;

CHAP. II.

How the step-mother of Sir Tristram had ordained poison for to have poisoned Sir Tristram.

THEN certain of them would have slain the child, because they would have been lords of the country of Liones. But then through the fair speech of the gentlewoman, and by the means that she made, the most part of the barons would not assent thereto. And then they let carry home the dead queen, and much dole was made for her. Then this meanwhile Merlin delivered king Meliodas out of prison, on the morn after his queen was dead. And so when the king was come home, the most part of the barons made great joy. But the sorrow that the king made for his queen that might no tongue tell. So then the king let inter her richly. And after he let christen his child as his wife had commanded afore her death. And then he let call him Tristram, the sorrowful born child. Then the king Meliodas endured seven years without a wife, and all this time the young Tristram was nourished well. Then it befel that king Meliodas wedded king Howell's daughter of Britany, and anon she had children of king Meliodas, then was she heavy and wroth that her children should not enjoy the country of Liones, wherefore this queen ordained for to poison young Tristram. So she let poison to be put into a piece of silver in the chamber where as Tristram and her children were together, unto that intent that when Tristram was thirsty he should drink that drink. And so it fell upon a day, the queen's son, as he was in that chamber, espied the cup with poison, and he wend it had been good drink, and because the child was thirsty, he took the cup with poison and drank freely, and therewithall suddenly the child brast, and was dead. When the queen wist of the death of her son, wit ye well that she was heavy. But yet the king understood nothing of her treason. Notwithstanding the queen would not leave this, but eft she let ordain more poison, and put it in a cup. And by fortune king Meliodas her husband found the cup with wine where was the poison, and he that was much thirsty took the cup for to drink thereout. And as he would have drunken thereof, the queen espied him, and then she ran unto him and pulled the cup from him suddenly. The king marvelled why she did so, and remembered him how her son was suddenly slain with poison. And then he took her by the hand, and said, Thou false traitress, thou shalt tell me what manner· of drink this is, or else I shall slay thee. And therewith he pulled out his sword, and swore a great oath that he should slay her but if she told him truth. Ah mercy my lord, said she, and I shall tell you all. And then she told him why she would have slain Tristram, because her children should enjoy his land. Well, said king Meliodas, and therefore shall ye have the law. And so she was condemned by the assent of the barons to be burnt, and then was there made a great fire. And right as she was at the fire to take her execution young Tristram kneeled afore king Meliodas, and besought him to give him a boon. I will well, said the king again. Then said young Tristram, Give me the life of thy queen, my stepmother. That is unrightfully asked, said king Meliodas, for thou ought of right to hate her, for she would have slain thee with that poison and she might have had her will; and for thy sake most is my cause that she should die. Sir, said Tristram, as for that, I beseech you of your mercy that ye will forgive it her, and as for my part God forgive it her, and I do, and so much it liked your highness to grant me my boon for God's love I require you hold your promise. Since it is so, said the king, I will that ye have her life. Then said the king, I give her to you, and go ye to the fire and take her and do with her what ye will. So Sir Tristram went to the fire, and by the commandment of the king delivered her from the death. But after that king Meliodas would never have ado with her as at bed and board. But by the good means of young Tristram he made the king and her accorded. But then the king would not suffer young Tristram ·to abide no longer in his court.

CHAP. III.

How Sir Tristram was sent into France, and had one to govern him named Gouvernail, and how he learned to harp, hawk, and hunt.

AND then he let ordain a gentleman that was well learned and taught; his name was Gouvernail; and then he sent young Tristram with Gouvernail into France, to learn the language, and nurture, and deeds of arms. And there was Tristram more than seven years. And then when he well could speak the language, and had learned all that he might learn in that country, then he came home to his father king Meliodas again. And so Tristram learned to be an harper passing all other, that there was none such called in no country, and so in harping and on instruments of music he applied him in his youth for to learn. And after as he growed in might and strength he laboured ever in hunting and in hawking, so that never gentleman more, that ever we heard tell of. And as the book saith, he began good measures of blowing of beasts·of venery and beasts of chase, and all manner of vermains; and all these terms we have yet of hawking and hunting. And therefore the book of venery, of hawking, and hunting, is called the book of Sir Tristram. Wherefore, as me seemeth, all gentlemen that bear old arms ought of right to honour Sir Tristram for the goodly terms that gentlemen have and use, and shall to the day of doom, that thereby in a manner all men of worship may dissever a gentleman from a yeoman, and from a yeoman a villain. For he that gentle is will draw unto him gentle taches, and to follow the customs of noble gentlemen. Thus Sir Tristram endured in Cornwall until he was big and strong, of the age of nineteen years. And then the king Meliodas had great joy of Sir Tristram, and so had the queen his wife. For ever after in her life, because Sir Tristram saved her from the fire, she did never hate him more after, but loved him ever after, and gave Tristram many great gifts; for every estate loved him where that he went.

CHAP. IV.

How Sir Marhaus came out of Ireland for to ask truage of Cornwall, or else he would fight therefore.

THEN it befel that king Anguish of Ireland sent to king Mark of Cornwall for his truage, that Cornwall had paid many winters. And all that time king Mark was behind of the truage for seven years. And king Mark and his barons gave unto the messager of Ireland these words and answer, that they would none pay; and bad the messager go unto his king Anguish, and tell him we will pay him no truage, but tell your lord, and he will always have truage of us of Cornwall, bid him send a trusty knight of his land that will fight for his right, and we shall find another for to defend our right. With this answer the messagers departed into Ireland. And when king Anguish understood the answer of the messagers, he was wonderly wroth. And then he called unto him Sir Marhaus, the good knight, that was nobly proved, and a knight of the Table Round. And this Sir Marhaus was brother unto the queen of Ireland. Then the king said thus: Fair brother Sir Marhaus, I pray you go into Cornwall for my sake, and do battle for our truage that of right we ought to have, and whatsoever ye spend ye shall have sufficiently more than ye shall need. Sir, said Marhaus, wit ye well that I shall not be loth to do battle in the right of you and your land with the best knight of the Table Round, for I know them for the most part what be their deeds, and for to advance my deeds and to increase my worship, I will right gladly go unto this journey for our right.

So in all haste there was made purveyance for Sir Marhaus, and he had all things that to him needed, and so he departed out of Ireland, and arrived up in Cornwall, even fast by the castle of Tintagil. And when king Mark understood that he was there arrived to fight

for Ireland, then made king Mark great sorrow when he understood that the good and noble knight Sir Marhaus was come. For they knew no knight that durst have ado with him. For at that time Sir Marhaus was called one of the famousest and renowned knights of the world.

And thus Sir Marhaus abode in the sea, and every day he sent unto king Mark for to pay the truage that was behind of seven year, or else to find a knight to fight with him for the truage. This manner of message Sir Marhaus sent daily unto king Mark. Then they of Cornwall let make cries in every place, that what knight would fight for to save the truage of Cornwall he should be rewarded so that he should fare the better the term of his life. Then some of the barons said to king Mark, and counselled him to send to the court of king Arthur for to seek Sir Launcelot du Lake, that was that time named for the marvellousest knight of all the world. Then there were some other barons that counselled the king not to do so, and said that it was labour in vain, because Sir Marhaus was a knight of the Round Table, therefore any of them will be loth to have ado with other, but if it were any knight at his own request would fight disguised and unknown. So the king and all his barons assented that it was no boot to seek any knight of the Round Table. This meanwhile came the language and the noise unto king Meliodas, how that Sir Marhaus abode battle fast by Tintagil, and how king Mark could find no manner knight to fight for him. When young Tristram heard of this he was wroth and sore ashamed that there durst no knight in Cornwall have ado with Sir Marhaus of Ireland.

CHAP. V.

How Tristram enterprized the battle to fight for the truage of Cornwall, and how he was made knight.

THEREWITHAL Sir Tristram went unto his father king Meliodas, and asked him counsel what was best to do for to re-cover from Cornwall truage. For as me seemeth, said Sir Tristram, it were shame that Sir Marhaus, the queen's brother of Ireland, should go away, unless that he were fought withall. As for that, said Sir Meliodas, wit ye well son Tristram that Sir Marhaus is called one of the best knights of the world, and knight of the Table Round, and therefore I know no knight in this country that is able to match with him. Alas, said Sir Tristram, that I am not made knight: and if Sir Marhaus should thus depart into Ireland, may I never have worship, and I were made knight I should match him. And sir, said Tristram, I pray you give me leave to ride to king Mark, and so ye be not displeased of king Mark will I be made knight. I will well, said king Meliodas, that ye be ruled as your courage will rule you.

Then Sir Tristram thanked his father much. And then he made him ready to ride into Cornwall. In the mean-while there came a messenger with letters of love from king Faramon of France's daughter unto Sir Tris-tram, that were full piteous letters, and in them were written many complaints of love. But Sir Tristram had no joy of her letters, nor regard unto her. Also she sent him a little brachet that was passing fair. But when the king's daughter understood that Tris-tram would not love her, as the book saith, she died for sorrow. And then the same squire that brought the letter and the brachet came again unto Sir Tristram as after ye shall hear in the tale. So this young Sir Tristram rode unto his uncle king Mark of Cornwall. And when he came there he heard say that there would no knight fight with Sir Marhaus. Then went Sir Tristram unto his uncle and said, Sir, if ye will give me the order of knighthood I will do battle with Sir Marhaus. What are ye? said the king, and from whence be ye come? Sir, said Tristram, I come from king Meliodas that wedded your sister, and a gentleman wit ye well

I am. King Mark beheld Sir Tristram, and saw that he was but a young man of age, but he was passingly well made and big. Fair sir, said the king, what is your name, and where were ye born? Sir, said he again, my name is Tris-tram, and in the country of Liones was I born. Ye say well, said the king, and if ye will do this battle I shall make you knight. Therefore I come to you, said Sir Tristram, and for none other cause. But then king Mark made him knight. And therewithal anon as he had made him knight, he sent a messenger unto Sir Marhaus with letters that said that he had found a young knight ready for to take the battle to the uttermost. It may well be, said Sir Marhaus; but tell unto king Mark that I will not fight with no knight but if he be of blood royal, that is to say either king's son or queen's son, born of a prince or princess.

When king Mark understood that, he sent for Sir Tristram de Liones and told him what was the answer of Sir Marhaus. Then said Sir Tristram, Since that he sayeth so, let him wit that I am come of father's side and mother's side of as noble blood as he is. For, Sir, now shall ye know that I am king Meliodas' son, born of your own sister dame Elizabeth, that died in the forest in the birth of me. Yea! said king Mark, ye are welcome fair nephew to me. Then in all the haste the king let horse Sir Tristram and arm him in the best manner that might be had or gotten for gold or silver. And then king Mark sent unto Sir Marhaus, and did him to wit that a better born man than he was himself should fight with him, and his name is Sir Tristram de Liones, gotten of king Meliodas, and born of king Mark's sister. Then was Sir Marhaus glad and blithe that he should fight with such a gentleman. And so by the assent of king Mark and Sir Marhaus they let ordain that they should fight within an island nigh Sir Marhaus' ships; and so was Sir Tris-tram put into a vessel both his horse and he, and all that to him belonged both for his body and for his horse. Sir Tristram lacked nothing. And when king Mark and his barons of Cornwall beheld how young Sir Tristram departed with such a carriage to fight for the right of Cornwall, there was neither man nor woman of worship but they wept to see and understand so young a knight to jeopard himself for their right.

CHAP. VI.

How Sir Tristram arrived into the island for to furnish the battle with Sir Marhaus.

So to shorten this tale, when Sir Tristram was arrived within the island he looked to the further side, and there he saw at an anchor six ships nigh to the land, and under the shadow of the ships upon the land there hoved the noble knight Sir Marhaus of Ireland. Then Sir Tristram commanded his servant Gouvernail to bring his horse to the land, and dress his harness at all manner of rights. And then when he had so done he mounted upon his horse; and when he was in his saddle well apparelled, and his shield dressed upon his shoulder, Tristram asked Gouvernail, Where is this knight that I shall have ado withall? Sir, said Gouvernail, see ye him not? I wend ye had seen him, yonder he hoveth under the shadow of his ships upon horseback, with his spear in his hand, and his shield upon his shoulder. That is truth, said the noble knight Sir Tristram, now I see him well enough. Then he commanded his servant Gouvernail to go to his vessel again, and command me unto mine uncle king Mark, and pray him if that I be slain in this battle, for to inter my body as him seemeth best, and as for me let him wit that I will never yield me for cowardice; and if I be slain and flee not, then have they lost no truage for me; and if so be that I flee or yield me as recreant, bid mine uncle never bury me in christian burials. And upon thy life, said Sir Tristram to Gouvernail, come thou not nigh this island till that thou see me overcome or slain, or else that I win yonder knight. So either departed from other sore weeping.

CHAP. VII.

How Sir Tristram fought against Sir Marhaus and achieved his battle, and how Sir Marhaus fled to his Ship.

AND then Sir Marhaus perceived Sir Tristram, and said thus: Young knight Sir Tristram, what doest thou here? Me sore repenteth of thy courage, for wit thou well I have been assayed, and the best knights of this land have been assayed of my hands, and also I have matched with the best knights of the world, and therefore by my counsel return again unto thy vessel. And fair knight, and well proved knight, said Sir Tristram, thou shalt well wit I may not forsake thee in this quarrel, for I am for thy sake made knight. And thou shalt well wit that I am a king's son, born of a queen, and such promise I have made at mine uncle's request and mine own seeking, that I shall fight with thee unto the uttermost, and deliver Cornwall from the old truage. And also wit thou well, Sir Marhaus, that this is the greatest cause that thou couragest me to have ado with you, for thou art called one of the most renowned knights of the world, and because of that noise and fame that thou hast, thou givest me courage to have ado with thee, for never yet was I proved with good knight; and since I took the order of knighthood this day I am well pleased that I may have ado with so good a knight as thou art. And now wit thou well, Sir Marhaus, that I cast me to get worship on thy body, and if that I be not proved, I trust I shall be worshipfully proved upon thy body, and to deliver the country of Cornwall from all manner of truage from Ireland for ever. When Sir Marhaus had heard him say what he would, he said then thus again: Fair knight, since it is so that thou casteth to win worship of me, I let thee wit worship mayest thou none lose by me if thou mayest stand me three strokes, for I let thee wit for my noble deeds, proved and seen, king Arthur made me knight of the Table Round. Then they began to feuter their spears, and they met so fiercely together that they smote either other down both horse and all. But Sir Marhaus smote Sir Tristram a great wound in the side with his spear, and then they avoided their horses, and pulled out their swords, and threw their shields afore them, and then they lashed together as men that were wild and courageous. And when they had stricken so together long, then they left their strokes, and foined at their breathes and visors; and when they saw that that might not prevail them, then they hurtled together like rams to bear either other down. Thus they fought still more than half a day, and either were wounded passing sore, that the blood ran down freshly from them upon the ground. By then Sir Tristram waxed more fresher than Sir Marhaus, and better winded and bigger, and with a mighty stroke he smote Sir Marhaus upon the helm such a buffet, that it went through his helm, and through the coif of steel, and through the brain-pan, and the sword stuck so fast in the helm and in his brain-pan that Sir Tristram pulled thrice at his sword or ever he might pull it out from his head, and there Marhaus fell down on his knees, the edge of Tristram's sword left in his brain-pan. And suddenly Sir Marhaus rose groveling, and threw his sword and his shield from him, and so ran to his ships and fled his way, and Sir Tristram had ever his shield and his sword. And when Sir Tristram saw Sir Marhaus withdraw him, he said, Ah sir knight of the Round Table, why withdrawest thou thee; thou doest thyself and thy kin great shame, for I am but a young knight, or now I was never proved, and rather than I should withdraw me from thee, I had rather be hewn in an hundred pieces. Sir Marhaus answered no word, but went his way sore groaning. Well sir knight, said Sir Tristram, I promise thee thy sword and thy shield shall be mine, and thy shield shall I wear in all places where I ride on mine adventures, and in the sight of king Arthur and all the Round Table.

CHAP. VIII.

How Sir Marhaus, after he was arrived in Ireland, died of the stroke that Tristram had given him, and how Tristram was hurt.

ANON Sir Marhaus and his fellowship departed into Ireland. And as soon as he came to the king his brother he let search his wounds. And when his head was searched, a piece of Sir Tristram's sword was found therein, and might never be had out of his head for no surgeons, and so he died of Sir Tristram's sword, and that piece of the sword the queen his sister kept it for ever with her, for she thought to be revenged and she might.

Now turn we again unto Sir Tristram, that was sore wounded, and full sore bled, that he might not within a little while when he had taken cold scarcely stir him of his limbs. And then he set him down softly upon a little hill, and bled fast. Then anon came Gouvernail his man with his vessel, and the king and his barons came with procession against him, and when he was come to the land king Mark took him in his arms, and the king and Sir Dinas the Seneschal led Sir Tristram into the castle of Tintagil. And then was he searched in the best manner, and laid in his bed. And when king Mark saw his wounds he wept heartily, and so did all his lords. So God me help, said king Mark, I would not for all my lands that my nephew died. So Sir Tristram lay there a month and more, and ever he was like to die of that stroke that Sir Marhaus smote him first with the spear. For, as the French book saith, the spear's head was envenomed, that Sir Tristram might not be whole. Then was king Mark and all his barons passing heavy, for they deemed none other but that Sir Tristram should not recover. Then the king let send after all manner of leeches and surgeons, both unto men and women, and there was none that would behote him the life. Then came there a lady that was a right wise lady, and she said plainly unto king Mark and to Sir Tristram and to all his barons, that he should never be whole, but if Sir Tristram went in the same country that the venom came from, and in that country should he be holpen or else never. Thus said the lady unto the king. When king Mark understood that, he let purvey for Sir Tristram a fair vessel, well victualled, and therein was put Sir Tristram and Gouvernail with him, and Sir Tristram took his harp with him, and so he was put into the sea to sail into Ireland, and so by good fortune he arrived up in Ireland, even fast by a castle where the king and the queen was; and at his arrival he sat and harped in his bed a merry lay, such one heard they never none in Ireland afore that time. And when it was told the king and the queen of such a knight that was such an harper, anon the king sent for him, and let search his wounds, and then asked him his name. Then he answered, I am of the country of Liones, and my name is Tramtrist, that thus was wounded in a battle as I fought for a lady's right. Truly, said king Anguish, ye shall have all the help in this land that ye may have here. But I let you wit in Cornwall I had a great loss as ever had king, for there I lost the best knight of the world, his name was Marhaus, a full noble knight, and knight of the Table Round; and there he told Sir Tristram wherefore Sir Marhaus was slain. Sir Tristram made semblant as he had been sorry, and better knew he how it was than the king.

CHAP. IX.

How Sir Tristram was put to the keeping of La Beale Isoud for to be healed of his wound.

THEN the king for great favour made Tramtrist to be put in his daughter's ward and keeping, because she was a noble surgeon. And when she had searched him she found in the bottom of his wound that therein was poison, and so she healed him within a while, and therefore Tramtrist cast great love to La Beale Isoud, for she was at that time the fairest maid and lady of the world. And there Tramtrist learned her to harp, and she began to have a great fancy unto him. And at that time Sir Palamides the Saracen was in that country, and well cherished with the king and the queen. And every day Sir Palamides drew unto La Beale Isoud, and proffered her many gifts, for he loved her passingly well. All that espied Tramtrist, and full well knew he Sir Palamides for a noble knight and a mighty man. And wit ye well Sir Tramtrist had great despite at Sir Palamides, for La Beale Isoud told Tramtrist that Sir Palamides was in will to be christened for her sake. Thus was there great envy betwixt Tramtrist and Sir Palamides. Then it befel that King Anguish let cry a great justs and a great tournament for a lady which was called the lady of the lawns, and she was nigh cousin unto the king. And what man won her, three days after he should wed her, and have all her lands. This cry was made in England, Wales, Scotland, and also in France and in Britany. It befel upon a day La Beale Isoud came unto Sir Tramtrist and told him of this tournament. He answered and said, Fair lady, I am but a feeble knight, and but late I had been dead had not your good ladyship been. Now, fair lady, what would ye I should do in this matter? Well ye wot, my lady, that I may not just. Ah Tramtrist, said La Beale Isoud, why will ye not have ado at that tournament? well I wot Sir Palamides shall be there and to do what he may, and therefore Tramtrist I pray you for to be there, for else Sir Palamides is like to win the degree. Madam, said Tramtrist, as for that it may be so, for he is a proved knight, and I am but a young knight and late made, and the first battle that I did it mishapped me to be sore wounded as ye see. But and I wist ye would be my better lady, at that tournament I will be, so that ye will keep my counsel, and let no creature have knowledge that I shall just but yourself, and such as ye will to keep your counsel; my poor person shall I jeopard there for your sake, that peradventure Sir Palamides shall know when that I come. Thereto, said La Beale Isoud, do your best, and as I can, said La Beale Isoud, I shall purvey horse and armour for you at my devise. As ye will so be it, said Sir Tramtrist, I will be at your commandment. So at the day of justs there came Sir Palamides with a black shield, and he overthrew many knights, that all the people had marvel of him. For he put to the worse Sir Gawaine, Gaheris, Agravaine, Bagdemagus, Kay, Dodias le Savage, Sagramore le Desirous, Gumret le Petit, and Griflet le Fise de Dieu. All these the first day Sir Palamides strake down to the earth. And then all manner of knights were adread of Sir Palamides, and many called him the knight with the black shield. So that day Sir Palamides had great worship. Then came king Anguish unto Tramtrist and asked him why he would not just. Sir, said he, I was but late hurt, and as yet I dare not adventure me. Then came there the same squire that was sent from the king's daughter of France unto Sir Tristram. And when he had espied Sir Tristram he fell flat to his feet. All that espied La Beale Isoud, what courtesy the squire made unto Sir Tristram. And therewith all suddenly Sir Tristram ran unto his squire, whose name was Hebes le Renoumes, and prayed him heartily in no wise to tell his name. Sir, said Hebes, I will not discover your name but if ye command me.

CHAP. X.

How Sir Tristram won the degree at a tournament in Ireland, and there made Palamides to bear no harness in a year.

THEN Sir Tristram asked him what he did in those countries. Sir, he said, I came hither with Sir Gawaine for to be made knight, and if it please you, of your hands that I may be made knight. Await upon me as to-morn, secretly, and in the field I shall make you a knight. Then had La Beale Isoud great suspicion unto Tramtrist that he was some man of worship proved, and therewith she comforted herself, and cast more love unto him than she had done tofore. And so on the morn Sir Palamides made him ready to come into the field as he did the first day. And there he smote down the king with the hundred knights, and the king of Scotland. Then had La Beale Isoud ordained and well arrayed Sir Tramtrist in white horse and harness. And right so she let put him out at a privy postern, and so he came into the field as it had been a bright angel. And anon Sir Palamides espied him, and therewith he feutered a spear unto Sir Tramtrist, and he again unto him. And there Sir Tristram smote down Sir Palamides unto the earth. And then there was a great noise of people: some said Sir Palamides had a fall, some said the knight with the black shield had a fall. And wit you well La Beale Isoud was passing glad. And then Sir Gawaine and his fellows nine had marvel what knight it might be that had smitten down Sir Palamides. Then would there none just with Tramtrist, but all that were there forsook him, most and least. Then Sir Tristram made Hebes a knight, and caused him to put himself forth, and did right well that day. So after Sir Hebes held him with Sir Tristram. And when Sir Palamides had received this fall, wit ye well he was sore ashamed: and as privily as he might he withdrew him out of the field. All that espied Sir Tristram, and lightly he rode after Sir Palamides, and overtook him, and bad him turn, for better he would assay him or ever he departed. Then Sir Palamides turned him, and either lashed at other with their swords. But at the first stroke Sir Tristram smote down Palamides, and gave him such a stroke upon the head that he fell to the earth. So then Tristram bad yield him and do his commandment, or else he would slay him. When Sir Palamides beheld his countenance, he dread his buffets so that he granted all his askings. Well said, said Sir Tristram, this shall be your charge. First upon pain of your life that ye forsake my lady La Beale Isoud, and in no manner wise that ye draw not to her. Also this twelvemonth and a day that ye bear none armour nor none harness of war. Now promise me this, or here shalt thou die. Alas, said Palamides, for ever am I ashamed. Then he sware as Sir Tristram had commanded him. Then for despite and anger Sir Palamides cut off his harness and threw them away. And so Sir Tristram turned again to the castle where was La Beale Isoud, and by the way he met with a damsel that asked after Sir Launcelot, that won the Dolorous Gard worshipfully, and this damsel asked Sir Tristram what he was: for it was told her that it was he that smote down Sir Palamides, by whom the ten knights of king Arthur were smitten down. Then the damsel prayed Sir Tristram to tell her what he was, and whether that he were Sir Launcelot du Lake, for she deemed that there was no knight in the world might do such deeds of arms, but if it were Launcelot. Fair damsel, said Sir Tristram, wit ye well that I am not Sir Launcelot, for I was never of such prowess, but in God is all, that he may make me as good a knight as the good knight Sir Launcelot. Now, gentle knight, said she, put up thy visor. And when she beheld his visage she thought she saw never a better man's visage, nor a better faring knight. And then when the damsel knew certainly that he was not Sir Launcelot, then she took her leave and departed from him. And then Sir Tristram rode privily unto the postern where kept him La Beale Isoud, and there she made him good cheer, and thanked God of his good speed. So anon within a while the king and the queen understood that it was Tramtrist that smote down Sir Palamides; then was he much made of more than he was before.

CHAP. XI.

How the queen espied that Sir Tristram had slain her brother Sir Marhaus by his sword, and in what jeopardy he was.

THUS was Sir Tramtrist long there well cherished with the king and the queen, and namely with La Beale Isoud. So upon a day the queen and La Beale Isoud made a bath for Sir Tramtrist, and when he was in his bath the queen and Isoud her daughter roamed up and down in the chamber, and there whiles Gouvernail and Hebes attended upon Tramtrist, and the queen beheld his sword there as it lay upon his bed. And then by unhap the queen drew out his sword and beheld it a long while, and both they thought it a passing fair sword, but within a foot and an half of the point there was a great piece thereof out broken of the edge. And when the queen espied that gap in the sword, she remembered her of a piece of a sword that was found in the brain-pan of Sir Marhaus, the good knight that was her brother. Alas, then said she unto her daughter La Beale Isoud, this is the same traitor knight that slew my brother thine uncle. When Isoud heard her say so she was passing sore abashed, for passing well she loved Sir Tramtrist, and full well she knew the cruelness of her mother the queen. Anon therewithal the queen went unto her own chamber and sought her coffer, and there she took out the piece of the sword that was pulled out of Sir Marhaus' head after that he was dead. And then she ran with that piece of iron to the sword that lay upon the bed. And when she put that piece of steel and iron unto the sword, it was as meet as it might be when it was new broken. And then the queen griped that sword in her hand fiercely, and with all her might she ran straight upon Tramtrist, where he sat in his bath, and there she had rived him through had not Sir Hebes gotten her in his arms, and pulled the sword from her, and else she had thrust him through. Then when she was letted of her evil will, she ran to the king Anguish her husband, and said on her knees, Oh my lord, here have ye in your house that traitor knight that slew my brother and your servant, that noble knight Sir Marhaus. Who is that, said king Anguish, and where is he ? Sir, she said, it is Sir Tramtrist, the same knight that my daughter healed. Alas, said the king, therefore am I right heavy, for he is a full noble knight as ever I saw in field. But I charge you, said the king to the queen, that ye have not ado with that knight, but let me deal with him. Then the king went into the chamber unto Sir Tramtrist, and then was he gone unto his chamber, and the king found him all ready armed to mount upon his horse. When the king saw him all ready armed to go unto horseback, the king said, Nay, Tramtrist, it will not avail to compare thee against me. But thus much I shall do for my worship and for thy love ; in so much as thou art within my court, it were no worship for me to slay thee, therefore upon this condition I will give thee leave to depart from this court in safety, so thou wilt tell me who was thy father, and what is thy name, and if thou slew Sir Marhaus, my brother.

CHAP. XII.

How Sir Tristram departed from the king and La Beale Isoud out of Ireland for to come into Cornwall.

Sir, said Tristram, now I shall tell you all the truth : my father's name is Meliodas, king of Liones, and my mother hight Elizabeth, that was sister unto king Mark of Cornwall ; and my mother died of me in the forest, and because thereof she commanded or she died that when I were christened that they should christen me Tristram, and because I would not be known in this country I turned my name, and let me call Tramtrist ; and for the truage of Cornwall I fought for mine uncle's sake, and for the right of Cornwall that ye had possessed many years. And wit

ye well, said Tristram unto the king, I did the battle for the love of mine uncle king Mark, and for the love of the country of Cornwall, and for to increase mine honour. For that same day that I fought with Sir Marhaus I was made knight, and never or then did I no battle with no knight, and from me he went alive, and left his shield and his sword behind. Truly, said the king, I may not say but ye did as a knight should, and it was your part to do for your quarrel, and to increase your worship as a knight should ; howbeit I may not maintain you in this country with my worship, unless that I should displease my barons, and my wife, and her kin. Sir, said Tristram, I thank you of your good lordship that I have had with you here, and the great goodness my lady your daughter hath shewed me, and therefore, said Sir Tristram, it may so happen that ye shall win more by my life than by my death, for in the parts of England it may happen I may do you service at some season that ye shall be glad that ever ye shewed me your good lordship. With more I promise you as I am true knight, that in all places I shall be my lady your daughter's servant and knight in right and in wrong, and I shall never fail her never to do as much as a knight may do. Also I beseech your good grace that I may take my leave at my lady your daughter, and at all the barons and knights. I will well, said the king. Then Sir Tristram went unto La Beale Isoud and took his leave of her. And then he told her all, what he was, and how he had changed his name because he would not be known, and how a lady told him that he should never be whole till he came into this country where the poison was made :—Where through I was near my death, had not your ladyship been. Oh gentle knight, said La Beale Isoud, full wo am I of thy departing, for I saw never man that I owed so good will to. And therewithal she wept heartily. Madam, said Sir Tristram, ye shall understand that my name is Sir Tristram de Liones, son of king Meliodas and of his queen. And I promise you faithfully that I shall be all the days of my life your knight. Gramercy, said La Beale Isoud, and I promise you there against that I shall not be married this seven years but by your assent, and to whom that ye will I shall be married, him will I have, and he will have me if ye will consent. And then Sir Tristram gave her a ring and she gave him another, and therewith he departed from her, leaving her making great dole and lamentation. And he straight went unto the court among all the barons, and there he took his leave at most and least, and openly he said among them all, Fair lords, now it is so that I must depart. If there be any man here that I have offended unto, or that any man be with me grieved, let complain him here afore me or that ever I depart, and I shall amend it unto my power. And if there be any that will proffer me wrong, or say of me wrong or shame behind my back, say it now or never, and here is my body to make it good, body against body. And all they stood still, there was not one that would say one word, yet were there some knights that were of the queen's blood, and of Sir Marhaus's blood, but they would not meddle with him.

CHAP. XIII.

How Sir Tristram and king Mark hurt each other for the love of a knight's wife.

So Sir Tristram departed, and took the sea, and with good wind he arrived up at Tintagil in Cornwall. And when king Mark was whole in his prosperity there came tidings that Sir Tristram was arrived and whole of his wounds; thereof was king Mark passing glad, and so were all the barons. And when he saw his time, he rode unto his father king Meliodas, and there he had all the cheer that the king and the queen could make him. And then largely king Meliodas and his queen parted of their lands and goods to Sir Tristram. Then by the licence of king Meliodas his father he returned again unto the court of king

Mark, and there he lived in great joy long time, until at the last there befel a jealousy and an unkindness between king Mark and Sir Tristram, for they loved both one lady, and she was an earl's wife, that hight Sir Segwarides. And this lady loved Sir Tristram passing well, and he loved her again, for she was a passing fair lady, and that espied Sir Tristram well. Then king Mark understood that, and was jealous, for king Mark loved her passingly well. So it fell upon a day, this lady sent a dwarf unto Sir Tristram, and bad him say that as he loved her that he would be with her the next day following. Also she charged you that ye come not to her but if ye be well armed, for her lover was called a good knight. Sir Tristram answered to the dwarf, Recommend me unto my lady, and tell her I will not fail but I will be with her the term that she hath set me. And with this answer the dwarf departed. And king Mark espied that the dwarf was with Sir Tristram, upon message from Sir Segwarides's wife; then king Mark sent for the dwarf. And when he was come he made the dwarf by force to tell him all, why and wherefore that he came on message to Sir Tristram. Now, said king Mark, go where thou wilt, and upon pain of death that thou say no word that thou spakest with me. So the dwarf departed from the king. And that same time that was set betwixt Sir Segwarides's wife and Sir Tristram, king Mark armed him, and made him ready, and took two knights of his council with him, and so he rode afore, for to abide by the way, to await upon Sir Tristram. And as Sir Tristram came riding upon his way, with his spear in his hand, king Mark came hurtling upon him with his two knights suddenly. And all three smote him with their spears, and king Mark hurt Sir Tristram on the breast right sore; and then Sir Tristram feutered his spear, and smote his uncle king Mark such a stroke that he rashed him to the earth, and bruised him that he lay still in a swoon, and it was long or he might move himself; and then he ran to the one knight, and oft to the other, and smote them to the cold earth, that they lay still. And therewithal Sir Tristram rode forth sore wounded to the lady, and found her abiding him at a postern.

CHAP. XIV.
How Sir Tristram came to the lady, and how her husband fought with Sir Tristram.

AND there she welcomed him fair, and so she let put up his horse in the best wise, and then she unarmed him: and so they supped lightly, and within a while there came one that warned her that her lord was near hand, within a bow draft. So she made Sir Tristram to arise, and so he armed him, and took his horse, and so departed. By then was come Sir Segwarides, and when he found that there had been a knight, Ah, false traitress, then he said, why hast thou betrayed me? And therewithal he swung out a sword, and said, But if thou tell me who hath been here, here thou shalt die. Ah, my lord, mercy, said the lady, and held up her hands, saying, Slay me not, and I shall tell you all who hath been here. Tell anon, said Sir Segwarides, to me all the truth. Anon for dread she said, Here was Sir Tristram with me, and by the way as he came to me ward he was sore wounded. Ah, thou false traitress, said Sir Segwarides, where is he become? Sir, she said, he is armed, and departed on horseback, not yet hence half-a-mile. Ye say well, said Segwarides. Then he armed him lightly, and gat his horse, and rode after Sir Tristram, that rode straightway unto Tintagil. And within a while he overtook Sir Tristram, and then he bad him turn, false traitor knight, and Sir Tristram anon turned him against him. And therewithal Segwarides smote Sir Tristram with a spear that it all to-brast; and then he swung out his sword, and smote fast at Sir Tristram. Sir knight, said Sir Tristram, I counsel you that ye smite no more, howbeit, for the wrongs that I have done you,

I will forbear you as long as I may. Nay, said Segwarides, that shall not be, for either thou shalt die or I. Then Sir Tristram drew out his sword, and hurtled his horse unto him fiercely, and through the waist of the body he smote Sir Segwarides that he fell to the earth in a swoon. And so Sir Tristram departed and left him there, and so he rode unto Tintagil, and took his lodging secretly, for he would not be known that he was hurt. Also, Sir Segwarides's men rode after their master, whom they found lying in the field sore wounded, and brought him home on his shield, and there he lay long or that he were whole, but at the last he recovered. Also king Mark would not be aknown of, that Sir Tristram and he had met that time. And as for Sir Tristram, he wist not that it had been king Mark that had met with him. And so the king's assistance came to Sir Tristram, to comfort him as he lay sick in his bed. But as long as king Mark lived he loved never Sir Tristram after that: though there was fair speech, love was there none. And thus it passed many weeks and days, and all was forgiven and forgotten. For Sir Segwarides durst not have ado with Sir Tristram, because of his noble prowess, and also because he was nephew unto king Mark, therefore he let it over slip, for he that hath a privy hurt is loth to have a shame outward.

CHAP. XV.
How Sir Bleoberis demanded the fairest lady in king Mark's court, whom he took away, and how he was fought with.

THEN it befel upon a day, that the good knight Bleoberis de Ganis, brother to Blamore de Ganis, and nigh cousin unto the good knight Sir Launcelot du Lake,—this Bleoberis came unto the court of king Mark, and there he asked of king Mark a boon, to give him what gift he would ask in his court. When the king heard him ask so, he marvelled of his asking, but because he was a knight of the Round Table, and of a great renown, king Mark granted him his whole asking. Then, said Sir Bleoberis, I will have the fairest lady in your court that me list to choose. I may not say nay, said king Mark; now choose at your adventure. And so Sir Bleoberis did chose Sir Segwarides's wife, and took her by the hand, and so went his way with her, and so he took his horse and let set her behind his squire, and rode upon his way. When Sir Segwarides heard tell that his lady was gone with a knight of king Arthur's court, then anon he armed him, and rode after that knight for to rescue his lady. So when Bleoberis was gone with this lady, king Mark and all the court was wroth that she was away. Then were there certain ladies that knew that there was great love between Sir Tristram and her, and also that lady loved Sir Tristram above all other knights. Then there was one lady that rebuked Sir Tristram in the horriblest wise, and called him coward knight, that he would for shame of his knighthood see a lady so shamefully taken away from his uncle's court. But Sir Tristram answered her thus: Fair lady, it is not my part to have ado in such matters, while her lord and husband is present here. And if it had been that her lord had not been here in this court, then for the worship of this court peradventure I would have been her champion, and if so be Sir Segwarides speed not well, it may happen that I will speak with that good knight or ever he pass from this country. Then within awhile came one of Sir Segwarides's squires, and told in the court that Sir Segwarides was beaten sore and wounded to the point of death: as he would have rescued his lady Sir Bleoberis overthrew him, and sore hath wounded him. Then was king Mark heavy thereof, and all the court. When Sir Tristram heard of this he was ashamed and sore grieved. And then was he soon armed and on horseback, and Gouvernail his servant bare his shield and spear. And so as Sir Tristram rode fast he met with Sir Andret his cousin, that by the commandment of king Mark was sent to bring forth, and ever it lay

in his power two knights of king Arthur's court, that rode by the country to seek their adventures. When Sir Tristram saw Sir Andret he asked him what tidings. Truly, said Sir Andret, there was never worse with me, for here by the commandment of king Mark I was sent to fetch two knights of king Arthur's court, and that one beat me and wounded me, and set nought by my message. Fair cousin, said Sir Tristram, ride on your way, and if I may meet them it may happen I shall revenge you. So Sir Andret rode into Cornwall, and Sir Tristram rode after the two knights, the which one hight Sagramore le Desirous, and that other hight Dodinas le Savage.

CHAP. XVI.
How Sir Tristram fought with two knights of the Round Table.

THEN within awhile Sir Tristram saw them afore him two likely knights. Sir, said Gouvernail unto his master, Sir, I would counsel you not to have ado with them, for they be two proved knights of Arthur's court. As for that, said Sir Tristram, have ye no doubt but I will have ado with them to encrease my worship, for it is many day sithen I did any deeds of arms. Do as ye list, said Gouvernail. And therewithal anon Sir Tristram asked them from whence they came, and whither they would, and what they did in those marches. Sir Sagramore looked upon Sir Tristram, and had scorn of his words, and asked him again, Fair knight, be ye a knight of Cornwall? Whereby ask ye it? said Sir Tristram. For it is seldom seen, said Sir Sagramore, that ye Cornish knights be valiant men of arms: for within these two hours there met us, one of you Cornish knights, and great words he spake, and anon with little might he was laid to the earth. And, as I trow, said Sir Sagramore, ye shall have the same handsel that he had. Fair lords, said Sir Tristram, it may so happen that I may better withstand than he did, and whether ye will or nill I will have ado with you, because he was my cousin that ye beat. And therefore here do your best; and wit ye well but if ye quit you the better here upon this ground one knight of Cornwall shall beat you both. When Sir Dodinas le Savage heard him say so, he gat a spear in his hand, and said, Sir knight, keep well thyself. And then they departed, and came together as it had been thunder. And Sir Dodinas' spear brast in sunder, but Sir Tristram smote him with a more might, that he smote him clean over the horse croup, that nigh he had broken his neck. When Sir Sagramore saw his fellow have such a fall he marvelled what knight he might be, and he dressed his spear with all his might, and Sir Tristram against him, and they came together as the thunder, and there Sir Tristram smote Sir Sagramore a strong buffet, that he bare his horse and him to the earth, and in the falling he brake his thigh. When this was done Sir Tristram asked them, Fair knights, will ye any more? Be there no bigger knights in the court of king Arthur? It is to you shame to say of us knights of Cornwall dishonour, for it may happen a Cornish knight may match you. That is truth, said Sir Sagramore, that have we well proved; but I require thee, said Sir Sagramore, tell us your right name, by the faith and truth that ye owe to the high order of knighthood. Ye charge me with a great thing, said Sir Tristram, and sithen ye list to wit it, ye shall know and understand that my name is Sir Tristram de Liones, king Meliodas' son, and nephew unto king Mark. Then were they two knights fain that they had met with Sir Tristram, and so they prayed him to abide in their fellowship. Nay, said Sir Tristram, for I must have ado with one of your fellows, his name is Sir Bleoberis de Ganis. God speed you well, said Sir Sagramore and Dodinas. Sir Tristram departed, and rode onward on his way, and then was he ware before him in a valley where rode Sir Bleoberis with Sir Segwarides's lady, that rode behind his squire upon a palfrey.

CHAP. XVII.

How Sir Tristram fought with Sir Bleoberis for a lady, and how the lady was put to choice to whom she would go.

THEN Sir Tristram rode more than a pace until that he had overtaken him. Then spake Sir Tristram: Abide, he said, knight of Arthur's court, bring again that lady, or deliver her to me. I will do neither, said Sir Bleoberis, for I dread no Cornish knight so sore that me list to deliver her. Why, said Sir Tristram, may not a Cornish knight do as well as another knight? This same day two knights of your court, within this three mile met with me, and or ever we departed they found a Cornish knight good enough for them both. What were their names? said Bleoberis. They told me, said Sir Tristram, that the one of them hight Sir Sagramore le Desirous, and the other hight Dodinas le Savage. Ah, said Sir Bleoberis, have ye met with them? Truly they were two good knights, and men of great worship, and if ye have beat them both ye must needs be a good knight: but if it so be that ye have beat them both, yet shall ye not fear me, but ye shall beat me or ever ye have this lady. Then defend you, said Sir Tristram. So they departed and came together like thunder, and either bare other down, horse and all, to the earth. Then they avoided their horses and lashed together eagerly with swords, and mightily, now tracing and traversing on the right hand and on the left hand more than two hours. And sometimes they rushed together with such a might that they lay both groveling on the ground. Then Sir Bleoberis de Ganis start aback, and said thus: Now, gentle good knight, a while hold your hands and let us speak together. Say what ye will, said Sir Tristram, and I will answer you. Sir, said Bleoberis, I would wit of whence ye be, and of whom ye be come, and what is your name? Truly, said Sir Tristram, I fear not to tell you my name: wit ye well I am king Meliodas' son, and my mother is king Mark's sister, and my name is Sir Tristram de Liones, and king Mark is mine uncle. Truly, said Bleoberis, I am right glad of you, for ye are he that slew Marhaus, knight, hand for hand in an island for the truage of Cornwall; also ye overcame Sir Palamides the good knight at a tournament in an island, where ye beat Sir Gawaine and his nine fellows. Wit ye well, said Sir Tristram, that I am the same knight. Now I have told you my name, tell me yours with good will. Wit ye well that my name is Sir Bleoberis de Ganis, and my brother hight Sir Blamor de Ganis, that is called a good knight, and we be sister's children unto my lord Sir Launcelot du Lake, that we call one of the best knights of the world. That is truth, said Sir Tristram; Sir Launcelot is called peerless of courtesy and of knighthood; and for his sake, said Sir Tristram, I will not with my good will fight no more with you, for the great love I have to Sir Launcelot du Lake. In good faith, said Bleoberis, as for me, I will be loth to fight with you. But since ye follow me here to have this lady, I shall proffer you kindness, courtesy, and gentleness, right here upon this ground. This lady shall be betwixt us both, and to whom that she will go, let him have her in peace. I will well, said Tristram, for, as I deem, she will leave you and come to me. Ye shall prove it anon, said Bleoberis.

CHAP. XVIII.

How the lady forsook Sir Tristram and abode with Sir Bleoberis, and how she desired to go to her husband.

So when she was set betwixt them both, she said these words unto Sir Tristram: Wit ye well, Sir Tristram de Liones, that but late thou was the man in the world that I most loved and trusted, and I wend thou haddest loved me again above all ladies. But when thou sawest this knight lead me away, thou madest no cheer to rescue me, but suffered my lord Sir Segwarides to ride after me, but until that time I

wend thou haddest loved me, and therefore now I will leave thee, and never love thee more. And therewithal she went unto Sir Bleoberis. When Sir Tristram saw her do so, he was wonderly wroth with that lady, and ashamed to come to the court. Sir Tristram, said Sir Bleoberis, ye are in the default, for I hear, by this lady's words, she, before this day, trusted you above all earthly knights, and, as she saith, ye have deceived her; therefore, wit ye well, there may no man hold that will away, and rather than ye should be heartily displeased with me, I would ye had her and she would abide with you. Nay, said the lady, I will never go with him, for he that I loved most I wend he had loved me. And therefore, Sir Tristram, she said, ride as thou came, for though thou haddest overcome this knight, as ye were likely, with thee never would I have gone. And I shall pray this knight so fair of his knighthood, that or ever he pass this country he will lead me to the abbey where my lord Sir Segwarides lieth. Truly, said Bleoberis, I let you wit, good knight Sir Tristram, because king Mark gave me the choice of a gift in this court, and so this lady liked me best, notwithstanding she is wedded and hath a lord, and I have fulfilled my quest, she shall be sent unto her husband again, and in especial most for your sake Sir Tristram: and if she would go with you I would ye had her. I thank you, said Sir Tristram, but for her love I shall be ware what manner of lady I shall love or trust. For had her lord Sir Segwarides been away from the court I should have been the first that should have followed you, but since ye have refused me, as I am a true knight I shall her know passingly well that I shall love or trust. And so they took their leave one from the other and departed. And so Sir Tristram rode unto Tintagil, and Sir Bleoberis rode unto the abbey where Sir Segwarides lay sore wounded, and there he delivered his lady and departed as a noble knight. And when Sir Segwarides saw his lady he was greatly comforted. And then she told him that

Sir Tristram had done great battle with Sir Bleoberis, and caused him to bring her again. These words pleased Sir Segwarides right well, that Sir Tristram would do so much; and so that lady told all the battle unto king Mark betwixt Sir Tristram and Sir Bleoberis.

CHAP. XIX.

How King Mark sent Sir Tristram for La Beale Isoud toward Ireland, and how by fortune he arrived into England.

THEN when this was done king Mark cast always in his heart how he might destroy Sir Tristram. And then he imagined in himself to send Sir Tristram into Ireland for La Beale Isoud. For Sir Tristram had so praised her beauty and her goodness that king Mark said he would wed her, whereupon he prayed Sir Tristram to take his way into Ireland for him on message. And all this was done to the intent to slay Sir Tristram. Notwithstanding, Sir Tristram would not refuse the message for no danger nor peril that might fall for the pleasure of his uncle, but to go he made him ready in the most goodliest wise that might be devised. For Sir Tristram took with him the most goodliest knights that he might find in the court, and they were arrayed after the guise that was then used in the goodliest manner. So Sir Tristram departed and took the sea with all his fellowship. And anon as he was in the broad sea, a tempest took him and his fellowship and drove them back into the coast of England, and there they arrived fast by Camelot, and full fain they were to take the land. And when they were landed Sir Tristram set up his pavilion upon the land of Camelot, and there he let hang his shield upon the pavilion. And that day came two knights of king Arthur's, that one was Sir Ector de Maris, and Sir Morganor. And they touched the shield and bad him come out of the pavilion for to just, and he would just. Ye shall be answered, said Sir Tristram, and ye will tarry a little while. So he made him ready, and first he smote down Sir Ector de Maris, and after he smote down Sir Morganor, all with one spear, and sore bruised them. And when they lay upon the earth they asked Sir Tristram what he was, and of what country he was knight. Fair lords, said Sir Tristram, wit ye well that I am of Cornwall. Alas, said Sir Ector, now am I ashamed that ever any Cornish knight should overcome me. And then for despite Sir Ector put off his armour from him, and went on foot, and would not ride.

CHAP. XX.

How king Anguish of Ireland was summoned to come unto king Arthur's court for treason.

THEN it fell that Sir Bleoberis and Sir Blamor de Ganis that were brethren, they had summoned the king Anguish of Ireland to come to Arthur's court, upon pain of forfeiture of king Arthur's good grace. And if the king of Ireland came not in at the day assigned and set, the king should lose his lands. So by it happened that at the day assigned, king Arthur neither Sir Launcelot might not be there for to give the judgment, for king Arthur was with Sir Launcelot at the castle Joyous Gard. And so king Arthur assigned king Carados and the king of Scots to be there that day as judges. So when the kings were at Camelot king Anguish of Ireland was come to know his accusers. Then was there Blamor de Ganis, and appealed the king of Ireland of treason, that he had slain a cousin of his in his court in Ireland by treason. The king was sore abashed of his accusation, for why? he was come at the summoning of king Arthur, and or that he came at Camelot he wist not wherefore he was sent after. And when the king heard Sir Blamor say his will, he understood full well there was none other remedy but to answer him knightly. For the custom was such in those days, that and any man were appealed of any treason or murder, he should fight body for body, or else to find another knight for him. And all manner of murderers in those days were called treason. So when king Anguish understood his accusing he was passing heavy, for he knew Sir Blamor de Ganis that he was a noble knight, and of noble knights come. Then the king of Ireland was simply purveyed of his answer, therefore the judges gave him respite by the third day to give his answer. So the ·king departed unto his lodging. The mean while there came a lady by Sir Tristram's pavilion making great dole. What aileth you, said Sir Tristram, that ye make such dole? Ah, fair knight, said the lady, I am ashamed unless that some good knight help me, for a great lady of worship sent by me a fair child and a rich unto Sir Launcelot du Lake, and hereby there met with me a knight and threw me down from my palfrey, and took away the child from me. Well my lady, said Sir Tristram, and for my lord Sir Launcelot's sake I shall get you that child again, or else I shall be beaten for it. And so Sir Tristram took his horse, and asked the lady which way the knight rode. And then she told him. And he rode after him, and within a mile he overtook that knight.· And then Sir Tristram bad him turn and give again the child.

CHAP. XXI.

How Sir Tristram rescued a child from a knight, and how Gouvernail told him of king Anguish.

THE knight turned his horse, and he made him ready for to fight. And then Sir Tristram smote him with a sword such a buffet that he tumbled to the earth. And then he yielded him unto Sir Tristram. Then come thy way, said Sir Tristram, and bring the child to the lady again. So he took his horse meekly and rode with Sir Tristram, and then by the way Sir Tristram asked him his name. Then he said, My name is Breuse Saunce Pité. So when he had delivered that child to the lady he said, Sir, as in this the child is well remedied. Then Sir Tristram let him go again, that sore repented him after, for he was

a great foe unto many good knights of king Arthur's court. Then when Sir Tristram was in his pavilion, Gouvernail his man came and told him how that king Anguish of Ireland was come thither, and he was put in great distress, and there Gouvernail told Sir Tristram how king Anguish was summoned and appealed of murder. Truly, said Sir Tristram, these be the best tidings that ever came to me this seven year, for now shall the king of Ireland have need of my help, for I dare say there is no knight in this country that is not of Arthur's court dare do battle with Sir Blamor de Ganis, and for to win the love of the king of Ireland I will take the battle upon me, and therefore Gouvernail bring me, I charge thee, to the king. Then Gouvernail went unto king Anguish of Ireland and saluted him fair. The king welcomed him and asked him what he would. Sir, said Gouvernail, here is a knight near hand that desireth to speak with you: he bad me say he would do you service. What knight is he, said the king. Sir, he said, it is Sir Tristram de Liones, that for your good grace ye shewed him in your lands will reward you in these countries. Come on fellow, said the king, with me anon, and shew me unto Sir Tristram. So the king took a little hackney and but few fellowship with him until he came unto Sir Tristram's pavilion. And when Sir Tristram saw the king, he ran unto him and would have holden his stirrup. But the king lept from his horse lightly, and either halsed other in arms. My gracious lord, said Sir Tristram, gramercy of your great goodnesses shewed unto me in your marches and lands: and at that time I promised you to do my service and ever it lay in my power. And gentle knight, said the king unto Sir Tristram, now have I great need of you; never had I so great need of no knight's help. How so, my good lord? said sir Tristram. I shall tell you, said the king. I am summoned and appealed from my country for the death of a knight that was kin unto the good knight Sir Launcelot, wherefore Sir Blamor de Ganis, brother to Sir Bleoberis, hath appealed me to fight with him, other to find a knight in my stead. And well I wot, said the king, these that are come of king Ban's blood, as Sir Launcelot and these other, are passing good knights, and hard men for to win in battle as any that I know now living. Sir, said Sir Tristram, for the good lordship ye shewed me in Ireland, and for my lady your daughter's sake, La Beale Isoud, I will take the battle for you upon this condition that ye shall grant me two things: that one is, that ye shall swear to me that ye are in the right, that ye were never consenting to the knight's death; Sir, then, said Sir Tristram, when that I have done this battle, if God give me grace that I speed, that ye shall give me a reward, what thing reasonable that I will ask of you. Truly, said the king, ye shall have whatsoever ye will ask. It is well said, said Sir Tristram.

CHAP. XXII.

How Sir Tristram fought for Sir Anguish and overcame his adversary, and how his adversary would never yield him.

Now make your answer that your champion is ready, for I shall die in your quarrel rather than to be recreant. I have no doubt of you, said the king, that and ye should have ado with Sir Launcelot du Lake. Sir, said Sir Tristram, as for Sir Launcelot, he is called the noblest knight of the world, and wit ye well that the knights of his blood are noble men and dread shame; and as for Sir Bleoberis, brother to Sir Blamor, I have done battle with him, therefore upon my head it is no shame to call him a good knight. It is noised, said the king, that Blamor is the hardier knight. Sir, as for that, let him be, he shall never be refused, and as he were the best knight that now beareth shield or spear. So king Anguish departed unto king Carados and the kings that were that time as judges, and told them that he had found his champion ready.

And then by the commandments of the kings Sir Blamor de Ganis and Sir Tristram were sent for, to hear the charge. And when they were come before the judges, there were many kings and knights beheld Sir Tristram, and much speech they had of him because he slew Sir Marhaus the good knight, and because he forjusted Sir Palamides the good knight. So when they had taken their charge they withdrew them for to make them ready to do battle. Then said Sir Bleoberis to his brother Sir Blamor, Fair dear brother, remember of what kin we be come of, and what a man is Sir Launcelot du Lake, neither further nor nearer but brothers' children, and there was never none of our kin that ever was shamed in battle, and rather suffer death, brother, than to be shamed. Brother, said Blamor, have ye no doubt of me, for I shall never shame none of my blood, how be it I am sure that yonder knight is called a passing good knight, as of his time one of the world, yet shall I never yield me, nor say the loth word: well may he happen to smite me down with his great might of chivalry, but rather shall he slay me than I shall yield me as recreant. God speed you well, said Bleoberis, for ye shall find him the mightiest knight that ever ye had ado withall, for I know him, for I have had ado with him. God me speed, said Blamor de Ganis. And therewith he took his horse at the one end of the lists, and Sir Tristram at the other end of the lists, and so they feutred their spears and came together as it had been thunder, and there Sir Tristram through great might smote down Sir Blamor and his horse to the earth. Then anon Sir Blamor avoided his horse, and pulled out his sword and threw his shield afore him, and bad Sir Tristram alight; for though an horse hath failed me, I trust the earth will not fail me. And then Sir Tristram alight and dressed him unto battle, and there they lashed together strongly as racing and tracing, foining and dashing many sad strokes, that the kings and knights had great wonder that they might stand, for ever they fought like wood men, so that there were never knights seen fight more fiercely than they did, for Sir Blamor was so hasty that he would have no rest, that all men wondered that they had breath to stand on their feet; and all the place was bloody that they fought in. And at the last, Sir Tristram smote Sir Blamor such a buffet upon the helm that he there fell down upon his side, and Sir Tristram stood and beheld him.

CHAP. XXIII.

How Sir Blamor desired Tristram to slay him, and how Sir Tristram spared him, and how they took appointment.

THEN when Sir Blamor might speak, he said thus: Sir Tristram de Liones, I require thee, as thou art a noble knight, and the best knight that ever I found, that thou wilt slay me out, for I would not live to be made lord of all the earth, for I had lever die with worship than live with shame; and needs, Sir Tristram, thou must slay me, or else thou shalt never win the field, for I will never say the loth word. And therefore if thou dare slay me, slay me I require thee. When Sir Tristram heard him say so knightly, he wist not what to do with him; he remembering him of both parties; of what blood he was come, and for Sir Launcelot's sake he would be full loth to slay him, and in the other party in no wise he might not choose but he must make him to say the loth word, or else to slay him. Then Sir Tristram start aback, and went to the kings that were judges, and there he kneeled down before them, and besought them for their worships, and for king Arthur's, and Sir Launcelot's sake, that they would take this matter in their hands. For my fair lords, said Sir Tristram, it were shame and pity that this noble knight that yonder lieth should be slain, for ye hear well shamed will he not be, and I pray to God that he never be slain nor shamed for me. And as for the king

for whom I fight for, I shall require him, as I am his true champion and true knight in this field, that he will have mercy upon this good knight. Truly, said king Anguish to Sir Tristram, I will for your sake be ruled as ye will have me. For I know you for my true knight. And therefore I will heartily pray the kings that be here as judges to take it in their hands. And the kings that were judges called Sir Bleoberis to them, and asked him his advice. My lords, said Bleoberis, though my brother be beaten, and hath the worse through might of arms, I dare say, though Sir Tristram hath beaten his body he hath not beaten his heart, and I thank God, he is not shamed this day. And rather than he should be shamed I require you, said Bleoberis, let Sir Tristram slay him out. It shall not be so, said the kings, for his part adversary, both the king and the champion, have pity of Sir Blamor's knighthood. My lords, said Bleoberis, I will right well as ye will.

Then the kings called the king of Ireland, and found him good and treatable. And then, by all their advices, Sir Tristram and Sir Bleoberis took up Sir Blamor, and the two brethren were accorded with king Anguish, and kissed and made friends for ever. And then Sir Blamor and Sir Tristram kissed together, and there they made their oaths that they would never none of them two brethren fight with Sir Tristram, and Sir Tristram made the same oath. And for that gentle battle all the blood of Sir Launcelot loved Sir Tristram for ever.

Then king Anguish and Sir Tristram took their leave, and sailed into Ireland with great nobleness and joy. So when they were in Ireland the king let make it known throughout all the land, how and in what manner Sir Tristram had done for him. Then the queen and all that there were made the most of him that they might. But the joy that La Beale Isoud made of Sir Tristram there might no tongue tell, for of men earthly she loved him most.

CHAP. XXIV.

How Sir Tristram demanded La Beale Isoud for king Mark, and how Sir Tristram and Isoud drank the love drink.

THEN upon a day king Anguish asked Sir Tristram why he asked not his boon, for whatsoever he had promised him he should have it without fail. Sir, said Sir Tristram, now is it time, this is all that I will desire, that ye will give me La Beale Isoud your daughter, not for myself, but for mine uncle king Mark, that shall have her to wife, for so have I promised him. Alas, said the king, I had lever than all the land that I have ye would wed her yourself. Sir, and I did, then were I shamed for ever in this world, and false of my promise. Therefore, said Sir Tristram, I pray you hold your promise that ye promised me, for this is my desire, that ye will give me La Beale Isoud to go with me into Cornwall, for to be wedded to king Mark mine uncle. As for that, said king Anguish, ye shall have her with you, to do with her what it please you, that is for to say if that ye list to wed her yourself, that is to me levest: and if ye will give her unto king Mark your uncle, that is in your choice.

So to make a short conclusion, La Beale Isoud was made ready to go with Sir Tristram, and dame Bragwaine went with her for her chief gentlewoman, with many other. Then the queen, Isoud's mother, gave to her and dame Bragwaine, her daughter's gentlewoman, and unto Gouvernail, a drink, and charged them that what day king Mark should wed, that same day they should give him that drink, so that king Mark should drink to La Beale Isoud; and then, said the queen, I undertake either shall love other the days of their life. So this drink was given unto dame Bragwaine and unto Gouvernail. And then anon Sir Tristram took the sea and La Beale Isoud; and when they were in their cabin, it happed so that

they were thirsty, and they saw a little flacket of gold stand by them, and it seemed by the colour and the taste that it was noble wine. Then Sir Tristram took the flacket in his hand, and said, Madam Isoud, here is the best drink that ever ye drank, that dame Bragwaine your maiden, and Gouvernail my servant, have kept for themselves. Then they laughed and made good cheer, and either drank to other freely, and they thought never drink that ever they drank to other was so sweet nor so good. But by that their drink was in their bodies, they loved either other so well that never their love departed for weal neither for woe. And thus it happed the love first betwixt Sir Tristram and La Beale Isoud, the which love never departed the days of their life. So then they sailed till by fortune they came nigh a castle that hight Pluere, and thereby arrived for to repose them, weening to them to have had good harbourage. But anon as Sir Tristram was within the castle they were taken prisoners, for the custom of the castle was such, who that rode by that castle, and brought any lady, he must needs fight with the lord, that hight Breunor. And if it were so that Breunor wan the field, then the knight stranger and his lady he put to death, what that ever they were; and if it were so that the strange knight wan the field of Sir Breunor, then should he die and his lady both. This custom was used many winters, for it was called the Castle Pluere, that is to say the weeping castle.

CHAP. XXV.

How Sir Tristram and Isoud were in prison, and how he fought for her beauty, and smote off another lady's head.

THUS as Sir Tristram and La Beale Isoud were in prison, it happed a knight and a lady came unto them where they were, to cheer them. I have marvel, said Tristram unto the knight and the lady, what is the cause the lord of this castle holdeth us in prison: it was never the custom of no place of worship that ever I came in, that when a knight and a lady asked harbour, and they to receive them, and after to destroy them that be his guests. Sir, said the knight, this is the old custom of this castle, that when a knight cometh here, he must needs fight with our lord, and he that is the weaker must lose his head. And when that is done, if his lady that he bringeth be fouler than our lord's wife, she must lose her head: and if she be fairer proved than is our lady, then shall the lady of this castle lose her head. Now, said Sir Tristram, this is a foul custom and a shameful. But one advantage have I, said Sir Tristram, I have a lady is fair enough, fairer saw I never in all my life days, and I doubt not for lack of beauty she shall not lose her head, and rather than I should lose my head I will fight for it on a fair field. Wherefore, sir knight, I pray you tell your lord that I will be ready as to-morn with my lady, and myself to battle, if it be so I may have my horse and mine armour. Sir, said that knight, I undertake that your desire shall be sped right well.

And then he said, Take your rest, and look that ye be up by times to make you ready and your lady, for ye shall want no thing that you behoveth. And therewith he departed, and on the morn betimes that same knight came to Sir Tristram and fetched him out and his lady, and brought him horse and armour that was his own, and bad him make him ready to the field, for all the estates and commons of that lordship were there ready to behold that battle and judgment. Then came Sir Breunor, the lord of that castle, with his lady in his hand muffled, and asked Sir Tristram where was his lady:—For and thy lady be fairer than mine, with thy sword smite off my lady's head, and if my lady be fairer than thine, with my sword I must strike off her head. And if I may win thee, yet shall thy lady be mine, and thou shalt lose thy head.

Sir, said Tristram, this is a foul custom and horrible; and rather than my lady should lose her head, yet had I lever lose my head. Nay, nay, said Sir Breunor, the ladies shall be first shewed together, and the one shall have her judgment. Nay, I will not so, said Sir Tristram, for here is none that will give righteous judgment. But I doubt not, said Sir Tristram, my lady is fairer than thine, and that will I prove and make good with my hand. And whosoever he be that will say the contrary I will prove it on his head. And therewith Sir Tristram shewed La Beale Isoud, and turned her thrice about with his naked sword in his hand. And when Sir Breunor saw that, he did the same wise turn his lady. But when Sir Breunor beheld La Beale Isoud, him thought he never saw a fairer lady, and then he dread his lady's head should be off. And so all the people that were there present gave judgment that La Beale Isoud was the fairer lady, and the better made. How now, said Sir Tristram, me seemeth it were pity that my lady should lose her head, but because that thou and she of long time have used this wicked custom, and by you both there have many good knights and ladies been destroyed, for that cause it were no loss to destroy you both. Truly, said Sir Breunor, for to say the sooth, thy lady is fairer than mine, and that me sore repenteth. And so I hear the people privily say; for of all women I saw none so fair, and therefore if thou wilt slay my lady, I doubt not but I shall slay thee and have thy lady. Thou shalt win her, said Sir Tristram, as dear as ever knight won lady, and because of thine own judgment, as thou wouldest have done to my lady if that she had been fouler, and because of the evil custom, give me thy lady, said Tristram. And therewithall Sir Tristram strode unto him and took his lady from him, and with an awk stroke he smote off her head clean. Well knight, said Sir Breunor, now hast thou done me a despite.

CHAP. XXVI.

*How Sir Tristram fought with Sir Breu-
nor, and at the last smote off his
head.*

Now take thy horse: since I am lady-
less I will win thy lady and I may.
Then they took their horses and came
together as it had been the thunder; and
Sir Tristram smote Sir Breunor clean
from his horse, and lightly he rose up;
and as Sir Tristram came again by him
he thrust his horse throughout both the
shoulders, that his horse hurled here and
there and fell dead to the ground. And
ever Sir Breunor ran after to have slain
Sir Tristram, but Sir Tristram was light
and nimble and voided his horse lightly.
And or ever Sir Tristram might dress
his shield and his sword, the other gave
him three or four sad strokes. Then
they rushed together like two boars,
tracing and traversing mightily and
wisely as two noble knights. For this
Sir Breunor was a proved knight, and
had been, or then, the death of many
good knights, that it was pity that he
had so long endured. Thus they fought,
hurling here and there nigh two hours,
and either were wounded sore. Then
at the last Sir Breunor rushed upon Sir
Tristram, and took him in his arms, for
he trusted much in his strength. Then
was Sir Tristram called the strongest
and the highest knight of the world, for
he was called bigger than Sir Launcelot,
but Sir Launcelot was better breathed.
So anon Sir Tristram thrust Sir Breunor
down groveling, and then he unlaced
his helm and strake off his head. And
then all they that longed to the castle
came to him and did him homage and
fealty, praying him that he would abide
there still a little while to fordo that
foul custom. Sir Tristram granted
thereto. The meanwhile one of the
knights of the castle rode unto Sir
Galahad, the haut prince, the which
was Sir Breunor's son, which was a
noble knight, and told him what misadventure his father had and his
mother.

CHAP. XXVII.

*How Sir Galahad fought with Sir Tris-
tram, and how Sir Tristram yielded
him and promised to fellowship with
Launcelot.*

Then came Sir Galahad and the king
with the hundred knights with him, and
this Sir Galahad proffered to fight with
Sir Tristram hand for hand. And so
they made them ready to go unto battle
on horseback with great courage. Then
Sir Galahad and Sir Tristram met together so hard that either bare other
down, horse and all, to the earth. And
then they avoided their horses as noble
knights, and dressed their shields and
drew their swords with ire and ran-
cour, and they lashed together many
sad strokes, and one while striking,
another while foining, tracing and traversing as noble knights, thus they
fought long, near half a day, and either
were sore wounded. At the last Sir
Tristram waxed light and big, and
doubled his strokes, and drove Sir Galahad aback on the one side and on the
other, so that he was like to have been
slain. With that came the king with
the hundred knights, and all that fellowship went fiercely upon Sir Tristram.
When Sir Tristram saw them coming
upon him, then he wist well he might
not endure. Then as a wise knight
of war, he said to Sir Galahad the
haut prince, Sir, ye shew to me no
knighthood, for to suffer all your men
to have ado with me all at once, and as
me seemeth ye be a noble knight of
your hands, it is a great shame to you.
Truly, said Sir Galahad, there is none
other way but thou must yield thee to
me, other else to die, said Sir Galahad
to Sir Tristram. I will rather yield me
to you than die, for that is more for
the might of your men than for the
might of your hands. And therewith
Sir Tristram took his own sword by
the point, and put the pommel in the
hand of Sir Galahad. Therewithall
came the king with the hundred
knights, and hard began to assail Sir
Tristram. Let be, said Sir Galahad, be

ye not so hardy to touch him, for I have given this knight his life. That is your shame, said the king with the hundred knights; hath he not slain your father and your mother? As for that, said Sir Galahad, I may not blame him greatly, for my father had him in prison, and enforced him to do battle with him, and my father had such a custom, that was a shameful custom, that what knight came there to ask harbour, his lady must needs die but if she were fairer than my mother, and if my father overcame that knight he must needs die. This was a shameful custom and usage, a knight for his harbour asking to have such harbourage. And for this custom I would never draw about him. Truly, said the king, this was a shameful custom. Yea, said Sir Galahad, so seemed me, and me seemed it had been great pity that this knight should have been slain, for I dare say he is the noblest man that beareth life, but if it were Sir Launcelot du Lake. Now fair knight, said Sir Galahad, I require thee tell me thy name, and of whence thou art, and whither thou wilt. Sir, he said, my name is Sir Tristram de Liones, and from king Mark of Cornwall I was sent on message unto king Anguish of Ireland, for to fetch his daughter to be his wife, and here she is ready to go with me into Cornwall, and her name is La Beale Isoud. And Sir Tristram, said Sir Galahad the haut prince, well be ye found in these marches, and so ye will promise me to go unto Sir Launcelot du Lake and accompany with him, ye shall go where ye will, and your fair lady with you. And I shall promise you never in all my days shall such customs be used in this castle as have been used. Sir, said Sir Tristram, now I let you wit I wend ye had been Sir Launcelot du Lake when I saw you first, and, therefore I dread you the more; and Sir, I promise you, said Sir Tristram, as soon as I may I will see Sir Launcelot and enfellowship me with him, for of all the knights of the world I most desire his fellowship.

CHAP. XXVIII.

How Sir Launcelot met with Sir Carados bearing away Sir Gawaine, and of the rescue of Sir Gawaine.

AND then Sir Tristram took his leave when he saw his time, and took the sea. And in the mean while word came unto Sir Launcelot and to Sir Tristram that Sir Carados the mighty king, that was made like a giant, had fought with Sir Gawaine, and gave him such strokes that he swooned in his saddle, and after that he took him by the collar and pulled him out of his saddle, and fast bound him to the saddle bow, and so rode his way with him towards his castle. And as he rode, by fortune Sir Launcelot met with Sir Carados, and anon he knew Sir Gawaine that lay bound after him. Ah, said Sir Launcelot unto Sir Gawaine, how stands it with you? Never so hard, said Sir Gawaine, unless that ye help me, for without ye rescue me I know no knight that may, but either you or Sir Tristram. Wherefore Sir Launcelot was heavy of Sir Gawaine's words. And then Sir Launcelot bad Sir Carados, Lay down that knight, and fight with me. Thou art but a fool, said Sir Carados, for I will serve you in the same wise. As for that, said Sir Launcelot, spare me not, for I warn thee I will not spare thee. And then he bound Sir Gawaine hand and foot, and so threw him to the ground. And then he gat his spear of his Squire and departed from Sir Launcelot to fetch his course. And so either met with other, and brake their spears to their hands, and then they pulled out swords and hurtled together on horseback more than an hour. And at the last Sir Launcelot smote Sir Carados such a buffet upon the helm that it perched his brain-pan. So then Sir Launcelot took Sir Carados by the collar and pulled him under his horse feet, and then he alight and pulled off his helm and strake off his head. And then Sir Launcelot unbound Sir Gawaine. So this same tale was told to Sir Galahad and to Sir Tristram:—

here may ye hear the nobleness that followeth Sir Launcelot. Alas, said Sir Tristram, and I had not this message in hand with this fair lady, truly I would never stint or I had found Sir Launcelot. Then Sir Tristram and La Beale Isoud went to the sea and came into Cornwall, and there all the barons met them.

CHAP. XXIX.

Of the wedding of king Mark to La Beale Isoud, and of Bragwaine her maid, and of Palamides.

AND anon they were richly wedded with great nobley. But ever, as the French book saith, Sir Tristram and La Beale Isoud loved ever together.

Then was there great justs and great tourneying, and many lords and ladies were at that feast, and Sir Tristram was most praised of all other. Thus dured the feast long, and after the feast was done, within a little while after, by the assent of two ladies that were with queen Isoud, they ordained for hate and envy to destroy dame Bragwaine, that was maiden and lady unto La Beale Isoud, and she was sent into the forest for to fetch herbs, and there she was met, and bound feet and hand to a tree, and so she was bounden three days. And by fortune Sir Palamides found dame Bragwaine and there he delivered her from the death, and brought her to a nunnery there beside to be recovered. When Isoud the queen missed her maiden wit ye well she was right heavy as ever was any queen, for of all earthly women she loved her best, the cause was for she came with her out of her country.

And so upon a day the queen Isoud walked into the forest to put away her thoughts, and there she went herself unto a well and made great moan. And suddenly there came Sir Palamides to her, and had heard all her complaint, and said, Madame Isoud, and if ye will grant me my boon I shall bring to you dame Bragwaine safe and sound. And the queen was so glad of his proffer that suddenly unadvised she granted all his asking. Well madam, said Sir Pala-

mides, I trust to your promise, and if ye will abide here half an hour I shall bring her to you. I shall abide you, said La Beale Isoud. Then Sir Palamides rode forth his way to that nunnery, and lightly he came again with dame Bragwaine; but by her good will she would not have come again, because for love of the queen she stood in adventure of her life. Notwithstanding, half against her will, she went with Sir Palamides unto the queen. And when the queen saw her she was passing glad. Now madam, said Palamides, remember upon your promise, for I have fulfilled my promise. Sir Palamides, said the queen, I wot not what is your desire, but I will that ye wit howbeit I promised you largely I thought none evil, nor I warn you none ill will I do. Madam, said Sir Palamides, as at this time ye shall not know my desire, but before my lord your husband there shall ye know that I will have my desire that ye have promised me. And therewith the queen departed and rode home to the king, and Sir Palamides rode after her. And when Sir Palamides came before the king he said, Sir king, I require you as ye be a righteous king, that ye will judge me the right. Tell me the cause, said the king, and ye shall have right.

CHAP. XXX.

How Palamides demanded queen Isoud, and how Lambegus rode after to rescue her, and of the escape of Isoud.

SIR, said Palamides, I promised your queen Isoud to bring again dame Bragwaine that she had lost, upon this covenant, that she should grant me a boon that I would ask, and without grudging other advisement she granted me. What say ye, my lady? said the king. It is truly as he saith, said the queen, to say the sooth I promised him his asking for love and joy that I had to see her. Well madam, said the king, and if ye were hasty to grant him what boon he would ask, I will well that ye perform your promise. Then said Sir Palamides, I will that ye wit that I will have your queen to lead her and govern her where as me list. Therewith the king stood still, and bethought him of Sir Tristram, and deemed that he would rescue her. And then hastily the king answered, Take her with the adventures that shall fall of it, for Sir Palamides as I suppose thou wilt not keep her no while. As for that, said Sir Palamides, I dare right well abide the adventure. And so to make short tale, Sir Palamides took her by the hand and said, Madam, grudge not to go with me, for I desire nothing but your own promise. As for that, said the queen, I fear not greatly to go with thee, howbeit thou hast me at advantage upon my promise. For I doubt not I shall be worshipfully rescued from thee. As for that, said Sir Palamides, be it as it be may. So queen Isoud was set behind Palamides, and rode his way. Anon the king sent after Sir Tristram, but in no wise he could be found, for he was in the forest an hunting; for that was always his custom, but if he used arms, to chase and to hunt in the forests. Alas, said the king, now I am shamed for ever, that by mine own assent my lady and my queen shall be devoured. Then came forth a knight, his name was Lambegus, and he was a knight of Sir Tristram. My lord, said this knight, sith ye have trust in my lord Sir Tristram, wit ye well for his sake I will ride after your queen and rescue her, or else I shall be beaten. Gramercy, said the king, and I live, Sir Lambegus, I shall deserve it. And then Sir Lambegus armed him, and rode after as fast as he might. And then within awhile he overtook Sir Palamides: and then Sir Palamides left the queen. What art thou? said Sir Palamides, art thou Tristram? Nay, he said, I am his servant, and my name is Sir Lambegus. That me repenteth, said Sir Palamides, I had lever thou hadst been Sir Tristram. I believe you well, said Sir Lambegus, but when thou meetest with Sir Tristram thou shalt have thy hands full. And then they hurtled together and all to-brast their spears, and then they pulled out their swords and hewed on helms and hauberks. At the last Sir Palamides gave Sir Lambegus such a wound that he fell down like a dead knight to the earth. Then he looked after La Beale Isoud, and then she was gone he nist where. Wit ye well Sir Palamides was never so heavy. So the queen ran into the forest, and there she found a well, and therein she had thought to have drowned herself. And as good fortune would, there came a knight to her that had a castle thereby, his name was Sir Adtherp. And when he found the queen in that mischief he rescued her, and brought her to his castle. And when he wist what she was, he armed him and took his horse, and said he would be avenged upon Palamides, and so he rode till he met with him, and there Sir Palamides wounded him sore, and by force he made him to tell him the cause why he did battle with him, and how he had led the queen unto his castle. Now bring me there, said Palamides, or thou shalt die of my hands. Sir, said Sir Adtherp, I am so wounded I may not follow, but ride you this way, and it shall bring you into my castle, and there within is the queen. And then Sir Palamides rode still till he came to the castle, and at a window La Beale Isoud saw Sir Palamides, then she made the gates to be shut strongly. And when he saw he might not come within the castle, he put off his bridle and his saddle, and put his horse to pasture, and set himself down at the gate like a man that was out of his wit that recked not of himself.

CHAP. XXXI.

How Sir Tristram rode after Palamides, and how he found him and fought with him, and by the mean of Isoud the battle ceased.

Now turn we unto Sir Tristram, that when he was come home and wist La Beale Isoud was gone with Sir Palamides, wit ye well he was wroth out of measure. Alas, said Sir Tristram, I am this day shamed. Then he cried to Gouvernail his man, Haste thee that I were armed and on horseback, for well I wot Lambegus hath no might nor strength to withstand Sir Palamides: alas, that I had not been in his stead. So anon as he was armed and horsed Sir Tristram and Gouvernail rode after into the forest, and within a while he found his knight Lambegus almost wounded to the death, and Sir Tristram bare him to a forester, and charged him to keep him well. And then he rode forth, and there he found Sir Adtherp sore wounded, and he told him how the queen would have drowned herself and he had not been, and how for her sake and love he had taken upon him to do battle with Sir Palamides. Where is my lady? said Sir Tristram. Sir, said the knight, she is sure enough within my castle, and she can hold her within it. Gramercy, said Sir Tristram, of thy great goodness. And so he rode till he came nigh to that castle, and then Sir Tristram saw where Sir Palamides sat at the gate sleeping, and his horse pastured fast afore him. Now go thou Gouvernail, said Sir Tristram, and bid him awake and make him ready. So Gouvernail rode unto him and said, Sir Palamides, arise and take to thee thine harness. But he was in such a study that he heard not what Gouvernail said. So Gouvernail came again and told Sir Tristram that he slept, or else he was mad. Go thou again, said Sir Tristram, and bid him arise, and tell him that I am here his mortal foe. So Gouvernail rode again and put upon him the butt of his spear, and said, Sir Palamides make thee ready, for wit ye well Sir Tristram hoveth yonder, and sendeth thee word he is thy mortal foe. And therewithal Sir Palamides arose stilly without words, and gat his horse and saddled him and bridled him, and lightly he lept upon him, and gat his spear in his hand, and either feutred their spears, and hurtled fast together; and there Sir Tristram smote down Sir Palamides over his horse tail. Then lightly Sir Palamides put his shield afore him and drew his sword, and there began strong battle on both parties, for both

they fought for the love of one lady, and ever she lay on the walls and beheld them how they fought out of measure, and either were wounded passing sore, but Palamides was much sorer wounded. Thus they fought tracing and traversing more than two hours, that well nigh for dole and sorrow La Beale Isoud swooned. Alas, said she, that one I loved and yet do, and the other I love not, yet it were great pity that I should see Sir Palamides slain, for well I know by that time the end be done Sir Palamides is but a dead knight, and because he is not christened I would be loth that he should die a Saracen. And therewithal she came down and besought Sir Tristram to fight no more. Ah madam, said he, what mean you? will ye have me shamed? Well ye know I will be ruled by you. I will not your dishonour, said La Beale Isoud, but I would that ye would for my sake spare this unhappy Saracen Palamides. Madam, said Sir Tristram, I will leave fighting at this time for your sake.

Then she said to Sir Palamides: This shall be your charge, that thou shalt go out of this country while I am therein. I will obey your commandment, said Sir Palamides, the which is sore against my will. Then take thy way, said La Beale Isoud, unto the court of king Arthur, and there recommend me unto queen Guenever, and tell her that I send her word that there be within the land but four lovers, that is Sir Launcelot du Lake and queen Guenever, and Sir Tristram de Liones and queen Isoud.

CHAP. XXXII.

How Sir Tristram brought queen Isoud home, and of the debate of king Mark and Sir Tristram.

AND so Sir Palamides departed with great heaviness. And Sir Tristram took the queen and brought her again to king Mark, and then was there made great joy of her home coming. Who was cherished but Sir Tristram! Then Sir Tristram let fetch Sir Lambegus his knight from the forester's house, and it was long or he was whole, but at the last he was well recovered. Thus they lived with joy and play a long while. But ever Sir Andred, that was nigh cousin unto Sir Tristram, lay in a watch to wait betwixt Sir Tristram and La Beale Isoud, for to take them and slander them. So upon a day Sir Tristram talked with La Beale Isoud in a window, and that espied Sir Andred, and told it to the king. Then king Mark took a sword in his hand and came to Sir Tristram, and called him false traitor, and would have stricken him. But Sir Tristram was nigh him, and ran under his sword, and took it out of his hand. And then the king cried, Where are my knights and my men? I charge you slay this traitor. But at that time there was not one would move for his words. When Sir Tristram saw there was not one would be against him, he shook the sword to the king, and made countenance as though he would have stricken him. And then king Mark fled, and Sir Tristram followed him, and smote upon him five or six strokes flatling on the neck that he made him to fall upon the nose. And then Sir Tristram went his way and armed him, and took his horse and his man, and so he rode into that forest. And there upon a day Sir Tristram met with two brethren that were knights with king Mark, and there he strake off the head of the one, and wounded the other to the death, and he made him to bear his brother's head in his helm unto the king, and thirty more there he wounded. And when that knight came before the king to say his message, he there died afore the king and the queen. Then king Mark called his council unto him and asked advice of his barons what was best to do with Sir Tristram. Sir, said the barons, in especial Sir Dinas the seneschal, Sir, we will give you counsel for to send for Sir Tristram, for we will that ye wit many men will hold with Sir Tristram and he were hard bested. And sir, said Sir Dinas, ye shall understand that Sir Tristram is

called peerless and matchless of any christian knight, and of his might and his hardiness we knew none so good a knight, but if it be Sir Launcelot du Lake. And if he depart from your court and go to king Arthur's court, wit ye well he will get him such friends there that he will not set by your malice. And therefore, sir, I counsel you to take him to your grace. I will well, said the king, that he be sent for, that we may be friends. Then the barons sent for Sir Tristram under a safe conduct. And so when Sir Tristram came to the king, he was welcome, and no rehearsal was made, and there was game and play. And then the king and the queen went on hunting, and Sir Tristram.

CHAP. XXXIII.

How Sir Lamorak justed with thirty knights, and Sir Tristram at request of king Mark smote his horse down.

THE king and the queen made their pavilions and their tents in that forest beside a river, and there was daily hunting and justing, for there were ever thirty knights ready to just unto all them that came in at that time. And there by fortune came Sir Lamorak de Galis and Sir Driant, and there Sir Driant justed right well, but at the last he had a fall. Then Sir Lamorak proffered to just. And when he began he fared so with the thirty knights that there was not one of them but that he gave him a fall, and some of them were sore hurt. I marvel, said king Mark, what knight he is that doth such deeds of arms. Sir, said Sir Tristram, I know him for a noble knight as few now be living, and his name is Sir Lamorak de Galis. It were great shame, said the king, that he should go thus away, unless that some of you met with him better. Sir, said Sir Tristram, me seemeth it were no worship for a noble man for to have ado with him; and for because at this time he hath done overmuch for any mean knight living, therefore, as me seemeth, it were great shame and villainy to tempt him any more at this time, insomuch as he and his horse are weary both; for the deeds of arms that he hath done this day, and they be well considered, were enough for Sir Launcelot du Lake.

As for that, said king Mark, I require you as ye love me and my lady the queen La Beale Isoud, take your arms and just with Sir Lamorak de Galis. Sir, said Sir Tristram, ye bid me do a thing that is against knighthood, and well I can deem that I shall give him a fall, for it is no mastery, for my horse and I be fresh both, and so is not his horse and he; and wit ye well that he will take it for great unkindness, for ever one good is loth to take another at disadvantage. But because I will not displease you, as ye require me so will I do, and obey your commandment. And so Sir Tristram armed him anon and took his horse, and put him forth, and there Sir Lamorak met him mightily, and what with the might of his own spear, and of Sir Tristram's spear, Sir Lamorak's horse fell to the earth, and he sitting in the saddle. Then anon as lightly as he might he avoided the saddle and his horse, and put his shield afore him, and drew his sword. And then he bad Sir Tristram, Alight, thou knight, and thou darest. Nay, said Sir Tristram, I will no more have ado with thee, for I have done to thee overmuch unto my dishonour, and to thy worship. As for that, said Sir Lamorak, I can thee no thank: since thou hast forjusted me on horseback, I require thee, and I beseech thee, and thou be Sir Tristram, fight with me on foot. I will not so, said Sir Tristram; and wit ye well my name is Sir Tristram de Liones, and well I know ye be Sir Lamorak de Galis, and this that I have done to you was against my will, but I was required thereto; but to say that I will do at your request as at this time, I will have no more ado with you, for me shameth of that I have done. As for the shame, said Sir Lamorak, on thy part or on mine, bear thou it and thou wilt, for though a mare's son hath failed me, now a queen's son shall not fail thee; and therefore, and thou be

such a knight as men call thee, I require thee, alight, and fight with me. Sir Lamorak, said Sir Tristram, I understand your heart is great, and cause why ye have, to say the sooth: for it would grieve me and any knight should keep himself fresh and then to strike down a weary knight, for that knight nor horse was never formed that alway might stand or endure. And therefore, said Sir Tristram, I will not have ado with you, for me forthinketh of that I have done. As for that, said Sir Lamorak, I shall quit you and ever I see my time.

CHAP. XXXIV.

How Sir Lamorak sent an horn to king Mark in despite of Sir Tristram, and how Sir Tristram was driven into a chapel.

So he departed from him with Sir Driant, and by the way they met with a knight that was sent from Morgan le Fay unto king Arthur, and this knight had a fair horn harnessed with gold, and the horn had such a virtue that there might no lady nor gentlewoman drink of that horn but if she were true to her husband, and if she were false she should spill all the drink, and if she were true to her lord she might drink peaceably. And because of queen Guenever, and in the despite of Sir Launcelot, this horn was sent unto king Arthur, and by force Sir Lamorak made that knight to tell all the cause why he bare that horn. Now shalt thou bear this horn, said Lamorak unto king Mark, or else choose thou to die for it. For I tell thee plainly, in despite and reproof of Sir Tristram thou shalt bear that horn unto king Mark his uncle, and say thou to him that I sent it him for to assay his lady, and if she be true to him he shall prove her. So the knight went his way unto king Mark, and brought him that rich horn, and said that Sir Lamorak sent it him, and thereto he told him the virtue of that horn. Then the king made queen Isoud to drink thereof, and an hundred ladies, and there were but four ladies of all those that drank clean. Alas, said king Mark, this is a great despite; and sware a great oath that she should be burnt, and the other ladies. Then the barons gathered them together, and said plainly, they would not have those ladies burnt for an horn made by sorcery, that came from as false a sorceress and witch as then was living. For that horn did never good, but caused strife and debate, and always in her days she had been an enemy to all true lovers. So there were many knights made their avow, if ever they met with Morgan le Fay that they would shew her short courtesy. Also Sir Tristram was passing wroth that Sir Lamorak sent that horn unto king Mark, for well he knew that it was done in the despite of him; and therefore he thought to quit Sir Lamorak. Then, always, Sir Tristram used to go to queen Isoud when he might, and ever Sir Andred his cousin watched him night and day, for to take him with La Beale Isoud. And so, upon a day, Sir Andred his cousin espied the hour and the time when Sir Tristram went to his lady. And then Sir Andred gat unto him twelve knights, and he set upon Sir Tristram secretly and suddenly, and there Sir Tristram was taken with La Beale Isoud, and then was he bound hand and foot, and so was he kept until the next day. And then by assent of king Mark, and of Sir Andred, and of some of the barons, Sir Tristram was led unto a chapel which stood upon the sea rocks, there for to take his judgment; and so he was led bound with forty knights. And when Sir Tristram saw there was none other remedy but needs that he must die, then said he, Fair lords, remember what I have done for the country of Cornwall, and in what jeopardy I have been in for the weal of you all. For when I fought for the truage of Cornwall with Sir Marhaus the good knight, I was promised for to be better rewarded, when ye all refused to take the battle; therefore, as ye be good gentle knights, see me not thus shamefully to die, for it is shame to all knighthood thus to see me

die. For I dare well say, said Sir Tristram, that I never yet met with no knight but I was as good as he, or better. Fie upon thee, said Sir Andred, false traitor that thou art with thy vaunting, for all thy boast thou shalt die this day. O Andred, Andred, said Sir Tristram, thou shouldst be my kinsman, and now thou art to me full unfriendly, but and there were no more but thou and I, thou wouldst not put me to death. No! said Sir Andred, and therewith he drew his sword and would have slain him. When Sir Tristram saw him make such countenance, he looked upon both his hands that were fast bound unto two knights, and suddenly he pulled them both to him and unwrast his hands, and then he lept unto his cousin Andred and wrested his sword out of his hands, then he smote Sir Andred that he fell to the earth, and so Sir Tristram fought till he had killed ten knights. So then Sir Tristram gat the chapel and kept it mightily. Then the cry was great, and the people drew fast unto Sir Andred, more than an hundred. When Sir Tristram saw the people draw unto him, he remembered that he was naked, and shut fast the chapel door, and brake the bars of a window, and so he lept out and fell upon the crags in the sea. And so at that time Sir Andred nor none of his fellows might get to him at that time.

CHAP. XXXV.

How Sir Tristram was holpen by his men, and of queen Isoud which was put in a lazar-cote, and how Tristram was hurt.

So when they were departed, Gouvernail and Sir Lambegus, and Sir Sentraille de Lushon, that were Sir Tristram's men, sought their master. When they heard he was escaped, then they were passing glad, and on the rocks they found him, and with towels they pulled him up. And then Sir Tristram asked them where La Beale Isoud was, for he wend she had been had away of Andred's people. Sir, said Gouvernail, she is put in a lazar-cote. Alas, said Sir Tristram, this is a full ungoodly place for such a fair lady;

and if I may she shall not be long there. And so he took his men, and went there as was La Beale Isoud, and fetched her away, and brought her into a forest to a fair manor, and Sir Tristram there abode with her. So the good knight bad his men go from him,—For at this time I may not help you. So they departed all save Gouvernail. And so upon a day Sir Tristram went into the forest for to desport him, and then it happened that he fell there on sleep. And there came a man that Sir Tristram afore hand had slain his brother; and when this man had found him he shot him through the shoulder with an arrow, and Sir Tristram lept up and killed that man. And in the mean while it was told king Mark how Sir Tristram and La Beale Isoud were in that same manor, and as soon as ever he might thither he came with many knights to slay Sir Tristram. And when he came there he found him gone; and there he took La Beale Isoud home with him, and kept her strait that by no means never she might wit nor send unto Tristram, nor he unto her. And then when Sir Tristram came toward the old manor, he found the track of many horses, and thereby he wist his lady was gone. And then Sir Tristram took great sorrow, and endured with great pain long time, for the arrow that he was hurt withall was envenomed.

Then by the means of La Beale Isoud she told a lady that was cousin unto dame Bragwaine, and she came to Sir Tristram, and told him that he might not be whole by no means,—For thy lady La Beale Isoud may not help thee; therefore she biddeth you haste into Britanny to king Howel, and there ye shall find his daughter Isoud la Blanche Mains, and she shall help thee. Then Sir Tristram and Gouvernail gat them shipping, and so sailed into Britanny. And when king Howel wist that it was Sir Tristram he was full glad of him. Sir, he said, I am come into this country to have help of your daughter, for it is told me that there is none other may heal me but she. And so within a while she healed him.

CHAP. XXXVI.

How Sir Tristram served in war king Howel of Britanny and slew his adversary in the field.

THERE was an earl that hight Grip, and this earl made great war upon the king, and put the king to the worse, and besieged him. And on a time Sir Kehydius, that was son to king Howel, as he issued out he was sore wounded nigh to the death. Then Gouvernail went to the king and said, Sir, I counsel you to desire my lord, Sir Tristram, as in your need to help you. I will do by your counsel, said the king. And so he went unto Sir Tristram and prayed him in his wars for to help him, for my son Sir Kehydius may not go into the field. Sir, said Sir Tristram, I will go to the field, and do what I may. Then Sir Tristram issued out of the town with such fellowship as he might make, and did such deeds that all Britanny spake of him. And then at the last, by great might and force, he slew the earl Grip with his own hands, and more than an hundred knights he slew that day. And then Sir Tristram was received right worshipfully with procession. Then king Howel embraced him in his arms and said, Sir Tristram, all my kingdom I will resign to thee. God defend, said Sir Tristram, for I am beholden unto you for your daughter's sake to do for you. Then by the great means of king Howel and Kehydius his son, by great proffers there grew great love betwixt Isoud and Sir Tristram, for that lady was both good and fair, and a woman of noble blood and fame. And for because that Sir Tristram had such cheer and riches, and all other pleasance that he had, almost he had forsaken La Beale Isoud. And so upon a time Sir Tristram agreed to wed Isoud la Blanche Mains. And at the last they were wedded, and solemnly held their marriage.

And in the mean while there was a knight in Britanny, his name was Suppinabiles, and he came over the sea into England, and then he came unto the court of king Arthur, and there he met with Sir Launcelot du Lake, and told him of the marriage of Sir Tristram. Then said Sir Launcelot, Fie upon him, untrue knight to his lady, that so noble a knight as Sir Tristram is, should be found to his first lady false, La Beale Isoud, queen of Cornwall. But say ye him this, said Sir Launcelot, that of all knights in the world I loved him most, and had most joy of him, and all was for his noble deeds; and let him wit the love between him and me is done for ever, and that I give him warning from this day forth as his mortal enemy.

CHAP. XXXVII.

How Sir Suppinabiles told Sir Tristram how he was defamed in the court of king Arthur, and of Sir Lamorak.

Then departed Sir Suppinabiles unto Britanny again, and there he found Sir Tristram, and told him that he had been in king Arthur's court. Then said Sir Tristram, Heard ye any thing of me? Truly, said Sir Suppinabiles, there I heard Sir Launcelot speak of you great shame, and that ye be a false knight to your lady, and he bad me to do you to wit that he will be your mortal enemy in every place where he may meet you. That me repenteth, said Tristram, for of all knights I loved to be in his fellowship. So Sir Tristram made great moan, and was ashamed that noble knights should defame him for the sake of his lady. And in this mean while La Beale Isoud made a letter unto queen Guenever, complaining her of the untruth of Sir Tristram, and how he had wedded the king's daughter of Britanny. Queen Guenever sent her another letter, and bad her be of good cheer, for she should have joy after sorrow, for Sir Tristram was so noble a knight called, that by crafts of sorcery ladies would make such noble men to wed them, but in the end, queen Guenever said, it shall be thus, that he shall hate her, and love you better than ever he did tofore.

So leave we Sir Tristram in Britanny,

and speak we of Sir Lamorak de Galis, that as he sailed his ship fell on a rock and perished all, save Sir Lamorak and his squire, and there he swam mightily, and fishers of the Isle of Servage took him up, and his squire was drowned, and the shipmen had great labour to save Sir Lamorak's life for all the comfort that they could do. And the lord of that isle hight Sir Nabon le Noire, a great mighty giant. And this Sir Nabon hateth all the knights of king Arthur, and in no wise he would do them favor. And these fishers told Sir Lamorak all the guise of Sir Nabon, how there came never knight of king Arthur's but he destroyed him. And at the last battle that he did was slain Sir Nanowne le Petite, the which he put to a shameful death in despite of king Arthur, for he was drawn limb-meal. That forthinketh me, said Sir Lamorak, for that knight's death, for he was my cousin. And if I were at mine ease as well as ever I was, I would revenge his death. Peace, said the fishers, and make here no words, for, or ye depart from hence, Sir Nabon must know that ye have been here, or else we should die for your sake. So that I be whole, said Lamorak, of my disease that I have taken in the sea, I will that ye tell him that I am a knight of king Arthur's, for I was never afeard to deny my lord.

CHAP. XXXVIII.

How Sir Tristram and his wife arrived in Wales, and how he met there with Sir Lamorak.

Now turn we unto Sir Tristram, that upon a day he took a little barge, and his wife Isoud la Blanch Mains, with Sir Kehydius her brother, to play them in the coasts. And when they were from the land, there was a wind drove them into the coast of Wales upon this Isle of Servage, where as was Sir Lamorak, and there the barge all to-rove, and there dame Isoud was hurt, and as well as they might they gat into the forest, and there by a well he saw Segwarides and a damsel. And then either saluted other. Sir, said Segwarides, I know you for Sir Tristram de Liones, the man in the world that I have the most cause to hate, because ye departed the love between me and my wife; but as for that, said Segwarides, I will never hate a noble knight for a light lady, and therefore I pray you be my friend, and I will be yours unto my power, for wit ye well ye are hard bested in this valley, and we shall have enough to do either of us to succour other. And then Sir Segwarides brought Sir Tristram unto a lady thereby that was born in Cornwall, and she told him all the perils of that valley, and how there came never knight there but he were taken prisoner or slain. Wit you well fair lady, said Sir Tristram, that I slew Sir Marhaus, and delivered Cornwall from the truage of Ireland, and I am he that delivered the king of Ireland from Sir Blamor de Ganis, and I am he that beat Sir Palamides, and wit ye well, I am Sir Tristram de Liones, that by the grace of God shall deliver this woful Isle of Servage. So Sir Tristram was well eased; then one told him there was a knight of king Arthur's that was wrecked on the rocks. What is his name? said Sir Tristram. We wot not, said the fishers, but he keepeth it no counsel but that he is a knight of king Arthur's, and by the mighty lord of this isle he setteth nought by. I pray you, said Sir Tristram, and ye may bring him hither that I may see him; and if he be any of the knights of Arthur's I shall know him. Then the lady prayed the fishers to bring him to her place. So, on the morrow they brought him thither in a fisher's raiment. And as soon as Sir Tristram saw him he smiled upon him and knew him well, but he knew not Sir Tristram. Fair knight, said Sir Tristram, me seemeth by your cheer ye have been diseased but late, and also me thinketh I should know you heretofore. I will well, said Sir Lamorak, that ye have seen me and met with me. Fair sir, said Sir Tristram, tell me your name. Upon a covenant I will tell you, said Sir Lamorak, that

is, that ye will tell me whether ye be lord of this island or no, that is called Nabon le Noire. For sooth, said Sir Tristram, I am not he, nor I hold not of him, I am his foe as well ye be, and so shall I be found or I depart out of this isle. Well, said Sir Lamorak, since ye have said so largely unto me, my name is Sir Lamorak de Galis, son unto king Pellinore. For sooth, I trow well, said Sir Tristram, for, and ye said other, I know the contrary. What are ye, said Sir Lamorak, that knoweth me? I am Sir Tristram de Liones. Ah, sir, remember ye not of the fall ye did give me once, and after ye refused me to fight on foot. That was not for fear I had of you, said Sir Tristram, but me shamed at that time to have more ado with you, for me seemed ye had enough; but, Sir Lamorak, for my kindness many ladies ye put to a reproof, when ye sent the horn from Morgan le Fay to king Mark, where as ye did this in despite of me. Well, said he, and it were to do again, so would I do, for I had lever strife and debate fell in king Mark's court rather than Arthur's court, for the honour of both courts be not alike. As to that, said Sir Tristram, I know well. But that that was done, it was for despite of me, but all your malice hurt not greatly. Therefore, said Sir Tristram, ye shall leave all your malice and so will I, and let us assay how we may win worship between you and me upon this giant Sir Nabon le Noire, that is lord of this island, to destroy him. Sir, said Sir Lamorak, now I understand your knighthood, it may not be false that all men say, for of your bounty, nobless, and worship, of all knights ye are peerless; and for courtesy and gentleness I shewed you ungentleness, and that now me repenteth.

CHAP. XXXIX.

How Sir Tristram fought with Sir Nabon and overcame him, and made Sir Lamorak lord of the isle.

In the mean time came word that Sir Nabon had made a cry that all the people of that isle should be at his castle the fifth day after. And the same day the son of Nabon should be made knight, and all the knights of that valley and thereabout should be there to just, and all those of the realm of Logris should be there to just with them of North Wales; and thither came five hundred knights, and they of the country brought there Sir Lamorak, and Sir Tristram, and Sir Kehydius, and Sir Segwarides, for they durst none otherwise do. And then Sir Nabon lent Sir Lamorak horse and armour at Sir Lamorak's desire, and Sir Lamorak justed and did such deeds of arms that Nabon and all the people said there was never knight that ever they saw do such deeds of arms. For, as the French book saith, he forjusted all that were there, for the most part of five hundred knights, that none abode him in his saddle. Then Sir Nabon proffered to play with him his play:— For I saw never no knight do so much upon a day. I will well, said Sir Lamorak, play as I may, but I am weary and sore bruised: and there either gat a spear, but Nabon would not encounter with Sir Lamorak, but smote his horse in the forehead and so slew him, and then Sir Lamorak went on foot and turned his shield and drew his sword, and there began strong battle on foot. But Sir Lamorak was so sore bruised and short breathed, that he traced and traversed somewhat aback. Fair fellow, said Sir Nabon, hold thy hand, and I shall shew thee more courtesy than ever I shewed knight, because I have seen this day thy noble knighthood. And therefore stand thou by, and I will wit whether any of thy fellows will have ado with me. Then when Sir Tristram heard that, he stept forth and said, Nabon, lend me horse and sure armour, and I will have ado with thee. Well fellow, said Sir Nabon, go thou to yonder pavilion, and arm thee of the best thou findest there, and I shall play a marvellous play with thee. Then, said Sir Tristram, look ye play well, or else peradventure I shall learn you a new play. That is well said, fellow, said Sir Nabon. So when Sir Tristram was armed as him liked best, and well shielded and sworded, he dressed to him on foot, for well he knew that Sir Nabon would not abide a stroke with a spear, therefore he would slay all knights' horses. Now fair fellow, said Sir Nabon, let us play. So then they fought long on foot, tracing and traversing, smiting and foining long without any rest. At the last Sir Nabon prayed him to tell him his name. Sir Nabon, I tell thee my name is Sir Tristram de Liones, a knight of Cornwall under king Mark. Thou art welcome, said Sir Nabon, for of all knights I have most desired to fight with thee or with Sir Launcelot. So then they went eagerly together, and Sir Tristram slew Sir Nabon, and so forthwith he lept to his son and strake off his head. And then all the country said they would hold of Sir Tristram. Nay, said Sir Tristram, I will not so: here is a worshipful knight Sir Lamorak de Galis that for me he shall be lord of this country, for he hath done here great deeds of arms. Nay, said Sir Lamorak, I will not be lord of this country, for I have not deserved it as well as ye, therefore give ye it where ye will, for I will none have. Well, said Sir Tristram, since ye nor I will not have it, let us give it to him that hath not so well deserved it. Do as ye list, said Sir Lamorak, for the gift is yours, for I will none have and I had deserved it. So it was given to Segwarides, wherefore he thanked him, and so was he lord, and worshipfully he did govern it. And then Sir Segwarides delivered all prisoners, and set good governance in that valley; and so he returned into Cornwall, and told king Mark and La Beale Isoud how Sir Tristram had advanced him to the Isle of Servage, and there he proclaimed in all Cornwall of all the adventures of these two knights, so was it openly known. But full woe was La Beale Isoud when she heard tell that Sir Tristram was wedded to Isoud La Blanche Mains.

CHAP. XL.

How Sir Lamorak departed from Sir Tristram, and how he met with Sir Frol, and after with Sir Launcelot.

So turn we unto Sir Lamorak, that rode toward Arthur's court; and Sir Tristram and his wife and Kehydius took a vessel and sailed into Britanny unto king Howel, where he was welcome. And when he heard of these adventures they marvelled of his noble deeds. Now turn we unto Sir Lamorak, that when he was departed from Sir Tristram, he rode out of the forest till he came to an hermitage. When the hermit saw him he asked him from whence he came. Sir, said Sir Lamorak, I come from this valley. Sir, said the hermit, thereof I greatly marvel, for this twenty winter I saw never no knight pass this country but he was either slain or villainously wounded, or passed as a poor prisoner. Those ill customs, said Sir Lamorak, are fordone; for Sir Tristram slew your lord Sir Nabon, and his son. Then was the hermit glad, and all his brethren, for he said there was never such a tyrant among Christian men,—and therefore, said the hermit, this valley and franchise we will hold of Sir Tristram. So on the morrow Sir Lamorak departed. And as he rode he saw four knights fight against one, and that one knight defended him well, but at the last the four knights had him down. And then Sir Lamorak went betwixt them, and asked them why they would slay that one knight, and said it was shame four against one. Thou shalt well wit, said the four knights, that he is false. That is your tale, said Sir Lamorak, and when I hear him also speak I will say as ye say. Then said Lamorak, Ah knight, can ye not excuse you but that ye are a false knight? Sir, said he, yet can I excuse me both with my words and with my hands, that I will make good upon one of the best of them, my body to his body. Then spake they all at once: We will not jeopard our bodies as for thee; but wit thou well, they said,

and king Arthur were here himself, it should not lie in his power to save his life. That is too much said, said Sir Lamorak, but many speak behind a man more than they will say to his face. And because of your words, ye shall understand that I am one of the simplest of king Arthur's court: in the worship of my lord now do your best, and in despite of you I shall rescue him. And then they lashed all at once to Sir Lamorak; but anon at two strokes Sir Lamorak had slain two of them, and then the other two fled. So then Sir Lamorak turned again to that knight and asked him his name. Sir, he said, my name is Sir Frol of the Out Isles. Then he rode with Sir Lamorak and bare him company; and as they rode by the way they saw a seemly knight riding against them, and all in white. Ah, said Frol, yonder knight justed late with me, and smote me down, therefore I will just with him. Ye shall not do so, said Sir Lamorak, by my counsel, and ye will tell me your quarrel, whether ye justed at his request, or he at yours. Nay, said Sir Frol, I justed with him at my request. Sir, said Lamorak, then will I counsel you deal no more with him, for me seemeth by his countenance he should be a noble knight and no jester, for me thinketh he should be of the Table Round. Therefore I will not spare, said Sir Frol; and then he cried and said, Sir knight, make thee ready to just. That needeth not, said the knight, for I have no lust to just with thee. But yet they feutred their spears, and the white knight overthrew Sir Frol, and then he rode his way a soft pace. Then Sir Lamorak rode after him, and prayed him to tell him his name, For me seemeth ye should be of the fellowship of the Round Table. Upon a covenant, said he, I will tell you my name, so that ye will not discover my name, and also that ye will tell me yours. Then, said he, my name is Sir Lamorak de Galis. And my name is Sir Launcelot du Lake. Then they put up their swords, and kissed heartily together, and either made great joy of other. Sir, said Sir Lamorak, and it please you I will do you service. God defend, said Sir Launcelot, that any of so noble blood as ye be should do me service. Then he said more, I am in a quest that I must do myself alone. Now God speed you, said Sir Lamorak, and so they departed. Then Sir Lamorak came to Sir Frol and horsed him again. What knight is that? said Sir Frol. Sir, said he, it is not for you to know, nor it is no point of my charge. Ye are the more uncourteous, said Sir Frol, and therefore I will depart from you. Ye may do as ye list, said Sir Lamorak, and yet by my company you have saved the fairest flower of your garland. So they departed.

CHAP. XLI.

How Sir Lamorak slew Sir Frol, and of the courteous fighting with Sir Belliance his brother.

THEN within two or three days Sir Lamorak found a knight at a well sleeping, and his lady sat with him and waked. Right so came Sir Gawaine and took the knight's lady, and set her up behind his squire. So Sir Lamorak rode after Sir Gawaine, and said, Sir Gawaine, turn again. And then said Sir Gawaine, What will ye do with me? for I am nephew to king Arthur. Sir, said he, for that cause I will spare you, else that lady should abide with me, or else ye should just with me. Then Sir Gawaine turned him and ran to him that owned the lady with his spear. But the knight with pure might smote down Sir Gawaine, and took his lady with him. All this Sir Lamorak saw, and said to himself, But I revenge my fellow, he will say of me dishonour in king Arthur's court. Then Sir Lamorak returned and proffered that knight to just. Sir, said he, I am ready. And so they came together with all their might, and there Sir Lamorak smote the knight through both sides, that he fell to the earth dead. Then the lady rode to that knight's brother that hight Sir Belliance le Orgulous, that dwelled

fast thereby, and then she told him how his brother was slain. Alas, said he, I will be revenged. And so horsed him and armed him, and within a while he overtook Sir Lamorak, and bad him, Turn, and leave that lady, for thou and I must play a new play, for thou hast slain my brother Sir Frol, that was a better knight than ever were thou. It might well be, said Sir Lamorak, but this day in the field I was found the better. So they rode together, and unhorsed other, and turned their shields and drew their swords, and fought mightily as noble knights proved by the space of two hours. So then Sir Belliance prayed him to tell his name. Sir, said he, my name is Sir Lamorak de Galis. Ah, said Sir Belliance, thou art the man in the world that I most hate, for I slew my sons for thy sake, where I saved thy life, and now thou hast slain my brother Sir Frol. Alas, how should I be accorded with thee? therefore defend thee, for thou shalt die: there is none other remedy. Alas, said Sir Lamorak, full well me ought to know you, for ye are the man that most have done for me. And therewith Sir Lamorak kneeled down and besought him of grace. Arise, said Sir Belliance, or else there as thou kneelest I shall slay thee. That shall not need, said Sir Lamorak, for I will yield me unto you, not for fear of you, nor for your strength, but your goodness maketh me full loth to have ado with you; wherefore I require you, for God's sake, and for the honour of knighthood, forgive me all that I have offended unto you. Alas, said Belliance, leave thy kneeling, or else I shall slay thee without mercy. Then they went again unto battle, and either wounded other, that all the ground was bloody there as they fought. And at the last Belliance withdrew him aback and set him down softly upon a little hill, for he was so faint for bleeding that he might not stand. Then Sir Lamorak threw his shield upon his back, and asked him, What cheer? Well, said Sir Belliance. Ah sir, yet shall I shew you favour in your mal-ease. Ah knight, Sir Belliance said, Sir Lamorak thou art a fool, for and I had thee at such advantage as thou hast done me I should slay thee, but thy gentleness is so good and large that I must needs forgive thee mine evil will. And then Sir Lamorak kneeled down and unlaced first his umberere, and then his own. And then either kissed other with weeping tears. Then Sir Lamorak led Sir Belliance to an abbey fast by, and there Sir Lamorak would not depart from Belliance till he was whole. And then they swore together that none of them should never fight against other. So Sir Lamorak departed and went to the court of king Arthur.

Here leue we of sire Lamorak and of sir Tristram. And here begynneth the historye of La cote male tayle.

The Ninth Book.

CHAP. I.

How a young man came into the court of king Arthur, and how Sir Kay called him in scorn La Cote Male Taile.

At the court of king Arthur there came a young man and bigly made, and he was richly beseen, and he desired to be made knight of the king, but his over garment sat overthwartly, howbeit it was rich cloth of gold. What is your name? said king Arthur. Sir, said he, my name is Breunor le Noire, and within short space ye shall know that I am of good kin. It may well be, said Sir Kay the seneschal, but in mockage ye shall be called La Cote Male Taile, that is as much as to say, the evilshapen coat. It is a great thing that thou askest, said the king; and for what cause wearest thou that rich coat? tell me; for I can well think for some cause it is. Sir, said he, I had a father a noble knight, and as he rode on hunting, upon a day it happed him to lay him down to sleep. And there came a knight that had been long his enemy. And when he saw he was fast on sleep, he all tohewed him; and this same coat had my father on the same time, and that maketh this coat to sit so evil upon me, for the strokes be on it as I found it, and never shall be amended for me. Thus to have my father's death in remembrance I wear this coat till I be revenged; and because ye are called the most noblest king in the world I come to you that ye should make me knight. Sir, said Sir Lamorak and Sir Gaheris, it were well done to make him knight, for him beseemeth well of person and of countenance, that he shall prove a good man, and a good knight and a mighty; for Sir, and ye be remembered, even such one was Sir Launcelot du Lake when he came first into this court, and full few of us knew from whence he came, and now he is proved the most man of worship in the world, and all your court and all your Round Table is by Sir Launcelot worshipped and amended more than by any knight now living. That is truth, said the king, and tomorrow at your request I shall make him knight. So on the morrow there was an hart found, and thither rode king Arthur with a company of his knights to slay the hart. And this young man that Sir Kay named La Cote Male Taile was there left behind with queen Guenever, and by sudden adventure there was an horrible lion kept in a strong tower of stone, and it happened that he at that time brake loose, and came hurling afore the queen and her knights. And when the queen saw the lion, she cried, and fled, and prayed her knights to rescue her. And there was none of them all but twelve that abode, and all the other fled. Then said La Cote Male Taile, Now I see well that all coward knights be not dead: and therewithal he drew his sword and dressed him afore the lion. And that lion gaped wide, and came upon him ramping to have slain him. And he then smote him in the midst of the head such a mighty stroke that it clave his head in sunder, and dashed to the earth. Then was it told the queen how that the young man that Sir Kay named by scorn La Cote Male Taile had slain the lion. With that the king came home. And when the queen told him of that adventure he was well pleased, and said, Upon pain of mine head he shall prove a noble man, and a faithful knight, and true of his promise. Then the king forthwithal made him knight. Now Sir, said this young knight, I require you and all the knights of your court, that ye call me by none other name but La Cote Male Taile; insomuch as Sir Kay so hath named me, so will I be called. I assent me well thereto, said the king.

CHAP. II.

How a damsel came unto the court and desired a knight to take on him an inquest, which La Cote Male Taile emprized.

THEN that same day there came a damsel into the king's court, and she brought with her a great black shield, with a white hand in the midst holding a sword. Other picture was there none in that shield. When king Arthur saw her, he asked her from whence she came, and what she would. Sir, she said, I have ridden long and many a day with this shield many ways, and for this cause I am come to your court:—There was a good knight that owned this shield, and this knight had undertaken a great deed of arms to achieve it, and so it misfortuned him another strong knight

met with him by sudden adventure, and there they fought long, and either wounded other passing sore, and they were so weary that they left that battle even hand. So this knight that owned this shield saw none other way but he must die; and then he commanded me to bear this shield to the court of king Arthur, he requiring and praying some good knight to take this shield, and that he would fulfil the quest that he was in. Now what say ye to this quest? said king Arthur. Is there any of you here that will take upon him to weld this shield? Then was there not one that would speak one word. Then Sir Kay took the shield in his hands. Sir knight, said the damsel, what is your name? Wit ye well, said he, my name is Sir Kay the seneschal, that widewhere is known. Sir, said that damsel, lay down that shield, for wit ye well it falleth not for you, for he must be a better knight than ye that shall weld this shield. Damsel, said Sir Kay, wit ye well I took this shield in my hands by your leave for to behold it, not to that intent, but go wheresoever thou wilt, for I will not go with you. Then the damsel stood still a great while, and beheld many of those knights. Then spake the knight La Cote Male Taile, Fair damsel, I will take the shield and that adventure upon me, so I wist I should know whither ward my journey might be, for because I was this day made knight I would take this adventure upon me. What is your name, fair young man? said the damsel. My name is, said he, La Cote Male Taile. Well mayest thou be called so, said the damsel, the knight with the evil-shapen coat, but and thou be so hardy to take upon thee to bear that shield and to follow me, wit thou well thy skin shall be as well hewn as thy coat. As for that, said La Cote Male Taile, when I am so hewn I will ask you no salve to heal me withal. And forthwithal there came into the court two squires, and brought him great horses and his armour and his spears, and anon he was armed, and took his leave. I would not by my will, said the king, that ye took upon you that hard adventure. Sir, said he, this adventure is mine, and the first that ever I took upon me, and that will I follow whatsoever come of me. Then that damsel departed, and La Cote Male Taile followed first after. And within a while he overtook the damsel. And anon she missaid him in the foullest manner.

CHAP. III.

How La Cote Male Taile overthrew Sir Dagonet the king's fool, and of the rebuke that he had of the damsel.

THEN Sir Kay ordained Sir Dagonet, king Arthur's fool, to follow after La Cote Male Taile, and there Sir Kay ordained that Sir Dagonet was horsed and armed, and bad him follow La Cote Male Taile and proffer him to just, and so he did, and when he saw La Cote Male Taile he cried and bad him make him ready to just. So Sir La Cote Male Taile smote Sir Dagonet over his horse croup. Then the damsel mocked La Cote Male Taile, and said, Fie for shame, now art thou shamed in Arthur's court when they send a fool to have ado with thee, and specially at thy first justs. Thus she rode long and chid. And within a while there came Sir Bleoberis the good knight, and there he justed with La Cote Male Taile, and there Sir Bleoberis smote him so sore that horse and all fell to the earth. Then La Cote Male Taile arose up lightly and dressed his shield and drew his sword, and would have done battle to the utterance, for he was wood wroth. Not so, said Bleoberis de Ganis, as at this time I will not fight upon foot. Then the damsel Maledisant rebuked him in the foullest manner, and bad him, turn again coward. Ah damsel, he said, I pray you of mercy to missay me no more, my grief is enough though ye give me no more. I call myself never the worse knight when a mare's son faileth me, and also I count me never the worse knight for a fall of Sir Bleoberis. So thus he rode with her two days, and by fortune there came Sir

Palamides and encountered with him, and he in the same wise served him as did Bleoberis toforehand. What dost thou here in my fellowship, said the damsel Maledisant, thou canst not sit no knight nor withstand him one buffet, but if it were Sir Dagonet. Ah fair damsel, I am not the worse to take a fall of Sir Palamides, and yet great disworship have I none, for neither Bleoberis nor yet Palamides would not fight with me on foot. As for that, said the damsel, wit thou well they have disdain and scorn to light off their horses to fight with such a mean knight as thou art. So in the meanwhile there came Sir Mordred, Sir Gawaine's brother, and so he fell in the fellowship with the damsel Maledisant. And then they came afore the castle Orgulous, and there was such a custom that there might no knight come by that castle but either he must just or be prisoner, or at the least to lose his horse and his harness. And there came out two knights against them, and Sir Mordred justed with the foremost, and that knight of the castle smote Sir Mordred down off his horse. And then anon La Cote Male Taile justed with that other, and either of them smote other down, horse and all to the earth. And when they avoided their horses, then either of them took other's horses. And then La Cote Male Taile rode into that knight that smote down Sir Mordred, and justed with him; and there Sir La Cote Male Taile hurt and wounded him passing sore, and put him from his horse as he had been dead. So he turned unto him that met him afore, and he took the flight toward the castle, and Sir La Cote Male Taile rode after him into the castle Orgulous, and there La Cote Male Taile slew him.

CHAP. IV.

How La Cote Male Taile fought against an hundred knights, and how he escaped by the mean of a lady.

AND anon there came an hundred knights about him and assailed him; and when he saw his horse should be slain he alight and voided his horse, and put the bridle under his feet, and so put him out of the gate. And when he had so done, he hurled in among them, and dressed his back unto a lady's chamber-wall, thinking himself that he had lever die there with worship than to abide the rebukes of the damsel Maledisant. And in the mean time as he stood and fought, that lady whose was the chamber, went out slily at her postern, and without the gates she found La Cote Male Taile's horse, and lightly she gat him by the bridle and tied him to the postern. And then she went unto her chamber slily again for to behold how that one knight fought against an hundred knights. And so when she had beheld him long, she went to a window behind his back and said, Thou knight thou fightest wonderly well, but for all that at the last thou must needs die, but and thou canst through thy mighty prowess win unto yonder postern, for there have I fastened thy horse to abide thee; but wit thou well thou must think on thy worship and think not to die, for thou mayest not win unto that postern without thou do nobly and mightily. When La Cote Male Taile heard her say so, he griped his sword in his hands, and put his shield fair afore him, and through the thickest press he thrulled through them. And when he came to the postern he found there ready four knights, and at two the first strokes he slew two of the knights, and the other fled, and so he won his horse and rode from them. And all as it was, it was rehearsed in king Arthur's court, how he slew twelve knights within the castle Orgulous. And so he rode on his way. And in the mean while the damsel said to Sir Mordred, I ween my foolish knight be either slain or taken prisoner. Then were they ware where he came riding. And when he was come unto them, he told all how he had sped, and escaped in despite of them all, and some of the best of them will tell no tales. Thou liest falsely, said the damsel, that dare I make good, but as a fool and a dastard to all knighthood

they have let thee pass. That may ye prove, said La Cote Male Taile. With that she sent a courier of hers that rode alway with her, for to know the truth of this deed. And so he rode thither lightly, and asked how and in what manner that Sir La Cote Male Taile was escaped out of the castle. Then all the knights cursed him and said that he was fiend and no man; for he hath slain here twelve of our best knights, and we wend unto this day that it had been too much for Sir Launcelot du Lake, or for Sir Tristram de Liones. And in despite of us all he is departed from us, and maugre our heads.

With this answer the courier departed, and came to Maledisant his lady, and told her all how Sir La Cote Male Taile had sped at the castle Orgulous. Then she smote down her head, and said little. By my head, said Sir Mordred to the damsel, ye are greatly to blame so to rebuke him, for I warn you plainly he is a good knight, and I doubt not but he shall prove a noble knight, but as yet he may not sit sure on horseback: for he that shall be a good horseman it must come of usage and exercise. But when he cometh to the strokes of his sword he is then noble and mighty, and that saw Sir Bleoberis and Sir Palamides, for wit ye well they are wily men of arms, and anon they know when they see a young knight by his riding, how they are sure to give him a fall from his horse or a great buffet. But for the most part they will not light on foot with young knights, for they are wight and strongly armed. For in likewise Sir Launcelot du Lake when he was first made knight he was often put to the worse upon horseback, but ever upon foot he recovered his renown, and slew and defoiled many knights of the Round Table. And therefore the rebukes that Sir Launcelot did to many knights causeth them that be men of prowess to beware, for often I have seen the old proved knights rebuked and slain by them that were but young beginners. Thus they rode sure talking by the way together.

Here leave we off a while of this tale, and speak we of Sir Launcelot du Lake.

CHAP. V.

How Sir Launcelot came to the court and heard of La Cote Male Taile, and how he followed after him, and how La Cote Male Taile was prisoner.

THAT when he was come to the court of king Arthur, then heard he tell of the young knight La Cote Male Taile, how he slew the lion, and how he took upon him the adventure of the black shield, the which was named at that time the hardiest adventure of the world. Truly, said Sir Launcelot unto many of his fellows, it was shame to all the noble knights to suffer such a young knight to take such adventure upon him for his destruction: for I will that ye wit, said Sir Launcelot, that that damsel Maledisant hath borne that shield many a day for to seek the most proved knights, and that was she that Breuse Sance Pité took that shield from her, and after Tristram de Liones rescued that shield from him and gave it to the damsel again. A little afore that time Sir Tristram fought with my nephew Sir Blamor de Ganis for a quarrel that was betwixt the king of Ireland and him. Then many knights were sorry that Sir La Cote Male Taile was gone forth to that adventure. Truly, said Sir Launcelot, I cast me to ride after him. And within seven days Sir Launcelot overtook La Cote Male Taile. And then he saluted him and the damsel Maledisant. And when Sir Mordred saw Sir Launcelot then he left their fellowship. And so Sir Launcelot rode with them all a day, and ever that damsel rebuked La Cote Male Taile, and then Sir Launcelot answered for him; then she left off and rebuked Sir Launcelot. So this mean time Sir Tristram sent by a damsel a letter unto Sir Launcelot excusing him of the wedding of Isoud la Blanche Mains, and passing courteously and gently Sir Tristram wrote unto Sir Launcelot, ever beseeching him to be his good friend, and unto La

Beale Isoud of Cornwall, and that Sir Launcelot would excuse him if that ever he saw her. And within short time said Sir Tristram that he would speak with La Beale Isoud and with him right hastily. Then Sir Launcelot departed from the damsel and from Sir La Cote Male Taile, for to oversee that letter, and for to write another letter unto Sir Tristram de Liones. And in the mean while La Cote Male Taile rode with the damsel until they came unto a castle that hight Pendragon, and there were six knights stood afore him, and one of them proffered to just with La Cote Male Taile. And there La Cote Male Taile smote him over his horse croup. And then the five knights set upon him all at once with their spears, and there they smote La Cote Male Taile down, horse and man, and then they alight suddenly, and set their hands upon him all at once and took him prisoner, and so led him unto the castle and kept him as prisoner. And on the morn Sir Launcelot arose and delivered the damsel with letters unto Sir Tristram, and then he took his way after La Cote Male Taile, and by the way upon a bridge there was a knight proffered Sir Launcelot to just, and Sir Launcelot smote him down, and then they fought upon foot a noble battle together, and a mighty. And at the last Sir Launcelot smote him down groveling upon his hands and his knees; and then that knight yielded him, and Sir Launcelot received him fair. Sir, said the knight, I require thee tell me your name, for much my heart giveth unto you. Nay, said Sir Launcelot, as at this time I will not tell you my name, unless then that ye tell me your name. Certainly, said the knight, my name is Sir Nerovens, that was made knight of my lord Sir Launcelot du Lake. Ah, Nerovens de Lile, said Sir Launcelot, I am right glad that ye are proved a good knight, for now wit ye well my name is Sir Launcelot du Lake. Alas, said Nerovens de Lile, what have I done. And therewithall flatling he fell to his feet, and would have kissed them, but Sir Launcelot would not let him; and then either made great joy of other. And then Sir Nerovens told Sir Launcelot that he should not go by the castle of Pendragon, For there is a lord, a mighty knight, and many knights with him, and this night I heard say that they took a knight prisoner yesterday that rode with a damsel, and they say he is a knight of the Round Table.

CHAP. VI.

How Sir Launcelot fought with six knights, and after with Sir Brian, and how he delivered the prisoners.

AH, said Sir Launcelot, that knight is my fellow, and him shall I rescue, or else I shall lose my life therefore. And therewithal he rode fast till he came before the castle of Pendragon, and anon therewithal there came six knights, and all made them ready to set upon Sir Launcelot at once. Then Sir Launcelot feutred his spear, and smote the foremost that he brake his back in sunder, and three of them hit and three failed. And then Sir Launcelot past through them, and lightly he turned in again, and smote another knight through the breast and throughout the back, and more than an ell, and therewithal his spear brake. So then all the remnant of the four knights drew their swords, and lashed at Sir Launcelot, and at every stroke Sir Launcelot bestowed so his strokes that at four strokes sundry they avoided their saddles, passing sore wounded, and forthwithal he rode hurling into that castle. And, anon the lord of the castle that was that time called Sir Brian de les isles, the which was a noble man, and a great enemy unto king Arthur, within awhile he was armed and upon horseback: and then they feutred their spears, and hurled together so strongly that both their horses rashed to the earth. And then they avoided their saddles, and dressed their shields, and drew their swords, and flung together as wood men, and there were many strokes given in a while. At the last Sir Launcelot gave

to Sir Brian such a buffet that he kneeled upon his knees, and then Sir Launcelot rashed upon him, and with great force he pulled him off his helm, and when Sir Brian saw that he should be slain, he yielded him, and put him in his mercy and in his grace. Then Sir Launcelot made him to deliver all his prisoners that he had within his castle, and therein Sir Launcelot found of Arthur's knights thirty, and forty ladies, and so he delivered them and then he rode his way. And anon as La Cote Male Taile was delivered he gat his horse and his harness, and his damsel Maledisant. The mean while Sir Nerovens, that Sir Launcelot had fought withall afore at the bridge, he sent a damsel after Sir Launcelot for to wit how he sped at the castle of Pendragon. And then they within the castle marvelled what knight he was when Sir Brian and his knights delivered all those prisoners. Have ye no marvel, said the damsel, for the best knight in this world was here, and did this tourney, and wit ye well, she said, it was Sir Launcelot. Then was Sir Brian full glad, and so was his lady and all his knights that such a man should win them. And when the damsel and La Cote Male Taile understood that it was Sir Launcelot du Lake that had ridden with them in fellowship, and that she remembered her how she had rebuked him and called him coward, then was she passing heavy.

CHAP. VII.

How Sir Launcelot met with the damsel named Maledisant, and how he named her the damsel Bienpensant.

So then they took their horses and rode forth a pace after Sir Launcelot. And within two mile they overtook him, and saluted him, and thanked him, and the damsel cried Sir Launcelot mercy of her evil deed, and saying, For now I know the flower of all knighthood is parted even between Sir Tristram and you. For I have sought you my lord Sir Launcelot, and Sir Tristram, long, and now I thank God I have met with you; and once at Camelot, I met with Sir Tristram, and there he rescued this black shield with the white hand holding a naked sword, which Sir Breuse Sance Pité had taken away from me. Now, fair damsel, said Sir Launcelot, who told you my name? Sir, said she, there came a damsel from a knight that ye fought withall at the bridge, and she told me your name was Sir Launcelot du Lake. Blame have she then, said Sir Launcelot, but her lord Sir Nerovens hath told her. But damsel, said Sir Launcelot, upon this covenant I will ride with you, so that ye will not rebuke this knight Sir La Cote Male Taile no more, for he is a good knight, and I doubt not he shall prove a noble knight, and for his sake, and pity that he should not be destroyed, I followed him to succour him in this great need. Ah, God thank you, said the damsel, for now I will say unto you and to him both, I rebuked him never for no hate that I hated him, but for great love that I had to him: for ever I supposed that he had been too young and too tender to take upon him these adventures, and, therefore by my will I would have driven him away for jealousy that I had of his life; for it may be no young knight's deed that shall achieve this adventure to the end. Perdy, said Sir Launcelot, it is well said, and where ye are called the damsel Maledisant, I will call you the damsel Bienpensant. And so they rode forth a great while until they came to the border of the country of Surluse, and there they found a fair village with a strong bridge like a fortress. And when Sir Launcelot and they were at the bridge, there start forth afore them of gentlemen and yeomen many that said, Fair lords, ye may not pass this bridge and this fortress because of that black shield that I see one of you bear, and therefore there shall not pass but one of you at once; therefore choose which of you shall enter within this bridge first. Then Sir Launcelot proffered himself first to enter within this bridge. Sir, said La Cote Male Taile, I beseech you let me enter first within this fortress, and if I may speed well I will send for you, and if it happen that I be slain, there it goeth. And if so be that I am a prisoner taken, then may ye rescue me. I am loth, said Sir Launcelot, to let you pass this passage. Sir, said La Cote Male Taile, I pray you let me put my body in this adventure. Now go your way, said Sir Launcelot, and Jesu be your speed. So he entered, and anon there met with him two brethren, the one hight Sir Plaine de Force, and the other hight Sir Plaine de Amours; and anon they met with Sir La Cote Male Taile, and first La Cote Male Taile smote down Sir Plaine de Force, and soon after he smote down Plaine de Amours, and then they dressed them to their shields and swords, and bad La Cote Male Taile alight, and so he did, and there was dashing and foining with swords, and so they began to assail full hard La Cote Male Taile, and many great wounds they gave him upon his head and upon his breast and upon his shoulders. And as he might ever among he gave sad strokes again. And then the two brethren traced and traversed for to be of both hands of Sir La Cote Male Taile, but he by fine force and knightly prowess gat them afore him. And then when he felt himself so wounded then he doubled his strokes and gave them so many wounds that he felled them to the earth, and would have slain them had they not yielded them. And right so Sir La Cote Male Taile took the best horse that there was of them three, and so rode forth his way to the other fortress and bridge, and there he met with the third brother, whose name was Sir Plenorius, a full noble knight, and there they justed together, and either smote other down horse and man to the earth. And then they avoided their horses, and dressed their shields, and drew their swords, and gave many sad strokes, and one while the one knight was afore on the bridge, and another while the other. And thus they fought two hours and more, and never rested, and ever Sir Launcelot and the damsel beheld them. Alas, said the damsel, my knight fighteth passing sore and over long. Now may ye see, said Sir Launcelot, that he is a noble knight, for to consider his first battle, and his grievous wounds. And even forth with all so wounded as he is, it is great marvel that he may endure this long battle with that good knight.

CHAP. VIII.

How La Cote Male Taile was taken prisoner, and after rescued by Sir Launcelot, and how Sir Launcelot overcame four brethren.

THIS mean while Sir La Cote Male Taile sank right down upon the earth, what for-wounded and what for-bled he might not stand. Then the other knight had pity of him, and said, Fair young knight, dismay you not, for had ye been fresh when ye met with me, as I was, I well wot that I should not have endured so long as ye have done, and therefore for your noble deeds of arms I shall shew to you kindness and gentleness in all that I may. And forth withal this noble knight Sir Plenorius took him up in his arms, and led him into his tower. And then he commanded him the wine, and made to search him, and to stop his bleeding wounds. Sir, said La Cote Male Taile, withdraw you from me, and hie you to yonder bridge again, for there will meet you another manner knight than ever I was. Why, said Sir Plenorius, is there another manner knight behind of your fellowship? Yea, said La Cote Male Taile, there is a much better knight than I am. What is his name? said Plenorius. Ye shall not know for me, said La Cote Male Taile. Well, said the knight, he shall be encountered withal, whatsoever he be. Then Sir Plenorius heard a knight call that said, Sir Plenorius, where art thou? either thou must deliver me the prisoner that thou hast led unto thy tower, or else come and do battle with me. Then Sir Plenorius gat his horse, and came with a spear in his hand,

galloping towards Sir Launcelot, and then they began to feutre their spears, and came together as thunder, and smote either other so mightily that their horses fell down under them. And then they avoided their horses, and pulled out their swords, and like two bulls they lashed together with great strokes and foins, but ever Sir Launcelot recovered ground upon him, and Sir Plenorius traced to have gone about him. But Sir Launcelot would not suffer that, but bare him backer and backer till he came nigh his tower gate. And then said Sir Launcelot, I know thee well for a good knight, but wit thou well thy life and death is in my hand, and therefore yield thee to me, and thy prisoner. The other answered no word, but strake mightily upon Sir Launcelot's helm, that fire sprang out of his eyen; then Sir Launcelot doubled his strokes so thick, and smote at him so mightily, that he made him kneel upon his knees, and therewith Sir Launcelot lept upon him and pulled him groveling down. Then Sir Plenorius yielded him, and his tower, and all his prisoners, at his will. And then Sir Launcelot received him and took his troth, and then he rode to the other bridge, and there Sir Launcelot justed with other three of his brethren, the one hight Pillounes, and the other hight Pellogris, and the third Sir Pellandris. And first upon horseback Sir Launcelot smote them down, and afterward he beat them on foot, and made them to yield them unto him, and then he returned unto Sir Plenorius, and there he found in his prison king Carados of Scotland and many other knights, and all they were delivered. And then Sir La Cote Male Taile came to Sir Launcelot, and then Sir Launcelot would have given him all these fortresses and these bridges. Nay, said La Cote Male Taile, I will not have Sir Plenorius's livelihood: with that he will grant you, my lord Sir Launcelot, to come unto king Arthur's court, and to be his knight, and all his brethren, I will pray you, my lord, to let him have his livelihood. I will well, said Sir Launcelot, with this that he will come to the court of king Arthur, and become his man, and his brethren five. And as for you, Sir Plenorius, I will undertake, said Sir Launcelot, at the next feast, so there be a place voided, that ye shall be knight of the Round Table. Sir, said Sir Plenorius, at the next feast of Pentecost I will be at Arthur's court, and at that time I will be guided and ruled as king Arthur and ye will have me. Then Sir Launcelot and Sir La Cote Male Tail reposed them there unto the time that Sir La Cote Male Taile was whole of his wounds, and there they had merry cheer, and good rest, and many games, and there were many fair ladies.

CHAP. IX.

How Sir Launcelot made La Cote Male Taile lord of the castle of Pendragon, and after was made knight of the Round Table.

AND in the mean while there came Sir Kay the seneschal, and Sir Brandiles, and anon they fellowshipped with them. And then within ten days then departed those knights of king Arthur's court from these fortresses. And as Sir Launcelot came by the castle of Pendragon, there he put Sir Brian de les isles from his lands, because he would never be withold with king Arthur, and all that castle of Pendragon, and all the lands thereof, he gave to Sir La Cote Male Taile. And then Sir Launcelot sent for Sir Nerovens, that he made once knight, and he made him to have all the rule of that castle and of that country under La Cote Male Taile. And so they rode to Arthur's court all wholly together. And at Pentecost next following there was Sir Plenorius, and Sir La Cote Male Taile, called otherwise by right Sir Breunor le Noire, both made knights of the Table Round, and great lands king Arthur gave them; and there Breunor le Noire wedded that damsel Maledisant. And after she was called Beauvivante: but ever after for the more part he was called La Cote Male Taile, and he proved a passing noble knight and mighty, and many worship-

ful deeds he did after in his life, and Sir Plenorius proved a noble knight and full of prowess. And all the days of their life for the most part they awaited upon Sir Launcelot. And Sir Plenorius's brethren were ever knights of king Arthur. And also as the French book maketh mention, Sir La Cote Male Taile avenged his father's death.

CHAP. X.

How La Beale Isoud sent letters unto Sir Tristram by her maid Bragwaine, and of divers adventures of Sir Tristram.

Now leave we here Sir La Cote Male Taile, and turn we unto Sir Tristram de Liones that was in Britanny. When La Beale Isoud understood that he was wedded, she sent unto him by her maiden Bragwaine as piteous letters as could be thought and made, and her conclusion was, that, and it pleased Sir Tristram, that he would come to her court and bring with him Isoud la Blanche Mains, and they should be kept as well as she herself. Then Sir Tristram called unto him Sir Kehydius and asked him whether he would go with him into Cornwall secretly. He answered him that he was ready at all times. And then he let ordain prively a little vessel, and therein they went, Sir Tristram, Kehydius, dame Bragwaine, and Gouvernail Sir Tristram's squire. So when they were in the sea, a contrarious wind blew them on the coasts of North Wales, nigh the castle perilous. Then said Sir Tristram, Here shall ye abide me these ten days, and Gouvernail my squire with you. And if so be I come not again by that day, take the next way into Cornwall, for in this forest are many strange adventures as I have heard say, and some of them I cast me to prove or I depart: and when I may I shall hie me after you. Then Sir Tristram and Kehydius took their horses and departed from their fellowship. And so they rode within that forest a mile and more. And at the last Sir Tristram saw afore him a likely knight armed, sitting by a well, and a strong mighty horse passing nigh him tied to an oak, and a man hoving and riding by him, leading an horse laden with spears. And this knight that sat at the well seemed by his countenance to be passing heavy. Then Sir Tristram rode near him and said, Fair knight, why sit ye so drooping? Ye seem to be a knight errant by your arms and harness, and therefore dress you to just with one of us or with both. Therewithal that knight made no words, but took his shield and buckled it about his neck, and lightly he took his horse and lept upon him. And then he took a great spear of his squire, and departed his way a furlong. Sir Kehydius asked leave of Sir Tristram to just first. Do your best, said Sir Tristram. So they met together, and there Sir Kehydius had a fall, and was sore wounded on high above the breast. Then Sir Tristram said, Knight, that is well justed, now make you ready unto me. I am ready, said the knight. And then that knight took a greater spear in his hand and encountered with Sir Tristram, and there by great force that knight smote down Sir Tristram from his horse, and he had a great fall. Then Sir Tristram was sore ashamed, and lightly he avoided his horse and put his shield afore his shoulder, and drew his sword. And then Sir Tristram required that knight of his knighthood to alight upon foot and fight with him. I will well, said the knight. And so he alight upon foot and avoided his horse, and cast his shield upon his shoulder, and drew his sword, and there they fought a long battle together full nigh two hours.

Then Sir Tristram said, Fair knight, hold thy hand, and tell me of whence thou art, and what is thy name. As for that, said the knight, I will be advised, but and thou wilt tell me thy name, peradventure I will tell thee mine.

CHAP. XI.

How Sir Tristram met with Sir Lamorak de Galis, and how they fought, and after accorded never to fight together.

Now fair knight, he said, my name

is Sir Tristram de Liones. Sir, said the other knight, and my name is Sir Lamorak de Galis. Ah Sir Lamorak, said Sir Tristram, well be we met, and bethink thee now of the despite that thou didst me of the sending of the horn unto king Mark's court, to the intent to have slain or dishonoured my lady the queen La Beale Isoud. And therefore wit thou well, said Sir Tristram, the one of us shall die or we depart. Sir, said Sir Lamorak, remember that we were together in the isle of Servage, and at that time ye promised me great friendship. Then Sir Tristram would make no longer delays, but lashed at Sir Lamorak, and thus they fought long, till either were weary of other. Then Sir Tristram said to Sir Lamorak, In all my life met I never with such a knight that was so big and well breathed as ye be; therefore, said Sir Tristram, it were pity that any of us both should here be mischieved. Sir, said Sir Lamorak, for your renown and name I will that ye have the worship of this battle, and therefore I will yield me unto you. And therewith he took the point of his sword to yield him. Nay, said Sir Tristram, ye shall not do so, for I know well your proffers are more of your gentleness than for any fear or dread ye have of me. And therewithal Sir Tristram proffered him his sword, and said, Sir Lamorak, as an overcome knight I yield me unto you, as to a man of the most noble prowess that ever I met withal. Nay, said Sir Lamorak, I will do you gentleness. I require you let us be sworn together that never none of us shall after this day have ado with other. And there withal Sir Tristram and Sir Lamorak sware that never none of them should fight against other, nor for weal nor for woe.

CHAP. XII.

How Sir Palamides followed the questing beast, and he smote down both Sir Tristram and Sir Lamorak with one spear.

AND this mean while there came Sir Palamides the good knight following the questing beast that had in shape a head like a serpent's head, and a body like a libbard, haunches like a lion, and footed like a hart, and in his body there was such a noise as it had been the noise of thirty couple of hounds questing, and such a noise that beast made wheresover he went. And this beast evermore Sir Palamides followed, for it was called his quest. And right so as he followed this beast it came by Sir Tristram, and soon after came Palamides, and to brief this matter he smote down Sir Tristram and Sir Lamorak both with one spear, and so he departed after the beast Glatisant, that was called the questing beast, wherefore these two knights were passing wroth that Sir Palamides would not fight on foot with them.

Here men may understand that be of worship, that he was never formed that all times might stand, but some time he was put to the worse by mal-fortune. And at some time the worse knight put the better knight to a rebuke. Then Sir Tristram and Sir Lamorak gat Sir Kehydius upon a shield betwixt them both, and led him to a forester's lodge, and there they gave him in charge to keep him well, and with him they abode three days. Then the two knights took their horses and at the cross they parted. And then said Sir Tristram to Sir Lamorak, I require you if ye hap to meet with Sir Palamides, say him that he shall find me at the same well there I met him, and there I, Sir Tristram, shall prove whether he be better knight than I. And so either departed from other a sundry way, and Sir Tristram rode nigh there as was Sir Kehydius, and Sir Lamorak rode until he came to a chapel, and there he put his horse unto pasture. And anon there came Sir Meliagaunce that was king Bagdemagus's son, and he there put his horse to pasture, and was not ware of Sir Lamorak, and then this knight Sir Meliagaunce made his moan of the love that he had to queen Guenever, and there he made a woful complaint. All this heard Sir

Lamorak, and on the morn Sir Lamorak took his horse and rode unto the forest, and there he met two knights hoving under the wood shawe. Fair knights, said Sir Lamorak, what do ye hoving here and watching, and if ye be knights errant that will just, lo I am ready. Nay, sir knight, they said, not so, we abide not here for to just with you, but we lie here in await of a knight that slew our brother. What knight was that, said Sir Lamorak, that ye would fain meet withal. Sir, they said, it is Sir Launcelot that slew our brother, and if ever we may meet with him he shall not escape but we shall slay him. Ye take upon you a great charge, said Sir Lamorak, for Sir Launcelot is a noble proved knight. As for that we doubt not, for there is none of us but we are good enough for him. I will not believe that, said Sir Lamorak, for I heard never yet of no knight the days of my life but Sir Launcelot was too big for him.

CHAP. XIII.

How Sir Lamorak met with Sir Meliagaunce, and how they fought together for the beauty of queen Guenever.

RIGHT so as they stood talking thus, Sir Lamorak was ware how Sir Launcelot came riding straight toward them; then Sir Lamorak saluted him, and he him again. And then Sir Lamorak asked Sir Launcelot if there were any thing that he might do for him in these marches. Nay, said Sir Launcelot, not at this time, I thank you. Then either departed from other, and Sir Lamorak rode again there as he left the two knights, and then he found them hid in the leaved wood. Fie on you, said Sir Lamorak, false cowards, pity and shame it is that any of you should take the high order of knighthood. So Sir Lamorak departed from them, and within a while he met with Sir Meliagaunce, and then Sir Lamorak asked him why he loved queen Guenever as he did: For I was not far from you when ye made your complaint by the chapel. Did ye so, said Sir Meliagaunce, then will I abide by it : I love queen Guenever; what will ye with it? I will prove and make good that she is the fairest lady and most of beauty in the world. As to that, said Sir Lamorak, I say nay thereto, for queen Morgause of Orkney, mother to Sir Gawaine, and his mother is the fairest queen and lady that beareth the life. That is not so, said Sir Meliagaunce, and that will I prove with my hands upon thy body. Will ye so, said Sir Lamorak, and in a better quarrel keep I not to fight. Then they departed either from other in great wrath. And then they came riding together as it had been thunder, and either smote other so sore that their horses fell backward to the earth. And then they avoided their horses, and dressed their shields, and drew their swords. And then they hurtled together as wild boars, and thus they fought a great while. For Meliagaunce was a good man and of great might, but Sir Lamorak was hard big for him, and put him always aback; but either had wounded other sore. And as they stood thus fighting, by fortune came Sir Launcelot and Sir Bleoberis riding. And then Sir Launcelot rode betwixt them, and asked them for what cause they fought so together, and ye are both knights of king Arthur.

CHAP. XIV.

How Sir Meliagaunce told for what cause they fought, and how Sir Lamorak justed with king Arthur.

SIR, said Meliagaunce, I shall tell you for what cause we do this battle. I praised my lady queen Guenever, and said she was the fairest lady of the world, and Sir Lamorak said nay thereto, for he said queen Morgause of Orkney was fairer than she, and more of beauty. Ah Sir Lamorak, why sayest thou so? It is not thy part to dispraise thy princess that thou art under her obeisance and we all. And therewith he alight on foot, and said, For this quarrel make thee ready, for I will prove upon thee that queen Guenever is the fairest lady

and most of bounty in the world. Sir, said Sir Lamorak, I am loth to have ado with you in this quarrel. For every man thinketh his own lady fairest; and though I praise the lady that I love most, ye should not be wroth. For though my lady queen Guenever be fairest in your eye, wit ye well queen Morgause of Orkney is fairest in mine eye, and so every knight thinketh his own lady fairest; and, wit ye well, Sir, ye are the man in the world, except Sir Tristram, that I am most lothest to have ado withal. But and ye will needs fight with me, I shall endure you as long as I may. Then spake Sir Bleoberis, and said, My lord Sir Launcelot, I wist you never so misadvised as ye are now. For Sir Lamorak saith you but reason and knightly. For I warn you I have a lady, and me thinketh that she is the fairest lady of the world. Were this a great reason that ye should be wroth with me for such language? And well ye wot that Sir Lamorak is as noble a knight as I know, and he hath owed you and us ever good will, and therefore I pray you be good friends. Then Sir Launcelot said unto Sir Lamorak: I pray you forgive me mine evil will; and if I was misadvised I will amend it. Sir, said Sir Lamorak, the amends is soon made betwixt you and me. And so Sir Launcelot and Sir Bleoberis departed. And Sir Meliagaunce and Sir Lamorak took their horses, and either departed from other. And within a while came king Arthur, and met with Sir Lamorak, and justed with him, and there he smote down Sir Lamorak, and wounded him sore with a spear, and so he rode from him, wherefore Sir Lamorak was wroth that he would not fight with him on foot; how be it that Sir Lamorak knew not king Arthur.

CHAP. XV.

How Sir Kay met with Sir Tristram, and after of the shame spoken of the knights of Cornwall, and how they justed.

Now leave we of this tale, and speak we of Sir Tristram, that as he rode he met with Sir Kay the seneschal, and there Sir Kay asked Sir Tristram of what country he was. He answered that he was of the country of Cornwall. It may well be, said Sir Kay, for yet heard I never that ever good knight came out of Cornwall. That is evil spoken, said Sir Tristram, but and it please you to tell me your name I require you. Sir, wit ye well, said Sir Kay, that my name is Sir Kay the seneschal. Is that your name? said Sir Tristram; now wit ye well that ye are named the shamefullest knight of your tongue that now is living, how be it ye are called a good knight, but ye are called unfortunate, and passing overthwart of your tongue. And thus they rode together till they came to a bridge. And there was a knight would not let them pass till one of them justed with him. And so that knight justed with Sir Kay, and there that knight gave Sir Kay a fall; his name was Sir Tor, Sir Lamorak's half brother. And then they two rode to their lodging, and there they found Sir Brandiles; and Sir Tor came thither anon after.

And as they sat at supper, these four knights, three of them spake all shame by Cornish knights. Sir Tristram heard all that they said, and he said but little, but he thought the more; but at that time he discovered not his name. Upon the morn Sir Tristram took his horse and abode them upon their way; and there Sir Brandiles proffered to just with Sir Tristram, and Sir Tristram smote him down, horse and all, to the earth. Then Sir Tor le Fise de Vayshoure encountered with Sir Tristram, and there Sir Tristram smote him down. And then he rode his way, and Sir Kay followed him, but he would not of his fellowship. Then Sir Brandiles came to Sir Kay, and said, I would wit fain what is that knight's name. Come on with me, said Sir Kay, and we shall pray him to tell us his name. So they rode together till they came nigh him; and then they were ware where he sat by a well, and had put off his helm to drink at the well. And when

he saw them come, he laced on his helm lightly, and took his horse, and proffered them to just. Nay, said Sir Brandiles, we justed late enough with you; we come not in that intent. But for this we come, to require you of knighthood to tell us your name. My fair knights, since that is your desire, and to please you, ye shall wit that my name is Sir Tristram de Liones, nephew unto king Mark of Cornwall. In good time, said Sir Brandiles, and well ye be found; and wit ye well that we be right glad that we have found you, and we be of a fellowship that would be right glad of your company. For ye are the knight in the world that the noble fellowship of the Round Table most desireth to have the company of. I thank them, said Sir Tristram, of their great goodness; but as yet I feel well that I am unable to be of their fellowship. For I was never of such deeds of worthiness to be in the company of such a fellowship. Ah, said Sir Kay, and ye be Sir Tristram de Liones, ye are the man now called most of prowess, except Sir Launcelot du Lake. For he beareth not the life, christian ne heathen, that can find such another knight, to speak of his prowess, and of his hands, and his truth withal. For yet could there never creature say of him dishonour and make it good. Thus they talked a great while; and then they departed either from other, such ways as them seemed best.

CHAP. XVI.

How king Arthur was brought into the forest perilous, and how Sir Tristram saved his life.

Now shall ye hear what was the cause that king Arthur came into the forest perilous, that was in North Wales, by the means of a lady. Her name was Annowre, and this lady came to king Arthur at Cardiff, and she, by fair promise and fair behests, made king Arthur to ride with her into that forest perilous; and she was a great sorceress, and many days she had loved king Arthur, and therefore she came into that country. So when the king was gone with her, many of his knights followed after king Arthur when they missed him, as Sir Launcelot, Brandiles, and many other. And when she had brought him to her tower, she desired him to love her. And then the king remembered him of his lady, and would not love her for no craft that she could do. Then every day she would make him ride into that forest with his own knights, to the intent to have had king Arthur slain. For when this lady Annowre saw that she might not have him at her will, then she laboured by false means to have destroyed king Arthur and slain. Then the Lady of the lake, that was alway friendly to king Arthur, she understood by her subtle crafts that king Arthur was like to be destroyed. And therefore this Lady of the lake, that hight Nimue, came into that forest to seek after Sir Launcelot du Lake, or Sir Tristram, for to help king Arthur; for as that same day this Lady of the lake knew well that king Arthur should be slain, unless that he had help of one of these two knights. And thus she rode up and down till she met with Sir Tristram, and anon as she saw him she knew him. O my lord Sir Tristram, she said, well be ye met, and blessed be the time that I have met with you; for this same day, and within these two hours, shall be done the foulest deed that ever was done in this land. O fair damsel, said Sir Tristram, may I amend it? Come on with me, she said, and that in all the haste ye may, for ye shall see the most worshipfullest knight of the world hard bested. Then said Sir Tristram, I am ready to help such a noble man. He is neither better nor worse, said the Lady of the lake, but the noble king Arthur himself. God defend, said Sir Tristram, that ever he should be in such distress. Then they rode together a great pace, until they came to a little turret or castle, and underneath that castle they saw a knight standing upon foot fighting with two knights; and so Sir Tristram beheld them, and at the last the two knights smote down the

one knight, and that one of them unlaced his helm to have slain him. And the lady Annowre gat king Arthur's sword in her hand to have stricken off his head. And therewithal came Sir Tristram with all his might, crying, Traitress, traitress, leave that. And anon there Sir Tristram smote one of the knights through the body, that he fell dead; and then he rashed to the other and smote his back in sunder, and in the mean while the Lady of the lake cried to king Arthur, Let not that false lady escape. Then king Arthur overtook her, and with the same sword he smote off her head; and the Lady of the lake took up her head, and hung it up by the hair on her saddle bow. And then Sir Tristram horsed king Arthur, and rode forth with him, but he charged the Lady of the lake not to discover his name as at that time. When the king was horsed he thanked heartily Sir Tristram, and desired to wit his name; but he would not tell him, but that he was a poor knight adventurous. And so he bare king Arthur fellowship till he met with some of his knights. And within a mile he met with Sir Ector de Maris, and he knew not king Arthur nor Sir Tristram, and he desired to just with one of them. Then Sir Tristram rode unto Sir Ector, and smote him from his horse. And when he had done so he came again to the king, and said: My lord, yonder is one of your knights, he may bear you fellowship; and another day by that deed that I have done for you, I trust ye shall understand that I would do you service. Alas, said king Arthur, let me wit what ye are. Not at this time, said Sir Tristram. So he departed, and left king Arthur and Sir Ector together.

CHAP. XVII.

How Sir Tristram came to La Beale Isoud, and how Kehydius began to love La Beale Isoud, and of a letter that Tristram found.

AND then at a day set Sir Tristram and Sir Lamorak met at the well; and then they took Kehydius at the forester's house, and so they rode with him to the ship where they left dame Bragwaine and Gouvernail, and so they sailed into Cornwall all wholly together; and by assent and information of dame Bragwaine, when they were landed they rode unto Sir Dinas the seneschal, a trusty friend of Sir Tristram's. And so dame Bragwaine and Sir Dinas rode to the court of king Mark, and told the queen, La Beale Isoud, that Sir Tristram was nigh her in that country. Then for very pure joy La Beale Isoud swooned : and when she might speak, she said, Gentle knight seneschal, help that I might speak with him, or else my heart will brast.

Then Sir Dinas and dame Bragwaine brought Sir Tristram and Kehydius privily unto the court, unto a chamber whereas La Beale Isoud assigned it; and to tell the joy that was between La Beale Isoud and Sir Tristram, there is no tongue can tell it, nor heart think it, nor pen write it. And, as the French book maketh mention, at the first time that ever Sir Kehydius saw La Beale Isoud, he was so enamoured upon her that for very pure love he might never withdraw it. And at the last, as ye shall hear or the book be ended, Sir Kehydius died for the love of La Beale Isoud. And then privily he wrote unto her letters and ballads of the most goodliest that were used in those days. And when La Beale Isoud understood his letters, she had pity of his complaint, and unadvised she wrote another letter to comfort him withal. And Sir Tristram was all this while in a turret, at the commandment of La Beale Isoud, and when she might she came unto Sir Tristram. So on a day king Mark played at the chess under a chamber window; and at that time Sir Tristram and Sir Kehydius were within the chamber, over king Mark, and as it mishapped Sir Tristram found the letter that Kehydius sent to La Beale Isoud; also he had found the letter that she wrote unto Kehydius, and at that same time La Beale Isoud was in the same chamber. Then Sir Tristram came unto La Beale

Isoud, and said ; Madam, here is a letter that was sent unto you, and here is the letter that ye sent unto him that sent you that letter. Alas, madam, the good love that I have loved you, and many lands and riches have I forsaken for your love, and now ye are a traitress to me, the which doth me great pain. But as for thee, Sir Kehydius, I brought thee out of Britanny into this country, and thy father, king Howel, I won his lands; howbeit, I wedded thy sister, Isoud la Blanche Mains, for the goodness which she did to me : but wit thou well Sir Kehydius for this falsehood and treason thou hast done me, I will revenge it upon thee. And therewithal Sir Tristram drew out his sword, and said, Sir Kehydius keep thee, and then La Beale Isoud swooned to the earth. And when Sir Kehydius saw Sir Tristram come upon him, he saw none other boot, but lept out at a bay window, even over the head where sat king Mark playing at the chess. And when the king saw one come hurling over his head, he said, Fellow, what art thou, and what is the cause thou leapest out of that window? My lord the king, said Kehydius, it fortuned me that I was asleep in the window above your head, and as I slept I slumbered, and so I fell down. And thus Sir Kehydius excused him.

CHAP. XVIII.

How Sir Tristram departed from Tintagil, and how he sorrowed, and was so long in a forest till he was out of his mind.

THEN Sir Tristram dread sore lest he were discovered unto the king that he was there, wherefore he drew him to the strength of the tower, and armed him in such armour as he had, for to fight with them that would withstand him. And so when Sir Tristram saw there was no resistance against him, he sent Gouvernail for his horse and for his spear, and knightly he rode forth out of the castle openly that was called the castle of Tintagil. And even at the gate he met with Gingalin, Sir Gawaine's son. And anon Sir Gingalin put his spear in his rest, and ran upon Sir Tristram, and brake his spear, and Sir Tristram at that time had but a sword, and gave him such a buffet upon the helm that he fell down from his saddle, and his sword slid down and carved asunder his horse neck. And so Sir Tristram rode his way into the forest, and all this doing saw king Mark. And then he sent a squire unto the hurt knight, and commanded him to come to him, and so he did. And when king Mark wist that it was Sir Gingalin, he welcomed him, and gave him a horse, and asked him what knight it was that had encountered with him. Sir, said Sir Gingalin, I wot not what knight he was, but well I wot that he sigheth, and maketh great dole. Then Sir Tristram within a while met with a knight of his own, that hight Sir Fergus. And when he had met with him he made great sorrow, insomuch that he fell down off his horse in a swoon, and in such sorrow he was in three days and three nights. Then at the last Sir Tristram sent unto the court by Sir Fergus, for to ask what tidings. And so as he rode by the way he met with a damsel that came from Sir Palamides, to know and seek how Sir Tristram did. Then Sir Fergus told her how he was almost out of his mind. Alas, said the damsel, where shall I find him? In such a place, said Sir Fergus. Then Sir Fergus found queen Isoud sick in her bed, making the greatest dole that ever any earthly woman made. And when the damsel found Sir Tristram, she made great dole because she might not amend him; for the more she made of him the more was his pain. And at the last Sir Tristram took his horse and rode away from her. And then was it three days or that she could find him, and then she brought him meat and drink, but he would none. And then another time Sir Tristram escaped away from the damsel, and it happed him to ride by the same castle where Sir Palamides and Sir Tristram did battle when La Beale Isoud departed them. And there by for-

tune the damsel met with Sir Tristram again, making the greatest dole that ever earthly creature made, and she went to the lady of that castle, and told her of the misadventure of Sir Tristram. Alas, said the lady of that castle, where is my lord Sir Tristram? Right here by your castle, said the damsel. In good time, said the lady, is he so nigh me: he shall have meat and drink of the best, and a harp I have of his whereupon he taught me,—for of goodly harping he beareth the prize in the world. So this lady and the damsel brought him meat and drink, but he eat little thereof. Then upon a night he put his horse from him, and then he unlaced his armour, and then Sir Tristram would go into the wilderness, and brast down the trees and boughs; and otherwhile, when he found the harp that the lady sent him, then would he harp and play thereupon and weep together. And sometime when Sir Tristram was in the wood, that the lady wist not where he was, then would she sit her down and play upon that harp: then would Sir Tristram come to that harp and hearken thereto, and sometime he would harp himself. Thus he there endured a quarter of a year. Then at the last he ran his way. And then she wist not where he was become. And then was he naked, and waxed lean and poor of flesh, and so he fell into the fellowship of herdmen and shepherds, and daily they would give him of their meat and drink. And when he did any shrewd deed they would beat him with rods, and so they clipped him with shears and made him like a fool.

CHAP. XIX.

How Sir Tristram soused Dagonet in a well, and how Palamides sent a damsel to seek Tristram, and how Palamides met with king Mark.

AND upon a day Sir Dagonet, king Arthur's fool, came into Cornwall, with two squires with him, and as they rode through that forest they came by a fair well where Sir Tristram was wont to be, and the weather was hot, and they alight to drink of that well, and in the mean while their horses brake loose. Right so Sir Tristram came unto them, and first he soused Sir Dagonet in that well, and after his squires, and thereat laughed the shepherds, and forthwithal he ran after their horses, and brought them again one by one, and right so, wet as they were, he made them leap up and ride their ways. Thus Sir Tristram endured there an half year naked, and would never come in town nor village. The mean while the damsel that Sir Palamides sent to seek Sir Tristram she went unto Sir Palamides, and told him all the mischief that Sir Tristram endured. Alas, said Sir Palamides, it is great pity that ever so noble a knight should be so mischieved for the love of a lady. But nevertheless I will go and seek him, and comfort him and I may. Then a little before that time La Beale Isoud had commanded Sir Kehydius out of the country of Cornwall. So Sir Kehydius departed with a dolorous heart. And by adventure he met with Sir Palamides, and they enfellowshipped together, and either complained to other of their love, that they loved La Beale Isoud. Now let us, said Sir Palamides, seek Sir Tristram that loved her as well as we, and let us prove whether we may recover him. So they rode into that forest, and three days and three nights they would never take their lodging, but ever sought Sir Tristram. And upon a time by adventure they met with king Mark that was ridden from his men all alone. When they saw him, Sir Palamides knew him, but Sir Kehydius knew him not. Ah, false king, said Sir Palamides, it is pity thou hast thy life, for thou art a destroyer of all worshipful knights, and by thy mischief, and thy vengeance, thou hast destroyed that most noble knight Sir Tristram de Liones; and therefore defend thee, said Sir Palamides, for thou shalt die this day. That were shame, said king Mark, for ye two are armed, and I am unarmed. As for that, said Sir Palamides, I shall find a remedy therefore. Here is a knight with me, and thou shalt

have his harness. Nay, said king Mark, I will not have ado with you, for cause have ye none to me. For all the misease that Sir Tristram hath was for a letter that he found; for, as to me, I did to him no displeasure, and I am full sorry for his disease and malady. So when the king had thus excused him, they were friends, and king Mark would have had them unto Tintagil, but Sir Palamides would not, but turned unto the realm of Logris, and Sir Kehydius said he would go into Britanny.

Now turn we unto Sir Dagonet again, then when he and his squires were upon horseback, he deemed that the shepherds had sent that fool to array them so because that they laughed at them, and so they rode unto the keepers of beasts, and all to beat them. Sir Tristram saw them beaten that were wont to give him meat and drink, then he ran thither and gat Sir Dagonet by the head, and gave him such a fall to the earth that he bruised him sore, so that he lay still. And then he wrast his sword out of his hand and therewith he ran to one of his squires and smote off his head, and the other fled. And so Sir Tristram took his way with that sword in his hand, running as he had been wild wood. Then Sir Dagonet rode to king Mark and told him how he had sped in that forest. And therefore, said Sir Dagonet, beware, king Mark, that thou come not about that well in the forest, for there is a fool naked, and that fool and I fool met together, and he had almost slain me. Ah, said king Mark, that is Sir Matto le Breune, that fell out of his wit because he lost his lady. For when Sir Gaheris smote down Sir Matto and won his lady of him, never since was he in his mind, and that was pity, for he was a good knight.

CHAP. XX.

How it was noised how Sir Tristram was dead, and how La Beale Isoud would have slain herself.

THEN Sir Andred that was cousin unto Sir Tristram, made a lady that was his paramour to say and noise it that she was with Sir Tristram or ever he died. And this tale she brought unto king Mark's court, that she buried him by a well, and that or he died he besought king Mark to make his cousin, Sir Andred, king of the country of Liones, of the which Sir Tristram was lord of. All this did Sir Andred because he would have had Sir Tristram's lands. And when king Mark heard tell that Sir Tristram was dead, he wept and made great dole. But when queen Isoud heard of these tidings, she made such sorrow that she was nigh out of her mind. And so upon a day she thought to slay herself, and never to live after Sir Tristram's death. And so upon a day La Beale Isoud gat a sword privily, and bare it into her garden, and there she pight the sword through a plum tree up to the hilts, so that it stack fast, and it stood breast high. And as she would have run upon the sword and to have slain herself, all this espied king Mark, how she kneeled down and said, Sweet Lord Jesu have mercy upon me, for I may not live after the death of Sir Tristram de Liones, for he was my first love, and he shall be the last. And with these words came king Mark and took her in his arms, and then he took up the sword, and bare her away with him into a strong tower, and there he made her to be kept, and watched her surely. And after that she lay long sick, nigh at the point of death. This mean while ran Sir Tristram naked in the forest with the sword in his hand, and so he came to an hermitage, and there he laid him down and slept, and in the mean while the hermit stale away his sword, and laid meat down by him. Thus was he kept there a ten days, and at the last he departed and came to the herdmen again. And there was a giant in that country that hight Tauleas, and for fear of Sir Tristram more than seven years he durst never much go at large, but for the most part he kept him in a sure castle of his own. And so this Tauleas heard tell that Sir Tristram was dead, by the

noise of the court of king Mark. Then this Tauleas went daily at large. And so it happed upon a day he came to the herdmen wandering and lingering, and there he set him down to rest among them. The mean while there came a knight of Cornwall that led a lady with him, and his name was Sir Dinant. And when the giant saw him, he went from the herdmen and hid him under a tree, and so the knight came to the well, and there he alight to repose him. And as soon as he was from his horse, the giant Tauleas came betwixt this knight and his horse, and took the horse and lept upon him. So forthwith he rode unto Sir Dinant and took him by the collar, and pulled him afore him upon his horse, and there would have stricken off his head. Then the herdmen said unto Sir Tristram, Help yonder knight. Help ye him, said Sir Tristram. We dare not, said the herdmen. Then Sir Tristram was ware of the sword of the knight there as it lay, and so thither he ran, and took up the sword and strake off Sir Tauleas's head, and so he went his way to the herdmen again.

CHAP. XXI.

How king Mark found Sir Tristram naked, and made him to be borne home to Tintagil, and how he was there known by a brachet.

THEN the knight took up the giant's head, and bare it with him unto king Mark, and told him what adventure betid him in the forest, and how a naked man rescued him from the grimly giant Tauleas. Where had ye this adventure? said king Mark. Forsooth, said Sir Dinant, at the fair fountain in your forest where many adventurous knights meet, and there is the mad man. Well, said king Mark, I will see that wild man. So within a day or two king Mark commanded his knights and his hunters, that they should be ready on the morn for to hunt, and on the morn he went unto that forest. And when the king came to that well, he found there lying by that well a fair naked man, and a sword by him. Then king Mark blew and straked, and therewith his knights came to him. And then the king commanded his knights to take that naked man with fairness, and bring him to my castle. So they did softly and fair, and cast mantles upon Sir Tristram, and so led him unto Tintagil; and there they bathed him and washed him, and gave him hot suppings, till they had brought him well to his remembrance. But all this while there was no creature that knew Sir Tristram, nor what man he was. So it fell upon a day that the queen La Beale Isoud heard of such a man that ran naked in the forest, and how the king had brought him home to the court. Then La Beale Isoud called unto her dame Bragwaine, and said, Come on with me, for we will go see this man that my lord brought from the forest the last day. So they passed forth, and asked where was the sick man. And then a squire told the queen that he was in the garden taking his rest, and reposing him against the sun. So when the queen looked upon Sir Tristram she was not remembered of him. But ever she said unto dame Bragwaine, Me seemeth I should have seen him heretofore in many places. But as soon as Sir Tristram saw her he knew her well enough, and then he turned away his visage and wept. Then the queen had always a little brachet with her, that Sir Tristram gave her the first time that ever she came into Cornwall, and never would that brachet depart from her, but if Sir Tristram was nigh there as was La Beale Isoud; and this brachet was sent from the king's daughter of France unto Sir Tristram for great love. And anon as this little brachet felt a savour of Sir Tristram, she leaped upon him, and licked his cheeks and his ears, and then she whined and quested, and she smelled at his feet and at his hands, and on all parts of his body that she might come to. Ah, my lady, said dame Bragwaine unto La Beale Isoud, alas, alas! said she, I see it is mine own lord, Sir Tristram. And thereupon Isoud fell down in a

swoon, and so lay a great while; and when she might speak, she said, My lord Sir Tristram, blessed be God ye have your life; and now I am sure ye shall be discovered by this little brachet, for she will never leave you: and also I am sure as soon as my lord king Mark do know you, he will banish you out of the country of Cornwall, or else he will destroy you. Therefore mine own lord, grant king Mark his will, and then draw you unto the court of king Arthur, for there are ye beloved. And ever when I may I shall send unto you, and when ye list ye may come to me, and at all times early and late I will be at your commandment to live as poor a life as ever did queen or lady. O madam, said Sir Tristram, go from me, for mickle anger and danger have I escaped for your love.

CHAP. XXII.

How king Mark, by the advice of his council, banished Sir Tristram out of Cornwall the term of ten years.

THEN the queen departed, but the brachet would not from him. And therewithal came king Mark, and the brachet sat upon him, and bayed at them all. Therewithal Sir Andred spake and said, Sir, this is Sir Tristram, I see by the brachet. Nay, said the king, I cannot suppose that. So the king asked him upon his faith what he was, and what was his name. Truly, said he, my name is Sir Tristram de Liones, now do by me what ye list. Ah, said king Mark, me repenteth of your recovery. And then he let call his barons to judge Sir Tristram to death. Then many of his barons would not assent thereto, and in especial Sir Dinas the seneschal and Sir Fergus. And so by the advice of them all Sir Tristram was banished out of the country for ten year, and thereupon he took his oath upon a book before the king and his barons. And so he was made to depart out of the country of Cornwall, and there were many barons brought him into his ship, of the which some were his friends, and some his foes. And in the mean while there came a knight of king Arthur's, his name was Dinadan, and his coming was to seek after Sir Tristram. Then they shewed him where he was armed at all points, going to the ship. Now, fair knight, said Sir Dinadan, or ye pass this court, that ye will just with me I require you. With a good will, said Sir Tristram, and these lords will give me leave. Then the barons granted thereto, and so they ran together, and there Sir Tristram gave Sir Dinadan a fall. And then he prayed Sir Tristram to give him leave to go in his fellowship. Ye shall be right welcome, said then Sir Tristram. And so they took their horses and rode to their ships together. And when Sir Tristram was in the sea, he said, Greet well king Mark and all mine enemies, and say them I will come again when I may. And well am I rewarded for the fighting with Sir Marhaus, and delivering all this country from servage, and well I am rewarded for the fetching and costs. of La Beale Isoud out of Ireland, and the danger that I was in first and last, and by the way coming home what danger I had to bring again queen Isoud from the castle Pluere. And well am I rewarded when I fought with Sir Bleoberis for Sir Segwarides' wife. And well am I rewarded when I fought with Sir Blamor de Ganis for king Anguish, father unto La Beale Isoud. And well am I rewarded when I smote down the good knight Sir Lamorak de Galis at king Mark's request. And well am I rewarded when I fought with the king with the hundred knights, and the king of Northgalis, and both these would have put his land in servage, and by me they were put to a rebuke. And well am I rewarded for the slaying of Tauleas the mighty giant, and many more deeds have I done for him, and now have I my warison. And tell king Mark that many noble knights of the Table Round have spared the barons of this country for my sake. Also am I not well rewarded when I fought with the

good knight Sir Palamides, and rescued queen Isoud from him. And at that time king Mark said afore all his barons, I should have been better rewarded. And forthwithal he took the sea.

CHAP. XXIII.

How a damsel sought help to help Sir Launcelot against thirty knights, and how Sir Tristram fought with them.

AND at the next landing, fast by the sea, there met with Sir Tristram and with Sir Dinadan Sir Ector de Maris and Sir Bors de Ganis. And there Sir Ector justed with Sir Dinadan and he smote him and his horse down. And then Sir Tristram would have justed with Sir Bors, and Sir Bors said he would not just with no Cornish knights, for they are not called men of worship. And all this was done upon a bridge. And with this came Sir Bleoberis and Sir Driant, and Sir Bleoberis proffered to just with Sir Tristram, and there Sir Tristram smote down Sir Bleoberis. Then said Sir Bors de Ganis, I wist never Cornish knight of so great valour nor so valiant as that knight that beareth the trappours embroidered with crowns. And then Sir Tristram and Sir Dinadan departed from them into a forest, and there met them a damsel that came for the love of Sir Launcelot to seek after some noble knights of king Arthur's court for to rescue Sir Launcelot. And so Sir Launcelot was ordained, for by the treason of queen Morgan le Fay to have slain Sir Launcelot, and for that cause she ordained thirty knights for to lie in a wait for Sir Launcelot, and this damsel knew this treason. And for this cause the damsel came for to seek noble knights to help Sir Launcelot. For that night, or the day after, Sir Launcelot should come where these thirty knights were. And so this damsel met with Sir Bors, Sir Bleoberis, Sir Ector, and Sir Driant, and there she told them all four of the treason of Morgan le Fay. And then they promised her that they would be nigh where Sir Launcelot should meet with the thirty knights, and if so be they set upon him we will do rescues as we can. So the damsel departed, and by adventure the damsel met with Sir Tristram and with Sir Dinadan, and there the damsel told them all the treason that was ordained for Sir Launcelot. Fair damsel, said Sir Tristram, bring me to that same place where they should meet with Sir Launcelot. Then said Sir Dinadan, What will ye do? it is not for us to fight with thirty knights, and wit you well I will not thereof, as to match one knight two or three is enough, and they be men. But for to match fifteen knights, that will I never undertake. Fie for shame, said Sir Tristram, do but your part. Nay, said Sir Dinadan, I will not thereof, but if ye will lend me your shield, for ye bear a shield of Cornwall, and for the cowardice that is named to the knights of Cornwall, by your shields ye be ever forborn. Nay, said Sir Tristram, I will not depart from my shield for her sake that gave it me. But one thing, said Sir Tristram, I promise thee Sir Dinadan, but if thou wilt promise me to abide with me, here I shall slay thee: for I desire no more of thee but to answer one knight, and if thy heart will not serve thee, stand by and look upon me and them. Sir, said Sir Dinadan, I promise you to look upon and to do what I may to save myself, but I would I had not met with you. So then anon these thirty knights came fast by these four knights, and they were ware of them, and either of other. And so these thirty knights let them pass for this cause, that they would not wrath them if cause be that they had ado with Sir Launcelot, and the four knights let them pass to this intent, that they would see and behold what they would do with Sir Launcelot. And so the thirty knights past on, and came by Sir Tristram and Sir Dinadan. And then Sir Tristram cried on high, Lo here is a knight against you for the love of Sir Launcelot. And there he slew two with one spear, and ten with his sword. And then came in Sir Dinadan, and he

did passing well. And so of the thirty knights there went but ten away, and they fled. All this battle saw Sir Bors de Ganis, and his three fellows. And then they saw well it was the same knight that justed with them at the bridge. Then they took their horses and rode unto Sir Tristram, and praised him, and thanked him of his good deeds, and they all desired Sir Tristram to go with them to their lodging. And he said nay, he would not go to no lodging. Then they all four knights prayed him to tell them his name. Fair lords, said Sir Tristram, as at this time I will not tell you my name.

CHAP. XXIV.

How Sir Tristram and Sir Dinadan came to a lodging where they must just with two knights.

THEN Sir Tristram and Sir Dinadan rode forth their way till they came to the shepherds and to the herdmen, and there they asked them if they knew any lodging or harbour there nigh hand. Forsooth sirs, said the herdmen, hereby is good lodging in a castle, but there is such a custom that there shall no knight be harboured but if he just with two knights, and if he be but one knight he must just with two. And as ye be therein, soon shall ye be matched. There is shrewd harbour, said Sir Dinadan, lodge where ye will, for I will not lodge there. Fie for shame, said Sir Tristram, are ye not a knight of the Table Round, wherefore ye may not with your worship refuse your lodging. Not so, said the herdmen, for and ye be beaten and have the worse ye shall not be lodged there, and if ye beat them ye shall be well harboured. Ah, said Sir Dinadan, they are two sure knights. Then Sir Dinadan would not lodge there in no manner, but as Sir Tristram required him of his knighthood, and so they rode thither. And to make short tale, Sir Tristram and Sir Dinadan smote them down both, and so they entered into the castle, and had good cheer as they could think or devise. And when they were unarmed, and thought to be merry and in good rest, there came in at the gates Sir Palamides and Sir Gaheris, requiring to have the custom of the castle. What array is this? said Sir Dinadan, I would have my rest. That may not be, said Sir Tristram; now must we needs defend the custom of this castle, insomuch as we have the better of the lords of this castle, and therefore, said Sir Tristram, needs must ye make you ready. In the devil's name, said Sir Dinadan, came I into your company. And so they made them ready. And Sir Gaheris encountered with Sir Tristram, and Sir Gaheris had a fall, and Sir Palamides encountered with Sir Dinadan, and Sir Dinadan had a fall; then was it fall for fall. So then must they fight on foot. That would not Sir Dinadan, for he was so sore bruised of the fall that Sir Palamides gave him. Then Sir Tristram unlaced Sir Dinadan's helm, and prayed him to help him. I will not, said Sir Dinadan, for I am sore wounded of the thirty knights that we had but late ago to do withal. But ye fare, said Sir Dinadan unto Sir Tristram, as a mad man, and as a man that is out of his mind, that would cast himself away, and I may curse the time that ever I saw you. For in all the world are not two such knights that be so wood as is Sir Launcelot and ye Sir Tristram: for once I fell in the fellowship of Sir Launcelot as I have now done with you, and he set me a work that a quarter of a year I kept my bed. Defend me, said Sir Dinadan, from such two knights, and specially from your fellowship. Then, said Sir Tristram, I will fight with them both. Then Sir Tristram bad them come forth both, for I will fight with you. Then Sir Palamides and Sir Gaheris dressed them and smote at them both. Then Dinadan smote at Sir Gaheris a stroke or two, and turned from him. Nay, said Sir Palamides, it is too much shame for us two knights to fight with one. And then he did bid Sir Gaheris stand aside with that knight that hath no list to

fight. Then they rode together and fought long, and at the last Sir Tristram doubled his strokes and drove Sir Palamides aback more than three strides. And then by one assent Sir Gaheris and Sir Dinadan went betwixt them and departed them in sunder. And then by assent of Sir Tristram, they would have lodged together. But Sir Dinadan would not lodge in that castle, and then he cursed the time that ever he came in their fellowship. And so he took his horse and his harness and departed. Then Sir Tristram prayed the lords of that castle to lend him a man to bring him to a lodging. And so they did, and overtook Sir Dinadan, and rode to their lodging two miles thence with a good man in a priory, and there they were well at ease. And that same night, Sir Bors, and Sir Bleoberis, and Sir Ector, and Sir Driant, abode still in the same place there as Sir Tristram fought with the thirty knights, and there they met with Sir Launcelot the same night, and had made promise to lodge with Sir Colgrevance the same night.

CHAP. XXV.

How Sir Tristram justed with Sir Kay and Sir Sagramor le Desirous, and how Sir Gawaine turned Sir Tristram from Morgan le Fay.

BUT anon as the noble knight Sir Launcelot heard of the shield of Cornwall, then wist he well that it was Sir Tristram that fought with his enemies. And then Sir Launcelot praised Sir Tristram, and called him the man of most worship in the world. So there was a knight in that priory that hight Pellinore, and he desired to wit the name of Sir Tristram, but in no wise he could not. And so Sir Tristram departed and left Sir Dinadan in the priory, for he was so weary and so sore bruised that he might not ride. Then this knight, Sir Pellinore, said to Sir Dinadan, Sithen that ye will not tell me that knight's name, I will ride after him and make him to tell me his name, or he shall die therefore. Beware, sir knight, said Sir Dinadan, for and ye follow him ye shall repent it. So that knight, Sir Pellinore, rode after Sir Tristram, and required him of justs. Then Sir Tristram smote him down, and wounded him through the shoulder, and so he past on his way. And on the next day following Sir Tristram met with pursuivants, and they told him that there was made a great cry of tournament between king Carados of Scotland and the king of North Wales, and either should just against other at the Castle of Maidens. And these pursuivants sought all the country after the good knights, and in especial king Carados let make seeking for Sir Launcelot, and the king of Northgalis let seek after Sir Tristram de Liones. And at that time Sir Tristram thought to be at that justs, and so by adventure they met with Sir Kay the seneschal and Sir Sagramor le Desirous, and Sir Kay required Sir Tristram to just, and Sir Tristram in a manner refused him, because he would not be hurt nor bruised against the great justs that should be before the Castle of Maidens, and therefore he thought to repose him, and to rest him. And alway Sir Kay cried, Sir knight of Cornwall, just with me, or else yield thee to me as recreant. When Sir Tristram heard him say so, he turned to him, and then Sir Kay refused him, and turned his back. Then Sir Tristram said, As I find thee shall I take thee. Then Sir Kay turned with evil will, and Sir Tristram smote Sir Kay down, and so he rode forth. Then Sir Sagramor le Desirous rode after Sir Tristram and made him to just with him. And there Sir Tristram smote down Sir Sagramor le Desirous from his horse, and rode his way, and the same day he met with a damsel that told him that he should win great worship of a knight adventurous, that did much harm in all that country.

When Sir Tristram heard her say so, he was glad to go with her to win worship. So Sir Tristram rode with that damsel a six mile, and then met him Sir Gawaine, and therewithal Sir Gawaine knew the damsel, that she was a damsel of queen-Morgan le Fay. Then Sir Gawaine understood that she led that knight to some mischief. Fair knight, said Sir Gawaine, whither ride you now with that damsel? Sir, said Sir Tristram, I wot not whither I shall ride, but as the damsel will lead me. Sir, said Sir Gawaine, ye shall not ride with her, for she and her lady did never good, but ill. And then Sir Gawaine pulled out his sword, and said, Damsel, but if thou tell me anon for what cause thou leadest this knight with thee, thou shalt die for it right anon. I know all your lady's treason and yours. Mercy, Sir Gawaine, she said, and if ye will save my life I will tell you. Say on, said Sir Gawaine, and thou shalt have thy life. Sir, she said, queen Morgan le Fay, my lady, hath ordained a thirty ladies to seek and espy after Sir Launcelot or Sir Tristram, and by the trains of these ladies, who that may first meet with any of these two knights, they should turn them unto Morgan le Fay's castle, saying that they should do deeds of worship, and if any of those two knights came there, there be thirty knights lying and watching in a tower to wait upon Sir Launcelot, or upon Sir Tristram. Fie for shame, said Sir Gawaine, that ever such false treason should be wrought or used in a queen and a king's sister, and a king and queen's daughter.

CHAP. XXVI.

How Sir Tristram and Sir Gawaine rode to have fought against the thirty knights, but they durst not come out.

Sir, said Sir Gawaine, will ye stand with me, and we will see the malice of these thirty knights? Sir, said Sir Tristram, go ye to them and it please you, and ye shall see I will not fail you, for it is not long ago since I and a fellow met with thirty knights of that queen's fellowship; and God speed us so that we may win worship. So then Sir Gawaine and Sir Tristram rode toward the castle where Morgan le Fay was, and ever Sir Gawaine deemed well that he was Sir Tristram de Liones, because he heard that two knights had slain and beaten thirty knights. And when they came afore the castle Sir Gawaine spake on high, and said, Queen Morgan le Fay, send out your knights that ye have laid in a watch for Sir Launcelot, and for Sir Tristram. Now, said Sir Gawaine, I know your false treason, and through all places where that I ride men shall know of your false treason. And now let see Sir Gawaine whether ye dare come out of your castle ye thirty knights. Then the queen spake and all the thirty knights at once, and said, Sir Gawaine, full well wotest thou what thou dost and sayest; for we know thee passing well; but all that thou speakest and dost thou sayest it upon pride of that good knight that is there with thee. For there be some of us that know full well the hands of that knight over all well, and wit thou well, Sir Gawaine, it is more for his sake than for thine that we will not come out of this castle. For wit ye well, Sir Gawaine, that knight that beareth the arms of Cornwall we know him, and what he is. Then Sir Gawaine and Sir Tristram departed, and rode on their ways a day or two together, and there by adventure they met with Sir Kay and Sir Sagramor le Desirous. And then they were glad of Sir Gawaine, and he of them, but they wist not what he was with the shield of Cornwall but by deeming. And thus they rode together a day or two. And then they were ware of Sir Breuse Sance Pité chasing a lady for to have slain her, for he had slain her lover before. Hold you all still, said Sir Gawaine, and shew none of you forth, and ye shall see me reward yonder false knight, for and he espy you he is so well horsed that he will escape away. And then Sir Gawaine rode betwixt Sir Breuse and the lady, and said, False knight, leave her and have ado with me. When Sir Breuse saw no more but Sir Gawaine he feutred his spear, and Sir Gawaine against him, and there Sir Breuse overthrew Sir Gawaine, and then he rode over him and overthwart him twenty

times, to have destroyed him; and when Sir Tristram saw him do so villainous a deed, he hurled out against him. And when Sir Breuse saw him with the shield of Cornwall, he knew him well that it was Sir Tristram, and then he fled, and Sir Tristram followed after him. And Sir Breuse Sance Pité was so horsed that he went his way quite. And Sir Tristram followed him long, for he would fain have been avenged upon him. And so when he had long chased him he saw a fair well, and thither he rode to repose him, and tied his horse to a tree.

CHAP. XXVII.

How damsel Bragwaine found Tristram sleeping by a well, and how she delivered letters to him from La Beale Isoud.

AND then he pulled off his helm, and washed his visage and his hands, and so he fell on sleep. In the mean while came a damsel that had sought Sir Tristram many ways and days within this land. And when she came to the well she looked upon him, and had forgotten him as in remembrance of Sir Tristram, but by his horse she knew him, that hight Passe-Brewel, that had been Sir Tristram's horse many years. For when he was mad in the forest, Sir Fergus kept him. So this lady dame Bragwaine abode still till he was awake. So when she saw him wake she saluted him, and he her again, for either knew other of old acquaintance. Then she told him how she had sought him long and broad, and there she told him how she had letters from queen La Beale Isoud. Then anon Sir Tristram read them, and wit ye well he was glad, for therein was many a piteous complaint. Then Sir Tristram said, Lady Bragwaine, ye shall ride with me till that tournament be done at the Castle of Maidens; and then shall ye bear letters and tidings with you. And then Sir Tristram took his horse and sought lodging, and there he met with a good ancient knight that prayed him to lodge with him. Right so came Gouvernail unto

Sir Tristram, that was glad of that lady. So this old knight's name was Sir Pellounes, and he told of the great tournament that should be at the Castle of Maidens. And there Sir Launcelot and thirty-two knights of his blood had ordained shields of Cornwall. And right so there came one unto Sir Pellounes and told him that Sir Persides de Bloise was come home, and then that knight held up his hands and thanked God of his coming home, and there Sir Pellounes told Sir Tristram that in two years he had not seen his son Sir Persides. Sir, said Sir Tristram, I know your son well enough for a good knight. So on a time Sir Tristram and Sir Persides came to their lodging both at once, and so they unarmed them, and put upon them their clothing. And then these two knights each welcomed other. And when Persides understood that Sir Tristram was of Cornwall, he said he was once in Cornwall,—and there I justed afore king Mark, and so it happed me at that time to overthrow ten knights, and then came to me Sir Tristram de Liones and overthrew me, and took my lady from me, and that I shall never forget, but I shall remember me and ever I see my time. Ah, said Sir Tristram, now I understand that ye hate Sir Tristram. What deem ye, ween ye that Sir Tristram is not able to withstand your malice? Yes, said Sir Persides, I know well that Sir Tristram is a noble knight, and a much better knight than I, yet shall I not owe him my good will. Right as they stood thus talking at a bay window of that castle, they saw many knights riding to and fro toward the tournament. And then was Sir Tristram ware of a likely knight riding upon a great black horse, and a black covered shield. What knight is that, said Sir Tristram, with the black horse and the black shield? He seemeth to be a good knight. I know him well, said Sir Persides, he is one of the best knights of the world. Then is it Sir Launcelot, said Sir Tristram. Nay, said Sir Persides, it is Sir Palamides, that is yet unchristened.

CHAP. XXVIII.

How Sir Tristram had a fall of Sir Palamides, and how Launcelot overthrew two knights.

THEN they saw much people of the country salute Sir Palamides. And within a while after there came a squire of the castle that told Sir Pellounes, that was lord of that castle, that a knight with a black shield had smitten down thirteen knights. Fair brother, said Sir Tristram unto Sir Persides, let us cast upon us our cloaks, and let us go see the play. Not so, said Sir Persides, we will not go like knaves thither, but we will ride like men and good knights to withstand our enemies. So they armed them, and took their horses, and great spears, and thither they went, there as many knights assayed themselves before the tournament. And anon Sir Palamides saw Sir Persides, and then he sent a squire unto him, and said, Go thou to the yonder knight with a green shield and therein a lion of gold, and say to him I require him to just with me, and tell him that my name is Sir Palamides. When Sir Persides understood that request of Sir Palamides he made him ready. And there anon they met together, but Sir Persides had a fall. Then Sir Tristram dressed him to be revenged upon Sir Palamides. And that saw Sir Palamides, that was ready, and so was not Sir Tristram, and took him at advantage, and smote him over his horse tail when he had no spear in his rest. Then start up Sir Tristram, and took his horse lightly, and was wroth out of measure, and sore ashamed of that fall. Then Sir Tristram sent unto Sir Palamides by Gouvernail his squire, and prayed him to just with him at his request. Nay, said Sir Palamides, as at this time I will not just with that knight, for I know him better than he weeneth. And if he be wroth, he may right it to-morn at the Castle of Maidens, where he may see me and many other knights. With that came Sir Dinadan, and when he saw Sir Tristram wroth he list not to jest. Lo, said Sir Dinadan, here may a man prove, be a man never so good yet may he have a fall, and he was never so wise but he might be overseen, and he rideth well that never fell. So Sir Tristram was passing wroth, and said to Sir Persides and Sir Dinadan, I will revenge me. Right so as they stood talking there, there came by Sir Tristram a likely knight, riding passing soberly and heavily, with a black shield. What knight is that? said Sir Tristram unto Sir Persides. I know him well, said Sir Persides, for his name is Sir Briant of North Wales : so he past on among other knights of North Wales. And there came in Sir Launcelot du Lake with a shield of the arms of Cornwall, and he sent a squire unto Sir Briant, and required him to just with him. Well, said Sir Briant, since I am required to just I will do what I may. And there Sir Launcelot smote down Sir Briant from his horse a great fall. And then Sir Tristram marvelled what knight he was that bare the shield of Cornwall. Whatsoever he be, said Sir Dinadan, I warrant you he is of king Ban's blood, the which be knights of the most noble prowess in the world, for to account so many for so many. Then there came two knights of Northgalis, the one hight Hew de la Montaine, and the other Sir Madok de la Montaine, and they challenged Sir Launcelot foot hot. Sir Launcelot not refusing them, but made him ready, with one spear he smote them down both over their horse croups, and so Sir Launcelot rode his way. By my faith, said Sir Tristram, he is a good knight that beareth the shield of Cornwall, and me seemeth he rideth in the best manner that ever I saw knight ride. Then the king of Northgalis rode unto Sir Palamides, and prayed him heartily for his sake to just with that knight that hath done us of Northgalis despite. Sir, said Sir Palamides, I am full loth to have ado with that knight, and cause why is for as to-morn the great tournament shall be, and therefore I will keep myself fresh by my will. Nay, said the king of Northgalis, I pray you require him of justs. Sir, said Sir Palamides, I will just at your request, and require that knight to just with me ; and often I have seen a man have a fall at his own request.

CHAP. XXIX.

How Sir Launcelot justed with Palamides and overthrew him, and after he was assailed with twelve knights.

THEN Sir Palamides sent unto Sir Launcelot a squire, and required him of justs. Fair fellow, said Sir Launcelot, tell me thy lord's name. Sir, said the squire, my lord's name is Sir Palamides the good knight. In good hour, said Sir Launcelot, for there is no knight that I saw this seven years that I had lever have ado withal than with him. And so either knights made them ready with two great spears. Nay, said Sir Dinadan, ye shall see that Sir Palamides will quit him right well. It may be so, said Sir Tristram, but I undertake that knight with the shield of Cornwall shall give him a fall. I believe it not, said Sir Dinadan. Right so they spurred their horses, and feutred their spears, and either hit other, and Sir Palamides brake a spear upon Sir Launcelot, and he sat and moved not, but Sir Launcelot smote him so lightly that he made his horse to avoid the saddle, and the stroke brake his shield and the hauberk, and had he not fallen he had been slain. How now, said Sir Tristram, I wist well by the manner of their riding both that Sir Palamides should have a fall. Right so Sir Launcelot rode his way, and rode to a well to drink and to repose him, and they of Northgalis espied him whither he rode, and then there followed him twelve knights for to have mischieved him, for this cause, that upon the morn, at the tournament of the Castle of Maidens, that he should not win the victory. So they came upon Sir Launcelot suddenly, and scarcely he might put upon him his helm and take his horse but they were in hands with him. And then Sir Launcelot gat his spear and rode through them, and there he slew a knight, and brake his spear in his body. Then he drew his sword and smote upon the right hand and upon the left hand, so that within a few strokes he had slain other three knights, and the remnant that abode he wounded them sore, all that did abide. Thus Sir Launcelot escaped from his enemies of North Wales, and then he rode forth on his way to a friend, and lodged him till on the morn, for he would not the first day have ado in the tournament, because of his great labour. And on the first day he was with king Arthur, there as he was set on high upon a scaffold, to discern who was best worthy of his deeds. So Sir Launcelot was with king Arthur, and justed not the first day.

CHAP. XXX.

How Sir Tristram behaved him the first day of the tournament, and there he had the prize.

Now turn we unto Sir Tristram de Liones, that commanded Gouvernail his servant to ordain him a black shield with none other remembrance therein. And so Sir Persides and Sir Tristram departed from their host Sir Pellounes and they rode early toward the tournament, and then they drew them to king Carados' side of Scotland: and anon knights began the field, what of the king of Northgalis' part, and what of king Carados' part, and there began great party. Then there was hurling and rashing. Right so came in Sir Persides and Sir Tristram, and so they did fare that they put the king of Northgalis aback. Then came in Sir Bleoberis de Ganis and Sir Gaheris with them of Northgalis, and then was Sir Persides smitten down and almost slain, for more than forty horsemen went over him. For Sir Bleoberis did great deeds of arms, and Sir Gaheris failed him not. When Sir Tristram beheld them, and saw them do such deeds of arms, he marvelled what they were. Also Sir Tristram thought shame that Sir Persides was so

done to; and then he gat a great spear in his hand, and then he rode to Sir Gaheris and smote him down from his horse. And then was Bleoberis wroth, and gat a spear and rode against Sir Tristram in great ire, and there Sir Tristram met with him, and smote Sir Bleoberis from his horse. So then the king with the hundred knights was wroth, and he horsed Sir Bleoberis and Sir Gaheris again, and there began a great meddle ; and ever Sir Tristram held them passing short, and ever Sir Bleoberis was passing busy upon Sir Tristram. And there came Sir Dinadan against Sir Tristram, and Sir Tristram gave him such a buffet that he swooned in his saddle. Then anon Sir Dinadan came to Sir Tristram, and said, Sir, I know thee better than thou weenest, but here I promise thee my troth I will never come against thee more, for I promise thee that sword of thine shall never come on my helm. With that came Sir Bleoberis, and Sir Tristram gave him such a buffet that down he laid his head : and then he caught him so sore by the helm that he pulled him under his horse feet. And then king Arthur blew to lodging. Then Sir Tristram departed to his pavilion, and Sir Dinadan rode with him. And Sir Persides and king Arthur then, and the kings upon both parties, marvelled what knight that was with the black shield. Many said their advice, and some knew him for Sir Tristram, and held their peace, and would nought say. So that first day king Arthur and all the kings and lords that were judges gave Sir Tristram the prize, how be it they knew him not, but named him the knight with the black shield.

CHAP. XXXI.

How Sir Tristram returned against king Arthur's party, because he saw Sir Palamides on that party.

THEN upon the morn Sir Palamides returned from the king of Northgalis, and rode to king Arthur's side, where was king Carados, and the king of Ireland, and Sir Launcelot's kin, and Sir Gawaine's kin. So Sir Palamides sent the damsel unto Sir Tristram that he sent to seek him when he was out of his mind in the forest; and this damsel asked Sir Tristram what he was, and what was his name. As for that, said Sir Tristram, tell Sir Palamides he shall not wit as at this time, unto the time I have broken two spears upon him. But let him wit thus much, said Sir Tristram, that I am the same knight that he smote down in over evening at the tournament, and tell him plainly, on what part that Sir Palamides be I will be on the contrary part. Sir, said the damsel, ye shall understand that Sir Palamides will be on king Arthur's side, where the most noble knights of the world be. Then, said Sir Tristram, will I be with the king of Northgalis, because Sir Palamides will be on king Arthur's side, and else I would not but for his sake. So when king Arthur was come they blew unto the field, and then there began a great party, and so king Carados justed with the king with the hundred knights, and there king Carados had a fall; then there was hurling and rashing, and right so came in knights of king Arthur's, and they bare back the king of Northgalis' knights. Then Sir Tristram came in, and began so roughly and so bigly that there was none might withstand him, and thus Sir Tristram endured long. And at the last Sir Tristram fell among the fellowship of king Ban, and there fell upon him Sir Bors de Ganis, and Sir Ector de Maris, and Sir Blamor de Ganis, and many other knights. And then Sir Tristram smote on the right hand and on the left hand, that all lords and ladies spake of his noble deeds. But at the last Sir Tristram should have had the worse had not the king with the hundred knights been. And then he came with his fellowship and rescued Sir Tristram, and brought him away from those knights that bare the shields of Cornwall. And then Sir Tristram saw another fellowship by themselves, and there were a forty knights together, and Sir Kay the seneschal was their governor. Then Sir Tristram rode in amongst them, and there he smote down Sir Kay from his horse, and there he fared among those knights like a grey hound among conies. Then Sir Launcelot found a knight that was sore wounded upon the head. Sir, said Sir Launcelot, who wounded you so sore? Sir, he said, a knight that beareth a black shield, and I may curse the time that ever I met with him, for he is a devil and no man. So Sir Launcelot departed from him, and thought to meet with Sir Tristram, and so he rode with his sword drawn in his hand to seek Sir Tristram, and then he espied him how he hurled here and there, and at every stroke Sir Tristram well nigh smote down a knight. O mercy, said the king, sith the time I bare arms saw I never no knight do so marvellous deeds of arms. And if I should set upon this knight, said Sir Launcelot to himself, I did shame to myself; and therewithal Sir Launcelot put up his sword. And then the king with the hundred knights and a hundred more of North Wales set upon the twenty of Sir Launcelot's kin: and they twenty knights held them ever together as wild swine, and none would fail other. And so when Sir Tristram beheld the noblesse of these twenty knights, he marvelled of their good deeds, for he saw by their fare and by their rule, that they had lever die than avoid the field. Now, said Sir Tristram, well may he be valiant and full of prowess that hath such a sort of noble knights unto his kin, and full like is he to be a noble man that is their leader and governor. He meant it by Sir Launcelot du Lake. So when Sir Tristram had beholden them long, he thought shame to see two hundred knights battering upon twenty knights. Then Sir Tristram rode unto the king with the hundred knights and said, Sir, leave your fighting with those twenty knights, for ye win no worship of them, ye be so many, and they so few; and wit ye well they will not out of the field, I see by their cheer and countenance; and worship get ye none and ye slay them. Therefore leave your fighting with them, for I to increase my worship I will ride to the twenty knights and help them with all my might and power. Nay, said the king with the hundred knights, ye shall not do so. Now I see your courage and courtesy I will withdraw my knights for your pleasure, for evermore a good knight will favour another, and like will draw to like.

CHAP. XXXII.

How Sir Tristram found Palamides by a well, and brought him with him to his lodging.

THEN the king with the hundred knights withdrew his knights. And all this while, and long tofore, Sir Launcelot had watched upon Sir Tristram with a very purpose to have fellowshipped with him. And then suddenly Sir Tristram, Sir Dinadan, and Gouvernail his man, rode their way into the forest, that no man perceived where they went. So then king Arthur blew unto lodging, and gave the king of Northgalis the prize, because Sir Tristram was upon his side. Then Sir Launcelot rode here and there, so wood as lion that wanted his fill, because he had lost Sir Tristram, and so he returned unto king Arthur. And then in all the field was a noise that with the wind it might be heard two mile thence, how the lords and ladies cried, The knight with the black shield hath won the field. Alas, said king Arthur, where is that knight become? It is shame to all those in the field so to let him escape away from you; but with gentleness and courtesy ye might have brought him unto me to the Castle of Maidens. Then the noble king Arthur went unto his knights, and comforted them in the best wise that he could, and said, My fair fellows be not dismayed, howbeit ye have lost the field this day. And many were hurt and sore wounded, and many were whole. My fellows, said king Arthur, look that ye be of good cheer, for to-morrow I will be in the field with you, and revenge you of your enemies.

So that night king Arthur and his knights reposed themselves. The damsel that came from La Beale Isoud unto Sir Tristram, all the while the tournament was a doing she was with queen Guenever, and ever the queen asked her for what cause she came into that country. Madam, she answered, I come for none other cause but from my lady La Beale Isoud to wit of your welfare. For in no wise she would not tell the queen that she came for Sir Tristram's sake. So this lady, dame Bragwaine, took her leave of queen Guenever, and she rode after Sir Tristram. And as she rode through the forest she heard a great cry, then she commanded her squire to go into that forest to wit what was that noise. And so he came to a well, and there he found a knight bound to a tree, crying as he had been wood, and his horse and his harness standing by him. And when he espied the squire, therewith he started and brake himself loose, and took his sword in his hand, and ran to have slain that squire. Then he took his horse and fled all that ever he might unto dame Bragwaine again, and told her of his adventure. Then she rode unto Sir Tristram's pavilion, and told Sir Tristram what adventure she had found in the forest. Alas, said Sir Tristram, upon my head there is some good knight at mischief. Then Sir Tristram took his horse and his sword and rode thither, and there he heard how the knight complained unto himself, and said, I, woeful knight, Sir Palamides, what misadventure befalleth me, that thus am defoiled with falsehood and treason, through Sir Bors and Sir Ector. Alas, he said, why live I so long! And then he gat his sword in his hands, and made many strange signs and tokens, and so through his raging he threw his sword into that fountain. Then Sir Palamides wailed and wrang his hands. And at the last, for pure sorrow, he ran into that fountain over his middle, and sought after his sword. Then Sir Tristram saw that, and ran upon Sir Palamides, and held him in his arms fast. What art thou, said Sir Palamides, that holdeth me so? I am a man of this forest that would thee none harm. Alas, said Sir Palamides, I may never win worship where Sir Tristram is, for ever where he is and I be there then get I no worship, and if he be away for the most part I have the gree, unless that Sir Launcelot du Lake be there or Sir Lamorak. Then Sir Palamides said: Once in Ireland Sir Tristram put me to the worse, and another time in Cornwall, and in other places in this land. What would ye do, said Sir Tristram, and ye had Sir Tristram? I would fight with him, said Sir Palamides, and ease my heart upon him, and yet, to say the sooth, Sir Tristram is the gentlest knight in this world living. What will ye do? said Sir Tristram, will ye go with me to your lodging? Nay, said he, I will go to the king with the hundred knights, for he rescued me from Sir Bors de Ganis and Sir Ector, and else had I been slain traitourly. Sir Tristram said him such kind words that Sir Palamides went with him to his lodging. Then Gouvernail went tofore and charged dame Bragwaine to go out of the way to her lodging, and bid ye Sir Persides that he make him no quarrels. And so they rode together till they came to Sir Tristram's pavilion, and there Sir Palamides had all the cheer that might be had all that night. But in no wise Sir Palamides might not know what was Sir Tristram. And so after supper they went to rest, and Sir Tristram for great travail slept till it was day: And Sir Palamides might not sleep for anguish, and in the dawning of the day he took his horse privily and rode his way unto Sir Gaheris and to Sir Sagramor le Desirous, where they were in their pavilions, for they three were fellows at the beginning of the tournament. And then upon the morn the king blew unto the tournament upon the third day.

CHAP. XXXIII.

How Sir Tristram smote down Sir Palamides, and how he justed with king Arthur, and other feats.

So the king of Northgalis and the king with the hundred knights, they two encountered with king Carados and with the king of Ireland, and there the king with the hundred knights smote down king Carados, and the king of Northgalis smote down the king of Ireland. With that came in Sir Palamides, and when he came he made great work, for by his indented shield he was well known. So came in king Arthur and did great deeds of arms together, and put the king of Northgalis and the king with the hundred knights to the worse. With this came in Sir Tristram with his black shield, and anon he justed with Sir Palamides, and there by fine force Sir Tristram smote Sir Palamides over his horse croup. Then king Arthur cried, Knight with the black shield make thee ready to me. And in the same wise Sir Tristram smote king Arthur. And then by force of king Arthur's knights the king and Sir Palamides were horsed again. Then king Arthur with a great eager heart gat a spear in his hand, and there upon the one side he smote Sir Tristram over his horse. Then foot-hot Sir Palamides came upon Sir Tristram as he was on foot, to have over-ridden him. Then Sir Tristram was ware of him, and there he stooped aside, and with great ire he gat him by the arm, and pulled him down from his horse. Then Sir Palamides lightly arose, and then they dashed together mightily with their swords, and many kings, queens, and lords stood and beheld them. And at the last Sir Tristram smote Sir Palamides upon the helm three mighty strokes, and at every stroke that he gave him he said, Have this for Sir Tristram's sake. With that Sir Palamides fell to the earth groveling. And then came the king with the hundred knights and brought Sir Tristram an horse, and so was he horsed again. By then was Sir Palamides horsed, and with great ire he justed upon Sir Tristram with his spear as it was in the rest, and gave him a great dash with his spear. Then Sir Tristram avoided his spear and gat him by the neck with his both hands, and pulled him clean out of his saddle, and so he bare him afore him the length of ten spears, and then in the presence of them all he let him fall at his adventure. Then Sir Tristram was ware of king Arthur with a naked sword in his hand, and with his spear Sir Tristram ran upon king Arthur, and then king Arthur boldly abode him, and with his sword he smote a-two his spear, and therewithal Sir Tristram was astonished, and so king Arthur gave him three or four great strokes or he might get out his sword, and at the last Sir Tristram drew his sword and assailed other passing hard. With that the great press parted, then Sir Tristram rode here and there and did his great pain, that eleven of the good knights of the blood of king Ban, that was of Sir Launcelot's kin, that day Sir Tristram smote down, that all the estates marvelled of his great deeds, and all cried upon the knight with the black shield.

CHAP. XXXIV.

How Sir Launcelot hurt Sir Tristram, and how after Sir Tristram smote down Palamides.

THEN this cry was so large that Sir Launcelot heard it. And then he gat a great spear in his hand, and came towards the cry. Then Sir Launcelot cried, The knight with the black shield, make thee ready to just with me. When Sir Tristram heard him say so, he gat his spear in his hand, and either abashed down their heads, and came together as thunder, and Sir Tristram's spear brake in pieces, and Sir Launcelot by mal-fortune struck Sir Tristram on the side a deep wound nigh to the death. But yet Sir Tristram avoided not his saddle, and so the spear brake: therewithal Sir Tristram that was wounded gat out his sword, and he rashed to Sir Launcelot,

and gave him three great strokes upon the helm that the fire spang there out, and Sir Launcelot abashed his head lowly toward his saddle-bow. And therewithal Sir Tristram departed from the field, for he felt him so wounded that he wend he should have died. And Sir Dinadan espied him, and followed him into the forest. Then Sir Launcelot abode and did many marvellous deeds. So when Sir Tristram was departed by the forest side, he alight, and unlaced his harness and refreshed his wound. Then wend Sir Dinadan that he should have died. Nay, nay, said Sir Tristram, Dinadan never dread thee, for I am heart whole, and of this wound I shall soon be whole by the mercy of God. By that Sir Dinadan was ware where came Sir Palamides riding straight upon them. And then Sir Tristram was ware that Sir Palamides came to have destroyed him. And so Sir Dinadan gave him warning and said, Sir Tristram, my lord, ye are so sore wounded that ye may not have ado with him, therefore I will ride against him and do to him what I may; and if I be slain ye may pray for my soul, and in the meanwhile ye may withdraw you and go into the castle, or into the forest, that he shall not meet with you. Sir Tristram smiled and said, I thank you, Sir Dinadan, of your good will, but ye shall wit that I am able to handle him. And then anon hastily he armed him and took his horse and gat a great spear in his hand, and said to Sir Dinadan, Adieu, and rode toward Sir Palamides a soft pace.

Then when Sir Palamides saw that, he made countenance to amend his horse; but he did it for this cause, for he abode Sir Gaheris that came after him. And when he was come, he rode toward Sir Tristram. Then Sir Tristram sent unto Sir Palamides and required him to just with him; and if he smote down Sir Palamides he would do no more to him; and if it so happened that Sir Palamides smote down Sir Tristram he bad him do his utterance. So they were accorded. Then they met together, and Sir Tristram smote down Sir

Palamides, that he had a grievous fall, so that he lay still as he had been dead. And then Sir Tristram ran upon Sir Gaheris, and he would not have justed, but whether he would or not Sir Tristram smote him over his horse croup, that he lay still as though he had been dead. And then Sir Tristram rode his way, and left Sir Persides' squire within the pavilions, and Sir Tristram and Sir Dinadan rode to an old knight's place to lodge them. And that old knight had five sons at the tournament, for whom he prayed heartily for their coming home. And so, as the French book saith, they came home all five well beaten.

And when Sir Tristram departed into the forest, Sir Launcelot held alway the fight like hard as a man enraged that took no heed to himself, and wit ye well there was many a noble knight against him. And when king Arthur saw Sir Launcelot do so marvellous deeds of arms, he then armed him, and took his horse and armour, and rode into the field to help Sir Launcelot, and so many knights came in with king Arthur. And to make short tale, in conclusion, the king of Northgalis and the king of the hundred knights were put to the worse, and because Sir Launcelot abode and was the last in the field, the prize was given him. But Sir Launcelot would neither for king, queen, nor knight have the prize. But where the cry was cried through the field, Sir Launcelot, Sir Launcelot, hath won the field this day, Sir Launcelot let make another cry contrary, Sir Tristram hath won the field, for he began first, and last he hath endured, and so hath he done the first day, the second, and the third day.

CHAP. XXXV.

How the prize of the third day was given to Sir Launcelot, and Sir Launcelot gave it unto Sir Tristram.

THEN all the estates and degrees high and low said of Sir Launcelot great worship for the honour that he did unto Sir Tristram, and for that honour doing to Sir Tristram he was at that time more praised and renowned than if he had overthrown five hundred knights: and all the people wholly for this gentleness, first the estates both high and low, and after the commonalty, cried at once, Sir Launcelot hath won the field, whosoever say nay. Then was Sir Launcelot wroth and ashamed, and so therewithal he rode to king Arthur. Alas, said the king, we are all dismayed that Sir Tristram is thus departed from us. Truly, said king Arthur, he is one of the noblest knights that ever I saw hold spear or sword in hand, and the most courteyest knight in his fighting, for full hard I saw him, said king Arthur, when he smote Sir Palamides upon his helm, thrice that he abashed his helm with his strokes, and also he said, here is a stroke for Sir Tristram, and thus thrice he said. Then king Arthur, Sir Launcelot, and Sir Dodinas le Savage took their horses to seek Sir Tristram, and by the means of Sir Persides he had told king Arthur where Sir Tristram was in his pavilion, but when they came there Sir Tristram and Sir Dinadan were gone. Then king Arthur and Sir Launcelot were heavy, and returned again to the Castle of Maidens making great dole for the hurt of Sir Tristram, and his sudden departing. Truly, said king Arthur, I am more heavy that I cannot meet with him than for all the hurts that all my knights have had at the tournament. Right so came Sir Gaheris and told to king Arthur how Sir Tristram had smitten down Sir Palamides, and it was at Sir Palamides's own request. Alas, said king Arthur, that was great dishonour to Sir Palamides, inasmuch as Sir Tristram was sore wounded, and now may we all, kings, and knights, and men of worship, say that Sir Tristram may be called a noble knight, and one of the best knights that ever I saw the days of my life. For I will that ye all kings and knights know, said king Arthur, that I never saw knight do so marvellously as he hath done these three days, for he was the first that began, and that longest held on, save this last day. And though he was hurt, it was a manly adventure of two noble knights : and when two noble men encounter needs must the one have the worse, like as God will suffer at that time. As for me, said Sir Launcelot, for all the lands that ever my father left me I would not have hurt Sir Tristram and I had known him at that time. That I hurt him was for I saw not his shield, for if I had seen his black shield I would not have meddled with him for many causes, for late he did as much for me as ever knight did, and that is well known that he had ado with thirty knights, and no help save Sir Dinadan. And one thing shall I promise, said Sir Launcelot, Sir Palamides shall repent it, as in his unkindly dealing for to follow that noble knight that I by mishap hurt thus. Sir Launcelot said all the worship that might be said by Sir Tristram. Then king Arthur made a great feast to all that would come.

And thus let we pass king Arthur, and a little we will turn unto Sir Palamides, that, after he had a fall of Sir Tristram, he was nigh hand enraged out of his wit for despite of Sir Tristram. And so he followed him by adventure. And as he came by a river in his woodness he would have made his horse to have lept over; and the horse failed footing and fell in the river, wherefore Sir Palamides was adread lest he should have been drowned, and then he avoided his horse and swam to the land, and let his horse go down by adventure.

CHAP. XXXVI.

How Sir Palamides came to the castle where Sir Tristram was, and of the quest that Sir Launcelot and ten knights made for Sir Tristram.

AND when he came to the land he took off his harness, and sat roaring and crying as a man out of his mind. Right so came a damsel even by Sir Palamides, that was sent from Sir Gawaine and his brother unto Sir Mordred, that lay sick in the same place with that old knight where Sir Tristram was. For,

as the French book saith, Sir Persides hurt so Sir Mordred a ten days afore ; and had it not been for the love of Sir Gawaine and his brother, Sir Persides had slain Sir Mordred. And so this damsel came by Sir Palamides, and she and he had language together, the which pleased neither of them : and so the damsel rode her ways till she came to the old knight's place, and there she told that old knight how she had met with the woodest knight by adventure that ever she met withal. What bare he in his shield ? said Sir Tristram. It was indented with white and black, said the damsel. Ah, said Sir Tristram, that was Sir Palamides the good knight, for well I know him, said Sir Tristram, for one of the best knights living in this realm. Then that old knight took a little hackney, and rode for Sir Palamides, and brought him unto his own manor ; and then full well knew Sir Tristram Sir Palamides, but he said but little, for at that time Sir Tristram was walking upon his feet, and well amended of his hurts, and always when Sir Palamides saw Sir Tristram he would behold him full marvellously. And ever him seemed that he had seen him. Then would he say to Sir Dinadan, And ever I may meet with Sir Tristram, he shall not escape my hands. I marvel, said Sir Dinadan, that ye boast behind Sir Tristram, for it is but late that he was in your hands, and ye in his hands ; why would ye not hold him when ye had him ? for I saw myself twice or thrice that ye gat but little worship of Sir Tristram. Then was Sir Palamides ashamed. So leave we them a little while in the castle with the old knight Sir Darras.

Now shall we speak of king Arthur, that said to Sir Launcelot, Had not ye been, we had not lost Sir Tristram, for he was here daily unto the time ye met with him, and in an evil time, said Arthur, ye encountered with him. My lord Arthur, said Launcelot, ye put upon me that I should be cause of his departure : truly it was against my will. But when men be hot in deeds of arms, often they hurt their friends as well as their foes ;

and my lord, said Sir Launcelot, ye shall understand that Sir Tristram is a man that I am loth to offend, for he hath done for me more than ever I did for him as yet. But then Sir Launcelot made to bring forth a book, and then Sir Launcelot said, Here we are ten knights that will swear upon a book never to rest one night where we rest another, this twelvemonth, until that we find Sir Tristram. And as for me, said Sir Launcelot, I promise you upon this book that and I may meet with him, either by fairness or foulness I shall bring him to this court, or else I shall die therefore. And the names of these ten knights that had undertaken this quest were these following. First was Sir Launcelot; Sir Ector de Maris, Sir Bors de Ganis, and Bleoberis, and Sir Blamor de Ganis, and Lucan the butler, Sir Uwaine, Sir Galihud, Sir Lionel, and Galiodin. So these ten noble knights departed from the court of king Arthur; and so they rode upon their quest together until they came to a cross where departed four highways, and there departed the fellowship in four, to seek Sir Tristram. And as Sir Launcelot rode by adventure he met with dame Bragwaine, that was sent into that country to seek Sir Tristram, and she fled as fast as her palfrey might go. So Sir Launcelot met with her, and asked her why she fled. Ah, fair knight, said dame Bragwaine, I flee for dread of my life, for here followeth me Sir Breuse Sance Pité to slay me. Hold you nigh me, said Sir Launcelot. Then when Sir Launcelot saw Sir Breuse Sance Pité, Sir Launcelot cried unto him and said, False knight, destroyer of ladies and damsels, now thy last days be come. When Sir Breuse Sance Pité saw Sir Launcelot's shield he knew it well, for at that time he bare not the arms of Cornwall, but he bare his own shield. And then Sir Breuse fled, and Sir Launcelot followed after him. But Sir Breuse was so well horsed, that when him list to flee he might well flee, and also abide when him list. And then Sir Launcelot returned unto dame Bragwaine, and she thanked him of his great labour.

CHAP. XXXVII.

How Sir Tristram, Sir Palamides, and Sir Dinadan were taken and put in prison.

Now will we speak of Sir Lucan the butler, that by fortune came riding to the same place there as was Sir Tristram, and in he came in none other intent but to ask harbour. Then the porter asked what was his name. Tell your lord that my name is Sir Lucan the butler, a knight of the Round Table. So the porter went unto Sir Darras, lord of the place, and told him who was there to ask harbour. Nay, nay, said Sir Daname, that was nephew unto Sir Darras, say him that he shall not be lodged here. But let him wit that I Sir Daname will meet with him anon, and bid him make him ready. So Sir Daname came forth on horseback, and there they met together with spears, and Sir Lucan smote down Sir Daname over his horse croup, and then he fled into that place, and Sir Lucan rode after him, and asked after him many times. Then Sir Dinadan said to Sir Tristram, It is shame to see the lord's cousin of this place defoiled. Abide, said Sir Tristram, and I shall redress it. And in the mean while Sir Dinadan was on horseback, and he justed with Lucan the butler, and there Sir Lucan smote Dinadan through the thick of the thigh, and so he rode his way, and Sir Tristram was wroth that Sir Dinadan was hurt, and followed after, and thought to avenge him. And within a mile he overtook Sir Lucan and bade him turn: and so they met together, so that Sir Tristram hurt Sir Lucan passing sore, and gave him a fall. With that came Sir Uwaine, a gentle knight, and when he saw Sir Lucan so hurt, he called Sir Tristram to just with him. Fair knight, said Sir Tristram, tell me your name I require you. Sir knight, wit ye well my name is Sir Uwaine le Fisc de Roy Ureine. Ah, said Sir Tristram, by my will I would not have ado with you at no time. Ye shall not so, said Sir Uwaine, but ye shall have ado with me. And then Sir Tristram saw none other boot, but rode against him, and overthrew Sir Uwaine, and hurt him in the side, and so he departed unto his lodging again. And when Sir Dinadan understood that Sir Tristram had hurt Sir Lucan, he would have ridden after Sir Lucan to have slain him, but Sir Tristram would not suffer him.

Then Sir Uwaine let ordain an horselitter, and brought Sir Lucan to the abbey of Ganis, and the castle thereby hight the castle of Ganis, of the which Sir Bleoberis was lord. And at that castle Sir Launcelot promised all his fellows to meet in the quest of Sir Tristram. So when Sir Tristram was come to his lodging, there came a damsel that told Sir Darras that three of his sons were slain at that tournament, and two grievously wounded that they were never like to help themselves, and all this was done by a noble knight that bare the black shield, and that was he that bare the prize. Then came there one and told Sir Darras that the same knight was within him that bare the black shield. Then Sir Darras went unto Sir Tristram's chamber, and there he found his shield and shewed it to the damsel. Ah, sir, said the damsel, that same is he that slew your three sons. Then without any tarrying Sir Darras put Sir Tristram, and Sir Palamides, and Sir Dinadan within a strong prison, and there Sir Tristram was like to have died of great sickness, and every day Sir Palamides would reprove Sir Tristram of old hate betwixt them. And ever Sir Tristram spake fair and said little. But when Sir Palamides saw the falling of sickness of Sir Tristram then was he heavy for him, and comforted him in all the best wise he could. And, as the French book saith, there came forty knights to Sir Darras that were of his own kin, and they would have slain Sir Tristram and his two fellows, but Sir Darras would not suffer that, but kept them in prison, and meat and drink

they had. So Sir Tristram endured there great pain, for sickness had undertaken him, and that is the greatest pain a prisoner may have. For all the while a prisoner may have his health of body, he may endure under the mercy of God, and in hope of good deliverance; but when sickness toucheth a prisoner's body, then may a prisoner say all wealth is him bereft, and then he hath cause to wail and to weep. And so did Sir Tristram when sickness had undertaken him, for then he took such sorrow that he had almost slain himself.

CHAP. XXXVIII.

How king Mark was sorry for the good renown of Sir Tristram: some of king Arthur's knights justed with knights of Cornwall.

Now will we speak, and leave Sir Tristram, Sir Palamides, and Sir Dinadan in prison, and speak we of other knights that sought after Sir Tristram many divers parts of this land. And some went into Cornwall, and by adventure Sir Gaheris, nephew unto king Arthur, came unto king Mark, and there he was well received, and sat at king Mark's own table and eat of his own mess. Then king Mark asked Sir Gaheris what tidings there were in the realm of Logris. Sir, said Sir Gaheris, the king reigneth as a noble knight, and now but late there was a great justs and tournament as ever I saw any in the realm of Logris, and the most noble knights were at that justs. But there was one knight that did marvellously three days, and he bare a black shield, and of all knights that ever I saw he proved the best knight. Then said king Mark, That was Sir Launcelot, or Sir Palamides the Paynim. Not so, said Sir Gaheris, for both Sir Launcelot and Sir Palamides were on the contrary part against the knight with the black shield. Then it was Sir Tristram, said the king. Yea, said Sir Gaheris. And therewith the king smote down his head, and in his heart he feared sore that Sir Tristram should get him such worship in the realm of

Logris, where through that he himself should not be able to withstand him. Thus Sir Gaheris had great cheer with king Mark, and with queen La Beale Isoud, the which was glad of Sir Gaheris' words; for well she wist by his deeds and manners that it was Sir Tristram. And then the king made a feast royal, and unto that feast came Sir Uwaine le Fise de Roy Ureine, and some folk called him Uwaine le Blanche Mains. And this Sir Uwaine challenged all the knights of Cornwall. Then was the king wood wroth that he had no knights to answer him. Then Sir Andred, nephew unto king Mark, lept up and said, I will encounter with Sir Uwaine. Then he went and armed him, and horsed him in the best manner. And there Sir Uwaine met with Sir Andred and smote him down, that he swooned on the earth. Then was king Mark sorry and wroth out of measure that he had no knight to revenge his nephew Sir Andred. So the king called unto him Sir Dinas the seneschal, and prayed him for his sake to take upon him to just with Sir Uwaine. Sir, said Sir Dinas, I am full loth to have ado with any knight of the Round Table. Yet, said the king, for my love take upon thee to just. So Sir Dinas made him ready, and anon they encountered together with great spears, but Sir Dinas was overthrown, horse and man, a great fall. Who was wroth but king Mark? Alas, he said, have I no knight that will encounter with yonder knight. Sir, said Sir Gaheris, for your sake I will just. So Sir Gaheris made him ready, and when he was armed he rode into the field. And when Sir Uwaine saw Sir Gaheris' shield, he rode unto him and said, Sir, ye do not your part; for, sir, the first time ye were made knight of the Round Table ye sware that ye should not have ado with your fellowship wittingly. And pardy Sir Gaheris, ye knew me well enough by my shield, and so do I know you by your shield, and though ye would break your oath I would not break mine, for there is not one here,

nor ye, that shall think I am afraid of you, but I durst right well have ado with you, but we be sisters' sons. Then was Sir Gaheris ashamed. And so therewithal every knight went his way, and Sir Uwaine rode into the country. Then king Mark armed him and took his horse and his spear, with a squire with him. And then he rode afore Sir Uwaine, and suddenly at a gap he ran upon him as he that was not ware of him, and there he smote him almost through the body, and there left him. So within a while there came Sir Kay, and found Sir Uwaine, and asked him how he was hurt. I wot not, said Sir Uwaine, why, nor wherefore, but by treason I am sure I gat this hurt, for here came a knight suddenly upon me or that I was ware, and suddenly hurt me. Then there was come Sir Andred to seek king Mark. Thou traitor knight, said Sir Kay, and I wist it were thou that thus traitourly hast hurt this noble knight, thou shouldst never pass my hands. Sir, said Sir Andred, I did never hurt him, and that I will report me to himself. Fie on you, false knights, said Sir Kay, for ye of Cornwall are nought worth. So Sir Kay made carry Sir Uwaine to the abbey of the black cross, and there he was healed. And then Sir Gaheris took his leave of king Mark. But or he departed he said, Sir king, ye did a foul shame unto you and your court when ye banished Sir Tristram out of this country, for ye needed not to have doubted no knight and he had been here. And so he departed.

CHAP. XXXIX.

Of the treason of king Mark, and how Sir Gaheris smote him down and Andred his cousin.

THEN there came Sir Kay the seneschal unto king Mark, and there he had good cheer shewing outward. Now fair lords, said he, will ye prove any adventures in the forest of Morris, in the which I know well is as hard an adventure as I know any. Sir, said Sir Kay, I will prove it. And Sir Gaheris said he would be advised, for king Mark was ever full of treason. And therewithal Sir Gaheris departed and rode his way. And by the same way that Sir Kay should ride he laid him down to rest, charging his squire to wait upon Sir Kay,—and warn me when he cometh. So within a while Sir Kay came riding that way. And then Sir Gaheris took his horse and met him, and said, Sir Kay, ye are not wise to ride at the request of king Mark, for he dealeth all with treason. Then said Sir Kay, I require you let us prove this adventure. I shall not fail you, said Sir Gaheris. And so they rode that time till a lake that was that time called the perilous lake, and there they abode under the shawe of the wood. The mean while king Mark within the castle of Tintagil avoided all his barons, and all other save such as were privy with him were all avoided out of his chamber. And then he let call his nephew Sir Andred, and bad arm him and horse him lightly, and by that time it was midnight. And so king Mark was armed in black, horse and all. And so at a privy postern they two issued out with their varlets with them, and rode till they came to that lake. Then Sir Kay espied them first, and gat his spear, and proffered to just. And king Mark rode against him, and smote each other full hard, for the moon shone as the bright day. And there at that justs Sir Kay's horse fell down, for his horse was not so big as the king's horse was, and Sir Kay's horse bruised him full sore. Then Sir Gaheris was wroth that Sir Kay had a fall. Then he cried, Knight, sit thou fast in thy saddle, for I will revenge my fellow. Then king Mark was afeard of Sir Gaheris, and so with evil will king Mark rode against him: and Sir Gaheris gave him such a stroke that he fell down. So then forthwithal Sir Gaheris ran unto Sir Andred, and smote him from his horse quite that his helm smote in the earth and nigh had broken his neck. And therewith Sir Gaheris alight, and gat up Sir Kay. And then they went both on foot to them, and bad them yield them and tell

their names, or else they should die. Then with great pain Sir Andred spake first and said, It is king Mark of Cornwall, therefore beware what ye do, and I am Sir Andred his cousin. Fie on you both, said Sir Gaheris, for a false traitor, and false treason hast thou wrought and he both, under the feigned cheer that ye made us. It were pity, said Sir Gaheris, that thou shouldst live any longer. Save my life, said king Mark, and I will make amends; and consider that I am a king anointed. It were the more shame, said Sir Gaheris, to save thy life; thou art a king anointed with crism, and therefore thou shouldest hold with all men of worship; and therefore thou art worthy to die. With that he lashed at king Mark without saying any more; and he covered him with his shield, and defended him as he might. And then Sir Kay lashed at Sir Andred. And therewithal king Mark yielded him unto Sir Gaheris, and then he kneeled down, and made his oath upon the cross of the sword that never while he lived he would be against errant knights. And also he sware to be good friend unto Sir Tristram, if ever he came into Cornwall. By then Sir Andred was on the earth, and Sir Kay would have slain him. Let be, said Sir Gaheris, slay him not I pray you. It were pity, said Sir Kay, that he should live any longer, for this is nigh cousin unto Sir Tristram, and ever he hath been a traitor unto him, and by him he was exiled out of Cornwall, and therefore I will slay him, said Sir Kay. Ye shall not, said Sir Gaheris; sithen I have given the king his life, I pray you give him his life. And therewithal Sir Kay let him go. And so Sir Kay and Sir Gaheris rode forth their way unto Dinas the seneschal, for because they heard say that he loved well Sir Tristram. So they reposed them there. And soon after they rode unto the realm of Logris. And so within a little while they met with Sir Launcelot, that had always dame Bragwaine with him, to that intent he wend to have met sooner with Sir Tristram, and Sir Launcelot asked what tidings in Cornwall, and whether they heard of Sir Tristram or not. Sir Kay and Sir Gaheris answered and said that they heard not of him. Then they told Sir Launcelot word by word of their adventure. Then Sir Launcelot smiled, and said, Hard it is to take out of the flesh that is bred in the bone. And so made them merry together.

CHAP. XL.

How after that Sir Tristram, Sir Palamides, and Sir Dinadan had been long in prison they were delivered.

Now leave we off this tale and speak we of Sir Dinas that loved a lady within the castle, and she loved another knight better than him. And so when Sir Dinas went out on hunting she slipped down by a towel, and took with her two brachets, and so she went to the knight that she loved. And when Sir Dinas came home and missed his lady, and his brachets, then was he more wroth for his brachets than for the lady. So then he rode after the knight that had his lady, and bad him turn and just. So Sir Dinas smote him down, that with the fall he brake his leg and his arm. And then his lady cried Sir Dinas mercy, and said she would love him better than ever she did. Nay, said Sir Dinas, I shall never trust them that once betrayed me, and therefore as ye have begun so end, for I will never meddle with you. And so Sir Dinas departed and took his brachets with him, and so rode to his castle.

Now will we turn unto Sir Launcelot, that was right heavy that he could never hear no tidings of Sir Tristram, for all this while he was in prison with Sir Darras, Palamides, and Dinadan. Then dame Bragwaine took her leave to go into Cornwall, and Sir Launcelot, Sir Kay, and Sir Gaheris rode to seek Sir Tristram in the country of Surluse. Now speaketh this tale of Sir Tristram and of his two fellows, for every day Sir Palamides brawled and said language against Sir Tristram. I marvel, said Sir Dinadan, of thee Sir Palamides:

and thou hadst Sir Tristram here thou wouldst do him no harm; for and a wolf and a sheep were together in prison, the wolf would suffer the sheep to be in peace. And wit thou well, said Sir Dinadan, this same is Sir Tristram at a word, and now mayest thou do thy best with him, and let see now how ye can shift it with your hands. Then was Sir Palamides abashed and said little. Sir Palamides, said Sir Tristram, I have heard much of your ill-will against me, but I will not meddle with you as at this time by my will, because I dread the lord of this place that hath us in governance, for and I dread him more than I do thee, soon should it be shift. So they appeased themselves. Right so came in a damsel and said, Knights, be of good cheer, for ye are sure of your lives, and that I heard say my lord Sir Darras. Then were they glad all three, for daily they wend they should have died. Then soon after this Sir Tristram fell sick, that he wend to have died. Then Sir Dinadan wept, and so did Sir Palamides under them both making great sorrow. So a damsel came into them, and found them mourning. Then she went to Sir Darras and told him how that mighty knight that bare the black shield was likely to die. That shall not be, said Sir Darras, for God defend when any knights come to me for succour that I should suffer them to die within my prison. Therefore, said Sir Darras to the damsel, fetch that knight and his fellows afore me. And then anon when Sir Darras saw Sir Tristram afore him, he said, Sir knight, me repenteth of thy sickness, for thou art called a full noble knight, and so it seemeth by thee. And wit ye well, it shall never be said that Sir Darras shall destroy such a noble knight as thou art in prison, howbeit that thou hast slain three of my sons, whereby I was greatly agrieved. But now shalt thou go and thy fellows, and your harness and horses have been fair and clean kept, and ye shall go where it liketh you, upon this covenant, that thou, knight, will promise me to be good friend to my sons two that be now on live, and also that thou tell me thy name. Sir, said he, as for me, my name is Sir Tristram de Liones, and in Cornwall was I born, and nephew I am unto king Mark. And as for the death of your sons, I might not do withal, for and they had been the next kin that I have, I might have done none otherwise. And if I had slain them by treason or treachery, I had been worthy to have died. All this I consider, said Sir Darras, that all that ye did was by force of knighthood, and that was the cause I would not put you to death. But since ye be Sir Tristram the good knight, I pray. you heartily to be my good friend and to my sons. Sir, said Sir Tristram, I promise you by the faith of my body ever while I live I will do you service, for ye have done to us but as a natural knight ought to do. Then Sir Tristram reposed him there till that he was amended of his sickness. And when he was big and strong they took their leave, and every knight took their horses and so departed, and rode together till they came to a cross way. Now fellows, said Sir Tristram, here will we depart in sundry ways. And because Sir Dinadan had the first adventure, of him I will begin.

CHAP. XLI.

How Sir Dinadan rescued a lady from Sir Breuse Sance Pité, and how Sir Tristram received a shield of Morgan le Fay.

So as Sir Dinadan rode by a well, he found a lady making great dole. What aileth you? said Sir Dinadan. Sir knight, said the lady, I am the wofullest lady of the world, for within these five days here came a knight called Sir Breuse Sance Pité, and he slew mine own brother, and ever since he hath kept me at his own will, and of all men in the world I hate him most. And therefore I require you of knighthood to avenge me, for he will not tarry but be here anon. Let him come,

said Sir Dinadan, and because of honour of all women I will do my part. With this came Sir Breuse, and when he saw a knight with his lady, he was wood wroth. And then he said, Sir knight, keep thee from me. So they hurled together as thunder, and either smote other passing sore. But Sir Dinadan put him through the shoulder a grievous wound, and or ever Sir Dinadan might turn him, Sir Breuse was gone and fled. Then the lady prayed him to bring her to a castle there beside but four mile thence. And so Sir Dinadan brought her there, and she was welcome, for the lord of that castle was her uncle. And so Sir Dinadan rode his way upon his adventure.

Now turn we this tale unto Sir Tristram, that by adventure he came to a castle to ask lodging, wherein was queen Morgan le Fay. And so when Sir Tristram was let into that castle he had good cheer all that night. And upon the morn when he would have departed, the queen said, Wit ye well ye shall not depart lightly, for ye are here as a prisoner. God defend, said Sir Tristram, for I was but late a prisoner. Fair knight, said the queen, ye shall abide with me till that I wit what ye are, and from whence ye come. And ever the queen would set Sir Tristram on her side, and her paramour on the other side, and ever queen Morgan would behold Sir Tristram, and thereat the knight was jealous, and was in will suddenly to have run upon Sir Tristram with a sword, but he left it for shame. Then the queen said to Sir Tristram, Tell me thy name, and I shall suffer you to depart when you will. Upon that covenant I tell you my name is Sir Tristram de Liones. Ah, said Morgan le Fay, and I had wist that thou shouldst not have departed so soon as thou shalt: but sithen I have made a promise I will hold it, with that thou wilt promise me to bear upon thee a shield that I shall deliver thee, unto the castle of the Hard Rock, where king Arthur hath cried a great tournament, and there I pray you that ye will be, and to do for me as much deeds of arms as ye may do. For at that Castle of Maidens, Sir Tristram, ye did marvellous deeds of arms as ever I heard knight do. Madam, said Sir Tristram, let me see the shield that I shall bear. So the shield was brought forth, and the shield was goldish, with a king and a queen therein painted, and a knight standing above them, with one foot upon the king's head, and the other upon the queen's. Madam, said Sir Tristram, this is a fair shield and a mighty; but what signifieth this king and this queen and that knight standing upon both their heads. I shall tell you, said Morgan le Fay, it signifieth king Arthur and queen Guenever, and a knight that holdeth them both in bondage and servage. Who is that knight? said Sir Tristram. That shall ye not wit as at this time, said the queen. But, as the French book saith, queen Morgan loved Sir Launcelot best, and ever she desired him, and he would never love her, nor do nothing at her request, and therefore she held many knights together for to have taken him by strength. And because she deemed that Sir Launcelot loved queen Guenever, and she him again, therefore queen Morgan le Fay ordained that shield to put Sir Launcelot to a rebuke, to that intent that king Arthur might understand the love between them. Then Sir Tristram took that shield and promised her to bear it at the tournament at the castle of the Hard Rock. But Sir Tristram knew not that shield was ordained against Sir Launcelot, but afterward he knew it.

CHAP. XLII.

How Sir Tristram took with him the shield, and also how he slew the paramour of Morgan le Fay.

So then Sir Tristram took his leave of the queen, and took the shield with him. Then came the knight that held queen Morgan le Fay, his name was Sir Hemison, and he made him ready to follow Sir Tristram. Fair friend, said Morgan, ride not after that knight, for

ye shall win no worship of him. Fie on him, coward, said Sir Hemison, for I wist never good knight come out of Cornwall, but if it were Sir Tristram de Liones. What and that be he, said she. Nay, nay, said he, he is with La Beale Isoud, and this is but a daffish knight. Alas my fair friend, ye shall find him the best knight that ever ye met withal, for I know him better than ye do. For your sake, said Sir Hemison, I shall slay him. Ah, fair friend, said the queen, me repenteth that ye will follow that knight, for I fear me sore of your again coming. With this, this knight rode his way wood wroth, and he rode after Sir Tristram as fast as he had been chased with knights. When Sir Tristram heard a knight come after him so fast, he returned about, and saw a knight coming against him. And when he came nigh to Sir Tristram, he cried on high, Sir knight, keep thee from me. Then they rushed together as it had been thunder, and Sir Hemison bruised his spear upon Sir Tristram, but his harness was so good that he might not hurt him. And Sir Tristram smote him harder, and bare him through the body, and he fell over his horse croup. Then Sir Tristram turned to have done more with his sword, but he saw so much blood go from him, that him seemed he was likely to die: and so he departed from him and came to a fair manor to an old knight, and there Sir Tristram lodged.

CHAP. XLIII.

How Morgan le Fay buried her paramour, and how Sir Tristram praised Sir Launcelot and his kin.

Now leave we to speak of Sir Tristram, and speak we of the knight that was wounded to the death. Then his varlet alight, and took off his helm; and then he asked his master whether there were any life in him. There is in me life, said the knight, but it is but little, and therefore leap thou up behind me, when thou hast holpen me up; and hold me fast that I fall not, and bring me to queen Morgan le Fay, for deep draughts of death draw to my heart, that I may not live, for I would fain speak with her or I died. For else my soul will be in great peril and I die. And with great pain his varlet brought him to the castle, and there Sir Hemison fell down dead. When Morgan le Fay saw him dead, she made great sorrow out of reason. And then she let despoil him unto his shirt, and so she let him put into a tomb. And about the tomb she let write: Here lieth Sir Hemison, slain by the hands of Sir Tristram de Liones. Now turn we unto Sir Tristram, that asked the knight, his host, if he saw late any knights adventurous. Sir, he said, the last night here lodged with me Sir Ector de Maris and a damsel with him, and that damsel told me that he was one of the best knights of the world. That is not so, said Sir Tristram, for I know four better knights of his own blood; and the first is Sir Launcelot du Lake, call him the best knight; and Sir Bors de Ganis, Sir Bleoberis, Sir Blamor de Ganis, and Sir Gaheris. Nay, said his host, Sir Gawaine is a better knight than he. That is not so, said Sir Tristram, for I have met with them both, and I felt Sir Gaheris for the better knight; and Sir Lamorak, I call him as good as any of them, except Sir Launcelot. Why name ye not Sir Tristram, said his host, for I account him as good as any of them. I know not Sir Tristram, said Tristram. Thus they talked and jested as long as them list, and then went to rest. And on the morn Sir Tristram departed and took his leave of his host, and rode towards the Roche-dure, and none adventure had Sir Tristram but that, and so he rested not till he came to the castle, where he saw five hundred tents.

CHAP. XLIV.

How Sir Tristram at a tournament bare the shield that Morgan le Fay had delivered him.

THEN the king of Scots and the king of Ireland held against king Arthur's knights, and there began a great meddle. So came in Sir Tristram and did marvellous deeds of arms, for there he smote down many knights. And ever he was afore king Arthur with that shield. And when king Arthur saw that shield, he marvelled greatly in what intent it was made. But queen Guenever deemed as it was, wherefore she was heavy. Then was there a damsel of queen Morgan in a chamber by king Arthur, and when she heard king Arthur speak of that shield, then she spake openly unto king Arthur, Sir king, wit ye well this shield was ordained for you, to warn you of your shame and dishonour, and that longeth to you and to your queen. And then anon the damsel piked her away privily, that no man wist where she was become. Then was king Arthur sad and wroth, and asked from whence came that damsel. There was not one that knew her, nor wist where she was become. Then queen Guenever called to her Sir Ector de Maris, and there she made her complaint to him, and said, I wot well this shield was made by Morgan le Fay, in despite of me and Sir Launcelot, wherefore I dread sore lest I should be destroyed. And ever the king beheld Sir Tristram that did so marvellous deeds of arms, that he wondered sore what knight he might be, and well he wist it was not Sir Launcelot. And it was told him that Sir Tristram was in Petit Britain with Isoud la Blanche Mains, for he deemed, and he had been in the realm of Logris, Sir Launcelot or some of his fellows that were in the quest of Sir Tristram, that they should have found him or that time. So king Arthur had marvel what knight he might be. And ever Sir Arthur's eye was on that shield. All that espied the queen, and that made her sore afeard. Then ever Sir Tristram smote down knights, wonderly to behold, what upon the right hand and upon the left hand, that unneth no knight might withstand him. And the king of Scots and the king of Ireland began to withdraw them. When Arthur espied that, he thought that that knight with the strange shield should not escape him. Then he called unto him Sir Uwaine la Blanche Mains, and bade him arm him and make him ready. So anon king Arthur and Sir Uwaine dressed them before Sir Tristram, and required him to tell them where he had that shield. Sir, he said, I had it of queen Morgan le Fay, sister unto king Arthur.

Soo here endeth this history of this book, for it is the firste book of sire Tristram de Lyones, and the second book of sir tristram foloweth.

Here begynneth the second book of sire Tristram. Howe syre Tristram smote doune kyng Arthur and sir Uwayne, by cause he wold not telle hem wherfor that shelde was made. But to say the sothe sire Tristram coude not telle the cause, for he knewe it not.

The Tenth Book.

CHAP. I.

How Sir Tristram justed and smote down king Arthur, because he told him not the cause why he bare that shield.

AND if so be ye can describe what ye bear, ye are worthy to bear the arms. As for that, said Sir Tristram, I will answer you. This shield was given me, not desired, of queen Morgan le Fay. And as for me, I cannot describe these arms, for it is no point of my charge, and yet I trust to bear them with worship. Truly, said king Arthur, ye ought to bear none arms but if ye wist what ye bear. But I pray you tell me your name. To what intent? said Sir Tristram. For I would wit, said king Arthur. Sir, ye shall not wit as at this time. Then shall ye and I do battle together, said king Arthur. Why, said Sir Tristram, will ye do battle with me but if I tell you my name? and that little needeth you and ye were a man of worship, for ye have seen me this day have had great travail; and therefore ye are a villainous knight to ask battle of me, considering my great travail, howbeit I will not fail you, and have ye no doubt that I fear not you; though ye think ye have me at a great advantage, yet shall I right well endure you. And therewithal king Arthur dressed his shield and his spear, and Sir Tristram against him, and they came so eagerly together. And there king Arthur brake his spear all to pieces upon Sir Tristram's shield. But Sir Tristram hit king Arthur again, that horse and man fell to the earth. And there was king Arthur wounded on the left side a great wound and a perilous. Then when Sir Uwaine saw his lord Arthur lie on the ground sore wounded he was passing heavy. And then he dressed his shield and spear, and cried aloud unto Sir Tristram, and said, Knight, defend thee. So they came together as thunder, and Sir Uwaine brake his spear all to pieces upon Sir Tristram's shield. And Sir Tristram smote him harder and sorer, with such a might that he bare him clean out of his saddle to the earth.

With that Sir Tristram turned about and said, Fair knights, I had no need to just with you, for I have had enough to do this day. Then arose Arthur and went to Sir Uwaine, and said to Sir Tristram, We have as we have deserved, for through our pride we demanded battle of you, and yet we knew not your name. Nevertheless, said Sir Uwaine, by saint cross he is a strong knight at mine advice as any is now living.

Then Sir Tristram departed, and in every place he asked and demanded after Sir Launcelot, but in no place he could not hear of him whether he were dead or on live, wherefore Sir Tristram made great dole and sorrow. So Sir Tristram rode by a forest, and then was he ware of a fair tower by a marsh on that one side, and on that other side a fair meadow. And there he saw ten knights fighting together. And ever the nearer he came he saw how there was but one knight did battle against nine knights, and that one knight did so marvellously that Sir Tristram had great wonder that ever one knight might do so great deeds of arms. And then within a little while he had slain half their horses and unhorsed them, and their horses ran in the fields and forest. Then Sir Tristram had so great pity upon that one knight that endured so great pain, and ever he thought it should be Sir Palamides by his shield. And so he rode unto the knights and cried unto them, and bad them cease of their battle, for they did themselves great shame, so many knights to fight with one. Then answered the master of those knights, his name was called Breuse Sance Pité, that was at that time the most mischievousest knight living, and said thus : Sir knight, what have ye ado with us to meddle ; and therefore and ye be wise depart on your way as ye came, for this knight shall not escape us. That were pity, said Sir Tristram, that so good a knight as he is should be slain so cowardly. And therefore I warn you I will succour him with all my puissance.

CHAP. II.

How Sir Tristram saved Sir Palamides' life, and how they promised to fight together within a fortnight.

So Sir Tristram alight off his horse because they were on foot, that they should not slay his horse, and then dressed his shield with his sword in his hand : and he smote on the right hand and on the left hand passing sore, that well nigh at every stroke he strake down a knight. And when they espied his strokes they fled all with Breuse Sance Pité unto the tower : and Sir Tristram followed fast after with his sword in his hand. But they escaped into the tower and shut Sir Tristram without the gate. And when Sir Tristram saw this he returned back unto Sir Palamides, and found him sitting under a tree sore wounded. Ah, fair knight, said Sir Tristram, well be ye found. Gramercy, said Sir Palamides, of your great goodness, for ye have rescued me of my life, and saved me from my death. What is your name? said Sir Tristram. He said, my name is Sir Palamides. Oh, said Sir Tristram, thou hast a fair grace of me this day that I should rescue thee, and thou art the man in the world that I most hate. But now make thee ready, for I will do battle with thee. What is your name? said Sir Palamides. My name is Sir Tristram, your mortal enemy. It may be so, said Sir Palamides, but ye have done overmuch for me this day that I should fight with you, for inasmuch as ye have saved my life, it will be no worship for you to have ado with me, for ye are fresh, and I am wounded sore. And therefore and ye will needs have ado with me, assign me a day, and then I shall meet with you without fail. Ye say well, said Sir Tristram. Now, I assign you to meet me in the meadow by the river of Camelot, where Merlin set the peron. So they were agreed. Then Sir Tristram asked Sir Palamides why the ten knights did battle with him. For this cause, said Sir Palamides, as I rode on mine adventures in a forest here beside, I espied where lay a dead knight, and a lady weeping beside him. And when I saw her making such dole, I asked her who slew her lord? Sir, she said, the falsest knight of the world now living: and he is the most villain that ever man heard speak of, and his name is Sir Breuse Sance Pité. Then for pity I made the damsel to leap on her palfrey, and I promised her to be her warrant, and to help her to inter her lord. And so, suddenly, as I came riding by this tower, there came out Sir Breuse Sance Pité, and suddenly he strake me from my horse. And then or I might recover my horse, this Sir Breuse slew the damsel. And so I took my horse again, and I was sore ashamed, and so began the meddle betwixt us. And this is the cause wherefore we did this battle. Well, said Sir Tristram, now I understand the manner of your battle. But in any wise have remembrance of your promise that ye have made with me to do battle with me this day fortnight. I shall not fail you, said Sir Palamides. Well, said Sir Tristram, as at this time I will not fail you till that ye be out of the danger of your enemies. So they mounted upon their horses, and rode together unto that forest, and there they found a fair well, with clear water burbling. Fair sir, said Sir Tristram, to drink of that water have I courage. And then they alight off their horses. And then were they ware by them where stood a great horse tied to a tree, and ever he neighed. And then were they ware of a fair knight armed under a tree, lacking no piece of harness, save his helm lay under his head. Truly, said Sir Tristram, yonder lieth a wellfaring knight, what is best to do? Awake him, said Sir Palamides. So Sir Tristram wakened him with the butt of his spear. And so the knight arose up hastily, and put his helm upon his head, and gat a great spear in his hand, and without any more words he hurled unto Sir Tristram, and smote him clean from his saddle to the earth, and hurt him on the left side, that Sir Tristram lay in great peril. Then he galloped

farther, and fet his course, and came hurling upon Sir Palamides, and there he strake him a part through the body, that he fell from his horse to the earth. And then this strange knight left them there, and took his way through the forest. With this Sir Palamides and Sir Tristram were on foot, and gat their horses again, and either asked counsel of other what was best to do. By my head, said Sir Tristram, I will follow this strong knight that thus hath shamed us. Well, said Sir Palamides, and I will repose me hereby with a friend of mine. Beware, said Sir Tristram unto Palamides, that ye fail not that day that ye have set with me to do battle, for, as I deem, ye will not hold your day, for I am much bigger than ye. As for that, said Sir Palamides, be it as it be may, for I fear you not: for and I be not sick nor prisoner I will not fail you. But I have cause for to have more doubt of you that ye will not meet with me, for ye ride after yonder strong knight, and if ye meet with him it is an hard adventure and ever ye escape his hands. Right so Sir Tristram and Sir Palamides departed, and either took their ways diverse.

CHAP. III.

How Sir Tristram sought a strong knight that had smitten him down, and many other knights of the Round Table.

So Sir Tristram rode long after this strong knight. And at the last he saw where lay a lady overthwart a dead knight. Fair lady, said Sir Tristram, who hath slain your lord? Sir, said she, there came a knight riding as my lord and I rested us here, and asked him of whence he was, and my lord said of Arthur's court. Therefore, said the strong knight, I will just with thee, for I hate all these that be of Arthur's court. And my lord that lieth here dead mounted upon his horse, and the strong knight and my lord encountered together, and there he smote my lord through out with his spear. And thus he hath brought me in great woe and damage. That me repenteth, said Sir

Tristram, of your great anger; and it please you tell me your husband's name? Sir, said she, his name was Galardoun, that would have proved a good knight. So departed Sir Tristram from that dolorous lady, and had much evil lodging. Then on the third day Sir Tristram met with Sir Gawaine and with Sir Bleoberis in a forest at a lodge: and either were sore wounded. Then Sir Tristram asked Sir Gawaine and Sir Bleoberis if they met with such a knight, with such a cognisance, with a covered shield. Fair sir, said these knights, such a knight met with us to our great damage. And first he smote down my fellow Sir Bleoberis, and sore wounded him because he bad me I should not have ado with him, for why, he was over strong for me. That strong knight took his words at scorn, and said he said it for mockery. And then they rode together, and so he hurt my fellow. And when he had done so, I might not for shame but I must just with him. And at the first course, he smote me down and my horse to the earth. And there he had almost slain me, and from us he took his horse and departed, and in an evil time we met with him. Fair knights, said Sir Tristram, so he met with me and with another knight that hight Palamides, and he smote us both down with one spear, and hurt us right sore. By my faith, said Sir Gawaine, by my counsel ye shall let him pass and seek him no farther, for at the next feast of the Round Table upon pain of my head ye shall find him there. By my faith, said Sir Tristram, I shall never rest till that I find him. And then Sir Gawaine asked him his name. Then he said, My name is Sir Tristram. And so either told other their names. And then departed Sir Tristram, and rode his way. And by fortune in a meadow Sir Tristram met with Sir Kay the seneschal and Sir Dinadan. What tidings with you, said Sir Tristram,—with you knights? Not good, said these knights. Why so? said Sir Tristram, I pray you tell me, for I ride to seek a knight. What cog-

nisance beareth he? said Sir Kay. He beareth, said Sir Tristram, a covered shield close with a cloth. By my head, said Sir Kay, that is the same knight that met with us, for this night we were lodged within a widow's house, and there was that knight lodged. And when he wist we were of Arthur's court, he spake great villainy by the king, and specially by the queen Guenever. And then on the morrow we waged battle with him for that cause. And at the first recounter, said Sir Kay, he smote me down from my horse, and hurt me passing sore. And when my fellow Sir Dinadan saw me smitten down and hurt, he would not revenge me, but fled from me. And thus is he departed. And then Sir Tristram required them to tell him their names, and so either told other their names. And so Sir Tristram departed from Sir Kay and from Sir Dinadan, and so he passed through a great forest into a plain, till he was ware of a priory, and there he reposed him with a good man six days.

CHAP. IV.

How Sir Tristram smote down Sir Sagramor le Desirous, and Sir Dodinas le Savage.

AND then he sent his man that hight Gouvernail, and commanded him to go to a city there by to fetch him new harness; for it was long time afore that that Sir Tristram had been refreshed; his harness was bruised and broken. And when Gouvernail his servant was come with his apparel, he took his leave at the widow, and mounted upon his horse, and rode his way early on the morn. And, by sudden adventure Sir Tristram met with Sir Sagramor le Desirous, and with Sir Dodinas le Savage. And these two knights met with Sir Tristram and questioned with him, and asked him if he would just with them. Fair knights, said Sir Tristram, with a good will I would just with you, but I have promised at a day set near hand to do battle with a strong knight. And therefore I am loth to have ado with you, for and it misfortuned me here to be hurt, I should not be able to do my battle which I promised. As for that, said Sir Sagramor, maugre your head ye shall just with us or ye pass from us. Well, said Sir Tristram, if ye enforce me thereto, I must do what I may. And then they dressed their shields, and came running together with great ire. But through Sir Tristram's great force, he strake Sir Sagramor from his horse. Then he hurled his horse farther, and said to Sir Dodinas, Knight, make thee ready. And so through fine force Sir Tristram strake Dodinas from his horse. And when he saw them lie on the earth he took his bridle, and rode forth on his way, and his man Gouvernail with him. Anon as Sir Tristram was past, Sir Sagramor and Sir Dodinas gat again their horses, and mounted up lightly, and followed after Sir Tristram. And when Sir Tristram saw them come so fast after him, he returned with his horse to them, and asked them what they would. It is not long ago since I smote you down to the earth at your own request and desire : I would have ridden by you but ye would not suffer me, and now me seemeth ye would do more battle with me. That is truth, said Sir Sagramor and Sir Dodinas, for we will be revenged of the despite that ye have done to us. Fair knights, said Sir Tristram, that shall little need you, for all that I did to you ye caused it, wherefore I require you of your knighthood leave me as at this time, for I am sure and I do battle with you I shall not escape without great hurts, and as I suppose ye shall not escape all lotless. And this is the cause why I am so loth to have ado with you. For I must fight within these three days with a good knight and as valiant as any is now living, and if I be hurt I shall not be able to do battle with him. What knight is that, said Sir Sagramor, that ye shall fight withal? Sir, said he, it is a good knight called Sir Palamides. By my head, said Sir Sagramor and Sir Dodinas, ye have cause to dread

him, for ye shall find him a passing good knight and a valiant. And because ye shall have ado with him we will forbear you as at this time, and else ye should not escape us lightly. But fair knight, said Sir Sagramor, tell us your name. Sir, said he, my name is Sir Tristram de Liones. Ah, said Sagramor and Sir Dodinas, well be ye found, for much worship have we heard of you. And then either took leave of other, and departed on their way.

CHAP. V.

How Sir Tristram met at the peron with Sir Launcelot, and how they fought together unknown.

THEN departed Sir Tristram and rode straight unto Camelot, to the peron that Merlin had made tofore, where Sir Lanceor, that was the king's son of Ireland, was slain by the hands of Balin. And in that same place was the fair lady Columbe slain, that was love unto Sir Lanceor, for after he was dead she took his sword and thrust it through her body. And by the craft of Merlin he made to inter this knight Sir Lanceor and his lady Columbe under one stone. And at that time Merlin prophesied that in that same place should fight two the best knights that ever were in Arthur's days, and the best lovers. So when Sir Tristram came to the tomb where Lanceor and his lady were buried, he looked about him after Sir Palamides. Then was he ware of a seemly knight came riding against him all in white, with a covered shield. When he came nigh Sir Tristram, he said on high, Ye be welcome, Sir knight, and well and truly have ye holden your promise. And then they dressed their shields and spears, and came together with all their mights of their horses. And they met so fiercely that both their horses and knights fell to the earth. And as fast as they might they avoided their horses, and put their shields before them, and they strake together with bright swords, as men that were of might, and either wounded other wonderly sore, that the blood ran out upon the grass. And thus they two fought the space of four hours, that never one would speak to other one word, and of their harness they had hewn off many pieces. Oh, said Gouvernail, I have marvel greatly of the strokes my master hath given to your master. By my head, said Sir Launcelot's servant, your master hath not given so many but your master hath received as many or more. Oh, said Gouvernail, it is too much for Sir Palamides to suffer, or Sir Launcelot, and yet pity it were that either of these good knights should destroy other's blood. So they stood and wept both, and made great dole when they saw the bright swords over covered with blood of their bodies. Then at the last spake Sir Launcelot and said: Knight, thou fightest wonderly well as ever I saw knight, therefore and it please you tell me your name. Sir, said Sir Tristram, that is me loth to tell any man my name. Truly, said Sir Launcelot, and I were required, I was never loth to tell my name. It is well said, quoth Sir Tristram, then I require you to tell me your name. Fair knight, he said, my name is Sir Launcelot du Lake. Alas, said Sir Tristram, what have I done, for ye are the man in the world that I love best. Fair knight, said Sir Launcelot, tell me your name. Truly, said he, my name is Sir Tristram de Liones. Oh, said Sir Launcelot, what adventure is befallen me! And therewith Sir Launcelot kneeled down and yielded him up his sword. And therewithal Sir Tristram kneeled adown, and yielded him up his sword. And so either gave other the degree. And then they both forthwithal went to the stone, and set them down upon it, and took off their helms to cool them, and either kissed other an hundred times. And then anon after they took their helms and rode to Camelot. And there they met with Sir Gawaine and with Sir Gaheris that had made promise to Arthur never to come again to the court till they had brought Sir Tristram with them.

CHAP. VI.

How Sir Launcelot brought Sir Tristram to the court, and of the great joy that the king and other made for the coming of Sir Tristram.

RETURN again, said Sir Launcelot, for your quest is done, for I have met with Sir Tristram: lo here is his own person. Then was Sir Gawaine glad, and said to Sir Tristram, Ye are welcome, for now have ye eased me greatly of my labour. For what cause, said Sir Gawaine, came ye into this court? Fair sir, said Sir Tristram, I came into this country because of Sir Palamides, for he and I had assigned at this day to have done battle together at the peron, and I marvel I hear not of him. And thus by adventure my lord Sir Launcelot and I met together. With this came king Arthur. And when he wist that there was Sir Tristram, then he ran unto him and took him by the hand and said, Sir Tristram, ye be as welcome as any knight that ever came to this court. And when the king had heard how Sir Launcelot and he had foughten, and either had wounded other wonderly sore, then the king made great dole. Then Sir Tristram told the king how he came thither for to have had ado with Sir Palamides. And then he told the king how he had rescued him from the nine knights and Breuse Sance Pité, and how he found a knight lying by a well, and that knight smote down Sir Palamides and me, but his shield was covered with a cloth. So Sir Palamides left me, and I followed after that knight. And in many places I found where he had slain knights, and forjusted many. By my head, said Sir Gawaine, that same knight smote me down and Sir Bleoberis, and hurt us sore both, he with the covered shield. Ah, said Sir Kay, that knight smote me adown and hurt me passing sore, and fain would I have known him, but I might not. Mercy, said Arthur, what knight was that with the covered shield? I know not, said Sir Tristram; and so said they all. Now, said king

Arthur, then wot I, for it is Sir Launcelot. Then they all looked upon Sir Launcelot and said, Ye have beguiled us with your covered shield. It is not the first time, said Arthur, he hath done so. My lord, said Sir Launcelot, truly wit ye well I was the same knight that bare the covered shield. And because I would not be known that I was of your court I said no worship of your house. That is truth, said Sir Gawaine, Sir Kay, and Sir Bleoberis. Then king Arthur took Sir Tristram by the hand, and went to the Table Round. Then came queen Guenever and many ladies with her, and all the ladies said at one voice, Welcome, Sir Tristram. Welcome, said the damsels : Welcome, said the knights : Welcome, said Arthur, for one of the best knights and the gentlest of the world, and the man of most worship. For of all manner of hunting thou bearest the prize, and of all measures of blowing thou art the beginning, and of all the terms of hunting and hawking ye are the beginner : of all instruments of music ye are the best; therefore, gentle knight, said Arthur, ye are welcome to this court. And also I pray you, said Arthur, grant me a boon. It shall be at your commandment, said Tristram. Well, said Arthur, I will desire of you that ye will abide in my court. Sir, said Sir Tristram, thereto is me loth, for I have ado in many countries. Not so, said Arthur, ye have promised me, ye may not say nay. Sir, said Sir Tristram, I will as ye will. Then went Arthur unto the sieges about the Round Table, and looked in every siege the which were void that lacked knights. And then the king saw in the siege of Marhaus letters that said, This is the siege of the noble knight Sir Tristram. And then Arthur made Sir Tristram knight of the Table Round with great nobley and great feast as might be thought. For Sir Marhaus was slain afore by the hands of Sir Tristram in an island, and that was well known at that time in the court of Arthur ; for this Marhaus was a worthy knight. And for evil deeds

that he did unto the country of Cornwall Sir Tristram and he fought. And they fought so long tracing and traversing till they fell bleeding to the earth, for they were so sore wounded that they might not stand for bleeding. And Sir Tristram by fortune recovered, and Sir Marhaus died through the stroke on the head. So leave we of Sir Tristram, and speak we of king Mark.

CHAP. VII.

How for the despite of Sir Tristram king Mark came with two knights into England, and how he slew one of the knights.

Then king Mark had great despite of the renown of Sir Tristram, and then he chased him out of Cornwall : yet was he nephew unto king Mark, but he had great suspicion unto Sir Tristram, because of his queen, La Beale Isoud : for him seemed that there was too much love between them both. So when Sir Tristram departed out of Cornwall into England, king Mark heard of the great prowess that Sir Tristram did there, the which grieved him sore. So he sent on his party men to espy what deeds he did. And the queen sent privily on her part spies to know what deeds he had done, for great love was between them twain. So when the messagers were come home, they told the truth as they had heard, that he passed all other knights, but if it were Sir Launcelot. Then king Mark was right heavy of these tidings, and as glad was La Beale Isoud. Then in great despite he took with him two good knights and two squires, and disguised himself, and took his way into England, to the intent for to slay Sir Tristram. And one of these two knights hight Sir Bersules, and the other knight was called Sir Amant. So as they rode, king Mark asked a knight that he met where he should find king Arthur. He said, at Camelot. Also he asked that knight after Sir Tristram, whether he heard of him in the court of king Arthur. Wit you well, said that knight, ye shall find

Sir Tristram there for a man of as great worship as is now living, for through his prowess he won the tournament of the Castle of Maidens, that standeth by the Hard Rock. And sithen he hath won with his own hands thirty knights that were men of great honour. And the last battle that ever he did he fought with Sir Launcelot, and that was a marvellous battle. And not by force Sir Launcelot brought Sir Tristram to the court, and of him king Arthur made passing great joy, and so made him knight of the Table Round, and his seat was where the good knight's Sir Marhaus seat was. Then was king Mark passing sorry when he heard of the honour of Sir Tristram, and so they departed. Then said king Mark unto his two knights, Now will I tell you my counsel; ye are the men that I trust most to on live; and I will that ye wit my coming hither is to this intent, for to destroy Sir Tristram by wiles or by treason; and it shall be hard if ever he escape our hands. Alas, said Bersules, what mean you? for ye be set in such a way ye are disposed shamefully. For Sir Tristram is the knight of most worship that we know living, and therefore I warn you plainly I will never consent to do him to the death; and therefore I will yield my service, and forsake you. When king Mark heard him say so, suddenly he drew his sword, and said, A traitor! and smote Sir Bersules on the head, that the sword went to his teeth. When Amant the knight saw him do that villainous deed, and his squires, they said it was foul done and mischievously, wherefore we will do thee no more service; and wit ye well we will appeach thee of treason afore Arthur. Then was king Mark wonderly wroth, and would have slain Amant; but he and the two squires held them together, and set nought by his malice. When king Mark saw he might not be revenged on them, he said thus unto the knight Amant, Wit thou well, and thou appeach me of treason I shall thereof defend me afore king Arthur; but I require thee that thou tell not my name that I am king Mark, whatsoever come of me. As for that, said Sir Amant, I will not discover your name. And so they parted; and Amant and his fellows took the body of Bersules and buried it.

CHAP. VIII.

How king Mark came to a fountain where he found Sir Lamorak complaining for the love of king Lot's wife.

THEN king Mark rode till he came to a fountain, and there he rested him, and stood in a doubt whether he would ride to Arthur's court or none, or return again to his country. And as he thus rested him by that fountain, there came by him a knight well armed on horseback, and he alight and tied his horse unto a tree, and set him down by the brink of the fountain, and there he made great languor and dole, and made the dolefullest complaint of love that ever man heard; and all this while was he not ware of king Mark. And this was a great part of his complaint, he cried and wept, saying, O fair queen of Orkney, king Lot's wife, and mother of Sir Gawaine, and to Sir Gaheris, and mother to many other, for thy love I am in great pains. Then king Mark arose, and went near him, and said, Fair knight, ye have made a piteous complaint. Truly, said the knight, it is an hundred part more rueful than my heart can utter. I require you, said king Mark, tell me your name. Sir, said he, as for my name, I will not hide it from no knight that beareth a shield, and my name is Sir Lamorak de Galis. But when Sir Lamorak heard king Mark speak, then wist he well by his speech that he was a Cornish knight. Sir, said Sir Lamorak, I understand by your tongue ye be of Cornwall, wherein there dwelleth the shamefullest king that is now living, for he is a great enemy to all good knights; and that proveth well, for he hath chased out of that country Sir Tristram, that is the worshipfullest knight that now is living, and all knights speak of him worship, and for jealousy of his queen he hath chased him out of his country. It is pity, said Sir Lamorak, that ever any such false knight-coward as king Mark is should be matched with such a fair lady and good as La Beale Isoud is, for all the world of him speaketh shame, and of her worship that any queen may have. I have not ado in this matter, said king Mark, neither nought will I speak thereof. Well said, said Sir Lamorak. Sir, can ye tell me any tidings? I can tell you, said Sir Lamorak, that there shall be a great tournament in haste beside Camelot, at the castle of Jagent. And the king with the hundred knights, and the king of Ireland, as I suppose, make that tournament.

Then there came a knight, that was called Sir Dinadan, and saluted them both. And when he wist that king Mark was a knight of Cornwall, he reproved him for the love of king Mark a thousand fold more than did Sir Lamorak. Then he proffered to just with king Mark. And he was full loth thereto; but Sir Dinadan edged him so, that he justed with Sir Lamorak. And Sir Lamorak smote king Mark so sore that he bare him on his spear end over his horse tail. And then king Mark arose again, and followed after Sir Lamorak. But Sir Dinadan would not just with Sir Lamorak, but he told king Mark that Sir Lamorak was Sir Kay the seneschal. That is not so, said king Mark, for he is much bigger than Sir Kay. And so he followed and overtook him, and bad him abide. What will ye do? said Sir Lamorak. Sir, he said, I will fight with a sword, for ye have shamed me with a spear. And therewith they dashed together with swords, and Sir Lamorak suffered him and forbare him. And king Mark was passing hasty, and smote thick strokes. Sir Lamorak saw he would not stint, and waxed somewhat wroth, and doubled his strokes, for he was one of the noblest knights of the world, and he beat him so on the helm that his head hung nigh on the saddle bow.

When Sir Lamorak saw him fare so, he said, Sir knight, what cheer? me seemeth ye have nigh your fill of fighting; it were pity to do you any more harm for ye are but a mean knight, therefore I give you leave to go where ye list. Gramercy, said king Mark, for ye and I be not matches. Then Sir Dinadan mocked king Mark and said, Ye are not able to match a good knight. As for that, said king Mark, at the first time that I justed with this knight ye refused him. Think ye that it is a shame to me? said Sir Dinadan: nay, sir, it is ever worship to a knight to refuse that thing that he may not attain: therefore your worship had been much more, to have refused him as I did: for I warn you plainly he is able to beat five such as ye and I be; for ye knights of Cornwall are no men of worship, as other knights are. And because ye are no men of worship, ye hate all men of worship; for never was bred in your country such a knight as Sir Tristram.

CHAP. IX.

How king Mark, Sir Lamorak, and Sir Dinadan came to a castle, and how king Mark was known there.

THEN they rode forth all together, king Mark, Sir Lamorak, and Sir Dinadan, till that they came unto a bridge. And at the end thereof stood a fair tower. Then saw they a knight on horseback, well armed, brandishing a spear, crying and proffering himself to just. Now, said Sir Dinadan unto king Mark, yonder are two brethren, that one hight Allein, and that other hight Trian, that will just with any that passeth this passage. Now proffer yourself, said Dinadan to king Mark, for ever ye be laid to the earth. Then king Mark was ashamed, and therewith he feutred his spear, and hurtled to Sir Trian, and either brake their spears all to pieces, and passed through anon. Then Sir Trian sent king Mark another spear to just more; but in no wise he would not just no more. Then they came to the castle, all three knights, and they prayed the lord of the castle for harbour. Ye are right welcome, said the knights of the castle, for the love of the lord of this castle, the which hight Sir Tor le Fise Aries. And then they came into a fair court, well repaired. And they had passing good cheer till the lieutenant of this castle that hight Berluse espied king Mark of Cornwall. Then said Berluse, Sir knight, I know you better than ye ween, for ye are king Mark, that slew my father afore mine own eyes, and me had ye slain had I not escaped into a wood; but wit ye well for the love of my lord of this castle, I will neither hurt you ne harm you, nor none of your fellowship. But wit ye well when ye are past this lodging I shall hurt you and I may, for ye slew my father traitourly. But first for the love of my lord Sir Tor, and for the love of Sir Lamorak the honourable knight that here is lodged, ye shall have none ill lodging. For it is pity that ever ye should be in the company of good knights, for ye are the most villainous knight or king that is now known on live; for ye are a destroyer of good knights, and all that ye do is but treason.

CHAP. X.

How Sir Berluse met with king Mark, and how Sir Dinadan took his part.

THEN was king Mark sore ashamed, and said but little again. But when Sir Lamorak and Sir Dinadan wist that he was king Mark they were sorry of his fellowship. So after supper they went to lodging. So on the morn they arose early, and king Mark and Sir Dinadan rode together; and three mile from their lodging there met with them three knights, and Sir Berluse was one, and the other his two cousins. Sir Berluse saw king Mark, and then he cried on high, Traitor, keep thee from me, for wit thou well that I am Berluse. Sir knight, said Sir Dinadan, I counsel you to leave off at this time, for he is riding to king Arthur; and because I

have promised to conduct him to my lord king Arthur, needs must I take a part with him, howbeit I love not his condition, and fain I would be from him. Well Dinadan, said Sir Berluse, me repenteth that ye will take part with him, but now do your best. And then he hurtled to king Mark, and smote him sore upon the shield that he bare him clean out of his saddle to the earth. That saw Sir Dinadan, and he feutred his spear, and ran to one of Berluse's fellows, and smote him down off his saddle. Then Dinadan turned his horse, and smote the third knight in the same wise to the earth, for Sir Dinadan was a good knight on horseback. And there began a great battle, for Berluse and his fellows held them together strongly on foot. And so through the great force of Sir Dinadan, king Mark had Sir Berluse to the earth, and his two fellows fled; and had not been Sir Dinadan, king Mark would have slain him; and so Sir Dinadan rescued him of his life, for king Mark was but a murderer. And then they took their horses and departed, and left Sir Berluse there sore wounded. Then king Mark and Sir Dinadan rode forth a four leagues English till that they came to a bridge, where hoved a knight on horseback, armed and ready to just. Lo, said Sir Dinadan unto king Mark, yonder hoveth a knight that will just, for there shall none pass this bridge but he must just with that knight. It is well, said king Mark, for this justs falleth with thee. Sir Dinadan knew the knight well that he was a noble knight, and fain he would have justed, but he had lever king Mark had justed with him, but by no mean king Mark would not just. Then Sir Dinadan might not refuse him in no manner. And then either dressed their spears and their shields and smote together, so that through fine force Sir Dinadan was smitten to the earth. And lightly he arose up, and gat his horse, and required that knight to do battle with swords. And he answered and said, Fair knight, as at this time I may not have ado with you no more; for the custom of this passage is such. Then was Sir Dinadan passing wroth, that he might not be revenged of that knight; and so he departed. And in no wise would that knight tell his name; but ever Sir Dinadan thought that he should know him by his shield that it should be Sir Tor.

CHAP. XI.

How king Mark mocked Sir Dinadan, and how they met with six knights of the Round Table.

So as they rode by the way, king Mark then began to mock Sir Dinadan, and said, I wend you knights of the Table Round might in no wise find their matches. Ye say well, said Sir Dinadan, as for you, on my life I call you none of the best knights; but sith ye have such a despite at me, I require you to just with me, to prove my strength. Not so, said king Mark, for I will not have ado with you in no manner. But I require you of one thing, that when ye come to Arthur's court, discover not my name, for I am there so hated. It is shame to you, said Sir Dinadan, that ye govern yourself so shamefully; for I see by you ye are full of cowardice, and ye are a murderer, and that is the greatest shame that a knight may have, for never a knight being a murderer hath worship, nor never shall have. For I saw but late through my force ye would have slain Sir Berluse, a better knight than ye, or ever ye shall be, and more of prowess.

Thus they rode forth talking, till they came to a fair place where stood a knight, and prayed them to take their lodging with him. So at the request of that knight they reposed them there, and made them well at ease, and had great cheer. For all errant knights were welcome to him, and especially all those of Arthur's court. Then Sir Dinadan demanded his host, what was the knight's name that kept the bridge. For what cause ask you it? said his host. For it is not long ago, said Sir Dinadan, since he gave me a fall. Ah, fair knight,

said his host, thereof have ye no marvel, for he is a passing good knight, and his name is Sir Tor, the son of Aries le Vaysher. Ah, said Sir Dinadan, was that Sir Tor, for truly so ever me thought. Right as they stood thus talking together, they saw come riding to them over a plain six knights of the court of king Arthur, well armed at all points. And there by their shields Sir Dinadan knew them well. The first was the good knight Sir Uwaine, the son of king Uriens; the second was the noble knight Sir Brandiles; the third was Ozana le Cure Hardy; the fourth was Uwaine les Adventurous; the fifth was Sir Agravaine; the sixth Sir Mordred, brother to Sir Gawaine. When Sir Dinadan had seen these six knights, he thought in himself he would bring king Mark by some wile to just with one of them. And anon they took their horses and ran after these knights well a three mile English. Then was king Mark ware where they sat all six about a well, and eat and drank such meats as they had, and their horses walking and some tied, and their shields hung in divers places about them. Lo, said Sir Dinadan, yonder are knights errant that will just with us. God forbid, said king Mark, for they be six, and we but two. As for that, said Sir Dinadan, let us not spare, for I will assay the foremost. And therewith he made him ready. When king Mark saw him do so, as fast as Sir Dinadan rode toward them king Mark rode froward them with all his menial company. So when Sir Dinadan saw king Mark was gone, he set the spear out of the rest, and threw his shield upon his back, and came riding to the fellowship of the Table Round. And anon Sir Uwaine knew Sir Dinadan, and welcomed him, and so did all his fellowship.

CHAP. XII.

How the six knights sent Sir Dagonet to just with king Mark, and how king Mark refused him.

AND then they asked him of his adventures, and whether he had seen Sir

Tristram, or Sir Launcelot. Truly, said Sir Dinadan, I saw none of them since I departed from Camelot. What knight is that, said Sir Brandiles, that so suddenly departed from you, and rode over yonder field? Sir, said he, it was a knight of Cornwall, and the most horrible coward that ever bestrode horse. What is his name? said all the knights. I wot not, said Sir Dinadan. So when they had reposed them, and spoken together, they took their horses and rode to a castle where dwelled an old knight that made all knights errant good cheer. Then in the mean while that they were talking came into the castle Sir Griflet le Fise de Dieu, and there was he welcome, and they asked him whether he had seen Sir Launcelot or Sir Tristram? Sirs, he answered, I saw him not since he departed from Camelot. So as Sir Dinadan walked and beheld the castle, thereby in a chamber he espied king Mark, and then he rebuked him, and asked him why he departed so? Sir, said he, for I durst not abide because they were so many. But how escaped ye? said king Mark. Sir, said Sir Dinadan, they were better friends than I wend they had been. Who is captain of that fellowship? said the king. Then for to fear him Sir Dinadan said it was Sir Launcelot. Oh, said the king, might I know Sir Launcelot by his shield? Yea, said Dinadan, for he beareth a shield of silver and black bends. All this he said to fear the king, for Sir Launcelot was not in his fellowship. Now I pray you, said king Mark, that ye will ride in my fellowship? That is me loth to do, said Sir Dinadan, because ye forsook my fellowship. Right so Sir Dinadan went from king Mark and went to his own fellowship. And so they mounted upon their horses, and rode on their ways, and talked of the Cornish knight, for Dinadan told them that he was in the castle where they were lodged. It is well said, said Sir Griflet, for here have I brought Sir Dagonet king Arthur's fool, that is the best fellow and the merriest in the world. Will ye do well? said Sir Dinadan; I have told the Cornish knight

that here is Sir Launcelot, and the Cornish knight asked me what shield he bare. Truly I told him that he bare the same shield that Sir Mordred beareth. Will ye do well? said Sir Mordred; I am hurt and may not well bear my shield nor harness, and therefore put my shield and my harness upon Sir Dagonet, and let him set upon the Cornish knight. That shall be done, said Sir Dagonet, by my faith. Then anon was Dagonet armed in Mordred's harness and his shield, and he was set on a great horse and a spear in his hand. Now, said Dagonet, shew me the knight, and I trow I shall bear him down. So all these knights rode to a wood side, and abode till king Mark came by the way. Then they put forth Sir Dagonet, and he came on all the while his horse might run, straight upon king Mark. And when he came nigh king Mark, he cried as he were wood, and said, Keep thee, knight of Cornwall, for I will slay thee. Anon as king Mark beheld his shield he said to himself, Yonder is Sir Launcelot: alas, now am I destroyed. And therewithal he made his horse to run as fast as it might through thick and thin. And ever Sir Dagonet followed king Mark crying and rating him as a wood man through a great forest. When Sir Uwaine and Sir Brandiles saw Dagonet so chase king Mark, they laughed all as they were wood. And then they took their horses and rode after to see how Sir Dagonet sped. For they would not for no good that Sir Dagonet were hurt, for king Arthur loved him passing well, and made him knight with his own hands. And at every tournament he began to make king Arthur to laugh. Then the knights rode here and there crying and chasing after king Mark, that all the forest rang of the noise.

CHAP. XIII.

How Sir Palamides by adventure met king Mark flying, and how he overthrew Dagonet and other knights.

So king Mark rode by fortune by a

well in the way where stood a knight errant on horseback armed at all points with a great spear in his hand. And when he saw king Mark coming flying he said, Knight, return again for shame, and stand with me, and I shall be thy warrant. Ah, fair knight, said king Mark, let me pass, for yonder cometh after me the best knight of the world, with the black bended shield. Fie for shame, said the knight, he is none of the worthy knights. And if he were Sir Launcelot or Sir Tristram I should not doubt to meet the better of them both. When king Mark heard him say that word he turned his horse and abode by him. And then that strong knight bare a spear to Dagonet, and smote him so sore that he bare him over his horse tail, and nigh he had broken his neck. And anon after him came Sir Brandiles, and when he saw Dagonet have that fall he was passing wroth, and cried, Keep thee knight! And so they hurtled together wonderous sore. But the knight smote Sir Brandiles so sore that he went to the earth, horse and man. Sir Uwaine came after and saw all this. Truly, said he, yonder is a strong knight. And then they feutred their spears, and this knight came so eagerly that he smote down Sir Uwaine. Then came Ozana with the hardy heart, and he was smitten down. Now, said Sir Griflet, by my counsel let us send to yonder errant knight, and wit whether he be of Arthur's court, for, as I deem, it is Sir Lamorak de Galis. So they sent unto him, and prayed the strange knight to tell his name, and whether he were of Arthur's court or not. As for my name they shall not wit, but tell them I am a knight errant as they are: and let them wit that I am no knight of king Arthur's court. And so the squire rode again to them, and told them his answer of him. By my head, said Sir Agravaine, he is one of the strongest knights that ever I saw, for he hath overthrown three noble knights, and needs we must encounter with him for shame. So Sir Agravaine feutred his spear, and that other was ready, and

smote him down over his horse to the earth. And in the same wise he smote Sir Uwaine les Avoutres and also Sir Griflet. Then had he served them all but Sir Dinadan, for he was behind, and Sir Mordred was unarmed, and Dagonet had his harness. So when this was done this strong knight rode on his way a soft pace, and king Mark rode after him praising him much, but he would answer no words, but sighed wonderly sore, hanging down his head, taking no heed to his words. Thus they rode well a three mile English, and then this knight called to him a varlet and bad him, Ride until yonder fair manor, and recommend me to the lady of that castle and place, and pray her to send me refreshing of good meats and drinks. And if she ask thee what I am, tell her that I am the knight that followeth the glatisant beast,—that is in English to say the questing beast. For that beast wheresoever he went he quested with such a noise as it had been a thirty couple of hounds.

Then the varlet went his way, and came to the manor and saluted the lady, and told her from whence he came. And when she understood that he came from the knight that followed the questing beast, O sweet Lord Jesu, she said, when shall I see that noble knight, my dear son Palamides. Alas, he will not abide with me! And therewith she swooned and wept and made passing great dole. And then all so soon as she might she gave the varlet all that he asked. And the varlet returned unto Sir Palamides, for he was a varlet of king Mark. And as soon as he came he told the knight's name was Sir Palamides. I am well pleased, said king Mark, but hold thee still and say nothing. Then they alight, and set them down and reposed them awhile. Anon withal king Mark fell on sleep. When Sir Palamides found him sound asleep he took his horse and rode his way, and said to them, I will not be in the company of a sleeping knight. And so he rode forth a great pace.

CHAP. XIV.

How king Mark and Sir Dinadan heard Sir Palamides making great sorrow and mourning for La Beale Isoud.

Now turn we unto Sir Dinadan that found these seven knights passing heavy. And when he wist how that they sped, as heavy was he. My lord Uwaine, said Dinadan, I dare lay my head it is Sir Lamorak de Galis; I promise you all I shall find him and he may be found in this country. And so Sir Dinadan rode after this knight. And so did king Mark, that sought him through the forest. So as king Mark rode after Sir Palamides, he heard a noise of a man that made great dole. Then king Mark rode as nigh that noise as he might and as he durst. Then was he ware of a knight that was descended off his horse and had put off his helm, and there he made a piteous complaint and a dolorous of love.

Now leave we that, and talk we of Sir Dinadan, that rode to seek Sir Palamides. And as he came within a forest, he met with a knight a chaser of a deer. Sir, said Sir Dinadan, met ye with a knight with a shield of silver and lions' heads? Yea, fair knight, said the other, with such a knight met I with but a while ago, and straight yonder way he went. Gramercy, said Sir Dinadan, for might I find the track of his horse, I should not fail to find that knight. Right so as Sir Dinadan rode in the even late, he heard a doleful noise, as it were of a man. Then Sir Dinadan rode toward that noise. And when he came nigh that noise, he alight off his horse and went near him on foot. Then was he ware of a knight that stood under a tree, and his horse tied by him, and the helm off his head. And ever that knight made a doleful complaint as ever made knight. And always he made his complaint of La Beale Isoud the queen of Cornwall, and said, Ah fair lady, why love I thee, for thou art fairest of all other, and yet shewest thou never love to me nor bounty. Alas, yet must I love thee. And I may not blame thee

fair lady, for mine eyes be cause of this sorrow. And yet to love thee I am but a fool, for the best knight of the world loveth thee, and ye him again, that is Sir Tristram de Liones. And the falsest king and knight is your husband, and the most coward and full of treason is your lord king Mark. Alas, that ever so fair a lady and peerless of all other should be matched with the most villainous knight of the world. All this language heard king Mark what Sir Palamides said by him. Wherefore he was adread when he saw Sir Dinadan, lest, and he espied him, that he would tell Sir Palamides that he was king Mark; and therefore he withdrew him, and took his horse and rode to his men where he commanded them to abide. And so he rode as fast as he might unto Camelot. And the same day he found there Amant the knight ready, that before king Arthur had appealed him of treason. And so lightly the king commanded them to do battle. And by misadventure king Mark smote Amant through the body. And yet was Amant in the righteous quarrel. And right so he took his horse and departed from the court for dread of Sir Dinadan, that he would tell Sir Tristram and Sir Palamides what he was. Then were there maidens that La Beale Isoud had sent to Sir Tristram that knew Sir Amant well.

CHAP. XV.

How king Mark had slain Sir Amant wrongfully tofore king Arthur, and Sir Launcelot fetched king Mark to king Arthur.

THEN by the licence of king Arthur they went to him, and spake with him, for while the truncheon of the spear stuck in his body he spake: Ah, fair damsels, said Amant, recommend me unto La Beale Isoud, and tell her that I am slain for the love of her and of Sir Tristram. And there he told the damsels how cowardly king Mark had slain him and Sir Bersules his fellow:—And for that deed I appealed him of treason, and here I am slain in a righteous quarrel; and all was because Sir Bersules and I would not consent by treason to slay the noble knight Sir Tristram. Then the two maidens cried aloud that all the court might hear it, and said, O sweet Lord Jesu that knoweth all hid things, why sufferest thou so false a traitor to vanquish and slay a true knight that fought in a righteous quarrel! Then anon it was sprung to the king and the queen, and to all lords and ladies, that it was king Mark that had slain Sir Amant, and Sir Bersules afore hand, wherefore they did their battle. Then was king Arthur wroth out of measure, and so were all the other knights.

But when Sir Tristram knew all the matter, he made great dole out of measure, and wept for sorrow for loss of the noble knights Sir Bersules and Sir Amant. When Sir Launcelot espied Sir Tristram weep, he went hastily to king Arthur, and said, Sir, I pray you give me leave to return again to yonder false king and knight. I pray you, said king Arthur, fetch him again, but I would not that ye slew him for my worship. Then Sir Launcelot armed him in all haste, and mounted upon a great horse, and took a spear in his hand and rode after king Mark. And from thence a three mile English Sir Launcelot overtook him, and bad him—Turn recreant king and knight: for whether thou wilt or not thou shalt go with me to king Arthur's court. King Mark returned and looked upon Sir Launcelot and said, Fair sir, what is your name? Wit thou well, said he, my name is Sir Launcelot, and therefore defend thee. And when king Mark wist that it was Sir Launcelot, and came so fast upon him with a spear, he cried then aloud, I yield me to thee Sir Launcelot, honourable knight. But Sir Launcelot would not hear him, but came fast upon him. King Mark saw that, and made no defence, but tumbled down out of his saddle to the earth as a sack, and there he lay still, and cried Sir Launcelot mercy.—Arise, recreant knight and king.—I will not fight, said king Mark; but whither that

ye will I will go with you. Alas, alas, said Sir Launcelot, that I may not give thee one buffet for the love of Sir Tristram and of La Beale Isoud, and for the two knights that thou hast slain traitourly. And so he mounted upon his horse, and brought him to king Arthur. And there king Mark alight in that same place, and threw his helm from him upon the earth, and his sword, and fell flat to the earth of king Arthur's feet, and put him in his grace and mercy. Truly, said Arthur, ye are welcome in a manner, and in a manner ye are not welcome. In this manner ye are welcome, that ye come hither maugre your head, as I suppose. That is truth, said king Mark, and else I had not been here: for my lord Sir Launcelot brought me hither through his fine force, and to him am I yielden to as recreant. Well, said Arthur, ye understand ye ought to do me service, homage, and fealty, and never would ye do me none, but ever ye have been against me, and a destroyer of my knights: now how will ye acquit you? Sir, said king Mark, right as your lordship will require me, unto my power I will make a large amends. For he was a fair speaker and false there under. Then for great pleasure of Sir Tristram, to make them twain accorded, the king withheld king Mark as at that time, and made a broken love day between them.

CHAP. XVI.

How Sir Dinadan told Sir Palamides of the battle between Sir Launcelot and Sir Tristram.

Now turn we again unto Sir Palamides, how Sir Dinadan comforted him in all that he might from his great sorrow. What knight are ye? said Sir Palamides. Sir, I am a knight errant as ye be, that hath sought you long by your shield. Here is my shield, said Sir Palamides, wit ye well, and ye will aught therewith, I will defend it. Nay, said Sir Dinadan, I will not have ado with you but in good manner. And if ye will ye shall find me soon ready,

Sir, said Sir Dinadan, whitherward ride you this way? By my head, said Sir Palamides, I wot not, but as fortune leadeth me. Heard ye or saw ye ought of Sir Tristram?—Truly of Sir Tristram I both heard and saw, and not for then we loved not inwardly well together, yet at my mischief Sir Tristram rescued me from my death: and yet or he and I departed, by both our assents we assigned a day that we should have met at the stony grave that Merlin set beside Camelot, and there to have done battle together, howbeit I was letted, said Sir Palamides, that I might not hold my day, the which grieveth me sore; but I have a large excuse, for I was prisoner with a lord, and many other more, and that shall Sir Tristram right well understand, that I brake it not of fear of cowardice. And then Sir Palamides told Sir Dinadan the same day that they should have met. Truly, said Sir Dinadan, that same day met Sir Launcelot and Sir Tristram at the same grave of stone. And there was the most mightiest battle that ever was seen in this land betwixt two knights, for they fought more than two hours, and there they both bled so much blood that all men marvelled that ever they might endure it. And so at the last by both their assents they were made friends and sworn brethren for ever, and no man can judge the better knight. And now is Sir Tristram made a knight of the Round Table, and he sitteth in the siege of the noble knight Sir Marhaus. By my head, said Sir Palamides, Sir Tristram is far bigger than Sir Launcelot, and the hardier knight. Have ye assayed them both? said Sir Dinadan. I have seen Sir Tristram fight, said Sir Palamides, but never Sir Launcelot to my witting.—But at the fountain where Sir Launcelot lay on sleep, there with one spear he smote down Sir Tristram and Sir Palamides, but at that time they knew not either other. Fair knight, said Sir Dinadan, as for Sir Launcelot and Sir Tristram let them be, for the worst of them will not be lightly matched of no knight that I know

living. No, said Sir Palamides; but and I had a quarrel to the better of them both, I would with as good a will fight with him as with you. Sir, said Sir Dinadan, I require you tell me your name, and in good faith I shall hold you company till that we come to Camelot, and there ye shall have great worship now at this great tournament; for there shall be queen Guenever and La Beale Isoud of Cornwall. Wit you well, Sir knight, said Sir Palamides, for the love of La Beale Isoud I will be there, and else not, but I will not have ado in king Arthur's court. Sir, said Dinadan, I shall ride with you and do you service, so ye will tell me your name. Sir knight, ye shall understand that my name is Sir Palamides, brother to Sir Safere, the good and noble knight, and Sir Segwarides and I we be Saracens born of father and mother. Sir, said Sir Dinadan, I thank you much for the telling of your name. For I am glad of that I know your name, and I promise you by the faith of my body ye shall not be hurt by me by my will, but rather be advanced. And thereto will I help you with all my power I promise you, doubt ye not. And certainly on my life ye shall win great worship in the court of king Arthur, and be right welcome. So then they dressed on their helms and put on their shields, and mounted upon their horses, and took the broad way toward Camelot. And then were they ware of a castle that was fair and rich, and also passing strong as any was within this realm.

CHAP. XVII.

How Sir Lamorak justed with divers knights of the castle wherein was Morgan le Fay.

Sir Palamides, said Dinadan, here is a castle that I know well, and therein dwelleth queen Morgan le Fay, king Arthur's sister, and king Arthur gave her this castle, the which he hath repented him since a thousand times; for since king Arthur and she have been at debate and strife; but this castle could he never get nor win of her by no manner of engine; and ever as she might she made war on king Arthur. And all dangerous knights she withholdeth with her for to destroy all these knights that king Arthur loveth. And there shall no knight pass this way but he must just with one knight, or with two or with three. And if it hap that king Arthur's knight be beaten, he shall lose his horse and his harness and all that he hath, and hard if that he escape but that he shall be prisoner. Truly, said Palamides, this is a shameful custom, and a villainous usage for a queen to use, and, namely, to make such war upon her own lord that is called the flower of chivalry that is christian or heathen, and with all my heart I would destroy that shameful custom. And I will that all the world wit she shall have no service of me. And if she send out any knights, as I suppose she will, for to just, they shall have both their hands full. And I shall not fail you, said Sir Dinadan, unto my puissance, upon my life. So as they stood on horseback afore the castle there came a knight with a red shield, and two squires after him. And he came straight unto Sir Palamides the good knight, and said to him, Fair and gentle knight errant, I require thee for the love thou owest unto knighthood, that ye will not have ado here with these men of this castle. (For this was Sir Lamorak that thus said.) For I came hitherto to seek this deed, and it is my request. And therefore I beseech you, knight, let me deal, and if I be beaten revenge me. Well, said Palamides, let see how ye will speed, and we shall behold you. Then anon came forth a knight of the castle, and proffered to just with the knight with the red shield. Anon they encountered together, and he with the red shield smote him so hard that he bare him over to the earth. Therewith anon came another knight of the castle, and he was smitten so sore that he avoided his saddle. And forthwith came the third knight, and the knight with the red shield smote him to the earth.

Then came Sir Palamides and besought him that he might help him to just. Fair knight, said he unto him, suffer me as at this time to have my will, for and they were twenty knights I shall not doubt them. And ever there were upon the walls of the castle many lords and ladies that cried and said, Well have ye justed, knight with the red shield. But as soon as the knight had smitten them down, his squire took their horses and avoided the saddles and bridles of their horses, and turned them into the forest, and made the knights to be kept to the end of the justs. Right so came out of the castle the fourth knight, and freshly proffered to just with the knight with the red shield. And he was ready, and he smote him so hard that horse and man fell to the earth, and the knight's back brake with the fall, and his neck also. Truly, said Sir Palamides, that yonder is a passing good knight, and the best juster that ever I saw. By my head, said Sir Dinadan, he is as good as ever was Sir Launcelot or Sir Tristram, what knight somever he be.

CHAP. XVIII.

How Sir Palamides would have justed for Sir Lamorak with the knights of the castle.

THEN forthwithal came out a knight of the castle with a shield bended with black and with white. And anon the knight with the red shield and he encountered together so hard that he smote the knight of the castle through the bended shield and through the body, and brake the horse's back. Fair knight, said Sir Palamides, ye have overmuch in hand, therefore I pray you let me just, for ye had need to be reposed. Why sir, said the knight, seem ye that I am weak and feeble? and, sir, me thinketh ye proffer me wrong, and to me shame, when I do well enough. I tell you now as I told you erst, for and they were twenty knights I shall beat them. And if I be beaten or slain then may ye revenge me. And if ye think that I be weary, and ye have an appetite to just with me, I shall find you justing enough. Sir, said Palamides, I said it not because I would just with you, but me seemeth that ye have overmuch on hand. And therefore, and ye were gentle, said the knight with the red shield, ye should not proffer me shame; therefore I require you to just with me, and ye shall find that I am not weary. Sith ye require mè, said Sir Palamides, take keep to yourself. Then they two knights came together as fast as their horses might run, and the knight smote Sir Palamides so sore on the shield that the spear went into his side, a great wound and a perilous. And therewithal Sir Palamides voided his saddle. And that knight turned unto Sir Dinadan. And when he saw him coming, he cried aloud and said, Sir, I will not have ado with you. But for that he let it not, but came straight upon him. So Sir Dinadan for shame put forth his spear and all to-shivered it upon the knight. But he smote Sir Dinadan again so hard that he smote him clean from his saddle; but their horses he would not suffer his squires to meddle with, and because they were knights errant. Then he dressed him again to the castle, and justed with seven knights more, and there was none of them might withstand him, but he bare him to the earth. And of these twelve knights he slew in plain justs four. And the eight knights he made them to swear on the cross of a sword that they should never use the evil customs of the castle. And when he had made them to swear that oath, he let them pass. And ever stood the lords and the ladies on the castle walls crying and saying, Knight with the red shield, ye have marvellously well done, as ever we saw knight do. And therewith came a knight out of the castle unarmed, and said, Knight with the red shield, overmuch damage hast thou done to us this day, therefore return whither thou wilt, for here are no more that will have ado with thee, for we repent sore that ever thou camest here, for by thee is fordone the old custom of this castle. And with that word he turned again into the castle, and shut the gates. Then the knight with the red shield turned and called his squires, and so past forth on his way, and rode a great pace. And when he was past, Sir Palamides went to Sir Dinadan and said, I had never such a shame of one knight that ever I met, and therefore I cast me to ride after him, and to be revenged with my sword. For a horseback I deem I shall get no worship of him. Sir Palamides, said Dinadan, ye shall not meddle with him by my counsel, for ye shall get no worship of him, and for this cause,—ye have seen him this day have had overmuch to do, and overmuch travailed. Truly, said Sir Palamides, I shall never be at ease till that I have had ado with him. Sir, said Dinadan, I shall give you my beholding. Well, said Sir Palamides, then shall ye see how we shall redress our mights. So they took their horses of their varlets, and rode after the knight with the red shield; and down in a valley beside a fountain they were ware where he was alight to repose him, and had done off his helm for to drink at the well.

CHAP. XIX.

How Sir Lamorak justed with Sir Palamides and hurt him grievously.

Then Palamides rode fast till he came nigh him. And then he said, Knight, remember ye of the shame ye did to me right now at the castle, therefore dress thee, for I will have ado with thee. Fair knight, said he unto Sir Palamides, of me ye win no worship, for ye have seen this day that I have been travailed sore. As for that, said Palamides, I will not let; for wit ye well I will be revenged. Well, said the knight, I may happen to endure you. And therewithal he mounted upon his horse, and took a great spear in his hand, ready for to just. Nay, said Palamides, I will not just, for I am sure at justing I get no prize. Fair knight, said that knight, it would beseem a knight to just and to fight on horseback. Ye shall see what I will do, said Palamides. And therewith he alight down upon foot, and dressed his shield afore him, and pulled out his sword. Then the knight with the red shield descended down from his horse, and dressed his shield afore him, and so he drew out his sword. And then they came together a soft pace, and wonderly they lashed together passing thick, the mountenance of an hour, or ever they breathed. Then they traced and traversed, and waxed wonderly wroth, and either behight other death. They hewed so fast with their swords, that they cut in down half their swords and mails, that the bare flesh in some places stood above their harness. And when Sir Palamides beheld his fellow's sword over covered with his blood, it grieved him sore. Somewhile they foined, somewhile they strake as wild men. But at the last Sir Palamides waxed faint, because of his first wound that he had at the castle with a spear, for that wound grieved him wonderly sore. Fair knight, said Palamides, me seemeth we have assayed either other passing sore, and if it may please thee I require thee of thy knighthood tell me thy name. Sir, said the knight to Palamides, that is me loth to do, for thou hast done me wrong and no knighthood to proffer me battle, considering my great travail: but and thou wilt tell me thy name, I will tell thee mine. Sir, said he, wit thou well my name is Palamides. Ah sir, ye shall understand my name is Sir Lamorak de Galis, son and heir unto the good knight and king, king Pellinore; and Sir Tor the good knight is my half brother. When Sir Palamides heard him say so, he kneeled down and asked mercy: For outrageously have I done to you this day, considering the great deeds of arms I have seen you do, shamefully and unknightly I have required you to do battle. Ah, Sir Palamides, said Sir Lamorak, over much have ye done and said to me. And therewith he embraced him with both his hands, and said, Palamides the worthy knight, in all this land is no

better than ye, nor of more prowess, and me repenfed sore that we should fight together. So it doth not me, said Sir Palamides, and yet am I sorer wounded than ye be; but as for that, I shall soon thereof be whole. But certainly I would not for the fairest castle in this land but if thou and I had met, for I shall love you the days of my life afore all other knights, except my brother Sir Safere. I say the same, said Sir Lamorak, except my brother Sir Tor. Then came Sir Dinadan, and he made great joy of Sir Lamorak. Then their squires dressed both their shields and their harness, and stopped their wounds. And thereby at a priory they rested them all night.

CHAP. XX.

How it was told Sir Launcelot that Dagonet chased king Mark, and how a knight overthrew him and six knights.

Now turn we again, when Sir Uwaine and Sir Brandiles with his fellows came to the court of king Arthur: they told the king, Sir Launcelot, and Sir Tristram how Sir Dagonet the fool chased king Mark through the forest, and how the strong knight smote them down all seven with one spear. There was great laughing and jesting at king Mark and at Sir Dagonet. But all these knights could not tell what knight it was that rescued king Mark. Then they asked king Mark if that he knew him. And he answered and said, He named himself the knight that followed the questing beast, and on that name he sent one of my varlets to a place where was his mother, and when she heard from whence he came, she made passing great dole, and discovered to my varlet his name, and said, O my dear son, Sir Palamides, why wilt thou not see me? and therefore, Sir, said king Mark, it is to understand his name is Sir Palamides, a noble knight. Then were all these seven knights glad that they knew his name. Now turn we again, for on the morn they took their horses, both Sir Lamorak, Palamides, and Dinadan, with their squires and varlets, till they saw a fair castle that stood on a mountain well closed. And thither they rode, and there they found a knight that hight Galahalt, that was lord of that castle. And there they had great cheer, and were well eased. Sir Dinadan, said Sir Lamorak, what will ye do? O sir, said Dinadan, I will to-morrow to the court of king Arthur. By my head, said Sir Palamides, I will not ride these three days, for I am sore hurt and much have I bled, and therefore I will repose me here. Truly, said Sir Lamorak, and I will abide here with us. And when ye ride then will I ride, unless that ye tarry over long, then will I take my horse. Therefore I pray you, Sir Dinadan, abide and ride with us. Faithfully, said Dinadan, I will not abide, for I have such a talent to see Sir Tristram that I may not abide long from him. Ah, Dinadan, said Sir Palamides, now do I understand that ye love my mortal enemy, and therefore how should I trust you? Well, said Dinadan, I love my lord Sir Tristram above all other, and him will I serve and do honour. So shall I, said Sir Lamorak, in all that may lie in my power. So on the morn Sir Dinadan rode unto the court of king Arthur. And by the way as he rode he saw where stood an errant knight, and made him ready for to just. Not so, said Sir Dinadan, for I have no will to just. With me shall ye just, said the knight, or that ye pass this way. Whether ask ye justs? by love or by hate? The knight answered, Wit ye well I ask it for love, and not for hate. It may well be so, said Sir Dinadan, but ye proffer me hard love, when ye will just with me with a sharp spear. But fair knight, said Sir Dinadan, sith ye will just with me, meet with me in the court of king Arthur, and there shall I just with you. Well, said the knight, sith ye will not just with me, I pray you tell me your name. Sir knight, said he, my name is Sir Dinadan. Ah, said the knight, full well know I you for a good knight and a gentle, and wit you well I love you heartily. Then shall here be no justs, said Dinadan, betwixt us. So they departed. And the same day he came to Camelot where lay king Arthur. And there he saluted the king and the queen, Sir Launcelot and Sir Tristram. And all the court was glad of Sir Dinadan, for he was gentle, wise, and courteous, and a good knight. And in especial the valiant knight Sir Tristram loved Sir Dinadan passing well above all other knights save Sir Launcelot. Then the king asked Sir Dinadan what adventures he had seen. Sir, said Dinadan, I have seen many adventures, and of some king Mark knoweth, but not all. Then the king hearkened Sir Dinadan how he told that Sir Palamides and he were afore the castle of Morgan le Fay, and how Sir Lamorak took the justs afore them, and how he forjusted twelve knights, and of them four he slew, and how after he smote down Sir Palamides and me both. I may not believe that, said the king, for Sir Palamides is a passing good knight. That is very truth, said Sir Dinadan, but yet I saw him better proved hand for hand. And then he told the king all that battle, and how Sir Palamides was more weaker and more hurt, and more lost of his blood. And without doubt, said Sir Dinadan, had the battle longer lasted Palamides had been slain. Oh, said king Arthur, this is to me a great marvel. Sir, said Tristram, marvel ye no thing thereof, for at mine advice there is not a valianter knight in all the world living, for I know his might. And now I will say you, I was never so weary of knight but if it were Sir Launcelot. And there is no knight in the world except Sir Launcelot I would did so well as Sir Lamorak. Truly, said the king, I would that knight Sir Lamorak came to this court. Sir, said Dinadan, he will be here in short space and Sir Palamides both. But I fear that Palamides may not yet travel.

CHAP. XXI.

How king Arthur let do cry a justs, and how Sir Lamorak came in and overthrew Sir Gawaine and many other.

THEN within three days after the king let make a justing at a priory.

And there made them ready many knights of the Round Table. For Sir Gawaine and his brethren made them ready to just. But Tristram, Launcelot, nor Dinadan, would not just, but suffered Sir Gawaine, for the love of king Arthur, with his brethren, to win the gree if they might. Then on the morn they apparelled them to just, Sir Gawaine and his four brethren, and did there great deeds of arms. And Sir Ector de Maris did marvellously well; but Sir Gawaine passed all that fellowship, wherefore king Arthur and all the knights gave Sir Gawaine the honour at the beginning. Right so king Arthur was ware of a knight and two squires the which came out of a forest side, with a shield covered with leather, and then he came slily and hurtled here and there, and anon with one spear he had smitten down two knights of the Round Table. Then with his hurtling he lost the covering of his shield. Then was the king and all other ware that he bare a red shield. Oh, said king Arthur, see where rideth a stout knight, he with the red shield. And there was noise and crying, Beware the knight with the red shield. So within a little while he had overthrown three brethren of Sir Gawaine's. Truly, said king Arthur, me seemeth yonder is the best juster that ever I saw. With that he saw him encounter with Sir Gawaine, and he smote him down with so great force, that he made his horse to avoid his saddle. How now, said the king, Sir Gawaine hath a fall, well were me and I knew what knight he were with the red shield. I know him well, said Dinadan, but as at this time ye shall not know his name. By my head, said Sir Tristram, he justed better than Sir Palamides, and if ye list to know his name, wit ye well his name is Sir Lamorak de Galis. As they stood thus talking, Sir Gawaine and he encountered together again, and there he smote Sir Gawaine from his horse, and bruised him sore. And in the sight of king Arthur he smote down twenty knights beside Sir Gawaine and

his brethren. And so clearly was the prize given him as a knight peerless. Then slily and marvellously Sir Lamorak withdrew him from all the fellowship into the forest side. All this espied king Arthur, for his eye went never from him.

Then the king, Sir Launcelot, Sir Tristram, and Sir Dinadan took their hacknies and rode straight after the good knight Sir Lamorak de Galis, and there found him. And thus said the king, Ah fair knight, well be ye found. When he saw the king he put off his helm and saluted him. And when he saw Sir Tristram he alight down off his horse, and ran to him for to take him by the thighs; but Sir Tristram would not suffer him, but he alight or that he came, and either took other in arms, and made great joy of other. The king was glad, and also was all the fellowship of the Round Table, except Sir Gawaine and his brethren. And when they wist that he was Sir Lamorak, they had great despite at him, and were wonderly wroth with him, that he had put them to dishonour that day. Then Gawaine called privily in counsel all his brethren, and to them said thus: Fair brethren, here may ye see whom that we hate king Arthur loveth, and whom that we love he hateth. And wit ye well, my fair brethren, that this Sir Lamorak will never love us, because we slew his father king Pellinore, for we deemed that he slew our father, king of Orkney. And for the despite of Pellinore Sir Lamorak did us a shame to our mother, therefore I will be revenged. Sir, said Sir Gawaine's brethren, let see how ye will or may be revenged, and ye shall find us ready. Well, said Sir Gawaine, hold you still, and we shall espy our time.

CHAP. XXII.

How king Arthur made king Mark to be accorded with Sir Tristram, and how they departed toward Cornwall.

Now pass we our matter, and leave we Sir Gawaine, and speak of king

Arthur that on a day said unto king Mark, Sir, I pray you to give me a gift that I shall ask you. Sir, said king Mark, I will give you whatsoever ye desire, and it be in my power. Sir, gramercy, said king Arthur: this I will ask you, that ye will be good lord unto Sir Tristram, for he is a man of great honour; and that ye will take him with you into Cornwall, and let him see his friends, and there cherish him for my sake. Sir, said king Mark, I promise you by the faith of my body, and by the faith I owe to God and to you, I shall worship him for your sake in all that I can or may. Sir, said Arthur, and I will forgive you all the evil will that ever I owed you, and so be that ye swear that upon a book afore me. With a good will, said king Mark. And so he there sware upon a book afore him and all his knights, and therewith king Mark and Sir Tristram took either other by the hands hard knit together. But for all this king Mark thought falsely, as it proved after, for he put Sir Tristram in prison, and cowardly would have slain him. Then soon after king Mark took his leave to ride into Cornwall, and Sir Tristram made him ready to ride with him, wherefore the most part of the Round Table were wroth and heavy; and in especial Sir Launcelot, and Sir Lamorak, and Sir Dinadan were wroth out of measure. For well they wist king Mark would slay or destroy Sir Tristram. Alas, said Dinadan, that my lord Sir Tristram shall depart. And Sir Tristram took such sorrow that he was amazed like a fool. Alas, said Sir Launcelot unto king Arthur, what have ye done, for ye shall lose the most man of worship that ever came into your court? It was his own desire, said Arthur, and therefore I might not do withal; for I have done all that I can, and made them at accord. Accord, said Sir Launcelot, fie upon that accord, for ye shall hear that he shall slay Sir Tristram, or put him in a prison, for he is the most coward and the villainest king and knight that is now living. And therewith Sir

Launcelot departed, and came to king Mark, and said to him thus: Sir king, wit thou well, the good knight Sir Tristram shall go with thee. Beware, I counsel thee, of treason; for and thou mischieve that knight, by any manner of falsehood or treason, by the faith I owe to God and to the order of knighthood, I shall slay thee with mine own hands. Sir Launcelot, said the king, over much have ye said to me; and I have sworn and said over largely afore king Arthur, in hearing of all his knights, that I shall not slay nor betray him. It were to me overmuch shame to break my promise. Ye say well, said Sir Launcelot, but ye are called so false and full of treason that no man may believe you. Forsooth, it is known well wherefore ye came into this country, and for none other cause but for to slay Sir Tristram. So with great dole king Mark and Sir Tristram rode together; for it was by Sir Tristram's will and his means to go with king Mark, and all was for the intent to see La Beale Isoud; for without the sight of her Sir Tristram might not endure.

CHAP. XXIII.

How Sir Percivale was made knight of king Arthur, and how a dumb maid spake, and brought him to the Round Table.

Now turn we again unto Sir Lamorak, and speak we of his brethren. Sir Tor, which was king Pellinore's first son; and Sir Aglavale was his next son; Sir Lamorak, Dornar, Percivale, these were his sons too. So when king Mark and Sir Tristram were departed from the court, there was made great dole and sorrow for the departing of Sir Tristram. Then the king and his knights made no manner of joys eight days after. And at the eight days' end, there came to the court a knight, with a young squire with him; and when this knight was unarmed, he went to the king, and required him to make the young squire a knight. Of what lineage is he come? said king Arthur. Sir, said the knight, he is the son of king

Pellinore, that did you sometime good service, and he is brother unto Lamorak de Galis the good knight. Well, said the king, for what cause desire ye that of me, that I should make him knight? Wit you well, my lord the king, that this young squire is brother to me, as well as to Sir Lamorak, and my name is Aglavale. Sir Aglavale, said Arthur, for the love of Sir Lamorak, and for his father's love, he shall be made knight to-morrow. Now tell me, said Arthur, what is his name? Sir, said the knight, his name is Percivale de Galis.

So on the morn the king made him knight in Camelot. But the king and all the knights thought it would be long or that he proved a good knight. Then at the dinner when the king was set at the table, and every knight after he was of prowess, the king commanded him to be set among mean knights; and so was Sir Percivale set as the king commanded. Then was there a maiden in the queen's court that was come of high blood; and she was dumb, and never spake word. Right so she came straight into the hall, and went unto Sir Percivale, and took him by the hand, and said aloud, that the king and all the knights might hear it, Arise, Sir Percivale the noble knight and God's knight, and go with me; and so he did. And there she brought him to the right side of the siege-perilous, and said, Fair knight, take here thy siege, for that siege appertaineth to thee, and to none other. Right so she departed and asked a priest. And as she was confessed and houselled; then she died. Then the king and all the court made great joy of Sir Percivale.

CHAP. XXIV.

How Sir Lamorak visited king Lot's wife, and how Sir Gaheris slew her which was his own mother.

Now turn we unto Sir Lamorak, that much was there praised. Then, by the mean of Sir Gawaine and his brethren, they sent for their mother there besides fast by a castle beside Camelot; and all was to that intent to slay Sir Lamorak.

The queen of Orkney was there but a while, but Sir Lamorak wist of her being, and was full fain; and for to make an end of this matter he sent unto her, and there betwixt them was a time assigned that Sir Lamorak should come to her. Thereof was ware Sir Gaheris, and there he rode afore, the same time, and waited upon Sir Lamorak. And then he saw where he came all armed; and where Sir Lamorak alight, he tied his horse to a privy postern, and so he went into a parlour and unarmed him; and then he went unto the queen, and she made of him passing great joy, and he of her again, for either loved other passing sore. So when the knight, Sir Gaheris, saw his time, he came unto them, all armed, with his sword naked, and suddenly gat his mother by the hair, and strake off her head. When Sir Lamorak saw the blood dash upon him all hot, the which he loved passing well, wit you well he was sore abashed and dismayed of that dolorous knight. And therewithal Sir Lamorak leaped up as a knight dismayed, saying thus: Ah Sir Gaheris, knight of the Table Round, foul and evil have ye done, and to you great shame. Alas, why have ye slain your mother that bare you; with more right ye should have slain me. The offence hast thou done, said Gaheris, notwithstanding a man is born to offer his service, but yet shouldest thou beware with whom thou meddlest, for thou hast put me and my brethren to a shame, and thy father slew our father; and thou to love our mother is too much shame for us to suffer. And as for thy father king Pellinore, my brother Sir Gawaine and I slew him. Ye did him the more wrong, said Sir Lamorak, for my father slew not your father; it was Balan le Savage; and as yet my father's death is not revenged. Leave those words, said Gaheris, for and thou speak feloniously I will slay thee, but because thou art unarmed I am ashamed to slay thee. But wit thou well, in what place I may get thee I shall slay thee; and now my mother is quit of thee; and therefore withdraw thee and take thine armour, that thou were gone. Sir Lamorak saw there was none other boot, but fast armed him, and took his horse, and rode his way, making great sorrow. But for the shame and dolour he would not ride to king Arthur's court, but rode another way. But when it was known that Gaheris had slain his mother, the king was passing wroth, and commanded him to go out of his court. Wit ye well, Sir Gawaine was wroth that Gaheris had slain his mother, and let Sir Lamorak escape. And for this matter was the king passing wroth, and so was Sir Launcelot, and many other knights. Sir, said Sir Launcelot, here is a great mischief befallen by felony, and by forecast treason, that your sister is thus shamefully slain. And I dare say that it was wrought by treason, and I dare say ye shall lose that good knight Sir Lamorak, the which is great pity. I wote well and am sure, and Sir Tristram wist it he would never more come within your court, the which should grieve you much more, and all your knights. God defend, said the noble king Arthur, that I should lose Sir Lamorak or Sir Tristram, for then twain of my chief knights of the Table Round were gone. Sir, said Sir Launcelot, I am sure that ye shall lose Sir Lamorak, for Sir Gawaine and his brethren will slay him by one mean or other, for they among them have concluded and sworn to slay him and ever they may see their time. That shall I let, said Arthur.

CHAP. XXV.

How Sir Agravaine and Sir Mordred met with a knight fleeing, and how they both were overthrown, and of Sir Dinadan.

Now leave we of Sir Lamorak, and speak of Sir Gawaine's brethren, and specially of Sir Agravaine and Sir Mordred. As they rode on their adventures, they met with a knight flying sore wounded, and they asked him what tidings? Fair knights, said he, here cometh a knight after me that will slay me. With that came Sir Dinadan, riding to them by adventure, but he would promise them no help. But Sir Agravaine and Sir Mordred promised him to rescue him. Therewithal came that knight straight unto them. And anon he proffered to just. That saw Sir Mordred, and rode to him; but he strake Sir Mordred over his horse tail. That saw Sir Agravaine, and straight he rode toward that knight. And right so as he served Mordred, so he served Agravaine, and said to them, Sirs, wit ye well both, that I am Breuse Sance Pité, that hath done this to you. And yet he rode over Agravaine five or six times. When Dinadan saw this, he must needs just with him for shame. And so Dinadan and he encountered together, that with pure strength Sir Dinadan smote him over his horse tail. Then he took his horse and fled. For he was on foot one of the valiantest knights in Arthur's days, and a great destroyer of all good knights. Then rode Sir Dinadan unto Sir Mordred and unto Sir Agravaine. Sir knight, said they all, well have ye done, and well have ye revenged us; wherefore we pray you tell us your name. Fair sirs, ye ought to know my name, the which is called Sir Dinadan. When they understood that it was Dinadan, they were more wroth than they were before, for they hated him out of measure, because of Sir Lamorak. For Dinadan had such a custom that he loved all good knights that were valiant, and he hated all those that were destroyers of good knights. And there were none that hated Dinadan but those that ever were called murderers. Then spake the hurt knight that Breuse Sance Pité had chased, his name was Dalan, and said, If thou be Dinadan, thou slewest my father. It may well be so, said Dinadan, but then it was in my defence, and at his request. By my head, said Dalan, thou shalt die therefore. And therewith he dressed his spear and his shield. And to make the shorter tale, Sir Dinadan smote him down off his horse, that his neck was nigh broken. And in the same wise he smote Sir Mordred and

Sir Agravaine. And after, in the quest of the Sancgreal, cowardly and feloniously they slew Dinadan, the which was great damage, for he was a great jester and a passing good knight. And so Sir Dinadan rode to a castle that hight Beale-Valet, and there he found Sir Palamides, that was not yet whole of the wound that Sir Lamorak gave him. And there Dinadan told Palamides all the tidings that he heard and saw of Sir Tristram, and how he was gone with king Mark, and with him he hath all his will and desire. Therewith Sir Palamides waxed wroth, for he loved La Beale Isoud, and then he wist well that Sir Tristram should see her.

CHAP. XXVI.

How king Arthur, the queen, and Launcelot received letters out of Cornwall, and of the answer again.

Now leave we Sir Palamides and Sir Dinadan, in the Castle of Beale-Valet, and turn we again unto king Arthur. There came a knight out of Cornwall, his name was Fergus, a fellow of the Round Table, and there he told the king and Sir Launcelot good tidings of Sir Tristram, and there were brought goodly letters, and how he left him in the Castle of Tintagil. Then came the damsel that brought goodly letters unto king Arthur and unto Sir Launcelot; and there she had passing good cheer of the king and of the queen Guenever, and of Sir Launcelot. Then they wrote goodly letters again. But Sir Launcelot bad ever Sir Tristram beware of king Mark; for ever he called him in his letters king Fox, as who saith, He fareth all with wiles and treason: whereof Sir Tristram in his heart thanked Sir Launcelot. Then the damsel went unto La Beale Isoud, and bare her letter from the king and from Sir Launcelot, whereof she was in passing great joy. Fair damsel, said La Beale Isoud, how fareth my lord Arthur, and the queen Guenever, and the noble knight, Sir Launcelot du Lake? She answered, and to make short tale, Much the better that ye and Sir Tristram be

in joy. Truly, said La Beale Isoud, Sir Tristram suffereth great pain for me, and I for him. So the damsel departed, and brought letters to king Mark. And when he had read them, and understood them, he was wroth with Sir Tristram, for he deemed that he had sent the damsel unto king Arthur; for Arthur and Launcelot in a manner threatened king Mark. And as king Mark read these letters he deemed treason by Sir Tristram. Damsel, said king Mark, will ye ride again, and bear letters from me unto king Arthur? Sir, she said, I will be at your commandment to ride when ye will. Ye say well, said the king; come again, said the king, to-morn, and fetch your letters. Then she departed, and told them how she should ride again with letters unto Arthur. Then, we pray you, said La Beale Isoud and Sir Tristram, that when ye have received your letters, that ye would come by us, that we may see the privity of your letters. All that I may do, madam, ye wot well I must do for Sir Tristram, for I have been long his own maiden. So on the morn the damsel went to king Mark, to have had his letters, and to depart. I am not advised, said king Mark, at this time to send my letters. Then privily and secretly he sent letters unto king Arthur, and unto queen Guenever, and unto Sir Launcelot. So the varlet departed, and found the king and queen in Wales, at Carlion. And as the king and the queen were at mass the varlet came with the letters; and when mass was done the king and the queen opened the letters privily by themselves. And the beginning of the king's letters spake wonderly short unto king Arthur, and bade him intermeddle with himself, and with his wife, and of his knights, for he was able enough to rule and keep his wife.

CHAP. XXVII.

How Sir Launcelot was wroth with the letter that he received from king Mark, and of Dinadan which made a lay of king Mark.

When king Arthur understood the letter he mused of many things, and thought on his sister's words, queen Morgan le Fay, that she had said betwixt queen Guenever and Sir Launcelot. And in this thought he studied a great while. Then he bethought him again how his sister was his own enemy, and that she hated the queen and Sir Launcelot, and so he put all that out of his thought. Then king Mark read the letter again, and the latter clause said that king Mark took Sir Tristram for his mortal enemy, wherefore he put Arthur out of doubt he would be revenged of Sir Tristram. Then was king Arthur wroth with king Mark. And when queen Guenever read her letter, and understood it, she was wroth out of measure, for the letter spake shame by her, and by Sir Launcelot. And so privily she sent the letter unto Sir Launcelot. And when he wist the intent of the letter, he was so wroth that he laid him down on his bed to sleep, whereof Sir Dinadan was ware, for it was his manner to be privy with all good knights. And as Sir Launcelot slept he stole the letter out of his hand, and read it word by word; and then he made great sorrow for anger. And so Sir Launcelot awaked, and went to a window, and read the letter again, the which made him angry. Sir, said Dinadan, wherefore be ye angry? discover your heart to me. For sooth ye wot well I owe you good will, howbeit I am a poor knight, and a servitor unto you and to all good knights. For though I be not of worship myself, yet I love all those that be of worship. It is truth, said Sir Launcelot, ye are a trusty knight, and for great trust I will shew you my counsel. And when Dinadan understood all; he said, This is my counsel: set you right nought by these threats, for king Mark is so villainous that by fair speech shall never man get of him. But ye shall see what I shall do. I will make a lay for him, and when it is made I shall make an harper to sing it afore him. So anon he went and made it, and taught it an harper that hight Eliot, and when he knew it, he taught it to many harpers.

And so by the will of Sir Launcelot, and of Arthur, the harpers went straight into Wales and into Cornwall, to sing the lay that Sir Dinadan made by king Mark, which was the worst lay that ever harper sang with harp or with any other instruments.

CHAP. XXVIII.

How Sir Tristram was hurt, and of a war made to king Mark; and of Sir Tristram, how he promised to rescue him.

Now turn we again unto Sir Tristram and to king Mark. As Sir Tristram was at justs and at tournament it fortuned he was sore hurt, both with a spear and with a sword. But yet he wan always the degree. And for to repose him he went to a good knight that dwelled in Cornwall in a castle, whose name was Sir Dinas the seneschal. Then by misfortune there came out of Sessoin a great number of men of arms, and an hideous host; and they entered nigh the castle of Tintagil; and their captain's name was Elias, a good man of arms. When king Mark understood his enemies were entered into his land, he made great dole and sorrow, for in no wise by his will king Mark would not send for Sir Tristram, for he hated him deadly. So when his council was come, they devised and cast many perils of the strength of their enemies; and then they concluded all at once, and said thus unto king Mark, Sir, wit ye well ye must send for Sir Tristram the good knight, or else they will never be overcome. For by Sir Tristram they must be fought withal, or else we row against the stream. Well, said king Mark, I will do by your counsel. But yet he was full loth thereto, but need constrained him to send for him. Then was he sent for in all haste that might be, that he should come to king Mark. When Sir Tristram understood that the king had sent for him, he mounted upon a soft ambler and rode to king Mark. And when he was come, the king said thus: Fair nephew Sir Tristram, this is all: here be come our enemies of Sessoin, that are here nigh hand; and without tarrying they must be met with shortly, or else they will destroy this country. Sir, said Sir Tristram, wit ye well, all my power is at your commandment; and wit ye well Sir, these eight days may I bear none arms, for my wounds be not yet whole. And by that day I shall do what I may. Ye say well, said king Mark: then go ye again, and repose you, and make you fresh; and I shall go and meet the Sessoins with all my power. So the king departed unto Tintagil, and Sir Tristram went to repose him. And the king made a great host, and departed them in three. The first part led Sir Dinas the seneschal, and Sir Andred led the second part, and Sir Arguis led the third part, and he was of the blood of king Mark. And the Sessoins had three great battles, and many good men of arms. And so king Mark, by the advice of his knights, issued out of the castle of Tintagil upon his enemies. And Dinas the good knight rode out afore, and slew two knights with his own hands; and then began the battles. And there was marvellous breaking of spears, and smiting of swords, and slew down many good knights, and ever was Sir Dinas the seneschal the best of king Mark's part. And thus the battle endured long with great mortality. But at the last king Mark and Sir Dinas, were they never so loth, they withdrew them to the castle of Tintagil, with great slaughter of people, and the Sessoins followed on fast, that ten of them were put within the gates, and four slain with the portcullis. Then king Mark sent for Sir Tristram by a varlet, that told him all the mortality. Then he sent the varlet again, and bade him, Tell king Mark that I will come as soon as I am whole, for erst I may do him no good. Then king Mark had his answer. Therewith came Elias, and bade the king yield up the castle, for ye may not hold it no while. Sir Elias, said the king, so will I yield up the castle, if I be not soon rescued. Anon king Mark sent again for rescue to Sir Tris-

tram. By then Sir Tristram was whole, and he had gotten him ten good knights of Arthur's, and with them he rode unto Tintagil. And when he saw the great host of Sessoins he marvelled wonder greatly. And then Sir Tristram rode by the woods and by the ditches as secretly as he might, till he came nigh the gates. And there dressed a knight to him, when he saw that Sir Tristram would enter; and Sir Tristram smote him down dead. And so he served three more. And every each of these ten knights slew a man of arms. So Sir Tristram entered into the castle of Tintagil. And when king Mark wist that Sir Tristram was come, he was glad of his coming, and so was all the fellowship, and of him they made great joy.

CHAP. XXIX.

How Sir Tristram overcame the battle, and how Elias desired a man to fight body for body.

So on the morn, Elias the captain came and bade king Mark come out and do battle, For now the good knight Sir Tristram is entered, it will be a shame to thee, said Elias, for to keep thy walls. When king Mark understood this, he was wroth, and said no word, but went unto Sir Tristram and asked him his counsel. Sir, said Sir Tristram, will ye that I give him his answer? I will well, said king Mark. Then Sir Tristram said thus to the messager, Bear thy lord word from the king and me, that we will do battle with him to-morn in the plain field. What is your name? said the messager. Wit thou well my name is Sir Tristram de Liones. Therewithal the messager departed, and told his lord Elias all that he had heard. Sir, said Sir Tristram unto king Mark, I pray you give me leave to have the rule of the battle. I pray you take the rule, said king Mark. Then Sir Tristram let devise the battle in what manner that it should be. He let depart his host in six parts, and ordained Sir Dinas the seneschal to have the fore ward, and other knights to rule the remnant: and the same night Sir Tristram burnt all the Sessoins' ships unto the cold water. Anon as Elias wist that, he said, It was of Sir Tristram's doing, for he casteth that we shall never escape, mother's son of us; therefore, fair fellows, fight freely to-morrow, and miscomfort you nought for any knight, though he be the best knight in the world: he may not have ado with us all. Then they ordained their battles in four parts, wonderly well apparelled and garnished with men of arms. Thus they within issued, and they without set freely upon them; and there Sir Dinas did great deeds of arms. Not for then Sir Dinas and his fellowship were put to the worse. With that came Sir Tristram, and slew two knights with one spear. Then he slew on the right hand and on the left hand, that men marvelled that ever he might do such deeds of arms. And then he might see sometime the battle was driven a bow draught from the castle, and sometime it was at the gates of the castle. Then came Elias the captain rashing here and there, and hit king Mark so sore upon the helm that he made him to avoid the saddle; and then Sir Dinas gat king Mark again to horseback. Therewithal came in Sir Tristram like a lion, and there he met with Elias, and he smote him so sore upon the helm that he avoided his saddle. And thus they fought till it was night, and for great slaughter, and for wounded people, evereach party drew to their rest. And when king Mark was come within the castle of Tintagil, he lacked of his knights an hundred; and they without lacked two hundred: and they searched the wounded men on both parties. And then they went to council; and wit you well, either party were loth to fight more, so that either might escape with their worship.

When Elias the captain understood the death of his men, he made great dole; and when he wist that they were loth to go to battle again he was wroth out of measure. Then Elias sent word unto king Mark in great despite, whether

he would find a knight that would fight for him, body for body, and if that he might slay king Mark's knight, he to have the truage of Cornwall yearly: and if that his knight slay mine, I fully release my claim for ever. Then the messager departed unto king Mark, and told him how that his lord Elias had sent him word to find a knight to do battle with him, body for body. When king Mark understood the messager he bad him abide, and he should have his answer. Then called he all the baronage together, to wit what was the best counsel. They said, all at once, To fight in a field we have no lust, for had not been Sir Tristram's prowess, it had been likely that we never should have escaped. And therefore, sir, as we deem, it were well done to find a knight that would do battle with him, for he knightly proffereth.

CHAP. XXX.

How Sir Elias and Sir Tristram fought together for the truage, and how Sir Tristram slew Elias in the field.

NOT for then, when all this was said, they could find no knight that would do battle with him. Sir king, said they all, here is no knight that dare fight with Elias. Alas, said king Mark, then am I utterly shamed, and utterly destroyed, unless that my nephew Sir Tristram will take the battle upon him. Wit ye well, they said all, he had yesterday over much on hand, and he is weary for travail, and sore wounded. Where is he? said king Mark. Sir, said they, he is in his bed to repose him. Alas, said king Mark, but I have the succour of my nephew Sir Tristram I am utterly destroyed for ever. Therewith one went to Sir Tristram where he lay, and told him what king Mark had said. And therewith Sir Tristram arose lightly, and put on him a long gown, and came afore the king and all the lords. And when he saw them all so dismayed, he asked the king and the lords what tidings were with them. Never worse, said the king. And therewith he told him all how he had word of Elias to find a knight to fight for the truage of Cornwall, and none can I find; and as for you, said the king and all the lords, we may ask no more of you for shame, for through your hardiness yesterday ye saved all our lives. Sir, said Sir Tristram, now I understand ye would have my succour, reason would that I should do all that lieth in my power to do, saving my worship and my life, howbeit I am sore bruised and hurt. And sithen Sir Elias proffereth so largely, I shall fight with him, or else I will be slain in the field, or else I will deliver Cornwall from the old truage. And therefore lightly call his messenger, and he shall be answered: for as yet my wounds be green, and they will be sorer a seven night after than they be now, and therefore he shall have his answer, that I will do battle to-morn with him. Then was the messenger departed brought before king Mark. Hark my fellow, said Sir Tristram, go fast unto thy lord, and bid him make true assurance on his part, for the truage, as the king here shall make on his part; and then tell thy lord Sir Elias, that I, Sir Tristram, king Arthur's knight, and knight of the Table Round, will as to-morn meet with thy lord on horseback, and do battle as long as my horse may endure, and after that to do battle with him on foot to the utterance. The messenger beheld Sir Tristram from the top to the toe; and therewithal he departed, and came to his lord, and told him how he was answered of Sir Tristram. And therewithal was made hostage on both parties, and made it as sure as it might be, that whether party had the victory, so to end. And then were both hosts assembled, on both parts of the field without the castle of Tintagil, and there was none but Sir Tristram and Sir Elias armed. So when the appointment was made, they departed in sunder, and they came together with all the might that their horses might run. And either knight smote other so hard that both horses and knights went to the earth.

Not for then they both lightly arose, and dressed their shields on their shoulders, with naked swords in their hands, and they dashed together that it seemed a flaming fire about them. Thus they traced and traversed, and hewed on helms and hauberks, and cut away many cantels of their shields, and either wounded other passing sore, so that the hot blood fell freshly upon the earth. And by then they had fought the mountenance of an hour Sir Tristram waxed faint and for-bled, and gave sore aback. That saw Sir Elias, and followed fiercely upon him, and wounded him in many places. And ever Sir Tristram traced and traversed, and went froward him here and there, and covered him with his shield as he might all weakly, that all men said he was overcome. For Sir Elias had given him twenty strokes against one. Then was there laughing of the Sessoins' party, and great dole on king Mark's party. Alas, said the king, we are ashamed and destroyed all for ever. For, as the book saith, Sir Tristram was never so matched, but if it were Sir Launcelot. Thus as they stood and beheld both parties, that one party laughing, and the other part weeping, Sir Tristram remembered him of his lady, La Beale Isoud, that looked upon him, and how he was likely never to come in her presence. Then he pulled up his shield, that erst hung full low; and then he dressed up his shield unto Elias, and gave him many sad strokes, twenty against one, and all to-brake his shield and his hauberk, that the hot blood ran down to the earth. Then began king Mark to laugh and all Cornish men, and that other party to weep. And ever Sir Tristram said to Sir Elias, Yield thee! Then when Sir Tristram saw him so staggering on the ground, he said, Sir Elias, I am right sorry for thee, for thou art a passing good knight as ever I met withal, except Sir Launcelot. Therewithal Sir Elias fell to the earth, and there died. What shall I do? said Sir Tristram unto king Mark, for this battle is at an end. Then they of Elias's party departed;

and king Mark took of them many prisoners, to redress the harms and the scathes that he had of them, and the remnant he sent into their country to ransom out their fellows. Then was Sir Tristram searched and well healed. Yet for all this king Mark would fain have slain Sir Tristram. But for all that ever Sir Tristram saw or heard by king Mark, yet would he never beware of his treason, but ever he would be there as La Beale Isoud was.

CHAP. XXXI.

How at a great feast that king Mark made, an harper came and sang the lay that Dinadan had made.

Now will we pass of this matter, and speak we of the harper that Sir Launcelot and Sir Dinadan had sent into Cornwall. And at the great feast that king Mark made for joy that the Sessoins were put out of his country, then came Eliot the harper, with the lay that Dinadan had made, and secretly brought it unto Sir Tristram, and told him the lay that Dinadan had made by king Mark. And when Sir Tristram heard it, he said: That Dinadan can make wonderly well and ill, there as it shall be. Sir, said Eliot, dare I sing this song afore king Mark? Yea, on my peril, said Sir Tristram, for I shall be thy warrant. Then at the meat came in Eliot the harper, and because he was a curious harper men heard him sing the same lay that Dinadan had made, the which spake the most villainy by king Mark of his treason that ever man heard. When the harper had sung his song to the end, king Mark was wonderly wroth, and said, Thou harper, how durst thou be so bold on thy head to sing this song before me? Sir, said Eliot, wit you well I am a minstrel, and I must do as I am commanded of these lords that I bear the arms of. And, sir, wit you well that Sir Dinadan, a knight of the Table Round, made this song, and made me to sing it afore you. Thou sayest well, said king Mark, and because thou art a minstrel thou shalt go quit, but I charge thee hie thee fast out of my sight. So the harper departed, and went to Sir Tristram, and told him how he had sped. Then Sir Tristram let make letters, as goodly as he could, to Launcelot, and to Sir Dinadan. And so he let conduct the harper out of the country. But to say that king Mark was wonderly wroth, he was; for he deemed that the lay that was sung afore him was made by Sir Tristram's counsel, wherefore he thought to slay him and all his well-willers in that country.

CHAP. XXXII.

How king Mark slew by treason his brother Boudwin, for good service that he had done to him.

Now turn we to another matter, that fell between king Mark and his brother that was called the good prince Sir Boudwin, that all the people of the country loved passing well. So it befell upon a time, that the miscreants Saracens landed in the country of Cornwall, soon after these Sessoins were gone. And then the good prince Sir Boudwin, at the landing, he raised the country privily and hastily. And or it were day he let put wild-fire in three of his own ships, and suddenly he pulled up the sail, and with the wind he made those ships to be driven among the navy of the Saracens; and to make short tale, those three ships set on fire all the ships, that none were saved. And at the point of the day the good prince Boudwin, with all his fellowship, set on the miscreants, with shouts and cries, and slew to the number of forty thousand, and left none alive. When king Mark wist this, he was wonderly wroth that his brother should win such worship. And because this prince was better beloved than he in all that country, and that also Sir Boudwin loved well Sir Tristram, therefore he thought to slay him. And thus hastily as a man out of his wit, he sent for prince Boudwin, and Anglides his wife, and bad them bring their young son with them, that he might see him. All this he did to the intent to slay the child as well as his father, for he was the falsest traitor that ever was born. Alas, for his goodness and for his good deeds this gentle prince Boudwin was slain. So when he came with his wife Anglides, the king made them fair semblant till they had dined. And when they had dined, king Mark sent for his brother, and said thus: Brother, how sped you when the miscreants arrived by you? Me seemeth it had been your part to have sent me word, that I might have been at that journey, for it had been reason that I had had the honour, and not you. Sir, said the prince Boudwin, it was so that and I had tarried till that I had sent for you, those miscreants had destroyed my country. Thou liest, false traitor, said king Mark, for thou art ever about for to win worship from me, and put me to dishonour, and thou cherishest that I hate. And therewith he struck him to the heart with a dagger, that he never after spake word. Then the lady Anglides made great dole and swooned, for she saw her lord slain afore her face. Then was there no more to do, but prince Boudwin was despoiled and brought to burial. But Anglides privily got her husband's doublet and his shirt, and that she kept secretly. Then was there much sorrow and crying, and great dole made Sir Tristram, Sir Dinas, Sir Fergus, and so did all the knights that were there, for that prince was passingly well beloved. So La Beale Isoud sent unto Anglides, the prince Boudwin's wife, and bad her avoid lightly, or else her young son Alisander le Orphelin should be slain. When she heard this, she took her horse and her child, and rode her way with such poor men as durst ride with her.

CHAP. XXXIII.

How Anglides, Boudwin's wife, escaped with her young son, Alisander le Orphelin, and came to the castle of Arundel.

NOTWITHSTANDING, when king Mark had done this deed, yet he thought to do more vengeance; and with his sword in his hand he sought from chamber to chamber, to find Anglides and her young son. And when she was missed, he called a good knight that hight Sir Sadok, and charged him, by pain of death, to fetch Anglides again, and her young son. So Sir Sadok departed, and rode after Anglides. And within ten mile he overtook her, and bade her turn again, and ride with him to king Mark. Alas, fair knight, she said, what shall ye win by my son's death, or by mine? I have had over much harm, and too great a loss. Madam, said Sadok, of your loss is dole and pity; but, madam, said Sadok, would ye depart out of this country with your son, and keep him till he be of age, that he may revenge his father's death, then would I suffer you to depart from me, so ye promise me for to revenge the death of prince Boudwin. Ah, gentle knight, Jesu thank thee, and if ever my son Alisander le Orphelin live to be a knight, he shall have his father's doublet and his shirt with the bloody marks; and I shall give him such a charge that he shall remember it while he liveth. And therewithal Sadok departed from her, and either betook other to God. And when Sadok came to king Mark, he told him faithfully that he had drowned young Alisander, her son; and thereof king Mark was full glad.

Now turn we unto Anglides, that rode both night and day by adventure out of Cornwall, and little and in few places she rested. But ever she drew southward to the sea side, till by fortune she came to a castle that is called Magouns, and now it is called Arundel in Southsex. And the constable of the castle welcomed her, and said she was welcome to her own castle; and there was Anglides worshipfully received, for the constable's wife was nigh her cousin. And the constable's name was Bellangere, and that same constable told Anglides that the same castle was hers by right inheritance. Thus Anglides endured years and winters, till

Alisander was big and strong. There was none so wight in all that country, neither there was none that might do no manner of mastery afore him.

CHAP. XXXIV.

How Anglides gave the bloody doublet to Alisander her son the same day that he was made knight, and the charge withal.

THEN upon a day Bellangere the constable came to Anglides and said, Madam, it were time that my lord Alisander were made knight, for he is a passing strong young man. Sir, said she, I would he were made knight; but then must I give him the most charge that ever sinful mother gave to her child. Do as ye list, said Bellangere, and I shall give him warning that he shall be made knight. Now it will be well done that he may be made knight at our Ladyday in Lent. Be it so, said Anglides, and I pray you make ready therefore. So came the constable to Alisander, and told him that he should at our Ladyday in Lent be made knight. I thank God, said Alisander, these are the best tidings that ever came to me. Then the constable ordained twenty of the greatest gentlemen's sons, and the best born men of the country, that should be made knights that same day that Alisander was made knight. So on the same day that Alisander and his twenty fellows were made knights, at the offering of the mass there came Anglides unto her son, and said thus: O fair sweet son, I charge thee upon my blessing, and of the high order of chivalry that thou takest here this day, that thou understand what I shall say and charge thee withal. Therewithal she pulled out a bloody doublet and a bloody shirt, that were be-bled with old blood. When Alisander saw this, he start back and waxed pale, and said, Fair mother, what may this mean? I shall tell thee, fair son; this was thine own father's doublet and shirt that he ware upon him that same day that he was slain. And there she told him why and wherefore: and how

for his goodness king Mark slew him with his dagger afore mine own eyes. And therefore this shall be your charge, that I shall give thee. Now I require thee and charge thee upon my blessing, and upon the high order of knighthood, that thou be revenged upon king Mark for the death of thy father. And therewithal she swooned. Then Alisander leaped to his mother, and took her up in his arms, and said, Fair mother, ye have given me a great charge, and here I promise you I shall be avenged upon king Mark when that I may, and that I promise to God and to you. So this feast was ended. And the constable, by the advice of Anglides, let purvey that Sir Alisander was well horsed and harnessed. Then he justed with his twenty fellows that were made knights with him. But, for to make a short tale, he overthrew all those twenty, that none might withstand him a buffet.

CHAP. XXXV.

How it was told to king Mark of Sir Alisander, and how he would have slain Sir Sadok for saving of his life.

THEN one of those knights departed unto king Mark, and told him all how Alisander was made knight, and all the charge that his mother gave him, as ye have heard afore time. Alas, false treason, said king Mark, I wend that young traitor had been dead. Alas, whom may I trust? And therewithal king Mark took a sword in his hand, and sought Sir Sadok from chamber to chamber to slay him. When Sir Sadok saw king Mark come with his sword in his hand, he said thus: Beware, king Mark, and come not nigh me, for wit thou well that I saved Alisander his life, of which I never repent me, for thou falsely and cowardly slewest his father Boudwin traitorly for his good deeds. Wherefore I pray almighty Jesu send Alisander might and strength to be revenged upon thee. And now beware king Mark of young Alisander, for he is made a knight. Alas, said king Mark, that ever I should hear a traitor say so afore me. And therewith four knights of king Mark drew their swords to slay Sir Sadok. But anon Sir Sadok slew them all in king Mark's presence. And then Sir Sadok passed forth into his chamb̃er, and took his horse and his harness, and rode on his way a good pace. For there was neither Sir Tristram, neither Sir Dinas, nor Sir Fergus, that would Sir Sadok any evil will. Then was king Mark wroth, and thought to destroy Sir Alisander, and Sir Sadok that had saved him, for king Mark dread and hated Sir Alisander most of any man living. When Sir Tristram understood that Alisander was made knight, anon forthwithal he sent him a letter, praying him and charging him that he would draw him to the court of king Arthur, and that he put him in the rule and in the hands of Sir Launcelot. So this letter was sent to Alisander from his cousin Sir Tristram. And at that time he thought to do after his commandment. Then king Mark called a knight that brought him the tidings from Alisander, and bade him abide still in that country. Sir, said that knight, so must I do, for in mine own country I dare not come. No force, said king Mark. I shall give thee here double as much lands as thou haddest of thine own. But within short space Sir Sadok met with that false knight and slew him. Then was king Mark wood wroth out of measure. Then he sent unto queen Morgan le Fay and to the queen of Northgalis, praying them in his letters that they two sorceresses would set all the country in fire, with ladies that were enchantresses, and by such that were dangerous knights, as Malgrin, and Breuse Sance Pité; that by no means Alisander le Orphelin should escape, but either he should be taken or slain. This ordinance made king Mark for to destroy Alisander.

CHAP. XXXVI.

How Sir Alisander wan the prize at a tournament, and of Morgan le Fay. And how he fought with Sir Malgrin and slew him.

Now turn we again unto Sir Alisander, that at his departing from his mother took with him his father's bloody shirt. So that he bare with him always till his death day, in tokening to think on his father's death. So was Alisander purposed to ride to London by the counsel of Sir Tristram to Sir Launcelot. And by fortune he went by the sea-side, and rode wrong. And there he won at a tournament the gree, that king Carados made. And there he smote down king Carados, and twenty of his knights, and also Sir Safere a good knight, that was Sir Palamides' brother, the good knight. All this saw a damsel, and saw the best knight just that ever she saw. And ever as he smote down knights he made them to swear to wear no harness in a twelvemonth and a day. This is well said, said Morgan le Fay, this is the knight that I would fain see. And so she took her palfrey and rode a great while, and then she rested her in her pavilion. So there came four knights: two were armed, and two were unarmed, and they told Morgan le Fay their names. The first was Elias de Gomeret, the second was Car de Gomeret; those were armed: that other twain were of Camiliard, cousins unto queen Guenever, and that one hight Sir Guy, and that other hight Garaunt; those were unarmed. There these four knights told Morgan le Fay how a young knight had smitten them down before a castle. For the maiden of that castle said that he was but late made knight and young. But as we suppose, but if it were Sir Tristram, or Sir Launcelot, or Sir Lamorak the good knight, there is none that might sit him a buffet with a spear. Well, said Morgan le Fay, I shall meet that knight or it be long time, and he dwell in that country.

So turn we to the damsel of the castle, that when Alisander le Orphelin had forjusted the four knights, she called him to her, and said thus: Sir knight, wilt thou for my sake just and fight with a knight of this country, that is and hath been long time an evil neighbour to me, his name is Malgrin, and he will not suffer me to be married in no manner wise for all that I can do, or any knight for my sake. Damsel, said Alisander, and he come while I am here I will fight with him, and my poor body for your sake I will jeopard. And therewithal she sent for him, for he was at her commandment. And when either had a sight of other they made them ready for to just, and they came together eagerly, and Malgrin bruised his spear upon Alisander, and Alisander smote him again so hard that he bare him quite from his saddle to the earth. But this Malgrin arose lightly and dressed his shield and drew his sword, and bad him alight, saying, Though thou have the better of me on horseback, shalt thou find that I shall endure like a knight on foot. It is well said, said Alisander. And so lightly he voided his horse, and betook him to his varlet. And then they rashed together like two boars, and laid on their helms and shields long time by the space of three hours, that never man could say which was the better knight. And in the meanwhile came Morgan le Fay to the damsel of the castle, and they beheld the battle. But this Malgrin was an old roted knight, and he was called one of the dangerous knights of the world to do battle on foot: but on horseback there were many better. And ever this Malgrin awaited to slay Alisander, and so wounded him wonderly sore, that it was marvel that ever he might stand, for he had bled so much blood: for Alisander fought wildly and not wittily. And that other was a felonious knight, and awaited him, and smote him sore. And sometime they rashed together with their shields like two boars or rams, and fell groveling both to the earth. Now knight, said Malgrin, hold thy hand awhile, and tell me what thou art. I will not, said Alisander, but if me list. But tell me thy name, and why thou keepest this country, or else thou shalt die of my hands. Wit thou well, said Malgrin, that for this maiden's love of this castle I have slain ten good knights by mishap; and by outrage and pride of

myself I have slain ten other knights. Truly, said Alisander, this is the foulest confession that ever I heard knight make, nor never heard I speak of other men of such a shameful confession; wherefore it were great pity and great shame to me that I should let thee live any longer; therefore keep thee as well as ever thou mayest, for as I am true knight, either thou shalt slay me or else I shall slay thee, I promise thee faithfully. Then they lashed together fiercely. And at the last Alisander smote Malgrin to the earth, and then he raced off his helm, and smote off his head lightly. And when he had done and ended this battle, anon he called to him his varlet, the which brought him his horse. And then he weening to be strong enough would have mounted. And so she laid Sir Alisander in a horse-litter, and led him into the castle, for he had no foot nor might to stand upon the earth. For he had sixteen great wounds, and in especial one of them was like to be his death.

CHAP. XXXVII.

How queen Morgan le Fay had Alisander in her castle, and how she healed his wounds.

THEN queen Morgan le Fay searched his wounds, and gave such an ointment unto him that he should have died. And on the morn when she came to him, he complained him sore; and then she put other ointments upon him, and then he was out of his pain. Then came the damsel of the castle, and said unto Morgan le Fay, I pray you help me that this knight might wed me, for he hath won me with his hands. Ye shall see, said Morgan le Fay, what I shall say. Then Morgan le Fay went to Sir Alisander and bad in any wise that he should refuse this lady—if she desire to wed you, for she is not for you. So the damsel came and desired of him marriage. Damsel, said Orphelin, I thank you, but as yet I cast me not to marry in this country. Sir, said she, sithen ye will not marry me, I pray you, insomuch as ye have won me, that ye will give me to a knight of this country that hath been my friend and loved me many years. With all my heart, said Alisander, I will assent thereto. Then was the knight sent for; his name was Sir Gerine le Grose. And anon he made them handfast and wedded them. Then came queen Morgan le Fay to Alisander, and bad him arise, and put him in a horse-litter: and gave him such a drink that in three days and three nights he waked never but slept: and so she brought him to her own castle, that at that time was called La Beale Regard. Then Morgan le Fay came to Alisander, and asked him if he would fain be whole. Who would be sick, said Alisander, and he might be whole? Well, said Morgan le Fay, then shall ye promise me by your knighthood that this day twelvemonth and a day ye shall not pass the compass of this castle, and without doubt ye shall lightly be whole. I assent, said Sir Alisander. And there he made her a promise. Then was he soon whole. And when Alisander was whole then he repented him of his oath, for he might not be revenged upon king Mark. Right so there came a damsel that was cousin to the Earl of Pase, and she was cousin to Morgan le Fay. And by right that castle of La Beale Regard should have been hers by true inheritance. So this damsel entered into this castle where lay Alisander, and there she found him upon his bed, passing heavy and all sad.

CHAP. XXXVIII.

How Alisander was delivered from the queen Morgan le Fay by the means of a damsel.

Sir knight, said the damsel, and ye would be merry, I could tell you good tidings. Well were me, said Alisander, and I might hear of good tidings, for now I stand as a prisoner by my promise. Sir, said she, wit you well that ye be a prisoner, and worse than ye ween. For my lady, my cousin queen Morgan le Fay, keepeth you here for none other intent but for to do her pleasure with you, when it liketh her. Defend me, said Alisander, from such pleasure, for I had lever die than I would do her such pleasure. Truly, said the damsel, and ye would love me and be ruled by me, I shall make your deliverance with your worship. Tell me, said Alisander, by what mean, and ye shall have my love. Fair knight, said she, this castle of right ought to be mine, and I have an uncle the which is a mighty earl, he is earl of Pase, and of all folks he hateth most Morgan le Fay, and I shall send unto him, and pray him for my sake to destroy this castle for the evil customs that be used therein; and then will he come and set wild fire on every part of the castle, and I shall get you out at a privy postern, and there shall ye have your horse and your harness. Ye say well, damsel, said Alisander. And then she said, Ye may keep the room of this castle this twelvemonth and a day, then break ye not your oath. Truly, fair damsel, said Alisander, ye say sooth. And then he kissed her. So anon she sent unto her uncle, and bad him come and destroy that castle; for as the book saith, he would have destroyed that castle afore time, had not that damsel been. When the earl understood her letters he sent her word again, that on such a day he would come and destroy that castle. So when that day came, she shewed Alisander a postern where through he should flee into a garden, and there he should find his armour and his horse. When the day came that was set, thither came the earl of Pase with four hundred knights, and set on fire all the parts of the castle, that, or they ceased, they left not a stone standing. And all this while that the fire was in the castle, he abode in the garden. And when the fire was done, he let make a cry that he would keep that piece of earth, there as the castle of La Beale Regard was, a twelvemonth and a day, from all manner knights that would come.

So it happed there was a duke that

hight Ansirus, and he was of the kin of Sir Launcelot. And this knight was a great pilgrim, for every third year he would be at Jerusalem. And because he used all his life to go in pilgrimage, men called him duke Ansirus the pilgrim. And this duke had a daughter that hight Alice, that was a passing fair woman, and because of her father she was called Alice La Beale Pilgrim. And anon as she heard of this cry, she went unto Arthur's court, and said openly in hearing of many knights, That what knight may overcome that knight that keepeth that piece of earth shall have me and all my lands. When the knights of the Round Table heard her say thus, many were glad, for she was passing fair, and of great rents. Right so she let cry in castles and towns as fast on her side as Sir Alisander did on his side. Then she dressed her pavilion straight by the piece of earth that Alisander kept. So she was not so soon there but there came a knight of Arthur's court, that hight Sagramor le Desirous, and he proffered to just with Alisander, and they encountered, and Sagramor le Desirous bruised his spear upon Sir Alisander, but Sir Alisander smote him so hard that he avoided his saddle. And when La Beale Alice saw him just so well, she thought him a passing goodly knight on horseback. And then she lept out of her pavilion and took Sir Alisander by the bridle, and thus she said: Fair knight, I require thee of thy knighthood, shew me thy visage. I dare well, said Alisander, shew my visage. And then he put off his helm; and when she saw his visage she said, Truly, thee I must love and never other. Then shew me your visage, said he.

CHAP. XXXIX.

How Alisander met with Alice la Beale Pilgrim, and how he justed with two knights; and after of him and of Sir Mordred.

THEN she unwimpled her visage. And when he saw her he said, Here have

I found my love and my lady. Truly, fair lady, said he, I promise you to be your knight, and none other that beareth the life. Now, gentle knight, said she, tell me your name. My name is, said he, Alisander le Orphelin. Now, damsel, tell me your name, said he. My name is, said she, Alice la Beale Pilgrim. And when we be more at our heart's ease, both ye and I shall tell each other of what blood we be come. So there was great love betwixt them. And as they thus talked, there came a knight that hight Harsouse le Berbuse, and asked part of Sir Alisander's spears. Then Sir Alisander encountered with him, and at the first Sir Alisander smote him over his horse croup. And then there came another knight that hight Sir Hewgon. And Sir Alisander smote him down as he did that other. Then Sir Hewgon proffered to do battle on foot. Sir Alisander overcame him with three strokes, and there would have slain him had he not yielded him. So then Alisander made both those knights to swear to wear none armour in a twelvemonth and a day. Then Sir Alisander alight down, and went to rest him and repose him. Then the damsel that halp Sir Alisander out of the castle, in her play told dame Alice altogether how he was prisoner of the castle of La Beale Regard: and there she told her how she gat him out of prison. Sir, said Alice la Beale Pilgrim, me seemeth ye are much beholden to this maiden. That is truth, said Sir Alisander. And there Alice told him of what blood she was come. Sir, wit ye well, she said, that I am of the blood of king Ban, that was father unto Sir Launcelot. Ye wis, fair lady, said Alisander, my mother told me that my father was brother unto a king, and I am nigh cousin to Sir Tristram. Then this while came there three knights, that one hight Vains, and that other hight Harvis de les Marches, and the third hight Perin de la Montaine. And with one spear Sir Alisander smote them down all three, and gave them such falls that they had no list to fight upon foot. So he made them to swear to wear no arms in a twelvemonth. So when they were departed, Sir Alisander beheld his lady Alice on horseback as he stood in her pavilion. And then he was so enamoured upon her, that he wist not whether he were on horseback or on foot. Right so came the false knight Sir Mordred, and saw Sir Alisander was assotted upon his lady: and therewithal he took his horse by the bridle and led him here and there, and had cast to have led him out of that place to have shamed him. When the damsel that halp him out of that castle saw how shamefully he was led, anon she let arm her, and set a shield upon her shoulder. And therewith she mounted upon his horse, and gat a naked sword in her hand, and she thrust unto Alisander with all her might, and she gave him such a buffet that he thought the fire flew out of his eyes. And when Alisander felt that stroke he looked about him, and drew his sword. And when she saw that, she fled, and so did Mordred into the forest, and the damsel fled into the pavilion. So when Sir Alisander understood himself how the false knight would have shamed him, had not the damsel been, then was he wroth with himself that Sir Mordred was so escaped his hands. But then Sir Alisander and dame Alice had good game at the damsel, how sadly she hit him upon the helm. Then Sir Alisander justed thus day by day, and on foot he did many battles with many knights of king Arthur's court, and with many knights strangers. Therefore to tell all the battles that he did it were overmuch to rehearse, for every day within that twelvemonth he had ado with one knight or with other, and some day he had ado with three or with four. And there was never knight that put him to the worse. And at the twelvemonth's end he departed with his lady Alice la Beale Pilgrim. And the damsel would never go from him: and so they went into their country of Benoye, and lived there in great joy.

CHAP. XL.

How Sir Galahalt did do cry a justs in Surluse, and queen Guenever's knights should just against all that would come.

But as the book saith, king Mark would never stint till he had slain him by treason. And by Alice he gat a child which hight Bellengerus le Beuse. And by good fortune he came to the court of king Arthur, and proved a passing good knight: and he revenged his father's death; for the false king Mark slew both Sir Tristram and Alisander falsely and feloniously. And it happed so that Alisander had never grace nor fortune to come unto king Arthur's court. For and he had come to Sir Launcelot, all knights said that knew him, he was one of the strongest knights that was in Arthur's days. And great dole was made for him.

So let us we of him pass, and turn we to another tale. So it befell that Sir Galahalt the haut prince was lord of the country of Surluse, whereof came many good knights. And this noble prince was a passing good man of arms, and ever he held a noble fellowship together. And then he came to Arthur's court, and told him his intent, how this was his will, how he would let cry a justs in the country of Surluse, the which country was within the lands of king Arthur, and there he asked leave to let cry a justs. I will give you leave, said king Arthur. But wit thou well, said king Arthur, I may not be there. Sir, said queen Guenever, please it you to give me leave to be at that justs. With right good will, said Arthur, for Sir Galahalt the haut prince shall have you in governance. Sir, said Galahalt, I will as ye will. Sir, then the queen I will take with me, and such knights as please me best. Do as ye list, said king Arthur. So anon she commanded Sir Launcelot to make him ready with such knights as he thought best. So in every good town and castle of this land was made a cry, that in the country of Surluse Sir Galahalt should make a justs that should last eight days:

and how the haut prince with the help of queen Guenever's knights should just against all manner of men that would come. When this cry was known, kings and princes, dukes and earls, barons and noble knights, made them ready to be at that justs. And at the day of justing there came in Sir Dinadan disguised, and did many great deeds of arms.

CHAP. XLI.

How Sir Launcelot fought in the tournament, and how Sir Palamides did arms there for a damsel.

THEN at the request of queen Guenever and of king Bagdemagus, Sir Launcelot came into the range, but he was disguised, and that was the cause that few folk knew him. And there met with him Sir Ector de Maris his own brother, and either brake their spears upon other to their hands. And then either gat another spear, and then Sir Launcelot smote down Sir Ector de Maris his own brother. That saw Sir Bleoberis, and he smote Sir Launcelot such a buffet upon the helm that he wist not well where he was. Then Sir Launcelot was wroth, and smote Sir Bleoberis so sore upon the helm that his head bowed down backward. And he smote eft another buffet that he avoided his saddle. And so he rode by and thrust forth to the thickest. When the king of Northgalis saw Sir Ector and Sir Bleoberis lie on the ground, then he was wonderous wroth, for they came on his part against them of Surluse. So the king of Northgalis ran to Sir Launcelot, and brake a spear upon him all to pieces. Therewith Sir Launcelot overtook the king of Northgalis and smote him such a buffet on the helm with his sword that he made him to avoid his horse; and anon the king was horsed again. So both the king Bagdemagus and the king of Northgalis party hurled together: and then began a strong meddle, but they of Northgalis were far bigger.

When Sir Launcelot saw his party go to the worst, he thronged into the thickest press with a sword in his hand, and there he smote down on the right hand and on the left hand, and pulled down knights, and rased off their helms, that all men had wonder that ever one knight might do such deeds of arms. When Sir Meliagant, that was son unto king Bagdemagus, saw how Sir Launcelot fared, he marvelled greatly. And when he understood that it was he, he wist well that he was disguised for his sake. Then Sir Meliagant prayed a knight to slay Sir Launcelot's horse, either with sword or with spear. At that time king Bagdemagus met with a knight that hight Sauseise, a good knight, to whom he said, Now fair Sauseise, encounter with my son Meliagant, and give him large payment; for I would he were well beaten of thy hands, that he might depart out of the field. And then Sir Sauseise encountered with Sir Meliagant, and either smote other down. And then they fought on foot, and there Sauseise had won Sir Meliagant had not there come rescues. So then the haut prince blew to lodging. And every knight unarmed him and went to the great feast. Then in the meanwhile there came a damsel unto the haut prince, and complained that there was a knight that hight Goneries, that withheld her all her lands. Then the knight was there present, and cast his glove to him, or to any that would fight in her name. So the damsel took up the glove all heavily for default of a champion. Then there came a varlet to her and said, Damsel, will ye do after me? Full fain, said the damsel. Then go ye unto such a knight that lyeth here beside in an hermitage, and that followeth the questing beast, and pray him to take the battle upon him, and anon I wot well he will grant you.

So anon she took her palfrey, and within awhile she found that knight, that was Sir Palamides. And when she required him, he armed him and rode with her, and made her to go to the haut prince, and to ask leave for her knight to do battle. I will well, said the haut prince. Then the knights were ready in the field to just on horse-back: and either gat a spear in their hands, and met so fiercely together that their spears all to-shivered. And then they flung out swords, and Sir Pala-mides smote Sir Goneries down to the earth, and then he rased off his helm, and smote off his head. Then they went to supper. And the damsel loved Sir Palamides, but the book saith she was of his kin. So then Sir Palamides disguised him in this manner; in his shield he bear the questing beast, and in all his trappings. And when he was thus ready, he sent to the haut prince to give him leave to just with other knights, but he was adoubted of Sir Launcelot. The haut prince sent him word again that he should be welcome, and that Sir Launcelot should not just with him. Then Sir Galahalt the haut prince let cry what knight soever he were that smote down Sir Palamides should have his damsel to himself.

CHAP. XLII.

How Sir Galahalt and Palamides fought together, and of Sir Dinadan and Sir Galahalt.

HERE beginneth the second day. Anon as Sir Palamides came into the field, Sir Galahalt the haut prince was at the range end, and met with Sir Palamides, and he with him, with great spears. And then they came so hard together that their spears all to-shivered. But Sir Galahalt smote him so hard that he bare him backward over his horse, but yet he lost not his stirrups. Then they drew their swords and lashed together many sad strokes that many worshipful knights left their business to behold them. But at the last Sir Gala-halt the haut prince smote a stroke of might unto Sir Palamides sore upon the helm, but the helm was so hard that the sword might not bite, but slipped and smote off the head of the horse of Sir Palamides. When the haut prince wist, and saw the good knight fall unto the earth, he was ashamed of that stroke. And therewith he alighted down off his own horse, and prayed the good knight Sir Palamides to take that horse of his gift, and to forgive him that deed. Sir, said Palamides, I thank you of your great goodness, for ever of a man of worship a knight shall never have dis-worship. And so he mounted upon that horse, and the haut prince had another anon. Now, said the haut prince, I release to you that maiden, for ye have won her. Ah, said Palamides, the damsel and I be at your commandment. So they departed, and Sir Galahalt did great deeds of arms. And right so came Dinadan and encountered with Sir Galahalt, and either came to other so fast with their spears, that their spears brake to their hands. But Dina-dan had wend the haut prince had been more weary than he was. And then he smote many sad strokes at the haut prince. But when Dinadan saw he might not get him to the earth, he said, My lord, I pray you leave me and take another. The haut prince knew not Dinadan, and left goodly for his fair words, and so they departed. But soon there came another, and told the haut prince that it was Dinadan. For-sooth, said the prince, therefore am I heavy that he is so escaped from me: for with his mocks and jests now shall I never have done with him. And then Galahalt rode fast after him, and bad him, Abide, Dinadan, for king Arthur's sake. Nay, said Sir Dinadan, we meet no more together this day. Then in that wrath the haut prince met with Meliagant, and he smote him in the throat, that and he had fallen his neck had broken, and with the same spear he smote down another knight. Then came in they of Northgalis, and many strangers, and were like to have put them of Surluse to the worse, for Sir Galahalt the haut prince had ever much in hand. So there came in the good knight Semound the Valiant, with forty knights, and he beat them all aback. Then the queen Guenever and Sir Laun-celot let blow to lodging: and every knight unarmed him, and dressed him to the feast.

CHAP. XLIII.

How Sir Archade appealed Sir Palamides of treason, and how Sir Palamides slew him.

WHEN Palamides was unarmed, he asked lodging for himself and the damsel. Anon the haut prince commanded them to lodging. And he was not so soon in his lodging, but there came a knight that hight Archade; he was brother unto Goneries, that Sir Palamides slew afore in the damsel's quarrel. And this knight Archade called Sir Palamides traitor, and appealed him for the death of his brother. By the leave of the haut prince, said Sir Palamides, I shall answer thee. When the haut prince understood their quarrel, he bad them go to dinner, and as soon as ye have dined, look that either knight be ready in the field. So when they had dined, they were armed both, and took their horses; and the queen, and the prince, and Sir Launcelot, were set to behold them. And so they let run their horses, and there Sir Palamides bare Archade on his spear over his horse tail. And then Palamides alight, and drew his sword; but Sir Archade might not arise, and there Sir Palamides rased off his helm, and smote off his head. Then the haut prince and queen Guenever went to supper. Then king Bagdemagus sent away his son Meliagant, because Sir Launcelot should not meet with him, for he hated Sir Launcelot, and that knew he not.

CHAP. XLIV.

Of the third day, and how Sir Palamides justed with Sir Lamorak, and other things.

Now beginneth the third day of justing, and at that day king Bagdemagus made him ready, and there came against him king Marsil, that had in gift an island of Sir Galahalt the haut prince; and this island had the name Pomitain. Then it befell that king Bagdemagus and king Marsil of Pomi-

tain met together with spears, and king Marsil had such a buffet that he fell over his horse croup. Then there came in a knight of king Marsil, to revenge his lord: and king Bagdemagus smote him down, horse and man, to the earth. So there came an earl that hight Arrouse, and Sir Breuse, and an hundred knights with them of Pomitain, and the king of Northgalis was with them; and all these were against them of Surluse. And then there began great battle, and many knights were cast under horse feet. And ever king Bagdemagus did best, for he first began, and ever he held on. Gaheris, Gawaine's brother, smote ever at the face of king Bagdemagus: and at, the last king Bagdemagus hurtled down Gaheris, horse and man. Then, by adventure, Sir Palamides, the good knight, met with Sir Blamor de Ganis, Sir Bleoberis' brother, and there either smote other with great spears, that both their horses and knights fell to the earth. But Sir Blamor had such a fall that he had almost broken his neck; for the blood brast out at nose, mouth, and his ears; but at the last he recovered well by good surgeons. Then there came in duke Chaleins of Clarance, and in his governance there came a knight that hight Elis la Noire; and there encountered with him king Bagdemagus, and he smote Elis that he made him to avoid his saddle. So the duke Chaleins of Clarance did there great deeds of arms; and of so late as he came in the third day there was no man did so well, except king Bagdemagus and Sir Palamides; that the prize was given that day unto king Bagdemagus. And then they blew unto lodging, and unarmed them, and went to the feast. Right so there came Sir Dinadan, and mocked and jested with king Bagdemagus, that all knights laughed at him; for he was a fine jester, and well loving all good knights. So anon as they had dined there came a varlet, bearing four spears on his back, and he came to Palamides and said thus: Here is a knight by hath sent you the choice of four spears, and requireth you for your lady's sake to take that one half of these spears, and just with him in the field. Tell him, said Palamides, I will not fail him. When Sir Galahalt wist of this, he bad Palamides make him ready. So the queen Guenever, the haut prince, and Sir Launcelot, they were set upon scaffolds to give the judgment of these two knights.

Then Sir Palamides and the strange knight ran so eagerly together that their spears brake to their hands. Anon withal either of them took a great spear in his hand and all to-shivered them in pieces. And then either took a greater spear. And then the knight smote down Sir Palamides, horse and man, to the earth. And as he would have passed over him, the strange knight's horse stumbled, and fell down upon Palamides. Then they drew their swords, and lashed together wonderly sore a great while. Then the haut prince and Sir Launcelot said they saw never two knights fight better than they did. But ever the strange knight doubled his strokes, and put Palamides aback. Therewith the haut prince cried, Ho; and then they went to lodging. And when they were unarmed they knew it was the noble knight Sir Lamorak. When Sir Launcelot knew that it was Sir Lamorak he made much of him; for above all earthly men he loved him best except Sir Tristram. Then queen Guenever commended him, and so did all other good knights make much of him, except Sir Gawaine's brethren. Then queen Guenever said unto Sir Launcelot, Sir, I require you that and ye just any more, that ye just with none of the blood of my lord Arthur. So he promised he would not as at that time.

CHAP. XLV.

Of the fourth day, and of many great feats of arms.

HERE beginneth the fourth day. Then came into the field the king with the hundred knights, and all they of Northgalis, and the duke Chaleins of Cla-

rance, and king Marsil of Pomitain. And there came Safere, Palamides' brother, and there he told him tidings of his mother, and how he appealed an earl before king Arthur:—For he made war upon our father and mother, and there I slew him in plain battle. So they went into the field, and the damsel with them; and there came to encounter against them Sir Bleoberis de Ganis, and Sir Ector de Maris. Sir Palamides encountered with Sir Bleoberis, and either smote other down; and in the same wise did Sir Safere and Sir Ector, and those two couples did battle on foot. Then came in Sir Lamorak, and he encountered with the king with the hundred knights, and smote him quite over his horse tail; and in the same wise he served the king of Northgalis, and also he smote down king Marsil. And so, or ever he stint, he smote down with his spear and with his sword thirty knights. When duke Chaleins saw Lamorak do so great prowess, he would not meddle with him for shame; and then he charged all his knights in pain of death that none of you touch him, for it were shame to all good knights and that knight were shamed. Then the two kings gathered them together, and all they set upon Sir Lamorak, and he failed them not, but rashed here and there, smiting on the right hand and on the left, and rased off many helms, so that the haut prince and queen Guenever said they saw never knight do such deeds of arms on horseback. Alas, said Launcelot to king Bagdemagus, I will arm me and help Sir Lamorak. And I will ride with you, said king Bagdemagus. And when they two were horsed, they came to Sir Lamorak, that stood among thirty knights, and well was him that might reach him a buffet : and ever he smote again mightily. Then came there into the press Sir Launcelot, and he threw down Sir Mador de la Porte, and with the truncheon of that spear he threw down many knights. And king Bagdemagus smote on the left hand and on the right hand marvellously well. And then the three kings

fled aback. Therewithal then Sir Galahalt let blow to lodging, and all the
heralds gave Sir Lamorak the prize.
And all this while fought Palamides,
Sir Bleoberis, Sir Safere, Sir Ector, on
foot. Never were there four knights
evener matched. And then they were
parted, and had unto their lodging, and
unarmed them, and so they went to the
great feast.

But when Sir Lamorak was come
unto the court, queen Guenever took
him in her arms, and said, Sir, well
have ye done this day. Then came the
haut prince, and he made of him great
joy, and so did Dinadan, for he wept
for joy. But the joy that Sir Launcelot
made of Sir Lamorak there might no
man tell. Then they went unto rest ;
and on the morn the haut prince let
blow unto the field.

CHAP. XLVI.

Of the fifth day, and how Sir Lamorak behaved him.

HERE beginneth the fifth day. So it
befell that Sir Palamides came in the
morn-tide and proffered to just there as
king Arthur was, in a castle there beside Surluse ; and there encountered
with him a worshipful duke, and there
Sir Palamides smote him over his horse
croup. And this duke was uncle unto
king Arthur. Then Sir Elise's son
rode unto Palamides, and Palamides
served Elise in the same wise. When Sir
Uwaine saw this, he was wroth. Then
he took his horse, and encountered with
Sir Palamides, and Palamides smote
him so hard that he went to the earth,
horse and man. And for to make a
short tale, he smote down three brethren .of Sir Gawaine's, that is for to
say, Mordred, Gaheris, and Agravaine.
Truly, said Arthur, this is a great
despite of a Saracen, that he shall smite
down my · blood. And therewithal
king Arthur was wood wroth, and
thought to have made him ready to
just. That espied Sir Lamorak, that
Arthur and his blood were discomfited.
And anon he was ready, and asked
Palamides if he would any more just.

Why should I not ? said Palamides.
Then they hurtled together, and brake
their spears and all to-shivered them,
that all the castle rang of their dints.
Then either gat a greater spear in his
hand, and they came so fiercely together ; but Sir Palamides' spear all
to-brast, and Sir Lamorak's did hold.
Therewithal Sir Palamides lost his
stirrups and lay upright on his horse's
back. And then Sir Palamides returned
again, and took his damsel, and Sir
Safere returned his way. So when he
was departed, king Arthur came to Sir
Lamorak, and thanked him of his goodness, and prayed him to tell him his
name. Sir, said Lamorak, wit you well,
I owe you my service : but as at this
time I will not abide here, for I see of
mine enemies many about me. Alas,
said Arthur, now wot I well it is Sir
Lamorak de Galis. O, Lamorak, abide
with me, and by my crown I shall never
fail thee : and not so hardy in Gawaine's head, nor none of his brethren,
to do thee any wrong. Sir, said Sir Lamorak, wrong have they done me and
to you both. That is truth, said king
Arthur, for they slew their own mother
and my sister, which me sore grieveth.
It had been much fairer and better
that ye had wedded her, for ye are a
king's son as well as they. Truly, said
the noble knight Sir Lamorak unto
Arthur, her death shall I never forget ;
I promise you and make mine avow I
shall avenge her death as soon as I see
time convenient. And if it were not at
the reverence of your highness I should
now have been revenged upon Sir Gawaine and his brethren. Truly, said
Arthur, I will make you at accord. Sir,
said Lamorak, as at this time I may
not abide with you, for I must to the
justs, where is Sir Launcelot and the
haut prince Sir Galahalt.

Then there was a damsel that was
daughter to king Bandes; and there was
a Saracen knight that hight Corsabrin,
and he loved the damsel, and in no wise
he would suffer her to be married. For
ever this Sir Corsabrin defamed her,
and named her that she was out of her

mind; and thus he let her that she might not be married.

CHAP. XLVII.

How Sir Palamides fought with Corsabrin for a lady, and how Palamides slew Corsabrin.

So by fortune this damsel heard tell that Palamides did much for damsels' sakes; so she sent to him a pensel, and prayed him to fight with Sir Corsabrin for her love, and he should have her, and her lands of her father's that should fall to her. Then the damsel sent unto Corsabrin, and bad him go unto Sir Palamides, that was a Paynim as well as he: and she gave him warning that she had sent him her pensel; and if he might overcome Palamides she would wed him. When Corsabrin wist of her deeds, then was he wood wroth and angry, and rode unto Surluse, where the haut prince was, and there he found Sir Palamides ready, the which had the pensel. So there they waged battle either with other afore Galahalt. Well, said the haut prince, this day must noble knights just, and at after dinner we shall see how ye can speed. Then they blew to justs. And in came Dinadan, and met with Sir Gerin, a good knight, and he threw him down over his horse croup: and Sir Dinadan overthrew four knights more; and there he did great deeds of arms. For he was a good knight, but he was a scoffer, and a jester, and the merriest knight among fellowship that was that time living. And he had such a custom that he loved every good knight, and every good knight loved him again. So then when the haut prince saw Dinadan do so well, he sent unto Sir Launcelot, and bade him strike down Sir Dinadan :— And when that ye have done so, bring him afore me and the noble queen Guenever. Then Sir Launcelot did as he was required. Then Sir Lamorak and he smote down many knights, and rased off helms, and drove all the knights afore them. And so Sir Launcelot smote down Sir Dinadan, and made his men to unarm him, and so

brought him to the queen and the haut prince, and then laughed at Sir Dinadan so sore that they might not stand. Well, said Sir Dinadan, yet have I no shame, for the old shrew Sir Launcelot smote me down. So they went to dinner, and all the court had good sport at Dinadan. Then when the dinner was done, they blew to the field, to behold Sir Palamides and Corsabrin. Sir Palamides pight his pensel in the midst of the field, and then they hurtled together with their spears as it were thunder, and either smote other to the earth. And then they pulled their swords, and dressed their shields, and lashed together mightily as mighty knights, that well nigh there was no piece of harness would hold them. For this Corsabrin was a passing felonious knight. Corsabrin, said Palamides, wilt thou release me yonder damsel, and the pensel? Then was Corsabrin wroth out of measure, and gave Palamides such a buffet that he kneeled on his knee. Then Palamides arose lightly, and smote him upon the helm that he fell down right to the earth. And therewith he rased off his helm, and said, Corsabrin, yield thee, or else thou shalt die of my hands. Fie on thee, said Corsabrin, do thy worst. Then he smote off his head. And therewithal came a stench of his body when the soul departed, so that there might no body abide the savour. So was the corpse had away and buried in a wood, because he was a Paymin.

Then they blew unto lodging, and Palamides was unarmed. Then he went unto queen Guenever, to the haut prince, and to Sir Launcelot. Sir, said the haut prince, here have ye seen this day a great miracle by Corsabrin, what savour there was when the soul departed from the body. Therefore, Sir, we will require you to take the baptism upon you; and I promise you, all knights will set the more by you, and say more worship by you. Sir, said Palamides, I will that ye all know that into this land I came to be christened, and in my heart I am christened, and christened will I be. But I have made such an avow, that I may not be christened till I have done seven true battles for Jesus' sake. And then will I be christened. And I trust God will take mine intent, for I mean truly. Then Sir Palamides prayed queen Guenever and the haut prince to sup with him. And so they did both, Sir Launcelot, and Sir Lamorak, and many other good knights. So on the morn they heard their mass, and blew the field; and then knights made them ready.

CHAP. XLVIII.

Of the sixth day, and what then was done.

HERE beginneth the sixth day. Then came there in Sir Gaheris, and there encountered with him Sir Ossaise of Surluse, and Sir Gaheris smote him over his horse croup. And then either party encountered with other, and there was many spears broken, and many knights cast under feet. So there came Sir Dornard and Sir Aglovale, that were brethren unto Sir Lamorak, and they met with other two knights, and either smote other so hard that all four knights and horses fell to the earth. When Sir Lamorak saw his two brethren down he was wroth out of measure. And then he gat a great spear in his hand, and therewithal he smote down four good knights, and then his spear brake. Then he pulled out his sword, and smote about him on the right hand and on the left hand, and rased off helms and pulled down knights, that all men marvelled of such deeds of arms as he did, for he fared so that many knights fled. Then he horsed his brethren again, and said, Brethren, ye ought to be ashamed to fall so off your horses; what is a knight but when he is on horseback? I set not by a knight when he is on foot, for all battles on foot are but pelowres battles. For there should no knight fight on foot, but if it were for treason, or else he were driven thereto by force: therefore, brethren, sit fast upon your horses, or else fight never more afore me. With that came in duke Chaleins of Clarance; and there encountered with him the earl Ulbawes of Surluse, and either of them smote other down. Then the knights of both parties horsed their lords again; for Sir Ector and Bleoberis were on foot, waiting on the duke Chaleins; and the king with the hundred knights was with the earl of Ulbawes. With that came Gaheris, and lashed to the king with the hundred knights, and he to him again. Then came the duke Chaleins and departed them. Then they blew to lodging, and the knights unarmed them, and drew them to their dinner; and at the midst of their dinner in came Dinadan, and began to rail. Then he beheld the haut prince, that seemed wroth with some fault that he saw. For he had a custom he loved no fish; and because he was served with fish, the which he hated, therefore he was not merry. When Sir Dinadan had espied the haut prince, he espied where was a fish with a great head, and that he gat betwixt two dishes, and served the haut prince with that fish. And then he said thus: Sir Galahalt, well may I liken you to a wolf, for he will never eat fish, but flesh. Then the haut prince laughed at his words. Well, well, said Dinadan to Launcelot, what do ye in this country; for here may no mean knights win no worship for thee? Sir Dinadan, said Launcelot, I ensure thee that I shall no more meet with thee, nor with thy great spear, for I may not sit in my saddle when that spear hitteth me. And if I be happy, I shall beware of that boisterous body that thou bearest. Well, said Launcelot, make good watch ever. God forbid that ever we meet, but if it be at a dish of meat. Then laughed the queen and the haut prince, that they might not sit at their table. Thus they made great joy till on the morn. And then they heard mass, and blew to field. And queen Guenever and all the estates were set, and judges armed clean with their shields to keep the right.

CHAP. XLIX.

*Of the seventh battle, and how Sir Laun-
celot, being disguised like a maid, smote
down Sir Dinadan.*

Now beginneth the seventh battle.
There came in the duke Cambines, and
there encountered with him Sir Aris-
tance, that was counted a good knight,
and they met so hard that either bare
other down, horse and man. Then came
there the earl of Lambaile, and helped
the duke again to horse. Then came
there Sir Ossaise of Surluse, and he
smote the earl Lambaile down from his
horse. Then began they to do great
deeds of arms, and many spears were
broken, and many knights were cast to
the earth. Then the king of Northgalis
and the earl Ulbawes smote together,
that all the judges thought it was like
mortal death. This mean while queen
Guenever and the haut prince and Sir
Launcelot made there Sir Dinadan make
him ready to just. I would, said Sir
Dinadan, ride into the field, but then
one of you twain will meet with me.
Perdy, said the haut prince, ye may see
how we sit here as judges with our
shields, and always mayest thou behold
whether we sit here or not. So Sir
Dinadan departed, and took his horse,
and met with many knights, and did
passing well. And as he was departed,
Sir Launcelot disguised himself, and put
upon his armour a maiden's garment
freshly attired. Then Sir Launcelot
made Sir Galihodin to lead him through
the range, and all men had wonder
what damsel it was. And so as Sir
Dinadan came into the range, Sir Launcelot, that was in the damsel's array,
gat Galihodin's spear, and ran unto
Sir Dinadan. And always Sir Dinadan
looked up there as Sir Launcelot was,
and then he saw one sit in the stead
of Sir Launcelot, armed. But when
Dinadan saw a manner of a damsel, he
dread perils that it was Sir Launcelot
disguised. But Sir Launcelot came
on him so fast that he smote him
over his horse croup. And then with
great scorns they gat Sir Dinadan into

the forest there beside, and there they
despoiled him unto his shirt, and put
upon him a woman's garment, and so
brought him into the field, and so they
blew unto lodging. And every knight
went and unarmed him. Then was Sir
Dinadan brought in among them all.
And when queen Guenever saw Sir
Dinadan brought so among them all,
then she laughed that she fell down,
and so did all that were there. Well,
said Dinadan to Launcelot, thou art so
false that I can never beware of thee.
Then, by all the assent, they gave Sir
Launcelot the prize: the next was Sir
Lamorak de Galis; the third was Sir
Palamides; the fourth was king Bagdemagus. So these four knights had the
prize. And there was great joy and
great nobley in all the court. And
on the morn queen Guenever and Sir
Launcelot departed unto king Arthur;
but in no wise Sir Lamorak would not
go with them. I shall undertake, said
Sir Launcelot, that, and ye will go with
us king Arthur shall charge Sir Gawaine
and his brethren never to do you hurt.
As for that, said Sir Lamorak, I will
not trust Sir Gawaine, nor none of his
brethren; and wit ye well Sir Launcelot, and it were not for my lord king
Arthur's sake, I should match Sir Gawaine and his brethren well enough.
But to say that I should trust them,
that shall I never. And therefore I
pray you recommend me unto my lord
Arthur, and unto all my lords of the
Round Table. And in what place that
ever I come I shall do you service to
my power: and, sir, it is but late that
I revenged that when my lord Arthur's kin were put to the worse by
Sir Palamides. Then Sir Lamorak departed from Sir Launcelot, and either
wept at their departing.

CHAP. L.

*How by treason Sir Tristram was brought
to a tournament for to have been slain,
and how he was put in prison.*

Now turn we from this matter, and
speak we of Sir Tristram, of whom this

book is principally of; and leave we the king and the queen, Sir Launcelot, and Sir Lamorak. And here beginneth the treason of king Mark that he ordained against Sir Tristram. There was cried by the coasts of Cornwall a great tour-nament and justs. And all was done by Sir Galahalt the haut prince, and king Bagdemagus, to the intent to slay Sir Launcelot, or else utterly destroy him and shame him, because Sir Laun-celot had always the higher degree: therefore this prince and this king made this justs against Sir Launcelot. And thus their counsel was discovered unto king Mark, whereof he was full glad. Then king Mark bethought him that he would have Sir Tristram unto that tour-nament disguised that no man should know him, to that intent that the haut prince should ween that Sir Tristram were Sir Launcelot. So at these justs came in Sir Tristram. And at that time Sir Launcelot was not there, but when they saw a knight disguised so such deeds of arms, they wend it had been Sir Launcelot. And in especial king Mark said it was Sir Launcelot plainly. Then they set upon him, both king Bagdemagus and the haut prince, and their knights, that it was wonder that ever Sir Tristram might endure that pain. Notwithstanding for all the pain that he had, Sir Tristram wan the de-gree at that tournament, and there he hurt many knights, and bruised them, and they hurt him, and bruised him wonderly sore. So when the justs were all done they knew well that it was Sir Tristram de Liones. And all that were on king Mark's party were glad that Sir Tristram was hurt, and the remnant were sorry of his hurt; for Sir Tristram was not so behated as was Sir Launce-lot within the realm of England. Then came king Mark unto Sir Tristram, and said, Fair nephew, I am sorry of your hurts. Gramercy, my lord, said Sir Tristram. Then king Mark made Sir Tristram for to be put in a horse bier, in great sign of love, and said, Fair cousin, I shall be your leech myself. And so he rode forth with Sir Tristram,

and brought him to a castle by day-light. And then king Mark made Sir Tristram to eat, and then after he gave him a drink, the which as soon as he had drunk he fell on sleep; and when it was night he made him to be carried to another castle, and there he put him in a strong prison, and there he ordained a man and a woman to give him his meat and drink. So there he was a great while. Then was Sir Tristram missed, and no creature wist where he was become. When La Beale Isoud heard how he was missed, privily she went unto Sir Sadok, and prayed him to espy where was Sir Tristram. Then when Sadok wist how Sir Tristram was missed, and anon espied that he was put in prison by king Mark and the traitors of Magons, then Sadok and two of his cousins laid them in an am-bushment, fast by the castle of Tintagil, in arms. And as by fortune there came riding king Mark and four of his nephews, and a certain of the traitors of Magons. When Sir Sadok espied them he brake out of the bushment, and set there upon them. And when king Mark espied Sir Sadok he fled as fast as he might. And there Sir Sadok slew all the four nephews unto king Mark. But these traitors of Magons slew one of Sadok's cousins, with a great wound in the neck, but Sadok smote the other to death. Then Sir Sadok rode upon his way unto a castle that was called Liones, and there he espied of the treason and felony of king Mark. So they of that castle rode with Sir Sadok till that they came to a castle that hight Arbray. And there in the town they found Sir Dinas the seneschal, that was a good knight. But when Sir Sadok had told Sir Dinas of all the treason of king Mark, he defied such a king, and said he would give up his lands that he held of him. And when he said these words all manner knights said as Sir Dinas said. Then by his advice, and of Sir Sadok's, he let stuff all the towns and castles within the country of Liones, and assembled all the people that they might make.

CHAP. LI.

How king Mark let do counterfeit letters from the Pope, and how Sir Percivale delivered Sir Tristram out of prison.

Now turn we unto king Mark, that when he was escaped from Sir Sadok he rode unto the castle of Tintagil, and there he made great cry and noise, and cried unto harness all that might bear arms. Then they sought and found where were dead four cousins of king Mark's, and the traitors of Magons. Then the king let inter them in a chapel. Then the king let cry in all the country that held of him, to go unto arms, for he understood to the war he must needs. When king Mark heard and understood how Sir Sadok and Sir Dinas were risen in the country of Liones, he remembered of wiles and treason. Lo, thus he did: he let make and counterfeit letters from the Pope, and did make a strange clerk to bear them unto king Mark. The which letters specified, that king Mark should make him ready, upon pain of cursing, with his host to come to the Pope, to help to go to Jerusalem, for to make war upon the Saracens. When this clerk was come by the mean of the king, anon withal king Mark sent these letters unto Sir Tristram, and bad him say thus; That and he would go war upon the miscreants, he should be had out of prison, and to have all his power. When Sir Tristram understood this letter, then he said thus to the clerk: Ah, king Mark, ever hast thou been a traitor, and ever wilt be: but clerk, said Sir Tristram, say thou thus unto king Mark. Since the apostle Pope hath sent for him, bid him go thither himself, for tell him, traitor king as he is, I will not go at his command, get I out of my prison as I may. For I see I am well rewarded for my true service. Then the clerk returned unto king Mark, and told him of the answer of Sir Tristram. Well, said king Mark, yet shall he be beguiled. So he went into his chamber, and counterfeited letters, and the letters specified that the Pope desired Sir Tristram to come himself to make war upon the miscreants. When the clerk was come again unto Sir Tristram and took him these letters, then Sir Tristram beheld these letters, and anon espied they were of king Mark's counterfeiting. Ah, said Sir Tristram, false hast thou been ever, king Mark, and so wilt thou end. Then the clerk departed from Sir Tristram, and came to king Mark again. By then there were come four wounded knights within the castle of Tintagil, and one of them his neck was nigh broken in twain, another had his arm stricken away, the third was borne through with a spear, the fourth had his teeth stricken in twain. And when they came afore king Mark they cried and said, King, why fleest thou not, for all this country is arisen clearly against thee. Then was king Mark wroth out of measure. And in the mean while there came into the country Sir Percivale de Galis, to seek Sir Tristram. And when he heard that Sir Tristram was in prison, Sir Percivale made clearly the deliverance of Sir Tristram by his knightly means. And when he was so delivered he made great joy of Sir Percivale, and so each one of other. Sir Tristram said unto Sir Percivale, And ye will abide in these marches, I will ride with you. Nay, said Percivale, in this country may I not tarry, for I must needs into Wales. So Sir Percivale departed from Sir Tristram, and rode straight unto king Mark, and told him how he had delivered Sir Tristram. And also he told the king that he had done himself great shame for to put Sir Tristram in prison, for he is now the knight of most renown in all this world living. And wit thou well the most noble knights of the world love Sir Tristram, and if he will make war upon you ye may not abide it. That is truth, said king Mark, but I may not love Sir Tristram because he loveth my queen and my wife, La Beale Isoud. Ah fie for shame, said Sir Percivale, say ye never so more. Are ye not uncle unto Sir Tristram, and he your nephew? Ye should never think that so noble a knight as Sir Tristram is, that he would do himself so great a villany to hold his uncle's wife, howbeit, said Sir Percivale, he may love your queen sinless, because she is called one of the fairest ladies of the world. Then Sir Percivale departed from king Mark. So when he was departed king Mark bethought him of more treason, notwithstanding king Mark granted Sir Percivale never by no manner of means to hurt Sir Tristram. So anon king Mark sent unto Sir Dinas the seneschal, that he should put down all the people that he had raised, for he sent him an oath that he would go himself unto the Pope of Rome to war upon the miscreants, and this is a fairer war than thus to raise the people against your king. When Sir Dinas the seneschal understood that king Mark would go upon the miscreants, then Sir Dinas in all the haste put down all the people; and when the people were departed every man to his home, then king Mark espied where was Sir Tristram with La Beale Isoud. And there by treason king Mark let take him and put him in prison, contrary to his promise that he made unto Sir Percivale. When queen Isoud understood that Sir Tristram was in prison she made as great sorrow as ever made lady or gentlewoman. Then Sir Tristram sent a letter unto La Beale Isoud, and prayed her to be his good lady; and if it pleased her to make a vessel ready for her and him, he would go with her unto the realm of Logris, that is this land. When La Beale Isoud understood Sir Tristram's letters and his intent, she sent him another, and bad him be of good comfort, for she would do make the vessel ready, and all things to purpose. Then La Beale Isoud sent unto Sir Dinas, and to Sadok, and prayed them in any wise to take king Mark and put him in prison, unto the time that she and Sir Tristram were departed unto the realm of Logris. When Sir Dinas the seneschal understood the treason of king Mark, he promised her again, and sent to her word that king Mark should be

put in prison. And as they devised it so it was done. And then Sir Tristram was delivered out of prison, and anon in all the haste queen Isoud and Sir Tristram went and took their counsel with that they would have with them when they departed.

CHAP. LII.
How Sir Tristram and La Beale Isoud came into England, and how Sir Launcelot brought them to Joyous Gard.

THEN La Beale Isoud and Sir Tristram took their vessel, and came by water into this land. And so they were not in this land four days but there came a cry of a justs and tournament that king Arthur let make. When Sir Tristram heard tell of that tournament, he disguised himself and La Beale Isoud, and rode unto that tournament. And when he came there he saw many knights just and tourney, and so Sir Tristram dressed him to the range. And to make short conclusion, he overthrew fourteen knights of the Round Table. When Sir Launcelot saw these knights thus overthrown Sir Launcelot dressed him to Sir Tristram. That saw La Beale Isoud, how Sir Launcelot was come into the field. Then La Beale Isoud sent unto Sir Launcelot a ring, and bad him wit that it was Sir Tristram de Liones. When Sir Launcelot understood that there was Sir Tristram, he was full glad, and would not just. Then Sir Launcelot espied whither Sir Tristram went, and after him he rode, and then either made of other great joy. And so Sir Launcelot brought Sir Tristram and La Beale Isoud unto Joyous Gard, that was his own castle that he had won with his own hands. And there Sir Launcelot put them in to weld for their own. And wit ye well that castle was garnished and furnished for a king and a queen royal there to have sojourned. And Sir Launcelot charged all his people to honour them and love them as they would do himself. So Sir Launcelot departed unto king Arthur; and then he told queen Guenever how he that justed so well at the last tournament was Sir Tristram. And there he told her how he had with him La Beale Isoud, maugre king Mark; and so queen Guenever told all this unto king Arthur. When king Arthur wist that Sir Tristram was escaped, and come from king Mark, and had brought La Beale Isoud with him, then was he passing glad. So because of Sir Tristram king Arthur let make a cry, that on May-day should be a justs, before the castle of Lonazep; and that castle was fast by Joyous Gard. And thus king Arthur devised, that all the knights of this land, and of Cornwall, and of North Wales, should just against all these countries,—Ireland, Scotland, and the remnant of Wales, and the country of Gore, and Surluse, and of Listinoise, and they of Northumberland, and all they that held lands of king Arthur on this half the sea. When this cry was made, many knights were glad and many were unglad. Sir, said Launcelot unto Arthur, by this cry that ye have made, ye will put us that be about you in great jeopardy, for there be many knights that have great envy to us, therefore when we shall meet at the day of justs, there will be hard shift among us. As for that, said Arthur, I care not, there shall we prove who shall be the best of his hands. So when Sir Launcelot understood wherefore king Arthur made this justing, then he made such purveyance that La Beale Isoud should behold the justs in a secret place that was honest for her estate.

Now turn we unto Sir Tristram and La Beale Isoud, how they made great joy daily together with all manner of mirths that they could devise; and every day Sir Tristram would go ride on hunting, for Sir Tristram was that time called the best chaser of the world, and the noblest blower of an horn of all manner of measures. For, as books report, of Sir Tristram came all the good terms of venery and hunting, and all the sizes and measures of blowing of an horn; and of him we had first all the terms of hawking, and which were beasts of chase, and beasts of venery,

and which were vermins; and all the blasts that belong to all manner of games. First to the uncoupling, to the seeking, to the rechate, to the flight, to the death, and to strake; and many other blasts and terms, that all manner of gentlemen have cause to the world's end to praise Sir Tristram and to pray for his soul.

CHAP. LIII.

How by the counsel of La Beale Isoud Sir Tristram rode armed, and how he met with Sir Palamides.

So on a day La Beale Isoud said unto Sir Tristram, I marvel me much, said she, that ye remember not yourself, how that ye be here in a strange country, and here be many perilous knights, and well ye wote that king Mark is full of treason, and that ye will ride thus to chase and hunt unarmed; ye might be destroyed. My fair lady and my love, I cry you mercy, I will no more do so. So then Sir Tristram rode daily on hunting armed, and his men bearing his shield and his spear. So on a day, a little afore the month of May, Sir Tristram chased an hart passing eagerly, and so the hart passed by a fair well. And then Sir Tristram alighted, and put off his helm to drink of that burbley water. Right so he heard and saw the questing beast come to the well. When Sir Tristram saw that beast, he put on his helm, for he deemed he should hear of Sir Palamides, for that beast was his quest. Right so Tristram saw where came a knight armed, upon a noble courser, and he saluted him, and they spake of many things; and this knight's name was Breuse Sance Pité. And right so withal there came unto them the noble knight Sir Palamides, and either saluted other, and spake fair to other. Fair knights, said Sir Breuse Sance Pité, I can tell you tidings. What is that? said those knights. Sirs, wit ye well that king Mark is put in prison by his own knights, and all was for love of Sir Tristram: for king Mark had put Sir Tristram twice in prison; and once

Sir Percivale delivered the noble knight Sir Tristram out of prison; and at the last time queen La Beale Isoud delivered him, and went clearly away with him into this realm: and all this while king Mark the false traitor is in prison. Is this truth? said Sir Palamides; then shall we hastily hear of Sir Tristram. And as for to say that I love La Beale Isoud, I dare make good that I do, and that she hath my service above all other ladies, and shall have the term of my life. And right so as they stood talking they saw afore them where came a knight, all armed on a great horse, and one of his men bare his shield, and the other his spears. And anon as that knight espied them, he gat his shield and his spear, and dressed him to just. Fair fellows, said Sir Tristram, yonder is a knight will just with us; let see which of us shall encounter with him, for I see well he is of the court of king Arthur. It shall not be long or he be met withal, said Sir Palamides, for I found never no knight in my quest of this glasting beast but, and he would just, I never refused him. As well may I, said Breuse Sance Pité, follow that beast as ye. Then shall ye do battle with me, said Sir Palamides. So Sir Palamides dressed him unto the other knight, Sir Bleoberis, that was a full noble knight, nigh kin unto Sir Launcelot. And so they met so hard that Sir Palamides fell to the earth, horse and all. Then Sir Bleoberis cried aloud, and said thus: Make thee ready, thou false traitor knight, Breuse Sance Pité, for wit thou certainly I will have ado with thee to the utterance, for the noble knights and ladies that thou hast falsely betrayed. When this false knight and traitor, Breuse Sance Pité, heard him say so, he took his horse by the bridle, and fled his way as fast as his horse might run, for sore he was of him afeard. When Sir Bleoberis saw him flee, he followed fast after him, through thick and through thin. And by fortune as Sir Breuse fled, he saw even afore him three knights of the Table Round, of the which the one hight Sir Ector de Maris, the other hight Sir Percivale de Galis, the third hight Sir Harry le Fise Lake, a good knight and an hardy. And as for Sir Percivale, he was called that time of his time one of the best knights of the world, and the best assured. When Breuse saw these knights, he rode straight unto them, and cried unto them, and prayed them of rescues. What need have ye? said Sir Ector. Ah, fair knights, said Sir Breuse, here followeth me the most traitor knight and most coward, and most of villainy: his name is Breuse Sance Pité; and if he may get me, he will slay me without mercy and pity. Abide with us, said Sir Percivale, and we shall warrant you. Then were they ware of Sir Bleoberis, that came riding all that he might. Then Sir Ector put himself forth for to just afore them all. When Sir Bleoberis saw that they were four knights, and he but himself, he stood in a doubt whether he would turn or hold his way. Then he said to himself, I am a knight of the Table Round, and rather than I should shame mine oath and my blood I will hold my way whatsoever fall thereof. And then Sir Ector dressed his spear, and smote either other passing sore, but Sir Ector fell to the earth. That saw Sir Percivale, and he dressed his horse toward him all that he might drive; but Sir Percivale had such a stroke that horse and man fell to the earth. When Sir Harry saw that they were both to the earth, then he said to himself, Never was Breuse of such prowess. So Sir Harry dressed his horse, and they met together so strongly that both the horses and knights fell to the earth; but Sir Bleoberis's horse began to recover again. That saw Sir Breuse, and he came hurtling, and smote him over and over, and would have slain him as he lay on the ground. Then Sir Harry le Fise Lake arose lightly, and took the bridle of Sir Breuse's horse, and said, Fie for shame, strike never a knight when he is at the earth; for this knight may be called no shameful knight of his deeds: for yet as men may see there as he lieth on the ground, he hath done worshipfully, and put to the worse passing good knights. Therefore will I not let, said Sir Breuse. Thou shalt not choose, said Sir Harry, as at this time. Then when Sir Breuse saw that he might not choose, nor have his will, he spake fair. Then Sir Harry let him go. And then anon he made his horse to run over Sir Bleoberis, and rashed him to the earth like if he would have slain him. When Sir Harry saw him do so villainously, he cried, Traitor knight, leave off for shame. And as Sir Harry would have taken his horse to fight with Sir Breuse, then Sir Breuse ran upon him as he was half upon his horse, and smote him down horse and man to the earth, and had near slain Sir Harry the good knight. That saw Sir Percivale, and then he cried, Traitor knight what dost thou? And when Sir Percivale was upon his horse, Sir Breuse took his horse, and fled all that ever he might, and Sir Percivale and Sir Harry followed after him fast, but ever the longer they chased the further were they behind. Then they turned again, and came to Sir Ector de Maris and to Sir Bleoberis. Ah fair knights, said Bleoberis, why have ye succoured that false knight and traitor? Why, said Sir Harry, what knight is he? for well I wot it is a false knight, said Sir Harry, and a coward, and a felonious knight. Sir, said Bleoberis, he is the most coward knight, and a devourer of ladies, and a destroyer of good knights, and specially of Arthur's. What is your name? said Sir Ector. My name is Sir Bleoberis de Ganis. Alas, fair cousin, said Ector, forgive it me, for I am Sir Ector de Maris. Then Sir Percivale and Sir Harry made great joy that they met with Bleoberis, but all they were heavy that Sir Breuse was escaped them, whereof they made great dole.

CHAP. LIV.

Of Sir Palamides, and how he met with Sir Bleoberis and with Sir Ector, and of Sir Percivale.

RIGHT so as they stood thus, there came Sir Palamides; and when he saw the shield of Bleoberis lie on the earth, then said Palamides, He that owneth that shield, let him dress him to me, for he smote me down here fast by at a fountain, and therefore I will fight with him on foot. I am ready, said Sir Bleoberis, here to answer thee; for wit thou well, sir knight, it was I, and my name is Bleoberis de Ganis. Well art thou met, said Palamides, and wit thou well my name is Sir Palamides the Saracen. And either of them hated other to the death. Sir Palamides, said Ector, wit thou well, there is neither thou, nor none knight that beareth the life, that slayeth any of our blood, but he shall die for it; therefore, and thou list to fight, go seek Sir Launcelot, or Sir Tristram, and there shall ye find your match. With them have I met, said Palamides, but I had never no worship of them. Was there never no manner of knight, said Sir Ector, but they, that ever matched with you? Yes, said Palamides, there was the third, a good knight as any of them, and of his age he was the best that ever I found; for, and he might have lived till he had been an hardier man, there liveth no knight now such, and his name was Sir Lamorak de Galis. And as he had justed at a tournament, there he overthrew me and thirty knights more, and there he won the degree. And at his departing, there met him Sir Gawaine and his brethren, and with great pain they slew him feloniously, unto all good knights' great damage. And when Sir Percivale heard that his brother was dead, Sir Lamorak, he fell over his horse's mane swooning, and there he made the greatest dole that ever made knight. And when Sir Percivale arose, he said, Alas, my good and noble brother Sir Lamorak, now shall we never meet, and I trow in all the wide world a man might not find such a knight as he was of his age; and it is too much to suffer the death of our father king Pellinore, and now the death of our good brother Sir Lamorak. Then in the mean while there came a varlet from the court of king Arthur, and told them of the great tournament that should be at Lonazep, and how these lands, Cornwall, and Northgalis, should be against all them that would come.

CHAP. LV.

How Sir Tristram met with Sir Dinadan, and of their devices, and what he said to Sir Gawaine's brethren.

Now turn we unto Sir Tristram, that as he rode on hunting he met with Sir Dinadan, that was come into that country to seek Sir Tristram. Then Sir Dinadan told Sir Tristram his name, but Sir Tristram would not tell his name, wherefore Sir Dinadan was wrōth. For such a foolish knight as ye are, said Sir Dinadan, I saw but late this day lying by a well, and he fared as he slept, and there he lay like a fool grinning, and would not speak, and his shield lay by him, and his horse stood by him, and well I wot he was a lover. Ah, fair sir, said Sir Tristram, are ye not a lover? Marry, fie on that craft, said Sir Dinadan. That is evil said, said Sir Tristram, for a knight may never be of prowess, but if he be a lover. It is well said, said Sir Dinadan: now tell me your name, sith ye be a lover, or else I shall do battle with you. As for that, said Sir Tristram, it is no reason to fight with me but I tell you my name: and as for that, my name shall ye not wit as at this time. Fie for shame, said Dinadan, art thou a knight, and darest not tell thy name to me? therefore I will fight with thee. As for that, said Sir Tristram, I will be advised, for I will not fight but if me list; and if I do battle, said Sir Tristram, ye are not able to withstand me. Fie on thee, coward, said Sir Dinadan. And thus as they hoved still, they saw a knight came riding against them. Lo, said Sir Tristram, see where cometh a knight riding will just with you. Anon as Sir Dinadan beheld him, he said, That is the same doted knight that I saw lie by the well, neither sleeping nor waking. Well, said Sir Tristram, I

know that knight well with the covered shield of azure, he is the king's son of Northumberland, his name is Epinegris, and he is as great a lover as I know, and he loveth the king's daughter of Wales, a full fair lady. And now I suppose, said Sir Tristram, and ye require him he will just with you; and then shall ye prove whether a lover be a better knight or ye that will not love no lady. Well, said Sir Dinadan, now shalt thou see what I shall do. Therewithal Sir Dinadan spake on high and said, Sir knight, make thee ready to just with me, for it is the custom of errant knights one to just with other. Sir, said Epinegris, is it the rule of you errant knights for to make a knight to just will he or nill? As for that, said Dinadan, make thee ready, for here is for me. And therewithal they spurred their horses, and met together so hard that Epinegris smote down Sir Dinadan. Then Sir Tristram rode to Sir Dinadan, and said, How now? me seemeth the lover hath well sped. Fie on thee coward, said Sir Dinadan, and if thou be a good knight revenge me. Nay, said Sir Tristram, I will not just as at this time, but take your horse, and let us go hence. Defend me, said Sir Dinadan, from thy fellowship, for I never sped well since I met with thee. And so they departed. Well, said Sir Tristram, peradventure I could tell you tidings of Sir Tristram. Defend me, said Dinadan, from thy fellowship, for Sir Tristram were mickle the worse and he were in thy company. And then they departed. Sir, said Sir Tristram, yet it may happen I shall meet with you in other places. So rode Sir Tristram unto Joyous Gard, and there he heard in that town great noise and cry. What is this noise, said Sir Tristram. Sir, said they, here is a knight of this castle that hath been long among us, and right now he is slain with two knights, and for none other cause but that our knight said that Sir Launcelot were a better knight than Sir Gawaine. That was a simple cause, said Sir Tristram, for to slay a good knight for to say well by his master. That is little remedy to us, said the men of the town, for and Sir Launcelot had been here, soon we should have been revenged upon the false knights. When Sir Tristram heard them say so, he sent for his shield and for his spear, and lightly within a little while he had overtaken them, and bade them turn and amend what they had misdone. What amends wouldest thou have? said the one knight. And therewith they took their course, and either met other so hard, that Sir Tristram smote down that knight over his horse tail. Then the other knight dressed him to Sir Tristram; and in the same wise he served the other knight. And then they gat off their horses as well as they might, and dressed their shields and swords to do their battle to the utterance. Knights, said Sir Tristram, ye shall tell me of whence ye are and what be your names; for such men ye might be ye should hard escape my hands; and ye might be such men of such a country that for all your evil deeds ye should pass quit. Wit thou well, sir knight, said they, we fear us not to tell thee our names, for my name is Sir Agravaine, and my name is Gaheris, brethren unto the good knight Sir Gawaine, and we be nephews unto king Arthur. Well, said Sir Tristram, for king Arthur's sake I shall let you pass as at this time. But it is shame, said Sir Tristram, that Sir Gawaine and ye that be come of so great a blood, that ye four brethren are so named as ye be. For ye be called the greatest destroyers and murderers of good knights that be now in this realm; for it is but as I heard say, that Sir Gawaine and ye slew among you a better knight than ever ye were, that was the noble knight Sir Lamorak de Galis; and it had pleased God, said Sir Tristram, I would I had been by Sir Lamorak at his death. Then shouldest thou have gone the same way, said Sir Gaheris. Fair knight, said Sir Tristram, there must have been many more knights than ye are. And therewithal Sir Tristram departed from them toward Joyous

Gard. And when he was departed they took their horses, and the one said to the other, We will overtake him and be revenged upon him in the despite of Sir Lamorak.

CHAP. LVI.

How Sir Tristram smote down Sir Agravaine and Sir Gaberis, and bow Sir Dinadan was sent for by La Beale Isoud.

So when they had overtaken Sir Tristram, Sir Agravaine bade him, Turn, traitor knight. That is evil said, said Sir Tristram; and therewith he pulled out his sword, and smote Sir Agravaine such a buffet upon the helm that he tumbled down off his horse in a swoon, and he had a grievous wound. And then he turned to Gaheris, and Sir Tristram smote his sword and his helm together with such a might that Gaheris fell out of his saddle; and so Sir Tristram rode unto Joyous Gard, and there he alight and unarmed him. So Sir Tristram told La Beale Isoud of all his adventure as ye have heard tofore. And when she heard him tell of Sir Dinadan, Sir, she said, is not that he that made the song by king Mark? That same is he, said Sir Tristram, for he is the best joker and jester, and a noble knight of his hands, and the best fellow that I know, and all good knights love his fellowship. Alas, Sir, said she, why brought ye not him with you? Have ye no care, said Sir Tristram, for he rideth to seek me in this country, and therefore he will not away till he have met with me. And there Sir Tristram told La Beale Isoud how Sir Dinadan held against all lovers. Right so there came in a varlet and told Sir Tristram how there was come an errant knight into the town with such colours upon his shield. That is Sir Dinadan, said Sir Tristram. Wit ye what ye shall do? said Sir Tristram; send ye for him, my lady Isoud, and I will not be seen, and ye shall hear the merriest knight that ever ye spake withal, and the maddest talker, and I pray you heartily that ye make him good cheer. Then anon La Beale Isoud sent into the town, and prayed Sir Dinadan that he would come into the castle and repose him there, with a lady. With a good will, said Sir Dinadan. And so he mounted upon his horse, and rode into the castle, and there he alight, and was unarmed, and brought into the castle. Anon La Beale Isoud came unto him, and either saluted other. Then she asked him of whence that he was. Madam, said Dinadan, I am of the court of king Arthur, and knight of the Table Round, and my name is Sir Dinadan. What do ye in this country? said La Beale Isoud. Madam, said he, I seek Sir Tristram the good knight, for it was told me that he was in this country. It may well be, said La Beale Isoud, but I am not aware of him. Madam, said Dinadan, I marvel of Sir Tristram and more other lovers, what aileth them to be so mad and so sotted upon women. Why, said La Beale Isoud, are ye a knight and be no lover? It is shame to you : wherefore ye may not be called a good knight but if ye make a quarrel for a lady. Nay, said Sir Dinadan, for the joy of love is too short, and the sorrow thereof, and what cometh thereof, dureth over long. Ah, said La Beale Isoud, say ye not so, for here fast by was the good knight Sir Bleoberis, that fought with three knights at once for a damsel's sake, and he wan her afore the king of Northumberland. It was so, said Sir Dinadan, for I know him well for a good knight and a noble, and come of noble blood, for all be noble knights of whom he is come of, that is Sir Launcelot du Lake. Now I pray you, said La Beale Isoud, tell me will ye fight for my love with three knights that done me great wrong? and in so much as ye be a knight of king Arthur's I require you to do battle for me. Then Sir Dinadan said, I shall say you be as fair a lady as ever I saw any, and much fairer than is my lady queen Guenever, but, wit ye well at one word, I will not fight for you with three knights, Heaven defend me. Then Isoud laughed, and had good game at him. So he had all the cheer that she

might make him; and there he lay all that night. And on the morn early Sir Tristram armed him, and La Beale Isoud gave him a good helm; and then he promised her that he would meet with Sir Dinadan, and they two would ride together unto Lonazep, where the tournament should be;—and there shall I make ready for you, where ye shall see the tournament. Then departed Sir Tristram with two squires that bare his shield and his spears that were great and long.

CHAP. LVII.

How Sir Dinadan met with Sir Tristram, and with justing with Sir Palamides Sir Dinadan knew him.

THEN after that, Sir Dinadan departed and rode his way a great pace until he had overtaken Sir Tristram. And when Sir Dinadan had overtaken him, he knew him anon, and he hated the fellowship of him above all other knights. Ah, said Sir Dinadan, art thou that coward knight that I met with yesterday, keep thee, for thou shalt just with me, maugre thy head. Well, said Sir Tristram, and I am loth to just. And so they let their horses run, and Sir Tristram missed of him a purpose, and Sir Dinadan brake a spear upon Sir Tristram; and therewith Sir Dinadan dressed him to draw out his sword. Not so, said Sir Tristram, why are ye so wroth? I will not fight. Fie on thee, coward, said Sir Dinadan, thou shamest all knights. As for that, said Sir Tristram, I care not, for I will wait upon you and be under your protection, for because ye are so good a knight ye may save me. The devil deliver me of thee, said Sir Dinadan, for thou art as goodly a man of arms and of thy person as ever I saw, and the most coward that ever I saw. What wilt thou do with those great spears that thou carriest with thee? I shall give them, said Sir Tristram, to some good knight when I come to the tournament : and if I see you do best I shall give them to you. So thus as they rode talking they saw where came an errant knight afore them, that dressed him to just. Lo, said Sir Tristram, yonder is one will just, now dress thee to him. A shame betide thee, said Sir Dinadan. Nay not so, said Tristram, for that knight beseemeth a shrew. Then shall I, said Sir Dinadan. And so they dressed their shields and their spears, and they met together so hard that the other knight smote down Sir Dinadan from his horse. Lo, said Sir Tristram, it had been better ye had left. Fie on thee, coward, said Sir Dinadan. Then Sir Dinadan started up, and gat his sword in his hand, and proffered to do battle on foot. Whether in love or in wrath, said the other knight. Let us do battle in love, said Sir Dinadan. What is your name? said that knight, I pray you tell me. Wit ye well my name is Sir Dinadan. Ah Dinadan, said that knight, and my name is Gareth, the youngest brother unto Sir Gawaine. Then either made of other great cheer, for this Gareth was the best knight of all the brethren, and he proved a good knight. Then they took their horses, and there they spake of Sir Tristram, how such a coward he was: and every word Sir Tristram heard, and laughed them to scorn. Then were they ware where there came a knight afore them well horsed and well armed, and he made him ready to just. Fair knights, said Sir Tristram, look betwixt you who shall just with yonder knight, for I warn you I will not have ado with him. Then shall I, said Sir Gareth : and so they encountered together, and there that knight smote down Sir Gareth over his horse croup. How now, said Sir Tristram unto Sir Dinadan, dress thee now, and revenge the good knight Gareth. That shall I not, said Sir Dinadan, for he hath stricken down a much bigger knight than I am. Ah, said Sir Tristram, now Sir Dinadan I see and feel well your heart faileth you, therefore now shall ye see what I shall do. And then Sir Tristram hurtled unto that knight, and smote him quite from his horse. And when Sir Dinadan saw that he marvelled greatly : and then he deemed that it was Sir Tristram. Then

this knight that was on foot pulled out his sword to do battle. What is your name? said Sir Tristram. Wit ye well, said the knight, my name is Sir Palamides. What knight hate ye most? said Sir Tristram. Sir knight, said he, I hate Sir Tristram to the death, for and I may meet with him the one of us shall die. Ye say well, said Sir Tristram, and wit ye well that I am Sir Tristram de Liones, and now do your worst. When Sir Palamides heard him say so he was astonished, and then he said thus, I pray you, Sir Tristram, forgive me all mine evil will, and if I live I shall do you service above all other knights that be living, and there as I have owed you evil will me sore repenteth. I wot not what aileth me, for me seemeth that ye are a good knight, and none other knight that named himself a good knight should not hate you ; therefore I require you, Sir Tristram, take no displeasure at mine unkind words. Sir Palamides, said Sir Tristram, ye say well, and well I wot ye are a good knight, for I have seen you proved, and many great enterprises have ye taken upon you, and well achieved them ; therefore, said Sir Tristram, and ye have any evil will to me, now may ye right it, for I am ready at your hand. Not so, my lord Sir Tristram ; I will do you knightly service in all things as ye will command. And right so I will take you, said Sir Tristram. And so they rode forth on their ways, talking of many things. O my lord Sir Tristram, said Dinadan, foul have ye mocked me, for truly I came into this country for your sake, and by the advice of my lord Sir Launcelot, and yet would not Sir Launcelot tell me the certainty of you, where I should find you. Truly, said Sir Tristram, Sir Launcelot wist well where I was, for I abode within his own castle.

CHAP. LVIII.

How they approached the castle Lonazep, and of other devices of the death of Sir Lamorak.

Thus they rode until they were ware

of the castle Lonazep: and then were they ware of four hundred tents and pavilions, and marvellous great ordinance. Truly, said Sir Tristram, yonder I see the greatest ordinance that ever I saw. Sir, said Palamides, me seemeth there was as great an ordinance at the castle of Maidens upon the rock where ye won the prize, for I saw myself where ye forjusted thirty knights. Sir, said Dinadan, and in Surluse at that tournament that Sir Galahalt of the Long Isles made, the which there dured seven days, was as great a gathering as is here, for there were many nations. Who was the best? said Sir Tristram. Sir, it was Sir Launcelot du Lake and the noble knight Sir Lamorak de Galis. And Sir Launcelot won the degree. I doubt not, said Sir Tristram, but he won the degree, so he had not been overmatched with many knights. And of the death of Sir Lamorak, said Sir Tristram, it was over great pity, for I dare say he was the cleanest mighted man and the best winded of his age that was on live, for I knew him that he was the biggest knight that ever I met withal, but if it were Sir Launcelot. Alas, said Sir Tristram, full woe is me for his death. And if they were not the cousins of my lord Arthur that slew him, they should die for it, and all those that were consenting to his death. And for such things, said Sir Tristram, I fear to draw unto the court of my lord Arthur: I will that ye wit it, said Sir Tristram unto Gareth. Sir, I blame you not, said Gareth, for well I understand the vengeance of my brethren Sir Gawaine, Sir Agravaine, Gaheris, and Mordred. But as for me, said Sir Gareth, I meddle not of their matters, therefore is none of them that loveth me; and for I understand they be murderers of good knights I left their company, and God would I had been by, said Gareth, when the noble knight Sir Lamorak was slain. Now, truly, said Sir Tristram, it is well said of you, for I had lever than all the gold betwixt this and Rome I had been there. Yea, said Sir Palamides, and so would I had been there,

and yet had I never the degree at no justs nor tournament there as he was, but he put me to the worse or on foot or on horseback, and that day that he was slain he did the most deeds of arms that ever I saw knight do in all my life days. And when him was given the degree by my lord Arthur, Sir Gawaine and his three brethren, Agravaine, Gaheris, and Sir Mordred, set upon Sir Lamorak in a privy place, and there they slew his horse, and so they fought with him on foot more than three hours, both before him and behind him; and Sir Mordred gave him his death's wound behind him at his back, and all to-hewed him: for one of his squires told me that saw it. Fie upon treason, said Sir Tristram, for it killeth my heart to hear this tale. So doth it mine, said Gareth; brethren as they be mine I shall never love them, nor draw in their fellowship, for that deed. Now speak we of other deeds, said Sir Palamides, and let him be, for his life ye may not get again. That is the more pity, said Dinadan, for Sir Gawaine and his brethren, except you, Sir Gareth, hate all the good knights of the Round Table for the most part; for well I wot, and they might privily, they hate my lord Sir Launcelot, and all his kin, and great privy despite they have at him; and that is my lord Sir Launcelot well ware of, and that causeth him to have the good knights of his kin about him.

CHAP. LIX.

How they came to Humber bank, and how they found a ship there, wherein lay the body of king Hermance.

SIR, said Palamides, let us leave off this matter, and let us see how we shall do at this tournament. By mine advice, said Palamides, let us four hold together against all that will come. Not by my counsel, said Sir Tristram, for I see by their pavilions there will be four hundred knights, and doubt ye not, said Sir Tristram, but there will be many good knights, and be a man never so valiant nor so big yet he may be overmatched. And so have I seen knights done many times : and when they wend best to have won worship they lost it. For manhood is not worth but if it be meddled with wisdom : and as for me, said Sir Tristram, it may happen I shall keep mine own head as well as another. So thus they rode until that they came to Humber bank, where they heard a cry and a doleful noise. Then were they ware in the wind where came a rich vessel covered over with red silk, and the vessel landed fast by them. Therewith Sir Tristram alight and his knights. And so Sir Tristram went afore and entered into that vessel. And when he came within, he saw a fair bed richly covered, and thereupon lay a dead seemly knight, all armed, save the head was all be-bled, with deadly wounds upon him : the which seemed to be a passing good knight. How may this be, said Sir Tristram, that this knight is thus slain ? Then Sir Tristram was ware of a letter in the dead knight's hand. Master mariners, said Sir Tristram, what meaneth that letter ? Sir, said they, in that letter ye shall hear and know how he was slain, and for what cause, and what was his name ; but sir, said the mariners, wit ye well that no man shall take that letter and read it but if he be a good knight, and that he will faithfully promise to revenge his death, else shall there no knight see that letter open. Wit ye well, said Sir Tristram, that some of us may revenge his death as well as others, and if it be so as ye mariners say, his death shall be revenged. And therewith Sir Tristram took the letter out of the knight's hand ; and it said thus :—Hermance king and lord of the Red City, I send unto all knights errant recommending unto you noble knights of Arthur's court, I beseech them all among them to find one knight that will fight for my sake with two brethren that I brought up of nought, and feloniously and traitorly they have slain me, wherefore I beseech one good knight to revenge my death. And he that revengeth my death, I will that he

have my Red City and all my castles. Sir, said the mariners, wit ye well this king and knight that here lieth was a full worshipful man, and of full great prowess, and full well he loved all manner of knights errant. Truly, said Sir Tristram, here is a piteous case, and full fain I would take this enterprise upon me, but I have made such a promise that needs I must be at this great tournament or else I am shamed. For well I wot for my sake in especial my lord Arthur let make this justs and tournament in this country ; and well I wot that many worshipful people will be there at that tournament for to see me. Therefore I fear me to take this enterprise upon me, that I shall not come again betimes to this justs. Sir, said Palamides, I pray you give me this enterprise, and ye shall see me achieve it worshipfully, or else I shall die in this quarrel. Well, said Sir Tristram, and this enterprise I give you, with this that ye be with me at this tournament, that shall be as at this day seven night. Sir, said Palamides, I promise you that I shall be with you by that day if I be unslain or unmaimed.

CHAP. LX.

How Sir Tristram with his fellowship came and were with an host which after fought with Sir Tristram ; and other matters.

THEN departed Sir Tristram, Gareth, and Sir Dinadan, and left Sir Palamides in the vessel ; and so Sir Tristram beheld the mariners how they sailed over long Humber. And when Sir Palamides was out of their sight, they took their horses, and beheld about them. And then were they ware of a knight that came riding against them unarmed, and nothing about him but a sword. . And when this knight came nigh them he saluted them, and they him again. Fair knights, said that knight, I pray you insomuch as ye be knights errant, that ye will come and see my castle, and take such as ye find there ; I pray you heartily. And so they rode with him into his castle; and there they were brought into the hall, that was well apparelled, and so they were there unarmed and set at a board. And when this knight saw Sir Tristram, anon he knew him; and then this knight waxed pale and wroth at Sir Tristram. When Sir Tristram saw his host make such cheer, he marvelled and said, Sir, mine host, what cheer make you? Wit thou well, said he, I fare the worse for thee, for I know thee, Sir Tristram de Liones, thou slewest my brother. And therefore I give thee summons I will slay thee, and ever I may get thee at large. Sir knight, said Sir Tristram, I am never advised that ever I slew any brother of yours; and if ye say that I did I will make you amends unto my power. I will none amends, said the knight, but keep thee from me. So when he had dined, Sir Tristram asked his arms and departed. And so they rode on their ways; and within a little while Sir Dinadan saw where came a knight well armed, and well horsed, without shield. Sir Tristram, said Sir Dinadan, take keep to yourself, for I undertake yonder cometh your host that will have ado with you. Let him come, said Sir Tristram, I shall abide him as well as I may. Anon the knight, when he came nigh Sir Tristram, he cried and bade him abide and keep him. So they hurtled together, but Sir Tristram smote the other knight so sore that he bare him over his horse croup. That knight arose lightly and took his horse again, and so rode fiercely to Sir Tristram, and smote him twice hard upon the helm. Sir knight, said Sir Tristram, I pray you leave off and smite me no more, for I would be loth to deal with you and I might choose, for I have your meat and your drink within my body. For all that he would not leave, and then Sir Tristram gave him such a buffet upon the helm, that he fell up so down from his horse, that the blood burst out at the ventails of his helm, and so he lay still, likely to have been dead. Then Sir Tristram said, Me repenteth sore of this buffet that I smote so sore, for as I suppose he is dead.

And so they left him and rode on their ways. So they had not ridden but a while, but they saw coming against them two full likely knights, well armed and well horsed, and goodly servants about them. The one was Berrant le Apres, and he was called the king with the hundred knights, and the other was Sir Segwarides, which were renowned two noble knights. So as they came either by other, the king looked upon Sir Dinadan, that at that time had Sir Tristram's helm upon his shoulder, the which helm the king had seen before with the queen of Northgalis, and that queen the king loved, and that helm the queen of Northgalis had given unto La Beale Isoud, and the queen La Beale Isoud gave it to Sir Tristram. Sir knight, said Berrant, where had ye that helm? What would ye? said Sir Dinadan. For I will have ado with thee, said the king, for the love of her that owned that helm, and therefore keep you. So they departed and came together with all the mights of their horses; and there the king with the hundred knights smote Sir Dinadan, horse and all, to the earth; and then he commanded his servant, Go and take thou his helm off, and keep it. So the varlet went to unbuckle his helm. What helm? What wilt thou do? said Sir Tristram; leave that helm. To what intent, said the king, will ye, sir knight, meddle with that helm? Wit you well, said Sir Tristram, that helm shall not depart from me, or it be dearer bought. Then make you ready, said Sir Berrant unto Sir Tristram. So they hurtled together, and there Sir Tristram smote him down over his horse tail. And then the king arose lightly, and gat his horse lightly again, and then he strake fiercely at Sir Tristram many great strokes. And then Sir Tristram gave Sir Berrant such a buffet upon the helm that he fell down over his horse, sore stunned. Lo, said Sir Dinadan, that helm is unhappy to us twain, for I had a fall for it, and now, sir king, have ye another fall. Then Segwarides asked, Who shall just with me? I pray thee, said Sir Gareth unto Dinadan, let me have this justs. Sir, said Dinadan, I pray you take it as for me. That is no reason, said Tristram, for this justs should be yours. At a word, said Sir Dinadan, I will not thereof. Then Gareth dressed him to Sir Segwarides, and there Sir Segwarides smote Sir Gareth and his horse to the earth. Now, said Sir Tristram to Dinadan, just with yonder knight. I will not thereof, said Dinadan. Then will I, said Sir Tristram. And then Sir Tristram ran to him and gave him a fall, and so they left them on foot. And Sir Tristram rode unto Joyous Gard, and there Sir Gareth would not of his courtesy have gone into this castle, but Sir Tristram would not suffer him to depart. And so they alight and unarmed them, and had great cheer. But when Dinadan came afore La Beale Isoud, he cursed the time that ever he bare Sir Tristram's helm, and there he told her how Sir Tristram had mocked him. Then was there laughing and jesting at Sir Dinadan, that they wist not what to do with him.

CHAP. LXI.

How Palamides went for to fight with two brethren for the death of king Hermance.

Now will we leave them merry within Joyous Gard, and speak we of Sir Palamides. Then Sir Palamides sailed even along Humber to the coasts of the sea, where was a fair castle. And at that time it was early in the morning afore day. Then the mariners went unto Sir Palamides, that slept fast. Sir knight, said the mariners, ye must arise, for here is a castle, there ye must go into. I assent me, said Sir Palamides. And therewithal he arrived. And then he blew his horn, that the mariners had given him. And when they within the castle heard that horn, they put forth many knights, and there they stood upon the walls, and said with one voice, Welcome be ye to this castle. And then it waxed clear day,

and Sir Palamides entered into the castle. And within a while he was served with many divers meats. Then Sir Palamides heard about him much weeping and great dole. What may this mean? said Sir Palamides: I love not to hear such a sorrow, and fain I would know what it meaneth. Then there came afore him one whose name was Sir Ebel, that said thus, Wit ye well, sir knight, this dole and sorrow is here made every day, and for this cause: we had a king that hight Hermance, and he was king of the Red City, and this king that was lord was a noble knight, large and liberal of his expense. And in the world he loved nothing so much as he did errant knights of king Arthur's court, and all justing, hunting, and all manner of knightly games; for so kind a king and knight had never the rule of poor people as he was; and because of his goodness and gentleness we bemoan him and ever shall. And all kings and estates may beware by our lord, for he was destroyed in his own default, for had he cherished them of his blood he had yet lived with great riches and rest; but all estates may beware of our king. But alas, said Ebel, that we shall give all other warning by his death. Tell me, said Palamides, in what manner was your lord slain, and by whom? Sir, said Sir Ebel, our king brought up of children two men that now are perilous knights, and these two knights our king had so in charity, that he loved no man nor trusted no man of his blood, nor none other that was about him. And by these two knights our king was governed: and so they ruled him peaceably, and his lands, and never would they suffer none of his blood to have no rule with our king. And also he was so free and so gentle, and they so false and deceivable, that they ruled him peaceably; and that espied the lords of our king's blood, and departed from him unto their own livelihood. Then when these two traitors understood that they had driven all the lords of his blood from him, they were not pleased with that rule, but then they thought to have more, as ever it is an old saw, Give a churl rule, and thereby he will not be sufficed ; for whatsoever he be that is ruled by a villain born, and the lord of the soil to be a gentleman born, the same villain shall destroy all the gentlemen about him ; therefore all estates and lords beware whom ye take about you. And if ye be a knight of king Arthur's court, remember this tale, for this is the end and conclusion. My lord and king rode unto the forest hereby, by the advice of these false traitors; and there he chased at the red deer, armed at all pieces full like a good knight ; and so for labour he waxed dry, and then he alight and drank at a well ; and when he was alight, by the assent of these two traitors, that one that hight Helius he suddenly smote our king through the body with a spear, and so they left him there. And when they were departed, then by fortune I came to the well, and found my lord and king wounded to the death. And when I heard his complaint, I let bring him to the water side, and in that same ship I put him alive; and when my lord king Hermance was in that vessel, he required me for the true faith I owed unto him for to write a letter in this manner :—

CHAP. LXII.

The copy of the letter written for to revenge the king's death, and how Sir Palamides fought for to have the battle.

RECOMMENDING unto king Arthur and to all his knights errant, beseeching them all that insomuch as I king Hermance, king of the Red City, thus am slain by felony and treason through two knights of mine own, and of mine own bringing up, and of mine own making, that some worshipful knight will revenge my death, insomuch I have been ever to my power well willing unto Arthur's court; and who that will adventure his life with these two traitors for my sake in one battle, I king Hermance, king of the Red City, freely give him all my lands and rents that ever I held in

my life. This letter, said Ebel, I wrote by my lord's commandment ; and then he received his Creator, and when he was dead he commanded me or ever he was cold to put that letter fast in his hand ; and then he commanded me to put forth that same vessel down Humber, and I should give these mariners in commandment never to stint until that they came unto Logris, where all the noble knights shall assemble at this time;—And there shall some good knight have pity on me to revenge my death, for there was never king nor lord falselyer ne traitorlyer slain than I am here to my death. Thus was the complaint of our king Hermance. Now, said Sir Ebel, ye know all how our lord was betrayed, and we require you for God's sake have pity upon his death, and worshipfully revenge his death, and then may ye hold all these lands. For we all wit well that, and ye may slay these two traitors, the Red City and all those that be therein will take you for their lord. Truly, said Sir Palamides, it grieveth my heart for to hear you tell this doleful tale. And to say the truth, I saw the same letter that ye speak of ; and one of the best knights on the earth read that letter to me, and by his commandment I came hither to revenge your king's death ; and therefore have done, and let me wit where I shall find those traitors, for I shall never be at ease in my heart till that I be in hands with them. Sir, said Sir Ebel, then take your ship again, and that ship must bring you unto the Delectable Isle, fast by the Red City, and we in this castle shall pray for you and abide your again-coming ; for this same castle, and ye speed well, must needs be yours ; for our king Hermance let make this castle for the love of the two traitors, and so we kept it with strong hand, and therefore full sore are we threated. Wot ye what ye shall do, said Sir Palamides ; whatsoever come of me, look ye keep well this castle. For, and it misfortune me so to be slain in this quest, I am sure there will come one of the best knights of the world for to revenge my death, and that is Sir Tristram de Liones, or else Sir Launcelot du Lake.

Then Sir Palamides departed from that castle. And as he came nigh the city, there came out of a ship a goodly knight armed against him, with his shield on his shoulder, and his hand upon his sword. And anon as he came nigh Sir Palamides he said, Sir knight, what seek ye here? Leave this quest, for it is mine, and mine it was or ever it was yours, and therefore I will have it. Sir knight, said Palamides, it may well be that this quest was yours or it was mine, but when the letter was taken out of the dead king's hand, at that time by likelihood there was no knight had undertaken to revenge the death of the king. And so at that time I promised to revenge his death. And so I shall, or else I am ashamed. Ye say well, said the knight, but wit ye well then will I fight with you, and who be the better knight of us both, let him take the battle upon hand. I assent me, said Sir Palamides. And then they dressed their shields and pulled out their swords, and lashed together many sad strokes as men of might; and this fighting was more than an hour; but at the last Sir Palamides waxed big and better winded, so that then he smote that knight such a stroke that he made him to kneel upon his knees. Then that knight spake on high and said, Gentle knight, hold thy hand. Sir Palamides was goodly, and withdrew his hand. Then this knight said, Wit ye well, knight, that thou art better worthy to have this battle than I, and I require thee of knighthood tell me thy name. Sir, my name is Palamides, a knight of king Arthur, and of the Table Round, that hither I came to revenge the death of this dead king.

CHAP. LXIII.

Of the preparation of Sir Palamides and the two brethren that should fight with him.

WELL be ye found, said the knight to Palamides, for of all knights that be on live, except three, I had levest have you. The first is Sir Launcelot du Lake, the second is Sir Tristram de Liones, the third is my nigh cousin Sir Lamorak de Galis. And I am brother unto king Hermance that is dead, and my name is Sir Hermind. Ye say well, said Sir Palamides, and ye shall see how I shall speed. And if I be there slain go ye to my lord Sir Launcelot, or else to my lord Sir Tristram, and pray them to revenge my death, for as for Sir Lamorak, him shall ye never see in this world. Alas, said Sir Hermind, how may that be? He is slain, said Sir Palamides, by Sir Gawaine and his brethren. Truly, said Hermind, there was not one for one that slew him. That is truth, said Sir Palamides, for they were four dangerous knights that slew him, as Sir Gawaine, Sir Agravaine, Sir Gaheris, and Sir Mordred; but Sir Gareth the fifth brother was away, the best knight of them all. And so Sir Palamides told Hermind all the manner, and how they slew Sir Lamorak all only by treason. So Sir Palamides took his ship, and arrived up at the Delectable Isle. And in the meanwhile Sir Hermind, that was the king's brother, he arrived up at the Red City, and there he told them how there was come a knight of king Arthur's to avenge king Hermance's death; and his name is Sir Palamides the good knight, that for the most part he followeth the beast Glatisant. Then all the city made great joy. For mickle had they heard of Sir Palamides, and of his noble prowess. So let they ordain a messenger and sent unto the two brethren, and bade them to make them ready, for there was a knight come that would fight with them both. So the messenger went unto them where they were at a castle there beside. And there he told them how there was a knight come of king Arthur's court to fight with them both at once. He is welcome, said they. But tell us, we pray you, if it be Sir Launcelot, or any of his blood. He is none of that blood, said the messenger. Then we care the less, said the two brethren, for with none of the blood of Sir Launcelot we keep not to have ado withal. Wit ye well, said the messenger, that his name is Sir Palamides, that yet is unchristened, a noble knight. Well, said they, and he be now unchristened he shall never be christened. So they appointed to be at the city within two days.

And when Sir Palamides was come to the city, they made passing great joy of him: and then they beheld him and saw that he was well made, cleanly and bigly, and unmaimed of his limbs, and neither too young nor too old; and so all the people praised him. And though he was not christened, yet he believed in the best manner, and was full faithful and true of his promise, and well conditioned. And because he made his avow that he would never be christened until the time that he had achieved the beast Glatisant, which was a wonderful beast, and a great signification, for Merlin prophesied much of that beast. And also Sir Palamides avowed never to take full christendom unto the time that he had done seven battles within the lists. So within the third day there came to the city these two brethren, the one hight Helius, the other hight Helake, the which were men of great prowess, howbeit that they were false and full of treason, and but poor men born, yet were they noble knights of their hands. And with them they brought forty knights to that intent that they should be big enough for the Red City. Thus came the two brethren with great boasting and pride, for they had put the Red City in fear and damage. Then they were brought to the lists. And Sir Palamides came into the place, and said thus: Be ye the two brethren, Helius and Helake, that slew your king and lord, Sir Hermance, by felony and treason, for whom that I am come hither to revenge his death? Wit thou well, said Sir Helius and Sir Helake, that we are the same knights that slew king Hermance. And wit thou well Sir Palamides, Saracen, that we shall handle thee so or thou depart

that thou shalt wish that thou werest christened. It may well be, said Sir Palamides, for yet I would not die or I were christened, and yet so am I not afeard of you both, but I trust to God that I shall die a better christian man than any of you both; and doubt ye not, said Sir Palamides, either ye or I shall be left dead in this place.

CHAP. LXIV.

Of the battle between Sir Palamides and the two brethren, and how the two brethren were slain.

THEN they departed, and the two brethren came against Sir Palamides, and he against them, as fast as their horses might run. And by fortune Sir Palamides smote Helake through his shield, and through the breast more than a fathom. All this while Sir Helius held up his spear, and for pride and presumption he would not smite Sir Palamides with his spear. But when he saw his brother lie on the earth, and saw he might not help himself, then he said unto Sir Palamides, Help thyself: and therewith he came hurtling unto Sir Palamides with his spear, and smote him quite from his saddle. Then Sir Helius rode over Sir Palamides twice or thrice. And therewith Sir Palamides was ashamed, and gat the horse of Sir Helius by the bridle, and therewithal the horse areared, and Sir Palamides halp after, and so they fell both to the earth, but anon Sir Helius start up lightly, and there he smote Sir Palamides a mighty stroke upon the helm, so that he kneeled upon his own knee. Then they lashed together many sad strokes, and traced and traversed, now backward, now sideling, hurtling together like two boars, and that same time they fell both groveling to the earth. Thus they fought still without any reposing two hours, and never breathed, and then Sir Palamides waxed faint and weary, and Sir Helius waxed passing strong, and doubled his strokes, and drove Sir Palamides overthwart and endlong all the field, that they of the city, when they saw Sir Palamides in this case, they wept, and cried, and made great dole, and the other party made as great joy. Alas, said the men of the city, that this noble knight should thus be slain for our king's sake. And as they were thus weeping and crying, Sir Palamides that had suffered an hundred strokes, that it was wonder that he stood upon his feet, at the last, Sir Palamides beheld as he might the common people how they wept for him, and then he said to himself, Ah, fie for shame, Sir Palamides, why hangest thou thy head so low? And therewith he bear up his shield, and looked Sir Helius in the visage, and he smote him a great stroke upon the helm, and after that another and another. And then he smote Sir Helius with such a might that he fell to the earth groveling, and then he rased off his helm from his head, and there he smote him such a buffet that he departed his head from the body. And then were the people of the city the joyfullest people that might be. So they brought him to his lodging with great solemnity, and there all the people became his men. And then Sir Palamides prayed them all to take keep unto all the lordship of king Hermance;—For, fair sirs, wit ye well, I may not as at this time abide with you, for I must in all haste be with my lord king Arthur at the castle of Lonazep, the which I have promised.

Then were the people full heavy at his departing. For all that city proffered Sir Palamides the third part of their goods so that he would abide with them: but in no wise as at that time he would not abide. And so Sir Palamides departed. And so he came unto the castle, there as Sir Ebel was lieutenant. And when they in the castle wist how Sir Palamides had sped there was a joyful company. And so Sir Palamides departed, and came to the castle of Lonazep. And when he wist that Sir Tristram was not there, he took his way over Humber, and came unto Joyous Gard where as Sir Tristram was, and La Beale Isoud. Sir Tristram had commanded that what knight errant came

within the Joyous Gard, as in the town, that they should warn Sir Tristram. So there came a man of the town, and told Sir Tristram how there was a knight in the town a passing goodly man. What manner of man is he? said Sir Tristram, and what sign beareth he? So the man told Sir Tristram all the tokens of him. That is Palamides, said Dinadan. It may well be, said Sir Tristram: go ye to him, said Sir Tristram unto Dinadan. So Dinadan went unto Sir Palamides, and there either made of other great joy, and so they lay together that night, and on the morn early came Sir Tristram and Sir Gareth, and took them in their beds, and so they arose and brake their fast.

CHAP. LXV.

How Sir Tristram and Sir Palamides met Breuse Sance Pité, and how Sir Tristram and La Beale Isoud went unto Lonazep.

AND then Sir Tristram desired Sir Palamides to ride into the fields and woods; so they were accorded to repose them in the forest. And when they had played them a great while, they rode unto a fair well, and anon they were ware of an armed knight that came riding against them, and there either saluted other. Then this armed knight spake to Sir Tristram, and asked what were those knights that were lodged in Joyous Gard. I wot not what they are, said Sir Tristram. What knights be ye, said that knight, for me seemeth that ye be no knights errant, because ye ride unarmed? Whether we be knights or not, we list not to tell thee our name. Wilt thou not tell me thy name, said that knight, then keep thee, for thou shalt die of my hands. And therewith he gat his spear in his hands, and would have run Sir Tristram through. That saw Sir Palamides, and smote his horse traverse in midst of the side, that man and horse fell to the earth. And therewith Sir Palamides alight, and pulled out his sword to have slain him. Let be, said Sir Tristram, slay him not, the knight is but a fool, it were shame to slay him. But take away his spear, said Sir Tristram, and let him take his horse and go where that he will. So when this knight arose he groaned sore of the fall, and so he took his horse, and when he was up, he turned then his horse, and required Sir Tristram and Sir Palamides to tell him what knights they were. Now wit ye well, said Sir Tristram, that my name is Sir Tristram de Liones, and this knight's name is Sir Palamides. When he wist what they were, he took his horse with the spurs because they should not ask him his name, and so rode fast away through thick and thin. Then came there by them a knight with a bended shield of azure, whose name was Epinogris, and he came toward them a great wallop. Whither are ye riding? said Sir Tristram. My fair lords, said Epinogris, I follow the falsest knight that beareth the life, wherefore I require tell me whether ye saw him, for he beareth a shield with a case of red over it. Truly, said Tristram, such a knight departed from us not a quarter of an hour ago; we pray you tell us his name. Alas, said Epinogris, why let ye him escape from you, and he is so great a foe unto all errant knights: his name is Breuse Sance Pité. Ah fie for shame, said Sir Palamides, alas that ever he escaped my hands, for he is the man in the world that I hate most. Then every knight made great sorrow to other, and so Epinogris departed, and followed the chase after him. Then Sir Tristram and his three fellows rode unto Joyous Gard, and there Sir Tristram talked unto Sir Palamides of his battle, how he sped at the Red City; and as ye have heard afore, so was it ended. Truly, said Sir Tristram, I am glad ye have well sped, for ye have done worshipfully. Well, said Sir Tristram, we must forward to-morn. And then he devised how it should be, and Sir Tristram devised to send his two pavilions to set them fast by the well of Lonazep,—and therein shall be the queen La Beale Isoud. It is well said, said Sir Dinadan.

But when Sir Palamides heard of that, his heart was ravished out of measure: notwithstanding he said but little. So when they came to Joyous Gard, Sir Palamides would not have gone into the castle, but as Sir Tristram took him by the finger, and led him into the castle. And when Sir Palamides saw La Beale Isoud, he was so ravished so that he might scarcely speak. So they went unto meat, but Palamides might not eat, and there was all the cheer that might be had. And on the morn they were apparelled to ride towards Lonazep.

So Sir Tristram had three squires, and La Beale Isoud had three gentlewomen, and both the queen and they were richly apparelled; and other people had they none with them, but varlets to bear their shields and their spears. And thus they rode forth. So as they rode they saw afore them a rout of knights: it was the knight Galihodin with twenty knights with him. Fair fellows, said Galihodin, yonder come four knights, and a rich and a well fair lady: I am in will to take that lady from them. That is not of the best counsel, said one of Galihodin's men, but send ye to them and wit what they will say. And so it was done. There came a squire to Sir Tristram and asked him whether they would just, or else to lose their lady? Not so, said Sir Tristram, tell your lord, I bid him come as many as we be, and win her and take her. Sir, said Palamides, and it please you, let me have this deed, and I shall undertake them all four. I will that ye have it, said Sir Tristram, at your pleasure. Now go and tell your lord Galihodin, that this same knight will encounter with him and his fellows.

CHAP. LXVI.

How Sir Palamides justed with Sir Gali-bodin and after with Sir Gawaine, and smote them down.

THEN this squire departed and told Galihodin, and then he dressed his shield, and put forth a spear, and Sir Palamides another, and there Sir Palamides smote Galihodin so hard that he smote both horse and man to the earth. And there he had an horrible fall. And then came there another knight, and in the same wise he served him, and so he served the third and the fourth, that he smote them over their horse croups: and always Sir Palamides' spear was whole. Then came six knights more of Galihodin's men, and would have been avenged upon Sir Palamides. Let be, said Sir Galihodin, not so hardy! None of you all meddle with this knight, for he is a man of great bounty and honour; and if he would, ye were not able to meddle with him. And right so they held them still. And ever Sir Palamides was ready to just. And when he saw they would no more, he rode unto Sir Tristram. Right well have ye done, said Sir Tristram, and worshipfully have ye done as a good knight should. This Galihodin was nigh cousin unto Galahalt the haut prince. And this Galihodin was a king within the country of Surluse. So as Sir Tristram, Sir Palamides, and La Beale Isoud rode together, they saw afore them four knights, and every man had his spear in his hand. The first was Sir Gawaine, the second Sir Uwaine, the third Sir Sagramor le Desirous, and the fourth was Dodinas le Savage. When Sir Palamides beheld them, that the four knights were ready to just, he prayed Sir Tristram to give him leave to have ado with them all so long as he might hold him on horseback:—And if that I be smitten down, I pray you revenge me. Well, said Sir Tristram, I will as ye will, and ye are not so fain to have worship, but I would as fain increase your worship. And there withal Sir Gawaine put forth his spear, and Sir Palamides another, and so they came so eagerly together that Sir Palamides smote Sir Gawaine to the earth, horse and all; and in the same wise he served Uwaine, Sir Dodinas, and Sagramor. All these four knights Sir Palamides smote down with divers spears. And then Sir Tristram departed toward Lonazep. And when they were departed, then came thither Galihodin with his ten knights unto Sir Gawaine,

and there he told him all how he had sped. I marvel, said Sir Gawaine, what knights they be that are so arrayed in green. And that knight upon the white horse smote me down, said Galihodin, and my three fellows. And so he did to me, said Gawaine, and well I wot, said Sir Gawaine, that either he upon the white horse is Sir Tristram, or else Sir Palamides, and that gaybeseen lady is queen Isoud. Thus they talked of one thing and of other. And in the mean while Sir Tristram passed on, till that he came to the well where his two pavilions were set, and there they alighted, and there they saw many pavilions and great array. Then Sir Tristram left there Sir Palamides and Sir Gareth with La Beale Isoud; and Sir Tristram and Sir Dinadan rode to Lonazep to hearken tidings; and Sir Tristram rode upon Sir Palamides' white horse. And when he came into the castle, Sir Dinadan heard a great horn blow, and to the horn drew many knights. Then Sir Tristram asked a knight, What meaneth the blast of that horn? Sir, said that knight, it is all those that shall hold against king Arthur at this tournament. The first is the king of Ireland, and the king of Surluse, the king of Listinoise, the king of Northumberland, and the king of the best part of Wales, with many other countries: and these draw them to a council, to understand what governance they shall be of. But the king of Ireland, whose name was Marhalt, and father to the good knight Sir Marhaus that Sir Tristram slew, had all the speech, that Sir Tristram might hear it. He said: Lords and fellows, let us look to ourselves, for wit ye well king Arthur is sure of many good knights, or else he would not with so few knights have ado with us; therefore, by my counsel, let every king have a standard and a cognizance by himself, that every knight draw to his natural lord, and then may every king and captain help his knights, if they have need. When Sir Tristram had heard all their counsel, he rode unto king Arthur for to hear of his counsel.

CHAP. LXVII.

How Sir Tristram and his fellowship came unto the tournament of Lonazep; and of divers justs and matters.

But Sir Tristram was not so soon come into the place, but Sir Gawaine and Sir Galihodin went to king Arthur, and told him, That same green knight in the green harness, with the white horse, smote us two down, and six of our fellows, this same day. Well, said Arthur; and then he called Sir Tristram, and asked him what was his name. Sir, said Sir Tristram, ye shall hold me excused as at this time, for ye shall not wit my name. And there Sir Tristram returned and rode his way. I have marvel, said Arthur, that yonder knight will not tell me his name, but go thou, Griflet le Fise de Dieu, and pray him to speak with me betwixt us. Then Sir Griflet rode after him, and overtook him, and said to him that king Arthur prayed him for to speak with him secretly apart. Upon this covenant, said Sir Tristram, I will speak with him that I will turn again, so that ye will ensure me not to desire to hear my name. I shall undertake, said Sir Griflet, that he will not greatly desire it of you. So they rode together until they came to king Arthur. Fair sir, said king Arthur, what is the cause ye will not tell me your name? Sir, said Sir Tristram, without a cause I will not hide my name. Upon what party will ye hold? said king Arthur. Truly, my lord, said Sir Tristram, I wot not yet on what party I will be on until I come to the field; and there as my heart giveth me there will I hold: but to-morrow ye shall see and prove on what party I shall come. And therewithal he returned and went to his pavilions. And upon the morn they armed them all in green, and came into the field; and there young knights began to just, and did many worshipful deeds. Then spake Gareth unto Sir Tristram, and prayed him to give him leave to break his spear, for him thought shame to bear his spear whole again. When Sir Tris-

tram heard him say so he laughed, and said, I pray you, do your best. Then Sir Gareth gat a spear, and proffered to just. That saw a nephew unto the king of the hundred knights, his name was Selises, and a good man of arms. So this knight Selises then dressed him unto Sir Gareth, and they two met together so hard that either smote other down, horse and all, to the earth; so they were both bruised and hurt, and there they lay till the king with the hundred knights halp Selises up; and Sir Tristram and Sir Palamides halp up Gareth again; and so they rode with Sir Gareth unto their pavilions, and then they pulled off his helm. And when La Beale Isoud saw Sir Gareth bruised in the face, she asked him what ailed him. Madam, said Sir Gareth, I had a great buffet, and, as I suppose, I gave another, but none of my fellows would not rescue me. Forsooth, said Palamides, it longed not to none of us as this day to just, for there have not this day justed no proved knights; and needs ye would just, and when the other party saw ye preferred yourself to just, they sent one to you, a passing good knight of his age, for I know him well, his name is Selises, and worshipfully ye met with him, and neither of you are dishonoured; and therefore refresh yourself, that ye may be ready and whole to just to-morrow. As for that, said Sir Gareth, I shall not fail you, and I may bestride my horse.

CHAP. LXVIII.

How Sir Tristram and his fellowship justed, and of the noble feats that they did in that tourneying.

Now upon what party, said Sir Tristram, is it best we be withal as to-morn? Sir, said Palamides, ye shall have mine advice to be against king Arthur as to-morn, for on his party will be Sir Launcelot, and many good knights of his blood with him. And the more men of worship that they be, the more worship we shall win. That is full knightly spoken, said Sir Tristram, and right so as ye counsel me, so will we do. So be it, said they all. So that night they were lodged with the best. And on the morn when it was day, they were arrayed in green trappings, shields, and spears; and La Beale Isoud in the same colour, and her three damsels. And right so these four knights came into the field endlong and through. And so they led La Beale Isoud thither as she should stand and behold all the justs in a bay window; but always she wimpled that no man might see her visage. And then these three knights rode straight unto the party of the king of Scots.

When king Arthur had seen them do all this, he asked Sir Launcelot what were these knights and that queen? Sir, said Sir Launcelot, I cannot say you in certain, but if Sir Tristram be in this country, or Sir Palamides, wit ye well it be they in certain, and La Beale Isoud. Then Arthur called to him Sir Kay, and said, Go lightly and wit how many knights there be here lacking of the Table Round, for by the sieges thou mayest know. So went Sir Kay, and saw by the writing in the sieges that there lacked ten knights,—And these be their names that be not here, Sir Tristram, Sir Palamides, Sir Percivale, Sir Gaheris, Sir Epinogris, Sir Mordred, Sir Dinadan, Sir La Cote Male Taile, and Sir Pelleas the noble knight. Well, said Arthur, some of these I dare undertake are here this day against us. Then came therein two brethren, cousins unto Sir Gawaine, the one hight Sir Edward, that other hight Sir Sadok, the which were two good knights, and they asked of king Arthur that they might have the first justs, for they were of Orkney. I am pleased, said king Arthur. Then Sir Edward encountered with the king of Scots, in whose party was Sir Tristram and Sir Palamides; and Sir Edward smote the king of Scots quite from his horse; and Sir Sadok smote down the king of North Wales, and gave him a wonder great fall, that there was a great cry on king Arthur's party, and that made Sir Palamides passing wroth; and so Sir Palamides

dressed his shield and his spear, and with all his might he met with Sir Edward of Orkney, that he smote him so hard that his horse might not stand on his feet, and so they hurtled to the earth: and then with the same spear Sir Palamides smote down Sir Sadok over his horse croup. Oh, said Arthur, what knight is that arrayed all in green? he justeth mightily. Wit you well, said Sir Gawaine, he is a good knight, and yet shall ye see him just better or he depart; and yet shall ye see, said Sir Gawaine, another bigger knight in the same colour than he is, for that same knight, said Sir Gawaine, that smote down right now my two cousins, he smote me down within these two days, and seven fellows more. This meanwhile, as they stood thus talking, there came into the place Sir Tristram upon a black horse, and or ever he stint he smote down with one spear four good knights of Orkney, that were of the kin of Sir Gawaine; and Sir Gareth and Sir Dinadan every each of them smote down a good knight. Truly, said Arthur, yonder knight upon the black horse doth mightily and marvellously well. Abide you, said Sir Gawaine; that knight with the black horse began not yet. Then Sir Tristram made to horse again the two kings that Edward and Sadok had unhorsed at the beginning. And then Sir Tristram drew his sword, and rode into the thickest of the press against them of Orkney, and there he smote down knights, and rashed off helms, and pulled away their shields, and hurtled down many knights: he fared so that Sir Arthur and all knights had great marvel, when they saw one knight do so great deeds of arms. And Sir Palamides failed not upon the other side, but did so marvellously well that all men had wonder. For there king Arthur likened Sir Tristram, that was on the black horse, like to a wood lion, and likened Sir Palamides, upon the white horse, unto a wood libbard, and Sir Gareth and Sir Dinadan unto eager wolves. But the custom was such among them, that none of the kings would help other, but all the fellowship of every standard to help other as they might. But ever Sir Tristram did so much deeds of arms that they of Orkney waxed weary of him, and so withdrew them unto Lonazep.

CHAP. LXIX.

How Sir Tristram was unhorsed and smitten down by Sir Launcelot, and after that Sir Tristram smote down king Arthur.

THEN was the cry of heralds and all manner of common people, The green knight hath done marvellously, and beaten all them of Orkney. And there the heralds numbered that Sir Tristram, that sat upon the black horse, had smitten down twenty knights; and Sir Palamides had smitten down twenty knights; and the most part of these fifty knights were of the house of king Arthur, and proved knights. Truly, said Arthur unto Sir Launcelot, this is a great shame to us to see four knights beat so many knights of mine; and therefore make you ready, for we will have ado with them. Sir, said Sir Launcelot, wit ye well that there are two passing good knights, and great worship were it not to us now to have ado with them, for they have this day sore travailed. As for that, said Arthur, I will be avenged, and therefore take with you Sir Bleoberis and Sir Ector, and I will be the fourth, said Arthur. Sir, said Launcelot, ye shall find me ready, and my brother Sir Ector, and my cousin Sir Bleoberis. And so when they were ready and on horseback, Now choose, said Sir Arthur unto Sir Launcelot, with whom that ye will encounter withal. Sir, said Launcelot, I will meet with the green knight upon the black horse (that was Sir Tristram), and my cousin Sir Bleoberis shall match the green knight upon the white horse (that was Sir Palamides), and my brother Sir Ector shall match with the green knight upon the white horse (that was Sir Gareth). Then must I, said Sir Arthur, have ado

with the green knight upon the grisled horse (and that was Sir Dinadan). Now every man take heed to his fellow, said Sir Launcelot. And so they trotted on together; and there encountered Sir Launcelot against Sir Tristram. So Sir Launcelot smote Sir Tristram so sore upon the shield that he bare horse and man to the earth: but Sir Launcelot wend it had been Sir Palamides, and so he passed forth. And then Sir Bleoberis encountered with Sir Palamides, and he smote him so hard upon the shield that Sir Palamides and his white horse rustled to the earth. Then Sir Ector de Maris smote Sir Gareth so hard that down he fell off his horse. And the noble king Arthur encountered with Sir Dinadan, and he smote him quite from his saddle. And then the noise turned awhile how the green knights were slain down. When the king of Northgalis saw that Sir Tristram had a fall, then he remembered him how great deeds of arms Sir Tristram had done. Then he made ready many knights, for the custom and cry was such, that what knight were smitten down, and might not be horsed again by his fellows, or by his own strength, that as that day he should be prisoner unto the party that had smitten him down. So came in the king of Northgalis, and he rode straight unto Sir Tristram. And when he came nigh him he alight down suddenly, and betook Sir Tristram his horse, and said thus: Noble knight, I know thee not of what country thou art, but for the noble deeds that thou hast done this day take there my horse, and let me do as well as I may; for truly thou art better worthy to have mine horse than I myself. Gramercy, said Sir Tristram, and if I may I shall requite you. Look that ye go not far from us, and, as I suppose, I shall win you another horse. And therewith Sir Tristram mounted upon his horse, and there he met with king Arthur, and he gave him such a buffet upon the helm with his sword that king Arthur had no power to keep his saddle. And then Sir Tristram gave the king of Northgalis king Arthur's horse. Then was there great press about king Arthur for to horse him again. But Sir Palamides would not suffer king Arthur to be horsed again: but ever Sir Palamides smote on the right hand and on the left hand mightily as a noble knight. And this mean while Sir Tristram rode through the thickest of the press, and smote down knights on the right and on the left hand, and rased off helms, and so passed forth unto his pavilions, and left Sir Palamides on foot. And Sir Tristram changed his horse, and disguised himself all in red, horse and harness.

CHAP. LXX.

How Sir Tristram changed his harness and it was all red, and how he demeaned him, and how Sir Palamides slew Launcelot's horse.

AND when the queen La Beale Isoud saw that Sir Tristram was unhorsed, and she wist not where he was, then she wept greatly. But Sir Tristram, when he was ready, came dashing lightly into the field, and then La Beale Isoud espied him. And so he did great deeds of arms, with one spear that was great Sir Tristram smote down five knights or ever he stint. Then Sir Launcelot espied him readily that it was Sir Tristram, and then he repented him that he had smitten him down. And so Sir Launcelot went out of the press to repose him, and lightly he came again. And now when Sir Tristram came unto the press, through his great force he put Sir Palamides upon his horse, and Sir Gareth, and Sir Dinadan, and then they began to do marvellously. But Sir Palamides nor none of his two fellows knew not who had holpen them on horseback again. But ever Sir Tristram was nigh them and succoured them, and they not him, because he was changed into red armour. And all this while Sir Launcelot was away. So when La Beale Isoud knew Sir Tristram again upon his horse back she was passing glad, and then she laughed and

made good cheer. And as it happened Sir Palamides looked up toward her, where she lay in the window, and he espied how she laughed: and therewith he took such a rejoicing that he smote down, what with his spear and with his sword, all that ever he met; for through the sight of her he was so enamoured in her love, that he seemed at that time that, and both Sir Tristram and Sir Launcelot had been both against him, they should have won no worship of him. And in his heart, as the book saith, Sir Palamides wished that with his worship he might have ado with Sir Tristram before all men because of La Beale Isoud. Then Sir Palamides began to double his strength, and he did so marvellously that all men had wonder of him. And ever he cast up his eye unto La Beale Isoud, and when he saw her make such cheer he fared like a lion, that there might no man withstand him. And then Sir Tristram beheld him how that Sir Palamides bestirred him, and then he said unto Sir Dinadan, Truly, Sir Palamides is a passing good knight, and a well enduring: but such deeds saw I him never do, nor never heard I tell that ever he did so much in one day. It is his day, said Sir Dinadan: and he would say no more unto Sir Tristram; but to himself he said, And if ye knew for whose love he doth all these deeds of arms, soon would Sir Tristram abate his courage. Alas, said Sir Tristram, that Sir Palamides is not christened. So said king Arthur, and so said all those that beheld him. Then all people gave him the prize as for the best knight that day, that he passed Sir Launcelot or Sir Tristram. Well, said Dinadan to himself, all this worship that Sir Palamides hath here this day, he may thank the queen Isoud; for had she been away this day, Sir Palamides had not gotten the prize this day.

Right so came into the field Sir Launcelot du Lake, and saw and heard the noise and cry and the great worship that Sir Palamides had. He dressed him against Sir Palamides with a great mighty spear, and a long, and thought to smite him down. And when Sir Palamides saw Sir Launcelot come upon him so fast, he ran upon Sir Launcelot as fast with his sword as he might. And as Sir Launcelot should have stricken him he smote his spear on side, and smote it atwo with his sword. And Sir Palamides rashed unto Sir Launcelot and thought to have put him to a shame, and with his sword he smote his horse's neck that Sir Launcelot rode upon, and then Sir Launcelot fell to the earth. Then was the cry huge and great ;—See how Sir Palamides the Saracen hath smitten down Sir Launcelot's horse. Right then were there many knights wroth with Sir Palamides, because he had done that deed. Therefore many knights held there against that it was unknightly done in a tournament to kill a horse wilfully, but that it had been done in plain battle, life for life.

CHAP. LXXI.

How Sir Launcelot said to Sir Palamides, and how the prize of that day was given unto Sir Palamides.

WHEN Sir Ector de Maris saw Sir Launcelot his brother have such a despite, and so set on foot, then he gat a spear eagerly and ran against Sir Palamides, and he smote him so hard that he bare him quite from his horse. That saw Sir Tristram that was in red harness, and he smote down Sir Ector de Maris quite from his horse. Then Sir Launcelot dressed his shield upon his shoulder, and with his sword naked in his hand, and so came straight upon Sir Palamides fiercely, and said, Wit thou well, thou hast done me this day the greatest despite that ever any worshipful knight did to me in tournament or in justs, and therefore I will be avenged upon thee, therefore take keep to yourself. Ah mercy, noble knight, said Palamides, and forgive me mine unkindly deeds, for I have no power nor might to withstand you. And I have done so much this day, that well I wot I did never so much nor never

shall in my life days. And therefore, most noble knight, I require thee spare me as at this day, and I promise you I shall ever be your knight while I live. And ye put me from my worship now, ye put me from the greatest worship that ever I had, or ever shall have, in my life days. Well, said Sir Launcelot, I see, for to say the sooth, ye have done marvellously well this day, and I understand a part for whose love ye do it, and well I wot that love is a great mistress. And if my lady were here as she is not, wit you well that ye should not bear away the worship. But beware your love be not discovered ; for and Sir Tristram may know it ye will repent it. And since my quarrel is not here, ye shall have this day the worship as for me ; considering the great travail and pain that ye have had this day, it were no worship for me to put you from it. And therewithal Sir Launcelot suffered Sir Palamides to depart. Then Sir Launcelot by great force and might gat his own horse, maugre twenty knights. So when Sir Launcelot was horsed he did many marvels, and so did Sir Tristram, and Sir Palamides in likewise. Then Sir Launcelot smote down with a spear Sir Dinadan, and the king of Scotland, and the king of Wales, and the king of Northumberland, and the king of Listinoise. So then Sir Launcelot and his fellows smote down well a forty knights. Then came the king of Ireland and the king of the Straight Marches to rescue Sir Tristram and Sir Palamides. There began a great meddle, and many knights there were smitten down on both parties, and always Sir Launcelot spared Sir Tristram, and he spared him. And Sir Palamides would not meddle with Sir Launcelot. And so there was hurtling here and there. And then king Arthur sent out many knights of the Table Round. And Sir Palamides was ever in the foremost front. And Sir Tristram did so strongly well that the king and all other had marvel. And then the king let blow to lodging. And because Sir Palamides began first, and never he went nor rode out of the field to repose, but ever he was doing marvellously well, either on foot or on horseback, and longest enduring, king Arthur and all the kings gave Sir Palamides the 'honour and the gree as for that day. Then Sir Tristram commanded Sir Dinadan to fetch the queen La Beale Isoud, and bring her to his two pavilions that stood by the well. And so Dinadan did as he was commanded. But when Sir Palamides understood and wist that Sir Tristram was in the red armour, and on the red horse, wit ye well that he was glad, and so was Sir Gareth, and Sir Dinadan. For they all wend that Sir Tristram had been taken prisoner.

And then every knight drew to his inn. And then king Arthur and every knight spake of those knights. But above all men they gave Sir Palamides the prize, and all knights that knew Sir Palamides had wonder of his deeds. Sir, said Sir Launcelot unto Arthur, as for Sir Palamides, and he be the green knight, I dare say as for this day he is best worthy to have the degree, for he reposed him never, ne never changed his weeds. And he began first and longest held on. And yet well I wot, said Sir Launcelot, that there was a better knight than he, and that shall be proved or we depart, upon pain of my life. Thus they talked on either party, and so Sir Dinadan railed with Sir Tristram and said, What the devil is upon thee this day, for Sir Palamides' strength feebled never this day, but ever he doubled his strength.

CHAP. LXXII.

How Sir Dinadan provoked Sir Tristram to do well.

AND thou Sir Tristram faredst all this day as though thou hadst been asleep, and therefore I call thee coward. Well, Dinadan, said Sir Tristram, I was never called coward or now, of none earthly knight, in my life: and, wit thou well, sir, I call myself never the more coward though Sir Launcelot gave me a fall,

for I outcept him of all knights. And doubt ye not, Sir Dinadan, and Sir Launcelot have a quarrel good, he is too over good for any knight that now is living; and yet of his sufferance, largesse, bounty, and courtesy, I call him knight peerless. And so Sir Tristram was in manner wroth with Sir Dinadan. But all this language Sir Dinadan said because he would anger Sir Tristram, for to cause him to awake his spirits, and to be wroth. For well knew Sir Dinadan that and Sir Tristram were thoroughly wroth, Sir Palamides should not get the prize upon the morn. And for this intent Sir Dinadan said all this railing and language against Sir Tristram. Truly, said Sir Palamides, as for Sir Launcelot, of his noble knighthood, courtesy, and prowess, and gentleness, I know not his peer: for this day, said Sir Palamides, I did full uncourteously unto Sir Launcelot, and full unknightly, and full knightly and courteously he did to me again: for and he had been as ungentle to me as I was to him, this day I had won no worship. And therefore, said Palamides, I shall be Sir Launcelot's knight whiles my life lasteth. This talking was in the houses of kings. But all kings, lords, and knights said, of clear knighthood and pure strength, of bounty, and courtesy, Sir Launcelot and Sir Tristram bare the prize above all knights that ever were in Arthur's days. And there were never knights in Arthur's days did half so many deeds as they did: as the book saith, no ten knights did not half the deeds that they did; and there was never knight in their days that required Sir Launcelot or Sir Tristram of any quest, so it were not to their shame, but they performed their desire.

CHAP. LXXIII.

How king Arthur and Sir Launcelot came to see La Beale Isoud, and how Palamides smote down king Arthur.

So on the morn Sir Launcelot departed, and Sir Tristram was ready, and La Beale Isoud with Sir Palamides and

Sir Gareth. And so they rode all in green, full freshly beseen, unto the forest. And Sir Tristram left Sir Dinadan sleeping in his bed. And so as they rode, it happed the king and Launcelot stood in a window, and saw Sir Tristram ride and Isoud. Sir, said Sir Launcelot, yonder rideth the fairest lady of the world, except your queen dame Guenever. Who is that? said Sir Arthur. Sir, said he, it is queen Isoud, that, outtaken my lady your queen, she is matchless. Take your horse, said Arthur, and array you at all rights, as I will do, and I promise you, said the king, I will see her. Then anon they were armed and horsed, and either took a spear and rode unto the forest. Sir, said Launcelot, it is not good that ye go too nigh them, for wit ye well there are two as good knights as now are living; and therefore, Sir, I pray you be not too hasty. For peradventure there will be some knights be displeased and we come suddenly upon them. As for that, said Arthur, I will see her, for I take no force whom I grieve. Sir, said Launcelot, ye put yourself in great jeopardy. As for that, said the king, we will take the adventure. Right so anon the king rode even to her, and saluted her, and said, God you save. Sir, said she, ye are welcome. Then the king beheld her, and liked her wonderly well. With that came Sir Palamides unto Arthur and said, Uncourteous knight, what seeketh thou here? Thou art uncourteous, to come upon a lady thus suddenly; therefore withdraw thee. Sir Arthur took none heed of Sir Palamides' words, but ever he looked still upon queen Isoud. Then was Sir Palamides wroth, and therewith he took a spear and came hurtling upon king Arthur, and smote him down with a spear. When Sir Launcelot saw that despite of Sir Palamides, he said to himself, I am loth to have ado with yonder knight, and not for his own sake but for Sir Tristram. And one thing I am sure of, if I smite down Sir Palamides I must have ado with Sir Tristram, and that were over much for me to match them both, for

they are two noble knights: notwithstanding, whether I live or die, needs must I revenge my lord, and so will I whatsoever befal of me. And therewith Sir Launcelot cried to Sir Palamides, Keep thee from me! And then Sir Launcelot and Sir Palamides rashed together with two spears strongly. But Sir Launcelot smote Sir Palamides so hard that he went quite out of his saddle, and had a great fall. When Sir Tristram saw Sir Palamides have that fall, he said to Sir Launcelot, Sir knight keep thee, for I must just with thee. As for to just with me, said Sir Launcelot, I will not fail you for no dread I have of you, but I am loth to have ado with you and I might choose: for I will that ye wit that I must revenge my special lord, that was unhorsed unwarily and unknightly. And therefore, though I have revenged that fall, take ye no displeasure therein, for he is to me such a friend that I may not see him shamed. Anon Sir Tristram understood by his person and by his knightly words that it was Sir Launcelot du Lake, and verily Sir Tristram deemed that it was king Arthur, he that Sir Palamides had smitten down.

And then Sir Tristram put his spear from him, and put Sir Palamides again on horseback; and Sir Launcelot put king Arthur on horseback, and so departed. Truly, said Sir Tristram unto Palamides, ye did not worshipfully when ye smote down that knight so suddenly as ye did. And wit ye well ye did yourself great shame: for the knights came hither of their gentleness to see a fair lady, and that is every good knight's part to behold a fair lady, and ye had not ado to play such masteries afore my lady. Wit thou well it will turn to anger, for he that ye smote down was king Arthur, and that other was the good knight Sir Launcelot. But I shall not forget the words of Sir Launcelot, when that he called him a man of great worship: thereby I wist that it was king Arthur. And as for Sir Launcelot, and there had been five hundred knights in the meadow he would not have refused them, and yet he said he would refuse me : by that again I wist that it was Sir Launcelot, for ever he forbeareth me in every place, and sheweth me great kindness ; and of all knights—I out-take none, say what men will say—he beareth the flower of all chivalry, say it him whosoever will, and he be well angered, and that him list to do his utterance without any favour, I know him not on live but Sir Launcelot is over hard for him, be it on horseback or on foot. I may never believe, said Sir Palamides, that king Arthur will ride so privily as a poor errant knight. Ah, said Sir Tristram, ye know not my lord Arthur, for all knights may learn to be a knight of him. And therefore ye may be sorry, said Sir Tristram, of your unkindly deeds to so noble a king. And a thing that is done may not be undone, said Sir Palamides. Then Sir Tristram sent queen Isoud unto her lodging in the priory, there to behold all the tournament.

CHAP. LXXIV.

How the second day Palamides forsook Sir Tristram, and went to the contrary part against him.

THEN there was a cry unto all knights, that when they heard an horn blow they should make justs as they did the first day. And like as the brethren Sir Edward and Sir Sadok began the justs the first day, Sir Uwaine, the king's son Urein, and Sir Lucanere de Buttelere, began the justs the second day. And at the first encounter Sir Uwaine smote down the king's son of Scots, and Sir Lucanere ran against the king of Wales, and they brake their spears all to pieces, and they were so fierce both, that they hurtled together that both fell to the earth. Then they of Orkney horsed again Sir Lucanere. And then came in Sir Tristram de Liones ; and then Sir Tristram smote down Sir Uwaine and Sir Lucanere ; and Sir Palamides smote down other two knights ; and Sir Gareth smote down other two knights. Then said Sir Arthur unto Sir Launcelot, See yonder three knights do

passing well, and namely the first that justed. Sir, said Launcelot, that knight began not yet, but ye shall see him this day do marvellously. And then came into the place the duke's son of Orkney, and then they began to do many deeds of arms. When Sir Tristram saw them so begin, he said to Palamides, How feel ye yourself ? may ye do this day as ye did yesterday ? Nay, said Palamides, I feel myself so weary and so sore bruised of the deeds of yesterday, that I may not endure as I did yesterday. That me repenteth, said Sir Tristram, for I shall lack you this day. Sir Palamides said, Trust not to me, for I may not do as I did. All these words said Palamides for to beguile Sir Tristram. Sir, said Sir Tristram unto Sir Gareth, then must I trust upon you ; wherefore I pray you be not far from me to rescue me. And need be, said Gareth, I shall not fail you in all that I may do.

Then Sir Palamides rode by himself, and then in despite of Sir Tristram he put himself in the thickest press among them of Orkney : and there he did so marvellous deeds of arms that all men had wonder of him, for there might none stand him a stroke. When Sir Tristram saw Sir Palamides do such deeds he marvelled, and said to himself, He is weary of my company. So Sir Tristram beheld him a great while, and did but little else, for the noise and cry was so huge and great that Sir Tristram marvelled from whence came the strength that Sir Palamides had there in the field. Sir, said Sir Gareth unto Sir Tristram, remember ye not of the words that Sir Dinadan said to you yesterday, when he called you coward ? For sooth, Sir, he said it for none ill ; for ye are the man in the world that he most loveth, and all that he said was for your worship. And therefore, said Sir Gareth to Sir Tristram, let me know this day what ye be ; and wonder ye not so upon Sir Palamides, for he enforceth himself to win all the worship and honour from you. I may well believe it, said Sir Tristram, and since I understand his evil will and his envy ye shall see, if that I enforce myself, that the noise shall be left that now is upon him.

Then Sir Tristram rode into the thickest of the press, and then he did so marvellously well, and did so great deeds of arms, that all men said that Sir Tristram did double so much deeds of arms that Sir Palamides had done aforehand. And then the noise went plain from Sir Palamides, and all the people cried upon Sir Tristram. See, said the people, how Sir Tristram smiteth down with his spear so many knights. And see, said they all, how many knights he smiteth down with his sword, and of how many knights he rashed off their helms and their shields. And so he beat them all of Orkney afore him. How now, said Sir Launcelot unto king Arthur, I told you that this day there would a knight play his pageant. Yonder rideth a knight ye may see he doth knightly, for he hath strength and wind. Truly, said Arthur to Launcelot, ye say sooth, for I saw never a better knight, for he passeth far Sir Palamides. Sir, wit ye well, said Launcelot, it must be so of right, for it is himself that noble knight Sir Tristram. I may right well believe it, said Arthur. But when Sir Palamides heard the noise and the cry was turned from him he rode out on a part, and beheld Sir Tristram. And when Sir Palamides saw Sir Tristram do so marvellously well, he wept passingly sore for despite, for he wist well he should no worship win that day. For well knew Sir Palamides, when Sir Tristram would put forth his strength and his manhood, he should get but little worship that day.

CHAP. LXXV.

How Sir Tristram departed out of the field, and awaked Sir Dinadan, and changed his array into black.

THEN came king Arthur, and the king of Northgalis, and Sir Launcelot du Lake, and Sir Bleoberis, Sir Bors de Ganis, Sir Ector de Maris, these three knights came into the field with Sir Launcelot. And then Sir Launcelot with the three knights of his kin did so great deeds of arms, that all the noise began upon Sir Launcelot. And so they beat the king of Wales and the king of Scots far aback, and made them to avoid the field. But Sir Tristram and Sir Gareth abode still in the field, and endured all that ever there came, that all men had wonder that any knight might endure so many strokes. But ever Sir Launcelot and his three kinsmen, by the commandment of Sir Launcelot, forbare Sir Tristram. Then said Sir Arthur, Is that Sir Palamides that endureth so well? Nay, said Sir Launcelot, wit ye well it is the good knight Sir Tristram, for yonder ye may see Sir Palamides beholdeth, and hoveth, and doth little or nought. And, sir, ye shall understand that Sir Tristram weeneth this day to beat us all out of the field. And as for me, said Sir Launcelot, I shall not beat him, beat him who so will. Sir, said Launcelot unto Arthur, ye may see how Sir Palamides hoveth yonder as though he were in a dream; wit ye well he is full heavy that Tristram doth such deeds of arms. Then is he but a fool, said Arthur, for never was Sir Palamides, nor never shall be, of such prowess as Sir Tristram. And if he have any envy at Sir Tristram, and cometh in with him upon his side, he is a false knight. As the king and Sir Launcelot thus spake, Sir Tristram rode privily out of the press, that none espied him but La Beale Isoud and Sir Palamides, for they two would not let of their eyes upon Sir Tristram.

And when Sir Tristram came to his pavilions, he found Sir Dinadan in his bed asleep. Awake, said Tristram, ye ought to be ashamed so to sleep, when knights have ado in the field. Then Sir Dinadan arose lightly, and said, What will ye that I shall do? Make you ready, said Sir Tristram, to ride with me into the field. So when Sir Dinadan was armed he looked upon Sir Tristram's helm and on his shield, and when he saw so many strokes upon his helm and upon his shield, he said, In good time was I thus asleep; for had I been with you I must needs for shame there have followed you, more for shame than any prowess that is in me, that I see well now by those strokes, that I should have been truly beaten as I was yesterday. Leave your jests, said Sir Tristram, and come off, that we were in the field again. What, said Sir Dinadan, is your heart up? Yesterday ye fared as though ye had dreamed. So then Sir Tristram was arrayed in black harness. Oh, said Sir Dinadan, what aileth you this day? me seemeth ye be wilder than ye were yesterday. Then smiled Sir Tristram, and said to Dinadan, Await well upon me: if ye see me over-matched look that ye be ever behind me, and I shall make you ready way. So Sir Tristram and Sir Dinadan took their horses. All this espied Sir Palamides, both their going and their coming, and so did La Beale Isoud, for she knew Sir Tristram above all other.

CHAP. LXXVI.

How Sir Palamides changed his shield and his armour for to hurt Sir Tristram, and how Sir Launcelot did to Sir Tristram.

THEN when Sir Palamides saw that Sir Tristram was disguised, then he thought to do him a shame. So Sir Palamides rode to a knight that was sore wounded, that sat under a fair well from the field. Sir knight, said Sir Palamides, I pray you to lend me your armour and your shield, for mine is over well known in this field, and that hath done me great damage, and ye shall have mine armour and my shield, that is as sure as yours. I will well, said the knight, that ye have mine armour and my shield, if they may do you any avail. So Sir Palamides armed him hastily in that knight's armour, and his shield that shone as any crystal or silver, and so he came riding into the field. And then there was neither Sir Tristram nor none of king Arthur's party that knew Sir Palamides.

And right so as Sir Palamides was come into the field Sir Tristram smote down three knights, even in the sight of Sir Palamides. And then Sir Palamides rode against Sir Tristram, and either met other with great spears, that they brast to their hands. And then they dashed together with swords eagerly. Then Sir Tristram had marvel what knight he was that did battle so knightly with him. Then was Sir Tristram wroth, for he felt him passing strong, so that he deemed he might not have ado with the remnant of the knights, because of the strength of Sir Palamides. So they lashed together, and gave many sad strokes together, and many knights marvelled what knight he might be that so encountered with the black knight, Sir Tristram. Full well knew La Beale Isoud that there was Sir Palamides that fought with Sir Tristram, for she espied all in her window where that she stood, as Sir Palamides changed his harness with the wounded knight. And then she began to weep so heartily for the despite of Sir Palamides that there she swooned. Then came in Sir Launcelot with the knights of Orkney; and when the other party had espied Sir Launcelot they cried, Return, return, here cometh Sir Launcelot du Lake. So there came knights and said, Sir Launcelot, ye must needs fight with yonder knight in the black harness (that was Sir Tristram), for he hath almost overcome that good knight that fighteth with him with the silver shield (that was Sir Palamides). Then Sir Launcelot rode betwixt Sir Tristram and Sir Palamides, and Sir Launcelot said to Palamides, Sir knight, let me have the battle, for ye have need to be reposed. Sir Palamides knew Sir Launcelot well, and so did Sir Tristram. But because Sir Launcelot was a far hardier knight than himself therefore he was glad, and suffered Sir Launcelot to fight with Sir Tristram. For well wist he that Sir Launcelot knew not Sir Tristram, and there he hoped that Sir Launcelot should beat or shame Sir Tristram, whereof Sir Palamides was full fain. And so Sir

Launcelot gave Sir Tristram many sad strokes, but Sir Launcelot knew not Sir Tristram, but Sir Tristram knew well Sir Launcelot. And thus they fought long together, that La Beale Isoud was well out of her mind for sorrow. Then Sir Dinadan told Sir Gareth how that knight in the black harness was Sir Tristram, and this is Launcelot that fighteth with him, that must needs have the better of him, for Sir Tristram hath had too much travail this day. Then let us smite him down, said Sir Gareth. So it is better that we do, said Sir Dinadan, than Sir Tristram be shamed. For yonder hoveth the strong knight with the silver shield to fall upon Sir Tristram if need be. Then forthwithal Gareth rushed upon Sir Launcelot, and gave him a great stroke upon his helm so hard that he was astonied. And then came Sir Dinadan with a spear, and he smote Sir Launcelot such a buffet that horse and all fell to the earth. Alas, said Sir Tristram to Sir Gareth and Sir Dinadan, fie for shame, why did ye smite down so good a knight as he is, and namely when I had ado with him? Now ye do yourself great shame, and him no dis-worship: for I held him reasonable hot though ye had not holpen me. Then came Sir Palamides that was disguised, and smote down Sir Dinadan from his horse. Then Sir Launcelot, because Sir Dinadan had smitten him aforehand, then Sir Launcelot assailed Sir Dinadan passing sore, and Sir Dinadan defended him mightily. But well understood Sir Tristram that Sir Dinadan might not endure Sir Launcelot, wherefore Sir Tristram was sorry. Then came Sir Palamides fresh upon Sir Tristram. And when Sir Tristram saw him come, he thought to deliver him at once, because that he would help Sir Dinadan, because he stood in great peril with Sir Launcelot. Then Sir Tristram hurtled unto Sir Palamides, and gave him a great buffet, and then Sir Tristram gat Sir Palamides, and pulled him down underneath him. And so fell Sir Tristram with him, and Sir Tristram lept up lightly, and left Sir Palamides, and went betwixt Sir Launcelot and Dinadan, and then they began to do battle together. Right so Sir Dinadan gat Sir Tristram's horse, and said on high, that Sir Launcelot might hear it, My lord Sir Tristram, take your horse. And when Sir Launcelot heard him name Sir Tristram, Alas, said Sir Launcelot, what have I done? I am dishonoured. Ah, my lord Sir Tristram, said Launcelot, why were ye disguised? ye have put yourself in great peril this day. But, I pray you, noble knight, to pardon me, for and I had known you we had not done this battle. Sir, said Sir Tristram, this is not the first kindness ye shewed me. So they were both horsed again. Then all the people on the one side gave Sir Launcelot the honour and the degree, and on the other side all the people gave to the noble knight Sir Tristram the honour and the degree. But Launcelot said nay thereto:—For I am not worthy to have this honour, for I will report me unto all knights that Sir Tristram hath been longer in the field than I, and he hath smitten down many more knights this day than I have done; and therefore I will give Sir Tristram my voice and my name, and so I pray all my lords and fellows so to do. Then there was the whole voice of dukes and earls, barons and knights, that Sir Tristram this day is proved the best knight.

CHAP. LXXVII.

How Sir Tristram departed with La Beale Isoud, and how Palamides followed and excused him.

THEN they blew unto lodging, and queen Isoud was led unto her pavilions. But wit you well she was wroth out of measure with Sir Palamides, for she saw all his treason from the beginning to the ending. And all this while neither Sir Tristram, neither Sir Gareth, nor Dinadan, knew not of the treason of Sir Palamides. But afterward ye shall hear that there befel the greatest debate betwixt Sir Tristram and Sir Palamides that might be. So when the tournament was done, Sir Tristram, Gareth, and Dinadan rode with La Beale Isoud to these pavilions. And ever Sir Palamides rode with them in their company disguised as he was. But when Sir Tristram had espied him, that he was the same knight with the shield of silver that held him so hot that day, Sir knight, said Sir Tristram, wit you well here is none that hath need of your fellowship, and therefore I pray you depart from us. Sir Palamides answered again, as though he had not known Sir Tristram, Wit ye well, sir knight, from this fellowship will I never depart, for one of the best knights of the world commanded me to be in this company, and till he discharge me of my service I will not be discharged. By that Sir Tristram knew that it was Sir Palamides. Ah Sir Palamides, said the noble knight Sir Tristram, are ye such a knight? Ye have been named wrong, for ye have long been called a gentle knight, and as this day ye have shewed me great ungentleness, for ye had almost brought me unto my death. But as for you I suppose I should have done well enough, but Sir Launcelot with you was overmuch, for I know no knight living but Sir Launcelot is over good for him, and he will do his uttermost. Alas, said Sir Palamides, are ye my lord Sir Tristram? Yea, sir, and that ye know well enough. By my knighthood, said Palamides, until now I knew you not, for I wend that ye had been the king of Ireland; for well I wot that ye bare his arms. His arms I bare, said Sir Tristram, and that will I stand by, for I won them once in a field of a full noble knight, his name was Sir Marhaus, and with great pain I won that knight, for there was none other recover, but Sir Marhaus died through false leeches, and yet was he never yielden to me. Sir, said Palamides, I wend ye had been turned upon Sir Launcelot's party, and that caused me to turn. Ye say well, said Sir Tristram, and so I take you, and I forgive you. So then they rode into their pavilions, and when they were alight they un-

armed them, and washed their faces and hands, and so went to meat, and were set at their table. But when Isoud saw Sir Palamides she changed then her colours, and for wrath she might not speak. Anon Sir Tristram espied her countenance, and said, Madam, for what cause make ye us such cheer? we have been sore travailed this day. Mine own lord, said La Beale Isoud, be ye not displeased with me, for I may none otherwise do, for I saw this day how ye were betrayed, and nigh brought to your death. Truly, sir, I saw every deal, how, and in what wise; and therefore, sir, how should I suffer in your presence such a felon and traitor as Sir Palamides. For I saw him with mine eyes how he beheld you when ye went out of the field. For ever he hoved still upon his horse till he saw you come in againward. And then forthwithal I saw him ride to the hurt knight, and change harness with him, and then straight I saw him how he rode into the field. And anon as he had found you he encountered with you, and thus wilfully Sir Palamides did battle with you, and as for him, sir, I was not greatly afeard, but I dread sore Launcelot, that knew you not. Madam, said Palamides, ye may say what so ye will, I may not contrary you, but by my knighthood I knew not Sir Tristram. Sir Palamides, said Sir Tristram, I will take your excuse, but well I wot ye spared me but little, but all is pardoned on my part. Then La Beale Isoud held down her head, and said no more at that time.

CHAP. LXXVIII.

How king Arthur and Sir Launcelot came into their pavilions as they sat at supper; and of Palamides.

AND therewithal two knights armed came unto the pavilion, and there they alight both, and came in armed at all pieces. Fair knights, said Sir Tristram, ye are to blame to come thus armed at all pieces upon me while we are at our meat. If ye would anything, when we were in the field there might ye have eased your hearts. Not so, said the one of those knights, we come not for that intent; but wit ye well, Sir Tristram, we be come hither as your friends. And I am come here, said the one, for to see you, and this knight is come for to see La Beale Isoud. Then, said Sir Tristram, I require you do off your helms, that I may see you. That will we do at your desire, said the knights. And when their helms were off, Sir Tristram thought he should know them. Then said Sir Dinadan privily unto Sir Tristram, Sir, that is Sir Launcelot du Lake that spake unto you first, and the other is my lord king Arthur. Then said Sir Tristram unto La Beale Isoud, Madam, arise, for here is my lord king Arthur. Then the king and the queen kissed, and Sir Launcelot and Sir Tristram braced either other in arms, and then there was joy without measure, and at the request of La Beale Isoud king Arthur and Launcelot were unarmed. And then there was merry talking.

Madam, said Sir Arthur, it is many a day sithen that I have desired to see you. For ye have been praised so far, and now I dare say ye are the fairest that ever I saw; and Sir Tristram is as fair and as good a knight as any that I know, therefore me beseemeth ye are well beset together. Sir, I thank you, said the noble knight Sir Tristram, and Isoud; of your great goodness and largesse ye are peerless. Thus they talked of many things, and of all the whole justs. But for what cause, said king Arthur, were ye, Sir Tristram, against us? Ye are a knight of the Table Round; of right we should have been with us. Sir, said Sir Tristram, here is Dinadan and Sir Gareth your own nephew caused me to be against you. My lord Arthur, said Gareth, I may well bear the blame, but it were Sir Tristram's own deeds. That may I repent, said Sir Dinadan, for this unhappy Sir Tristram brought us to this tournament, and many great buffets he caused us to have. Then the king and Launcelot laughed that they might not

sit. What knight was that, said Arthur, that held you so short, this with the shield of silver? Sir, said Sir Tristram, here he sitteth at this board. What, said Arthur, was it Sir Palamides? Wit ye well it was he, said La Beale Isoud. Truly, said Arthur, that was unknightly done of you of so good a knight, for I have heard many people call you a courteous knight. Sir, said Palamides, I knew not Sir Tristram, for he was so disguised. Truly, said Launcelot, it may well be, for I knew not Sir Tristram, but I marvel why ye turned on our party. That was done for the same cause, said Launcelot. As for that, said Sir Tristram, I have pardoned him, and I would be right loth to leave his fellowship, for I love right well his company. So they left off, and talked of other things. And in the evening king Arthur and Sir Launcelot departed unto their lodging. But wit ye well Sir Palamides had envy heartily, for all that night he had never rest in his bed, but wailed and wept out of measure. So on the morn Sir Tristram, Gareth, and Dinadan arose early, and then they went unto Sir Palamides' chamber, and there they found him fast on sleep, for he had all night watched. And it was seen upon his cheeks that he had wept full sore. Say nothing, said Sir Tristram, for I am sure he hath taken anger and sorrow for the rebuke that I gave to him, and La Beale Isoud.

CHAP. LXXIX.

How Sir Tristram and Sir Palamides did the next day, and how king Arthur was unhorsed.

THEN Sir Tristram let call Sir Palamides, and bade him make him ready, for it was time to go to the field. When they were ready they were armed and clothed all in red, both Isoud and all they. And so they led her passing freshly through the field, into the priory where was her lodging. And then they heard three blasts blow, and every king and knight dressed him unto the field; and the first that was ready to just was Sir Palamides and Sir Kainus le Strange, a knight of the Table Round. And so they two encountered together, but Sir Palamides smote Sir Kainus so hard, that he smote him quite over his horse croup: and forth withal Sir Palamides smote down another knight, and brake then his spear, and pulled out his sword and did wonderly well. And then the noise began greatly upon Sir Palamides. Lo, said king Arthur, yonder Palamides beginneth to play his pageant. Truly, said Arthur, he is a passing good knight. And right as they stood talking thus, in came Sir Tristram as thunder, and he encountered Sir Kay the seneschal, and there he smote him down quite from his horse, and with that same spear Sir Tristram smote down three knights more; and then he pulled out his sword and did marvellously. Then the noise and cry changed from Sir Palamides and turned to Sir Tristram, and all the people cried, O Tristram! O Tristram! And then was Sir Palamides clean forgotten. How now, said Launcelot unto Arthur, yonder rideth a knight that playeth his pageants. Truly, said Arthur to Launcelot, ye shall see this day that yonder two knights shall here do this day wonders. Sir, said Launcelot, the one knight waiteth upon the other, and enforceth himself through envy to pass the noble knight Sir Tristram, and he knoweth not of the privy envy the which Sir Palamides hath to him. For all that the noble Sir Tristram doth is through clean knighthood. And then Sir Gareth and Dinadan did wonderly great deeds of arms as two noble knights, so that king Arthur spake of them great honour and worship; and the kings and knights of Sir Tristram's side did passing well, and held them truly together. Then Sir Arthur and Sir Launcelot took their horses and dressed them, and gat into the thickest of the press. And there Sir Tristram unknowing smote down king Arthur, and then Sir Launcelot would have rescued him, but there were so many upon Sir Launcelot that they pulled him down from his horse. And then the king of Ireland and the king of Scots, with their knights, did their pain to take king Arthur and Sir Launcelot prisoner. When Sir Launcelot heard them say so, he fared as it had been an hungry lion, for he fared so that no knight durst nigh him. Then came Sir Ector de Maris, and he bare a spear against Sir Palamides, and brake it upon him all to shivers. And then Sir Ector came again, and gave Sir Palamides such a dash with a sword that he stooped down upon his saddle-bow. And forth withal Sir Ector pulled down Sir Palamides under his feet. And then Sir Ector de Maris gat Sir Launcelot du Lake an horse, and brought it to him, and bad him mount upon him. But Sir Palamides lept afore, and gat the the horse by the bridle, and lept into the saddle. Truly, said Launcelot, ye are better worthy to have that horse than I. Then Sir Ector brought Sir Launcelot another horse. Gramercy, said Launcelot unto his brother. And so when he was horsed again, with one spear he smote down four knights. And then Sir Launcelot brought to king Arthur one of the best of the four horses. Then Sir Launcelot with king Arthur and a few of his knights of Sir Launcelot's kin, did marvellous deeds; for that time, as the book recordeth, Sir Launcelot smote down and pulled down thirty knights. Notwithstanding, the other part held them so fast together that king Arthur and his knights were overmatched. And when Sir Tristram saw that, what labour king Arthur and his knights, in especial the noble deeds that Sir Launcelot did with his own hands, he marvelled greatly.

CHAP. LXXX.

How Sir Tristram turned to king Arthur's side, and how Sir Palamides would not.

THEN Sir Tristram called unto him Sir Palamides, Sir Gareth, and Sir Dinadan, and said thus to them, My fair fellows, wit ye well that I will turn unto king Arthur's party, for I saw never so few men do so well, and it will be shame unto us knights that be of the Round Table to see our lord king Arthur, and that noble knight Sir Launcelot, to be dishonoured. It will be well done, said Sir Gareth and Sir Dinadan. Do your best, said Palamides, for I will not change my party that I came in withal. That is for my sake, said Sir Tristram : speed you well in your journey. And so departed Sir Palamides from them. Then Sir Tristram, Sir Gareth, and Sir Dinadan, turned with Sir Launcelot. And then Sir Launcelot smote down the king of Ireland quite from his horse; and so Sir Launcelot smote down the king of Scots, and the king of Wales. And then Sir Arthur ran unto Sir Palamides, and smote him quite from his horse. And then Sir Tristram bare down all that he met. Sir Gareth and Sir Dinadan did there as noble knights. Then all the parties began to flee. Alas, said Palamides, that ever I should see this day, for now have I lost all the worship that I wan. And then Sir Palamides went his way wailing, and so withdrew him till he came to a well, and there he put his horse from him, and did off his armour, and wailed and wept like as he had been a wood man.

Then many knights gave the prize to Sir Tristram, and there were many that gave the prize unto Sir Launcelot. Fair lords, said Sir Tristram, I thank you of the honour ye would give me, but I pray you heartily that ye would give your voice to Sir Launcelot, for by my faith, said Sir Tristram, I will give Sir Launcelot my voice. But Sir Launcelot would not have it. And so the prize was given betwixt them both. Then every man rode to his lodging. And Sir Bleoberis and Sir Ector rode with Sir Tristram and La Beale Isoud unto her pavilions. Then as Sir Palamides was at the well, wailing and weeping, there came by him fleeing the king of Wales, and of Scotland, and they saw Sir Palamides in that rage. Alas, said they, that so noble a man as ye be should be in this array. And then those kings gat Sir Palamides' horse again, and made him to arm him and mount upon his horse, and so he rode with them, making great dole. So when Sir Palamides came

nigh the pavilions there as Sir Tristram and La Beale Isoud were in, then Sir Palamides prayed the two kings to abide him there the while that he spake with Sir Tristram. And when he came to the port of the pavilions, Sir Palamides said on high, Where art thou, Sir Tristram de Liones? Sir, said Dinadan, that is Palamides. What, Sir Palamides, will ye not come in here among us? Fie on thee traitor, said Sir Palamides, for wit you well, and it were daylight as it is night, I would slay thee with mine own hands. And if ever I may get thee, said Palamides, thou shalt die for this day's deed. Sir Palamides, said Sir Tristram, ye blame me with wrong, for had ye done as I did ye had won worship. But since ye give me so large warning I shall be well ware of you. Fie on thee traitor, said Palamides, and therewith departed. Then on the morn Sir Tristram, Bleoberis, and Sir Ector de Maris, Sir Gareth, Sir Dinadan, what by water and what by land, they brought La Beale Isoud unto Joyous Gard, and there reposed them a seven night, and made all the mirths and disports that they could devise. And king Arthur and his knights drew unto Camelot, and Sir Palamides rode with the two kings; and ever he made the greatest dole that any man could think. For he was not all only so dolorous for the departing from La Beale Isoud, but he was a part as sorrowful to depart from the fellowship of Sir Tristram, for Sir Tristram was so kind and so gentle that when Sir Palamides remembered him thereof he might never be merry.

CHAP. LXXXI.

How Sir Bleoberis and Sir Ector reported to queen Guenever of the beauty of La Beale Isoud.

So at the seven night's end Sir Bleoberis and Sir Ector departed from Sir Tristram and from the queen, and these two good knights had great gifts, and Sir Gareth and Sir Dinadan abode with Sir Tristram. And when Sir Bleoberis and Sir Ector were come there as the queen Guenever was lodged in a castle by the sea side, and through the grace of God the queen was recovered from her malady, then she asked the two knights from whence they came. They said they came from Sir Tristram and from La Beale Isoud. How doth Sir Tristram, said the queen, and La Beale Isoud? Truly, said those two knights, he doth as a noble knight should do, and as for the queen Isoud, she is peerless of all ladies; for to speak of her beauty, bounty, and mirth, and of her goodness, we saw never her match as far as we have ridden and gone. Oh mercy, said queen Guenever, so saith all the people that have seen her and spoken with her. Would that I had part of her conditions. And it is misfortuned me of my sickness while that tournament endured; and, as I suppose, I shall never see in all my life such an assembly of knights and ladies as ye have done. Then the knights told her how Sir Palamides wan the degree at the first day with great noblesse; and the second day Sir Tristram wan the degree; and the third day Sir Launcelot wan the degree. Well, said queen Guenever, who did best all these three days? Truly, said these knights, Sir Launcelot and Sir Tristram had least dishonour: And wit ye well Sir Palamides did passing well and mightily, but he turned against the party that he came in withal, and that caused him to lose a great part of his worship, for it seemed that Sir Palamides is passing envious. Then shall he never win worship, said queen Guenever, for, and it happeth an envious man once to win worship, he shall be dishonoured twice therefore. And for this cause all men of worship hate an envious man, and will shew him no favour. And he that is courteous, kind, and gentle, hath favour in every place.

CHAP. LXXXII.

How Sir Palamides complained by a well, and how Epinogris came and found him, and of their both sorrows.

Now leave we of this matter, and speak we of Sir Palamides that rode and lodged him with the two kings, whereof the kings were heavy. Then the king of Ireland sent a man of his to Sir Palamides, and gave him a great courser. And the king of Scotland gave him great gifts, and fain they would have had Sir Palamides to have abiden with them, but in no wise he would abide, and so he departed and rode as adventures would guide him, till it was nigh noon. And then in a forest by a well Sir Palamides saw where lay a fair wounded knight, and his horse bound by him, and that knight made the greatest dole that ever he heard man make, for ever he wept and sighed as though he would die. Then Sir Palamides rode near him, and saluted him mildly and said, Fair knight, why wail ye so? let me lie down and wail with you, for doubt ye not I am much more heavier than ye are; for I dare say, said Palamides, that my sorrow is an hundred fold more than yours is, and therefore let us complain either to other. First, said the wounded knight, I require you tell me your name, for and thou be none of the noble knights of the Round Table thou shalt never know my name, whatsoever come of me. Fair knight, said Palamides, such as I am, be it better or be it worse, wit thou well that my name is Sir Palamides, son and heir unto king Astlabor, and Sir Safere and Sir Segwarides are my two brethren, and wit thou well as for myself I was never christened, but my two brethren are truly christened. Oh noble knight, said that knight, well is me that I have met with you, and wit ye well my name is Epinogris, the king's son of Northumberland. Now sit down, said Epinogris, and let us either complain to other. Then Sir Palamides began his complaint. Now shall I tell you, said Palamides, what woe I endure. I love the fairest queen and lady that ever bare life, and wit ye well her name is La Beale Isoud, king Mark's wife of Cornwall. That is great folly, said Sir Epinogris, for to love queen Isoud, for one of the best knights of the world loveth her, that is Sir Tristram de Liones. That is truth, said Palamides, for no man knoweth that matter better than I do, for I have been in Sir Tristram's fellowship this month, and with La Beale Isoud together; and alas, said Palamides, unhappy man that I am, now have I lost the fellowship of Sir Tristram for ever, and the love of La Beale Isoud for ever, and I am never like to see her more, and Sir Tristram and I be either to other mortal enemies. Well, said Epinogris, sith that ye loved La Beale Isoud, loved she you ever again, by anything that ye could think or wit? Nay, by my knighthood, said Palamides, I never espied that ever she loved me more than all the world. But the last day she gave me the greatest rebuke that ever I had, the which shall never go from my heart, and yet I well deserved that rebuke, for I had not done knightly, and therefore I have lost the love of her and of Sir Tristram for ever. And I have many times enforced myself to do many deeds for La Beale Isoud's sake, and she was the causer of my worship winning. Alas, said Sir Palamides, now have I lost all the worship that ever I wan, for never shall me befal such prowess as I had in the fellowship of Sir Tristram.

CHAP. LXXXIII.

How Sir Palamides brought to Sir Epinogris his lady; and how Sir Palamides and Sir Safere were assailed.

NAY, nay, said Epinogris, your sorrow is but a jest to my sorrow, for I rejoiced my lady and wan her with my hands, and lost her again, alas that day. Thus first I wan her, said Epinogris: my lady was an earl's daughter, and as the earl and two knights came from the tournament of Lonazep, for her sake I set upon this earl and on his two knights, my lady there being present, and so by fortune there I slew the earl and one of the knights, and the other knight fled, and so I had my lady. And on the morn, as she and I reposed us at this well side, there came there to me an errant knight, his name was Sir Helior le Preuse, an hardy knight; and this Sir Helior challenged me to fight for my lady. And then we went to battle, first upon horse and after on foot. But at the last Sir Helior wounded me so that he left me for dead, and so he took my lady with him. And thus my sorrow is more than yours, for I have rejoiced, and ye rejoiced never. That is truth, said Sir Palamides, but sith I can never recover myself, I shall promise you, if I can meet with Sir Helior I shall get you your lady again, or else he shall beat me. Then Sir Palamides made Sir Epinogris to take his horse, and so they rode to an hermitage, and there Sir Epinogris rested him. And in the mean while Sir Palamides walked privily out, to rest him under the leaves; and there beside he saw a knight come riding with a shield that he had seen Sir Ector de Maris bear aforehand, and there came after him a ten knights, and so these ten knights hoved under the leaves for heat. And anon after there came a knight, with a green shield and therein a white lion, leading a lady upon a palfrey. Then this knight with the green shield, that seemed to be master of the ten knights, he rode fiercely after Sir Helior; for it was he that hurt Sir Epinogris. And when he came nigh Sir Helior he bad him defend his lady. I will defend her, said Helior, unto my power. And so they ran together so mightily that either of these two knights smote other down, horse and all, to the earth, and then they wan up lightly and drew their swords and their shields, and lashed together mightily more than an hour. All this Sir Palamides saw and beheld, but ever at the last the knight with Sir Ector's shield was bigger, and at the last this knight smote Sir Helior down, and then that knight unlaced his helm to have stricken off his head. And then he cried mercy, and prayed him to save his life, and bad him take his lady.

Then Sir Palamides dressed him up, because he wist well that that same lady was Epinogris' lady, and he promised him to help him. Then Sir Palamides went straight to that lady, and took her by the hand, and asked her whether she knew a knight that hight Epinogris. Alas, she said, that ever he knew me, or I him, for I have for his sake lost my worship, and also his life grieveth me most of all. Not so, lady, said Palamides, come on with me, for here is Epinogris in this hermitage. Ah, well is me, said the lady, and he be on live. Whither wilt thou with that lady? said the knight with Sir Ector's shield. I will do with her what me list, said Palamides. Wit you well, said that knight, thou speakest over large, though thou seemest me to have at advantage, because thou sawest me do battle but late. Thou weenest, sir knight, to have that lady away from me so lightly; nay, think it never not, and thou were as good a knight as is Sir Launcelot, or as is Sir Tristram, or Sir Palamides, but thou shalt win her dearer than ever did I. And so they went unto battle upon foot, and there they gave many sad strokes, and either wounded other passing sore; and thus they fought still more than an hour. Then Sir Palamides had marvel what knight he might be that was so strong and so well breathed during, and thus said Palamides: Knight, I require thee tell me thy name. Wit thou well, said that knight, I dare tell thee my name, so that thou wilt tell me thy name. I will, said Palamides. Truly, said that knight, my name is Safere, son of king Astlabor, and Sir Palamides and Sir Segwarides are my brethren. Now, and wit thou well my name is Sir Palamides. Then Sir Safere kneeled down upon his knees, and prayed him of mercy; and then they unlaced their helms, and either kissed other weeping. And in the mean while Sir Epinogris arose out of his bed, and heard them by the strokes, and so he armed him to help Sir Palamides if need were.

CHAP. LXXXIV.

How Sir Palamides and Sir Safere conducted Sir Epinogris to his castle, and of other adventures.

THEN Sir Palamides took the lady by the hand and brought her to Sir Epinogris, and there was great joy betwixt them, for either swooned for joy. When they were met,—Fair knight and lady, said Sir Safere, it were pity to depart you, Heaven send you joy either of other. Gramercy, gentle knight, said Epinogris, and much more thank be to my lord Sir Palamides, that thus hath through his prowess made me to get my lady. Then Sir Epinogris required Sir Palamides and Sir Safere his brother to ride with them unto his castle, for the safeguard of his person. Sir, said Palamides, we will be ready to conduct you, because that ye are sore wounded. And so was Epinogris and his lady horsed, and his lady behind him, upon a soft ambler.

And then they rode unto his castle, where they had great cheer, and joy as great as ever Sir Palamides and Sir Safere ever had in their life days. So on the morn Sir Safere and Sir Palamides departed, and rode as fortune led them: and so they rode all that day until afternoon. And at the last they heard a great weeping and a great noise down in a manor. Sir, said then Sir Safere, let us wit what noise this is. I will well, said Sir Palamides. And so they rode forth till that they came to a fair gate of a manor, and there sat an old man saying his prayers and beads. Then Sir Palamides and Sir Safere alight, and left their horses, and went within the gates, and there they saw full many goodly men weeping. Fair sirs, said Sir Palamides, wherefore weep ye, and make this sorrow? Anon one of the knights of the castle beheld Sir Palamides and knew him, and then went to his fellows and said, Fair fellows, wit ye well all, we have in this castle the same knight that slew our lord at Lonazep, for I know him well, it is Sir Palamides. Then they went unto harness all that might bear harness, some on horseback and some on foot, to the number of threescore. And when they were ready, they came freshly upon Sir Palamides and upon Sir Safere with a great noise, and said thus, Keep thee,

Sir Palamides, for thou art known, and by right thou must be dead, for thou hast slain our lord, and therefore, wit ye well, we will slay thee, therefore defend thee. Then Sir Palamides and Sir Safere the one set his back to other, and gave many great strokes, and took many great strokes; and thus they fought with a twenty knights and forty gentlemen and yeomen, nigh two hours. But at the last, though they were loth, Sir Palamides and Sir Safere were taken and yielden, and put in a strong prison. And within three days twelve knights passed upon them, and they found Sir Palamides guilty, and Sir Safere not guilty, of their lord's death. And when Sir Safere should be delivered, there was great dole betwixt Sir Palamides and him, and many piteous complaints that Sir Safere made at his departing, that there is no maker can rehearse the tenth part. Fair brother, said Palamides, let be thy dolour and thy sorrow: and if I be ordained to die a shameful death, welcome be it; but and I had wist of this death that I am doomed unto, I should never have been yielden. So Sir Safere departed from his brother with the greatest dolour and sorrow that ever made knight. And on the morn they of the castle ordained twelve knights to ride with Sir Palamides unto the father of the same knight that Sir Palamides slew; and so they bound his legs under an old steed's belly. And then they rode with Sir Palamides unto a castle by the sea side, that hight Pelownes, and there Sir Palamides should have justice: thus was their ordinance. And so they rode with Sir Palamides fast by the castle of Joyous Gard; and as they passed by that castle, there came riding out of that castle by them one that knew Sir Palamides; and when that knight saw Sir Palamides bounden upon a crooked courser, the knight asked Sir Palamides for what cause he was led so. Ah, my fair fellow and knight, said Palamides, I ride toward my death, for the slaying of a knight at a tournament of Lonazep; and if I had not departed from my lord Sir Tristram, as I ought not to have done, now might I have been sure to have had my life saved. But I pray you, sir knight, recommand me unto my lord Sir Tristram, and unto my lady queen Isoud, and say to them, if ever I trespassed to them I ask them forgiveness. And also, I beseech you, recommand me unto my lord king Arthur, and unto all the fellowship of the Round Table, unto my power. Then that knight wept for pity of Sir Palamides; and therewithal he rode unto Joyous Gard as fast as his horse might run. And lightly that knight descended down off his horse, and went unto Sir Tristram, and there he told him all as ye have heard: and ever the knight wept as he had been mad.

CHAP. LXXXV.

How Sir Tristram made him ready to rescue Sir Palamides, but Sir Launcelot rescued him or he came.

WHEN Sir Tristram heard how Sir Palamides went to his death, he was heavy to hear that, and said, Howbeit that I am wrath with Sir Palamides, yet will not I suffer him to die so shameful a death, for he is a full noble knight. And then anon Sir Tristram was armed, and took his horse, and two squires with him, and rode a great pace toward the castle of Pelownes, where Sir Palamides was judged to death. And these twelve knights that led Sir Palamides passed by a well whereas Sir Launcelot was, which was alight there, and had tied his horse to a tree, and taken off his helm to drink of that well; and when he saw these knights, Sir Launcelot put on his helm, and suffered them to pass by him. And then was he ware of Sir Palamides bounden, and led shamefully to his death. Oh, mercy, said Launcelot, what misadventure is befallen him, that he is thus led toward his death? Forsooth, said Launcelot, it were shame to me to suffer this noble knight so to die and I might help him, therefore I will help him whatsoever come of it, or else I shall die for Sir Palamides' sake.

And then Sir Launcelot mounted upon his horse, and gat his spear in his hand, and rode after the twelve knights that led Sir Palamides. Fair knights, said Sir Launcelot, whither lead ye that knight? it beseemeth him full ill to ride bounden. Then these twelve knights suddenly turned their horses, and said to Sir Launcelot, Sir knight, we counsel thee not to meddle with this knight, for he hath deserved death, and unto death he is judged. That me repenteth, said Launcelot, that I may not ransom him with fairness, for he is over good a knight to die such a shameful death. And therefore, fair knights, said Sir Launcelot, keep you as well as ye can, for I will rescue that knight, or die for it. Then they began to dress their spears, and Sir Launcelot smote the foremost down, horse and man; and so he served three more with one spear, and then that spear brake; and therewithal Sir Launcelot drew his sword, and then he smote on the right hand and on the left hand: then within awhile he left none of those twelve knights but he had laid them to the earth, and the most part of them were sore wounded. And then Sir Launcelot took the best horse that he found, and loosed Sir Palamides, and set him upon that horse, and so they returned again unto Joyous Gard. And then was Sir Palamides ware of Sir Tristram how he came riding; and when Sir Launcelot saw him he knew him right well; but Sir Tristram knew not him, because Sir Launcelot had on his shoulder a golden shield. So Sir Launcelot made him ready to just with Sir Tristram, that Sir Tristram should not wend that he were Sir Launcelot. Then Sir Palamides cried on loud unto Sir Tristram, O my lord, I require you just not with this knight, for this good knight hath saved me from my death. When Sir Tristram heard him say so, he came a soft trotting pace toward them. And then Sir Palamides said, My lord Sir Tristram, much am I beholding unto you of your great goodness that would proffer your noble body to rescue me undeserved, for I have

greatly offended you. Notwithstanding, said Sir Palamides, here met we with this noble knight, that worshipfully and manly rescued me from twelve knights, and smote them down all, and wounded them sore.

CHAP. LXXXVI.

How Sir Tristram and Sir Launcelot, with Palamides, came to Joyous Gard; and of Palamides and Sir Tristram.

FAIR knight, said Sir Tristram unto Sir Launcelot, of whence be ye? I am a knight errant, said Sir Launcelot, that rideth to seek many adventures. What is your name? said Sir Tristram. Sir, at this time I will not tell you. Then Sir Launcelot said unto Sir Tristram and to Palamides, Now either of you are met together, I will depart from you. Not so, said Sir Tristram, I pray you of knighthood to ride with me unto my castle. Wit you well, said Sir Launcelot, I may not ride with you, for I have many deeds to do in other places, that at this time I may not abide with you. Truly, said Sir Tristram, I require you, as ye be a true knight to the order of knighthood, play you with me this night. Then Sir Tristram had a grant of Sir Launcelot: howbeit, though he had not desired him he would have ridden with them, or soon would come after them; for Sir Launcelot came for none other cause into that country but for to see Sir Tristram. And when they were come within Joyous Gard they alight, and their horses were led into a stable, and then they unarmed them. And when Sir Launcelot was unhelmed, Sir Tristram and Sir Palamides knew him. Then Sir Tristram took Sir Launcelot in arms, and so did La Beale Isoud; and Sir Palamides kneeled down upon his knees and thanked Sir Launcelot. When Sir Launcelot saw Sir Palamides kneel, he lightly took him up, and said thus; Wit thou well, Sir Palamides, I, and any knight in this land of worship, ought of very right succour and rescue so noble a knight as ye are proved and renowned throughout all this realm, endlong and overthwart. And then was there joy among them; and the oftener that Sir Palamides saw La Beale Isoud, the heavier he waxed day by day. Then Sir Launcelot within three or four days departed; and with him rode Sir Ector de Maris: and Dinadan and Sir Palamides were there left with Sir Tristram a two months and more. But ever Sir Palamides faded and mourned, that all men had marvel wherefore he faded so away. So upon a day, in the dawning Sir Palamides went into the forest by himself alone, and there he found a well, and then he looked into the well, and in the water he saw his own visage, how he was disturbed and defaded, nothing like that he was. What may this mean? said Sir Palamides. And thus he said to himself: Ah, Palamides, Palamides, why art thou diffaded, thou that was wont be called one of the fairest knights of the world? I will no more lead this life, for I love that I may never get nor recover. And therewithal he laid him down by the well. And then he began to make a rhyme of La Beale Isoud and him. And in the meanwhile Sir Tristram was that same day ridden into the forest to chase the hart of greese. But Sir Tristram would not ride on hunting never more unarmed because of Sir Breuse Sance Pité. And so as Sir Tristram rode into that forest up and down, he heard one sing marvellously loud; and that was Sir Palamides, that lay by the well. And then Sir Tristram rode softly thither, for he deemed there was some knight errant that was at the well.

And when Sir Tristram came nigh him, he descended down from his horse, and tied his horse fast till a tree, and then he came near him on foot. And anon he was ware where lay Sir Palamides by the well, and sang loud and merrily. And ever the complaints were of that noble queen La Beale Isoud, the which was marvellously and wonderfully well said, and full dolefully and piteously made. And all the whole song the noble knight Sir Tristram heard from the beginning to the ending, the which grieved and troubled him sore. But then at the last, when Sir Tristram had heard all Sir Palamides' complaints, he was wroth out of measure, and thought for to slay him there as he lay. Then Sir Tristram remembered himself that Sir Palamides was unarmed, and of the noble name that Sir Palamides had, and the noble name that himself had, and then he made a restraint of his anger, and so he went unto Sir Palamides a soft pace, and said, Sir Palamides, I have heard your complaint, and of thy treason that thou hast owed me so long. And wit thou well therefore thou shalt die. And if it were not for shame of knighthood thou shouldest not escape my hands, for now I know well thou hast awaited me with treason. Tell me, said Sir Tristram, how·thou wilt acquit thee. Sir, said Palamides, thus I will acquit me:—as for queen La Beale Isoud, ye shall wit well that I love her above all other ladies of the world; and well I wot it shall befal me as for her love as befel to the noble knight Sir Kehidius, that died for the love of La Beale Isoud; and now, Sir Tristram, I will that ye wit that I have loved La Beale Isoud many a day, and she hath been the causer of my worship. And else I had been the most simplest knight in the world. For by her, and because of her, I have won the worship that I have: for when I remembered me of La Beale Isoud, I wan the worship wheresoever I came, for the most part; and yet had I never reward nor bounty of her the days of my life, and yet have I been her knight guerdonless; and therefore Sir Tristram, as for any death I dread not, for I had as lief die as to live. And if I were armed as thou art, I should lightly do battle with thee. Well have ye uttered your treason, said Tristram. I have done to you no treason, said Sir Palamides, for love is free for all men, and though I have loved your lady she is my lady as well as yours: howbeit I have wrong if any wrong be, for ye rejoice her, and have her love, and so had I never, nor never am like to have. And yet shall I love her to the uttermost days of my life as well as ye.

CHAP. LXXXVII.

How there was a day set between Sir Tristram and Sir Palamides for to fight, and how Sir Tristram was hurt.

THEN, said Sir Tristram, I will fight with you unto the uttermost. I grant, said Palamides, for in a better quarrel keep I never to fight, for, and I die of your hands, of a better knight's hands may I not be slain. And sithen I understand that I shall never rejoice La Beale Isoud, I have as good will to die as to live. Then set ye a day, said Sir Tristram, that we shall do battle. This day fifteen days, said Palamides, will I meet with you here by, in the meadow under Joyous Gard. Fie for shame, said Sir Tristram, will ye set so long day? let us fight to-morn. Not so, said Palamides, for I am meagre, and have been long sick for the love of La Beale Isoud, and therefore I will repose me till I have my strength again. So then Sir Tristram and Sir Palamides promised faithfully to meet at the well that day fifteen days. I am remembered, said Sir Tristram to Palamides, that ye brake me once a promise when that I rescued you from Breuse Sance Pité and nine knights, and then ye promised me to meet at the peron and the grave beside Camelot, whereas at that time ye failed of your promise. Wit you well, said Palamides unto Sir Tristram, I was at that day in prison, so that I might not hold my promise. Truly, said Sir Tristram, and ye had holden your promise, this work had not been here now at this time. Right so departed Sir Tristram and Sir Palamides. And so Sir Palamides took his horse and his harness, and he rode unto king Arthur's court, and there Sir Palamides gat him four knights and four serjeants of arms, and so he returned againward unto Joyous Gard. And in the mean while Sir Tristram chased and hunted at all

manner of venery, and about three days afore the battle should be, as Sir Tristram chased an hart, there was an archer shot at the hart, and by misfortune he smote Sir Tristram in the thick of the thigh, and the arrow slew Sir Tristram's horse, and hurt him. When Sir Tristram was so hurt, he was passing heavy, and wit ye well he bled sore. And then he took another horse, and rode unto Joyous Gard with great heaviness, more for the promise he had made with Sir Palamides, as to do battle with him within three days after, than for any hurt of his thigh. Wherefore there was neither man nor woman that could cheer him with anything that they could make to him, neither queen La Beale Isoud, for ever he deemed that Sir Palamides had smitten him so that he should not be able to do battle with him at the day set.

CHAP. LXXXVIII.

How Sir Palamides kept his day to have foughten, but Sir Tristram might not come; and other things.

BUT in no wise there was no knight about Sir Tristram that would believe that ever Sir Palamides would hurt Sir Tristram, neither by his own hands nor by none other consenting. Then when the fifteenth day was come, Sir Palamides came to the well with four knights with him of Arthur's court, and three serjeants of arms. And for this intent Sir Palamides brought the knights with him and the serjeants of arms, for they should bear record of the battle betwixt Sir Tristram and Sir Palamides. And the one serjeant brought in his helm, the other his spear, the third his sword. So thus Sir Palamides came into the field, and there he abode nigh two hours. And then he sent a squire unto Sir Tristram, and desired him to come into the field to hold his promise. When the squire was come to Joyous Gard, anon as Sir Tristram heard of his coming, he let command that the squire should come to his presence there as he lay in his bed. My lord

Sir Tristram, said Palamides' squire, wit you well, my lord Palamides abideth you in the field, and he would wit whether ye would do battle or not. Ah, my fair brother, said Sir Tristram, wit thou well that I am right heavy for these tidings, therefore tell Sir Palamides and I were well at ease I would not lie here, nor he should have no need to send for me, and I might either ride or go: and for thou shalt say that I am no liar—Sir Tristram shewed him his thigh, that the wound was six inches deep:—And now thou hast seen my hurt, tell thy lord that this is no feigned matter; and tell him that I had lever than all the gold of king Arthur that I were whole: and tell Palamides, as soon as I am whole I shall seek him endlong and overthwart, and that I promise you as I am true knight: and if ever I may meet with him he shall have battle of me his fill. And with this the squire departed. And when Sir Palamides wist that Tristram was hurt, he was glad, and said, Now I am sure I shall have no shame, for I wot well I should have had hard handling of him, and by likely I must needs have had the worse. For he is the hardest knight in battle that now is living except Sir Launcelot. And then departed Sir Palamides where as fortune led him. And within a month Sir Tristram was whole of his hurt. And then he took his horse, and rode from country to country, and all strange adventures he achieved wheresoever he rode, and always he enquired for Sir Palamides, but of all that quarter of summer Sir Tristram could never meet with Sir Palamides. But thus as Sir Tristram sought and enquired after Sir Palamides, Sir Tristram achieved many great battles, wherethrough all the noise fell to Sir Tristram, and it ceased of Sir Launcelot; and therefore Sir Launcelot's brethren and his kinsmen would have slain Sir Tristram, because of his fame. But when Sir Launcelot wist how his kinsmen were set, he said to them openly, Wit you well, that and the envy of you all be so hardy to wait upon my lord Sir Tristram with any hurt, shame, or villainy, as I am true knight I shall slay the best of you with mine own hands. Alas, fie for shame, should ye for his noble deeds await upon him to slay him. Jesu defend, said Launcelot, that ever any noble knight as Sir Tristram is should be destroyed with treason. Of this noise and fame sprang into Cornwall, and among them of Liones, whereof they were passing glad and made great joy. And then they of Liones sent letters unto Sir Tristram of recommendation, and many great gifts to maintain Sir Tristram's estate. And ever between Sir Tristram resorted unto Joyous Gard, where as La Beale Isoud was, that loved him as her life.

Here endeth the tenthe book which is of syr Tristram.

And here foloweth the Enleuenth book whiche is of sir launcelot.

The Eleventh Book.

CHAP. I.

How Sir Launcelot rode on his adventure, and how he holpe a dolorous lady from her pain, and how that he fought with a dragon.

Now leave we Sir Tristram de Liones, and speak we of Sir Launcelot du Lake, and Sir Galahad, Sir Launcelot's son, how he was born, and in what manner, as the book of French rehearseth. Afore the time that Sir Galahad was born, there came in an hermit unto king Arthur, upon Whitsunday, as the knights sat at the Table Round. And when the hermit saw the siege perilous, he asked the king and all the knights why that siege was void. Sir Arthur and all the knights answered, There shall never none sit in that seige but one, but if he be destroyed. Then, said the hermit, wot ye what is he? Nay, said Arthur and all the knights, we wot not who is he that shall sit therein. Then wot I, said the hermit, for he that shall sit there is unborn, and this same year he shall be born that shall sit there in that siege perilous, and he shall win the Sangreal. When this hermit had made this mention he departed from the court of king Arthur. And then after this feast Sir Launcelot rode on his adventures, till on a time by adventure he passed over the bridge of Corbin, and there he saw the fairest tower that ever he saw, and thereunder was a fair town full of people, and all the people, men and women, cried at once, Welcome Sir Launcelot du Lake, the flower of all knighthood, for by thee all we shall be holpen out of danger. What mean ye, said Sir Launcelot, that ye cry so upon me? Ah, fair knight, said they all, here is within this tower a dolorous lady that hath been there in pains many winters: for ever she boileth in scalding water. And but late, said all the people, Sir Gawaine was here, and he might not help her, and so he left her in pain. So may I, said Sir Launcelot, leave her in pain as well as Sir Gawaine did. Nay, said the people, we know well that it is Sir Launcelot that shall deliver her. Well, said Launcelot, then show me what I shall do. Then they brought Sir Launcelot into the tower. And when he came to the chamber there as this lady was, the doors of iron unlocked and unbolted. And so Sir Launcelot went into the chamber that was as hot as any stew, and there Sir Launcelot took the fairest lady by the hand that ever he saw, and she was naked as a needle, and by enchantment queen Morgan le Fay and the queen of Northgalis had put her there in that pains because she was called the fairest lady of that country. And there she had been five years, and never might she be delivered

out of her great pains unto the time the best knight of the world had taken her by the hand. Then the people brought her clothes. And when she was arrayed, Sir Launcelot thought she was the fairest lady of the world, but if it were queen Guenever. Then this lady said to Sir Launcelot, Sir, if it please you will ye go with me hereby into a chapel that we may give loving and thanking to God? Madam, said Sir Launcelot, cometh on with me, I will go with you. So when they came there, and gave thankings to God, all the people, both learned and lay, gave thankings unto God and him, and said, Sir knight, since ye have delivered this lady, ye shall deliver us from a serpent that is here in a tomb. Then Sir Launcelot took his shield, and said, Bring me thither, and what I may do unto the pleasure of God and you, I will do. So when Sir Launcelot came thither, he saw written upon the tomb letters of gold that said thus: Here shall come a libbard of king's blood, and that shall slay this serpent, and this libbard shall engender a lion in this foreign country, the which lion shall pass all other knights. So then Sir Launcelot lift up the tomb, and there came out an horrible and a fiendly dragon spitting fire out of his mouth. Then Sir Launcelot drew out his sword and fought with the dragon long, and at last with great pain Sir Launcelot slew that dragon. Therewithal came king Pelles, the good and noble knight, and saluted Sir Launcelot, and he him again. Fair knight, said the king, what is your name? I require you of your knighthood tell me.

CHAP. II.

How Sir Launcelot came to Pelles, and of the Sangreal, and of Elaine, king Pelles' daughter.

Sir, said Launcelot, wit you well my name is Sir Launcelot du Lake. And my name is, said the king, Pelles, king of the foreign country, and cousin nigh unto Joseph of Arimathie. And then either of them made much of other, and so they went into the castle to take their repast. And anon there came in a dove at a window, and in her mouth there seemed a little censer of gold. And therewithal there was such a savour as all the spicery of the world had been there. And forthwithal there was upon the table all manner of meats and drinks that they could think upon. So came in a damsel passing fair and young, and she bare a vessel of gold betwixt her hands, and thereto the king kneeled devoutly, and said his prayers, and so did all that were there. Then said Sir Launcelot, What may this mean? This is, said the king, the richest thing that any man hath living. And when this thing goeth about, the Round Table shall be broken. And wit thou well, said the king, this is the holy Sancgreal that ye have here seen. So the king and Sir Launcelot led their life the most part of that day. And fain would king Pelles have found the mean to have had Sir Launcelot to love his daughter fair Elaine, and for this intent: the king knew well that Sir Launcelot should have a child by his daughter, the which should be named Sir Galahad, the good knight, by whom all the foreign country should be brought out of danger, and by him the holy Graale should be achieved. Then came forth a lady that hight dame Brisen, and she said unto the king, Sir, wit ye well, Sir Launcelot loveth no lady in the world but all only queen Guenever, and therefore work ye by counsel, and I shall make him to see your daughter Elaine, and he shall not wit but that he seeth queen Guenever. Oh, fair lady, dame Brisen, said the king, hope ye to bring this about? Sir, said she, upon pain of my life let me deal. For this Brisen was one of the greatest enchantresses that was that time in the world living.

Then anon by dame Brisen's wit she made one to come to Sir Launcelot that he knew well. And this man brought him a ring from queen Guenever like as it had come from her, and such one as she was wont for the most

part to wear. And when Sir Launcelot saw that token, wit ye well he was never so fain. Where is my lady? said Sir Launcelot. She is in the castle of Case, said the messager, but five mile hence. Then Sir Launcelot thought to be there the same night. And then this Brisen, by the commandment of king Pelles, let send Elaine to this castle with twenty-five knights unto the castle of Case. Then Sir Launcelot rode unto that castle, and there anon he was received worshipfully with such people to his seeming as were about queen Guenever. So when Sir Launcelot was alight, then dame Brisen brought him a cup full of wine, and as soon as he had drank that wine he was so assotted that he wend that maiden Elaine had been queen Guenever. Wit ye well that Sir Launcelot was glad, and so was that lady Elaine, for well she knew that of them should be born Sir Galahad, that should prove the best knight of the world. And then Sir Launcelot remembered him, and he arose up and went to the window.

CHAP. III.

How Sir Launcelot was displeased when he knew that he had been deceived, and how Galahad was born.

AND anon as he had unshut the window, the enchantment was gone, then he knew himself that he had been deceived. Alas, said he, that I have lived so long; now am I shamed. So then he gat his sword in his hand, and said, Thou traitress, who art thou? thou shalt die right here of my hands. Then this fair lady, Elaine, kneeled down afore Sir Launcelot and said, Fair courteous knight, come of king's blood, I require you have mercy upon me; and as thou art renowned the most noble knight of the world, slay me not, for I shall have a son by thee that shall be the most noblest knight of the world. Ah, false traitress, said Sir Launcelot, why hast thou betrayed me? Anon tell me what thou art. Sir, she said, I am Elaine, the daughter of king Pelles.

Well, said Sir Launcelot, I will forgive you this deed. And therewith he took her up in his arms and kissed her, for she was as fair a lady, and thereto young, and as wise as any was that time living. Truly, said Sir Launcelot, I may not blame this to you, but her that made this enchantment upon me, as between you and me ; and I may find her, that same lady Brisen, she shall lose her head for witchcraft, for there was never knight deceived so as I am. And so Sir Launcelot armed him, and took his leave mildly at that lady, young Elaine, and so he departed. Then she said, My lord Sir Launcelot, I beseech you see me as soon as you may, for I have obeyed me unto the prophecy that my father told me, and by his commandment to fulfil this prophecy I have given the greatest riches and the fairest flower that ever I had, and that is my maiden love and faith, and therefore, gentle knight, owe me your good will. And so Sir Launcelot arrayed him, and was armed, and took his leave mildly of that young lady Elaine, and so he departed, and rode till he came to the castle of Corbin where her father was. And as soon as her time came she was delivered of a fair child, and they christened him Galahad. And wit ye well that child was well kept and well nourished, and he was named Galahad, because Sir Launcelot was so named at the fontain stone; and after that, the Lady of the lake confirmed him Sir Launcelot du Lake. Then after this lady was delivered and churched there came a knight unto her, his name was Sir Bromel la Pleche, the which was a great lord, and he had loved that lady long, and he evermore desired her to wed her, and so by no means she could put him off, till on a day she said to Sir Bromel, Wit thou well, sir knight, I will not love you, for my love is set upon the best knight of the world. Who is he? said Sir Bromel. Sir, said she, it is Sir Launcelot du Lake that I love, and none other, and therefore woo me no longer. Ye say well, said Sir Bromel, and since ye have told me so much, ye shall have but little

joy of Sir Launcelot, for I shall slay him wheresoever I meet him. Sir, said the lady Elaine, do to him no treason. Wit ye well, my lady, said Bromel, and I promise you this twelvemonth I shall keep the bridge of Corbin for Sir Launcelot's sake, that he shall neither come nor go unto you but I shall meet with him.

CHAP. IV.

How Sir Bors came to dame Elaine, and saw Galahad, and how he was fed with the Sangreal.

THEN, as it befel by fortune and adventure, Sir Bors de Ganis, that was nephew unto Sir Launcelot, came over that bridge, and there Sir Bromel and Sir Bors justed, and Sir Bors smote Sir Bromel such a buffet that he bare him over his horse croup. And then Sir Bromel, as an hardy knight, pulled out his sword and dressed his shield, to do battle with Sir Bors. And then Sir Bors alight and avoided his horse, and there they dashed together many sad strokes, and long thus they fought, till at the last Sir Bromel was laid to the earth, and there Sir Bors began to unlace his helm to slay him. Then Sir Bromel cried Sir Bors' mercy, and yielded him. Upon this covenant thou shalt have thy life, said Sir Bors, so thou go unto Sir Launcelot upon Whitsunday that next cometh, and yield thee unto him as knight recreant. I will do it, said Sir Bromel : and that he sware upon the cross of the sword, and so he let him depart. And Sir Bors rode unto king Pelles that was within Corbin. And when the king and Elaine his daughter wist that Sir Bors was nephew unto Sir Launcelot, they made him great cheer. Then said dame Elaine, We marvel where Sir Launcelot is, for he came never here but once. Marvel not, said Sir Bors, for this half year he hath been in prison with queen Morgan le Fay, king Arthur's sister. Alas, said dame Elaine, that me repenteth. And ever Sir Bors beheld that child in her arms, and ever him seemed it was passing like Sir Launcelot. Truly, said dame Elaine, wit ye well this is his child. Then Sir Bors wept for joy, and he prayed to God it might prove as good a knight as his father was. And so came in a white dove, and she bare a little censer of gold in her mouth, and there was all manner of meats and drinks, and a maiden bare that Sancgreal, and she said openly, Wit you well Sir Bors that this child is Galahad, that shall sit in the siege perilous, and achieve the Sancgreal, and he shall be much better than ever was Sir Launcelot du Lake, that is his own father. And then they kneeled down and made their devotions, and there was such a savour as all the spicery in the world had been there. And when the dove took her flight, the maiden vanished with the Sancgreal as she came. Sir, said Sir Bors unto king Pelles, this castle may be named the castle adventurous, for here be many strange adventures. That is soth, said the king. For well may this place be called the adventurous place, for there come but few knights here that go away with any worship; be he never so strong, here he may be proved, and but late Sir Gawaine the good knight gat but little worship here. For I let you wit, said king Pelles, here shall no knight win no worship but if he be of worship himself, and of good living, and that loveth God, and dreadeth God, and else he getteth no worship here, be he never so hardy. That is a wonderful thing, said Sir Bors. What ye mean in this country I wot not, for ye have many strange adventures, and therefore I will lie in this castle this night. Ye shall not do so, said king Pelles, by my counsel, for it is hard and ye escape without a shame. I shall take the adventure that will befal me, said Sir Bors. Then I counsel you, said the king, to be confessed clean. As for that, said Sir Bors, I will be shriven with a good will. So Sir Bors was confessed, and for all women Sir Bors was a virgin, save for one, that was the daughter of king Brangoris, and their child hight Helin, and save for her Sir Bors was a pure maiden. And so he was led unto bed in a fair large chamber, and many doors were shut about the chamber. When Sir Bors espied all those doors, he avoided all the people, for he might have nobody with him; but in no wise Sir Bors would unarm him, but so he laid him down upon the bed. And right so he saw come in a light that he might well see a spear great and long, that came straight upon him pointling, and to Sir Bors seemed that the head of the spear burnt like a taper. And anon, or Sir Bors wist, the spear head smote him into the shoulder an hand breadth in deepness, and that wound grieved Sir Bors passing sore. And then he laid him down again for pain, and anon therewithal came a knight armed with his shield on his shoulder, and his sword in his hand, and he bad Sir Bors, Arise sir knight, and fight with me. I am sore hurt, he said, but yet I shall not fail thee. And then Sir Bors start up and dressed his shield, and then they lashed together mightily a great while. And at the last Sir Bors bare him backward, until that he came unto a chamber door, and there that knight went into that chamber, and rested him a great while. And when he had reposed him he came out freshly again, and began new battle with Sir Bors mightily and strongly.

CHAP. V.

How Sir Bors made Sir Pedivere to yield him, and of marvellous adventures that he had, and how he achieved them.

THEN Sir Bors thought he should no more go into that chamber to rest him, and so Sir Bors dressed him betwixt the knight and that chamber door, and there Sir Bors smote him down, and then that knight yielded him. What is your name? said Sir Bors. Sir, said he, my name is Pedivere of the Straight Marches. So Sir Bors made him to swear at Whitsunday next coming to be at the court of king Arthur and yield him there as a prisoner, as an overcome knight by the hands of Sir Bors. So thus departed Sir Pedivere of the Straight Marches. And then Sir Bors laid him down to rest, and then he heard and felt much noise in that chamber; and then Sir Bors espied that there came in, he wist not whether at the doors or windows, shot of arrows and of quarels, so thick that he marvelled, and many fell upon him and hurt him in the bare places. And then Sir Bors was ware where came in an hideous lion; so Sir Bors dressed him unto the lion, and anon the lion bereft him of his shield, and with his sword Sir Bors smote off the lion's head.

Right so Sir Bors forthwithal saw a dragon in the court, passing horrible, and there seemed letters of gold written in his forehead; and Sir Bors thought that the letters made a signification of king Arthur. Right so there came an horrible libard and an old, and there they fought long, and did great battle together. And at the last the dragon spit out of his mouth as it had been an hundred dragons, and lightly all the small dragons slew the old dragon, and tare him all to pieces. Anon withal there came an old man into the hall, and he sat him down in a fair chair, and there seemed to be two adders about his neck, and then the old man had an harp, and there he sang an old song, how Joseph of Aramathie came into this land. Then when he had sung, the old man bad Sir Bors—Go from thence, for here shall ye have no more adventures, and full worshipfully have ye done, and better shall ye do hereafter. And then Sir Bors seemed that there came the whitest dove with a little golden censer in her mouth; and anon therewithal the tempest ceased and passed that afore was marvellous to hear. So was all that court full of good savours. Then Sir Bors saw four children bearing four fair tapers, and an old man in the midst of the children with a censer in his one hand, and a spear in his other hand, and that spear was called the spear of vengeance.

CHAP. VI.

How Sir Bors departed; and how Sir Launcelot was rebuked of queen Guenever, and of his excuse.

Now, said that old man to Sir Bors, go ye to your cousin Sir Launcelot, and tell him of this adventure, the which had been most convenient for him of all earthly knights, but sin is so foul in him he may not achieve such holy deeds; for, had not been his sin, he had passed all the knights that ever were in his days. And tell thou Sir Launcelot, of all worldly adventures he passeth in manhood and prowess all other, but in these spiritual matters he shall have many his better. And then Sir Bors saw four gentlewomen coming by him poorly beseen, and he saw where that they entered into a chamber where was great light, as it were a summer light, and the women kneeled down afore an altar of silver with four pillars, and as it had been a bishop kneeled down afore that table of silver. And as Sir Bors looked over his head, he saw a sword like silver, naked, hoving over his head, and the clearness thereof smote so in his eyes that at that time Sir Bors was blind, and there he heard a voice that said, Go hence, thou Sir Bors, for as yet thou art not worthy for to be in this place. And then he went backward to his bed till on the morn. And on the morn king Pelles made great joy of Sir Bors, and then he departed and rode to Camelot, and there he found Sir Launcelot du Lake, and told him of the adventures he had seen with king Pelles at Corbin. So the noise sprang in king Arthur's court that Sir Launcelot had a child by Elaine, the daughter of king Pelles, wherefore queen Guenever was wroth and gave many rebukes to Sir Launcelot, and called him false knight. And then Sir Launcelot told the queen all, and how he was made to meet her by enchantment, in likeness of the queen. So the queen held Sir Launcelot excused. And, as the book saith, king Arthur had been in France, and had made war upon the mighty king Claudas, and had won much of his lands; and when the king was come again he let cry a great feast, that all lords and ladies of all England should be there, but if it were such as were rebellious against him.

CHAP. VII.

How dame Elaine, Galahad's mother, came in great estate unto Camelot, and how Sir Launcelot behaved him there.

AND when dame Elaine, the daughter of king Pelles, heard of this feast, she went to her father, and required him that he would give her leave to ride to that feast. The king answered, I will well ye go thither; but in any wise, as ye love me and will have my blessing, that ye be well beseen in the richest wise; and look that ye spare not for no cost; ask, and ye shall have all that you needeth. Then, by the advice of dame Brisen her maiden, all thing was apparelled unto the purpose, and there was never no lady more richlier beseen. So she rode with twenty knights and ten ladies and gentlewomen to the number of an hundred horses. And when she came to Camelot, king Arthur and queen Guenever said, and all the knights, that dame Elaine was the fairest and the best beseen lady that ever was seen in that court.

And anon as king Arthur wist that she was come, he met her and saluted her, and so did the most part of all the knights of the Round Table, both Sir Tristram, Sir Bleoberis, and Sir Gawaine, and many more that I will not rehearse. But when Sir Launcelot saw her he was so ashamed, and that because he drew his sword on her, that he would not salute her nor speak to her, and yet Sir Launcelot thought she was the fairest woman that ever he saw in his life days. But when dame Elaine saw Sir Launcelot that would not speak to her, she was so heavy that she wend her heart would have to-brast. For wit ye well, out of measure she loved him. And then Elaine said unto her woman dame Brisen, The unkindness of Sir Launcelot slayeth me near. Ah peace, madam, said dame Brisen, I will undertake that he shall come to you, and ye would hold you still. That were me lever, said dame Elaine, than all the gold that is above the earth. Let me deal, said dame Brisen. So when Elaine

was brought unto queen Guenever, either made other good cheer by countenance, but nothing with hearts. But all men and women spake of the beauty of dame Elaine, and of her great riches. Then the queen commanded that dame Elaine should sleep in a chamber nigh unto her chamber, and all under one roof. And so it was done as the queen had commanded. Then the queen sent for Sir Launcelot, and bid him come to her, or else, I am sure, said the queen, that ye will go to your lady, dame Elaine, by whom ye had Galahad. Ah, madam, said Sir Launcelot, never say ye so; for that was against my will. Then, said the queen, look that ye come to me when I send for you. Madam, said Sir Launcelot, I shall not fail you, but I shall be ready at your commandment. This bargain was soon done and made between them, but dame Brisen knew it by her crafts, and told it to her lady dame Elaine. Alas, said she, how shall I do. Let me deal, said dame Brisen, for I shall bring him by the hand, even to you, and he shall ween that I am queen Guenever's messager. Now well is me, said dame Elaine, for all the world I love not so much as I do Sir Launcelot.

CHAP. VIII.

How dame Brisen by enchantment brought Sir Launcelot to dame Elaine, and how queen Guenever rebuked him.

So then dame Brisen came to Sir Launcelot and said, Sir Launcelot du Lake, my lady queen Guenever awaiteth upon you. O my fair lady, said Sir Launcelot, I am ready to go with you where ye will have me. So Sir Launcelot took his sword in his hand, and then dame Brisen took him by the finger and led him unto her lady, dame Elaine; and then she departed and left them together. Wit ye well the lady was glad, and so was Sir Launcelot, for he wend that it was the queen. Then queen Guenever sent one of her women unto Sir Launcelot; and when she came there, she found Sir Launcelot was away: so she came to the queen and told her all. Alas, said the queen, where is that false knight become? Then the queen was nigh out of her wit, and then she writhed and weltered as a mad woman; and at the last the queen met with Sir Launcelot, and thus she said, False traitor knight that thou art, look thou never abide in my court, and not so hardy, thou false traitor knight that thou art, that ever thou come in my sight. Alas, said Sir Launcelot: and therewith he took such an heartly sorrow at her words that he fell down to the floor in a swoon. And therewithal queen Guenever departed. And when Sir Launcelot awoke of his swoon he lept out at a bay window into a garden, and there with thorns he was all to-scratched in his visage and his body, and so he ran forth he wist not whither, and was wild wood as ever was man; and so he ran two year, and never man might have grace to know him.

CHAP. IX.

How dame Elaine was commanded by queen Guenever to avoid the court, and how Sir Launcelot became mad.

Now turn we unto queen Guenever and to the fair lady Elaine. When dame Elaine heard the queen so to rebuke Sir Launcelot, and also she saw how he swooned, and how he lept out at a bay window, then she said unto queen Guenever, Madam, ye are greatly to blame for Sir Launcelot, for now ye have lost him; for I saw and heard by his countenance that he is mad for ever. Alas, madam, ye do great sin, and to yourself great dishonour, for ye have a lord of your own, and therefore it is your part to love him; for there is no queen in this world hath such another king as ye have. And if ye were not, I might have the love of my lord Sir Launcelot; and cause I have to love him, for I am his, and by him I have borne a fair son, and his name is Galahad, and he shall be in his time the best knight of the world. Dame Elaine, said the queen, I charge you

and command you to avoid my court; and for the love ye owe unto Sir Launcelot discover not his counsel, for and ye do it will be his death. As for that, said dame Elaine, I dare undertake he is marred for ever, and that have ye made, for ye nor I are like to rejoice him; for he made the most piteous groans when he lept out at yonder bay window that ever I heard man make. Alas! said fair Elaine, and alas! said the queen Guenever, for now I wot well we have lost him for ever. So on the morn dame Elaine took her leave to depart, and she would no longer abide. Then king Arthur brought her on her way with more than an hundred knights through a forest. And by the way she told Sir Bors de Ganis all how it betid, and how Sir Launcelot lept out at a bay window araged out of his wit. Alas, said Sir Bors, where is my lord Sir Launcelot become? Sir, said Elaine, I wot never. Alas, said Sir Bors, betwixt you both ye have destroyed that good knight. As for me, said dame Elaine, I said never nor did never thing that should in any wise displease him; but with the rebuke that queen Guenever gave him I saw him swoon to the earth; and when he awoke he took his sword in his hand, and lept out at a window, with the grisliest groan that ever I heard man make. Now farewell, dame Elaine, said Sir Bors, and hold my lord Arthur with a tale as long as ye can, for I will turn again unto queen Guenever and give her a heat: and I require you as ever ye will have my service, make good watch, and espy if ever ye may see my lord Sir Launcelot. Truly, said fair Elaine, I shall do all that I may do, for as fain would I know and wit where he is become as you or any of his kin, or queen Guenever, and cause great enough have I thereto as well as any other. And wit ye well, said fair Elaine to Sir Bors, I would lose my life for him rather than he should be hurt: but alas, I cast me never for to see him; and the chief causer of this is dame Guenever. Madam, said dame Brisen, the which had made the enchantment before betwixt Sir Launcelot and her, I pray you heartily let Sir Bors depart and hie him with all his might, as fast as he may, to seek Sir Launcelot. For I warn you he is clean out of his mind, and yet he shall be well holpen, and but by miracle. Then wept dame Elaine, and so did Sir Bors de Ganis, and so they departed; and Sir Bors rode straight unto queen Guenever, and when she saw Sir Bors she wept as she were wood. Fie on your weeping, said Sir Bors, for ye weep never but when there is no boot. Alas, said Sir Bors, that ever Sir Launcelot's kin saw you. For now have ye lost the best knight of our blood, and he that was all our leader and our succour. And I dare say and make it good, that all kings, christian nor heathen, may not find such a knight, for to speak of his nobleness and courtesy with his beauty and his gentleness. Alas, said Sir Bors, what shall we do that be of his blood? Alas, said Ector de Maris. Alas, said Lionel.

CHAP. X.

What sorrow queen Guenever made for Sir Launcelot, and how he was sought by knights of his kin.

AND when the queen heard them say so, she fell to the earth in a dead swoon. And then Sir Bors took her up, and roused her, and when she was awaked she kneeled afore the three knights, and held up both her hands, and besought them to seek him, and spare not for no goods but that he be founden, for I wot he is out of his mind. And Sir Bors, Sir Ector, and Sir Lionel departed from the queen, for they might not abide no longer for sorrow. And then the queen sent them treasure enough for their expenses, and so they took their horses and their armour, and departed. And then they rode from country to country, in forests and in wildernesses and in wastes, and ever they laid watch as well both at forests and at all manner of men as they rode, to hearken and enquire after him, as he that was a naked man in his shirt, with a sword in his hand. And thus

they rode nigh a quarter of a year, endlong and overthwart, in many places, forests and wildernesses, and ofttimes were evil lodged for his sake, and yet for all their labour and seeking could they never hear word of him. And wit you well these three knights were passing sorry. Then at the last Sir Bors and his fellows met with a knight, that hight Sir Melion de Tartare. Now, fair knight, said Sir Bors, whither be ye away? for they knew either other aforetime. Sir, said Sir Melion, I am in the way toward the court of king Arthur. Then we pray you, said Sir Bors, that ye will tell my lord Arthur, and my lady queen Guenever, and all the fellowship of the Round Table, that we cannot in no wise hear tell where Sir Launcelot is become. Then Sir Melion departed from them, and said that he would tell the king and the queen and all the fellowship of the Round Table, as they had desired him. So when Sir Melion came to the court of king Arthur, he told the king and the queen and all the fellowship of the Round Table, what Sir Bors had said of Sir Launcelot. Then Sir Gawaine, Sir Uwaine, Sir Sagramor le Desirous, Sir Aglovale, and Sir Percivale de Galis, took upon them by the great desire of king Arthur, and in especial by the queen, to seek throughout all England, Wales, and Scotland, to find Sir Launcelot. And with them rode eighteen knights more to bear them fellowship. And wit ye well they lacked no manner of spending: and so were they three and twenty knights.

Now turn we to Sir Launcelot, and speak we of his care and woe and what pain he there endured, for cold, hunger, and thirst he had plenty. And thus as these noble knights rode together, they by one assent departed, and then they rode by two, by three, and by four, and by five; and ever they assigned where they should meet. And so Sir Aglovale and Sir Percivale rode together unto their mother that was a queen in those days. And when she saw her two sons, for joy she wept tenderly. And then she said, Ah, my dear sons, when your father was slain he left me four sons, of the which now be twain slain; and for the death of my noble son Sir Lamorak shall my heart never be glad. And then she kneeled down upon her knees tofore Aglovale and Sir Percivale, and besought them to abide at home with her. Ah, sweet mother, said Sir Percivale, we may not; for we be come of king's blood of both parties, and therefore, mother, it is our kind to haunt arms and noble deeds. Alas, my sweet sons, then she said, for your sakes I shall lose my liking and joy, and then wind and weather I may not endure, what for the death of your father king Pellinore, that was shamefully slain by the hands of Sir Gawaine and his brother Sir Gaheris, and they slew him not manly, but by treason. Ah, my dear sons, this is a piteous complaint for me of your father's death, considering also the death of Sir Lamorak, that of knighthood had but few fellows. Now, my dear sons, have this in your mind. Then there was but weeping and sobbing in the court when they should depart, and she fell in swooning in midst of the court.

CHAP. XI.

How a servant of Sir Aglovale's was slain, and what vengeance Sir Aglovale and Sir Percivale did therefore.

AND when she was awaked she sent a squire after them with spending enough. And so when the squire had overtaken them, they would not suffer him to ride with them, but sent him home again to comfort their mother, praying her meekly of her blessing. And so this squire was benighted, and by misfortune he happened to come unto a castle where dwelled a baron. And so when the squire was come into the castle, the lord asked him from whence he came, and whom he served? My lord, said the squire, I serve a good knight that is called Sir Aglovale. The squire said it to good intent, weening unto him to have been more forborne for Sir Aglo-

vale's sake than if he had said he had served the queen, Aglovale's mother. Well, my fellow, said the lord of that castle, for Sir Aglovale's sake thou shalt have evil lodging, for Aglovale slew my brother, and therefore thou shalt die on part of payment. And then that lord commanded his men to have him away, and so pulled him out of the castle, and there they slew him without mercy. Right so on the morn came Sir Aglovale and Sir Percivale riding by a church-yard, where men and women were busy, and beheld the dead squire, and they thought to bury him. What is there, said Sir Aglovale, that ye behold so fast? A good man start forth and said, Fair knight, here lieth a squire slain shamefully this night. How was he slain, fair fellow? said Sir Aglovale. My fair sir, said the man, the lord of this castle lodged this squire this night, and because he said he was servant unto a good knight that is with king Arthur, his name is Sir Aglovale, therefore the lord commanded to slay him, and for this cause is he slain. Gramercy, said Sir Aglovale, and ye shall see his death revenged lightly, for I am that same knight for whom this squire was slain. Then Sir Aglovale called unto him Sir Percivale, and bad him alight lightly, and so they alight both, and betook their horses to their men, and so they went on foot into the castle. And all so soon as they were within the castle gate Sir Aglovale bad the porter, Go thou unto thy lord and tell him that I am Sir Aglovale, for whom this squire was slain this night. Anon the porter told this to his lord, whose name was Goodewin: anon he armed him, and then he came into the court and said, Which of you is Sir Aglovale? Here I am, said Aglovale: for what cause slewest thou this night my mother's squire? I slew him, said Sir Goodewin, because of thee; for thou slewest my brother Sir Gawdelin. As for thy brother, said Sir Aglovale, I avow it, I slew him, for he was a false knight and a betrayer of ladies and of good knights; and for the death of my squire thou

shalt die. I defy thee, said Sir Goodewin. Then they lashed together as
eagerly as it had been two lions: and
Sir Percivale he fought with all the
remnant that would fight. And within
a while Sir Percivale had slain all that
would withstand him; for Sir Percivale
dealt so his strokes that were so rude
that there durst no man abide him.
And within a while Sir Aglovale had
Sir Goodewin at the earth, and there he
unlaced his helm and strake off his
head. And then they departed and took
their horses. And then they let carry
the dead squire unto a priory, and there
they interred him.

CHAP. XII.

*How Sir Percivale departed secretly from
his brother, and how he loosed a knight
bound with a chain, and of other things.*

AND when this was done, they rode
into many countries, ever enquiring after
Sir Launcelot, but never they could hear
of him. And at the last they came to a
castle that hight Cardican, and there
Sir Percivale and Sir Aglovale were
lodged together; and privily about
midnight Sir Percivale came to Aglovale's squire, and said, Arise and make
thee ready, for ye and I will ride away
secretly. Sir, said the squire, I would
full fain ride with you where ye would
have me, but, and my lord your brother
take me, he will slay me. As for that
care thou not, for I shall be thy warrant. And so Sir Percivale rode till it
was afternoon, and then he came upon
a bridge of stone, and there he found a
knight that was bounden with a chain
fast about the waist unto a pillar of
stone. O fair knight, said that bounden
knight, I require thee loose me of my
bonds. What knight are ye? said Sir
Percivale, and for what cause are ye so
bounden? Sir, I shall tell you, said
that knight; I am a knight of the Table
Round, and my name is Sir Persides,
and thus by adventure I came this way,
and here I lodged in this castle at the
bridge foot, and therein dwelleth an
uncourteous lady, and because she prof-

fered me to be her paramour and I refused her, she set her men upon me
suddenly or ever I might come to my
weapon, and thus they bound me, and
here I wot well I shall die, but if some
man of worship break my bands. Be
ye of good cheer, said Sir Percivale, and
because ye are a knight of the Round
Table as well as I, I trust to God to
break your bands. And therewith Sir
Percivale drew out his sword, and strake
at the chain with such a might that he
cut a-two the chain, and through Sir
Persides' hauberk, and hurt him a little.
Truly, said Sir Persides, that was a
mighty stroke as ever I felt one, for had
not the chain been, ye had slain me.
And therewithal Sir Persides saw a
knight coming out of the castle all that
ever he might flying. Beware Sir, said
Sir Persides, yonder cometh a man
that will have ado with you. Let him
come, said Sir Percivale, and so he met
with that knight in the midst of the
bridge, and Sir Percivale gave him such
a buffet that he smote him quite from
his horse, and over a part of the bridge,
that had not been a little vessel under
the bridge that knight had been drowned.
And then Sir Percivale took the knight's
horse, and made Sir Persides to mount
upon him, and so they rode unto the
castle, and bad the lady deliver Sir
Persides' servants, or else he would slay
all that ever he found. And so for fear
she delivered them all. Then was Sir
Percivale ware of a lady that stood in
that tower. Ah, madam, said Sir Percivale, what use and custom is that in
a lady to destroy good knights but if
they will be your paramour? forsooth
this is a shameful custom of a lady.
And if I had not a great matter in my
hand, I should foredo your evil customs.
And so Sir Persides brought Sir Percivale unto his own castle, and there he
made him great cheer all that night.
And on the morn, when Sir Percivale
had heard mass and broken his fast,
he bad Sir Persides, Ride unto king
Arthur, and tell the king how that ye
met with me, and tell my brother Sir
Aglovale how I rescued you, and bid

him seek not after me, for I am in the quest to seek Sir Launcelot du Lake. And though he seek me he shall not find me, and tell him I will never see him, nor the court, till I have found Sir Launcelot. Also tell Sir Kay the seneschal, and to Sir Mordred, that I trust to God to be of as great worthiness as either of them. For tell them I shall never forget their mocks and scorns that they did to me that day that I was made knight. And tell them I will never see that court till men speak more worship of me than ever men did of any of them both. And so Sir Persides departed from Sir Percivale, and then he rode unto king Arthur, and told there of Sir Percivale. And when Sir Aglovale heard him speak of his brother Sir Percivale, he said, He departed from me unkindly. Sir, said Sir Persides, on my life he shall prove a noble knight as any now is living. And when he saw Sir Kay and Sir Mordred, Sir Persides said thus: My fair lords both, Sir Percivale greeteth you well both, and he sent you word by me that he trusteth to God or ever he come to the court again to be of as great nobleness as ever were ye both, and more men to. speak of his nobleness than ever they did you. It may well be, said Sir Kay and Sir Mordred, but at that time when he was made knight he was full unlikely to prove a good knight. As for that, said king Arthur, he must needs prove a good knight, for his father and his brethren were noble knights.

CHAP. XIII.

How Sir Percivale met with Sir Ector, and how they fought long, and each had almost slain other.

AND now will we turn unto Sir Percivale that rode long, and in a forest he met a knight with a broken shield and a broken helm, and as soon as either saw other readily, they made them ready to just, and so hurtled together with all the might of their horses, and met together so hard that Sir Percivale was smitten to the earth. And then Sir Per-

civale arose lightly and cast his shield on his shoulder and drew his sword, and bad the other knight alight, and do we battle to the uttermost. Will ye more? said that knight, and therewith he alight and put his horse from him, and then they came together an easy pace, and there they lashed together with noble swords, and sometime they stroke, and sometime they foined, and either gave other many great wounds. Thus they fought near half a day, and never rested but right little, and there was none of them both that had less wounds than fifteen, and they bled so much that it was marvel they stood on their feet. But this knight that fought with Sir Percivale was a proved knight and a wise fighting knight, and Sir Percivale was young and strong, not knowing in fighting as the other was. Then Sir Percivale spake first, and said, Sir knight, hold thy hand a while still, for we have foughten for a simple matter and quarrel over long, and therefore I require thee tell me thy name, for I was never or this time matched. Truly, said that knight, and never or this time was there never knight that wounded me so sore as thou hast done, and yet have I foughten in many battles; and now shalt thou wit that I am a knight of the Table Round, and my name is Sir Ector de Maris, brother unto the good knight Sir Launcelot du Lake. Alas, said Sir Percivale, and my name is Sir Percivale de Galis, that hath made my quest to seek Sir Launcelot; now I am siker that I shall never finish my quest, for ye have slain me with your hands. It is not so, said Sir Ector, for I am slain by your hands, and may not live; therefore I require you, said Sir Ector unto Sir Percivale, ride ye hereby to a priory, and bring me a priest that I may receive my Saviour, for I may not live. And when ye come to the court of king Arthur, tell not my brother Sir Launcelot how that ye slew me, for then he would be your mortal enemy; but ye may say that I was slain in my quest as I sought him. Alas, said Sir Percivale, ye say that thing that never will be, for I am so faint for bleeding that I may scarcely stand; how should I then take my horse?

CHAP. XIV.

How by miracle they were both made whole, by the coming of the holy vessel of Sangreal.

THEN they made both great dole out of measure. This will not avail, said Percivale. And then he kneeled down and made his prayer devoutly unto Almighty Jesu; for he was one of the best knights of the world that at that time was, in whom the very faith stood most in. Right so there came by, the holy vessel of the Sancgreal with all manner of sweetness and savour, but they could not readily see who that bare that vessel, but Sir Percivale had a glimmering of the vessel, and of the maiden that bare it, for he was a perfect clean maiden. And forthwithal they both were as whole of hide and limb as ever they were in their life days; then they gave thankings to God with great mildness. O Jesu! said Sir Percivale, what may this mean that we be thus healed, and right now we were at the point of dying? I wot full well, said Sir Ector, what it is. It is an holy vessel that is borne by a maiden, and therein is a part of the holy blood of our Lord Jesus Christ, blessed might He be! but it may not be seen, said Sir Ector, but if it be by a perfect man. Truly, said Sir Percivale, I saw a damsel, as me thought, all in white, with a vessel in both her hands, and forthwithal I was whole. So then they took their horses and their harness, and amended their harness as well as they might that was broken, and so they mounted upon their horses and rode talking together. And there Sir Ector de Maris told Sir Percivale how he had sought his brother Sir Launcelot long, and never could hear witting of him :—In many strange adventures have I been in this quest. And so either told other of their adventures.

𝔥𝔢𝔯𝔢 𝔢𝔫𝔡𝔢𝔱𝔥 𝔱𝔥𝔢 𝔢𝔫𝔩𝔢𝔲𝔢𝔫𝔱𝔥 𝔟𝔬𝔬𝔨𝔢. 𝔄𝔫𝔡 𝔥𝔢𝔯𝔢 𝔣𝔬𝔩𝔬𝔴𝔢𝔱𝔥 𝔱𝔥𝔢 𝔱𝔴𝔢𝔩𝔣𝔱𝔥 𝔟𝔬𝔬𝔨.

𝔗𝔥𝔢 𝔗𝔴𝔢𝔩𝔣𝔱𝔥 𝔅𝔬𝔬𝔨.

CHAP. I.

How Sir Launcelot in his madness took a sword and fought with a knight, and after lept into a bed.

AND now leave we of a while of Sir Ector and of Sir Percivale, and speak we of Sir Launcelot, that suffered and endured many sharp showers, that ever ran wild wood from place to place, and lived by fruit and such as he might get, and drank water two year, and other clothing had he but little but his shirt and his breeches. Thus as Sir Launcelot wandered here and there, he came in a fair meadow where he found a pavilion, and there by upon a tree there hung a white shield, and two swords hung thereby, and two spears leaned there by a tree. And when Sir Launcelot saw the swords, anon he lept to the one sword, and took it in his hand and drew it out. And then he lashed at the shield that all the meadow rang of the dints, that he gave such a noise as ten knights had foughten together. Then came forth a dwarf and lept unto Sir Launcelot, and would have had the sword out of his hand, and then Sir Launcelot took him by the both shoulders, and threw him to the ground upon his neck, that he had almost broken his neck, and therewithal the dwarf cried, Help. Then came forth a likely knight, and well apparelled in scarlet furred with meniver. And anon as he saw Sir Launcelot, he deemed that he should be out of his wit : and then he said with fair speech, Good man, lay down that sword, for, as me seemeth, thou hast more need of sleep, and of warm clothes, than to wield that sword. As for that, said Sir Launcelot, come not too nigh; for, and thou do, wit thou well I will slay thee. And when the knight of the pavilion saw that, he start backward within the pavilion. And then the dwarf armed him lightly, and so the knight thought by force and might to take the sword from Sir Launcelot, and so he came stepping out, and when Sir Launcelot saw him come so all armed with his sword in his hand, then Sir Launcelot flew to him with such a might, and hit him upon the helm such a buffet that the stroke troubled his brains, and therewith the sword brake in three. And the knight fell to the earth as he had been dead, the blood brasting out of his mouth, the nose, and the ears. And then Sir Launcelot ran into the pavilion, and rushed even into the warm bed : and there was a lady in that bed, and she gat her smock, and ran out of the pavilion. And when she saw her lord lie on the ground like to be dead, then she cried and wept as she had been mad. Then with her noise the knight awaked out of his swoon, and looked up weakly with his eyes, and then he asked her where was that mad man that had given him such a buffet? for such a buffet had I never of man's hand. Sir, said the dwarf, it is not worship to hurt him, for he is a man out of his wit, and doubt ye not he hath been a man of great worship, and for some heartly sorrow that he hath taken he is fallen mad : and me seemeth, said the dwarf, he resembleth much unto Sir Launcelot; for him I saw at the great tournament beside Lonazep. Jesu defend, said that knight, that ever that noble knight Sir Launcelot should be in such a plight. But whatsoever he be, said that knight, harm

will I none do him. And this knight's name was Bliant. Then he said unto the dwarf, Go thou fast on horseback unto my brother Sir Selivant, that is at the Castle Blank, and tell him of mine adventure, and bid him bring with him an horse-litter, and then will we bear this knight unto my castle.

CHAP. II.

How Sir Launcelot was carried in a horse-litter, and how Sir Launcelot rescued Sir Bliant his host.

So the dwarf rode fast, and he came again and brought Sir Selivant with him, and six men with an horse-litter. And so they took up the feather-bed with Sir Launcelot, and so carried all away with them unto the Castle Blank, and he never awaked till he was within the castle. And then they bound his hands and his feet, and gave him good meats and good drinks, and brought him again to his strength and his fairness, but in his wit they could not bring him again, nor to know himself. Thus was Sir Launcelot there more than a year and an half, honestly arrayed, and fair fared withal. Then upon a day this lord of that castle, Sir Bliant, took his arms on horseback with a spear to seek adventures. And as he rode in a forest there met him two knights adventurous. The one was Breuse Sance Pité, and his brother, Sir Bertelot, and these two ran both at once upon Sir Bliant, and brake their spears upon his body. And then they drew out swords, and made great battle, and fought long together. But at the last Sir Bliant was sore wounded, and felt himself faint, and then he fled on horseback toward his castle. And they came hurling under the castle where as Sir Launcelot lay in a window, and saw how two knights laid upon Sir Bliant with their swords. And when Sir Launcelot saw that, yet as wood as he was, he was sorry for his lord Sir Bliant. And then Sir Launcelot brake his chains from his legs and off his arms, and in the breaking he hurt his hands sore : and so Sir Launcelot ran out at a postern, and there he met with the two knights that chased Sir Bliant, and there he pulled down Sir Bertelot with his bare hands from his horse, and therewithal he wrothe his sword out of his hands, and so he lept unto Sir Breuse, and gave him such a buffet upon the head that he tumbled backward over his horse croup. And when Sir Bertelot saw there his brother have such a fall, he gat a spear in his hand, and would have run Sir Launcelot through. That saw Sir Bliant, and strake off the hand of Sir Bertelot: and then Sir Breuse and Sir Bertelot gat their horses and fled away. When Sir Selivant came, and saw what Sir Launcelot had done for his brother, then he thanked God, and so did his brother, that ever they did him any good. But when Sir Bliant saw that Sir Launcelot was hurt with the breaking of his irons, then was he heavy that ever he bound him. Bind him no more, said Sir Selivant, for he is happy and gracious. Then they made great joy of Sir Launcelot, and they bound him no more. And so he abode there an half year and more. And on the morn early, Sir Launcelot was ware where came a great boar with many hounds nigh him. But the boar was so big there might no hounds tear him, and the hunters came after blowing their horns, both on horseback and on foot: and then Sir Launcelot was ware where one alight, and tied his horse to a tree, and leaned his spear against the tree.

CHAP. III.

How Sir Launcelot fought against a boar and slew him, and how he was hurt, and brought unto an hermitage.

So came Sir Launcelot, and found the horse bounden till a tree, and a spear leaning against a tree, and a sword tied to the saddle bow. And then Sir Launcelot lept into the saddle, and gat that spear in his hand, and then he rode after the boar. And then Sir Launcelot was ware where the boar set his back to a tree, fast by an hermitage. Then Sir Launcelot ran at the boar with his spear. And therewith the boar turned him nimbly, and rove out the lungs and the heart of the horse, so that Launcelot fell to the earth, and or ever Sir Launcelot might get from the horse, the boar rove him on the brawn of the thigh, up to the hough bone. And then Sir Launcelot was wroth, and up he gat upon his feet, and drew his sword, and he smote off the boar's head at one stroke. And therewithal came out the hermit; and saw him have such a wound; then the hermit came to Sir Launcelot and bemoaned him, and would have had him home unto his hermitage. But when Sir Launcelot heard him speak, he was so wroth with his wound that he ran upon the hermit to have slain him, and the hermit ran away, and when Sir Launcelot might not overget him he threw his sword after him, for Sir Launcelot might go no farther for bleeding. Then the hermit turned again, and asked Sir Launcelot how he was hurt. Fellow, said Sir Launcelot, this boar hath bitten me sore. Then come with me, said the hermit, and I shall heal you. Go thy way, said Sir Launcelot, and deal not with me. Then the hermit ran his way, and there he met with a good knight with many men. Sir, said the hermit, here is fast by my place the goodliest man that ever I saw, and he is sore wounded with a boar, and yet he hath slain the boar. But well I wot, said the hermit, and he be not holpen, that goodly man shall die of that wound, and that were great pity. Then that knight, at the desire of the hermit, gat a cart, and in that cart that knight put the boar and Sir Launcelot, for Sir Launcelot was so feeble that they might right easily deal with him. And so Sir Launcelot was brought unto the hermitage, and there the hermit healed him of his wound. But the hermit might not find Sir Launcelot's sustenance, and so he impaired and waxed feeble, both of his body and of his wit, for the default of his sustenance: he waxed more wooder than he was aforehand. And then, upon a day, Sir Launcelot ran his way into the forest, and by adventure he came to the city of Corbin where dame Elaine was, that bare Galahad, Sir Launcelot's son. And so when he was entered into the town, he ran through the town to the castle, and then all the young men of that city ran after Sir Launcelot, and there they threw turves at him, and gave him many sad strokes. And ever as Sir Launcelot might over-reach any of them he threw them, so that they would never come in his hands no more, for of some he brake the legs and arms, and so fled into the castle, and then came out knights and squires and rescued Sir Launcelot. And when they beheld him, and looked upon his person, they thought they saw never so goodly a man. And when they saw so many wounds upon him, all they deemed that he had been a man of worship. And then they ordained him clothes to his body, and straw underneath him, and a little house. And then every day they would throw him meat, and set him drink, but there was but few would bring meat to his hands.

CHAP. IV.

How Sir Launcelot was known by dame Elaine, and was borne into a chamber, and after healed by the Sangreal.

So it befel, that king Pelles had a nephew, his name was Castor, and so he desired of the king to be made knight, and so at the request of this Castor, the king made him knight at the feast of Candlemas. And when Sir Castor was made knight, that same day he gave many gowns. And then Sir Castor sent for the fool, that was Sir Launcelot. And when he was come afore Sir Castor, he gave Sir Launcelot a robe of scarlet and all that belonged unto him. And when Sir Launcelot was so arrayed like a knight, he was the seemliest man in all the court, and none so well made. So when he saw his time he went into the garden, and there Sir Launcelot laid him down by a well and slept. And so at afternoon, dame Elaine and her maidens came into the garden to play

them, and as they roamed up and down, one of dame Elaine's maidens espied where lay a goodly man by the well sleeping, and anon shewed him to dame Elaine. Peace, said dame Elaine, and say no word; and then she brought dame Elaine where he lay. And when that she beheld him, anon she fell in re-membrance of him, and knew him verily for Sir Launcelot, and therewithal she fell on weeping so heartily that she sank even to the earth. And when she had thus wept a great while, then she arose and called her maidens, and said she was sick. And so she went out of the garden, and she went straight to her father, and there she took him apart by herself, and then she said, Oh father, now have I need of your help, and but if that ye help me, farewell my good days for ever. What is that, daughter? said king Pelles. Sir, she said, thus is it: in your garden I went for to sport, and there by the well I found Sir Laun-celot du Lake sleeping. I may not be-lieve that, said king Pelles. Sir, she said, truly he is there, and me seemeth he should be distract out of his wit. Then hold you still, said the king, and let me deal. Then the king called to him such as he most trusted, a four persons, and dame Elaine his daughter. And when they came to the well and beheld Sir Launcelot, anon dame Brisen knew him. Sir, said dame Brisen, we must be wise how we deal with him, for this knight is out of his mind, and if we awake him rudely, what he will do we all know not. But ye shall abide, and I shall throw such an enchantment upon him that he shall not awake within the space of an hour; and so she did. Then within a little while after king Pelles commanded that all people should avoid, that none should be in that way there as the king would come. And so when this was done, these four men and these ladies laid hand on Sir Launcelot. And so they bare him into a tower, and so into a chamber where was the holy vessel of the Sancgreal, and by force Sir Launce-lot was laid by that holy vessel, and there came a holy man and uncovered that vessel, and so by miracle, and by virtue of that holy vessel, Sir Launcelot was healed and recovered. And when that he was awaked he groaned and sighed, and complained greatly that he was passing sore.

CHAP. V.

How Sir Launcelot, after that he was whole and had his mind, he was ashamed, and how that Elaine desired a castle for him.

AND when Sir Launcelot saw king Pelles and Elaine he waxed ashamed, and said thus: Oh Lord Jesu, how came I here? For God's sake, my lord, let me wit how I came here? Sir, said dame Elaine, into this country ye came like a mad man clean out of your wit. And here have ye been kept as a fool, and no creature here knew what ye were, until by fortune a maiden of mine brought me unto you, where as ye lay sleeping by a well, and anon, as I verily beheld you, I knew you. And then I told my father, and so were ye brought afore this holy vessel, and by the virtue of it thus were ye healed. O, said Sir Launcelot, if this be sooth, how many there be that know of my woodness. Truly, said Elaine, no more but my father and I and dame Brisen. Now, I pray you, said Sir Launcelot, keep it in counsel, and let no man know it in the world, for I am sore ashamed that I have been thus miscarried, for I am banished out of the country of Logris for ever, that is for to say, the country of England. And so Sir Launcelot lay more than a fortnight, or ever that he might stir for soreness. And then upon a day he said unto dame Elaine these words: Lady Elaine, for your sake I have had much travel, care, and anguish, it needeth not to rehearse it, ye know how. Notwithstanding I know well I have done foul to you, when that I drew my sword to you, for to have slain you. And all was the cause that ye and dame Brisen deceived me. That is truth, said dame Elaine. Now will ye for my love,

said Sir Launcelot, go unto your father, and get me a place of him wherein I may dwell: for in the court of king Arthur may I never come. Sir, said dame Elaine, I will live and die with you, and only for your sake, and if my life might not avail you, and my death might avail you, wit ye well I would die for your sake. And I will go to my father, and I am sure there is nothing that I can desire of him but I shall have it. And where ye be, my lord Sir Launcelot, doubt ye not but I will be with you with all the service that I may do. So forthwithal she went to her father, and said, Sir, my lord Sir Launcelot desireth to be here by you in some castle of yours. Well, daughter, said the king, sith it is his desire to abide in these marches, he shall be in the castle of Bliant, and there shall ye be with him, and twenty of the fairest ladies that be in this country, and they shall all be of the great blood; and ye shall have ten knights with you. For, daughter, I will that ye wit we all be honoured by the blood of Sir Launcelot.

CHAP. VI.

How Sir Launcelot came into the Joyous Isle, and there he named himself Le Chevaler Mal Fet.

THEN went dame Elaine unto Sir Launcelot, and told him all how her father had devised for him and her. Then came the knight Sir Castor, that was nephew unto king Pelles, unto Sir Launcelot, and asked him what was his name? Sir, said Sir Launcelot, my name is Le Chevaler Mal Fet, that is to say, the knight that hath trespassed. Sir, said Sir Castor, it may well be so, but ever me seemeth your name should be Sir Launcelot du Lake, for or now I have seen you. Sir, said Launcelot, ye are not as a gentle knight: I put case my name were Sir Launcelot, and that it list me not to discover my name; what should it grieve you here to keep my counsel, and ye not hurt thereby? But wit thou well, and ever it lie in my power I shall grieve you, and that I promise you truly. Then Sir Castor kneeled down and besought Sir Launcelot of mercy:—For I shall never utter what ye be while that ye be in these parts. Then Sir Launcelot pardoned him. And then after this king Pelles with ten knights, and dame Elaine and twenty ladies, rode unto the castle of Bliant, that stood in an island enclosed in iron, with a fair water, deep and large. And when they were there Sir Launcelot let call it the Joyous Isle, and there was he called none otherwise but Le Chevaler Mal Fet, the knight that hath trespassed. Then Sir Launcelot let make him a shield all of sable, and a queen crowned in the midst all of silver, and a knight, clean armed, kneeling before her; and every day once, for any mirths that the ladies might make him, he would once every day look towards the realm of Logris where king Arthur and queen Guenever were. And then would he fall upon a weeping as though his heart should to-brast. So it fell that time that Sir Launcelot heard of a justing fast by his castle, within three leagues. Then he called unto him a dwarf, and he bade him go unto that justing, and, or ever the knights depart, look thou make there a cry in the hearing of all the knights, that there is one knight in the Joyous Isle, that is the castle Bliant, and say that his name is Le Chevaler Mal Fet, that will just against knights that will come; and who that putteth that knight to the worse shall have a fair maid and a jerfalcon.

CHAP. VII.

Of a great tourneying in the Joyous Isle, and how Sir Percivale and Sir Ector came thither, and Sir Percivale fought with him.

So when this cry was made, unto Joyous Isle drew knights to the number of five hundred. And wit ye well there was never seen in Arthur's days one knight that did so much deeds of arms as Sir Launcelot did three days together. For, as the book maketh truly mention, he had the better of all the five hundred knights, and there was not one slain of them. And after that Sir Launcelot made them all a great feast. And in the meanwhile came Sir Percivale de Galis and Sir Ector de Maris under that castle that was called the Joyous Isle. And as they beheld that gay castle they would have gone to that castle, but they might not for the broad water, and bridge could they find none. Then they saw on the other side a lady with a sperhawk in her hand, and Sir Percivale called unto her, and asked that lady who was in that castle. Fair knight, she said, here within this castle is the fairest lady in this land, and her name is Elaine. Also we have in this castle the fairest knight and the mightiest man that is, I dare say, living, and he calleth himself Le Chevaler Mal Fet. How came he into these marches? said Sir Percivale. Truly, said the damsel, he came into this country like a mad man, with dogs and boys chasing him through the city of Corbin; and by the holy vessel of the Sancgreal he was brought into his wit again, but he will not do battle with no knight but by undorne or by noon. And if ye list to come into the castle, said the lady, ye must ride unto the further side of the castle, and there shall ye find a vessel that will bear you and your horse. Then they departed and came unto the vessel. And then Sir Percivale alight, and said to Sir Ector de Maris, Ye shall abide me here until that I wit what manner a knight he is. For it were shame unto us, inasmuch as he is but one knight, and we should both do battle with him. Do ye as ye list, said Sir Ector de Maris, and here I shall abide you until that I hear of you. Then passed Sir Percivale the water. And when he came to the castle-gate, he bad the porter, Go thou to the good knight within the castle, and tell him here is come an errant knight to just with him. Sir, said the porter, ride ye within the castle, and there is a common place for justing, that lords and ladies may behold you.

So anon as Sir Launcelot had warning, he was soon ready; and there Sir Percivale and Sir Launcelot encountered with such a might, and their spears were so rude, that both the horses and the knights fell to the earth. Then they avoided their horses and flang out noble swords, and hewed away cantels of their shields, and hurtled together with their shields like two boars, and either wounded other passing sore. At the last Sir Percivale spake first, when they had foughten there more than two hours. Fair knight, said Sir Percivale, I require thee tell me thy name, for I met never with such a knight. Sir, said Sir Launcelot, my name is Le Chevalier Mal Fet: now tell me your name, said Sir Launcelot, I require you gentle knight. Truly, said Sir Percivale, my name is Sir Percivale de Galis, that was brother unto the good knight Sir Lamorak de Galis, and king Pellinore was our father, and Sir Aglovale is my brother. Alas, said Sir Launcelot, what have I done to fight with you that art a knight of the Table Round, that sometime was your fellow!

CHAP. VIII.

How each of them knew other, and of their great courtesy. And how his brother Sir Ector came unto him, and of their joy.

AND therewithal Sir Launcelot kneeled down upon his knees, and threw away his shield and his sword from him. When Sir Percivale saw him do so, he marvelled what he meaned. And then thus he said, Sir knight, whatsoever thou be, I require thee upon the high order of knighthood tell me thy true name. Then he said, Truly my name is Sir Launcelot du Lake, king Ban's son of Benoy. Alas, said Sir Percivale, what have I done! I was sent by the queen for to seek you, and so I have sought you nigh this two year; and yonder is Sir Ector de Maris your brother abideth me on the other side of the yonder water. Now, said Sir Percivale, I pray you forgive me mine offence that

I have here done. It is soon forgiven, said Sir Launcelot. Then Sir Percivale sent for Sir Ector de Maris. And when Sir Launcelot had a sight of him, he ran unto him and took him in his arms, and then Sir Ector kneeled down and either wept upon other, that all had pity to behold them. Then came dame Elaine, and she there made them great cheer as might lie in her power; and there she told Sir Ector and Sir Percivale how and in what manner Sir Launcelot came into that country, and how he was healed. And there it was known how long Sir Launcelot was with Sir Bliant and with Sir Selivant, and how he first met with them, and how he departed from them because of a boar; and how the hermit healed Sir Launcelot of his great wound, and how that he came to Corbin.

CHAP. IX.

How Sir Bors and Sir Lionel came to king Brandegore, and how Sir Bors took his son Helin le Blank, and of Sir Launcelot.

Now leave we Sir Launcelot in the Joyous Isle with the lady dame Elaine, and Sir Percivale and Sir Ector playing with them, and turn we to Sir Bors de Ganis and Sir Lionel, that had sought Sir Launcelot nigh by the space of two years, and never could they hear of him. And as they thus rode by adventure, they came to the house of Brandegore, and there Sir Bors was well known, for he had a child of the king's daughter fifteen years before, and his name was Helin le Blank. And when Sir Bors saw that child it liked him passing well. And so those knights had good cheer of the king Brandegore. And on the morn Sir Bors came afore king Brandegore, and said, Here is my son Helin le Blank, that as it is said he is my son; and since it is so, I will that ye wit I will have him with me unto the court of king Arthur. Sir, said the king, ye may well take him with you, but he is over tender of age. As for that, said Sir Bors, I will have him with me, and bring him to the house of most worship of the world. So when Sir Bors should depart, there was made great sorrow for the departing of Helin le Blank, and great weeping was there made. But Sir Bors and Sir Lionel departed. And within a while they came to Camelot, where was king Arthur. And when king Arthur understood that Helin le Blank was Sir Bors' son, and nephew unto king Brandegore, then king Arthur let him make knight of the Round Table; and so he proved a good knight and an adventurous.

Now will we turn to our matter of Sir Launcelot. It befel upon a day Sir Ector and Sir Percivale came to Sir Launcelot and asked him what he would do, and whether he would go with them unto king Arthur or not? Nay, said Sir Launcelot, that may not be by no mean; for I was so entreated at the court that I cast me never to come there more. Sir, said Sir Ector, I am your brother, and ye are the man in the world that I love most, and if I understood that it were your disworship, ye may understand I would never counsel you thereto; but king Arthur and all his knights, and in especial queen Guenever, made such dole and sorrow that it was marvel to hear and see. And ye must remember the great worship and renown that ye be of, how that ye have been more spoken of than any other knight that is now living; for there is none that beareth the name now but ye and Sir Tristram; therefore, brother, said Sir Ector, make you ready to ride to the court with us, and I dare say there was never knight better welcome to the court than ye: and I wot well, and can make it good, said Sir Ector, it hath cost my lady the queen twenty thousand pound the seeking of you. Well, brother, said Sir Launcelot, I will do after your counsel, and ride with you. So then they took their horses, and made them ready, and took their leave at king Pelles and at dame Elaine. And when Sir Launcelot should depart, dame Elaine made great sorrow. My lord Sir Launcelot, said dame Elaine, at this same feast of Pentecost shall your son and mine, Galahad, be made knight, for he is fully now fifteen winter old. Do as ye list, said Sir Launcelot, God give him grace to prove a good knight. As for that, said dame Elaine, I doubt not he shall prove the best man of his kin, except one. Then shall he be a man good enough, said Sir Launcelot.

CHAP. X.

How Sir Launcelot with Sir Percivale and Sir Ector came to the court, and of the great joy of him.

THEN they departed, and within five days' journey they came to Camelot, that is called in English, Winchester. And when Sir Launcelot was come among them, the king and all the knights made great joy of him. And there Sir Percivale de Galis and Sir Ector de Maris began and told the whole adventures, that Sir Launcelot had been out of his mind the time of his absence, how he called himself Le Chevaler Mal Fet, the knight that had trespassed, and in three days Sir Launcelot smote down five hundred knights. And ever, as Sir Ector and Sir Percivale told these tales of Sir Launcelot, queen Guenever wept as she should have died. Then the queen made great cheer. Truly, said king Arthur, I marvel for what cause ye Sir Launcelot went out of your mind? I and many others deem it was for the love of fair Elaine, the daughter of king Pelles, by whom ye are noised that ye have a child, and his name is Galahad; and men say he shall do marvels. My lord, said Sir Launcelot, if I did any folly, I have that I sought. And therewithal the king spake no more; but all Sir Launcelot's kin knew for whom he went out of his mind. And then there were great feasts made and great joy. And many great lords and ladies, when they heard that Sir Launcelot was come to the court again, they made great joy.

CHAP. XI.

How La Beale Isoud counselled Sir Tristram to go unto the court to the great feast of Pentecost.

Now will we leave of this matter, and speak we of Sir Tristram and of Sir Palamides, that was the Saracen unchristened. When Sir Tristram was come home unto Joyous Gard from his adventures, all this while that Sir Launcelot was thus missed two year and more, Sir Tristram bare the renown through all the realm of Logris, and many strange adventures befel him, and full well and manly and worshipfully he brought them to an end. So when he was come home, La Beale Isoud told him of the great feast that should be at Pentecost next following; and there she told him how Sir Launcelot had been missed two years, and all that while he had been out of his mind, and how he was holpen by the holy vessel the Sancgreal. Alas, said Sir Tristram, that caused some debate betwixt him and queen Guenever. Sir, said dame Isoud, I know it all, for queen Guenever sent me a letter, in the which she wrote me all how it was, for to require you to seek him; and now, blessed be God, said La Beale Isoud, he is whole and sound, and come again to the court. Thereof am I glad, said Sir Tristram, and now shall ye and I make us ready, for both ye and I will be at the feast. Sir, said Isoud, and it please you I will not be there, for through me ye be marked of many good knights, and that causeth you to have much more labour for my sake than needeth you. Then will I not be there, said Sir Tristram, but if ye be there. Not so, said La Beale Isoud, for then shall I be spoken of shame among all queens and ladies of estate, for ye that are called one of the noblest knights of the world, and ye a knight of the Round Table, how may ye be missed at that feast? What shall be said among all knights?—See how Sir Tristram hunteth, and hawketh, and cowereth within a castle with his lady, and forsaketh your worship. Alas, shall some say, it is pity that ever he was made knight, or that ever he should have the love of a lady. Also what shall queens and ladies say of me?—It is pity that I have my life, that I will hold so noble a knight as ye are from his worship. Truly, said Sir Tristram unto La Beale Isoud, it is passing well said of you, and nobly counselled, and now I well understand that ye love me; and like as ye have counselled me, I will do a part thereafter. But there shall no man nor child ride with me, but myself. And so will I ride on Tuesday next coming, and no more harness of war but my spear and my sword.

CHAP. XII.

How Sir Tristram departed unarmed, and met with Sir Palamides, and how they smote each other, and how Sir Palamides forbare him.

AND so when the day came, Sir Tristram took his leave at La Beale Isoud; and she sent with him four knights, and within half a mile he sent them again: and within a mile after Sir Tristram saw afore him where Sir Palamides had stricken down a knight, and almost wounded him to the death. Then Sir Tristram repented him that he was not armed, and then he hoved still. With that Sir Palamides knew Sir Tristram, and cried on high, Sir Tristram, now be we met, for or we depart we will redress our old sores! As for that, said Sir Tristram, there was never yet Christian man that might make his boast that ever I fled from him; and wit ye well Sir Palamides, thou that art a Saracen shall never make thy boast that Sir Tristram de Liones shall flee from thee. And therewith Sir Tristram made his horse to run, and with all his might he came straight upon Sir Palamides, and brast his spear upon him in an hundred pieces. And forthwithal Sir Tristram drew his sword. And then he turned his horse and struck at Palamides six great strokes upon his helm, and then Sir Palamides stood still and beheld Sir Tristram, and marvelled of his woodness and of his folly. And then Sir Palamides said to himself, And Sir Tristram were armed it were hard to cease him of this battle, and if I turn again and slay him I am shamed wheresoever that I go. Then Sir Tristram spake, and said, Thou coward knight, what castest thou to do? why wilt thou not do battle with me, for have thou no doubt I shall endure all thy malice. Ah, Sir Tristram, said Sir Palamides, full well thou wotest I may not fight with thee for shame, for thou art here naked, and I am armed, and if I slay thee dishonour shall be mine. And well thou wotest, said Sir Palamides to Sir Tristram, I know thy strength and thy hardiness to endure against a good knight. That is truth, said Sir Tristram, I understand thy valiantness well. Ye say well, said Sir Palamides, now I require you tell me a question that I shall say to you. Tell me what it is, said Sir Tristram, and I shall answer you the truth. I put the case, said Sir Palamides, that ye were armed at all rights as well as I am, and I naked as ye be, what would ye do to me now by your true knighthood? Ah, said Sir Tristram, now I understand thee well, Sir Palamides, for now must I say my own judgment, and, as God me bless, that I shall say shall not be said for no fear that I have of thee. But this is all; wit, Sir Palamides, as at this time thou shouldest depart from me, for I would not have ado with thee. No more will I, said Sir Palamides, and therefore ride forth on thy way. As for that I may choose, said Sir Tristram, either to ride or to abide. But Sir Palamides, said Sir Tristram, I marvel of one thing, that thou that art so good a knight, that thou wilt not be christened, and thy brother Sir Safere hath been christened many a day.

CHAP. XIII.

How that Sir Tristram gat him harness of a knight which was hurt, and how he overthrew Sir Palamides.

As for that, said Sir Palamides, I may not yet be christened, for one avow that I have made many years agone; howbeit in my heart I believe in Jesus Christ and his mild mother Mary; but I have but one battle to do, and when that is done I will be baptised with a good will. By my head, said Sir Tristram, as for one battle thou shalt not seek it no longer. For God defend, said Sir Tristram, that through my default thou shouldest longer live thus a Saracen. For yonder is a knight that ye, Sir Palamides, have hurt and smitten down; now help me that I were armed in his armour, and I shall soon fulfil thine avows. As ye will, said Sir Palamides, so it shall be. So they rode unto that knight that sat upon a bank, and then Sir Tristram saluted him, and he weakly saluted him again. Sir knight, said Sir Tristram, I require you tell me your right name. Sir, he said, my name is Sir Galleron of Galway, and knight of the Table Round. Truly, said Sir Tristram, I am right heavy of your hurts: but this is all, I must pray you to lend me all your whole armour, for ye see I am unarmed, and I must do battle with this knight. Sir, said the hurt knight, ye shall have it with a good will; but ye must beware, for I warn you that knight is wight. Sir, said Galleron, I pray you tell me your name, and what is that knight's name that hath beaten me. Sir, as for my name, it is Sir Tristram de Liones, and as for the knight's name that hath hurt you, it is Sir Palamides, brother unto the good knight Sir Safere, and yet is Sir Palamides unchristened. Alas, said Sir Galleron, that is pity that so good a knight and so noble a man of arms should be unchristened. Truly, said Sir Tristram, either he shall slay me, or I him, but that he shall be christened or ever we depart in sunder. My lord Sir Tristram, said Sir Galleron, your renown and worship is well known through many realms, and God save you this day from shenship and shame. Then Sir Tristram unarmed Galleron, the which was a noble knight and had done many deeds of arms, and he was a large knight of flesh and bone. And when he was unarmed he stood upon his feet, for he was bruised in the back with a spear; yet, so as Sir Galleron might, he armed Sir Tristram. And then Sir Tristram mounted upon his own horse, and in his hand he gat Sir Galleron's spear. And therewithal Sir Palamides was ready, and so they came hurtling together, and either smote other in the midst of their shields, and therewithal Sir Palamides' spear brake, and Sir Tristram smote down the horse; and then Sir Palamides, as soon as he might, avoided his horse, and dressed his shield, and pulled out his sword. That saw Sir Tristram, and therewith he alight, and tied his horse to a tree.

CHAP. XIV.

How Sir Tristram and Sir Palamides fought long together, and after accorded; and how Sir Tristram made him to be christened.

AND then they came together as two wild boars, lashing together, tracing and traversing as noble men that oft had been well proved in battle; but ever Sir Palamides dread the might of Sir Tristram, and therefore he suffered him to breathe him. Thus they fought more than two hours; and often Sir Tristram smote such strokes at Sir Palamides that he made him to kneel; and Sir Palamides brake and cut away many pieces of Sir Tristram's shield, and then Sir Palamides wounded Sir Tristram, for he was a well fighting man. Then Sir Tristram was wood wrath out of measure, and rashed upon Sir Palamides with such a might that Sir Palamides fell groveling to the earth, and therewithal he leapt up lightly upon his feet, and then Sir Tristram wounded Sir Palamides sore through the shoulder. And ever Sir Tristram fought still in like hard, and Sir Palamides failed not, but gave him many sad strokes. And at the last Sir Tristram doubled his strokes, and by fortune Sir Tristram smote Sir Palamides' sword out of his hand, and if Sir Palamides had stooped for his sword, he had been slain. Then Palamides stood still and beheld his sword with a sorrowful heart. How

now, said Sir Tristram unto Palamides, now have I thee at advantage as thou hadst me this day, but it shall never be said in no court, nor among good knights, that Sir Tristram shall slay any knight that is weaponless, and therefore take thou thy sword, and let us make an end of this battle. As for to do this battle, said Palamides, I dare right well end it; but I have no great lust to fight no more, and for this cause, said Palamides, mine offence to you is not so great but that we may be friends. All that I have offended is and was for the love of La Beale Isoud. And as for her, I dare say she is peerless above all other ladies, and also I proffered her never no dishonour; and by her I have gotten the most part of my worship, and sithen I offended never as to her own person. And as for the offence that I have done, it was against your own person, and for that offence ye have given me this day many sad strokes, and some I have given you again; and now I dare say I felt never man of your might, nor so well breathed, but if it were Sir Launcelot du Lake. Wherefore I require you, my lord, forgive me all that I have offended unto you. And this same day have me to the next church, and first let me be clean confessed, and after see you now that I be truly baptized. And then will we all ride together unto the court of Arthur, that we be there at the high feast. Now take your horse, said Sir Tristram, and as ye say, so it shall be; and all your evil will God forgive it you, and I do. And here, within this mile, is the suffragan of Carlisle, that shall give you the sacrament of baptism. Then they took their horses, and Sir Galleron rode with them. And when they came to the suffragan Sir Tristram told him their desire. Then the suffragan let fill a great vessel with water. And when he had hallowed it, he then confessed clean Sir Palamides, and Sir Tristram and Sir Galleron were his godfathers. And then soon after they departed, riding towards Camelot, where king Arthur and queen Guenever was, and for the most part all the knights of the Round Table. And so the king and all the court were glad that Sir Palamides was christened. And at the same feast in came Galahad and sat in the Siege Perilous.

And so therewithal departed and dissevered all the knights of the Round Table. And Sir Tristram returned again unto Joyous Gard, and Sir Palamides followed the questing beast.

𝔥ere endeth the second book of syr 𝔗ristram that was drawen oute of 𝔉rensshe in to 𝔈nglysshe.

𝔅ut here is no rehersal of the thyrd book. 𝔄nd here foloweth the noble tale of the 𝔖ancgreal that called is the hooly bessel and the sygnefycacyon of the blessid blood of our lord 𝔍hesu 𝔆ryste, blessid mote it be, the which was brought in to this land by 𝔍oseph of 𝔄rmathye, therefor on al synful souls blessid lord haue thou mercy.

𝔈xplicit liber xii. 𝔈t incipit 𝔇ecimustercius.

𝔗he 𝔗hirteenth 𝔅ook.

CHAP. I.

How at the Vigil of the feast of Pentecost entered into the hall, before king Arthur, a damsel, and desired Sir Launcelot for to come and dub a knight, and how he went with her.

AT the vigil of Pentecost, when all the fellowship of the Round Table were comen unto Camelot, and there heard their service, and the tables were set ready to the meat, right so entered into the hall a full fair gentlewoman on horseback, that had ridden full fast, for her horse was all besweat. Then she there alight, and came before the king, and saluted him; and then he said, Damsel, God thee bless! Sir, said she, I pray you say me where Sir Launcelot is? Yonder ye may see him, said the king. Then she went unto Launcelot and said, Sir Launcelot, I salute you on king Pelles' behalf, and I require you come on with me hereby into a forest. Then Sir Launcelot asked her with whom she dwelled? I dwell, said she, with king Pelles. What will ye with me? said Sir Launcelot. Ye shall know, said she, when ye come thither. Well, said

he, I will gladly go with you. So Sir Launcelot bade his squire saddle his horse and bring his arms; and in all haste he did his commandment. Then came the queen unto Launcelot and said, Will ye leave us at this high feast? Madam, said the gentlewoman, wit ye well he shall be with you to-morrow by dinner-time. If I wist, said the queen, that he should not be with us here to-morn, he should not go with you by my good will.

Right so departed Sir Launcelot with the gentlewoman, and rode until that he came into a forest, and into a great valley, where they saw an abbey of nuns; and there was a squire ready, and opened the gates; and so they entered, and descended off their horses, and there came a fair fellowship about Sir Launcelot and welcomed him, and were passing glad of his coming. And then they led him intó the Abbess's chamber, and unarmed him, and right so he was ware upon a bed lying two of his cousins, Sir Bors and Sir Lionel, and then he waked them, and when they saw him they made great joy. Sir, said Sir Bors unto Sir Launcelot, what adventure hath brought thee hither, for we wend to-morrow to have found you at Camelot? Truly, said Sir Launcelot, a gentlewoman brought me hither, but I know not the cause. In the meanwhile, as they thus stood talking together, there came twelve nuns which brought with them Galahad, the which was passing fair and well made, that unneth in the world men might not find his match; and all those ladies wept. Sir, said the ladies, we bring you here this child, the which we have nourished, and we pray you to make him a knight; for of a more worthier man's hand may he not receive the order of knighthood. Sir Launcelot beheld that young squire, and saw him seemly and demure as a dove, with all manner of good features, that he wend of his age never to have seen so fair a man of form. Then said Sir Launcelot, Cometh this desire of himself? He and all they said, Yea. Then shall he, said Sir Launcelot, receive the high order of knighthood as to-morrow at the reverence of the high feast. That night Sir Launcelot had passing good cheer, and on the morn at the hour of prime, at Galahad's desire, he made him knight, and said, God make him a good man, For beauty faileth you not as any that liveth.

CHAP. II.

How the letters were found written in the siege perilous, and of the marvellous adventure of the sword in a stone.

Now, fair sir, said Sir Launcelot, will ye come with me unto the court of king Arthur? Nay, said he, I will not go with you as at this time. Then he departed from them and took his two cousins with him, and so they came unto Camelot by the hour of undorne on Whitsunday. By that time the king and the queen were gone to the minster to hear their service: then the king and the queen were passing glad of Sir Bors and Sir Lionel, and so was all the fellowship. So when the king and all the knights were come from service, the barons espied in the sieges of the Round Table, all about written with gold letters. Here ought to sit he, and he ought to sit here. And thus they went so long until that they came to the siege perilous, where they found letters newly written of gold, that said: Four hundred winters and fifty-four accomplished after the passion of our Lord Jesu Christ ought this siege to be fulfilled. Then all they said, This is a marvellous thing, and an adventurous. In the name of God, said Sir Launcelot; and then he accounted the term of the writing, from the birth of our Lord unto that day. It seemeth me, said Sir Launcelot, this siege ought to be fulfilled this same day, for this is the feast of Pentecost after the four hundred and four and fifty year; and if it would please all parties, I would none of these letters were seen this day, till he be come that ought to achieve this adventure. Then made they to ordain a cloth of silk for to cover these letters in the siege perilous. Then the king bad haste unto dinner. Sir, said Sir Kay the steward, if ye go now unto your meat, ye shall break your old custom of your court. For ye have not used on this day to sit at your meat or that ye have seen some adventure. Ye say sooth, said the king, but I had so great joy of Sir Launcelot and of his cousins, which be come to the court whole and sound, that I bethought me not of my old custom. So as they stood speaking, in came a squire, and said unto the king, Sir, I bring unto you marvellous tidings. What be they? said the king. Sir, there is here beneath at the river a great stone, which I saw fleet above the water, and therein saw I sticking a sword. The king said, I will see that marvel. So all the knights went with him, and when they came unto the river, they found there a stone fleeting, as it were of red marble, and therein stack a fair and a rich sword, and in the pomell thereof were precious stones, wrought with subtil letters of gold. Then the barons read the letters, which said in this wise: Never shall man take me hence but only he by whose side I ought to hang, and he shall be the best knight of the world. When the king had seen these letters, he said unto Sir Launcelot, Fair sir, this sword ought to be yours, for I am sure ye be the best knight of the world. Then Sir Launcelot answered full soberly : Certes, sir, it is not my sword : also, sir, wit ye well I have no hardiness to set my hand to, for it longed not to hang by my side. Also who that assayeth to take that sword, and faileth of it, he shall receive a wound by that sword, that he shall not be whole long after. And I will that ye wit that this same day will the adventures of the Sancgreal, that is called the holy vessel, begin.

CHAP. III.

How Sir Gawaine assayed to draw out the sword, and how an old man brought in Galabad.

Now, fair nephew, said the king unto Sir Gawaine, assay ye for my love. Sir, he said, save your good grace, I shall not do that. Sir, said the king, assay to take the sword, and at my commandment. Sir, said Gawaine, your commandment I will obey. And therewith he took up the sword by the handles, but he might not stir it. I thank you, said the king to Sir Gawaine. My lord Sir Gawaine, said Sir Launcelot, now wit ye well, this sword shall touch you so sore that ye shall will ye had never set your hand thereto, for the best castle of this realm. Sir, he said, I might not withsay mine uncle's will and commandment. But when the king heard this, he repented it much, and said unto Sir Percivale that he should assay for his love. And he said, Gladly, for to bear Sir Gawaine fellowship. And therewith he set his hand on the sword, and drew it strongly, but he might not move it. Then were there more that durst be so hardy to set their hands thereto. Now may ye go to your dinner, said Sir Kay unto the king, for a marvellous adventure have ye seen. So the king and all went unto the court,

and every knight knew his own place, and set him therein, and young men that were knights served them. So when they were served, and all sieges fulfilled, save only the siege perilous, anon there befell a marvellous adventure, that all the doors and the windows of the place shut by themself. Not for then the hall was not greatly darkened, and therewith they abashed both one and other. Then king Arthur spake first, and said, Fair fellows and lords, we have seen this day marvels, but or night I suppose we shall see greater marvels. In the mean while came in a good old man, and an ancient, clothed all in white, and there was no knight knew from whence he came. And with him he brought a young knight, both on foot, in red arms, without sword or shield, save a scabbard hanging by his side. And these words he said, Peace be with you, fair lords. Then the old man said unto Arthur, Sir, I bring here a young knight the which is of king's lineage, and of the kindred of Joseph of Arimathie, whereby the marvels of this court and of strange realms shall be fully accomplished.

CHAP. IV.

How the old man brought Galabad to the siege perilous and set him therein, and how all the knights marvelled.

THE king was right glad of his words, and said unto the good man, Sir, ye be right welcome, and the young knight with you. Then the old man made the young man to unarm him ; and he was in a coat of red sendel, and bare a mantle upon his shoulder that was furred with ermine, and put that upon him. And the old knight said unto the young knight, Sir, follow me. And anon he led him unto the siege perilous, where beside sat Sir Launcelot, and the good man lift up the cloth, and found there letters that said thus : This is the siege of Galahad the haut prince. Sir, said the old knight, wit ye well that place is yours. And then he set him down surely in that siege. And then he said to the old man, Sir, ye may now go your way, for well have ye done that ye were commanded to do. And recommend me unto my grandsire king Pelles, and unto my lord Petchere, and say them on my behalf, I shall come and see them as soon as ever I may. So the good man departed, and there met him twenty noble squires, and so took their horses and went their way. Then all the knights of the Table Round marvelled them greatly of Sir Galahad, that he durst sit there in that siege perilous, and was so tender of age, and wist not from whence he came, but all only by God, and said, This is he by whom the Sancgreal shall be achieved, for there sat never none but he, but he were mischieved. Then Sir Launcelot beheld his son, and had great joy of him. Then Sir Bors told his fellows, Upon pain of my life this young knight shall come unto great worship. This noise was great in all the court, so that it came to the queen. Then she had marvel what knight it might be that durst adventure him to sit in the siege perilous. Many said unto the queen, he resembled much unto Sir Launcelot. I may well suppose, said the queen, that he is son of Sir Launcelot and king Pelles' daughter, and his name is Galahad. I would fain see him, said the queen, for he must needs be a noble man, for so is his father; I report me unto all the Table Round. So when the meat was done, that the king and all were risen, the king went unto the siege perilous, and lift up the cloth, and found there the name of Galahad, and then he shewed it unto Sir Gawaine, and said, Fair nephew, now have we among us Sir Galahad the good knight, that shall worship us all, and upon pain of my life he shall achieve the Sancgreal, right so as Sir Launcelot hath done us to understand. Then came king Arthur unto Galahad, and said, Sir, ye be welcome, for ye shall move many good knights to the quest of the Sancgreal, and ye shall achieve that never knights might bring to an end. Then the king took him by the hand, and went down from the palace to shew Galahad the adventures of the stone.

CHAP. V.

How king Arthur shewed the stone, hoving on the water, to Galahad, and how he drew out the sword.

THE queen heard thereof, and came after with many ladies, and shewed them the stone where it hoved on the water. Sir, said the king unto Sir Galahad, here is a great marvel as ever I saw, and right good knights have assayed and failed. Sir, said Galahad, that is no marvel, for this adventure is not theirs, but mine, and for the surety of this sword I brought none with me; for here by my side hangeth the scabbard. And anon he laid his hand on the sword, and lightly drew it out of the stone, and put it in the sheath and said unto the king, Now it goeth better than it did aforehand. Sir, said the king, a shield God shall send you. Now have I, said Sir Galahad, that sword that sometime was the good knight's Balin le Savage, and he was a passing good man of his hands. And with this sword he slew his brother Balan, and that was great pity, for he was a good knight, and either slew other through a dolorous stroke that Balan gave unto my grandfather king Pelles, the which is not yet whole, nor not shall be till I heal him. Therewith the king and all espied where came riding down the river a lady on a white palfrey toward them. Then she saluted the king and the queen, and asked if that Sir Launcelot was there? And then he answered himself, I am here, fair lady. Then she said, all with weeping, How your great doing is changed sith this day in the morn. Damsel, why say ye so? said Launcelot. I say you sooth, said the damsel, for ye were this day the best knight of the world, but who should say so now should be a liar, for there is now one better than ye. And well it is proved by the adventures of the sword whereto ye durst not set your hand, and that is the change and leaving of your name; wherefore I make unto you a remembrance, that ye shall not ween from henceforth that ye be the best knight of the world. As touching unto that, said Launcelot, I know well I was never the best. Yes, said the damsel, that were ye, and are yet of any sinful man of the world. And sir king, Nacien the hermit sendeth thee word, that thee shall befall the greatest worship that ever befell king in Britain; and I say you wherefore, for this day the Sancgreal shall appear in thy house, and feed thee and all thy fellowship of the Round Table. So she departed and went that same way that she came.

CHAP. VI.

How king Arthur had all the knights together, for to just in the meadow beside Camelot or they departed.

Now, said the king, I am sure at this quest of the Sancgreal shall all ye of the Table Round depart, and never shall I see you again whole together, therefore I will see you all whole together in the meadow of Camelot, to just and to tourney, that after your death men may speak of it, that such good knights were wholly together such a day. As unto that counsel, and at the king's request, they accorded all, and took on their harness that longed unto justing. But all this moving of the king was for this intent, for to see Galahad proved, for the king deemed he should not lightly come again unto the court after his departing. So were they assembled in the meadow, both more and less. Then Sir Galahad, by the prayer of the king and the queen, did upon him a noble jesserance, and also he did on his helm, but shield would he take none for no prayer of the king. And then Sir Gawaine and other knights prayed him to take a spear. Right so he did; and the queen was in a tower with all her ladies for to behold that tournament. Then Sir Galahad dressed him in the midst of the meadow, and began to break spears marvellously, that all men had wonder

of him, for he there surmounted all other knights, for within a while he had thrown down many good knights of the Table Round save twain, that was Sir Launcelot and Sir Percivale.

CHAP. VII.

How the queen desired to see Galahad, and how after all the knights were replenished with the holy Sangreal, and how they avowed the enquest of the same.

THEN the king, at the queen's request, made him to alight and to unlace his helm, that the queen might see him in the visage. And when she beheld him she said, Soothly, I dare well say that Sir Launcelot is his father, for never two men resembled more in likeness, therefore it is no marvel though he be of great prowess. So a lady that stood by the queen said, Madam, ought he of right to be so good a knight? Yea, forsooth, said the queen, for he is of all parties come of the best knights of the world, and of the highest lineage; for Sir Launcelot is come but of the eighth degree from our Lord Jesu Christ, and Sir Galahad is of the ninth degree from our Lord Jesu Christ; therefore I dare say they be the greatest gentlemen of the world. And then the king and all estates went home unto Camelot, and so went to evensong to the great minster. And so after upon that to supper, and every knight sat in his own place as they were toforehand. Then anon they heard cracking and crying of thunder, that them thought the place should all to-drive. In the midst of this blast entered a sun-beam more clearer by seven times than ever they saw day, and all they were alighted of the grace of the Holy Ghost. Then began every knight to behold other, and either saw other by their seeming fairer than ever they saw afore. Not for then there was no knight might speak one word a great while, and so they looked every man on other, as they had been dumb. Then there entered into the hall the holy Graile covered with white samite, but there was none might see it, nor who bare it. And there was all the hall full filled with good odours, and every knight had such meats and drinks as he best loved in this world: and when the holy Graile had been borne through the hall, then the holy vessel departed suddenly, that they wist not where it became. Then had they all breath to speak. And then the king yielded thankings unto God of his good grace that he had sent them. Certes, said the king, we ought to thank our Lord Jesu greatly, for that he hath shewed us this day at the reverence of this high feast of Pentecost. Now, said Sir Gawaine, we have been served this day of what meats and drinks we thought on, but one thing beguiled us, we might not see the holy Graile, it was so preciously covered: wherefore I will make here avow, that to-morn, without longer abiding, I shall labour in the quest of the Sancgreal, that I shall hold me out a twelvemonth and a day, or more if need be, and never shall I return again unto the court till I have seen it more openly than it hath been seen here: and if I may not speed, I shall return again as he that may not be against the will of our Lord Jesu Christ. When they of the Table Round heard Sir Gawaine say so, they arose up the most party, and made such avows as Sir Gawaine had made.

Anon as king Arthur heard this he was greatly displeased, for he wist well that they might not againsay their avows. Alas! said king Arthur unto Sir Gawaine, ye have nigh slain me with the avow and promise that ye have made. For through you ye have bereft me of the fairest fellowship and the truest of knighthood that ever were seen together in any realm of the world. For when they depart from hence, I am sure they all shall never meet more in this world, for they shall die many in the quest. And so it forethinketh me a little, for I have loved them as well as my life, wherefore it shall grieve me right sore the departition of this fellowship. For I have had an old custom to have them in my fellowship.

CHAP. VIII.

How great sorrow was made of the king and the queen and ladies for the departing of the knights, and how they departed.

AND therewith the tears filled in his eyes. And then he said, Gawaine, Gawaine, ye have set me in great sorrow. For I have great doubt that my true fellowship shall never meet here more again. Ah, said Sir Launcelot, comfort yourself, for it shall be unto us as a great honour, and much more than if we died in any other places, for of death we be sure. Ah Launcelot, said the king, the great love that I have had unto you all the days of my life maketh me to say such doleful words; for never christian king had never so many worthy men at this table as I have had this day at the Round Table, and that is my great sorrow. When the queen, ladies, and gentlewomen wist these tidings, they had such sorrow and heaviness that there might no tongue tell it, for those knights had holden them in honour and charity. But among all other queen Guenever made great sorrow. I marvel, said she, my lord would suffer them to depart from him. Thus was all the court troubled, for the love of the departition of those knights. And many of those ladies that loved knights would have gone with their lovers; and so had they done, had not an old knight come among them in religious clothing, and then he spake all on high and said, Fair lords which have sworn in the quest of the Sancgreal, thus sendeth you Nacien the hermit word, that none in this quest lead lady nor gentlewoman with him, for it is not to do in so high a service as they labour in, for I warn you plain, he that is not clean of his sins he shall not see the mysteries of our Lord Jesu Christ; and for this cause they left these ladies and gentlewomen. After this the queen came unto Galahad, and asked him of whence he was, and of what country? He told her of whence he was. And son unto

Sir Launcelot, she said he was: as to that he said neither yea nor nay. Truly, said the queen, of your father ye need not to shame you, for he is the goodliest knight and of the best men of the world come, and of the stock, of all parties, of kings. Wherefore ye ought of right to be of your deeds a passing good man, and certainly, she said, ye resemble him much. Then Sir Galahad was a little ashamed, and said, Madam, sith ye know in certain, wherefore do ye ask it me? for he that is my father shall be known openly, and all betimes. And then they went to rest them. And in the honour of the highness of Galahad he was led into king Arthur's chamber, and there rested in his own bed. And as soon as it was day the king arose, for he had no rest of all that night for sorrow. Then he went unto Gawaine and to Sir Launcelot, that were arisen for to hear mass. And then the king again said, Ah Gawaine, Gawaine, ye have betrayed me. For never shall my court be amended by you, but ye will never be sorry for me, as I am for you. And therewith the tears began to run down by his visage. And therewith the king said, Ah knight, Sir Launcelot, I require thee thou counsel me, for I would that this quest were undone, and it might be. Sir, said Sir Launcelot, ye saw yesterday so many worthy knights that then were sworn, that they may not leave it in no manner of wise. That wot I well, said the king, but it shall so heavy me at their departing, that I wot well there shall no manner of joy remedy me. And then the king and the queen went unto the minster. So anon Launcelot and Gawaine commanded their men to bring their arms. And when they all were armed, save their shields and their helms, then they came to their fellowship, which all were ready in the same wise for to go to the minster to hear their service.

Then after the service was done, the king would wit how many had taken the quest of the holy Graile, and to account them he prayed them all. Then found they by tale an hundred and fifty, and all were knights of the Round Table. And then they put on their helms, and departed, and recommended them all wholly unto the queen, and there was weeping and great sorrow. Then the queen departed into her chamber so that no man should perceive her great sorrows. When Sir Launcelot missed the queen he went into her chamber, and when she saw him she cried aloud, O, Sir Launcelot, ye have betrayed me and put me to death, for to leave thus my lord. Ah, madam, said Sir Launcelot, I pray you be not displeased, for I shall come again as soon as I may with my worship. Alas, said she, that ever I saw you! but He that suffered death upon the cross for all mankind, be to your good conduct and safety, and all the whole fellowship. Right so departed Sir Launcelot, and found his fellowship that abode his coming. And so they mounted upon their horses, and rode through the streets of Camelot, and there was weeping of the rich and poor, and the king turned away, and might not speak for weeping. So within a while they came to a city and a castle that hight Vagon: there they entered into the castle, and the lord of that castle was an old man that hight Vagon, and he was a good man of his living, and set open the gates, and made them all the good cheer that he might. And so on the morrow they were all accorded that they should depart every each from other. And then they departed on the morrow with weeping and mourning cheer, and every knight took the way that him best liked.

CHAP. IX.

How Galahad gat him a shield, and how they sped that presumed to take down the said shield.

Now rideth Sir Galahad yet without shield, and so he rode four days without any adventure. And at the fourth day after even-song he came to a white abbey, and there he was received with great reverence, and led to a chamber, and then he was unarmed, and then was he ware of two knights of the Round Table, one was king Bagdemagus, and that other was Sir Uwaine. And when they saw him they went unto him and made of him great solace, and so they went to supper. Sirs, said Sir Galahad, what adventure brought you hither? Sir, said they, it is told us that within this place is a shield that no man may bear about his neck but that if he be mischieved or dead within three days, or else maimed for ever. Ah, sir, said king Bagdemagus, I shall bear it to-morrow for to assay this strange adventure. In the name of God, said Sir Galahad. Sir, said Bagdemagus, and I may not achieve the adventure of this shield ye shall take it upon you, for I am sure ye shall not fail. Sir, said Galahad, I agree right well thereto, for I have no shield. So on the morn they arose and heard mass. Then king Bagdemagus asked. where the adventurous shield was. Anon a monk led him behind an altar where the shield hung as white as any snow, but in the midst was a red cross. Sir, said the monk, this shield ought not to be hanged about no knight's neck, but he be the worthiest knight of the world, and therefore I counsel you knights to be well advised. Well, said king Bagdemagus, I wot well that I am not the best knight of the world, but yet shall I assay to bear it. And so he bare it out of the monastery; and then he said unto Sir Galahad, If it will please you, I pray you abide here still, till ye know how I shall speed. I shall abide you here, said Galahad. Then king Bagdemagus took with him a squire, the which should bring tidings unto Sir Galahad how he sped. Then when they had ridden a two mile, and came in a fair valley afore an hermitage, then they saw a goodly knight come from that part in white armour, horse and all, and he came as fast as his horse might run with his spear in the rest, and king Bagdemagus dressed his spear against him, and brake it upon the

white knight; but the other struck him so hard that he brake the mails, and thrust him through the right shoulder, for the shield covered him not as at that time, and so he bare him from his horse, and therewith he alighted and took the white shield from him, saying, Knight, thou hast done thyself great folly, for this shield ought not to be borne but by him that shall have no peer that liveth. And then he came to king Bagdemagus's squire and said, Bear this shield unto the good knight Sir Galahad, that thou left in the abbey, and greet him well from me. Sir, said the squire, what is your name? Take thou no heed of my name, said the knight, for it is not for thee to know, nor for none earthly man. Now, fair sir, said the squire, at the reverence of Jesu Christ tell me for what cause this shield may not be borne, but if the bearer thereof be mischieved. Now, sith thou hast conjured me so, said the knight, this shield behoveth to no man but unto Galahad. And the squire went unto Bagdemagus and asked him whether he were sore wounded or not? Yea forsooth, said he, I shall escape hard from the death. Then he fetched his horse, and brought him with great pain unto an abbey. Then was he taken down softly, and unarmed, and laid in a bed, and there was looked to his wounds. And, as the book telleth, he lay there long, and escaped hard with the life.

CHAP. X.

How Galahad departed with the shield. And how king Evelake had received the shield of Joseph of Aramathie.

Sir Galahad, said the squire, that knight that wounded Bagdemagus sendeth you greeting, and bad that ye should bear this shield, where through great adventures should befall. Now blessed be God and fortune, said Sir Galahad. And then he asked his arms, and mounted upon his horse, and hung the white shield about his neck, and commended them unto God. And Sir

Uwaine said he would bear him fellowship if it pleased him. Sir, said Galahad, that may ye not, for I must go alone, save this squire shall bear me fellowship : and so departed Uwaine. Then within a while came Galahad there as the white knight abode him by the hermitage, and every each saluted other courteously. Sir, said Galahad, by this shield been many marvels fallen. Sir, said the knight, it befell after the passion of our Lord Jesu Christ thirty-two year, that Joseph of Armathie, the gentle knight the which took down our Lord off the holy cross, at that time he departed from Jerusalem with a great party of his kindred with him. And so he laboured till that they came to a city that hight Sarras. And at that same hour that Joseph came to Sarras, there was a king that hight Evelake, that had great war against the Saracens, and in especially against one Saracen, the which was the king Evelake's cousin, a rich king and a mighty, which marched nigh this land, and his name was called Tolleme la Feintes. So on a day this two met to do battle. Then Joseph, the son of Joseph of Armathie, went to king Evelake, and told him he should be discomfit and slain, but if he left his belief of the old law, and believed upon the new law. And then there he shewed him the right belief of the Holy Trinity, to the which he agreed unto with all his heart, and there this shield was made for king Evelake, in the name of Him that died upon the cross. And then through his good belief he had the better of king Tolleme. For when Evelake was in the battle, there was a cloth set afore the shield, and when he was in the greatest peril he let put away the cloth, and then his enemies saw a figure of a man on the cross, where through they all were discomfit. And so it befell that a man of king Evelake's was smitten his hand off, and bare that hand in his other hand. And Joseph called that man unto him, and bad him, Go with good devotion, touch the cross. And as soon as that man

had touched the cross with his hand, it was as whole as ever it was tofore. Then soon after there fell a great marvel, that the cross of the shield at one time vanished away, that no man wist where it became. And then king Evelake was baptised, and for the most part all the people of that city. So soon after Joseph would depart, and king Evelake would go with him, whether he would or nould. And so by fortune they came into this land, that at that time was called Great Britain. And there they found a great felon paynim, that put Joseph into prison. And so by fortune tidings came unto a worthy man that hight Mondrames, and he assembled all his people, for the great renown he had heard of Joseph, and so he came into the land of Great Britain, and disherited this felon paynim and consumed him, and therewith delivered Joseph out of prison. And after that all the people were turned to the christian faith.

CHAP. XI.

How Joseph made a cross on the white shield with his blood, and how Galahad was by a monk brought to a tomb.

Not long after that Joseph was laid in his deadly bed. And when king Evelake saw that, he made much sorrow, and said, For thy love I have left my country, and sith ye shall depart out of this world leave me some token of yours, that I may think on you. Joseph said, that will I do full gladly. Now bring me your shield that I took you when ye went into battle against king Tolleme. Then Joseph bled sore at the nose that he might not by no means be staunched. And there upon that shield he made a cross of his own blood. Now may ye see a remembrance that I love you, for ye shall never see this shield but ye shall think on me, and it shall be always as fresh as it is now ; and never shall no man bear this shield about his neck but he shall repent it, unto the time that Galahad the good knight bear it, and the last of my lineage shall have it about his neck, that shall do many marvellous deeds. Now, said king Evelake, where shall I put this shield, that this worthy knight may have it? Ye shall leave it there as Nacien the hermit shall be put after his death. For thither shall that good knight come the fifteenth day after that he shall receive the order of knighthood. And so that day that they set is this time that ye have his shield. And in the same abbey lieth Nacien the hermit. And then the white knight vanished away. Anon, as the squire had heard these words, he alight off his hackney, and kneeled down at Galahad's feet, and prayed him that he might go with him till he had made him knight.—If I would not refuse you?—Then will ye make me a knight, said the squire, and that order, by the grace of God, shall be well set in me. So Sir Galahad granted him, and turned again unto the abbey there they came from. And there men made great joy of Sir Galahad. And anon as he was alight, there was a monk brought him unto a tomb in a church-yard, where that was such a noise that who that heard it should verily nigh be mad or lose his strength. And, sir, they said, we deem it is a fiend.

CHAP. XII.

Of the marvel that Sir Galahad saw and heard in the tomb, and how he made Melias knight.

Now lead me thither, said Galahad. And so they did, all armed save his helm. Now, said the good man, go to the tomb and lift it up. So he did, and heard a great noise, and piteously he said that all men might hear it, Sir Galahad, the servant of Jesu Christ, come thou not nigh me, for thou shalt make me go again there where I have been so long. But Galahad was nothing afraid, but lift up the stone, and there came out so foul a smoke, and after he saw the foulest figure leap thereout that

ever he saw in the likeness of a man; and then he blessed him, and wist well it was a fiend. Then heard he a voice say, Galahad, I see there environ about thee so many angels that my power may not dare thee. Right so Sir Galahad saw a body all armed lie in that tomb, and beside him a sword. Now, fair brother, said Galahad, let us remove this body, for it is not worthy to lie in this church-yard, for he was a false Christian man. And therewith they all departed and went to the abbey. And anon as he was unarmed, a good man came and set him down by him, and said, Sir, I shall tell you what betokeneth all that ye saw in the tomb: For that covered body betokeneth the duresse of the world, and the great sin that our Lord found in the world, for there was such wretchedness that the father loved not the son, nor the son loved not the father, and that was one of the causes that our Lord took flesh and blood of a clean maiden; for our sins were so great at that time that well nigh all was wickedness. Truly, said Galahad, I believe you right well. So Sir Galahad rested him there that night. And upon the morn he made the squire knight, and asked him his name, and of what kindred he was come. Sir, said he, men call me Melias de Lile, and I am the son of the king of Denmark. Now, fair sir, said Galahad, sith ye be come of kings and queens, now look that knighthood be well set in you, for ye ought to be a mirror unto all chivalry. Sir, said Melias, ye say sooth. But, sir, sithen ye have made me a knight, ye must of right grant me my first desire that is reasonable. Ye say sooth, said Galahad. Then Melias said, that ye will suffer me to ride with you in this quest of the Sancgreal till that some adventure depart us.—I grant you, sir. Then men brought Sir Melias his armour, and his spear, and his horse; and so Sir Galahad and he rode forth all that week ere they found any adventure. And then upon a Monday, in the morning, as they were departed from an abbey, they came to a cross which departed two ways; and in that cross were letters written, that said thus: Now ye knights errant, the which goeth to seek knights adventurous, see here two ways; that one way defendeth thee that thou ne go that way, for he shall not go out of the way again, but if he be a good man and a worthy knight; and if thou go on the left hand, thou shalt not there lightly win prowess, for thou shalt in this way be soon assayed. Sir, said Melias to Galahad, if it like you to suffer me to take the way on the left hand, tell me, for there I shall well prove my strength. It were better, said Galahad, ye rode not that way, for I deem I should better escape in that way than ye.—Nay, my lord, I pray you let me have that adventure.—Take it, in God's name, said Galahad.

CHAP. XIII.

Of the adventure that Melias had, and how Galahad revenged him, and how Melias was carried into an abbey.

AND then rode Melias into an old forest, and therein he rode two days and more. And then he came into a fair meadow, and there was a fair lodge of boughs. And then he espied in that lodge a chair, wherein was a crown of gold subtily wrought. Also there was clothes covered upon the earth, and many delicious meats were set thereon. Sir Melias beheld this adventure, and thought it marvellous, but he had no hunger, but of the crown of gold he took much keep, and therewith he stooped down, and took it up, and rode his way with it. And anon he saw a knight came riding after him that said, Knight, set down that crown which is not yours, and therefore defend you. Then Sir Melias blessed him, and said, Fair Lord of heaven, help and save thy new-made knight. And then they let their horses run as fast as they might, so that the other knight smote Sir Melias through hauberk and through the left side, that he fell to the earth

nigh dead. And then he took the crown and went his way, and Sir Melias lay still and had no power to stir. In the meanwhile by fortune there came Sir Galahad and found him there in peril of death. And then he said, Ah, Melias, who hath wounded you? therefore it had been better to have ridden that other way. And when Sir Melias heard him speak, Sir, he said, for God's love let me not die in this forest, but bear me unto the abbey here beside, that I may be confessed and have my rites. It shall be done, said Galahad, but where is he that hath wounded you? With that Sir Galahad heard in the leaves cry on high, Knight, keep thee from me! Ah sir, said Melias, beware, for that is he that hath slain me. Sir Galahad answered, Sir knight, come on your peril. Then either dressed to other, and came together as fast as their horses might run; and Galahad smote him so that his spear went through his shoulder, and smote him down off his horse, and in the falling Galahad's spear brake. With that came out another knight out of the leaves and brake a spear upon Galahad, or ever he might turn him. Then Galahad drew out his sword and smote off the left arm of him, so that it fell to the earth. And then he fled, and Sir Galahad sued fast after him. And then he turned again unto Sir Melias, and there he alight and dressed him softly on his horse tofore him, for the truncheon of his spear was in his body, and Sir Galahad start up behind him, and held him in his arms, and so brought him to the abbey, and there unarmed him and brought him to his chamber. And then he asked his Saviour. And when he had received Him he said unto Sir Galahad, Sir, let death come when it pleaseth him. And therewith he drew out the truncheon of the spear out of his body: and then he swooned. Then came there an old monk, which sometime had been a knight, and beheld Sir Melias. And anon he ransacked him, and then he said unto Sir Galahad, I shall heal him of this wound, by the grace of God, within the term of seven weeks. Then was Sir Galahad glad, and unarmed him, and said he would abide there three days. And then he asked Sir Melias how it stood with him. Then he said, he was turned unto helping, God be thanked.

CHAP. XIV.

How Sir Galabad departed, and bow he was commanded to go to the castle of maidens to destroy the wicked custom.

Now will I depart, said Galahad, for I have much on hand, for many good knights be full busy about it, and this knight and I were in the same quest of the Sancgreal. Sir, said a good man, for his sin he was thus wounded: and I marvel, said the good man, how ye durst take upon you so rich a thing as the high order of knighthood without clean confession, and that was the cause ye were bitterly wounded. For the way on the right hand betokeneth the high way of our Lord Jesu Christ, and the way of a true good liver. And the other way betokeneth the way of sinners and of misbelievers. And when the devil saw your pride and presumption for to take you in the quest of the holy Sancgreal, that made you to be overthrown, for it may not be achieved but by virtuous living. Also, the writing on the cross was a signification of heavenly deeds, and of knightly deeds in God's works, and no knightly deeds in worldly works; and pride is head of all deadly sins, that caused this knight to depart from Sir Galahad: and where thou tookest the crown of gold thou sinnedst in covetise and in theft. All this were no knightly deeds. And this Galahad the holy knight, the which fought with the two knights, the two knights signify the two deadly sins which were wholly in this knight Sir Melias, and they might not withstand you, for ye are without deadly sin. Now departed Galahad from thence, and betaught them all unto God. Sir Melias said, My lord Galahad, as soon as I may ride I shall seek you. God send you health,

said Galahad; and so took his horse and departed and rode many journeys forward and backward, as adventure would lead him. And at the last it happened him to depart from a place or a castle, the which was named Abblasoure, and he had heard no mass, the which he was wont ever to hear or that he departed out of any castle or place, and kept that for a custom. Then Sir Galahad came unto a mountain, where he found an old chapel, and found there nobody, for all all was desolate, and there he kneeled tofore the altar, and besought God of wholesome counsel. So, as he prayed, he heard a voice that said, Go thou now, thou adventurous knight, to the Castle of Maidens, and there do thou away the wicked customs.

CHAP. XV.

How Sir Galabad fougbt with the knights of the castle, and destroyed the wicked custom.

WHEN Sir Galahad heard this he thanked God, and took his horse, and he had not ridden but half a mile, he saw in a valley afore him a strong castle with deep ditches, and there ran beside it a fair river, that hight Severn, and there he met with a man of great age, and either saluted other, and Galahad asked him the castle's name? Fair sir, said he, it is the Castle of Maidens. That is a cursed castle, said Galahad, and all they that be conversant therein; for all pity is out thereof, and all hardiness and mischief is therein.—Therefore I counsel you, sir knight, to turn again. Sir, said Galahad, wit you well I shall not turn again. Then looked Sir Galahad on his arms that nothing failed him, and then he put his shield afore him, and anon there met him seven fair maidens, the which said unto him, Sir knight, ye ride here in a great folly, for ye have the water to pass over. Why should I not pass the water? said Galahad. So rode he away from them, and met with a squire that said, Knight, those knights in the castle defy you, and forbid you, ye go no further till that they wit what ye would. Fair sir, said Galahad, I come for to destroy the wicked custom of this castle.—Sir, and ye will abide by that, ye shall have enough to do.—Go you now, said Galahad, and haste my needs. Then the squire entered into the castle. And anon after there came out of the castle seven knights, and all were brethren. And when they saw Galahad, they cried, Knight, keep thee, for we assure thee nothing but death. Why, said Galahad, will ye all have ado with me at once? Yea, said they, thereto mayest thou trust. Then Galahad put forth his spear, and smote the foremost to the earth, that near he brake his neck. And therewith all the other smote him on his shield great strokes, so that their spears brake. Then Sir Galahad drew out his sword, and set upon them so hard that it was marvel to see it, and so, through great force, he made them to forsake the field; and Galahad chased them till they entered into the castle, and so passed through the castle at another gate. And there met Sir Galahad an old man, clothed in religious clothing, and said, Sir, have here the keys of this castle. Then Sir Galahad opened the gates, and saw so much people in the streets that he might not number them, and all said, Sir, ye be welcome, for long have we abiden here our deliverance. Then came to him a gentlewoman, and said, These knights be fled, but they will come again this night, and here to begin again their evil custom. What will ye that I shall do? said Galahad. Sir, said the gentlewoman, that ye send after all the knights hither that hold their lands of this castle, and make them to swear for to use the customs that were used heretofore of old time. I will well, said Galahad. And there she brought him an horn of ivory, bounden with gold richly, and said, Sir, blow this horn, which will be heard two mile about this castle. When Sir Galahad had blown the horn he set him down upon a bed. Then came a priest unto Gala-

had, and said, Sir, it is past a seven year agone that these seven brethren came into this castle, and harboured with the lord of this castle, that hight the duke Lianour, and he was lord of all this country. And when they espied the duke's daughter that was a full fair woman, then by their false covin they made debate betwixt themselves, and the duke of his goodness would have departed them; and there they slew him and his eldest son. And then they took the maiden, and the treasure of the castle. And then by great force they held all the knights of this castle against their will under their obeisance, and in great servage and truage, robbing and pilling the poor common people of all that they had. So it happened on a day the duke's daughter said, Ye have done unto me great wrong to slay mine own father and my brother, and thus to hold our lands: not for then, she said, ye shall not hold this castle for many years, for by one knight ye shall be overcome. Thus she prophesied seven years agone. Well, said the seven knights, sithen ye say so, there shall never lady nor knight pass this castle, but they shall abide maugre their heads, or die therefore, till that knight be come by whom we shall lose this castle. And therefore it is called the Maidens' Castle, for they have devoured many maidens. Now, said Sir Galahad, is she here for whom this castle was lost? Nay, said the priest, she was dead within these three nights after that she was thus enforced; and sithen have they kept her younger sister, which endureth great pains with many other ladies. By this were the knights of the country come. And then he made them do homage and fealty to the duke's daughter, and set them in great ease of heart. And in the morn there came one to Galahad, and told him how that Gawaine, Gareth, and Uwaine had slain the seven brethren. I suppose well, said Sir Galahad: and took his armour and his horse and commended them unto God.

CHAP. XVI.

*How Sir Gawaine came to the Abbey for
to follow Galahad, and how he was
shriven to a Hermit.*

Now, saith the tale, after Sir Gawaine
departed, he rode many journeys both
toward and froward. And at the last
he came to the abbey where Sir Galahad had the white shield. And there
Sir Gawaine learned the way to sue
after Sir Galahad, and so he rode to
the abbey where Melias lay sick, and
there Sir Melias told Sir Gawaine of
the marvellous adventure that Sir Galahad did. Certes, said Sir Gawaine, I
am not happy that I took not the way
that he went; for, and I may meet with
him, I will not depart from him lightly,
for all marvellous adventures Sir Galahad achieveth. Sir, said one of the
monks, he will not of your fellowship. Why? said Sir Gawaine. Sir,
said he, for ye be wicked and sinful,
and he is full blessed.

Right as they thus stood talking
together, there came in riding Sir Gareth. And then they made joy either
of other. And on the morn they heard
mass, and so departed. And by the
way they met with Sir Uwaine les
Avoutres. And there Sir Uwaine told
Sir Gawaine how he had met with none
adventure sith he departed from the
court. Nor we, said Sir Gawaine.
And either promised other of those
three knights not to depart while that
they were in that quest, but if fortune
caused it. So they departed and rode
by fortune till that they came by the
Castle of Maidens. And there the seven
brethren espied the three knights, and
said, Sithen we be banished by one
knight from this castle, we shall destroy
all the knights of king Arthur's that we
may overcome, for the love of Sir Galahad. And therewith the seven knights
set upon the three knights: and by
fortune Sir Gawaine slew one of the
brethren, and each one of his fellows
slew another, and so slew the remnant.
And then they took the way under the
castle; and there they lost the way that

Sir Galahad rode, and there every each
of them departed from other, and Sir
Gawaine rode till he came to an hermitage, and there he found the good
man saying his evensong of Our Lady.
And there Sir Gawaine asked harbour
for charity, and the good man granted
it him gladly. Then the good man
asked him what he was? Sir, he said, I
am a knight of king Arthur's, that am
in the quest of the Sancgreal, and my
name is Sir Gawaine. Sir, said the
good man, I would wit how it standeth
betwixt God and you? Sir, said Sir
Gawaine, I will with a good will shew
you my life, if it please you. And there
he told the hermit how a monk of
an abbey called me wicked knight.
He might well say it, said the hermit,
for when ye were first made knight, ye
should have taken you to knightly deeds
and virtuous living, and ye have done
the contrary, for ye have lived mischievously many winters, and Sir Galahad is a maid, and sinned never, and
that is the cause he shall achieve where
he goeth that ye nor none such shall not
attain, nor none in your fellowship;
for ye have used the most untruest life
that ever I heard knight live. For,
certes, had ye not been so wicked as ye
are, never had the seven brethren been
slain by you and your two fellows.
For Sir Galahad, himself alone, beat
them all seven the day before, but his
living is such he shall slay no man
lightly. Also I may say you, the Castle
of Maidens betokeneth the good souls
that were in prison afore the Incarnation of Jesu Christ. And the seven
knights betoken the seven deadly sins
that reigned that time in the world.
And I may liken the good Galahad unto
the Son of the High Father, that light
within a maid, and bought all the souls
out of thrall: so did Sir Galahad deliver
all the maidens out of the woful castle.
Now, Sir Gawaine, said the good man,
thou must do penance for thy sin.—Sir,
what penance shall I do?—Such as I
will give, said the good man. Nay,
said Sir Gawaine, I may do no penance;
for we knights adventurous often suffer

great woe and pain. Well, said the good man, and then he held his peace. And on the morn Sir Gawaine departed from the hermit, and betaught him unto God. And by adventure he met with Sir Aglovale and Sir Griflet, two knights of the Table Round. And they two rode four days without finding of any adventure, and at the fifth day they departed. And every each held as fell them by adventure.

Here leaveth the tale of Sir Gawaine and his fellows, and speak we of Sir Galahad.

CHAP. XVII.

How Sir Galahad met with Sir Launcelot and with Sir Percivale, and smote them down, and departed from them.

So when Sir Galahad was departed from the Castle of Maidens, he rode till he came to a waste forest, and there he met with Sir Launcelot and Sir Percivale, but they knew him not, for he was new disguised. Right so, Sir Launcelot his father dressed his spear, and brake it upon Sir Galahad, and Sir Galahad smote him so again, that he smote down horse and man. And then he drew his sword, and dressed him unto Sir Percivale, and smote him so on the helm that it rove to the coif of steel, and had not the sword swerved Sir Percivale had been slain, and with the stroke he fell out of his saddle. This justs was done tofore the hermitage where a recluse dwelled. And when she saw Sir Galahad ride, she said, God be with thee, best knight of the world. Ah certes, said she all aloud, that Launcelot and Percivale might hear it, and yonder two knights had known thee as well as I do, they would not have encountered with thee. When Sir Galahad heard her say so he was sore adread to be known : therewith he smote his horse with his spurs, and rode a great pace froward them. Then perceived they both that he was Galahad, and up they gat on their horses, and rode fast after him, but in a while he was out of their sight.

And then they turned again with heavy cheer. Let us spere some tidings, said Percivale, at yonder recluse. Do as ye list, said Sir Launcelot. When Sir Percivale came to the recluse, she knew him well enough, and Sir Launcelot both. But Sir Launcelot rode overthwart and endlong in a wild forest, and held no path, but as wild adventure led him. And at the last he came to a stony cross, which departed two ways in waste land, and by the cross was a stone that was of marble, but it was so dark that Sir Launcelot might not wit what it was. Then Sir Launcelot looked by him, and saw an old chapel, and there he wend to have found people. And Sir Launcelot tied his horse till a tree, and there he did off his shield, and hung it upon a tree. And then he went to the chapel door, and found it waste and broken. And within he found a fair altar full richly arrayed with cloth of clean silk, and there stood a fair clean candlestick which bare six great candles, and the candlestick was of silver. And when Sir Launcelot saw this light, he had great will for to enter into the chapel, but he could find no place where he might enter : then was he passing heavy and dismayed. Then he returned and came to his horse, and did off his saddle and bridle, and let him pasture ; and unlaced his helm, and ungirded his sword, and laid him down to sleep upon his shield tofore the cross.

CHAP. XVIII.

How Sir Launcelot, half sleeping and half waking, saw a sick man borne in a litter, and how he was healed with the Sangreal.

AND so he fell on sleep, and half waking and half sleeping he saw come by him two palfreys all fair and white, the which bare a litter, therein lying a sick knight. And when he was nigh the cross, he there abode still. All this Sir Launcelot saw and beheld, for he slept not verily ; and he heard him say, Oh, sweet Lord, when shall this sorrow leave me ? and when shall the holy vessel come by me where through I shall be blessed? For I have endured thus long for little trespass. A full great while complained the knight thus, and always Sir Launcelot heard it. With that Sir Launcelot saw the candlestick with the six tapers come before the cross, and he saw nobody that brought it. Also there came a table of silver, and the holy vessel of the Sancgreal, which Sir Launcelot had seen aforetime in king Peschour's house. And therewith the sick knight set him up, and held up both his hands, and said, Fair sweet Lord, which is here within this holy vessel, take heed unto me, that I may be whole of this malady. And therewith on his hands and on his knees he went so nigh that he touched the holy vessel, and kissed it, and anon he was whole, and then he said, Lord God I thank thee, for I am healed of this sickness. So when the holy vessel had been there a great while it went unto the chapel, with the chandelier and the light, so that Launcelot wist not where it was become, for he was overtaken with sin that he had no power to arise against the holy vessel; wherefore after that many men said of him shame, but he took repentance after that. Then the sick knight dressed him up, and kissed the cross. Anon his squire brought him his arms, and asked his lord how he did? Certes, said he, I thank God right well, through the holy vessel I am healed. But I have great marvel of this sleeping knight, that had no power to awake when this holy vessel was brought hither. I dare right well say, said the squire, that he dwelleth in some deadly sin, whereof he was never confessed. By my faith, said the knight, whatsoever he be he is unhappy, for as I deem he is of the fellowship of the Round Table, the which is entered into the quest of the Sancgreal. Sir, said the squire, here I have brought you all your arms, save your helm and your sword, and therefore by my assent now may ye take this knight's helm and his sword. And so he did. And when he was clean armed he took Sir Launcelot's horse, for he was better than his own: and so departed they from the cross.

CHAP. XIX.

How a voice spake to Sir Launcelot, and how he found his horse and his helm borne away, and after went afoot.

THEN anon Sir Launcelot waked, and set him up, and bethought him what he had seen there, and whether it were dreams or not. Right so heard he a voice that said, Sir Launcelot, more harder than is the stone, and more bitter than is the wood, and more naked and barer than is the leaf of the fig-tree, therefore go thou from hence, and withdraw thee from this holy place. And when Sir Launcelot heard this he was passing heavy, and wist not what to do, and so departed, sore weeping, and cursed the time that he was born. For then he deemed never to have had worship more. For those words went to his heart, till that he knew wherefore he was called so. Then Sir Launcelot went to the cross, and found his helm, his sword, and his horse, taken away. And then he called himself a very wretch, and most unhappy of all knights: and there he said, My sin and my wickedness have brought me unto great dishonour. For when I sought worldly adventures for worldly desires I ever achieved them, and had the better in every place, and never was I discomfit in no quarrel, were it right or wrong. And now I take upon me the adventures of holy things, and now I see and understand that mine old sin hindereth me, and shameth me, so that I had no power to stir nor to speak when the holy blood appeared afore me. So thus he sorrowed till it was day, and heard the fowls sing: then somewhat he was comforted. But when Sir Launcelot missed his horse and his harness, then he wist well God was displeased with him. Then he departed from the cross on foot into a forest. And so by prime he came to an high hill, and found an hermitage, and an hermit therein, which was going unto mass. And then Launcelot kneeled down and cried on our Lord mercy for his wicked works. So when mass was done, Launcelot called him, and prayed him for charity for to hear his life. With a good will, said the good man. Sir, said he, be ye of king Arthur's court, and of the fellowship of the Round Table? Yea forsooth, and my name is Sir Launclot du Lake, that hath been right well said of, and now my good fortune is changed, for I am the most wretch of the world. The hermit beheld him, and had marvel how he was so abashed. Sir, said the hermit, ye ought to thank God more than any knight living; for He hath caused you to have more worldly worship than any knight that now liveth. And for your presumption to take upon you in deadly sin for to be in His presence, where His flesh and His blood was, that caused you ye might not see it with worldly eyes, for He will not appear where such sinners be, but if it be unto their great hurt, and unto their great shame. And there is no knight living now that ought to give God so great thanks as ye; for He hath given you beauty, seemliness, and great strength, above all other knights, and therefore ye are the more beholding unto God than any other man to love Him and dread Him; for your strength and manhood will little avail you and God be against you.

CHAP. XX.

How Sir Launcelot was shriven, and what sorrow he made; and of the good ensamples which were shewed him.

THEN Sir Launcelot wept with heavy cheer, and said, Now I know well ye say me sooth. Sir, said the good man, hide none old sin from me. Truly, said Sir Launcelot, that were me full loth to discover. For this fourteen years I never discovered one thing that I have used, and that may I now blame my shame and my misadventure. And then he told there that good man all his life, and how he had loved a queen unmeasurably, and out of measure long;—and all my great deeds of arms that I have done, I did the most part for the queen's sake, and for her sake would I do battle were it right or wrong, and never did I battle all only for God's sake, but for to win worship, and to cause me to be the better beloved, and little or nought I thanked God of it. Then Sir Launcelot said, I pray you counsel me. I will counsel you, said the hermit, if ye will ensure me that ye will never come in that queen's fellowship, as much as ye may forbear. And then Sir Launcelot promised him he would not, by the faith of his body. Look that your heart and your mouth accord, said the good man, and I shall ensure you ye shall have more worship than ever ye had. Holy father, said Sir Launcelot, I marvel of the voice that said to me marvellous words, as ye have heard toforehand. Have ye no marvel, said the good man, thereof; for it seemeth well God loveth you; for men may understand a stone is hard of kind, and namely one more than another, and that is to understand by thee Sir Launcelot, for thou wilt not leave thy sin for no goodness that God hath sent thee, therefore thou art more than any stone, and never wouldest thou be made soft nor by water nor by fire, and that is, the heat of the Holy Ghost may not enter in thee. Now take heed; in all the world men shall not find one knight to whom our Lord hath given so much of grace as He hath given you: for He hath given you fairness with seemliness: He hath given thee wit, discretion to know good from evil: He hath given thee prowess and hardiness; and given thee to work so largely that thou hast had at all days the better wheresoever thou camest. And now our Lord will suffer thee no longer, but that thou shalt know Him, whether thou wilt or nilt. And why the voice called thee bitterer than wood, for where overmuch sin dwelleth, there may be but little sweetness, wherefore thou art likened to an old rotten tree. Now have I shewed thee why thou art harder than the stone, and bitterer than the tree. Now shall I shew thee why thou art more naked and barer than the fig-tree. It befell that our Lord on Palm-Sunday preached in Jerusalem, and there He found in the people that all hardness was harboured in them, and there He found in all the town not one that would harbour Him. And then He went without the town, and found in the midst of the way a fig-tree, the which was right fair and well garnished of leaves, but fruit had it none. Then our Lord cursed the tree that bare no fruit; that betokeneth the fig-tree unto Jerusalem, that had leaves and no fruit. So thou, Sir Launcelot, when the holy Graile was brought afore thee, He found in thee no fruit, nor

good thought nor good will, and defouled with lechery. Certes, said Sir Launcelot, all that ye have said is true, and from henceforward I cast me by the grace of God never to be so wicked as I have been, but as to follow knighthood, and to do feats of arms. Then the good man enjoined Sir Launcelot such penance as he might do, and to sue knighthood, and so he assoiled him and prayed Sir Launcelot to abide with him all that day. I will well, said Sir Launcelot, for I have neither helm, nor horse, nor sword. As for that, said the good man, I shall help you or to-morn at even of an horse, and all that longeth unto you. And then Sir Launcelot repented him greatly.

𝔥𝔢𝔯𝔢 𝔩𝔢𝔲𝔢𝔱𝔥 𝔬𝔣 𝔱𝔥𝔢 𝔥𝔦𝔰𝔱𝔬𝔯𝔶 𝔬𝔣 𝔰𝔶𝔯 𝔩𝔞𝔲𝔫𝔠𝔢𝔩𝔬𝔱. 𝔞𝔫𝔡 𝔥𝔢𝔯𝔢 𝔣𝔬𝔩𝔬𝔴𝔢𝔱𝔥 𝔬𝔣 𝔰𝔶𝔯 𝔭𝔢𝔯𝔠𝔶𝔲𝔞𝔩𝔢 𝔡𝔢 𝔤𝔞𝔩𝔶𝔰 𝔴𝔥𝔦𝔠𝔥 𝔦𝔰 𝔱𝔥𝔢 𝔵𝔦𝔦𝔦𝔦. 𝔟𝔬𝔬𝔨.

𝔗𝔥𝔢 𝔉𝔬𝔲𝔯𝔱𝔢𝔢𝔫𝔱𝔥 𝔅𝔬𝔬𝔨.

CHAP. I.

How Sir Percivale came to a recluse, and asked counsel; and how she told him that she was his aunt.

Now saith the tale, that when Sir Launcelot was ridden after Sir Galahad, the which had all these adventures above said, Sir Percivale turned again unto the recluse, where he deemed to have tidings of that knight that Launcelot followed. And so he kneeled at her window, and the recluse opened it, and asked Sir Percivale what he would? Madam, he said, I am a knight of king Arthur's court, and my name is Sir Percivale de Galis. When the recluse heard his name, she had great joy of him, for mickle she had loved him tofore any other knight, for she ought to do so, for she was his aunt. And then she commanded the gates to

be opened, and there he had all the cheer that she might make him, and all that was in her power was at his commandment. So, on the morn, Sir Percivale went to the recluse, and asked her if she knew that knight with the white shield? Sir, said she, why would ye wit? Truly, madam, said Sir Percivale, I shall never be well at ease till that I know of that knight's fellowship, and that I may fight with him, for I may not leave him so lightly, for I have the shame yet. Ah, Percivale, said she, would ye fight with him? I see well ye have great will to be slain as your father was, through outrageousness. Madam, said Sir Percivale, it seemeth by your words that ye know me? Yea, said she, I well ought to know you, for I am your aunt, although I be in a priory place. For some called me some time the queen of the Waste Lands, and I was called the queen of most riches in the world; and it pleased me never my riches so much as doth my poverty. Then Sir Percivale wept for very pity, when he knew it was his aunt. Ah, fair nephew, said she, when heard ye tidings of your mother? Truly, said he, I heard none of her, but I dream of her much in my sleep, and therefore I wot not whether she be dead or on live. Certes, fair nephew, said she, your mother is dead; for after your departing from her, she took such a sorrow that anon after she was confessed she died. Now God have mercy on her soul, said Sir Percivale, it sore forethinketh me; but all we must change the life. Now fair aunt, tell me what is the knight? I deem it be he that bare the red arms on Whitsunday. Wit you well, said she, that this is he, for otherwise ought he not to do, but to go in red arms, and that same knight hath no peer, for he worketh all by miracle, and he shall never be overcome of no earthly man's hand.

CHAP. II.

How Merlin likened the Round Table to the world, and how the knights that should achieve the Sangreal should be known.

ALSO Merlin made the Round Table in tokening of the roundness of the world, for by the Round Table is the world signified by right. For all the world, christian and heathen, repair unto the Round Table, and when they are chosen to be of the fellowship of the Round Table, they think them more blessed, and more in worship, than if they had gotten half the world; and ye have seen that they have lost their fathers and their mothers, and all their kin, and their wives and their children, for to be of your fellowship. It is well seen by you; for since ye departed from your mother ye would never see her, ye found such a fellowship at the Round Table. When Merlin had ordained the Round Table, he said, by them which should be fellows of the Round Table the truth of the Sancgreal should be well known.

And men asked him how men might know them that should best do, and to achieve the Sancgreal? then he said there should be three white bulls that should achieve it, and the two should be maidens, and the third should be chaste. And that one of the three should pass his father as much as the lion passeth the libard, both of strength and hardiness. They that heard Merlin say so, said thus unto Merlin: Sithen there shall be such a knight, thou shouldst ordain by thy crafts a siege that no man should sit in it but he all only that shall pass all other knights. Then Merlin answered that he would do so. And then he made the siege perilous, in the which Galahad sat in at his meat on Whitsunday last past. Now madam, said Sir Percivale, so much have I heard of you, that by my good will I will never have ado with Sir Galahad, but by way of kindness. And for God's love, fair aunt, can ye teach me some way where I may find him, for much would I love the fellowship of him? Fair nephew, said she, ye must ride unto a castle the which is called Goothe, where he hath a cousin german, and there may ye be lodged this night. And as he teacheth you, sue after as fast as ye can, and if he can tell you no tidings of him, ride straight unto the castle of Carbonek, where the maimed king is there lying, for there shall ye hear true tidings of him.

CHAP. III.

How Sir Percivale came into a monastery, where he found king Evelake, which was an old man.

THEN departed Sir Percivale from his aunt, either making great sorrow. And so he rode till evensong time. And then he heard a clock smite. And then he was ware of a house closed well with walls and deep ditches, and there he knocked at the gate, and was let in, and he alight, and was led unto a chamber, and soon he was unarmed. And there he had right good cheer all that night, and on the morn he heard his mass, and in the monastery he found a priest ready at the altar. And on the right side he saw a pew closed with iron, and behind the altar he saw a rich bed and a fair, as of cloth of silk and gold. Then Sir Percivale espied that therein was a man or a woman, for the visage was covered. Then he left off his looking, and heard his service. And when it came to the sacring, he that lay within that perclose dressed him up, and uncovered his head, and then him beseemed a passing old man, and he had a crown of gold upon his head, and his shoulders were naked and uncovered unto his middle. And then Sir Percivale espied his body was full of great wounds, both on the shoulders, arms, and visage. And ever he held up his hands unto our Lord's body, and cried, Fair sweet Father Jesu Christ, forget not me, and so he lay down, but always he was in his prayers and orisons: and him seemed to be of the age of three hundred winter. And when the mass was done, the priest took our Lord's body and bare it to the sick king. And when he had used it, he did off his crown, and commanded the crown to be set on the altar. Then Sir Percivale asked one of the brethren what he was. Sir, said the good man, ye have heard much of Joseph of Armathie, how he was sent by Jesu Christ into this land, for to teach and preach the holy christian faith, and therefore he suffered many persecutions, the which the enemies of Christ did unto him. And in the city of Sarras he converted a king whose name was Evelake. And so this king came with Joseph into this land: and always he was busy to be there as the Sancgreal was, and on a time he nighed it so nigh that our Lord was displeased with him, but ever he followed it more and more, till God struck him almost blind. Then this king cried mercy, and said, Fair Lord, let me never die till the good knight of my blood of the ninth degree be come, that I may see him openly that he shall achieve the Sancgreal, that I may kiss him.

CHAP. IV.

How Sir Percivale saw many men of arms, bearing a dead knight, and how he fought against them.

WHEN the king thus had made his prayers, he heard a voice that said, Heard be thy prayers, for thou shalt not die till he have kissed thee: and when that knight shall come, the clearness of your eyes shall come again, and thou shalt see openly, and thy wounds shall be healed, and erst shall they never close. And this befell of king Evelake: and this same king hath lived this three hundred winters this holy life. And men say the knight is in the court that shall heal him. Sir, said the good man, I pray you tell me what knight that ye be, and if ye be of king Arthur's court and of the Table Round? Yea, forsooth, said he, and my name is Sir Percivale de Galis. And when the good man understood his name, he made great joy of him. And then Sir Percivale departed, and rode till the hour of noon. And he met in a valley about twenty men of arms, which bear in a bier a knight deadly slain. And when they saw Sir Percivale, they asked him of whence he was? and he answered, Of the court of king Arthur. Then they cried all at once, Slay him. Then Sir Percivale smote the first to the earth, and his horse upon him. And then seven of the knights smote upon his shield all at once, and the remnant slew his horse, so that he fell to the earth. So had they slain him or taken him, had not the good knight Sir Galahad, with the red arms, come there by adventure into those parts. And when he saw all those knights upon one knight, he cried, Save me that knight's life. And then he dressed him toward the twenty men of arms as fast as his horse might drive, with his spear in the rest, and smote the foremost horse and man to the earth. And when his spear was broken he set his hand to his sword, and smote on the right hand and on the left hand, that it was marvel to see. And at every stroke he smote one down, or put him to a rebuke, so that they would fight no more, but fled to a thick forest, and Sir Galahad followed them. And when Sir Percivale saw him chase them so, he made great sorrow that his horse was away. And then he wist well it was Sir Galahad. And then he cried aloud, Ah fair knight, abide and suffer me to do thankings unto thee, for much have ye done for me! But ever Sir Galahad rode so fast, that at the last he passed out of his sight. And as fast as Sir Percivale might he went after him on foot, crying. And then he met with a yeoman riding upon an hackney, the which led in his hand a great black steed, blacker than any bear. Ah fair friend, said Sir Percivale, as ever I may do for you, and to be your true knight in the first place ye will require me, that ye will lend me that black steed, that I might overtake a knight, the which rideth afore me. Sir knight, said the yeoman, I pray you hold me excused of that, for that I may not do. For wit ye well, the horse is such a man's horse, that, and I lent it you or any other man, that he would slay me. Alas, said Sir Percivale, I had never so great sorrow as I have had for losing of yonder knight. Sir, said the yeoman, I am right heavy for you, for a good horse would beseem you well, but I dare not deliver you this horse, but if ye would take him from me. That will I not do, said Sir Percivale. And so they departed, and Sir Percivale sat him down under a tree, and made sorrow out of measure. And as he was there, there came a knight riding on the horse that the yeoman led, and he was clean armed.

CHAP. V.

How a yeoman desired him to get again an horse, and how Sir Percivale's backney was slain, and how he gat an horse.

And anon the yeoman came pricking after as fast as ever he might, and asked Sir Percivale if he saw any knight riding on his black steed? Yea sir, forsooth, said he, why ask ye me that? Ah, sir, that steed he hath taken from me with

strength, wherefore my lord will slay me in what place he findeth me. Well, said Sir Percivale, what wouldest thou that I did? thou seest well that I am on foot, but and I had a good horse I should bring him soon again. Sir, said the yeoman, take mine hackney and do the best ye can, and I shall follow you on foot, to wit how that ye shall speed. Then Sir Percivale alight upon that hackney, and rode as fast as he might. And at the last he saw that knight. And then he cried, Knight, turn again; and he turned, and set his spear against Sir Pereivale, and he smote the hackney in the midst of the breast, that he fell down dead to the earth, and there he had a great fall, and the other rode his way. And then Sir Percivale was wood wroth, and cried, Abide, wicked knight, coward and false-hearted knight, turn again and fight with me on foot. But he answered not, but past on his way. When Sir Percivale saw he would not turn, he cast away his helm and sword, and said, Now am I a very wretch, cursed, and most unhappy above all other knights. So in this sorrow he abode all that day till it was night, and then he was faint, and laid him down and slept till it was midnight. And then he awaked, and saw afore him a woman which said unto him right fiercely, Sir Percivale, what doest thou here? He answered and said, I do neither good nor great ill. If thou wilt ensure me, said she, that thou wilt fulfil my will when I summon thee, I shall lend thee mine own horse, which shall bear thee whither thou wilt. Sir Percivale was glad of her proffer, and ensured her to fulfil all her desire.—Then abide me here, and I shall go fetch you an horse. And so she came soon again, and brought an horse with her that was inly black. When Sir Percivale beheld that horse, he marvelled that it was so great and so well apparelled: and not for then he was so hardy, and he lept upon him, and took none heed of himself. And so anon as he was upon him he thrust to him with his spurs, and so rode by a forest, and the moon shone clear. And within an hour and less, he bare him four days' journey thence, till he came to a rough water the which roared, and his horse would have borne him into it.

CHAP. VI.

Of the great danger that Sir Percivale was in by his horse, and how he saw a serpent and a lion fight.

AND when Sir Percivale came nigh the brim, and saw the water so boisterous, he doubted to overpass it. And then he made a sign of the cross in his forehead. When the fiend felt him so charged, he shook off Sir Percivale, and he went into the water, crying and roaring, making great sorrow; and it seemed unto him that the water burnt. Then Sir Percivale perceived it was a fiend, the which would have brought him unto his perdition. Then he commended himself unto God, and prayed our Lord to keep him from all such temptations. And so he prayed all that night, till on the morn that it was day. Then he saw that he was in a wild mountain the which was closed with the sea nigh all about, that he might see no land about him which might relieve him, but wild beasts. And then he went into a valley, and there he saw a young serpent bring a young lion by the neck, and so he came by Sir Percivale. With that came a great lion crying and roaring after the serpent. And as fast as Sir Percivale saw this, he marvelled, and hied him thither, but anon the lion had overtaken the serpent, and began battle with him. And then Sir Percivale thought to help the lion, for he was the more natural beast of the two; and therewith he drew his sword, and set his shield afore him, and there gave the serpent such a buffet that he had a deadly wound. When the lion saw that, he made no resemblant to fight with him, but made him all the cheer that a beast might make a man. Then Sir Percivale perceived that, and cast down his shield, which was broken, and then he did off his helm for to gather wind, for he was greatly enchafed with the serpent. And the lion went alway about him fawning as a spaniel. And then he stroked him on the neck and on the shoulders. And then he thanked God of the fellowship of that beast. And about noon, the lion took his little whelp, and trussed him, and bare him there he came from. Then was Sir Percivale alone. And as the tale telleth, he was one of the men of the world at that time that most believed in our Lord Jesu Christ. For in these days there were few folks that believed in God perfectly. For in those days the son spared not the father no more than a stranger. And so Sir Percivale comforted himself in our Lord Jesu, and besought God that no temptation should bring him out of God's service, but to endure as his true champion. Thus when Sir Percivale had prayed, he saw the lion come toward him, and then he couched down at his feet. And so all that night the lion and he slept together: and when Sir Percivale slept he dreamed a marvellous dream, that there two ladies met with him, and that one sat upon a lion, and that other sat upon a serpent, and that one of them was young, and the other was old, and the youngest him thought said, Sir Percivale, my lord saluteth thee, and sendeth thee word that thou array thee and make thee ready, for to - morn thou must fight with the strongest champion of the world. And if thou be overcome, thou shalt not be quit for losing of any of thy members, but thou shalt be shamed for ever to the world's end. And then he asked her what was her lord. And she said, the greatest lord of all the world. And so she departed suddenly, that he wist not where.

CHAP. VII.

Of the vision that Sir Percivale saw, and how his vision was expounded, and of his lion.

THEN came forth the other lady that rode upon the serpent, and she said, Sir Percivale, I complain me of you that ye. have done unto me, and have not offended unto you. Certes, madam, said he, unto you nor no lady I never offended. Yes, said she, I shall tell you why. I have nourished in this place a great while a serpent, which served me a great while, and yesterday ye slew him as he gat his prey. Say me for what cause ye slew him, for the lion was not yours? Madam, said Sir Percivale, I know well the lion was not mine, but I did it, for the lion is of a more gentler nature than the serpent, and therefore I slew him; me seemeth I did not amiss against you. Madam, said he, what would ye that I did? I would, said she, for the amends of my beast that ye become my man. And then he answered, That will I not grant you. No, said she, truly ye were never but my servant, since ye received the homage of our Lord Jesu Christ. Therefore I ensure you in what place I may find you without keeping, I shall take you as he that sometime was my man. And so she departed from Sir Percivale, and left him sleeping, the which was sore travailed of his vision. And on the morn he rose and blessed him, and he was passing feeble. Then was Sir Percivale ware in the sea, and saw a ship come sailing toward him, and Sir Percivale went unto the ship, and found it covered within and without with white samite. And at the board stood an old man clothed in a surplice in likeness of a priest. Sir, said Sir Percivale, ye be welcome. God keep you, said the good man. Sir, said the old man, of whence be ye? Sir, said Sir Percivale, I am of king Arthur's court, and a knight of the Table Round, the which am in the quest of the Sancgreal, and here I am in great duresse, and never like to escape out of this wilderness. Doubt not, said the good man, and ye be so true a knight as the order of chivalry requireth, and of heart as ye ought to be, ye should not doubt that none enemy should slay you. What are ye? said Sir Percivale. Sir, said the old man, I am of a strange country, and hither I come to comfort you. Sir, said Sir Percivale, what signifieth my dream that I dreamed this night? And there he told him alto-

gether. She which rode upon the lion, said the good man, betokeneth the new law of holy Church, that is to understand faith, good hope, belief, and baptism. For she seemed younger than the other, it is great reason, for she was born in the resurrection and the passion of our Lord Jesu Christ. And for great love she came to thee, to warn thee of thy great battle that shall befall thee. With whom, said Sir Percivale, shall I fight? With the most champion of the world, said the old man, for, as the lady said, but if thou quit thee well, thou shalt not be quit by losing of one member, but thou shalt be shamed to the world's end. And she that rode upon the serpent signifieth the old law, and that serpent betokeneth a fiend. And why she blamed thee that thou slewest her servant, it betokeneth nothing: the serpent that thou slewest betokeneth the devil that thou rodest upon to the rock, and when thou madest a sign of the cross, there thou slewest him, and put away his power. And when she asked thee amends and to become her man, and thou saidest thou wouldest not, that was to make thee to believe on her and leave thy baptism. So he commanded Sir Percivale to depart. And so he lept over the board, and the ship and all went away he wist not whither. Then he went up unto the rock and found the lion, which alway kept him fellowship, and he stroked him upon the back, and had great joy of him.

CHAP. VIII.

How Sir Percivale saw a ship coming to him-ward, and how the lady of the ship told him of her disheritance.

By that Sir Percivale had abiden there till midday he saw a ship come rowing in the sea as all the wind of the world had driven it. And so it drove under that rock. And when Sir Percivale saw this, he hied him thither, and found the ship covered with silk more blacker than any bier, and therein was a gentlewoman of great beauty, and she was clothed richly that none might be better. And when she saw Sir Percivale, she said, Who brought you in this wilderness where ye be never like to pass hence? for ye shall die here for hunger and mischief. Damsel, said Sir Percivale, I serve the best man of the world, and in his service he will not suffer me to die, for who that knocketh shall enter, and who that asketh shall have, and who that seeketh him, he hideth him not. But then she said, Sir Percivale wot ye what I am? Yea, said he. Now who taught you my name? said she. Now, said Sir Percivale, I know you better than ye ween. And I came out of the waste forest, where I found the red knight with the white shield, said the damsel. Ah damsel, said he, with that knight would I meet passing fain. Sir, said she, and ye will ensure me, by the faith that ye owe unto knighthood, that ye shall do my will what time I summon you, I shall bring you unto that knight. Yea, said he, I shall promise you to fulfil your desire. Well, said she, now shall I tell you, I saw him in the forest chasing two knights to a water, the which is called Mortaise, and he drove them into that water for dread of death, and the two knights passed over, and the red knight passed after, and there his horse was drenched, and he through great strength escaped unto the land. Thus she told him, and Sir Percivale was passing glad thereof. Then she asked him if he had eaten any meat late? Nay madam, truly I ate no meat nigh these three days, but late here I spake with a good man that fed me with his good words and holy, and refreshed me greatly. Ah, sir knight, said she, that same man is an enchanter, and a multiplier of words. For, and ye believe him, ye shall plainly be shamed, and die in this rock for pure hunger, and be eaten with wild beasts, and ye be a young man and a goodly knight, and I shall help you and ye will. What are ye? said Sir Percivale, that proffereth me thus great kindness. I am, said she, a gentlewoman that am disherited, which was sometime the richest woman of the world. Damsel, said Sir Percivale, who

hath disherited you, for I have great pity of you? Sir, said she, I dwelled with the greatest man of the world, and he made me so fair and so clear that there was none like me, and of that great beauty I had a little pride, more than I ought to have had. Also, I said a word that pleased him not. And then he would not suffer me to be any longer in his company, and so drove me from mine heritage, and so disherited me, and he had never pity of me nor of none of my council, nor of my court. And sithen, sir knight, it hath befallen me so, and through me and mine I have taken from him many of his men, and made them to become my men. For they ask never nothing of me but I give it them, that and much more. Thus I and all my servants war against him night and day. Therefore I know now no good knight, nor no good man, but I get them on my side and I may. And for that I know that thou art a good knight, I beseech you to help me. And for ye be a fellow of the Round Table, wherefore ye ought not to fail no gentlewoman which is disherited, and she besought you of help.

CHAP. IX.

How Sir Percivale promised her help, and how he required her of love, and how he was saved from the fiend.

THEN Sir Percivale promised her all the help that he might. And then she thanked him. And at that time the weather was hot, and then she called unto her a gentlewoman, and bad her bring forth a pavilion; and so she did, and pight it upon the gravel. Sir, said she, now may ye rest you in this heat of the day. Then he thanked her, and she put off his helm and his shield, and there he slept a great while. And then he awoke, and asked her if she had any meat, and she said, Yea, also ye shall have enough; and so there was set enough upon the table, and thereon so much that he had marvel, for there was all manner of meats that he could think on. Also he drank there the strongest wine that ever he drank, him thought, and therewith he was a little heated more than he ought to be. With that he beheld the gentlewoman, and him thought that she was the fairest creature that ever he saw. And then Sir Percivale proffered her love, and prayed her that she would be his. Then she refused him in a manner when he required her, for the cause he should be the more ardent on her, and ever he ceased not to pray her of love. And when she saw him well enchafed, then she said, Sir Percivale, wit ye well, I shall not fulfil your will, but if ye swear from henceforth ye shall be my true servant, and to do nothing but that I shall command you : will ye ensure me this as ye be a true knight ? Yea, said he, fair lady, by the faith of my body. Well, said she, now shall ye do with me whatso it please you, and now wit ye well that ye are the knight in the world that I have most desire to. And then Sir Percivale came near to her, to proffer her love, and by adventure and grace he saw his sword lie upon the ground all naked, in whose pommel was a red cross, and the sign of the crucifix therein, and bethought him on his knighthood, and his promise made toforehand unto the good man. Then he made the sign of the cross in his forehead, and therewith the pavilion turned up so down, and then it changed unto a smoke and a black cloud, and then he was adread, and cried aloud,—

CHAP. X.

How Sir Percivale for penance rove himself through the thigh; and how she was known for the devil.

FAIR sweet Father, Jesu Christ, ne let me not be shamed, the which was near lost had not thy good grace been! And then he looked into a ship, and saw her enter therein, which said, Sir Percivale, ye have betrayed me. And so she went with the wind roaring and yelling, that it seemed that all the water burnt after

her. Then Sir Percivale made great sorrow, and drew his sword unto him, saying, Sithen my flesh will be my master, I shall punish it. And therewith he rove himself through the thigh, that the blood start about him, and said, O good Lord, take this in recompensation of that I have done against thee my Lord. So then he clothed him and armed him, and called himself a wretch, saying, How nigh was I lost, and to have lost that I should never have gotten again, that was my virginity, for that may never be recovered after it is once lost. And then he stopped his bleeding wound with a piece of his shirt. Thus as he made his moan, he saw the same ship come from the Orient that the good man was in the day before : and the noble knight was ashamed with himself, and therewith he fell in a swoon. And when he awoke he went unto him weakly, and there he saluted this good man. And then he asked Sir Percivale, How hast thou done sith I departed ? Sir, said he, here was a gentlewoman, and led me into deadly sin : and there he told him altogether. Knew ye not the maid ? said the good man. Sir, said he, nay : but well I wot the fiend sent her hither to shame me. Oh, good knight, said he, thou art a fool, for that gentlewoman was the master fiend of hell, the which hath power above all devils, and that was the old lady that thou sawest in thy vision riding on the serpent. Then he told Sir Percivale how our Lord Jesu Christ beat him out of heaven for his sin, the which was the most brightest angel of heaven, and therefore he lost his heritage, and that was the champion that thou foughtest withal, the which had overcome thee, had not the grace of God been : now beware, Sir Percivale, and take this for an ensample. And then the good man vanished away. Then Sir Percivale took his arms, and entered into the ship, and so departed from thence.

Here endeth the fourtenthe booke, whiche is of syr percyual. And here foloweth of syre launcelot whiche is the fyftenth book.

The Fifteenth Book.

CHAP. I.

How Sir Launcelot came into a chapel, where he found dead, in a white shirt, a man of religion of an hundred winter old.

WHEN the hermit had kept Sir Launcelot three days, the hermit gat him an horse, an helm, and a sword. And then he departed about the hour of noon. And then he saw a little house, and when he came near he saw a chapel, and there beside he saw an old man that was clothed all in white full richly, and then Sir Launcelot said, God save you. God keep you, said the good man, and make you a good knight. Then Sir Launcelot alight, and entered into the chapel, and there he saw an old man dead, in a white shirt of passing fine cloth. Sir, said the good man, this man that is dead ought not to be in such clothing as ye see him in, for in that he brake the oath of his order. For he hath been more than an hundred winters a man of a religion. And then the good man and Sir Launcelot went into the chapel, and the good man took a stole about his neck, and a book, and then he conjured on that book, and with that they saw in an hideous figure and an horrible, that there was no man so hardhearted nor so hard but he should have been afeard. Then said the fiend, Thou hast travailed me greatly, now tell me what thou wilt with me? I will, said the good man, that thou tell me how my fellow became dead, and whether he be saved or damned? Then he said with a horrible voice, He is not lost, but saved. How may that be? said the good man; it seemed to me that he lived not well, for he brake his order for to wear a shirt, where he ought to wear none: and who that trespasseth against our order doth not well. Not so, said the fiend, this man that lieth here dead was come of a great lineage. And there was a lord that hight the earl de Vale, that held great war against this man's nephew, the which hight Aguarus. And so this Aguarus saw the earl was bigger than he, then he went for to take counsel of his uncle, the which lieth here dead as ye may see. And then he asked leave, and went out of his hermitage for to maintain his nephew against the mighty earl. And so it happed that this man that lieth here dead did so much by his wisdom and hardiness that the earl was taken, and three of his lords, by force of this dead man.

CHAP. II.

Of a dead man, how men would have hewen him, and it would not be, and how Sir Launcelot took the hair of the dead man.

THEN was there peace betwixt the earl and this Aguarus, and great surety that the earl should never war against him. Then this dead man that here lieth came to this hermitage again, and then the earl made two of his nephews for to be avenged upon this man. So they came on a day, and found this dead man at the sacring of his mass, and they abode him till he had said mass. And then they set upon him and drew out swords to have slain him. But there would no sword bite on him, more than upon a gad of steel, for the high Lord which he served he him preserved. Then made they a great fire, and did off all his cloathes and the hair off his back; and then this dead man hermit said unto them, Ween ye to burn me? It shall not lie in your power, nor to perish me as much as a thread, and there were any on my body. No! said one of them, it shall be assayed. And then they despoiled him, and put upon him this shirt, and cast him in a fire, and there he lay all that night till it was day, in that fire, and was not dead. And so in the morn I came and found him dead, but I found neither thread nor skin perished ; and so took him out of the fire with great fear, and laid him here as ye may see. And now may ye suffer me to go my way, for I have said you the truth. And then he departed with a great tempest. Then was the good man and Sir Launcelot more gladder than they were tofore. And then Sir Launcelot dwelled with that good man that night. Sir, said the good man, be ye not Sir Launcelot du Lake? Yea, sir, said he. What seek ye in this country? Sir, said Sir Launcelot, I go to seek the adventures of the Sancgreal. Well, said he, seek it ye may well, but though it were here ye shall have no power to see it, no more than a blind man should see a bright sword, and that is long on your sin, and else ye were more abler than any man living. And then Sir Launcelot began to weep. Then said the good man, Were ye confessed sith ye entered into the quest of the Sancgreal? Yea, sir, said Sir Launcelot. Then upon the morn, when the good man had sung his mass, then they buried the dead man. Then Sir Launcelot said, Father, what shall I do? Now, said the good man, I require you take this hair that was this holy man's, and put it next thy skin, and it shall prevail thee greatly. Sir, and I will do it, said Sir Launcelot. Also I charge you that ye eat no flesh as long as ye be in the quest of the Sancgreal, nor ye shall drink no wine, and that ye hear mass daily and ye may do it. So he took the hair and put it upon him, and so departed at evensong time. And so rode he into a forest, and there he met with a gentlewoman riding upon a white palfrey, and then she asked him, Sir knight, whither ride ye? Certes damsel, said Launcelot, I wot not whither I ride, but as fortune leadeth me. Ah, Sir Launcelot, said she, I wot what adventure ye seek, for ye were aforetime nearer than ye be now, and yet shall ye see it more openly than ever

ye did, and that shall ye understand in short time. Then Sir Launcelot asked her where he might be harboured that night? Ye shall not find this day nor night, but to-morn ye shall find harbour good, and ease of that ye be in doubt of. And then he commended her unto God. Then he rode till that he came to a cross, and took that for his host as for that night.

CHAP. III.

Of a vision that Sir Launcelot had, and how he told it to an hermit, and desired counsel of him.

AND so he put his horse to pasture, and did off his helm and his shield, and made his prayers unto the cross that he never fall in deadly sin again. And so he laid him down to sleep. And anon as he was asleep it befell him there a vision, that there came a man afore him all by compass of stars, and that man had a crown of gold on his head, and that man led in his fellowship seven kings and two knights. And all these worshipped the cross, kneeling upon their knees, holding up their hands towards the heaven; and all they said, Fair sweet Father of heaven, come and visit us, and yield unto us every each as we have deserved. Then looked Launcelot up to the heaven, and him seemed the clouds did open, and an old man came down with a company of angels, and alight among them, and gave unto every each his blessing, and called them his servants, and good and true knights. And when this old man had said thus, he came to one of those knights and said, I have lost all that I have set in thee, for thou hast ruled thee against me as a warrior, and used wrong wars with vain glory, more for the pleasure of the world than to please me, therefore thou shalt be confounded without thou yield me my treasure. All this vision saw Sir Launcelot at the cross. And on the morn he took his horse and rode till mid day, and there, by adventure, he met with the same knight that took his horse, his helm, and his sword, when he slept when the Sancgreal appeared afore the cross. When Sir Launcelot saw him he saluted him not fair, but cried on high, Knight, keep thee, for thou hast done to me great unkindness. And then they put afore them their spears, and Sir Launcelot came so fiercely upon him that he smote him and his horse down to the earth, that he had nigh broken his neck. Then Sir Launcelot took the knight's horse, that was his own aforehand, and descended from the horse he sat upon, and tied the knight's own horse to a tree, that he might find that horse when that he was arisen.

Then Sir Launcelot rode till night, and by adventure he met an hermit, and each of them saluted other, and there he rested with that good man all night, and gave his horse such as he might get. Then said the good man unto Launcelot, Of whence be ye? Sir, said he, I am of Arthur's court, and my name is Sir Launcelot du Lake, that am in the quest of the Sancgreal. And therefore I pray you to counsel me of a vision, the which I had at the cross. And so he told him all.

CHAP. IV.

How the hermit expounded to Sir Launcelot his vision, and told him that Sir Galahad was his son.

Lo, Sir Launcelot, said the good man, there thou mightest understand the high lineage that thou art come of, and thy vision betokeneth: After the passion of Jesu Christ forty years, Joseph of Aramathie preached the victory of king Evelake, that he had in the battles the better of his enemies. And of the seven kings and the two knights: the first of them is called Nappus, an holy man; and the second hight Nacien, in remembrance of his grandsire, and in him dwelled our Lord Jesu Christ; and the third was called Hellias le Grose; and the fourth hight Lisais; and the fifth hight Jonas, he departed out of his country and went into Wales, and took the daughter of Manuel, whereby he

had the land of Gaul, and he came to dwell in this country, and of him came king Launcelot thy grandsire, which there wedded the king's daughter of Ireland, and he was as worthy a man as thou art, and of him came king Ban thy father, the which was the last of the seven kings. And by thee, Sir Launcelot, it signifieth that the angels said thou were none of the seven fellowships. And the last was the ninth knight, he was signified to a lion, for he should pass all manner of earthly knights, that is Sir Galahad, the which thou gat of king Pelles' daughter, and thou ought to thank God more than any other man living; for of a sinner earthly thou hast no peer as in knighthood, nor never shall be. But little thank hast thou given to God for all the great virtues that God hath lent thee.

Sir, said Launcelot, ye say that that good knight is my son. That oughtest thou to know, and no man better, said the good man, for by the daughter of king Pelles thou hadst Galahad, and that was he that at the feast of Pentecost sat in the siege perilous, and therefore make thou it known openly that he is thy son, for that will be your worship and honour, and to all thy kindred. And I counsel you in no place press not upon him to have ado with him. Well, said Launcelot, me seemeth that good knight should pray for me unto the high Father that I fall not to sin again. Trust thou well, said the good man, thou farest much the better for his prayer; but the son shall not bear the wickedness of the father, nor the father shall not bear the wickedness of the son, but every each shall bear his own burthen; and therefore beseek thou only God, and he will help thee in all thy needs. And then Sir Launcelot and he went to supper, and so laid him to rest, and the hair pricked so Sir Launcelot's skin, which grieved him full sore, but he took it meekly, and suffered the pain. And so on the morn he heard his mass, and took his arms, and so took his leave.

CHAP. V.

How Sir Launcelot justed with many knights, and how he was taken.

AND then he mounted upon his horse and rode into a forest, and held no highway. And as he looked afore him he saw a fair plain, and beside that a fair castle, and afore the castle were many pavilions of silk and of divers hue. And him seemed that he saw there five hundred knights riding on horseback, and there were two parties; they that were of the castle were all on black horses, and their trappings black. And they that were without were all on white horses and trappings: and every each hurtled to other, that it marvelled Sir Launcelot. And at the last him thought they of the castle were put to the worse. Then thought Sir Launcelot for to help there the weaker party, in increasing of his chivalry. And so Sir Launcelot thrust in among the party of the castle, and smote down a knight, horse and man, to the earth. And then he rashed here and there, and did marvellous deeds of arms. And then he drew out his sword and strake many knights to the earth, so that all those that saw him marvelled that ever one knight might do so great deeds of arms. But always the white knights held them nigh about Sir Launcelot, for to tire him and wind him.

But at the last, as a man may not ever endure, Sir Launcelot waxed so faint of fighting and travailing, and was so weary of his great deeds, that he might not lift up his arms for to give one stroke, so that he wend never to have borne arms: and then they all took him and led him away into a forest, and there made him to alight and to rest him. And then all the fellowship of the castle were overcome for the default of him, and then then they said all unto Sir Launcelot, Blessed be God that ye be now of our fellowship, for we shall hold you in our prison. And so they left him with few words. And then Sir Launcelot made great sorrow, —For never or now was I never at

tournament nor justs but I had the best, and now I am shamed. And then he said, Now I am sure that I am more sinfuller than ever I was. Thus he rode sorrowing, and half a day was he out of despair, till that he came into a deep valley, and when Sir Launcelot saw he might not ride up into the mountain, he there alight under an apple-tree, and there he left his helm and his shield, and put his horse unto pasture. And then he laid him down to sleep. And then him thought there came an old man afore him, the which said, Ah, Launcelot, of evil faith and poor belief, wherefore is thy will turned so lightly towards thy deadly sin? And when he had said thus he vanished away, and Launcelot wist not where he was become. Then he took his horse, and armed him. And as he rode by the way he saw a chapel, where was a recluse, which had a window that she might see up to the altar. And all aloud she called Launcelot, for that he seemed a knight errant. And then he came, and she asked him what he was, and of what place, and where about he went to seek.

CHAP. VI.

How Sir Launcelot told his vision unto a woman, and how she expounded it to him.

AND then he told her altogether word by word, and the truth how it befel him at the tournament. And after told her his vision, that he had had that night in his sleep, and prayed her to tell him what it might mean, for he was not well content with it. Ah, Launcelot, said she, as long as ye were knight of earthly knighthood, ye were the most marvellous man of the world, and most adventurous. Now, said the lady, since ye be set among the knights of heavenly adventures, if adventure fell the contrary at that tournament, have thou no marvel; for that tournament yesterday was but a tokening of our Lord. And not for then there was none enchantment, for they at the tournament were earthly knights. The tournament was a token for to see who should have most knights, either Eliazar the son of king Pelles, or Argustus the son of king Harlon; but Eliazar was all clothed in white, and Argustus was covered in black, the which were come. All what this betokeneth I shall tell you. The day of Pentecost, when king Arthur held his court, it befell that earthly kings and knights took a tournament together, that is to say, the quest of the Sancgreal. The earthly knights were they, the which were clothed all in black, and the covering betokeneth the sins whereof they be not confessed. And they with the covering of white betokeneth virginity, and they that chosen chastity. And thus was the quest begun in them. Then thou beheld the sinners and the good men, and when thou sawest the sinners overcome, thou inclinedst to that party, for boasting and pride of the world, and all that must be left in that quest. For in this quest thou shalt have many fellows and thy betters, for thou art so feeble of evil trust and good belief, this made it when thou were there where they took thee, and led thee into the forest. And anon there appeared the Sancgreal unto the white knights, but thou was so feeble of good belief and faith, that thou might not abide it, for all the teaching of the good man, but anon thou turnedst unto the sinners; and that caused thy misadventure, that thou shouldest know good from evil and vain glory of the world, the which is not worth a pear. And for great pride thou madest great sorrow that thou hadst not overcome all the white knights with the covering of white, by whom was betokened virginity and chastity, and therefore God was wroth with you, for God loveth no such deeds in this quest; and this vision signifieth that thou were of evil faith and of poor belief, the which will make thee to fall into the deep pit of hell, if thou keep thee not. Now have I warned thee of thy vain glory and of thy pride, that thou hast many times erred against thy Maker. Beware of everlasting pain, for of all earthly knights I have most pity of thee, for I know well thou hast not thy peer of any earthly sinful man. And so she commanded Sir Launcelot to dinner; and after dinner he took his horse and commended her to God, and so rode into a deep valley, and there he saw a river and an high mountain. And through the water he must needs pass, the which was hideous; and then in the name of God he took it with good heart. And when he came over he saw an armed knight, horse and man black as any bear: without any word he smote Sir Launcelot's horse to the earth, and so he passed on: he wist not where he was become. And then he took his helm and his shield, and thanked God of his adventure.

𝕳ere leueth of the story of syr launcelot. And speke we of sir Gawayne, the whiche is the xbi. book.

𝕿he 𝕾ixteenth 𝕭ook.

CHAP. I.

How Sir Gawaine was nigh weary of the quest of the Sangreal, and of his marvellous dream.

WHEN Sir Gawaine was departed from his fellowship, he rode long without any adventure. For he found not the tenth part of adventure as he was wont to do. For Sir Gawaine rode from Whitsunday unto Michaelmas, and found none adventure that pleased him. So on a day it befell Gawaine met with Sir Ector de Maris, and either made great joy of other, that it were marvel to tell. And so they told every each other, and complained them greatly that they could find none adventure.

Truly, said Sir Gawaine unto Sir Ector, I am nigh weary of this quest, and loth I am to follow further in strange countries. One thing marvelleth me, said Sir Ector, I have met with twenty knights, fellows of mine, and all they complain as I do. I marvel, said Sir Gawaine, where that Sir Launcelot your brother is. Truly, said Sir Ector, I cannot hear of him, nor of Sir Galahad, Percivale, nor Sir Bors. Let them be, said Sir Gawaine, for they four have no peers. And if one thing were not in Sir Launcelot, he had no fellow of none earthly man; but he is as we be, but if he took more pain upon him. But and these four be met together, they will be loth that any man meet with them; for, and they fail of the Sancgreal, it is in waste of all the remnant to recover it. Thus as Ector and Gawaine rode more than eight days. And on a Saturday they found an old chapel, the which was wasted that there seemed no man thither repaired, and there they alight, and set their spears at the door, and in they entered into the chapel, and there made their orisons a great while, and then set them down in the sieges of the chapel. And as they spake of one thing and other, for heaviness they fell on sleep, and there befell them both marvellous adventures. Sir Gawaine him seemed he came into a meadow full of herbs and flowers. And there he saw a rack of bulls an hundred and fifty, that were proud and black, save three of them were all white, and one had a black spot, and the other two were so fair and so white that they might be no whiter. And these three bulls which were so fair were tied with two strong cords. And the remnant of the bulls said among them, Go we hence to seek better pasture. And so some went, and some came again; but they were so lean that they might not stand upright; and of the bulls that were so white, that one came again, and no more. But when this white bull was come again among these other, there arose up a great cry for lack of wind that failed them; and so they departed, one here and another there. This vision befell Sir Gawaine that night.

CHAP. II.

Of the vision of Sir Ector, and how he justed with Sir Uwaine les Avoutres, his sworn brother.

BUT to Sir Ector de Maris befell another vision, the contrary. For it seemed him that his brother Sir Launcelot and he alight out of a chair and lept upon two horses, and the one said to the other, Go we seek that we shall not find. And him thought that a man beat Sir Launcelot and despoiled him, and clothed him in another array, the which was all full of knots, and set him upon an ass. And so he rode till he came to the fairest well that ever he saw, and Sir Launcelot alight, and would have drunk of that well. And when he stooped to drink of the water, the water sank from him. And when Sir Launcelot saw that, he turned and went thither as the head came from. And in the meanwhile he trowed that himself and Sir Ector rode till that they came to a rich man's house, where there was a wedding. And there he saw a king, the which said, Sir knight, here is no place for you: and then he turned again unto the chair that he came from. Thus within a while both Gawaine and Ector awaked, and either told other of their vision, the which marvelled them greatly. Truly, said Ector, I shall never be merry till I hear tidings of my brother Launcelot.

Now as they sat thus talking, they saw an hand shewing unto the elbow, and was covered with red samite, and upon that hung a bridle not rich, and held within the fist a great candle which burnt right clear, and so passed afore them, and entered into the chapel, and then vanished away, and they wist not where. And anon came down a voice which said, Knights full of evil faith and poor belief, these two things have failed you, and therefore ye may not come to the adventures of the Sancgreal. Then first spake Gawaine and said, Ector, have ye heard these words? Yea truly, said Sir Ector, I heard all. Now go we, said Sir Ector, unto some hermit that will tell us of our vision, for it seemeth me we labour all in vain. And so they departed and rode into a valley, and there met with a squire which rode on an hackney, and they saluted him fair. Sir, said Gawaine, can thou teach us to any hermit? Here is one in a little mountain, said the squire, but it is so rough that there may no horse go thither; and therefore ye must go on foot: there shall ye find a poor house, and there is Nacien the hermit, which is the holiest man in this country. And so they departed either from other. And then in a valley they met with a knight all armed, which proffered them to just as far as he saw them. Truly, said Sir Gawaine, sith I departed from Camelot there was none proffered me to just but once. And now, sir, said Ector, let me just with him. Nay, said Gawaine, ye shall not, but if I be beaten, it shall not forthink me then if ye go after me. And then either embraced other to just, and came together as fast as their horses might run, and brast their shields and the mails, and the one more than the other: and Gawaine was wounded in the left side, but the other knight was smitten through the breast, and the spear came out on the other side, and so they fell both out of their saddles, and in the falling they brake both their spears. Anon Gawaine arose, and set his hand to his sword, and cast his shield afore him. But all for nought was it, for the knight had no power to arise against him. Then said Gawaine, Ye must yield you as an overcome man, or else I may slay you. Ah, sir knight, said he, I am but dead; for God's sake, and of your gentleness, lead me here unto an abbey, that I may receive my Creator. Sir, said Gawaine, I know no house of religion hereby. Sir, said the knight, set me on an horse tofore you, and I shall teach you.

Gawaine set him up in the saddle, and he lept up behind him for to sustain him, and so came to an abbey, where they were well received; and anon he was unarmed, and received his Creator. Then he prayed Gawaine to draw the truncheon of the spear out of his body. Then Gawaine asked him what he was, that knew him not? I am, said he, of king Arthur's court, and was a fellow of the Round Table, and we were brethren sworn together, and now, Sir Gawaine, thou hast slain me, and my name is Uwaine les Avoutres, that sometime was son unto king Uriens, and was in the quest of the Sancgreal; and now forgive it thee God, for it shall ever be said that the one sworn brother hath slain the other.

CHAP. III.

How Sir Gawaine and Sir Ector came to an hermitage to be confessed, and how they told to the hermit their visions.

ALAS, said Sir Gawaine, that ever this misadventure is befallen me. No force, said Uwaine, sith I shall die this death, of a much more worshipfuller man's hands might I not die; but when ye come to the court, recommand me unto my lord king Arthur, and all those that be left onlive, and for old brotherhood think on me. Then began Gawaine to weep, and Ector also. And then Uwaine himself, and Sir Gawaine, drew out the truncheon of the spear; and anon departed the soul from the body. Then Sir Gawaine and Sir Ector buried him, as men ought to bury a king's son, and made written upon his name, and by whom he was slain.

Then departed Gawaine and Ector, as heavy as they might for their misadventure; and so rode till that they came unto the rough mountain, and there they tied their horses, and went on foot to the hermitage. And when they were come up, they saw a poor house, and beside the chapel a little courtlage, where Nacien the hermit gathered worts, as he which had tasted none other meat of a great while. And when he saw the errant knights, he came toward them and saluted them, and they him again. Fair lords, said he, what adventure brought you hither? Sir, said Gawaine, to speak with you, for to be confessed. Sir, said the hermit, I am ready. Then they told him so much that he wist well what they were, and then he thought to counsel them if he might. Then began Gawaine first, and told him of his vision that he had had in the chapel: and Ector told him all as it is afore rehearsed. Sir, said the hermit unto Sir Gawaine, the fair meadow and the rack therein ought to be understood the Round Table, and by the meadow ought to be understood humility and patience, those be the things which be always green and quick; for men may no time overcome humility and patience, therefore was the Round Table founded, and the chivalry hath been at all times, so by the fraternity which was there that she might not be overcome. For men said she was founded in patience and in humility. At the rack ate an hundred and fifty bulls, but they ate not in the meadow, for their hearts should be set in humility and patience, and the bulls were proud and black, save only three. By the bulls is to understand the fellowship of the Round Table, which for their sin and their wickedness be black. Blackness is to say without good or virtuous works. And the three bulls which were white, save only one which was spotted;—the two white betoken Sir Galahad and Sir Percivale, for they be maidens clean and without spot; and the third that had a spot signifieth Sir Bors de Ganis, which trespassed but once in his virginity, but since he kept himself so well in chastity that all is forgiven him, and his misdeeds. And why those three were tied by the necks, they be three knights in virginity and chastity, and there is no pride smitten in them. And the black bulls which said, Go we hence, they were those which at Pentecost, at the high feast, took upon them to go in the quest of the Sancgreal without confession: they

might not enter in the meadow of humility and patience. And therefore they returned into waste countries, that signifieth death, for there shall die many of them: every each of them shall slay other for sin, and they that shall escape shall be so lean 'that it shall be marvel to see them. And of the three bulls without spot, the one shall come again, and the other two never.

CHAP. IV.

How the hermit expounded their vision.

THEN spake Nacien unto Ector. Sooth it is that Launcelot and ye came down of one chair: the chair betokeneth mastership and lordship, which ye came down from. But ye two knights, said the hermit, ye go to seek that ye shall never find, that is the Sancgreal. For it is the secret thing of our Lord Jesu Christ. What is to mean, that Sir Launcelot fell down off his horse:—he hath left pride, and taken him to humility, for he hath cried mercy loud for his sin, and sore repented him, and our Lord hath clothed him in His clothing, which is full of knots, that is the hair which he weareth daily. And the ass that he rode upon is a beast of humility. For God would not ride upon no steed, nor upon no palfrey. So in ensample that an ass betokeneth meekness, that thou sawest Sir Launcelot ride on in thy sleep: and the well where as the water sank from him when he should have taken thereof, and when he saw he might not have it, he returned thither from whence he came, for the well betokeneth the high grace of God, the more men desire it to take it, the more shall be their desire. So when he came nigh the Sancgreal, he meeked him that he held him not a man worthy to be so nigh the holy vessel, for he had been so defouled in deadly sin by the space of many years, yet when he kneeled to drink of the well, there he saw great providence of the Sancgreal. And for he had served so long the devil, he shall have vengeance four and twenty days long, for that he hath been the devil's servant four and twenty years. And then soon after he shall return unto Camelot out of this country, and he shall say a part of such things as he hath found.

Now will I tell you what betokeneth the hand with the candle and the bridle; that is to understand the Holy Ghost, where charity is ever, and the bridle signifieth abstinence. For when she is bridled in christian man's heart, she holdeth him so short that he falleth not in deadly sin. And the candle which sheweth clearness and sight, signifieth the right way of Jesu Christ. And when he went, and said, Knights of poor faith and of wicked belief,—these three things failed, charity, abstinence, and truth, therefore ye may not attain that high adventure of the Sancgreal.

CHAP. V.

Of the good counsel that the hermit gave to him.

CERTES, said Gawaine, soothly have ye said, that I see it openly. Now I pray you, good man and holy father, tell me why we met not with so many adventures as we were wont to do, and commonly have the better. I shall tell you gladly, said the good man : The adventure of the Sancgreal, which ye and many other have undertaken the quest of it, and find it not, the cause is, for it appeareth not to sinners. Wherefore marvel not though ye fail thereof, and many other. For ye ، be an untrue knight, and a great murderer, and to good men signifieth other things than murder. For I dare say, as sinful as Sir Launcelot hath been, sith that he went into the quest of the Sancgreal he slew never man, nor nought shall till that he come unto Camelot again. For he hath taken upon him for to forsake sin. And were not that he is not stable, but by his thought he is likely to turn again, he should be next to achieve it, save Galahad his son. But God

knoweth his thought, and his unstableness, and yet shall he die right an holy man; and no doubt he hath no fellow of no earthly sinful man. Sir, said Gawaine, it seemeth me by your words, that for our sins it will not avail us to travail in this quest. Truly, said the good man, there be an hundred such as ye be, that never shall prevail but to have shame. And when they had heard these voices, they commanded him unto God.

Then the good man called Gawaine, and said, It is long time passed sith that ye were made knight, and never since thou servedst thy Maker, and now thou art so old a tree, that in thee there is neither life nor fruit ; wherefore bethink thee that thou yield unto our Lord the bare rind, sith the fiend hath the leaves and the fruit. Sir, said Gawaine, and I had leisure I would speak with you, but my fellow here, Sir Ector, is gone, and abideth me yonder beneath the hill. Well, said the good man, thou were better to be counselled. Then departed Gawaine, and came to Ector, and so took their horses, and rode till they came to a foster's house which harboured them right well. And on the morn they departed from their host, and rode long or they could find any adventure.

CHAP. VI.

How Sir Bors met with an hermit, and how he was confessed to him, and of his penance enjoined to him.

WHEN Bors was departed from Camelot, he met with a religious man riding on an ass, and Sir Bors saluted him. Anon the good man knew, him that he was one of the knights errant that was in the quest of the Sancgreal. What are ye ? said the good man. Sir, said he, I am a knight that fain would be counselled in the quest of the Sancgreal : for he shall have much earthly worship that may bring it to an end. Certes, said the good man, that is sooth, for he shall be the best knight of the world, and the fairest of all the fellowship. But wit you well, there shall none attain it but by cleanness, that is, pure confession. So rode they together till that they came to an hermitage. And there he prayed Bors to dwell all that night with him: and so he alight, and put away his armour, and prayed him that he might be confessed; and so they went into the chapel, and there he was clean confessed: and they eat bread, and drank water, together. Now, said the good man, I pray thee that thou eat none other, till that thou sit at the table where the Sancgreal shall be. Sir, said he, I agree me thereto; but how wit ye that I shall sit there? Yes, said the good man, that know I, but there shall be but few of your fellows with you. All is welcome, said Sir Bors, that God sendeth me. Also, said the good man, instead of a shirt, and in sign of chastisement, ye shall wear a garment; thereof I pray you do off all your clothes and your shirt, and so he did. And then he took him a scarlet coat, so that should be instead of his shirt, till he had fulfilled the quest of the Sancgreal. And the good man found him in so marvellous a life, and so stable, that he marvelled, and felt that he was never corrupt in fleshly lusts, but in one time that he begat Elian le Blank. Then he armed him, and took his leave, and so departed. And so a little from thence he looked up into a tree, and there he saw a passing great bird upon an old tree, and it was passing dry, without leaves, and the bird sat above, and had birds, the which were dead for hunger. So smote he himself with his beak, the which was great and sharp. And so the great bird bled till that he died among his birds. And the young birds took the life by the blood of the great bird. When Bors saw this, he wist well it was great tokening. For when he saw the great bird arose not, then he took his horse and went his way. So by evensong, by adventure he came to a strong tower, and an high, and there was he lodged gladly.

CHAP. VII.

How Sir Bors was lodged with a lady, and how he took on him for to fight against a champion for her land.

AND when he was unarmed, they led him into an high tower, where was a lady, young, lusty, and fair. And she received him with great joy, and made him to sit down by her, and so was he set to sup with flesh and many dainties. And when Sir Bors saw that, he bethought him on his penance, and bad a squire to bring him water. And so he brought him, and he made sops therein, and ate them. Ah, said the lady, I trow ye like not my meat. Yes, truly, said Sir Bors, God thank you madam, but I may eat none other meat this day. Then she spake no more as at that time, for she was loth to displease him.

Then after supper they spake of one thing and other. With that there came a squire, and said, Madam, ye must purvey you to-morn for a champion, for else your sister will have this castle, and also your lands, except ye can find a knight that will fight to-morn in your quarrel against Pridam le Noire. Then she made sorrow, and said, Ah Lord God, wherefore granted ye to hold my land, whereof I should now be disherited without reason and right. And when Sir Bors had heard her say thus, he said, I shall comfort you. Sir, said she, I shall tell you, there was here a king that hight Aniause, which held all this land in his keeping. So it mishapped he loved a gentlewoman, a great deal elder than I. So took he her all this land to her keeping, and all his men to govern, and she brought up many evil customs, whereby she put to death a great part of his kinsmen. And when he saw that, he let chase her out of this land, and betook it me, and all this land in my charge: but anon, as that worthy king was dead, this other lady began to war upon me, and hath destroyed many of my men, and turned them against me, that I have well nigh no man left me, and I have nought else but this high tower that she left me. And yet she hath promised me to have this tower, without I can find a knight to fight with her champion. Now tell me, said Sir Bors, what is that Pridam le Noire? Sir, said she, he is the most doubted man of this land.—Now may ye send her word that ye have found a knight that shall fight with that Pridam le Noire in God's quarrel and yours. Then that lady was not a little glad, and sent word that she was provided. And that night Sir Bors had good cheer, but in no bed he would come, but laid him on the floor, nor never would do otherwise till that he had met with the quest of Sancgreal.

CHAP. VIII.

Of a vision which Sir Bors had that night, and how he fought and overcame his adversary.

AND anon as he was asleep, him befell a vision, that there came to him two birds, the one as white as a swan, and the other was marvellous black, but it was not so great as the other, but in the likeness of a raven. Then the white bird came to him, and said, And thou wouldst give me meat and serve me, I should give thee all the riches of the world, and I shall make thee as fair and as white as I am. So the white bird departed, and there came the black bird to him, and said, And thou wilt serve me to-morrow, and have me in no despite, though I be black, for wit thou well that more availeth my blackness, than the other's whiteness. And then he departed. And he had another vision: him thought that he came to a great place, which seemed a chapel, and there he found a chair set on the left side, which was worm-eaten and feeble. And on the right hand were two flowers like a lily, and the one would have taken the other's whiteness, but a good man parted them, that the one touched not the other, and then out of every flower came out many flowers, and fruit great plenty. Then him thought the good man said, Should not he do great folly, that would let these two flowers perish for to succour the rotten tree, that it fell not to the earth? Sir, said he, it seemeth me that this wood might not avail. Now keep thee, said the good man, that thou never see such adventure befall thee. Then he awaked and made a sign of the cross in the midst of the forehead, and so rose and clothed him, and there came the lady of the place, and she saluted him, and he her again, and so went to a chapel, and heard their service. And there came a company of knights that the lady had sent for, to lead Sir Bors unto battle. Then asked he his arms. And when he was armed, she prayed him to take a little morsel to dine. Nay, madam, said he, that shall I not do, till I have done my battle, by the grace of God. And so he lept upon his horse, and departed all the knights and men with him. And as soon as these two ladies met together, she which Bors should fight for, complained her, and said, Madam, ye have done me wrong to bereave me of my lands that king Aniause gave me, and full loth I am there should be any battle. Ye shall not choose, said the other lady, or else your knight withdraw him. Then there was the cry made, which party had the better of those two knights, that this lady should enjoy all the land. Now departed the one knight here, and the other there. Then they came together with such force that they pierced their shields and their hauberks, and the spears flew in pieces, and they wounded either other sore. Then hurtled they together so that they fell both to the earth, and their horses betwixt their legs. And anon they arose, and set hands to their swords, and smote each one other upon the heads, that they made great wounds and deep, that the blood went out of their bodies. For there found Sir Bors greater defence in that knight more than he wend. For that Pridam was a passing good knight, and he wounded Sir Bors full evil, and he him again. But ever this Sir Pridam held the stour in like hard.

That perceived Sir Bors, and suffered him till he was nigh attaint, and then he ran upon him more and more, and the other went back for dread of death. So in his withdrawing he fell upright, and Sir Bors drew his helm so strongly that he rent it from his head, and gave him great strokes with the flat of his sword upon the visage, and bade him yield him, or he should slay him. Then he cried him mercy, and said, Fair knight, for God's love slay me not, and I shall ensure thee never to war against thy lady, but be alway toward her. Then Bors let him be. Then the old lady fled with all her knights.

CHAP. IX.

How the lady was restored to her lands by the battle of Sir Bors, and of his departing, and how he met Sir Lionel taken and beaten with thorns, and also of a maid which should have been dishonoured.

So then came Bors to all those that held lands of his lady, and said he should destroy them but if they did such service unto her as belonged to their lands. So they did their homage, and they that would not were chased out of their lands. Then befell that young lady to come to her estate again, by the mighty prowess of Sir Bors de Ganis. So when all the country was well set in peace, then Sir Bors took his leave and departed, and she thanked him greatly, and would have given him great riches, but he refused it. Then he rode all that day till night, and came to an harbour, to a lady which knew him well enough, and made of him great joy. Upon the morn, as soon as the day appeared, Bors departed from thence, and so rode into a forest unto the hour of mid-day, and there befell him a marvellous adventure. So he met at the departing of the two ways two knights, that led Lionel his brother all naked, bounden upon a strong hackney, and his hands bounden tofore his breast: and every each of them held in his hand thorns, wherewith they went

beating him so sore that the blood trailed down more than in an hundred places of his body, so that he was all blood tofore and behind, but he said never a word, as he which was great of heart; he suffered all that ever they did to him as though he had felt none anguish. Anon Sir Bors dressed him to rescue him that was his brother: and so he looked upon the other side of him, and saw a knight which brought a fair gentlewoman, and would have set her in the thickest place of the forest, for to have been the more surer out of the way from them that sought him. And she, which was nothing assured, cried with an high voice, Saint Mary, succour your maid!

And anon she espied where Sir Bors came riding. And when she came nigh him, she deemed him a knight of the Round Table, whereof she hoped to have some comfort; and then she conjured him, by the faith that he owed unto Him in whose service thou art entered in, and for the faith ye owe unto the high order of knighthood, and for the noble king Arthur's sake, that I suppose that made thee knight, that thou help me, and suffer me not to be shamed of this knight!

When Bors heard her say thus, he had so much sorrow there he nist not what to do. For if I let my brother be in adventure he must be slain, and that would I not for all the earth. And if I help not the maid, she is shamed for ever, and also she shall lose her honour, the which she shall never get again. Then lift he up his eyes, and said weeping, Fair sweet Lord Jesu Christ, whose liege man I am, keep Lionel my brother, that these knights slay him not; and for pity of you, and for Mary's sake, I shall succour this maid.

CHAP. X.

How Sir Bors left to rescue his brother, and rescued the damsel; and how it was told him that Lionel was dead.

THEN dressed he him unto the knight the which had the gentlewoman, and then he cried, Sir knight, let your hand off that maiden, or ye be but dead. And then he set down the maiden and was armed at all pieces, save he lacked his spear. Then he dressed his shield, and drew out his sword, and Bors smote him so hard that it went through his shield and haberjon on the left shoulder; and through great strength he beat him down to the earth; and at the pulling out of Bors' spear there he swooned.

Then came Bors to the maid, and said, How seemeth it you? Of this knight ye be delivered at this time. Now Sir, said she, I pray you lead me there as this knight had me.— So shall I do gladly: and took the horse of the wounded knight, and set the gentlewoman upon him, and so brought her as she desired. Sir knight, said she, ye have better sped than ye weened, for if ye had not saved me five hundred men should have died for it. —What knight was he that had you in the forest? — By my faith, said she, he is my cousin. So wot I never with what craft the fiend enchafed him, for yesterday he took me from my father privily; for I nor none of my father's men mistrusted him not. And if he had shamed me, he should have died for the sin, and his body shamed and dishonoured for ever. Thus as she stood talking with him, there came twelve knights seeking after her, and anon she told them all how Bors had delivered her; then they made great joy, and besought him to come to her father, a great lord, and he should be right welcome. Truly, said Bors, that may not be at this time, for I have a great adventure to do in this country. So he commended them unto God, and departed. Then Sir Bors rode after Lionel his brother by the trace of their horses. Thus he rode seeking a great while. Then he overtook a man clothed in a religious clothing, and rode on a strong black horse, blacker than a bery, and said, Sir knight, what seek you? Sir, said he, I seek my brother, that I saw within a while beaten with two knights. Ah Bors, discomfort you not, nor fall

into no vain hope, for I shall tell you tidings such as they be; for truly he is dead. Then shewed he him a new slain body, lying in a bush, and it seemed him well that it was the body of Lionel. And then he made such a sorrow that he fell to the earth all in a swoon, and lay a great while there. And when he came to himself he said, Fair brother, sith the company of you and me is parted, shall I never have joy in my heart; and now He which I have taken unto my Master, He be my help. And when he had said thus, he took his body lightly in his arms, and put it upon the bow of his saddle. And then he said to the man, Canst thou tell me unto some chapel, where that I may bury this body? Come on, said he, here is one fast by. And so long they rode till they saw a fair tower, and afore it there seemed an old feeble chapel. And then they alight both, and put him into a tomb of marble.

CHAP. XI.

How Sir Bors told his dream to a priest which he had dreamed, and of the counsel that the priest gave to him.

Now leave we him here, said the good man, and go we to harbour till to-morrow, we will come here again to do him service. Sir, said Bors, be ye a priest? Yea, forsooth, said he.—Then I pray you tell me a dream that befell to me the last night.— Say on, said he. Then he began so much to tell him of the great bird in the forest: and after told him of his birds, one white, another black; and of the rotten tree, and of the white flowers. Sir, said the priest, I shall tell you a part now, and the other deal to-morrow. The white fowl betokeneth a gentlewoman, fair and rich, which loveth thee, and hath loved thee long; and if thou refuse her love, she shall go die anon, if thou have no pity on her. That signifieth the great bird, the which shall make thee for to refuse her. Now, for no fear nor for no dread that thou hast of God, thou shalt not refuse her, but thou wouldest not do it for to be holden chaste, for to conquer the praise of the vain-glory of the world; for that shall befall thee now, and thou refuse her, that Launcelot, the good knight thy cousin, shall die. And therefore men shall now say that thou art a manslayer, both of thy brother Sir Lionel, and of thy cousin Sir Launcelot du Lake, the which thou mightest have saved and rescued full easily. But thou weenedst to rescue a maid, which pertained nothing to thee. Now look thou whether it had been greater harm of thy brother's death, or else to have suffered her for to have lost her honour. Then asked he him, Hast thou heard the tokens of thy dream, the which I have told to you? Yea forsooth, said Sir Bors, all your exposition and declaring of my dream I have well understood and heard. Then said the man in this black clothing, Then is it in thy default if Sir Launcelot thy cousin die. Sir, said Bors, that were me loth; for wit ye well there is nothing in the world but I had lever do it than to see my lord Sir Launcelot du Lake to die in my default. Choose ye now the one or the other, said the good man. And then he led Sir Bors into an high tower, and there he found knights and ladies. Those ladies said he was welcome, and so they unarmed him. And when he was in his doublet, men brought him a mantle furred with ermine, and put it about him, and then they made him such cheer that he had forgotten all his sorrow and anguish, and only set his heart in these delights and dainties, and took no more thought for his brother Sir Lionel, neither of Sir Launcelot du Lake his cousin. And anon came out of a chamber to him the fairest lady that ever he saw, and more richer beseen than ever he saw queen Guenever, or any other estate. Lo! said they, Sir Bors, here is the lady unto whom we all owe our service, and I trow she be the richest lady, and the fairest of all the world, and the which loveth you best above all other knights, for she will have no knight but you. And when he understood that language, he

was abashed. Not for then she saluted him, and he her; and then they sat down together, and spake of many things, insomuch that she besought him to be her love, for she had loved him above all earthly men, and she should make him richer than ever was man of his age. When Sir Bors understood her words he was right evil at ease, which in no manner would not break chastity, so wist not he how to answer her.

CHAP. XII.

How the devil in a woman's likeness would have tempted Sir Bors, and how by God's grace he escaped.

ALAS! said she, Bors, shall ye not do my will? Madam, said Sir Bors, there is no lady in this world whose will I will fulfil as of this thing, for my brother lieth dead which was slain right late. Ah, Bors, said she, I have loved you long for the great beauty I have seen in you, and great hardiness I have heard of you, that needs ye must give me your love, and, therefore, I pray you grant it me. Truly, said he, I shall not do it in no manner of wise. Then she made him such sorrow as though she would have died. Well, Bors, said she, unto this have ye brought me nigh to mine end. And therewith she took him by the hand, and bade him behold her,— And ye shall see how I shall die for your love. Ah, said then he, that shall I never see. Then she departed, and went up into a high battlement, and led with her twelve gentlewomen: and when they were above, one of the gentlewomen cried and said, Ah, Sir Bors, gentle knight, have mercy on us all, and suffer my lady to have her will: and if ye do not, we must suffer death with our lady, for to fall down off this high tower. And if ye suffer us thus to die for so little a thing, all ladies and gentlewomen will say of you dishonour. Then looked he upward: they seemed all ladies of great estate and richly and well beseen. Then had he of them great pity: not for that he was un-counselled within himself, that lever he had they all had lost their souls than he is: and with that they fell adown all at once unto the earth. And when he saw that, he was all abashed, and had thereof great marvel. With that he blessed his body and his visage; and anon he heard a great noise and a great cry, as though all the fiends of hell had been about him, and therewith he saw neither tower, ne lady, ne gentlewoman, nor no chapel where he brought his brother to. Then held he up both his hands to the heaven, and said, Fair Father God, I am grievously escaped. And then he took his arms and his horse, and rode on his way. Then he heard a clock smite on his right hand, and thither he came to an abbey on his right hand, closed with high walls, and there was let in. Then they supposed that he was one of the quest of the Sancgreal. So they led him into a chamber, and unarmed him. Sirs, said Sir Bors, if there be any holy man in this house, I pray you let me speak with him. Then one of them led him unto the abbot, which was in a chapel. And then Sir Bors saluted him, and he him again. Sir, said Bors, I am a knight errant, and told him all the adventure which he had seen. Sir knight, said the abbot, I wot not what ye be, for I wend never that a knight of your age might have been so strong in the grace of our Lord Jesu Christ. Not for then ye shall go unto your rest, for I will not counsel you this day, it is too late, and to-morrow I shall counsel you as I can.

CHAP. XIII.

Of the holy communication of an abbot to Sir Bors, and how the abbot counselled him.

AND that night was Sir Bors served richly, and on the morn early he heard mass, and the abbot came to him and bad him good morrow, and Bors to him again. And then he told him he was a fellow of the quest of the Sancgreal, and how he had charge of the holy man to eat bread and water. Then [said the abbot] our Lord Jesu Christ shewed Him unto you, in the likeness of a soul that suffered great anguish for us since He was put upon the cross, and bled His heart blood for mankind: there was the token and the likeness of the Sancgreal that appeared afore you, for the blood that the great fowl bled revived the chickens from death to life. And by the bare tree is betokened the world, which is naked and without fruit, but if it come of our Lord. Also the lady for whom ye fought for, and king Aniause, which was lord there tofore, betokeneth Jesu Christ, which is the King of the world; and that ye fought for the lady, this it betokeneth: for when ye took the battle for the lady, by her ye shall understand the new law of Jesu Christ and holy Church; and by the other lady ye shall understand the old law and the fiend, which all day warreth against holy Church, therefore ye did your battle with right. For ye be Jesu Christ's knights, therefore ye ought to be defenders of holy Church. And by the black bird might ye understand the holy Church, which saith I am black, but he is fair. And by the white bird might men understand the fiend. And I shall tell you how the swan is white without forth, and black within; it is hypocrisy which is without yellow or pale, and seemeth without forth the servants of Jesu Christ, but they be within so horrible of filth and sin, and beguile the world evil. Also when the fiend appeared to thee in likeness of a man of religion, and blamed thee that thou left thy brother for a lady, so led thee where thou seemed thy brother was slain, but he is yet on live, and all was for to put thee in error, and bring thee unto vain hope and lechery, for he knew thou were tender hearted, and all was for thou shouldest not find the blessed adventure of the Sancgreal. And the third fowl betokeneth the strong battle against the fair ladies which were all devils. Also the dry tree, and the white lily:—the dry tree betokeneth thy brother Sir Lionel, which is dry without virtue, and therefore many men ought to call him the rotten tree, and the worm-eaten tree, for he is a murderer and doth contrary to the order of knighthood. And the two white flowers signify two maidens, the one is a knight which was wounded the other day, and the other is the gentlewoman which ye rescued; and why the other flower drew nigh the other, that was the knight which would have dishonoured her, and himself both. And, Sir Bors, ye had been a great fool, and in great peril, to have seen those two flowers perish for to succour the rotten tree, for and they had sinned together they had been damned: and for that ye rescued them both, men might call you a very knight and servant of Jesu Christ.

CHAP. XIV.

How Sir Bors met with his brother Sir Lionel, and how Sir Lionel would have slain Sir Bors.

THEN went Sir Bors from thence, and commended the abbot unto God. And then he rode all that day, and harboured with an old lady. And on the morn he rode to a castle in a valley, and there he met with a yeoman going a great pace toward a forest. Say me, said Sir Bors, canst thou tell me of any adventure? Sir, said he, here shall be under this castle a great and a marvellous tournament. Of what folks shall it be? said Sir Bors. The earl of Plains (said he) shall be on the one party, and the lady's nephew of Hervin on the other party. Then Bors thought to be there, if he might meet with his brother Sir Lionel, or any other of his fellowship which were in the quest of the Sancgreal. And then he turned to an hermitage that was in the entry of the forest. And when he was come thither, he found there Sir Lionel his brother, which sat all armed at the entry of the chapel door, for to abide there harbour till on the morn that the tournament shall be. And when Sir Bors saw him he had great joy of him, that was it marvel to tell of his joy. And then he alight off his horse and said, Fair sweet brother, when came ye hither? Anon as Sir Lionel saw him he said, Ah Bors, ye may not make none avaunt, but, as for you, I might have been slain; when ye saw two knights leading me away, beating me, ye left me to succour a gentlewoman, and suffered me in peril of death: for never erst ne did no brother to another so great an untruth. And for that misdeed now I ensure you but death, for well have ye deserved it; therefore keep thee from henceforward, and that shall ye find as soon as I am armed. When Sir Bors understood his brother's wrath, he kneeled down to the earth, and cried him mercy, holding up both his hands, and prayed him to forgive him his evil will. Nay, said Lionel, that shall never be, and I may have the higher hand, that I make mine avow to God: thou shalt have death for it, for it were pity ye lived any longer. Right so he went in, and took his harness, and mounted upon his horse, and came tofore him and said, Bors, keep thee from me, for I shall to thee as I would to a felon or a traitor, for ye be the untruest knight that ever came out of so worthy an house as was king Bors de Ganis, which was our father; therefore start upon thy horse, and so shall ye be most at your advantage. And but if ye will, I will run upon thee there as ye stand upon foot, and so the shame shall be mine and the harm yours; but of that shame reck I nought. When Sir Bors saw that he must fight with his brother or else to die, he nist not what to do. Then his heart counselled him not thereto, in as much as Lionel was born or he, wherefore he ought to bear him reverence; yet kneeled he down afore Lionel's horse feet, and said, Fair sweet brother, have mercy upon me and slay me not, and have in remembrance the great love which ought to be between us twain. What Sir Bors said to Lionel he recked not, for the fiend had brought him in such a will that he should slay him. Then when Lionel saw he would none other, and that he would not have risen to give him battle, he rushed over him, so that he smote Bors with his horse feet upward to the earth, and hurt him so sore that he swooned of distress, the which he felt in himself to have died without confession. So when Lionel saw this, he alight off his horse, to have smitten off his head. And so he took him by the helm, and would have rent it from his head. Then came the hermit running unto him, which was a good man and of great age, and well had he heard all the words that were between them, and so fell down upon Sir Bors.

CHAP. XV.

How Sir Colgrevance fought against Sir Lionel for to save Sir Bors, and how the hermit was slain.

THEN he said to Lionel, Ah, gentle knight, have mercy upon me and on thy brother, for if thou slay him thou shalt be dead of sin, and that were sorrowful; for he is one of the worthiest knights of the world, and of the best conditions. So God me help, said Lionel, Sir priest, but if ye flee from him I shall slay you, and he shall never the sooner be quit. Certes, said the good man, I had lever ye slay me than him, for my death shall not be great harm, not half so much as of his. Well, said Lionel, I am agreed; and set his hand to his sword, and smote him so hard that his head went backward. Not for that he restrained him of his evil will, but took his brother by the helm, and unlaced it to have stricken off his head, and had slain him without fail, but so it happed, Colgrevance, a fellow of the Round Table, came at that time thither, as our Lord's will was. And when he saw the good man slain, he marvelled much what it might be. And then he beheld Lionel would have slain his brother, and knew Sir Bors which he loved right well. Then start he down and took Lionel by the shoulders, and drew him strongly aback from Bors, and said, Lionel, will ye slay your brother, the worthiest knight of the world one? and that should no good man suffer. Why, said

Sir Lionel, will ye let me? therefore if ye intermit you in this, I shall slay you, and him after. Why, said Colgrevance, is this sooth, that ye will slay him? Slay him will I, said he, who so say the contrary; for he hath done so much against me that he hath well deserved it; and so ran upon him, and would have smitten him through the head; and Sir Colgrevance ran betwixt them and said, And ye be so hardy to do so more, we two shall meddle together. When Lionel understood his words, he took his shield afore him, and asked him what he was; and he told him Colgrevance, one of his fellows. Then Lionel defied him, and gave him a great stroke through the helm. Then he drew his sword, for he was a passing good knight, and defended him right manfully. So long endured the battle that Sir Bors rose up all anguishly, and beheld Sir Colgrevance, the good knight, fight with his brother for his quarrel. Then was he full sorry and heavy, and thought, if Colgrevance slew him that was his brother he should never have joy, and if his brother slew Colgrevance the shame should ever be his. Then would he have risen to have departed them, but he had not so much might to stand on foot: so he abode him so long till Colgrevance had the worse, for Sir Lionel was of great chivalry and right hardy, for he had pierced the hauberk and the helm, that he abode but death. For he had lost much of his blood, that it was marvel that he might stand upright. Then beheld he Sir Bors, which sat dressing him upward, and said, Ah Bors, why come ye not to cast me out of peril of death, wherein I have put me to succour you, which were right now nigh the death? Certes, said Lionel, that shall not avail you, for none of you shall bear other's warrant, but that ye shall die both of my hand. When Bors heard that, he did so much he rose and put on his helm. Then perceived he first the hermit priest which was slain, then made he a marvellous sorrow upon him.

CHAP. XVI.

*How Sir Lionel slew Sir Colgrevance,
and how after he would have slain
Sir Bors.*

THEN oft Colgrevance cried upon Sir
Bors, Why will ye let me die here for
your sake? if it please you that I die for
you the death, it will please me the
better for to save a worthy man. With
that word Sir Lionel smote off the helm
from his head. Then Colgrevance saw
that he might not escape; then he said,
Fair sweet Jesu, that I have misdone
have mercy upon my soul; for such
sorrow that my heart suffereth for goodness, and for alms deed that I would
have done here, be to me aligement of
penance unto my soul's health. At
these words Lionel smote him so sore
that he bare him to the earth. So when
he had slain Colgrevance, he ran upon
his brother as a fiendly man, and gave
him such a stroke that he made him
stoop; and he, that was full of humility,
prayed him, for God's love to leave this
battle: For and it befell, fair brother,
that I slew you, or ye me, we should be
dead of that sin. Never God me help
but if I have on you mercy, and I may
have the better hand. Then drew Bors
his sword, all weeping, and said, Fair
brother, God knoweth mine intent. Ah,
fair brother, ye have done full evil this
day to slay such an holy priest, the
which never trespassed. Also ye have
slain a gentle knight, and one of our
fellows. And well wot ye that I am
not afeard of you greatly, but I dread
the wrath of God; and this is an unkindly war, therefore God shew miracle
upon us both. Now God have mercy
upon me, though I defend my life against
my brother. With that Bors lift up
his hand, and would have smitten his
brother.

CHAP. XVII.

*How there came a voice which charged Sir
Bors to touch not him, and of a cloud
that came between them.*

AND then he heard a voice that said,
Flee, Bors, and touch him not, or else

thou shalt slay him. Right so alight a
cloud betwixt them in likeness of a fire,
and a marvellous flame, that both their
two shields burnt. Then were they sore
afraid, that they fell both to the earth,
and lay there a great while in a swoon.
And when they came to themselves,
Bors saw that his brother had no harm:
then he held up both his hands, for he
dread God had taken vengeance upon
him. With that he heard a voice say,
Bors, go hence and bear thy brother no
longer fellowship, but take thy way
anon right to the sea, for Sir Percivale
abideth thee there. Then he said to his
brother, Fair sweet brother, forgive me,
for God's love, all that I have trespassed
unto you. Then he answered, God forgive it thee, and I do gladly. So Sir
Bors departed from him, and rode the
next way to the sea. And at the last,
by fortune he came to an abbey which
was nigh the sea. That night Bors
rested him there, and in his sleep there
came a voice to him, and bad him go to
the sea; then he start up, and made a
sign of the cross in the midst of his forehead, and took his harness, and made
ready his horse, and mounted upon him.
And at a broken wall he rode out, and
rode so long till that he came to the
sea. And on the strand he found a ship
covered all with white samite. And he
alight, and betook him to Jesu Christ.
And as soon as he entered into the
ship, the ship departed into the sea, and
went so fast that him seemed the ship
went flying, but it was soon dark, so
that he might know no man, and so he
slept till it was day. Then he awaked,
and saw in the midst of the ship a
knight lie, all armed save his helm.
Then knew he that it was Sir Percivale
of Wales, and then he made of him
right great joy. But Sir Percivale was
abashed of him, and he asked him what
he was. Ah, fair sir, said Bors, know ye
me not? Certes, said he, I marvel how
ye came hither, but if our Lord brought
you hither himself: then Sir Bors
smiled, and did off his helm. Then
Percivale knew him, and either made
great joy of other, that it was marvel to

hear. Then Bors told him how he came into the ship, and by whose admonishment. And either told other of their temptations, as ye have heard toforehand. So went they downward in the sea, one while backward another while forward, and every each comforted other, and oft were in their prayers. Then said Sir Percivale, We lack nothing but Galahad the good knight.

And thus endeth the syxteenth book whiche is of syre Gawayne, Ector de marys, and syre Bors de ganys and sir percyual.

And here foloweth the seuententh book whiche is of the noble knyghte syre Galahad.

The Seventeenth Book.

CHAP. I.

How Sir Galahad fought at a tournament, and how he was known of Sir Gawaine and Sir Ector de Maris.

Now saith this story, when Galahad had rescued Percivale from the twenty knights, he rode then into a vast forest, wherein he rode many journeys, and he found many adventures, the which he brought to an end, whereof the story maketh here no mention. Then he took his way to the sea on a day, and it befell as he passed by a castle where was a wonder tournament, but they without had done so much that they within were put to the worse, yet were they within good knights enough. When Galahad saw that those within were at so great a mischief that men slew them at the entry of the castle, then he thought to help them, and put a spear forth, and smote the first that he fell to the earth, and the spear brake to pieces. Then he drew his sword, and smote there as they were thickest, and so he did wonderful deeds of arms, that all they marvelled. Then it happed that Gawaine and Sir Ector de Maris were with the knights without; but when they espied the white shield with the red cross, the one said to the other, Yonder is the good knight Sir Galahad the haut

prince: now he should be a great fool which should meet with him to fight. So by adventure he came by Sir Gawaine, and he smote him so hard that he clave his helm, and the coif of iron unto his head, so that Gawaine fell to the earth: but the stroke was so great, that it slanted down to the earth, and carved the horse shoulder in two. When Ector saw Gawaine down, he drew him aside, and thought it no wisdom for to abide him, and also for natural love, that he was his uncle. Thus through his great hardiness he beat aback all the knights without. And then they within came out and chased them all about. But when Galahad saw there would none turn again, he stole away privily, so that none wist where he was become. Now by my head, said Gawaine to Ector, now are the wonders true that were said of Launcelot du Lake, that the sword which stuck in the stone should give me such a buffet that I would not have it for the best castle in this world, and soothly now it is proved true, for never before had I such a stroke of man's hand. Sir, said Ector, me seemeth your quest is done. And yours is not done, said Gawaine, but mine is done; I shall seek no further. Then Gawaine was borne into a castle, and unarmed him, and laid him in a rich bed, and a leech found that he might live, and to be whole within a month. Thus Gawaine and Ector abode together. For Sir Ector would not away till Gawaine were whole. And the good knight Galahad rode so long till he came that night to the castle of Carboneck; and it befell him thus that he was benighted in an hermitage. So the good man was fain when he saw he was a knight errant. Then when they were at rest, there came a gentlewoman knocking at the door, and called Galahad, and so the good man came to the door to wit what she would. Then she called the hermit, Sir Ulfin, I am a gentlewoman that would speak with the knight that is with you. Then the good man awaked Galahad, and bad him arise, and speak with a gentlewoman that seemeth hath great need of you. Then Galahad went to her, and asked her what she would. Galahad, said she, I will that ye arm you, and mount upon your horse, and follow me, for I shall shew you within these three days the highest adventure that ever any knight saw. Anon Galahad armed him, and took his horse and commended him to God, and bad the gentlewoman go, and he would follow there as she liked.

CHAP. II.

How Sir Galahad rode with a damsel, and came to the ship whereas Sir Bors and Sir Percivale were in.

So she rode as fast as her palfrey might bear her, till that she came to the sea the which was called Collibe. And at the night they came unto a castle in a valley, was closed with a running water, and with strong walls and high. And so she entered into the castle with Galahad, and there had he great cheer, for the lady of that castle was the damsel's lady. So when he was unarmed, then said the damsel, Madam, shall we abide here all this day? Nay, said she, but till he hath dined, and till he hath slept a little. So he eat and slept a while, till that the maid called him, and armed him by torchlight. And

when the maid was horsed, and he both, the lady took Galahad a fair child and rich, and so they departed from the castle, till they came to the sea-side, and there they found the ship where Bors and Percivale were in, the which cried on the ship's board, Sir Galahad, ye be welcome, we have abiden you long. And when he heard them, he asked them what they were. Sir, said she, leave your horse here, and I shall leave mine; and took their saddles and their bridles with them, and made a cross on them, and so entered into the ship. And the two knights received them both with great joy, and every each knew other. And so the wind arose, and drove them through the sea in a marvellous place. And within a while it dawned. Then did Galahad off his helm and his sword, and asked of his fellows from whence came that fair ship. Truly, said they, ye wot as well as we, but of God's grace. And then they told every each to other of all their hard adventures, and of their great temptation. Truly, said Galahad, ye are much bounden to God, for ye have escaped great adventures: and had not the gentlewoman been I had not come here; for as for you, I wend never to have found you in these strange countries. Ah, Galahad, said Bors, if Launcelot your father were here then were we well at ease, for then me seemeth we failed nothing. That may not be, said Galahad, but if it please our Lord. By then the ship went from the land of Logris, and by adventure it arrived up betwixt two rocks passing great and marvellous, but there they might not land, for there was a swallow of the sea, save there was another ship, and upon it they might go without danger. Go we thither, said the gentlewoman, and there shall we see adventures, for for so is our Lord's will. And when they came thither, they found the ship rich enough, but they found neither man nor woman therein. But they found in the end of the ship two fair letters written, which said a dreadful word and a marvellous:—Thou man which shall enter into this ship, beware thou be in steadfast belief, for I am Faith; and therefore beware how thou enterest, for and thou fail I shall not help thee. Then said the gentlewoman, Percivale, wot ye what I am? Certes, said he, nay, to my witting. Wit you well, said she, that I am thy sister, which am daughter of king Pellinore. And therefore wit ye well ye are the man in the world that I most love. And if ye be not in perfect belief of Jesu Christ, enter not in no manner of wise, for then should ye perish in the ship, for he is so perfect he will suffer no sin in him. When Percivale understood that she was his very sister, he was inwardly glad, and said, Fair sister, I shall enter therein, for if I be a mis-creature, or an untrue knight, there shall I perish.

CHAP. III.

How Sir Galahad entered into the ship, and of a fair bed therein, with other marvellous things, and of a sword.

In the mean while Galahad blessed him and entered therein, and then next the gentlewoman, and then Sir Bors and Sir Percivale. And when they were therein, it was so marvellous fair and rich that they marvelled. And in the midst of the ship was a fair bed, and Sir Galahad went thereto, and found there a crown of silk. And at the feet was a sword rich and fair, and it was drawn out of the sheath half a foot and more, and the sword was of divers fashions, and the pommel was of stone, and there was in him all manner of colours that any man might find, and every each of the colours had divers virtues, and the scales of the haft were of two ribs of divers beasts. The one beast was a serpent, which was conversant in Calidone, and is called the serpent of the fiend. And the bone of him is of such a virtue, that there is no hand that handleth him shall never be weary nor hurt : and the other beast is a fish, which is not right great, and haunteth the flood of Eufrates ; and that fish is called Ertanax, and his bones be of such a

manner of kind, that who that handleth them shall have so much will that he shall never be weary, and he shall not think on joy nor sorrow that he hath had, but only that thing that he beholdeth before him. And as for this sword there shall never man begripe it at the handle but one, but he shall pass all other. In the name of God, said Percivale, I shall essay to handle it. So he set his hand to the sword, but he might not begripe it. By my faith, said he, now have I failed. Bors set his hand thereto and failed. Then Galahad beheld the sword, and saw the letters like blood, that said, Let see who shall assay to draw me out of my sheath, but if he be more hardier than other, and who that draweth me, wit ye well that he shall never fail of shame of his body, or to be wounded to the death. By my faith, said Galahad, I would draw this sword out of the sheath, but the offending is so great, that I shall not set my hand thereto. Now sir, said the gentlewoman, wit ye well that the drawing of this sword is forbidden to all men, save all only unto you. Also this ship arrived in the realm of Logris, and that time was deadly war between king Labor, which was father unto the maimed king, and king Hurlame, which was a Saracen. But then was he newly christened, so that men held him afterwards one of the wittiest men of the world. And so upon a day it befell that king Labor and king Hurlame had assembled their folk upon the sea, where this ship was arrived, and there king Hurlame was discomfit, and his men slain, and he was afeard to be dead, and fled to his ship, and there found this sword, and drew it, and came out and found king Labor, the man in the world of all Christendom in whom was then the greatest faith. And when king Hurlame saw king Labor, he dressed this sword, and smote him upon the helm so hard, that he clave him and his horse to the earth with the first stroke of his sword. And it was in the realm of Logris ; and so befell great pestilence and great harm to both realms. For sithen increased neither corn nor grass, nor well nigh no fruit, nor in the water was no fish, wherefore men call it the lands of the two marches, the waste land, for that dolorous stroke. And when king Hurlame saw this sword so carving, he turned again to fetch the scabbard: and so came into this ship, and entered, and put up the sword in the sheath. And as soon as he had done it, he fell down dead afore the bed. Thus was the sword proved, that none ne drew it but he were dead or maimed. So lay he there till a maiden came into the ship, and cast him out, for there was no man so hardy of the world to enter into that ship for the defence.

CHAP. IV.

Of the marvels of the sword and of the scabbard.

AND then beheld they the scabbard; it seemed to be of a serpent's skin. And thereon were letters of gold and silver. And the girdle was but poorly to come to, and not able to sustain such a rich sword, and the letters said: He which shall wield me, ought to be more harder than any other, if he bear me as truly as I ought to be borne. For the body of him which I ought to hang by, he shall not be shamed in no place while he is gird with this girdle, nor never none be so hardy to do away this girdle for it ought not to be done away, but by the hands of a maid, and that she be a king's daughter, and queen's, and she must be a maid all the days of her life, both in will and in deed; and if she break her virginity, she shall die the most villainous death that ever did any woman. Sir, said Percivale, turn this sword, that we may see what is on the other side. And it was red as blood, with black letters as any coal, which said, He that shall praise me most, most shall he find me to blame at a great need, and to whom I should be most debonair shall I be most felon, and that shall be at one time. Fair brother, said she to Percivale, it befell about a forty year after the passion of Jesu Christ,

that Nacien, the brother-in-law of king Mordrains, was borne into a town more than fourteen days' journey from his country, by the commandment of our Lord, into an isle, into the parts of the west, that men call the Isle of Turnance. So befell it that he found this ship at the entry of a rock, and he found the bed, and this sword, as we have heard now. Not for then he had not so much hardiness to draw it: and there he dwelled an eight days, and at the ninth day there fell a great wind which departed him out of the isle, and brought him to another isle by a rock, and there he found the greatest giant that ever man might see. Therewith came that horrible giant to slay him, and then he looked about him, and might not fly, and he had nothing to defend him with. So he ran to his sword, and when he saw it naked he praised it much, and then he shook it, and therewith he brake it in the midst. Ah, said Nacien, the thing I most praised ought I now most to blame. And therewith he threw the pieces of his sword over his bed. And after he lept over the board to fight with the giant, and slew him. And anon he entered into the ship again, and the wind arose, and drove him through the sea, that by adventure he came to another ship where king Mordrains was, which had been tempted full evil with a fiend in the port of perilous rock. And when that one saw the other they made great joy of other, and either told other of their adventure, and how the sword failed him at his most need. When Mordrains saw the sword he praised it much,—but the breaking was not to do but by wickedness of thyself-ward, for thou art in some sin:—and there he took the sword, and set the pieces together, and they soldered as fair as ever they were tofore; and there he put the sword in the sheath, and laid it down on the bed. Then heard they a voice that said, Go out of this ship a little while, and enter into the other, for dread ye fall in deadly sin; for, and ye be found in deadly sin, ye may not escape but perish. And so

God's enemies. Now behoveth thee to go to the maimed king as soon as thou mayest, for he shall receive by thee health which he hath abiden so long. And therewith the soul departed from the body. And Galahad made him to be buried as he ought to be.

Right so departed the three knights, and Percivale's sister with them. And so they came into a waste forest, and there they saw afore them a white hart, which four lions led. Then they took them to assent for to follow after, for to know whither they repaired; and so they rode after, a great pace, till that they came to a valley, and thereby was an hermitage where a good man dwelled; and the hart and the lions entered also. So when they saw all this, they turned to the chapel, and saw the good man in a religious weed, and in the armour of our Lord, for he would sing mass of the Holy Ghost, and so they entered in and heard mass. And at the secrets of the mass, they three saw the hart become a man, the which marvelled them, and set him upon the altar in a rich siege, and saw the four lions were changed, the one to the form of a man, the other to the form of a lion, and the third to an eagle, and the fourth was changed unto an ox. Then took they their siege where the hart sat, and went out through a glass window, and there was nothing perished nor broken, and they heard a voice say, In such a manner entered the son of God in the womb of a maid, Mary. And when they heard these words, they fell down to the earth, and were astonied, and therewith was a great clearness. And when they were come to themselves again, they went to the good man, and prayed him that he would say them truth. What thing have ye seen? said he: and they told him all that they had seen. Ah, lords, said he, ye be welcome, now wot I well ye be the good knights the which shall bring the Sancgreal to an end; for ye be they unto whom our Lord shall shew great secrets. And well ought our Lord be signified to an hart; for the hart when

he is old he waxeth young again in his white skin: right so cometh again our Lord from death to life, for he lost earthly flesh, that was the deadly flesh which he had taken in the womb of the blessed virgin Mary; and for that cause appeared our Lord as a white hart without spot. And the four that were with him is to understand the four evangelists, which set in writing a part of Jesu Christ's deeds that he did some time when he was among you an earthly man. For wit ye well never erst might no knight know the truth, for, ofttimes or this, our Lord shewed him unto good men and unto good knights in likeness of an hart. But I suppose from henceforth ye shall see no more. And then they joyed much, and dwelled there all that day. And upon the morrow, when they had heard mass they departed, and commended the good man to God. And so they came to a castle, and passed by. So there came a knight armed after them, and said, Lords, hark what I shall say to you.

CHAP. X.

How they were desired of a strange custom, the which they would not obey; and how they fought and slew many knights.

THIS gentlewoman that ye lead with you is a maid? Sir, said she, a maid I am. Then he took her by the bridle and said, By the holy cross ye shall not escape me tofore ye have yielden the custom of this castle. Let her go, said Percivale; ye be not wise, for a maid in what place she cometh is free. So in the meanwhile there came out a ten or twelve knights armed, out of the castle, and with them came gentlewomen which held a dish of silver, and then they said, This gentlewoman must yield us the custom of this castle. Sir, said a knight, what maid passeth hereby shall give this dish full of blood of her right arm. Blame have ye, said Galahad, that brought up such customs, and I ensure you of this gentlewoman ye shall fail while that I live. Truly, said Sir Percivale, I had lever be slain. And

I also, said Sir Bors. By my truth, said the knight, then shall ye die, for ye may not endure against us, though ye were the best knights of the world. Then let them run each to other, and the three fellows beat the ten knights, and then set their hands to their swords, and beat them down and slew them. Then there came out of the castle well a threescore knights armed. Fair lords, said the three fellows, have mercy upon yourselves, and have not ado with us. Nay, fair lords, said the knights of the castle, we counsel you to withdraw you, for ye are the best knights of the world, and therefore do no more, for ye have done enough. We will let you go with this harm, but we must needs have the custom. Certes, said Galahad, for nought speak ye. Well, said they, will ye die? We be not yet come thereto, said Galahad. Then began they to meddle together, and Galahad drew his sword with the strange girdles, and smote on the right hand and on the left hand, and slew what that ever abode him, and did such marvels that there was none that saw him but they wend he had been none earthly man but a monster. And his two fellows halp him passing well, and so they held the journey every each in like hard, till it was night. Then must they needs part. So came a good knight and said to the three fellows, If ye will come in to night, and take such harbour as here is, ye shall be right welcome, and we shall ensure you by the faith of our bodies, as we are true knights, to leave you in such estate to-morrow as we find you, without any falsehood. And as soon as ye know of the custom we dare say ye will accord. Therefore, for God's love, said the gentlewoman, go thither, and spare not for me. Go we, said Galahad, and so they entered into the castle. And when they were alight, they made great joy of them. So within a while the three knights asked the custom of the castle, and wherefore it was. What it is, said they, we will say you sooth.

CHAP. XI.

How Sir Percivale's sister bled a dish full of blood for to heal a lady; wherefore she died; and how that the body was put in a ship.

THERE is in this castle a gentlewoman which we and this castle is hers, and many other. So it befell many years agone there fell upon her a malady. And when she had lain a great while, she fell into a measle, and of no leech she could have no remedy. But at the last an old man said, and she might have a dish full of blood of a maid and a clean virgin in will and in work, and a king's daughter, that blood should be her health, and for to anoint her withal: and for this thing was this custom made. Now, said Percivale's sister, Fair knights, I see well that this gentlewoman is but dead. Certes, said Galahad, and if ye bleed so much, ye may die. Truly, said she, and I die for to heal her, I shall get me great worship and soul's health, and worship to my lineage, and better is one harm than twain. And therefore there shall be no more battle, but to-morn I shall yield you your custom of this castle. And then there was great joy, more than there was tofore. For else had there been mortal war upon the morn; notwithstanding she would none other, whether they would or nold. That night were the three fellows eased with the best, and on the morn they heard mass, and Sir Percivale's sister bad bring forth the sick lady. So she was, the which was evil at ease. Then said she, Who shall let me blood? So one came forth and let her blood, and she bled so much that the dish was full. Then she lift up her hand and blessed her. And then she said to the lady, Madam, I am come to the death, for to make you whole; for God's love pray for me. With that she fell in a swoon. Then Galahad and his two fellows start up to her, and lift her up, and stanched her, but she had bled so much that she might not live. Then she said, when she was awaked, Fair brother

Percivale, I die for the healing of this lady. So I require you that ye bury not me in this country, but as soon as I am dead put me in a boat at the next haven, and let me go as adventure will lead me; and as soon as ye three come to the city of Sarras, there to achieve the holy Graile, ye shall find me under a tower arrived, and there bury me in the spiritual place, for I say you so much, there Galahad shall be buried, and ye also, in the same place. Then Percivale understood these words, and granted it her, weeping. And then said a voice, Lords and fellows, to-morrow at the hour of prime ye three shall depart every each from other, till the adventure bring you to the maimed king. Then asked she her Saviour, and as soon as she had received him the soul departed from the body. So the same day was the lady healed, when she was anointed withal. Then Sir Percivale made a letter of all that she had holpen them as in strange adventures, and put it in her right hand, and so laid her in a barge, and covered it with black silk; and so the wind arose, and drove the barge from the land, and all knights beheld it, till it was out of their sight.

Then they drew all to the castle, and so forthwith there fell a sudden tempest, and a thunder, lightning, and rain, as all the earth would have broken. So half the castle turned up so down. So it passed evensong or the tempest was ceased. Then they saw afore them a knight armed and wounded hard in the body and in the head, that said, Oh, God, succour me, for now it is need! After this knight came another knight and a dwarf which cried to them afar, Stand, ye may not escape. Then the wounded knight held up his hands to God, that he should not die in such tribulation. Truly, said Galahad, I shall succour him for His sake that he calleth upon. Sir, said Bors, I shall do it, for it is not for you, for he is but one knight. Sir, said he, I grant. So Sir Bors took his horse, and commended him to God, and rode after to rescue the wounded knight. Now turn we to the two fellows.

CHAP. XII.

How Galahad and Percivale found in a castle many tombs of maidens that had bled to death.

Now saith the story that all night Galahad and Percivale were in a chapel in their prayers, for to save Sir Bors. So on the morrow they dressed them in their harness toward the castle, to wit what was fallen of them therein. And when they came there, they found neither man nor woman that he ne was dead by the vengeance of our Lord. With that they heard a voice that said, This vengeance is for blood shedding of maidens. Also they found at the end of the chapel a churchyard, and therein might they see a threescore fair tombs, and that place was so fair and so delectable that it seemed them there had been none tempest. For there lay the bodies of all the good maidens which were martyred for the sick lady's sake. Also they found the names of every each, and of what blood they were come, and all were of kings' blood, and twelve of them were kings' daughters. Then they departed, and went into a forest. Now, said Percivale unto Galahad, we must depart; so pray we our Lord that we may meet together in short time. Then they did off their helms, and kissed together, and wept at their departing.

CHAP. XIII.

How Sir Launcelot entered into the ship where Sir Percivale's sister lay dead; and how he met with Sir Galahad his son.

Now saith the history, that when Launcelot was come to the water of Mortoise, as it is rehearsed before, he was in great peril, and so he laid him down and slept, and took the adventure that God would send him.

So when he was asleep, there came a vision unto him and said, Launcelot, arise up, and take thine armour, and enter into the first ship that thou shalt find. And when he had heard these words, he start up and saw great clearness about him. And then he lift up his hand and blessed him, and so took his arms, and made him ready; and so by adventure he came by a strand, and found a ship, the which was without sail or oar. And as soon as he was within the ship, there he felt the most sweetness that ever he felt; and he was fulfilled with all thing that he thought on or desired. Then said he, Fair sweet Father Jesu Christ, I wot not in what joy I am, for this joy passeth all earthly joys that ever I was in. And so in this joy he laid him down to the ship's board, and slept till day. And when he awoke, he found there a fair bed, and therein lying a gentlewoman dead, the which was Sir Percivale's sister. And as Launcelot devised her, he espied in her right hand a writ, the which he read, the which told him all the adventures that ye have heard tofore, and of what lineage she was come. So with this gentlewoman Sir Launcelot was a month and more. If ye would ask how he lived, He that fed the people of Israel with manna in the desert, so was he fed. For every day, when he had said his prayers, he was sustained with the grace of the Holy Ghost. So on a night he went to play him by the water side, for he was somewhat weary of the ship. And then he listened, and heard an horse come, and one riding upon him. And when he came nigh he seemed a knight. And so he let him pass, and went there as the ship was, and there he alight, and took the saddle and the bridle and put the horse from him, and went into the ship. And then Launcelot dressed unto him and said, Ye be welcome. And he answered and saluted him again, and asked him, What is your name? for much my heart giveth unto you. Truly, said he, my name is Launcelot du Lake. Sir, said he, then be ye welcome, for ye were the beginner of me in this world. Ah, said he, are ye Galahad? Yea forsooth, said he. And so he kneeled down and asked him his blessing, and after took off his helm and kissed him. And there was great joy between them, for there is no tongue can tell the joy that

they made either of other, and many a friendly word spoken between, as kind would, the which is no need here to be rehearsed. And there every each told other of their adventures and marvels that were befallen to them in many journeys, sith that they departed from the court. Anon as Galahad saw the gentlewoman dead in the bed, he knew her well enough, and told great worship of her, and that she was the best maid living, and it was great pity of her death. But when Launcelot heard how the marvellous sword was gotten, and who made it, and all the marvels rehearsed afore, then he prayed Galahad his son that he would shew him the sword, and so he did. And anon he kissed the pommel, and the hilts, and the scabbard. Truly, said Launcelot, never erst knew I of so high adventures done, and so marvellous and strange. So dwelled Launcelot and Galahad within that ship half a year, and served God daily and nightly with all their power. And often they arrived in isles far from folk, where there repaired none but wild beasts; and there they found many strange adventures and perilous, which they brought to an end. But because the adventures were with wild beasts, and not in the quest of the Sancgreal, therefore the tale maketh here no mention thereof, for it would be too long to tell of all those adventures that befell them.

CHAP. XIV.

How a knight brought unto Sir Galahad an horse, and bad him come from his father Sir Launcelot.

So after, on a Monday, it befell that they arrived in the edge of a forest, tofore a cross, and then saw they a knight, armed all in white, and was richly horsed, and led in his right hand a white horse. And so he came to the ship, and saluted the two knights on the high Lord's behalf, and said, Galahad, sir, ye have been long enough with your father, come out of the ship, and start upon this horse, and go where the adventures shall lead thee in the quest of the Sancgreal. Then he went to his father, and kissed him sweetly, and said, Fair sweet father, I wot not when I shall see you more, till I see the body of Jesu Christ. I pray you, said Launcelot, pray ye to the high Father that He hold me in his service. And so he took his horse; and there they heard a voice, that said, Think for to do well, for the one shall never see the other before the dreadful day of doom. Now, son Galahad, said Launcelot, since we shall depart, and never see other, I pray to the high Father to preserve both me and you both. Sir, said Galahad, no prayer availeth so much as yours. And therewith Galahad entered into the forest. And the wind arose, and drove Launcelot more than a month throughout the sea, where he slept but little, but prayed to God that he might see some tidings of the Sancgreal. So it befell on a night, at midnight he arrived afore a castle, on the back side, which was rich and fair. And there was a postern opened towards the sea, and was open without any keeping, save two lions kept the entry; and the moon shone clear. Anon Sir Launcelot heard a voice that said, Launcelot, go out of this ship, and enter into the castle, where thou shalt see a great part of thy desire. Then he ran to his arms, and so armed him, and so he went to the gate, and saw the lions. Then set he hand to his sword, and drew it. Then there came a dwarf suddenly, and smote him on the arm so sore that the sword fell out of his hand. Then heard he a voice say, Oh man of evil faith and poor belief, wherefore trowest thou more on thy harness than in thy Maker? for He might more avail thee than thine armour, in whose service thou art set. Then said Launcelot, Fair Father Jesu Christ, I thank thee of thy great mercy, that thou reprovest me of my misdeed. Now see I well that ye hold me for your servant. Then took he again his sword, and put it up in his sheath, and made a cross in his forehead, and came to the lions, and they made semblant to do him harm. Notwithstanding he passed by them without hurt, and entered into the castle to the chief fortress, and there

were they all at rest. Then Launcelot entered in so armed, for he found no gate nor door but it was open. And at the last he found a chamber whereof the door was shut, and he set his hand thereto to have opened it, but he might not.

CHAP. XV.

How Sir Launcelot was tofore the door of the chamber wherein the holy Sangreal was.

THEN he enforced him mickle to undo the door. Then he listened, and heard a voice which sang so sweetly that it seemed none earthly thing; and him thought the voice said, Joy and honour be to the Father of Heaven! Then Launcelot kneeled down tofore the chamber, for well wist he that there was the Sancgreal within that chamber. Then said he, Fair sweet Father Jesu Christ, if ever I did thing that pleased the Lord, for thy pity have me not in despite for my sins done aforetime, and that thou shew me something of that I seek! And with that he saw the chamber door open, and there came out a great clearness, that the house was as bright as all the torches of the world had been there. So came he to the chamber door, and would have entered. And anon a voice said to him, Flee Launcelot, and enter not, for thou oughtest not to do it: and if thou enter thou shalt forthink it. Then he withdrew him aback right heavy. Then looked he up in the midst of the chamber, and saw a table of silver, and the holy vessel covered with red samite, and many angels about it, whereof one held a candle of wax burning, and the other held a cross, and the ornaments of an altar. And before the holy vessel he saw a good man clothed as a priest, and it seemed that he was at the sacring of the mass. And it seemed to Launcelot that above the priest's hands there were three men, whereof the two put the youngest by likeness between the priest's hands, and so he lift it up right high, and it seemed to shew so to the people. And then Launcelot marvelled not a little, for him thought that the priest was so greatly charged of the figure, that him seemed that he should fall to the earth. And when he saw none about him that would help him, then came he to the door a great pace, and said, Fair Father Jesu Christ, ne take it for no sin though I help the good man, which hath great need of help. Right so entered he into the chamber, and came toward the table of silver ; and when he came nigh he felt a breath that him thought it was intermeddled with fire, which smote him so sore in the visage that him thought it burnt his visage; and therewith he fell to the earth, and had no power to arise, as he that was so araged that had lost the power of his body, and his hearing, and his saying. Then felt he many hands about him, which took him up and bare him out of the chamber door, without any amending of his swoon, and left him there seeming dead to all people. So upon the morrow, when it was fair day, they within were arisen, and found Launcelot lying afore the chamber door. All they marvelled how that he came in. And so they looked upon him, and felt his pulse, to wit whether there were any life in him ; and so they found life in him, but he might neither stand, nor stir no member that he had ; and so they took him by every part of the body, and bare him into a chamber, and laid him in a rich bed, far from all folk, and so he lay four days. Then the one said he was on live, and the other said nay. In the name of God, said an old man, for I do you verily to wit he is not dead, but he is so full of life as the mightiest of you all, and therefore I counsel you that he be well kept till God send him life again.

CHAP. XVI.

How Sir Launcelot had lain fourteen days and as many nights as a dead man, and other divers matters.

IN such manner they kept Launcelot four and twenty days, and also many nights, that ever he lay still as a dead man ; and at the twenty-fifth day befell him after midday that he opened his eyes. And when he saw folk he made great sorrow and said, Why have ye awaked me? for I was more at ease than I am now. Oh Jesu Christ, who might be so blessed that might see openly thy great marvels of secretness there where no sinner may be. What have ye seen? said they about him. I have seen, said he, so great marvels that no tongue may tell, and more than any heart can think, and had not my son been here afore me I had seen much more. Then they told him how he had lain there four and twenty days and nights. Then him thought it was punishment for the twenty-four years that he had been a sinner, wherefore our Lord put him in penance four and twenty days and nights. Then looked Sir Launcelot before him, and saw the hair which he had borne nigh a year, for that he forethought him right much that he had broken his promise unto the hermit, which he had avowed to do. Then they asked him how it stood with him. Forsooth, said he, I am whole of body, thanked be our Lord ; therefore, sirs, for God's love tell me where that I am? Then said they all that he was in the castle of Carbonek. Therewith came a gentlewoman, and brought him a shirt of small linen cloth, but he changed not there, but took the hair to him again. Sir, said they, the quest of the Sancgreal is achieved right now in you, that never shall ye see of the Sancgreal no more than ye have seen. Now I thank God, said Launcelot, of His great mercy, of that I have seen, for it sufficeth me, for, as I suppose, no man in this world hath lived better than I have done to achieve that I have done. And therewith he took the hair, and clothed him in it, and above that he put a linen shirt, and after a robe of scarlet, fresh and new. And when he was so arrayed, they marvelled all, for they knew him that he was Launcelot, the good knight. And then they said all, O my lord Sir Launcelot, be that ye? And he said, Truly they went into the other ship. And as Nacien went over the board, he was smitten with a sword on the right foot, that he fell down noseling to the ship's board, and therewith he said, O God, how am I hurt. And then there came a voice and said, Take thou that for thy forfeit that thou didst in drawing of this sword, therefore thou receivest a wound, for thou were never worthy to handle it, as the writing maketh mention. In the name of God, said Galahad, ye are right wise of these works.

CHAP. V.

How king Pelles was smitten through both thighs because he drew the sword, and other marvellous histories.

SIR, said she, there was a king that hight Pelles the maimed king. And while he might ride, he supported much Christendom, and holy Church. So upon a day he hunted in a wood of his which lasted unto the sea, and at the last he lost his hounds and his knights, save only one: and there he and his knight went till that they came toward Ireland, and there he found the ship. And when he saw the letters and understood them, yet he entered, for he was right perfect of his life: but his knight had none hardiness to enter, and there found he this sword, and drew it out as much as ye may see. So therewith entered a spear, wherewith he was smitten him through both the thighs, and never sith might he be healed, nor nought shall tofore we come to him. Thus, said she, was king Pelles, your grandsire, maimed for his hardiness. In the name of God, damsel, said Galahad. So they went toward the bed to behold all about it, and above the head there hung two swords. Also there were two spindles which were as white as any snow, and other that were as red as blood, and other above green as any emerald: of these three colours were the spindles, and of natural colour within, and without any painting. These spindles, said the damsel, were when sinful Eve came to gather fruit, for which Adam and she were put out of paradise, she took with her the bough on which the apple hung on. Then perceived she that the branch was fair and green, and she remembered her the loss which came from the tree. Then she thought to keep the branch as long as she might. And for she had no cofier to keep it in, she put it in the earth. So by the will of our Lord the branch grew to a great tree within a little while, and was as white as any snow, branches, boughs, and leaves, that was a token a maiden planted it. But after the tree which was white became green as any grass, and all that came out of it. And in the same time there was Abel begotten; thus was the tree long of green colour. And so it befell many days after, under the same tree Cain slew Abel, whereof befell great marvel. For anon as Abel had received the death under the green tree, it lost the green colour and became red, and that was in tokening of the blood. And anon all the plants died thereof, but the tree grew and waxed marvellously fair, and it was the fairest tree and the most delectable that any man might behold and see, and so died the plants that grew out of it tofore the time that Abel was slain under it. So long endured the tree till that Solomon king David's son reigned, and held the land after his father. This Solomon was wise, and knew all the virtues of stones and trees, and so he knew the course of the stars, and many other diverse things.

This Solomon had an evil wife, where through he wend that there had never been no good woman, and so he despised them in his books. So answered a voice him once, Solomon, if heaviness come to a man by a woman, ne reck thou never. For yet shall there come a woman whereof there shall come greater joy unto man an hundred times more than this heaviness giveth sorrow, and that woman shall be born of thy lineage. Then when Solomon heard these words, he held himself but a fool, and the truth he perceived by old books. Also the Holy Ghost shewed him the coming of the glorious Virgin Mary. Then asked he of the voice if it should be in the end of his lineage. Nay, said the voice, but there shall come a man which shall be a maid, and the last of your blood, and he shall be as good a knight as duke Josua thy brother-in-law.

CHAP. VI.

How Solomon took David's sword by the counsel of his wife, and of other matters marvellous.

Now have I certified thee of that thou stoodst in doubt. Then was Solomon glad that there should come any such of his lineage, but ever he marvelled and studied who that should be, and what his name might be. His wife perceived that he studied, and thought that she would know it at some season, and so she waited her time, and asked of him the cause of his studying, and there he told her altogether how the voice told him. Well, said she, I shall let make a ship of the best wood and most durable that men may find. So Solomon sent for all the carpenters of the land and the best. And when they had made the ship, the lady said to Solomon, Sir, said she, since it is so that this knight ought to pass all other knights of chivalry which have been tofore him, and shall come after him, moreover I shall tell you, said she, ye shall go into our Lord's temple, whereas is king David's sword, your father, the which is the marvellousest and sharpest that ever was taken in any knight's hand. Therefore take that, and take off the pommel, and thereto make ye a pommel of precious stones, that it be so subtilly made that no man perceive it but that they be all one. And after make there an hilt so marvellously and wonderly that no man may know it. And after make a marvellous sheath. And when ye have made all this, I shall let make a girdle thereto, such as shall please me. All this king Solomon did let make as she devised, both the ship and all the remnant. And when the ship was ready in the sea to sail, the lady let make a great bed, and

marvellous rich, and set her upon the bed's head covered with silk, and laid the sword at the feet, and the girdles were of hemp, and therewith the king was angry. Sir, wit ye well, said she, that I have none so high a thing which were worthy to sustain so high a sword, and a maid shall bring other knights thereto, but I wot not when it shall be, nor what time. And there she let make a covering to the ship, of cloth of silk that should never rot for no manner of weather. Yet went that lady, and made a carpenter to come to the tree which Abel was slain under. Now, said she, carve me out of this tree as much wood as will make me a spindle. Ah, madam, said he, this is the tree the which our first mother planted. Do it, said she, or else I shall destroy thee. Anon as he began to work there came out drops of blood, and then would he have left, but she would not suffer him, and so he took away as much wood as might make a spindle, and so she made him to take as much of the green tree, and of the white tree. And when these three spindles were shapen, she made them to be fastened upon the ceiling of the bed. When Solomon saw this, he said to his wife, Ye have done marvellously, for though all the world were here right now, they could not devise wherefore all this was made, but our Lord himself, and thou that hast done it wotest not what it shall betoken. Now let it be, said she, for ye shall hear tidings sooner than ye ween.

Now shall ye hear a wonderful tale of king Solomon and his wife.

CHAP. VII.

A wonderful tale of king Solomon and his wife.

THAT night lay Solomon before the ship with little fellowship. And when he was on sleep, him thought there came from heaven a great company of angels, and alight into the ship, and took water which was brought by an angel in a vessel of silver, and sprinkled all the ship. And after he came to the sword and drew letters on the hilt. And after went to the ship's board, and wrote there other letters, which said: Thou man that wilt enter within me, beware that thou be full within the faith, for I ne am but faith and belief. When Solomon espied these letters he was abashed, so that he durst not enter, and so drew him aback, and the ship was anon shoven in the sea, and he went so fast that he lost sight of him within a little while. And then a little voice said, Solomon, the last knight of thy lineage shall rest in this bed. Then went Solomon and awaked his wife, and told her of the adventures of the ship.

Now saith the history, that a great while the three fellows beheld the bed and the three spindles. Then they were at certain that they were of natural colours, without painting. Then they lift up a cloth which was above the ground, and there they found a rich purse by seeming. And Percivale took it, and found therein a writ, and so he read it, and devised the manner of the spindles, and of the ship, whence it came, and by whom it was made. Now, said Galahad, where shall we find the gentlewoman that shall make new girdles to the sword. Fair sir, said Percivale's sister, dismay you not, for by the leave of God I shall let make a girdle to the sword, such one as shall belong thereto. And then she opened a box, and took out girdles which were seemly wrought with golden threads, and upon that were set full precious stones, and a rich buckle of gold. Lo lords, said she, here is a girdle that ought to be set about the sword. And wit ye well the greatest part of this girdle was made of my hair, which I loved well while that I was a woman of the world. But as soon as I wist that this adventure was ordained me, I clipped off my hair and made this girdle in the name of God. Ye be well found, said Sir Bors, for certes you have put us out of great pain, wherein we should have entered ne had your tidings been. Then went

the gentlewoman and set it on the girdle of the sword. Now, said the fellowship, what is the name of the sword, and what shall we call it? Truly, said she, the name of the sword is, the sword with the strange girdles, and the sheath, mover of blood; for no man that hath blood in him shall never see the one part of the sheath which was made of the tree of life. Then they said to Galahad, In the name of Jesu Christ, and pray you that ye gird you with this sword, which hath been desired so much in the realm of Logris. Now let me begin, said Galahad, to gripe this sword for to give you courage: but wit ye well it belongeth no more to me then it doth to you. And then he griped about it with his fingers a great deal. And then she girt him about the middle with the sword:—Now reck I not though I die, for now I hold me one of the blessed maidens of the world, which hath made the worthiest knight of the world. Damsel, said Galahad, ye have done so much that I shall be your knight all the days of my life. Then they went from that ship, and went to the other. And anon the wind drove them into the sea a great pace, but they had no victual: but it befell that they came on the morn to a castle that men call Carteloise, that was in the marches of Scotland. And when they had passed the port, the gentlewoman said, Lords, here be men arriven that, and they wist that ye were of king Arthur's court, ye should be assailed anon. Damsel, said Galahad, he that cast us out of the rock shall deliver us from them.

CHAP. VIII.

How Galahad and his fellows came to a castle, and how they were fought withal, and how they slew their adversaries, and other matters.

So it befell, as they spake thus there came a squire by them, and asked what they were. And they said they were of king Arthur's house. Is that sooth? said he. Now by my head, said he, ye be ill arrayed; and then turned he again unto the cliff fortress. And within a while they heard a horn blow. Then a gentlewoman came to them, and asked them of whence they were, and they told her. Fair lords, said she, for God's love turn again if ye may, for ye be come unto your death. Nay, they said, we will not turn again, for He shall help us in whose service we be entered in. Then as they stood talking, there came knights well armed, and bad them yield them, or else to die. That yielding, said they, shall be noyous to you; and therewith they let their horses run, and Sir Percivale smote the foremost to the earth, and took his horse and mounted thereupon, and the same did Galahad. Also Sir Bors served another so. For they had no horses in that country, for they left their horses when they took their ship in other countries. And so when they were horsed then began they to set upon them. And they of the castle fled into the strong fortress, and the three knights after them, into the castle, and so alight on foot, and with their swords slew them down, and gat into the hall. Then when they beheld the great multitude of people they had slain, they held themselves great sinners. Certes, said Bors, I ween and God had loved them that we should not have had power to have slain them thus, but they have done so much against our Lord that he will not suffer them to reign no longer. Say ye not so, said Galahad, for if they misdid against God the vengeance is not ours, but to Him which hath power thereof. So came there out of a chamber a good man which was a priest, and bear God's body in a cup. And when he saw them which lay dead in the hall, he was all abashed. And Galahad did off his helm and kneeled down, and so did his two fellows. Sir, said they, have ye no dread of us, for we be of king Arthur's court. Then asked the good man how they were slain so suddenly; and they told it him. Truly, said the good man, and ye might live as long as the world might endure,

never might ye have done so great an alms-deed as this. Sir, said Galahad, I repent me much, inasmuch as they were christened. Nay, repent you not, said he, for they were not christened, and I shall tell you how that I wot of this castle. Here was lord earl Hernox not but one year, and he had three sons good knights of arms, and a daughter the fairest gentlewoman that men knew. So those three knights loved their sister so sore that they burnt in love, and so they dishonoured her, maugre her head. And for she cried to her father, they slew her, and took their father and put him in prison, and wounded him nigh to the death, but a cousin of hers rescued him. And then did they great untruth: they slew clerks and priests, and made beat down chapels, that our Lord's service might not be served nor said; and this same day their father sent to me for to be confessed and houseled, but such shame had never man as I had this day with the three brethren: but the earl bad me suffer, for he said they should not long endure, for three servants of our Lord should destroy them; and now it is brought to an end. And by this ye may wit that our Lord is not displeased with your deeds. Certes, said Galahad, and it had not pleased our Lord, never should we have slain so many men in so little a while. And then they brought the earl Hernox out of prison into the midst of the hall, that knew Galahad anon, and yet he saw him never afore but by revelation of our Lord.

CHAP. IX.

How the three knights, with Percivale's sister, came into the waste forest, and of an hart and four lions and other things.

THEN began he to weep right tenderly, and said, Long have I abiden your coming, but for God's love hold me in your arms, that my soul may depart out of my body in so good a man's arms as ye be. Gladly, said Galahad. And then one said on high that all heard, Galahad, well hast thou avenged me on

God's enemies. Now behoveth thee to go to the maimed king as soon as thou mayest, for he shall receive by thee health which he hath abiden so long. And therewith the soul departed from the body. And Galahad made him to be buried as he ought to be.

Right so departed the three knights, and Percivale's sister with them. And so they came into a waste forest, and there they saw afore them a white hart, which four lions led. Then they took them to assent for to follow after, for to know whither they repaired; and so they rode after, a great pace, till that they came to a valley, and thereby was an hermitage where a good man dwelled; and the hart and the lions entered also. So when they saw all this, they turned to the chapel, and saw the good man in a religious weed, and in the armour of our Lord, for he would sing mass of the Holy Ghost, and so they entered in and heard mass. And at the secrets of the mass, they three saw the hart become a man, the which marvelled them, and set him upon the altar in a rich siege, and saw the four lions were changed, the one to the form of a man, the other to the form of a lion, and the third to an eagle, and the fourth was changed unto an ox. Then took they their siege where the hart sat, and went out through a glass window, and there was nothing perished nor broken, and they heard a voice say, In such a manner entered the son of God in the womb of a maid, Mary. And when they heard these words, they fell down to the earth, and were astonied, and therewith was a great clearness. And when they were come to themselves again, they went to the good man, and prayed him that he would say them truth. What thing have ye seen? said he: and they told him all that they had seen. Ah, lords, said he, ye be welcome, now wot I well ye be the good knights the which shall bring the Sancgreal to an end; for ye be they unto whom our Lord shall shew great secrets. And well ought our Lord be signified to an hart; for the hart when

he is old he waxeth young again in his white skin: right so cometh again our Lord from death to life, for he lost earthly flesh, that was the deadly flesh which he had taken in the womb of the blessed virgin Mary; and for that cause appeared our Lord as a white hart without spot. And the four that were with him is to understand the four evangelists, which set in writing a part of Jesu Christ's deeds that he did some time when he was among you an earthly man. For wit ye well never erst might no knight know the truth, for, ofttimes or this, our Lord shewed him unto good men and unto good knights in likeness of an hart. But I suppose from henceforth ye shall see no more. And then they joyed much, and dwelled there all that day. And upon the morrow, when they had heard mass they departed, and commended the good man to God. And so they came to a castle, and passed by. So there came a knight armed after them, and said, Lords, hark what I shall say to you.

CHAP. X.

How they were desired of a strange custom, the which they would not obey; and how they fought and slew many knights.

THIS gentlewoman that ye lead with you is a maid? Sir, said she, a maid I am. Then he took her by the bridle and said, By the holy cross ye shall not escape me tofore ye have yielden the custom of this castle. Let her go, said Percivale; ye be not wise, for a maid in what place she cometh is free. So in the meanwhile there came out a ten or twelve knights armed, out of the castle, and with them came gentlewomen which held a dish of silver, and then they said, This gentlewoman must yield us the custom of this castle. Sir, said a knight, what maid passeth hereby shall give this dish full of blood of her right arm. Blame have ye, said Galahad, that brought up such customs, and I ensure you of this gentlewoman ye shall fail while that I live. Truly, said Sir Percivale, I had lever be slain. And

I also, said Sir Bors. By my truth, said the knight, then shall ye die, for ye may not endure against us, though ye were the best knights of the world. Then let them run each to other, and the three fellows beat the ten knights, and then set their hands to their swords, and beat them down and slew them. Then there came out of the castle well a threescore knights armed. Fair lords, said the three fellows, have mercy upon yourselves, and have not ado with us. Nay, fair lords, said the knights of the castle, we counsel you to withdraw you, for ye are the best knights of the world, and therefore do no more, for ye have done enough. We will let you go with this harm, but we must needs have the custom. Certes, said Galahad, for nought speak ye. Well, said they, will ye die? We be not yet come thereto, said Galahad. Then began they to meddle together, and Galahad drew his sword with the strange girdles, and smote on the right hand and on the left hand, and slew what that ever abode him, and did such marvels that there was none that saw him but they wend he had been none earthly man but a monster. And his two fellows halp him passing well, and so they held the journey every each in like hard, till it was night. Then must they needs part. So came a good knight and said to the three fellows, If ye will come in to night, and take such harbour as here is, ye shall be right welcome, and we shall ensure you by the faith of our bodies, as we are true knights, to leave you in such estate to-morrow as we find you, without any falsehood. And as soon as ye know of the custom we dare say ye will accord. Therefore, for God's love, said the gentlewoman, go thither, and spare not for me. Go we, said Galahad, and so they entered into the castle. And when they were alight, they made great joy of them. So within a while the three knights asked the custom of the castle, and wherefore it was. What it is, said they, we will say you sooth.

CHAP. XI.

How Sir Percivale's sister bled a dish full of blood for to heal a lady; wherefore she died; and how that the body was put in a ship.

THERE is in this castle a gentlewoman which we and this castle is hers, and many other. So it befell many years agone there fell upon her a malady. And when she had lain a great while, she fell into a measle, and of no leech she could have no remedy. But at the last an old man said, and she might have a dish full of blood of a maid and a clean virgin in will and in work, and a king's daughter, that blood should be her health, and for to anoint her withal: and for this thing was this custom made. Now, said Percivale's sister, Fair knights, I see well that this gentlewoman is but dead. Certes, said Galahad, and if ye bleed so much, ye may die. Truly, said she, and I die for to heal her, I shall get me great worship and soul's health, and worship to my lineage, and better is one harm than twain. And therefore there shall be no more battle, but to-morn I shall yield you your custom of this castle. And then there was great joy, more than there was tofore. For else had there been mortal war upon the morn; notwithstanding she would none other, whether they would or nold. That night were the three fellows eased with the best, and on the morn they heard mass, and Sir Percivale's sister bad bring forth the sick lady. So she was, the which was evil at ease. Then said she, Who shall let me blood? So one came forth and let her blood, and she bled so much that the dish was full. Then she lift up her hand and blessed her. And then she said to the lady, Madam, I am come to the death, for to make you whole; for God's love pray for me. With that she fell in a swoon. Then Galahad and his two fellows start up to her, and lift her up, and stanched her, but she had bled so much that she might not live. Then she said, when she was awaked, Fair brother

Percivale, I die for the healing of this lady. So I require you that ye bury not me in this country, but as soon as I am dead put me in a boat at the next haven, and let me go as adventure will lead me; and as soon as ye three come to the city of Sarras, there to achieve the holy Graile, ye shall find me under a tower arrived, and there bury me in the spiritual place, for I say you so much, there Galahad shall be buried, and ye also, in the same place. Then Percivale understood these words, and granted it her, weeping. And then said a voice, Lords and fellows, to-morrow at the hour of prime ye three shall depart every each from other, till the adventure bring you to the maimed king. Then asked she her Saviour, and as soon as she had received him the soul departed from the body. So the same day was the lady healed, when she was anointed withal. Then Sir Percivale made a letter of all that she had holpen them as in strange adventures, and put it in her right hand, and so laid her in a barge, and covered it with black silk; and so the wind arose, and drove the barge from the land, and all knights beheld it, till it was out of their sight.

Then they drew all to the castle, and so forthwith there fell a sudden tempest, and a thunder, lightning, and rain, as all the earth would have broken. So half the castle turned up so down. So it passed evensong or the tempest was ceased. Then they saw afore them a knight armed and wounded hard in the body and in the head, that said, Oh God, succour me, for now it is need! After this knight came another knight and a dwarf which cried to them afar, Stand, ye may not escape. Then the wounded knight held up his hands to God, that he should not die in such tribulation. Truly, said Galahad, I shall succour him for His sake that he calleth upon. Sir, said Bors, I shall do it, for it is not for you, for he is but one knight. Sir, said he, I grant. So Sir Bors took his horse, and commended him to God, and rode after to rescue the wounded knight. Now turn we to the two fellows.

CHAP. XII.

How Galahad and Percivale found in a castle many tombs of maidens that had bled to death.

Now saith the story that all night Galahad and Percivale were in a chapel in their prayers, for to save Sir Bors. So on the morrow they dressed them in their harness toward the castle, to wit what was fallen of them therein. And when they came there, they found neither man nor woman that he ne was dead by the vengeance of our Lord. With that they heard a voice that said, This vengeance is for blood shedding of maidens. Also they found at the end of the chapel a churchyard, and therein might they see a threescore fair tombs, and that place was so fair and so delectable that it seemed them there had been none tempest. For there lay the bodies of all the good maidens which were martyred for the sick lady's sake. Also they found the names of every each, and of what blood they were come, and all were of kings' blood, and twelve of them were kings' daughters. Then they departed, and went into a forest. Now, said Percivale unto Galahad, we must depart; so pray we our Lord that we may meet together in short time. Then they did off their helms, and kissed together, and wept at their departing.

CHAP. XIII.

How Sir Launcelot entered into the ship where Sir Percivale's sister lay dead; and how he met with Sir Galahad his son.

Now saith the history, that when Launcelot was come to the water of Mortoise, as it is rehearsed before, he was in great peril, and so he laid him down and slept, and took the adventure that God would send him.

So when he was asleep, there came a vision unto him and said, Launcelot, arise up, and take thine armour, and enter into the first ship that thou shalt find. And when he had heard these words, he start up and saw great clearness about him. And then he lift up his hand and blessed him, and so took his arms, and made him ready; and so by adventure he came by a strand, and found a ship, the which was without sail or oar. And as soon as he was within the ship, there he felt the most sweetness that ever he felt; and he was fulfilled with all thing that he thought on or desired. Then said he, Fair sweet Father Jesu Christ, I wot not in what joy I am, for this joy passeth all earthly joys that ever I was in. And so in this joy he laid him down to the ship's board, and slept till day. And when he awoke, he found there a fair bed, and therein lying a gentlewoman dead, the which was Sir Percivale's sister. And as Launcelot devised her, he espied in her right hand a writ, the which he read, the which told him all the adventures that ye have heard tofore, and of what lineage she was come. So with this gentlewoman Sir Launcelot was a month and more. If ye would ask how he lived, He that fed the people of Israel with manna in the desert, so was he fed. For every day, when he had said his prayers, he was sustained with the grace of the Holy Ghost. So on a night he went to play him by the water side, for he was somewhat weary of the ship. And then he listened, and heard an horse come, and one riding upon him. And when he came nigh he seemed a knight. And so he let him pass, and went there as the ship was, and there he alight, and took the saddle and the bridle and put the horse from him, and went into the ship. And then Launcelot dressed unto him and said, Ye be welcome. And he answered and saluted him again, and asked him, What is your name? for much my heart giveth unto you. Truly, said he, my name is Launcelot du Lake. Sir, said he, then be ye welcome, for ye were the beginner of me in this world. Ah, said he, are ye Galahad? Yea forsooth, said he. And so he kneeled down and asked him his blessing, and after took off his helm and kissed him. And there was great joy between them, for there is no tongue can tell the joy that

they made either of other, and many a friendly word spoken between, as kind would, the which is no need here to be rehearsed. And there every each told other of their adventures and marvels that were befallen to them in many journeys, sith that they departed from the court. Anon as Galahad saw the gentlewoman dead in the bed, he knew her well enough, and told great worship of her, and that she was the best maid living, and it was great pity of her death. But when Launcelot heard how the marvellous sword was gotten, and who made it, and all the marvels rehearsed afore, then he prayed Galahad his son that he would shew him the sword, and so he did. And anon he kissed the pommel, and the hilts, and the scabbard. Truly, said Launcelot, never erst knew I of so high adventures done, and so marvellous and strange. So dwelled Launcelot and Galahad within that ship half a year, and served God daily and nightly with all their power. And often they arrived in isles far from folk, where there repaired none but wild beasts; and there they found many strange adventures and perilous, which they brought to an end. But because the adventures were with wild beasts, and not in the quest of the Sancgreal, therefore the tale maketh here no mention thereof, for it would be too long to tell of all those adventures that befell them.

CHAP. XIV.

How a knight brought unto Sir Galahad an horse, and bad him come from his father Sir Launcelot.

So after, on a Monday, it befell that they arrived in the edge of a forest, tofore a cross, and then saw they a knight, armed all in white, and was richly horsed, and led in his right hand a white horse. And so he came to the ship, and saluted the two knights on the high Lord's behalf, and said, Galahad, sir, ye have been long enough with your father, come out of the ship, and start upon this horse, and go where the adventures shall lead thee in the quest of the Sancgreal. Then he went to his father, and kissed him sweetly, and said, Fair sweet father, I wot not when I shall see you more, till I see the body of Jesu Christ. I pray you, said Launcelot, pray ye to the high Father that He hold me in his service. And so he took his horse; and there they heard a voice, that said, Think for to do well, for the one shall never see the other before the dreadful day of doom. Now, son Galahad, said Launcelot, since we shall depart, and never see other, I pray to the high Father to preserve both me and you both. Sir, said Galahad, no prayer availeth so much as yours. And therewith Galahad entered into the forest. And the wind arose, and drove Launcelot more than a month throughout the sea, where he slept but little, but prayed to God that he might see some tidings of the Sancgreal. So it befell on a night, at midnight he arrived afore a castle, on the back side, which was rich and fair. And there was a postern opened towards the sea, and was open without any keeping, save two lions kept the entry; and the moon shone clear. Anon Sir Launcelot heard a voice that said, Launcelot, go out of this ship, and enter into the castle, where thou shalt see a great part of thy desire. Then he ran to his arms, and so armed him, and so he went to the gate, and saw the lions. Then set he hand to his sword, and drew it. Then there came a dwarf suddenly, and smote him on the arm so sore that the sword fell out of his hand. Then heard he a voice say, Oh man of evil faith and poor belief, wherefore trowest thou more on thy harness than in thy Maker? for He might more avail thee than thine armour, in whose service thou art set. Then said Launcelot, Fair Father Jesu Christ, I thank thee of thy great mercy, that thou reprovest me of my misdeed. Now see I well that ye hold me for your servant. Then took he again his sword, and put it up in his sheath, and made a cross in his forehead, and came to the lions, and they made semblant to do him harm. Notwithstanding he passed by them without hurt, and entered into the castle to the chief fortress, and there

were they all at rest. Then Launcelot entered in so armed, for he found no gate nor door but it was open. And at the last he found a chamber whereof the door was shut, and he set his hand thereto to have opened it, but he might not.

CHAP. XV.

How Sir Launcelot was tofore the door of the chamber wherein the holy Sangreal was.

THEN he enforced him mickle to undo the door. Then he listened, and heard a voice which sang so sweetly that it seemed none earthly thing; and him thought the voice said, Joy and honour be to the Father of Heaven! Then Launcelot kneeled down tofore the chamber, for well wist he that there was the Sancgreal within that chamber. Then said he, Fair sweet Father Jesu Christ, if ever I did thing that pleased the Lord, for thy pity have me not in despite for my sins done aforetime, and that thou shew me something of that I seek! And with that he saw the chamber door open, and there came out a great clearness, that the house was as bright as all the torches of the world had been there. So came he to the chamber door, and would have entered. And anon a voice said to him, Flee Launcelot, and enter not, for thou oughtest not to do it: and if thou enter thou shalt forthink it. Then he withdrew him aback right heavy. Then looked he up in the midst of the chamber, and saw a table of silver, and the holy vessel covered with red samite, and many angels about it, whereof one held a candle of wax burning, and the other held a cross, and the ornaments of an altar. And before the holy vessel he saw a good man clothed as a priest, and it seemed that he was at the sacring of the mass. And it seemed to Launcelot that above the priest's hands there were three men, whereof the two put the youngest by likeness between the priest's hands, and so he lift it up right high, and it seemed to shew so to the people. And then Launcelot marvelled not a little, for him thought that the priest was so greatly charged of the figure, that him seemed that he should fall to the earth. And when he saw none about him that would help him, then came he to the door a great pace, and said, Fair Father Jesu Christ, ne take it for no sin though I help the good man, which hath great need of help. Right so entered he into the chamber, and came toward the table of silver; and when he came nigh he felt a breath that him thought it was intermeddled with fire, which smote him so sore in the visage that him thought it burnt his visage; and therewith he fell to the earth, and had no power to arise, as he that was so araged that had lost the power of his body, and his hearing, and his saying. Then felt he many hands about him, which took him up and bare him out of the chamber door, without any amending of his swoon, and left him there seeming dead to all people. So upon the morrow, when it was fair day, they within were arisen, and found Launcelot lying afore the chamber door. All they marvelled how that he came in. And so they looked upon him, and felt his pulse, to wit whether there were any life in him; and so they found life in him, but he might neither stand, nor stir no member that he had; and so they took him by every part of the body, and bare him into a chamber, and laid him in a rich bed, far from all folk, and so he lay four days. Then the one said he was on live, and the other said nay. In the name of God, said an old man, for I do you verily to wit he is not dead, but he is so full of life as the mightiest of you all, and therefore I counsel you that he be well kept till God send him life again.

CHAP. XVI.

How Sir Launcelot had lain fourteen days and as many nights as a dead man, and other divers matters.

In such manner they kept Launcelot four and twenty days, and also many nights, that ever he lay still as a dead man; and at the twenty-fifth day befell him after midday that he opened his eyes. And when he saw folk he made great sorrow and said, Why have ye awaked me? for I was more at ease than I am now. Oh Jesu Christ, who might be so blessed that might see openly thy great marvels of secretness there where no sinner may be. What have ye seen? said they about him. I have seen, said he, so great marvels that no tongue may tell, and more than any heart can think, and had not my son been here afore me I had seen much more. Then they told him how he had lain there four and twenty days and nights. Then him thought it was punishment for the twenty-four years that he had been a sinner, wherefore our Lord put him in penance four and twenty days and nights. Then looked Sir Launcelot before him, and saw the hair which he had borne nigh a year, for that he forethought him right much that he had broken his promise unto the hermit, which he had avowed to do. Then they asked him how it stood with him. Forsooth, said he, I am whole of body, thanked be our Lord; therefore, sirs, for God's love tell me where that I am? Then said they all that he was in the castle of Carbonek. Therewith came a gentlewoman, and brought him a shirt of small linen cloth, but he changed not there, but took the hair to him again. Sir, said they, the quest of the Sancgreal is achieved right now in you, that never shall ye see of the Sancgreal no more than ye have seen. Now I thank God, said Launcelot, of His great mercy, of that I have seen, for it sufficeth me, for, as I suppose, no man in this world hath lived better than I have done to achieve that I have done. And therewith he took the hair, and clothed him in it, and above that he put a linen shirt, and after a robe of scarlet, fresh and new. And when he was so arrayed, they marvelled all, for they knew him that he was Launcelot, the good knight. And then they said all, O my lord Sir Launcelot, be that ye? And he said, Truly

I am he. Then came word to king Pelles, that the knight that had lain so long dead was Sir Launcelot; then was the king right glad, and went to see him. And when Launcelot saw him come, he dressed him against him, and there made the king great joy of him. And there the king told him tidings, that his fair daughter was dead. Then Launcelot was right heavy of it, and said, Sir, me forthinketh the death of your daughter, for she was a full fair lady, fresh and young. And well I wot she bare the best knight that is now on earth, or that ever was since God was born. So the king held him there four days. And on the morrow he took his leave at king Pelles, and at all the fellowship that were there, and thanked them of the great labour. Right so as they sat at dinner in the chief hall, then was it so befallen that the Sancgreal had fulfilled the tables with all manner of meats that any heart might think. So as they sat, they saw all the doors and windows of the place were shut without man's hand, whereof they were all abashed, and none wist what to do. And then it happed suddenly a knight came to the chief door, and knocked, and cried, Undo the door; but they would not. And ever he cried, Undo, but they would not. And at the last it annoyed them so much, that the king himself arose, and came to a window where the knight called. Then he said, Sir knight, ye shall not enter at this time, while the Sancgreal is here, and therefore go into another. For certes ye be none of the knights of the quest, but one of them which hath served the fiend, and hast left the service of our Lord. And he was passing wroth at the king's words. Sir knight, said the king, sin ye would so fain enter, say me of what country ye be? Sir, said he, I am of the realm of Logris, and my name is Ector de Maris, and brother unto my lord Sir Launcelot. Truly, said the king, me forthinketh of that I have said, for your brother is here within. And when Ector de Maris understood that his brother was there, for he was the man in the world that he most dread and loved, and then he said, Alas, now doubleth my sorrow and shame, full truly said the good man of the hill unto Gawaine and to me of our dreams. Then went he out of the court as fast as his courser might run, and so through out the castle.

CHAP. XVII.

How Sir Launcelot returned towards Logris, and of other adventures which he saw in the way.

Then king Pelles came to Sir Launcelot, and told him tidings of his brother, whereof he was sorry that he wist not what to do. So Sir Launcelot departed, and took his armour, and said that he would go see the realm of Logris— which I have not seen in a twelve-month. And therewith commended the king to God, and so rode through many realms. And at the last he came to a white abbey, and there they made him that night great cheer. And on the morn he arose and heard mass, and afore an altar he found a rich tomb which was newly made, and then he took heed, and saw the sides written with letters of gold, which said, Here lieth king Bagdemagus of Gore, the which king Arthur's nephew slew:— and named him Sir Gawaine. Then was not he a little sorry, for Launcelot loved him much more than any other, and had it been any other than Gawaine he should not have escaped from death to life:—said to himself, Alas, this is a great hurt to king Arthur's court, the loss of such a man. And then he departed, and came to the abbey where Galahad did the adventure of the tombs, and wan the white shield with the red cross, and there had he great cheer all that night. And on the morn he turned unto Camelot, where he found king Arthur and the queen. But many of the knights of the Round Table were slain and destroyed, more than half. And so three were come home, Ector, Gawaine, and Lionel, and many other that need not to be rehearsed.

And all the court was passing glad of Sir Launcelot; and the king asked him many tidings of his son Galahad. And there Launcelot told the king of his adventures that had befallen him since he departed. And also he told him of the adventures of Galahad, Percivale, and Bors, which that he knew by the letter of the dead damsel, and as Galahad had told him. Now, God would, said the king, that they were all three here. That shall never be, said Launcelot, for two of them shall ye never see, but one of them shall come again.

Now leave we this story, and speak we of Galahad.

CHAP. XVIII.

How Galahad came to king Mordrains, and of other matters and adventures.

Now saith the story that Galahad rode many journeys in vain. And at the last he came to the abbey where king Mordrains was, and when he heard that, he thought he would abide to see him. And upon the morn, when he had heard mass, Galahad came unto king Mordrains, and anon the king saw him, the which had lain blind of long time. And then he dressed him against him, and said, Galahad, the servant of Jesu Christ, whose coming I have abiden so long, now embrace me, and let me rest on thy breast, so that I may rest between thine arms, for thou art a clean virgin above all knights, as the flower of the lily, in whom virginity is signified, and thou art the rose, the which is the flower of all good virtue, and in colour of fire. For the fire of the Holy Ghost is taken so in thee, that my flesh, which was all dead of oldness, is become young again. When Galahad heard his words, then he embraced him and all his body. Then said he, Fair Lord Jesu Christ, now I have my will, now I require thee in this point that I am in, thou come and visit me. And anon our Lord heard his prayer. Therewith the soul departed from the body. And then Galahad put him in the earth as a king ought to be: and so departed, and came into a perilous forest, where he found

the well the which boiled with great waves, as the tale telleth tofore. And as soon as Galahad set his hand thereto it ceased, so that it burnt no more, and the heat departed: for that it burnt it was a sign of lust; but that heat might not abide his pure virginity. And this was taken in the country for a miracle, and so ever after was it called Galahad's well. Then by adventure he came into the country of Gore, and into the abbey where Sir Launcelot had been toforehand, and found the tomb of king Bagdemagus (but was founder thereof Joseph of Armathie's son) and the tomb of Simeon where Launcelot had failed. Then he looked into a croft under the minster, and there he saw a tomb which burnt full marvellously. Then asked he the brethren what it was? Sir, said they, a marvellous adventure that may not be brought unto none end, but by him that passeth of bounty and of knighthood all them of the Round Table. I would, said Galahad, that ye would lead me thereto. Gladly, said they: and so led him till a cave; and he went down upon steps and came nigh the tomb, and then the flaming failed and the fire staunched, the which many a day had been great. Then came there a voice that said, Much are ye beholden to thank our Lord, the which hath given you a good hour, that ye may draw out the souls of earthly pain, and to put them into the joys of paradise. I am of your kindred, the which have dwelled in this heat this three hundred winter and four and fifty, to be purged of the sin that I did against Joseph of Armathie. Then Galahad took the body in his arms, and bear it into the minster. And that night lay Galahad in the abbey: and on the morn he gave him service, and put him in the earth, afore the high altar.

CHAP. XIX.

How Sir Percivale and Sir Bors met with Sir Galahad, and how they came to the castle of Carbonek, and other matters.

So departed he from thence, and commended the brethren to God. And so he rode five days till that he came to the maimed king, and ever followed Percivale the five days, asking where he had been, and so one told him how the adventures of Logris were achieved. So on a day it befell that they came out of a great forest, and there they met at travers with Sir Bors, the which rode alone. It is no need to tell if they were glad, and them he saluted, and they yielded him honour and good adventure; and every each told other. Then said Bors, It is more than a year and a half that I ne lay ten times where men dwelled, but in wild forests and in mountains, but God was ever my comfort.

Then rode they a great while till that they came to the castle of Carbonek. And when they were entered within the castle king Pelles knew them. Then there was great joy, for they wist well by their coming that they had fulfilled the quest of the Sancgreal. Then Eliazar, king Pelles' son, brought afore them the broken sword wherewith Joseph was stricken through the thigh. Then Bors set his hand thereto, if he might have soldered it again, but it would not be. Then he took it to Percivale, but he had no more power thereto than he. Now have ye it again, said Percivale to Galahad, for and it be ever achieved by one bodily man, ye must do it. And then took he the pieces and set them together, and they seemed that they had never been broken, and as well as it had been first forged. And when they within espied that the adventure of the sword was achieved, then they gave the sword to Bors, for it might not be better set, for he was a good knight, and a worthy man. And a little afore even the sword arose great and marvellous, and was full of great heat, that many men fell for dread. And anon alight a voice among them, and said, They that ought not to sit at the table of Jesu Christ arise, for now shall very knights be fed. So they went thence all save king Pelles and Eliazar his son, the which were holy men, and a maid which was his niece. And so these three

fellows and they three were there; no more. Anon they saw knights all armed come in at the hall door, and did off their helms and their arms, and said unto Galahad, Sir, we have hied right much for to be with you at this table, where the holy meat shall be parted. Then said he, Ye be welcome: but of whence be ye? So three of them said they were of Gaul, and other three said they were of Ireland, and the other three said they were of Denmark. So as they sat thus, there came out a bed of tree of a chamber, the which four gentlewomen brought, and in the bed lay a good man sick, and a crown of gold upon his head; and there in the midst of the place they set him down, and went again their way. Then he lift up his head and said, Galahad, knight, ye be welcome, for much have I desired your coming, for in such pain and in such anguish I have been long. But now I trust to God the term is come that my pain shall be allayed, that I shall pass out of this world, so as it was promised me long ago. Therewith a voice said, There be two among you that be not in the quest of the Sancgreal, and therefore depart ye.

CHAP. XX.

How Galahad and his fellows were fed of the holy Sangreal, and how our Lord appeared to them, and other things.

THEN king Pelles and his son departed. And therewithal beseemed them that there came a man and four angels from heaven, clothed in likeness of a bishop, and had a cross in his hand, and these four angels bare him up in a chair, and set him down before the table of silver whereupon the Sancgreal was, and it seemed that he had in midst of his forehead letters that said, See ye here Joseph the first bishop of Christendom, the same which our Lord succoured in the city of Sarras, in the spiritual place. Then the knights marvelled, for that bishop was dead more than three hundred year tofore. Oh knights, said he, marvel not, for I was sometime an earthly man. With that they heard the chamber door open, and there they saw angels, and two bare candles of wax, and the third a towel, and the fourth a spear which bled marvellously, that three drops fell within a box which he held with his other hand. And they set the candles upon the table, and the third the towel upon the vessel, and the fourth the holy spear even upright upon the vessel. And then the bishop made semblant as though he would have gone to the sacring of the mass. And then he took an ubbly, which was made in likeness of bread; and at the lifting up there came a figure in likeness of a child, and the visage was as red and as bright as any fire, and smote himself into the bread, so that they all saw it, that the bread was formed of a fleshly man, and then he put it into the holy vessel again. And then he did that longed to a priest to do to a mass. And then he went to Galahad and kissed him, and bad him go and kiss his fellows, and so he did anon. Now, said he, servants of Jesu Christ, ye shall be fed afore this table with sweet meats, that never knights tasted. And when he had said, he vanished away; and they set them at the table in great dread, and made their prayers. Then looked they, and saw a man come out of the holy vessel, that had all the signs of the passion of Jesu Christ, bleeding all openly, and said, My knights and my servants and my true children, which be come out of deadly life into spiritual life, I will now no longer hide me from you, but ye shall see now a part of my secrets and of my hid things: now hold and receive the high meat which ye have so much desired. Then took he himself the holy vessel, and came to Galahad, and he kneeled down and there he received his Saviour, and after him so received all his fellows; and they thought it so sweet that it was marvellous to tell. Then said he to Galahad, Son, wotest thou what I hold betwixt my hands? Nay, said he, but if ye will tell me. This is, said he, the holy dish wherein I ate the lamb on Sher-thursday. And now hast thou seen that thou

most desiredst to see, but yet hast thou not seen it so openly as thou shalt see it in the city of Sarras, in the spiritual place. Therefore thou must go hence, and bear with thee this holy vessel, for this night it shall depart from the realm of Logris, that it shall never be seen more here, and wotest thou wherefore? for he is not served nor worshipped to his right, by them of this land, for they be turned to evil living, therefore I shall disherit them of the honour which I have done them. And therefore go ye three to-morrow unto the sea, where ye shall find your ship ready, and with you take the sword with the strange girdles, and no more with you, but Sir Percivale and Sir Bors. Also I will that ye take with you of the blood of this spear, for to anoint the maimed king, both his legs and all his body, and he shall have his health. Sir, said Galahad, why shall not these other fellows go with us?— For this cause, for right as I departed mine apostles, one here and another there, so I will that ye depart. And two of you shall die in my service, but one of you shall come again, and tell tidings. Then gave he them his blessing and vanished away.

CHAP. XXI.

How Galahad anointed with the blood of the spear the maimed king, and other adventures.

AND Galahad went anon to the spear which lay upon the table, and touched the blood with his fingers, and came after to the maimed king, and anointed his legs. And therewith he clothed him anon, and start upon his feet out of his bed as an whole man, and thanked our Lord that he had healed him. And that was not to the world-ward, for anon he yield him to a place of religion of white monks, and was a full holy man. That same night, about midnight came a voice among them, which said, My sons and not my chieftains, my friends and not my warriors, go ye hence, where ye hope best to do, and as I bad you.—

Ah, thanked be thou, Lord, that thou wilt vouchsafe to call us thy sinners. Now may we well prove that we have not lost our pains.

And anon in all haste they took their harness and departed. But the three knights of Gaul, one of them hight Claudine, king Claudas' son, and the other two were great gentlemen. Then prayed Galahad to every each of them, that if they come to king Arthur's court, that they should salute my lord Sir Launcelot my father, and of them of the Round Table, and prayed them if that they came on that part that they should not forget it. Right so departed Galahad, Percivale, and Bors with him. And so they rode three days, and then they came to a rivage, and found the ship whereof the tale speaketh of tofore. And when they came to the board, they found in the midst the table of silver which they had left with the maimed king, and the Sancgreal, which was covered with red samite. Then were they glad to have such things in their fellowship, and so they entered, and made great reverence thereto, and Galahad fell in his prayer long time to our Lord, that, at what time he asked, that he should pass out of this world : so much he prayed, till a voice said to him, Galahad, thou shalt have thy request, and when thou askest the death of thy body thou shalt have it, and then shalt thou find the life of the soul. Percivale heard this, and prayed him of fellowship that was between them, to tell him wherefore he asked such things. That shall I tell you, said Galahad : the other day when we saw a part of the adventures of the Sancgreal, I was in such a joy of heart that I trow never man was that was earthly, and therefore I wot well when my body is dead my soul shall be in great joy to see the blessed Trinity every day, and the majesty of our Lord Jesu Christ. So long were they in the ship that they said to Galahad, Sir, in this bed ought ye to lie, for so saith the scripture. And so he laid him down and slept a great while. And when he awaked he looked afore him, and saw the city of Sarras. And as they would have landed, they saw the ship wherein Percivale had put his sister in. Truly, said Percivale, in the name of God, well hath my sister holden us covenant. Then took they out of the ship the table of silver, and he took it to Percivale and to Bors to go tofore, and Galahad came behind, and right so they went to the city, and at the gate of the city they saw an old man crooked. Then Galahad called him, and bad him help to bear this heavy thing. Truly, said the old man, it is ten year ago that I might not go but with crutches. Care thou not, said Galahad, and arise up and shew thy good will. And so he assayed, and found himself as whole as ever he was. Then ran he to the table, and took one part against Galahad. And anon arose there great noise in the city, that a cripple was made whole by knights marvellous that entered into the city. Then anon after, the three knights went to the water, and brought up into the palace Percivale's sister, and buried her as richly as a king's daughter ought to be. And when the king of the city, which was cleped Estorause, saw the fellowship, he asked them of whence they were, and what thing it was that they had brought upon the table of silver. And they told him the truth of the Sancgreal, and the power which that God had set there. Then the king was a tyrant, and was come of the line of paynims, and took them, and put them in prison in a deep hole.

CHAP. XXII.

How they were fed with the Sangreal while they were in prison, and how Galahad was made king.

But as soon as they were there, our Lord sent them the Sancgreal, through whose grace they were alway fulfilled while that they were in prison. So at the year's end it befell that this king Estorause lay sick, and felt that he should die. Then he sent for the three knights, and they came afore him, and he cried them mercy of that he had done to them, and they forgave it him goodly, and he died anon. When the king was dead, all the city was dismayed, and'wist not who might be their king. Right so as they were in counsel, there came a voice among them, and bad them choose the youngest knight of them three to be their king, for he shall well maintain you and all yours. So they made Galahad king by all the assent of the whole city, and else they would have slain him. And when he was come to behold the land, he let make about the table of silver a chest of gold and of precious stones that covered the holy vessel, and every day early the three fellows would come afore it and make their prayers. Now at the year's end, and the self day after Galahad had borne the crown of gold, he arose up early, and his fellows, and came to the palace, and saw tofore them the holy vessel, and a man kneeling on his knees, in likeness of a bishop, that had about him a great fellowship of angels, as it had been Jesu Christ himself. And then he arose and began a mass of Our Lady. And when he came to the sacrament of the mass, and had done, anon he called Galahad, and said to him, Come forth, the servant of Jesu Christ, and thou shalt see that thou hast much desired to see. And then he began to tremble right hard, when the deadly flesh began to behold the spiritual things. Then he held up his hands toward heaven, and said, Lord, I thank thee, for now I see that that hath been my desire many a day. Now, blessed Lord, would I not longer live, if it might please thee Lord. And therewith the good man took our Lord's body betwixt his hands, and proffered it to Galahad, and he received it right gladly and meekly. Now, wotest thou what I am? said the good man. Nay, said Galahad. — I am Joseph of Armathie, which our Lord hath sent here to thee to bear thee fellowship. And wotest thou wherefore that he hath sent me more than any other? For thou hast resembled me in two things,

in that thou hast seen the marvels of the Sancgreal, and in that thou hast been a clean maiden, as I have been and am. And when he had said these words, Galahad went to Percivale and kissed him, and commanded him to God. And so he went to Sir Bors and kissed him, and commanded him to God, and said, Fair lord, salute me to my lord Sir Launcelot, my father, and as soon as ye see him bid him remember of this unstable world. And therewith he kneeled down tofore the table and made his prayers, and then suddenly his soul departed to Jesu Christ, and a great multitude of angels bare his soul up to heaven, that the two fellows might well behold it. Also the two fellows saw come from heaven an hand, but they saw not the body; and then it came right to the vessel, and took it and the spear, and so bare it up to heaven. Sithen was there never man so hardy to say that he had seen the Sancgreal.

CHAP. XXIII.

Of the sorrow that Percivale and Bors made when Galahad was dead; and of Percivale how he died, and other matters.

WHEN Percivale and Bors saw Galahad dead, they made as much sorrow as ever did two men: and if they had not been good men they might lightly have fallen in despair. And the people of the country and of the city were right heavy. And then he was buried. And as soon as he was buried, Sir Percivale yielded him to an hermitage out of the city, and took a religious clothing; and Bors was alway with him, but never changed he his secular clothing, for that he purposed him to go again into the realm of Logris. Thus a year and two months lived Sir Percivale in the hermitage a full holy life, and then passed out of this world. And Bors let bury him by his sister and by Galahad in the spiritualties. When Bors saw that he was in so far countries as in the parts of Babylon, he departed from Sarras, and armed him, and came to the sea, and entered into a ship, and so it befell him in good adventure he came into the realm of Logris. And he rode so fast till he came to Camelot where the king was. And then was there great joy made of him in the court, for they wend all he had been dead, forasmuch as he had been so long out of the country. And when they had eaten, the king made great clerks to come afore him, that they should chronicle of the high adventures of the good knights. When Bors had told him of the adventures of the Sancgreal, such as had befallen him and his three fellows, that was Launcelot, Percivale, Galahad and himself. There Launcelot told the adventures of the Sancgreal that he had seen. All this was made in great books, and put in almeries at Salisbury. And anon Sir Bors said to Sir Launcelot, Galahad your own son saluted you by me, and after you king Arthur, and all the court, and so did Sir Percivale: for I buried them with mine own hands in the city of Sarras. Also, Sir Launcelot, Galahad prayeth you to remember of this uncertain world, as ye behight him when ye were together more than half a year. This is true, said Launcelot; now I trust to God his prayer shall avail me. Then Launcelot took Sir Bors in his arms, and said, Gentle cousin, ye are right welcome to me, and all that ever I may do for you and for yours, ye shall find my poor body ready at all times whiles the spirit is in it, and that I promise you faithfully, and never to fail. And wit ye well, gentle cousin Sir Bors, that ye and I will never depart in sunder whilst our lives may last. Sir, said he, I will as ye will.

𝔗𝔥𝔲𝔰 𝔢𝔫𝔡𝔢𝔱𝔥 𝔱𝔥𝔦𝔰𝔱𝔬𝔯𝔶 𝔬𝔣 𝔱𝔥𝔢 𝔖𝔞𝔫𝔠𝔤𝔯𝔢𝔞𝔩 𝔱𝔥𝔞𝔱 𝔴𝔞𝔰 𝔟𝔯𝔢𝔲𝔢𝔩𝔶 𝔡𝔯𝔞𝔴𝔢𝔫 𝔬𝔲𝔱𝔢 𝔬𝔣 𝔉𝔯𝔢𝔫𝔰𝔰𝔥𝔢 𝔦𝔫 𝔱𝔬 𝔈𝔫𝔤𝔩𝔶𝔰𝔰𝔥𝔢, 𝔱𝔥𝔢 𝔴𝔥𝔦𝔠𝔥𝔢 𝔦𝔰 𝔞 𝔰𝔱𝔬𝔯𝔶 𝔠𝔯𝔬𝔫𝔶𝔠𝔩𝔢𝔡 𝔣𝔬𝔯 𝔬𝔫𝔢 𝔬𝔣 𝔱𝔥𝔢 𝔱𝔯𝔲𝔢𝔰𝔱 𝔞𝔫𝔡 𝔱𝔥𝔢 𝔥𝔬𝔩𝔶𝔢𝔰𝔱 𝔱𝔥𝔞𝔱 𝔦𝔰 𝔦𝔫 𝔱𝔥𝔶𝔰 𝔴𝔬𝔯𝔩𝔡, 𝔱𝔥𝔢 𝔴𝔥𝔦𝔠𝔥 𝔦𝔰 𝔱𝔥𝔢 𝔵𝔳𝔦𝔦 𝔟𝔬𝔬𝔨.

𝔄𝔫𝔡 𝔥𝔢𝔯𝔢 𝔣𝔬𝔩𝔬𝔴𝔢𝔱𝔥 𝔱𝔥𝔢 𝔢𝔶𝔤𝔥𝔱𝔢𝔫𝔱𝔥 𝔟𝔬𝔬𝔨.

𝔗𝔥𝔢 𝔈𝔦𝔤𝔥𝔱𝔢𝔢𝔫𝔱𝔥 𝔅𝔬𝔬𝔨.

CHAP. I.

Of the joy of king Arthur and the queen had of the achievement of the Sangreal; and how Launcelot fell to his old love again.

So after the quest of the Sancgreal was fulfilled, and all knights that were left on live were come again unto the Table Round, as the book of the Sancgreal maketh mention, then was there great joy in the court, and in especial king Arthur and queen Guenever made great joy of the remnant that were come home, and passing glad was the king and the queen of Sir Launcelot and of Sir Bors. For they had been passing long away in the quest of the Sancgreal. Then, as the book saith, Sir Launcelot began to resort unto queen Guenever again, and forgat the promise and the perfection that he made in the quest. For, as the book saith, had not Sir Launcelot been in his privy thoughts and in his mind so set inwardly to the queen, as he was in seeming outward to God, there had no knight passed him in the quest of the Sancgreal: but ever his thoughts were privily on the queen, and so they loved together more hotter

than they did toforehand, that many in
the court spake of it, and in especial Sir
Agravaine, Sir Gawaine's brother, for
he was ever open mouthed. So befell
that Sir Launcelot had many resorts of
ladies and damsels, that daily resorted
unto him, that besought him to be their
champion. And in all such matters of
right Sir Launcelot appealed him daily
to do for the pleasure of our Lord Jesu
Christ. And ever as much as he might
he withdrew him from the company
and fellowship of queen Guenever, for
to eschew the slander and noise: wherefore the queen waxed wroth with Sir
Launcelot, and upon a day she called
Sir Launcelot unto her chamber, and
said thus: Sir Launcelot, I see and feel
daily that thy love beginneth to slake,
for thou hast no joy to be in my presence, but ever thou art out of this
court, and quarrels and matters thou
hast now adays for ladies and gentlewomen, more than ever thou were wont
to have aforehand. Ah, madam, said
Launcelot, in this ye must hold me
excused for divers causes. One is, I
was but late in the quest of the Sancgreal, and I thank God, of his great
mercy, and never of my deserving, that
I saw in that my quest as much as ever
saw any sinful man, and so was it told
me. And if I had not had my privy
thoughts to return to your love again
as I do, I had seen as great mysteries as
ever saw my son Galahad, or Percivale,
or Sir Bors, and therefore, madam, I
was but late in that quest. Wit ye well,
madam, it may not be yet lightly forgotten the high service in whom I did
my diligent labour. Also, madam, wit
ye well that there be many men speak
of our love in this court, and have you
and me greatly in a wait, as Sir Agravaine, and Sir Mordred: and, madam,
wit ye well, I dread them more for your
sake than for any fear that I have of
them myself, for I may happen to escape and rid myself in a great need,
where ye must abide all that will be
said unto you. And then if that ye fall
in any distress through wilful folly, then
is there none other remedy or help but

by me and my blood. And wit ye well,
madam, the boldness of you and me will
bring us to great shame and slander,
and that were me loth to see you dishonoured. And that is the cause that
I take upon me more for to do for
damsels and maidens than ever I did
tofore, that men should understand my
joy and my delight is my pleasure to
have ado for damsels and maidens.

CHAP. II.

*How the queen commanded Sir Launcelot
to avoid the court, and of the sorrow
that Launcelot made.*

ALL this while the queen stood still,
and let Sir Launcelot say what he
would. And when he had all said, she
brast out on weeping, and so she sobbed
and wept a great while: and when she
might speak, she said, Launcelot, now
I well understand that thou art a false
recreant knight, and lovest and holdest
other ladies, and by me thou hast disdain and scorn. For wit thou well, she
said, now I understand thy falsehood,
and therefore shall I never love thee no
more, and never be thou so hardy to
come in my sight; and right here I discharge thee this court, that thou never
come within it, and I forsend thee my
fellowship, and upon pain of thy head
that thou see me no more. Right so
Sir Launcelot departed with great heaviness, that hardly he might sustain
himself for great dole making. Then
he called Sir Bors, Sir Ector de Maris,
and Sir Lionel, and told them how the
queen had forfend him the court, and
so he was in will to depart into his own
country. Fair sir, said Sir Bors de
Ganis, ye shall not depart out of this
land by mine advice; ye must remember
in what honour ye are renowned, and
called the noblest knight of the world,
and many great matters ye have in hand,
and women in their hastiness will do
oftimes that sore repenteth them, and
therefore by mine advice ye shall take
your horse, and ride to the good hermitage here beside Windsor, that sometime was a good knight, his name is Sir

Brasias, and there shall ye abide till I send you word of better tidings. Brother, said Sir Launcelot, wit ye well I am full loth to depart out of this realm, but the queen hath defended me so highly that me seemeth she will never be my good lady as she hath been. Say ye never so, said Sir Bors, for many times or this time she hath been wroth with you, and after it she was the first that repented it. Ye say well, said Launcelot, for now will I do by your counsel, and take mine horse and my harness, and ride to the hermit Sir Brasias, and there will I repose me until I hear some manner of tidings from you. But, fair brother, I pray you get me the love of my lady queen Guenever, and ye may. Sir, said Sir Bors, ye need not to move me of such matters, for well ye wot I will do what I may to please you. And then the noble knight Sir Launcelot departed with right heavy cheer, suddenly, that none earthly creature wist of him, nor where he was become, but Sir Bors. So when Sir Launcelot was departed, the queen made no manner of sorrow in shewing, to none of his blood, nor to none other: but, wit ye well, inwardly, as the book saith, she took great thought, but she bare it out with a proud countenance, as though she felt nothing nor danger.

CHAP. III.

How at a dinner that the queen made there was a knight poisoned, which Sir Mador laid on the queen.

AND then the queen let make a privy dinner in London unto the knights of the Round Table. And all was for to show outward that she had as great joy in all other knights of the Table Round as she had in Sir Launcelot. All only at that dinner she had Sir Gawaine and his brethren, that is to say, Sir Agravaine, Sir Gaheris, Sir Gareth, and Sir Mordred. Also there was Sir Bors de Ganis, Sir Blamor de Ganis, Sir Bleoberis de Ganis, Sir Galihud, Sir Galihodin, Sir Ector de Maris, Sir Lionel, Sir Palamides, Sir Safere his brother,

Sir La Cote Male Taile, Sir Persant, Sir Ironside, Sir Brandiles, Sir Kay le Seneschal, Sir Mador de la Porte, Sir Patrise, a knight of Ireland, Aliduk, Sir Astomore, and Sir Pinel le Savage, the which was cousin to Sir Lamorak de Galis, the good knight that Sir Gawaine and his brethren slew by treason. And so these four and twenty knights should dine with the queen in a privy place by themselves, and there was made a great feast of all manner of dainties. But Sir Gawaine had a custom that he used daily at dinner and at supper, that he loved well all manner of fruit, and in especial apples and pears. And therefore, whosoever dined or feasted Sir Gawaine would commonly purvey for good fruit for him; and so did the queen for to please Sir Gawaine, she let purvey for him of all manner of fruit, for Sir Gawaine was a passing hot knight of nature. And this Pinel hated Sir Gawaine because of his kinsman Sir Lamorak de Galis, and therefore for pure envy and hate Sir Pinel enpoisoned certain apples, for to enpoison Sir Gawaine. And so this was well unto the end of the meat: and so it befell by misfortune a good knight named Patrise, cousin unto Sir Mador de la Porte, to to take a poisoned apple. And when he had eaten it he swelled so till he brast, and there Sir Patrise fell down suddenly dead among them. Then every knight lept from the board ashamed and araged for wrath, nigh out of their wits. For they wist not what to say: considering queen Guenever made the feast and dinner, they all had suspicion unto her. My lady, the queen, said Gawaine, wit ye well, madam, that this dinner was made for me: for all folks that know my conditions understand that I love well fruit, and now I see well I had near been slain; therefore, madam, I dread lest ye will be shamed. Then the queen stood still, and was sore abashed, that she nist not what to say. This shall not so be ended, said Sir Mador de la Porte, for here have I lost a full noble knight of my blood, and therefore upon this shame and despite I will be revenged to the utterance. And there openly Sir Mador appealed the queen of the death of his cousin Sir Patrise. Then stood they all still, that none of them would speak a word against him. For they had a great suspicion unto the queen because she let make that dinner. And the queen was so abashed that she could none other ways do but wept so heartily that she fell in a swoon. With this noise and cry came to them king Arthur. And when he wist of that trouble, he was a passing heavy man.

CHAP. IV.

How Sir Mador appeached the queen of treason, and there was no knight would fight for her at the first time.

AND ever Sir Mador stood still afore the king, and ever he appealed the queen of treason: for the custom was such that time that all manner of shameful death was called treason. Fair lords, said king Arthur, me repenteth of this trouble, but the case is so I may not have ado in this matter, for I must be a rightful judge, and that repenteth me that I may not do battle for my wife: for, as I deem, this deed came never by her, and therefore I suppose she shall not be all distained, but that some good knight shall put his body in jeopardy, rather than she shall be burnt in a wrong quarrel. And therefore, Sir Mador, be not so hasty, for it may happen she shall not be all friendless, and therefore desire thou thy day of battle, and she shall purvey her of some good knight that shall answer you, or else it were to me great shame, and to all my court. My gracious lord, said Sir Mador, ye must hold me excused, for though ye be our king in that degree, ye are but a knight as we are, and ye are sworn unto knighthood as well as we, and therefore I beseech you that ye be not displeased. For there is none of the four and twenty knights that were bidden to this dinner but all they have great suspicion unto the queen. What say ye all, my lords? said Sir Mador. Then they answered by and by that

they could not excuse the queen, for why she made the dinner, and either it must come by her or by her servants. Alas, said the queen, I made this dinner for a good intent, and never for none evil; so Almighty God help me in my right as I was never purposed to do such evil deeds, and that I report me unto God. My lord the king, said Sir Mador, I require you, as ye be a righteous king, give me a day that I may have justice. Well, said the king, I give the day this day fifteen days, that thou be ready armed on horseback in the meadow beside Westminster. And if it so fall that there be any knight to encounter with you, there mayest thou do the best, and God speed the right. And if it so fall that there be no knight at that day, then must my queen be burnt, and there shall she be ready to have her judgment. I am answered, said Sir Mador; and every knight went where it liked him. So when the king and the queen were together, the king asked the queen how this case befell? The queen answered, So God me help I wot not how, nor in what manner. Where is Sir Launcelot? said king Arthur, and he were here, he would not grudge to do battle for you. Sir, said the queen, I wot not where he is, but his brother and his kinsmen deem that he is not within this realm. That me repenteth, said king Arthur, for and he were here he would soon stint this strife. Then I will counsel you, said the king, and unto Sir Bors—That ye will do battle for her for Sir Launcelot's sake,—and upon my life he will not refuse you. For well I see, said the king, that none of these four and twenty knights that were with you at your dinner, where Sir Patrise was slain, will do battle for you, nor none of them will say well of you, and that shall be great slander for you in this court. Alas, said the queen, and I may not do withal, but now I miss Sir Launcelot, for and he were here he would put me soon to my heart's ease. What aileth you, said the king, ye cannot keep Sir Launcelot on your side? For, wit ye well, said the king, who that hath Sir Launcelot upon his party hath the most man of worship in the world upon his side. Now go your way, said the king unto the queen, and require Sir Bors to do battle for you for Sir Launcelot's sake.

CHAP. V.

How the queen required Sir Bors to fight for her, and how he granted upon condition; and how he warned Sir Launcelot thereof.

So the queen departed from the king, and sent for Sir Bors into her chamber. And when he was come, she besought him of succour. Madam, said he, what would ye that I did, for I may not with my worship have ado in this matter, because I was at the same dinner, for dread that any of those knights would have me in suspicion. Also madam, said Sir Bors, now miss ye Sir Launcelot, for he would not have failed you neither in right nor in wrong, as ye have well proved when ye have been in danger, and now ye have driven him out of this country, by whom ye and all we were daily worshipped by. Therefore, madam, I marvel me how ye dare for shame require me to do any thing for you, in so much ye have chased him out of your country, by whom we were borne up and honoured. Alas, fair knight, said the queen, I put me wholly in your grace, and all that is done amiss I will amend as ye will counsel me. And therewith she kneeled down upon both her knees, and besought Sir Bors to have mercy upon her,—or I shall have a shameful death, and thereto I never offended. Right so came king Arthur, and found the queen kneeling afore Sir Bors. Then Sir Bors pulled her up, and said, Madam, ye do to me great dishonour. Ah, gentle knight, said the king, have mercy upon my queen, courteous knight, for I am now in certain she is untruly defamed. And therefore, courteous knight, said the king, promise her to do battle for her: I require you, for the love of Sir Launcelot. My lord, said Sir Bors, ye re-

quire me the greatest thing that any man may require me; and wit ye well, if I grant to do battle for the queen I shall wrath many of my fellowship of the Table Round; but as for that, said Bors, I will grant my lord, for my lord Sir Launcelot's sake, and for your sake, I will at that day be the queen's champion, unless that there come by adventure a better knight than I am to do battle for her. Will ye promise me this, said the king, by your faith? Yea sir, said Sir Bors, of that will I not fail you, nor her both, but if that there come a better knight than I am, and then shall he have the battle. Then was the king and the queen passing glad, and so departed, and thanked him heartily. So then Sir Bors departed secretly upon a day, and rode unto Sir Launcelot, there as he was with the hermit Sir Brasias, and told him of all their adventure. Ah, said Sir Launcelot, this is come happily as I would have it, and therefore I pray you make you ready to do battle, but look that ye tarry till ye see me come, as long as ye may. For I am sure Mador is an hot knight, when he is enchafed, for the more ye suffer him, the hastier will he be to battle. Sir, said Bors, let me deal with him; doubt ye not ye shall have all your will. Then departed Sir Bors from him, and came to the court again. Then was it noised in all the court that Sir Bors should do battle for the queen: wherefore many knights were displeased with him, that he would take upon him to do battle in the queen's quarrel, for there were but few knights in the court but they deemed the queen was in the wrong, and that she had done that treason. So Sir Bors answered thus unto his fellows of the Table Round: Wit ye well, my fair lords, it were shame to us all, and we suffered to see the most noble queen of the world to be shamed openly, considering her lord and our lord is the man of most worship in the world, and most christened, and he hath ever worshipped us all, in all places. Many answered him again:—As for our most noble king Arthur, we love him and honour him as well as ye do; but as for queen Guenever we love her not, because she is a destroyer of good knights. Fair lords, said Sir Bors, me seemeth ye say not as ye should say, for never yet in my days knew I never, nor heard say, that ever she was a destroyer of any good knight: but at all times, as far as I ever could know, she was always a maintainer of good knights, and always she hath been large and free of her goods to all good knights, and the most bounteous lady of her gifts and her good grace that ever I saw or heard speak of. And therefore it were shame, said Sir Bors, to us all to our most noble king's wife, and we suffered her to be shamefully slain. And wit ye well, said Sir Bors, I will not suffer it, for I dare say so much, the queen is not guilty of Sir Patrise's death, for she owed him never none ill will, nor none of the four and twenty knights that were at that dinner; for I dare say for good love she bad us to dinner, and not for no mal-engine; and that I doubt not shall be proved hereafter: for howsoever the game goeth, there was treason among us. Then some said to Sir Bors, We may well believe your words. And so some of them were well pleased, and some were not so.

CHAP. VI.

How at the day Sir Bors made him ready for to fight for the queen; and when he should fight how another discharged him.

THE day came on fast until the even that the battle should be. Then the queen sent for Sir Bors, and asked him how he was disposed. Truly madam, said he, I am disposed in likewise as I promised you; that is for to say, I shall not fail you, unless by adventure there come a better knight than I am, to do the battle for you: then, madam, am I discharged of my promise. Will ye, said the queen, that I tell my lord Arthur thus? Do as it shall please you, madam. Then the queen went unto the king, and told him the answer of Sir Bors. Have ye no doubt, said

the king, of Sir Bors, for I call him now one of the best knights of the world, and the most profitablest man. And thus it past on until the morn. And the king and the queen, and all manner of knights that were there at that time, drew them unto the meadow beside Westminster, where the battle should be. And so when the king was come with the queen, and many knights of the Round Table, then the queen was put there in the constable's ward, and a great fire made about an iron stake, that, and Sir Mador de la Porte had the better, she should be burnt. Such custom was used in those days, that neither for favour, neither for love, nor affinity, there should be none other but righteous judgment, as well upon a king as upon a knight, and as well upon a queen as upon another poor lady. So in this meanwhile came in Sir Mador de la Porte, and took his oath afore the king, That the queen did this treason until his cousin Sir Patrise, and unto his oath he would prove it with his body, hand for hand, who that would say the contrary. Right so came in Sir Bors de Ganis, and said, that as for queen Guenever, she is in the right, and that will I make good with my hands, that she is not culpable of this treason that is put upon her. Then make thee ready, said Sir Mador, and we shall prove whether thou be in the right or I. Sir Mador, said Sir Bors, wit thou well I know you for a good knight: not for then I shall not fear so greatly, but I trust to God I shall be able to withstand your malice: but thus much have I promised my lord Arthur, and my lady the queen, that I shall do battle for her in this case to the uttermost, unless that there come a better knight than I am, and discharge me. Is that all, said Sir Mador, either come thou off and do battle with me, or else say nay. Take your horse, said Sir Bors, and, as I suppose, ye shall not tarry long, but ye shall be answered. Then either departed to their tents, and made them ready to horseback as they thought best. And anon Sir

Mador came into the field with his shield on his shoulder, and his spear in his hand. And so rode about the place, crying unto king Arthur, Bid your champion come forth and he dare! Then was Sir Bors ashamed, and took his horse and came to the lists' end. And then was he ware where came from a wood there fast by a knight, all armed upon a white horse, with a strange shield of strange arms, and he came riding all that he might run. And so he came to Sir Bors, and said, Fair knight, I pray you be not displeased, for here must a better knight than ye are have this battle; therefore I pray you withdraw you. For wit ye well I have had this day a right great journey, and this battle ought to be mine, and so I promised you when I spake with you last, and with all my heart I thank you of your good will. Then Sir Bors rode unto king Arthur, and told him how there was a knight come that would have the battle for to fight for the queen. What knight is he? said the king. I wot not, said Sir Bors, but such covenant he made with me to be here this day. Now my lord, said Sir Bors, here am I discharged.

CHAP. VII.

How Sir Launcelot fought against Sir Mador for the queen, and how he overcame Sir Mador and discharged the queen.

THEN the king called to that knight, and asked him if he would fight for the queen. Then he answered to the king, Therefore came I hither, and therefore, Sir king, he said, tarry me no longer, for I may not tarry. For anon as I have finished this battle I must depart hence, for I have ado many matters elsewhere. For wit you well, said that knight, this is dishonour to you all knights of the Round Table, to see and know so noble a lady, and so courteous a queen, as queen Guenever is, thus to be rebuked and shamed amongst you. Then they all marvelled what knight that might be that so took the battle

upon him, for there was not one that knew him, but if it were Sir Bors. Then said Sir Mador de la Porte unto the king, Now let me wit with whom I shall have ado withal. And then they rode to the lists' end, and there they couched their spears, and ran together with all their mights. And Sir Mador's spear brake all to pieces, but the other's spear bare Sir Mador's horse and all backward to the earth a great fall. But mightily and suddenly he avoided his horse, and put his shield afore him, and then drew his sword, and bad the other knight alight and do battle with him on foot. Then that knight descended from his horse lightly like a valiant man, and put his shield afore him, and drew his sword, and so they came eagerly unto battle, and either gave other many great strokes, tracing and traversing, rasing and foining, and hurtling together with their swords, as it were wild boars. Thus were they fighting nigh an hour, for this Sir Mador was a strong knight, and mightily proved in many strong battles. But at last this knight smote Sir Mador groveling upon the earth, and the knight stept near him to have pulled Sir Mador flatling upon the ground; and therewith suddenly Sir Mador arose, and in his rising he smote that knight through the thick of the thighs, that the blood ran out fiercely. And when he felt himself so wounded, and saw his blood, he let him arise upon his feet; and then he gave him such a buffet upon the helm that he fell to the earth flatling, and therewith he strode to him for to have pulled off his helm off his head. And then Sir Mador prayed that knight to save his life, and so he yielded him as overcome, and released the queen of his quarrel. I will not grant thee thy life, said that knight, only that thou freely release the queen for ever, and that no mention be made upon Sir Patrise's tomb that ever queen Guenever consented to that treason. All this shall be done, said Sir Mador, I clearly discharge my quarrel for ever. Then the knights parters of the lists took up Sir Mador and led him to his tent. And the other knight went straight to the stair foot where sat king Arthur, and by that time was the queen come to the king, and either kissed other heartily. And when the king saw that knight, he stooped down to him and thanked him, and in likewise did the queen: and the king prayed him to put off his helmet, and to repose him, and to take a sop of wine, and then he put off his helm to drink, and then every knight knew him that it was Sir Launcelot du Lake. Anon as the king wist that, he took the queen in his hand, and went unto Sir Launcelot, and said, Sir, grant mercy of your great travail that ye have had this day for me and for my queen. My lord, said Sir Launcelot, wit ye well I ought of right ever to be in your quarrel, and in my lady the queen's quarrel to do battle, for ye are the man that gave me the high honour of knighthood, and that day my lady your queen did me great worship, and else I had been shamed; for that same day ye made me knight through my hastiness I lost my sword, and my lady your queen found it, and lapped it in her train, and gave me my sword when I had need thereto, and else had I been shamed among all knights. And therefore, my lord Arthur, I promised her at that day ever to be her knight in right or in wrong. Grant mercy, said king Arthur, for this journey, and wit ye well, said the king, I shall acquit your goodness. And ever the queen beheld Sir Launcelot, and wept so tenderly that she sank almost to the ground for sorrow that he had done to her so great goodness, where she shewed him great unkindness. Then the knights of his blood drew unto him, and there either of them made great joy of other. And so came all the knights of the Table Round that were there at that time, and welcomed him. And then Sir Mador was had to leech-craft, and Sir Launcelot was healed of his wound. And then there was made great joy and mirths in that court.

CHAP. VIII.

How the truth was known by the maiden of the lake, and of divers other matters.

AND so it befell that the damsel of the lake, her name was Nimue, the which wedded the good knight Sir Pelleas, and so she came to the court, for ever she did great goodness unto king Arthur, and to all his knights, through her sorcery and enchantments. And so when she heard how the queen was an angered for the death of Sir Patrise, then she told it openly that she was never guilty, and there she disclosed by whom it was done, and named him Sir Pinel, and for what cause he did it. There it was openly disclosed, and so the queen was excused, and the knight Pinel fled into his country. Then was it openly known that Sir Pinel enpoisoned the apples at the feast, to that intent to have destroyed Sir Gawaine, because Sir Gawaine and his brethren destroyed Sir Lamorak de Galis, to the which Sir Pinel was cousin unto. Then was Sir Patrise buried in the church of Westminster, in a tomb, and thereupon was written, Here lieth Sir Patrise of Ireland, slain by Sir Pinel le Savage, that enpoisoned apples to have slain Sir Gawaine, and by misfortune Sir Patrise eat one of those apples, and then suddenly he brast. Also there was written upon the tomb, that queen Guenever was appealed of treason of the death of Sir Patrise by Sir Mador de la Porte, and there was made mention how Sir Launcelot fought with him for queen Guenever, and overcame him in plain battle. All this was written upon the tomb of Sir Patrise, in excusing of the queen. And then Sir Mador sued daily and long to have the queen's good grace. And so by the means of Sir Launcelot he caused him to stand in the queen's grace, and all was forgiven. Thus it passed forth till our Lady day, Assumption. Within a fifteen days of that feast the king let cry a great justs and a tournament that should be at that day at Camelot, that is Winchester. And the king let cry that he and the king of Scots would just against all that would come against them. And when this cry was made, thither came many knights. So there came thither the king of Northgalis, and king Anguish of Ireland, and the king with the hundred knights, and Sir Galahalt the haut prince, and the king of Northumberland, and many other noble dukes and earls of divers countries. So king Arthur made him ready to depart to these justs, and would have had the queen with him : but at that time she would not, she said, for she was sick and might not ride at that time. That me repenteth, said the king, for this seven year ye saw not such a fellowship together, except at Whitsuntide when Galahad departed from the court. Truly, said the queen to the king, ye must hold me excused, I may not be there, and that me repenteth. And many deemed the queen would not be there because of Sir Launcelot du Lake, for Sir Launcelot would not ride with the king ; for he said that he was not whole of the wound the which Sir Mador had given him. Wherefore the king was heavy and passing wroth, and so he departed towards Winchester with his fellowship. And so by the way the king lodged in a town called Astolat, that is now in English called Gilford, and there the king lay in the castle. So when the king was departed, the queen called Sir Launcelot unto her, and said, Sir Launcelot ye are greatly to blame, thus to hold you behind my lord : what trow ye, what will your enemies and mine say and deem ? nought else but see how Sir Launcelot holdeth him ever behind the king, and so doth the queen, for that they would be together ; and thus will they say, said the queen to Sir Launcelot, have ye no doubt thereof.

CHAP. IX.

How Sir Launcelot rode to Astolat, and received a sleeve to bear upon his helm at the request of a maid.

MADAM, said Sir Launcelot, I allow your wit, it is of late come sin ye were wise, and therefore, madam, as at this time I will be ruled by your counsel, and this night I will take my rest, and to-morrow by time will take my way toward Winchester. But wit you well, said Sir Launcelot to the queen, that at that justs I will be against the king and all his fellowship. Ye may there do as ye list, said the queen, but by my counsel ye shall not be against your king and your fellowship, for therein be full many hardy knights of your blood, as ye wot well enough, it needeth not to rehearse them. Madam, said Sir Launcelot, I pray you that ye be not displeased with me, for I will take the adventure that God will send me. And so upon the morn early Sir Launcelot heard mass, and brake his fast, and so took his leave of the queen, and departed. And then he rode so much until he came to Astolat, that is Gilford; and there it happed him in the eventide he came to an old baron's place, that hight Sir Bernard of Astolat. And as Sir Launcelot entered into his lodging, king Arthur espied him as he did walk in a garden beside the castle, how he took his lodging, and knew him full well. It is well, said king Arthur unto the knights that were with him in that garden beside the castle, I have now espied one knight that will play his play at the justs to the which we be gone toward, I undertake he will do marvels. Who is that, we pray you tell us, said many knights that were there at that time. Ye shall not wit for me, said the king, at this time. And so the king smiled, and went to his lodging. So when Sir Launcelot was in his lodging, and unarmed him in his chamber, the old baron and hermit came unto him, making his reverence, and welcomed him in the best manner ; but the old knight knew not Sir Launcelot. Fair sir, said Sir Launcelot to his host, I would pray you to lend me a shield that were not openly known, for mine is well known. Sir, said his host, ye shall have your desire, for me seemeth ye be one of the likeliest knights of the world, and therefore I shall shew you friendship. Sir, wit you well I have two sons which were but late made knights, and the eldest hight Sir Tirre, and he was hurt that same day that he was made knight, that he may not ride, and his shield ye shall have, for that is not known, I dare say, but here and in no place else. And my youngest son hight Sir Lavaine, and if it please you he shall ride with you unto that justs, and he is of his age strong and wight. For much my heart giveth unto you that ye should be a noble knight, therefore, I pray you tell me your name, said Sir Bernard. As for that, said Sir Launcelot, ye must hold me excused as at this time, and if God give me grace to speed well at the justs I shall come again and tell you. But I pray you, said Sir Launcelot, in any wise let me have your son Sir Lavaine with me, and that I may have his brother's shield. Also this shall be done, said Sir Bernard.

This old baron had a daughter that time that was called that time the fair maid of Astolat. And ever she beheld Sir Launcelot wonderfully. And, as the book saith, she cast such a love unto Sir Launcelot that she could never withdraw her love, wherefore she died; and her name was Elaine le Blank. So thus as she came to and fro, she was so hot in her love that she besought Sir Launcelot to wear upon him at the justs a token of hers. Fair damsel, said Sir Launcelot, and if I grant you that, ye may say I do more for your love than ever I did for lady or damsel. Then he remembered him that he would go to the justs disguised, and for because he had never afore that time borne no manner of token of no damsel, then he bethought him that he would bear one of her, that none of his blood thereby might know him. And then he said, Fair maiden, I will grant you to wear a token of yours upon my helmet, and therefore what it is shew it me. Sir, she said, it is a red sleeve of mine, of scarlet well embroidered with great pearls. And so she brought it him. So Sir Launcelot received it and said, Never did I erst so much for

no damsel. And then Sir Launcelot betook the fair maiden his shield in keeping, and prayed her to keep that until that he came again. And so that night he had merry rest and great cheer. For ever the damsel Elaine was about Sir Launcelot, all the while she might be suffered.

CHAP. X.

How the tourney began at Winchester, and what knights were at the justs, and other things.

So upon a day on the morn, king Arthur and all his knights departed; for their king had tarried there three days to abide his noble knights. And so when the king was riden, Sir Launcelot and Sir Lavaine made them ready for to ride, and either of them had white shields, and the red sleeve Sir Launcelot let carry with him. And so they took their leave at Sir Bernard the old baron, and at his daughter the fair maiden of Astolat. And then they rode so long till they came to Camelot, that time called Winchester. And there was great press of kings, dukes, earls, and barons, and many noble knights. But there Sir Launcelot was lodged privily, by the means of Sir Lavaine, with a rich burgess, that no man in that town was ware what they were. And so they sojourned there till our Lady day, Assumption, as the great feast should be. So then trumpets blew unto the field, and king Arthur was set on high upon a scaffold, to behold who did best. But, as the French book saith, king Arthur would not suffer Sir Gawaine to go from him, for never had Sir Gawaine the better and Sir Launcelot were in the field; and many times was Sir Gawaine rebuked when Launcelot came into any justs disguised. Then some of the kings, as king Anguish of Ireland and the king of Scotland, were that time turned upon the side of king Arthur. And then on the other party was the king of Northgalis, and the king with the hundred knights, and the king of Northumberland, and Sir Galahalt the haut prince. But these three kings and this duke were passing weak to hold against king Arthur's party: for with him were the noblest knights of the world. So then they withdrew them either party from other, and every man made him ready in his best manner to do what he might. Then Sir Launcelot made him ready, and put the red sleeve upon his head, and fastened it fast; and so Sir Launcelot and Sir Lavaine departed out of Winchester privily, and rode until a little leaved wood, behind the party that held against king Arthur's party, and there they held them still till the parties smote together. And then came in the king of Scots and the king of Ireland on Arthur's party: and against them came the king of Northumberland; and the king with the hundred knights smote down the king of Northumberland, and the king with the hundred knights smote down king Anguish of Ireland. Then Sir Palamides, that was on Arthur's party, encountered with Sir Galahalt, and either of them smote down other, and either party halp their lords on horseback again. So there began a strong assail upon both parties. And then there came in Sir Brandiles, Sir Sagramor le Desirous, Sir Dodinas le Savage, Sir Kay le Seneschal, Sir Griflet le Fise de Dieu, Sir Mordred, Sir Meliot de Logris, Sir Ozanna le Cure Hardy, Sir Safere, Sir Epinogris, and Sir Galleron of Galway. All these fifteen knights were knights of the Table Round. So these with more others came in together, and beat on back the king of Northumberland, and the king of North Wales. When Sir Launcelot saw this, as he hoved in a little leaved wood, then he said unto Sir Lavaine, See yonder is a company of good knights, and they hold them together as boars that were chafed with dogs. That is truth, said Sir Lavaine.

CHAP. XI.

How Sir Launcelot and Sir Lavaine entered in the field against them of king Arthur's court, and how Launcelot was hurt.

Now, said Sir Launcelot, and ye will help me a little, ye shall see yonder fellowship which chaseth now these men in our side, that they shall go as fast backward as they went forward. Sir, spare not, said Sir Lavaine, for I shall do what I may. Then Sir Launcelot and Sir Lavaine came in at the thickest of the press, and there Sir Launcelot smote down Sir Brandiles, Sir Sagramor, Sir Dodinas, Sir Kay, Sir Griflet, and all this he did with one spear. And Sir Lavaine smote down Sir Lucan le Buttelere, and Sir Bedivere. And then Sir Launcelot gat another spear, and there he smote down Sir Agravaine, Sir Gaheris, and Sir Mordred, and Sir Meliot de Logris. And Sir Lavaine smote down Ozanna le Cure Hardy: and then Sir Launcelot drew his sword, and there he smote on the right hand and on the left hand, and by great force he unhorsed Sir Safere, Sir Epinogris, and Sir Galleron. And then the knights of the Table Round withdrew them aback, after they had gotten their horses as well as they might. O mercy, said Sir Gawaine, what knight is yonder, that doth so marvellous deeds of arms in that field? I wot what he is, said king Arthur. But as at this time I will not name him. Sir, said Sir Gawaine, I would say it were Sir Launcelot, by his riding and his buffets that I see him deal: but ever me seemeth it should not be he, for that he beareth the red sleeve upon his head, for I wist him never bear token, at no justs, of lady nor gentlewoman. Let him be, said king Arthur, he will be better known and do more or ever he depart. Then the party that were against king Arthur were well comforted, and then they held them together, that beforehand were sore rebuked. Then Sir Bors, Sir Ector de Maris, and Sir Lionel, called unto them the knights of their blood, as Sir Blamor de Ganis, Sir Bleoberis, Sir Aliduke, Sir Galihud, Sir Galihodin, Sir Bellangere le Beuse, so these nine knights of Sir Launcelot's kin thrust in mightily, for they were all noble knights. And they, of great hate and despite that they had unto him, thought to rebuke that noble knight Sir Launcelot, and Sir Lavaine, for they knew them not. And so they came hurtling together, and smote down many knights of Northgalis and of Northumberland. And when Sir Launcelot saw them fare so, he gat a spear in his hand, and there encountered with him all at once Sir Bors, Sir Ector, and Sir Lionel, and all they three smote him at once with their spears. And with force of themselves they smote Sir Launcelot's horse to the earth. And by misfortune Sir Bors smote Sir Launcelot through the shield into the side, and the spear brake, and the head left still in his side. When Sir Lavaine saw his master lie on the ground, he ran to the king of Scots, and smote him to the earth, and by great force he took his horse and brought him to Sir Launcelot, and maugre them all he made him to mount upon that horse. And then Launcelot gat a spear in his hand, and there he smote Sir Bors horse and man to the earth, in the same wise he served Sir Ector and Sir Lionel, and Sir Lavaine smote down Sir Blamor de Ganis. And then Sir Launcelot drew his sword, for he felt himself so sore and hurt that he wend there to have had his death. And then he smote Sir Bleoberis such a buffet on the helmet that he fell down to the earth in a swoon. And in the same wise he served Sir Aliduke and Sir Galihud. And Sir Lavaine smote down Sir Bellangere, that was the son of Alisander le Orphelin. And by this was Sir Bors horsed, and then he came with Sir Ector and Sir Lionel, and all they three smote with swords upon Sir Launcelot's helmet. And when he felt their buffets, and his wound the which was so grievous, then he thought to do what he might while he might endure; and then he gave Sir Bors such a buffet that he made him bow his head passing low, and therewithal he rased off his helm, and might have slain him, and so pulled him down. And in the same wise he served Sir Ector and Sir Lionel. For, as the book saith, he might have slain them, but when he saw their

visages his heart might not serve him thereto, but left them there.

And then afterward he hurled in the thickest press of them all, and did there the marvellousest deeds of arms that ever man saw or heard speak of; and ever Sir Lavaine the good knight with him. And there Sir Launcelot with his sword smote and pulled down, as the French book maketh mention, more than thirty knights, and the most party were of the Table Round. And Sir Lavaine did full well that day, for he smote down ten knights of the Table Round.

CHAP. XII.

How Sir Launcelot and Sir Lavaine departed out of the field, and in what jeopardy Launcelot was.

MERCY, said Sir Gawaine to Arthur, I marvel what knight that he is with the red sleeve. Sir, said king Arthur, he will be known or he depart. And then the king blew unto lodging, and the prize was given by heralds unto the knight with the white shield, that bare the red sleeve. Then came the king with the hundred knights, the king of Northgalis, and the king of Northumberland, and Sir Galahalt the haut prince, and said unto Sir Launcelot, Fair knight, God thee bless, for much have ye done this day for us, therefore we pray you that ye will come with us, that ye may receive the honour and the prize as ye have worshipfully deserved it. My fair lords, said Sir Launcelot, wit you well, if I have deserved thank I have sore bought it, and that me repenteth, for I am like never to escape with my life, therefore, fair lords, I pray you that ye will suffer me to depart where me liketh, for I am sore hurt. I take none force of none honour, for I had lever to repose me than to be lord of all the world. And therewithal he groaned piteously, and rode a great gallop away-ward from them, until he came under a wood's side; and when he saw that he was from the field nigh a mile, that he was sure he might not be seen, then he said with an high voice, O gentle knight Sir Lavaine, help me that this truncheon were out of my side, for it sticketh so sore that it nigh slayeth me. O mine own lord, said Sir Lavaine, I would fain do that might please you, but I dread me sore, and I draw out the truncheon, that ye shall be in peril of death. I charge you, said Sir Launcelot, as ye love me draw it out. And therewithal he descended from his horse, and right so did Sir Lavaine, and forthwith Sir Lavaine drew the truncheon out of his side. And he gave a great shriek, and a marvellous grisly groan, and his blood brast out nigh a pint at once, that at last he sank down, and so swooned pale and deadly. Alas, said Sir Lavaine, what shall I do? And then he turned Sir Launcelot into the wind, but so he lay there nigh half an hour as he had been dead. And so at the last Sir Launcelot cast up his eyes, and said, O Lavaine, help me that I were on my horse, for here is fast by within this two mile a gentle hermit, that sometime was a full noble knight and a great lord of possessions: and for great goodness he hath taken him to wilful poverty, and forsaken many lands, and his name is Sir Baudewin of Brittany, and he is a full noble surgeon, and a good leech. Now let see, help me up that I were there. For ever my heart giveth me that I shall never die of my cousin-german's hands. And then with great pain Sir Lavaine halp him upon his horse; and then they rode a great gallop together, and ever Sir Launcelot bled that it ran down to the earth. And so by fortune they came to that hermitage, which was under a wood, and a great cliff on the other side, and a fair water running under it. And then Sir Lavaine beat on the gate with the butt of his spear, and cried fast, Let in for Jesu's sake. And there came a fair child to them, and asked them what they would? Fair son, said Sir Lavaine, go and pray thy lord the hermit for God's sake to let in here a knight that is full sore wounded, and this day tell thy lord that I saw him do

more deeds of arms than ever I heard say that any man did. So the child went in lightly, and then he brought the hermit, the which was a passing good man. So when Sir Lavaine saw him, he prayed him for God's sake of succour. What knight is he? said the hermit, is he of the house of king Arthur or not? I wot not, said Sir Lavaine, what is he, nor what is his name, but well I wot I saw him do marvellously this day, as of deeds of arms. On whose party was he? said the hermit. Sir, said Sir Lavaine, he was this day against king Arthur, and there he wan the prize of all the knights of the Round Table. I have seen the day, said the hermit, I would have loved him the worse because he was against my lord king Arthur, for sometime I was one of the fellowship of the Round Table, but I thank God now I am otherwise disposed. But where is he? let me see him. Then Sir Lavaine brought the hermit to him.

CHAP. XIII.

How Launcelot was brought to an hermit for to be healed of his wound, and of other matters.

AND when the hermit beheld him as he sat leaning upon his saddle-bow, ever bleeding piteously, and ever the knight hermit thought that he should know him, but he could not bring him to knowledge, because he was so pale for bleeding, What knight are ye? said the hermit, and where were ye born? My fair lord, said Sir Launcelot, I am a stranger, and a knight adventurous that laboureth throughout many realms for to win worship. Then the hermit advised him better, and saw by a wound on his cheek that he was Sir Launcelot. Alas, said the hermit, mine own lord, why hide you your name from me: forsooth I ought to know you of right, for ye are the most noblest knight of the world; for well I know you for Sir Launcelot. Sir, said he, sith ye know me, help me and ye may, for God's sake; for I would be out of this pain at once, either to death or to life. Have ye no doubt, said the hermit, ye shall live and fare right well. And so the hermit called to him two of his servants, and so he and his servants bare him into the hermitage, and lightly unarmed him and laid him in his bed. And then anon the hermit stanched his blood, and made him to drink good wine, so that Sir Launcelot was well refreshed, and knew himself. For in those days it was not the guise of hermits as is now adays. For there were none hermits in those days but that they had been men of worship and of prowess, and those hermits held great household, and refreshed people that were in distress.

Now turn we unto king Arthur, and leave we Sir Launcelot in the hermitage. So when the kings were come together on both parties, and the great feast should be holden, king Arthur asked the king of Northgalis and their fellowship where was that knight that bare the red sleeve:—Bring him before me, that he may have his laud and honour and the prize, as it is right. Then spake Sir Galahalt the haut prince and the king with the hundred knights: We suppose that knight is mischieved, and that he is never like to see you, nor none of us all, and that is the greatest pity that ever we wist of any knight. Alas, said Arthur, how may this be? is he so hurt? What is his name? said king Arthur. Truly, said they all, we know not his name, nor from whence he came, nor whither he would. Alas, said the king, these be to me the worst tidings that came to me ·this seven year: for I would not for all the lands I hold, to know and wit it were so that that noble knight were slain. Know ye him? said they all. As for that, said Arthur, whether I know him or know him not, ye shall not know for me what man he is, but Almighty Jesu send me good tidings of him. And so said they all. By my head, said Sir Gawaine, if it be so, that the good knight be so sore hurt, it is great

damage and pity to all this land, for he is one of the noblest knights that ever I saw in a field handle a spear or a sword. And if he may be found I shall find him, for I am sure he is not far from this town. Bear you well, said king Arthur, and ye may find him, unless that he be in such a plight that he may not hold himself. Jesu defend, said Sir Gawaine, but wit I shall what he is, and I may find him. Right so, Sir Gawaine took a squire with him, upon hackneys, and rode all about Camelot within six or seven miles. But so he came again, and could hear no word of him.

Then within two days king Arthur and all the fellowship returned unto London again. And so as they rode by the way, it happed Sir Gawaine at Astolat to lodge with Sir Bernard, there as was Sir Launcelot lodged. And so as Sir Gawaine was in his chamber to repose him, Sir Bernard the old baron came unto him, and his daughter Elaine, for to cheer him, and to ask him what tidings, and who did best at that tournament of Winchester. Truly, said Sir Gawaine, there were two knights that bare two white shields; but the one of them bare a red sleeve upon his head, and certainly he was one of the best knights that ever I saw just in field. For I dare say, said Sir Gawaine, that one knight with the red sleeve smote down forty valiant knights of the Table Round, and his fellow did right well and worshipfully. Now blessed be God, said the fair maiden of Astolat, that that knight sped so well, for he is the man in the world that I first loved, and truly he shall be the last that ever I shall love. Now fair maid, said Sir Gawaine, is that good knight your love? Certainly, sir, said she, wit ye well he is my love. Then know ye his name, said Sir Gawaine. Nay, truly, said the damsel, I know not his name, nor from whence he cometh, but to say that I love him, I promise you and God that I love him. How had ye knowledge of him first? said Sir Gawaine.

CHAP. XIV.

How Sir Gawaine was lodged with the lord of Astolat, and there had knowledge that it was Sir Launcelot that bare the red sleeve.

THEN she told him as ye have heard tofore, and how her father betook him her brother to do him service, and how her father lent him her brother Sir Tirre's shield,—And here with me he left his own shield. For what cause did he so? said Sir Gawaine. For this cause, said the damsel, for his shield was too well known among many noble knights. Ah, fair damsel, said Sir Gawaine, please it you let me have a sight of that shield. Sir, said she, it is in my chamber covered with a case, and if ye will come with me, ye shall see it. Not so, said Sir Bernard, till his daughter let send for it. So when the shield was come, Sir Gawaine took off the case: and when he beheld that shield, he knew anon that it was Sir Launcelot's shield, and his own arms. Ah, mercy, said Sir Gawaine, now is my heart more heavier then ever it was tofore. Why? said Elaine. For I have great cause, said Sir Gawaine: is that knight that owneth this shield your love? Yea truly, said she, my love he is, God would I were his love. Truly, said Sir Gawaine, fair damsel, ye have right, for, and he be your love, ye love the most honourable knight of the world, and the man of most worship. So me thought ever, said the damsel, for never, or that time, for no knight that ever I saw loved I never none erst. God grant, said Sir Gawaine, that either of you may rejoice other, but that is in a great adventure. But truly, said Sir Gawaine unto the damsel, ye may say ye have a fair grace, for why, I have known that noble knight this four and twenty year, and never or that day I nor none other knight, I dare make it good, saw nor heard say that ever he bare token or sign of no lady, gentlewoman, nor maiden, at no justs nor tournament. And therefore, fair maiden, said Sir Gawaine, ye are much beholden to him to give him thanks. But I dread me, said Sir Gawaine, that ye shall never see him in this world, and that is great pity that ever was of earthly knight. Alas, said she, how may this be? Is he slain? I say not so, said Sir Gawaine, but wit ye well, he is grievously wounded, by all manner of signs, and by men's sight more likely to be dead then to be on live; and wit ye well he is the noble knight Sir Launcelot, for by this shield I know him. Alas, said the fair maiden of Astolat, how may this be, and what was his hurt? Truly, said Sir Gawaine, the man in the world that loved him best hurt him so, and I dare say, said Sir Gawaine, and that knight that hurt him knew the very certainty that he had hurt Sir Launcelot, it would be the most sorrow that ever came to his heart. Now, fair father, said then Elaine, I require you give me leave to ride and to seek him, or else I wot well I shall go out of my mind, for I shall never stint till that I find him and my brother Sir Lavaine. Do as it liketh you, said her father, for me right sore repenteth of the hurt of that noble knight. Right so the maid made her ready, and before Sir Gawaine making great dole. Then on the morn Sir Gawaine came to king Arthur, and told him how he had found Sir Launcelot's shield in the keeping of the fair maiden of Astolat. All that knew I aforehand, said king Arthur, and that caused me I would not suffer you to have ado at the great justs: for I espied, said king Arthur, when he came in till his lodging, full late in the evening in Astolat. But marvel have I, said Arthur, that ever he would bear any sign of any damsel: for, or now, I never heard say nor knew that ever he bare any token of none earthly woman. By my head, said Sir Gawaine, the fair maiden of Astolat loveth him marvellously well; what it meaneth I cannot say; and she is ridden after to seek him. So the king and all came to London, and there Sir Gawaine openly disclosed to all the court that it was Sir Launcelot that justed best.

CHAP. XV.

Of the sorrow that Sir Bors had for the hurt of Launcelot; and of the anger that the queen had because Launcelot bore the sleeve.

AND when Sir Bors heard that, wit ye well he was a heavy man, and so were all his kinsmen. But when queen Guenever wist that Sir Launcelot bare the red sleeve of the fair maiden of Astolat, she was nigh out of her mind for wrath. And then she sent for Sir Bors de Ganis in all the haste that might be. So when Sir Bors was come tofore the queen, then she said, Ah, Sir Bors, have ye heard say how falsely Sir Launcelot hath betrayed me? Alas, madam, said Sir Bors, I am afraid he hath betrayed himself, and us all. No force, said the queen, though he be destroyed, for he is a false traitor knight. Madam, said Sir Bors, I pray you say ye not so, for wit you well I may not hear such language of him. Why, Sir Bors, said she, should I not call him traitor, when he bare the red sleeve upon his head at Winchester, at the great justs? Madam, said Sir Bors, that sleeve-bearing repenteth me sore, but I dare say he did it to none evil intent, but for this cause he bare the red sleeve, that none of his blood should know him; for, or then, we nor none of us all never knew that ever he bare token or sign of maid, lady, ne gentlewoman. Fie on him, said the queen, yet for all his pride and boasting, there ye proved yourself his better. Nay, madam, say ye never more so, for he beat me and my fellows, and might have slain us, and he had would. Fie on him, said the queen, for I heard Sir Gawaine say before my lord Arthur, that it were marvel to tell the great love that is between the fair maiden of Astolat and him. Madam, said Sir Bors, I may not warn Sir Gawaine to say what it pleased him: but I dare say as for my lord Sir Launcelot, that he loveth no lady, gentlewoman, nor maid, but all he loveth in like much, and therefore, madam, said Sir Bors, ye may say what ye will, but wit ye well I

will haste me to seek him, and find him wheresoever he be, and God send me good tidings of him. And so leave we them there, and speak we of Sir Launcelot, that lay in great peril.

So as fair Elaine came to Winchester, she sought there all about, and by fortune Sir Lavaine was ridden to play him, to enchafe his horse. And anon as Elaine saw him she knew him, and then she cried onloud until him. And when he heard her, anon he came to her; and then she asked her brother, How did my lord, Sir Launcelot? Who told you, sister, that my lord's name was Sir Launcelot? Then she told him how Sir Gawaine by his shield knew him. So they rode together till that they came to the hermitage, and anon she alight. So Sir Lavaine brought her in to Sir Launcelot. And when she saw him lie so sick and pale in his bed, she might not speak, but suddenly she fell to the earth down suddenly in a swoon, and there she lay a great while. And when she was relieved she sighed, and said, My lord Sir Launcelot, alas, why be ye in this plight? and then she swooned again. And then Sir Launcelot prayed Sir Lavaine to take her up,— And bring her to me. And when she came to herself, Sir Launcelot kissed her, and said, Fair maiden, why fare ye thus? Ye put me to pain; wherefore make ye no more such cheer, for, and ye be come to comfort me, ye be right welcome, and of this little hurt that I have, I shall be right hastily whole, by the grace of God. But I marvel, said Sir Launcelot, who told you my name. Then the fair maiden told him all how Sir Gawaine was lodged with her father,— And there by your shield he discovered your name. Alas, said Sir Launcelot, that me repenteth, that my name is known, for I am sure it will turn unto anger. And then Sir Launcelot compassed in his mind that Sir Gawaine would tell queen Guenever how he bare the red sleeve, and for whom, that he wist well would turn unto great anger. So this maiden, Elaine, never went from Sir Launcelot, but watched him day and night, and did such attendance to him that the French book saith there was never woman did more kindlier for man than she. Then Sir Launcelot prayed Sir Lavaine to make espies in Winchester for Sir Bors if he came there, and told him by what tokens he should know him, by a wound in his forehead: For well I am sure, said Sir Launcelot, that Sir Bors will seek me, for he is the same good knight that hurt me.

CHAP. XVI.

How Sir Bors sought Launcelot and found him in the hermitage, and of the lamentation between them.

Now turn we unto Sir Bors de Ganis, that came unto Winchester to seek after his cousin, Sir Launcelot; and so when he came to Winchester, anon there were men that Sir Lavaine had made to lie in a watch for such a man; and anon Sir Lavaine had warning; and then Sir Lavaine came to Winchester, and found Sir Bors, and there he told him what he was, and with whom he was, and what was his name. Now, fair knight, said Sir Bors, I require you that ye will bring me to my lord Sir Launcelot. Sir, said Sir Lavaine, take your horse, and within this hour ye shall see him. And so they departed, and came to the hermitage.

And when Sir Bors saw Sir Launcelot lie in his bed, pale and discoloured, anon Sir Bors lost his countenance, and for kindness and pity he might not speak, but wept tenderly a great while. And then when he might speak he said thus: O my lord Sir Launcelot, God you bless, and send you hasty recovery; and full heavy am I of my misfortune and of mine unhappiness, for now I may call myself unhappy, and I dread me that God is greatly displeased with me, that he would suffer me to have such a shame for to hurt you, that are all our leader and all our worship, and therefore I call myself unhappy. Alas, that ever such a caitiff knight as I am should have power by unhappiness to hurt the most noblest knight of the world. Where I so shame-

fully set upon you and overcharged you, and where ye might have slain me, ye saved me, and so did not I: for I, and your blood, did to you our utterance. I marvel, said Sir Bors, that my heart or my blood would serve me, wherefore my lord Sir Launcelot, I ask your mercy. Fair cousin, said Sir Launcelot, ye be right welcome, and wit ye well overmuch ye say for to please me, the which pleaseth me not; for why? I have the same sought, for I would with pride have overcome you all, and there in my pride I was near slain, and that was in mine own default, for I might have given you warning of my being there. And then had I had no hurt; for it is an old said saw, there is hard battle there as kin and friends do battle either against other; there may be no mercy, but mortal war. Therefore, fair cousin, said Sir Launcelot, let this speech overpass, and all shall be welcome that God sendeth; and let us leave off this matter, and let us speak of some rejoicing: for this that is done may not be undone, and let us find a remedy how soon that I may be whole. Then Sir Bors leaned upon his bed's side, and told Sir Launcelot how the queen was passing wroth with him, because he ware the red sleeve at the great justs. And there Sir Bors told him all how Sir Gawaine discovered it by your shield that ye left with the fair maiden of Astolat. Then is the queen wroth, said Sir Launcelot, and therefore am I right heavy, for I deserved no wrath, for all that I did was because that I would not be known. Right so excused I you, said Sir Bors, but all was in vain, for she said more largely to me than I to you now. But is this she, said Sir Bors, that is so busy about you, that men call the fair maiden of Astolat? She it is, said Sir Launcelot, that by no means I cannot put from me. Why should ye put her from you? said Sir Bors, she is a passing fair damsel, and a well beseen and well taught; and God would, fair cousin, said Sir Bors, that ye could love her, but as to that I may not, nor I dare not, counsel you. But I see well, said Sir Bors, by her diligence about you, that she loveth you entirely. That me repenteth, said Sir Launcelot. Sir, said Sir Bors, she is not the first that hath lost her pain upon you, and that is the more pity. And so they talked of many more things. And so within three days or four, Sir Launcelot was big and strong again.

CHAP. XVII.

How Sir Launcelot armed him to assay if he might bear arms, and how his wound burst out again.

THEN Sir Bors told Sir Launcelot how there was sworn a great tournament and justs betwixt king Arthur and the king of Northgalis, that should be on All-hallowmass day, beside Winchester. Is that truth? said Sir Launcelot, then shall ye abide with me still a little while, until that I be whole, for I feel myself right big and strong. Blessed be God, said Sir Bors. Then were they there nigh a month together; and ever this maiden Elaine did ever her diligent labour, night and day, unto Sir Launcelot, that there was never child nor wife more meeker to father and husband, than was that fair maiden of Astolat. Wherefore Sir Bors was greatly pleased with her. So upon a day, by the assent of Sir Launcelot, Sir Bors and Sir Lavaine they made the hermit to seek in woods for divers herbs. And so Sir Launcelot made fair Elaine to gather herbs for him, to make him a bath. In the mean while, Sir Launcelot made him to arm him at all pieces, and there he thought to assay his armour and his spear, for his hurt or not. And so when he was upon his horse, he stirred him fiercely, and the horse was passing lusty and fresh, because he was not laboured a month before. And then Sir Launcelot couched that spear in the rest : that courser lept mightily when he felt the spurs ; and he that was upon him, the which was the noblest horse of the world, strained him mightily and stably, and kept still the spear in the rest. And therewith Sir Launcelot strained himself so straitly, with so great force, to get

the horse forward, that the bottom of the wound brast, both within and with-out, and therewithal the blood came out so fiercely that he felt himself so feeble that he might not sit upon his horse. And then Sir Launcelot cried unto Sir Bors, Ah, Sir Bors, and Sir Lavaine, help, for I am come to mine end. And therewith he fell down on the one side to the earth, like a dead corpse. And then Sir Bors and Sir Lavaine came to him, with sorrow making out of measure. And so by fortune the maiden Elaine heard their mourning, and then she came thither. And when she found Sir Launcelot there armed in that place, she cried and wept as she had been wood, and then she kissed him, and did what she might to awake him. And then she rebuked her brother and Sir Bors, and called them false traitors, why they would take him out of his bed ; then she cried, and said she would appeal them of his death. With this came the holy hermit, Sir Baudewin of Britanny ; and when he found Sir Launcelot in that plight he said but little, but wit ye well he was wroth ; and then he bade them, Let us have him in. And so they all bare him unto the hermitage, and unarmed him, and laid him in his bed, and evermore his wound bled pite-ously, but he stirred no limb of him. Then the knight hermit put a thing in his nose, and a little deal of water in his mouth, and then Sir Launcelot waked of his swoon, and then the her-mit stanched his bleeding. And when he might speak, he asked Sir Launcelot why he put his life in jeopardy. Sir, said Sir Launcelot, because I wend I had been strong, and also Sir Bors told me that there should be at Allhallow-mass a great justs betwixt king Arthur and the king of Northgalis, and therefore I thought to assay it myself, whether I might be there or not. Ah, Sir Laun-celot, said the hermit, your heart and your courage will never be done until your last day, but ye shall do now by my counsel ; let Sir Bors depart from you, and let him do at that tournament what he may, and by the grace of God, said the knight hermit, by that the tournament be done, and ye come hither again, Sir Launcelot shall be as whole as ye, so that he will be governed by me.

CHAP. XVIII.

How Sir Bors returned and told tidings of Sir Launcelot, and of the tourney, and to whom the prize was given.

THEN Sir Bors made him ready to depart from Sir Launcelot; and then Sir Launcelot said, Fair cousin, Sir Bors, recommend me unto all them unto whom me ought to recommend me unto, and I pray you enforce yourself at that justs, that ye may be best, for my love, and here shall I abide you, at the mercy of God, till ye come again. And so Sir Bors departed, and came to the court of king Arthur, and told them in what place he had left Sir Launcelot. That me repenteth, said the king, but sin he shall have his life, we may all thank God. And there Sir Bors told the queen in what jeopardy Sir Launcelot was, when he would essay his horse: and all that he did, madam, was for the love of you, because he would have been at this tournament. Fie on him, recreant knight, said the queen, for wit ye well I am right sorry and he shall have his life. His life shall he have, said Sir Bors, and who that would otherwise, except you, madam, we that be of his blood should help to short their lives. But, madam, said Sir Bors, ye have been oft-times displeased with my lord Sir Launcelot, but at all times at the end ye find him a true knight. And so he departed. And then every knight of the Round Table that was there present at that time, made them ready to be at that justs at Allhallowmass. And thither drew many knights of divers countries. And as Allhallowmass drew near, thither came the king of Northgalis, and the king with the hundred knights, and Sir Galahalt the haut prince of Surluse, and thither came king Anguish of Ireland, and the king of Scots. So these three

kings came on king Arthur's party. And so that day Sir Gawaine did great deeds of arms, and began first, and the heralds numbered that Sir Gawaine smote down twenty knights. Then Sir Bors de Ganis came in the same time, and he was numbered that he smote down twenty knights. And therefore the prize was given betwixt them both, for they began first, and the longest endured.

Also Sir Gareth, as the book saith, did that day great deeds of arms, for he smote down, and pulled down, thirty knights. But when he had done these deeds he tarried not, but so departed, and therefore he lost his prize. And Sir Palamides did great deeds of arms that day, for he smote down twenty knights, but he departed suddenly; and men deemed Sir Gareth and he rode together to some manner adventure. So when this tournament was done, Sir Bors departed, and rode till he came to Sir Launcelot his cousin, and then he found him walking on his feet, and there either made great joy of other. And so Sir Bors told Sir Launcelot of all the justs, like as ye have heard. I marvel, said Sir Launcelot, that Sir Gareth, when he had done such deeds of arms, that he would not tarry. Thereof we marvelled all, said Sir Bors, for, but if it were you, or Sir Tristram, or Sir Lamorak de Galis, I saw never knight bear down so many in so little a while as did Sir Gareth. And anon as he was gone, he wist not where. By my head, said Sir Launcelot, he is a noble knight, and a mighty man, and well breathed; and if he were well assayed, said Sir Launcelot, I would deem he were good enough for any man that beareth the life; and he is a gentle knight, courteous, true, and bounteous, meek and mild, and in him is no manner of mal-engine, but plain, faithful, and true. So then they made them ready to depart from the hermit. And so upon a morn they took their horses, and Elaine le Blank with them; and when they came to Astolat, there they were well lodged, and had great cheer of Sir Bernard the old baron, and of Sir Tirre his son. And so upon the morn, when Sir Launcelot should depart, fair Elaine brought her father with her, and Sir Tirre and Sir Lavaine, and thus she said:

CHAP. XIX.

Of the great lamentation of the fair maid of Astolat when Launcelot should depart, and how she died for his love.

My lord Sir Launcelot, now I see ye will depart, now, fair knight and courteous knight, have mercy upon me, and suffer me not to die for thy love. What would ye that I did? said Sir Launcelot. I would have you to my husband, said Elaine. Fair damsel, I thank you, said Sir Launcelot, but truly, said he, I cast me never to be wedded man. Then, fair knight, said she, will ye be my love? Jesu defend me, said Sir Launcelot, for then I rewarded to your father and your brother full evil for their great goodness. Alas, said she, then must I die for your love. Ye shall not so, said Sir Launcelot, for wit ye well, fair maiden, I might have been married and I had would, but I never applied me to be married yet. But because, fair damsel, that ye love me as ye say ye do, I will, for your good will and kindness, shew you some goodness, and that is this ; that wheresoever ye will beset your heart upon some good knight that will wed you, I shall give you together a thousand pound yearly, to you and to your heirs. Thus will I give you, fair madam, for your kindness, and always while I live to be your own knight. Of all this, said the maiden, I will none, for, but if ye will wed me, or else be my lover, wit you well, Sir Launcelot, my good days are done. Fair damsel, said Sir Launcelot, of these two things ye must pardon me. Then she shrieked shrilly, and fell down in a swoon ; and then women bare her into her chamber, and there she made overmuch sorrow. And then Sir Launcelot would depart; and there he asked Sir Lavaine what he

would do. What should I do, said Sir Lavaine, but follow you, but if ye drive me from you, or command me to go from you? Then came Sir Bernard to Sir Launcelot, and said to him, I cannot see but that my daughter Elaine will die for your sake. I may not do withal, said Sir Launcelot, for that me sore repenteth ; for I report me to yourself that my proffer is fair, and me repenteth, said Sir Launcelot, that she loveth me as she doth : I was never the causer of it, for I report me to your son, I early nor late proffered her bounty nor fair behests ; and as for me, said Sir Launcelot, I dare do all that a good knight should do, that she is a true maiden, both for deed and for will ; and I am right heavy of her distress, for she is a full fair maiden, good, and gentle, and well taught. Father, said Sir Lavaine, I dare make good she is pure and good as my lord Sir Launcelot hath said ; but she doth as I do, for since I first saw my lord Sir Launcelot I could never depart from him, nor nought I will and I may follow him. Then Sir Launcelot took his leave, and so they departed, and came unto Winchester. And when Arthur wist that Sir Launcelot was come, whole and sound, the king made great joy of him, and so did Sir Gawaine, and all the knights of the Round Table except Sir Agravaine and Sir Mordred. Also queen Guenever was wood wroth with Sir Launcelot, and would by no means speak with him, but estranged herself from him, and Sir Launcelot made all the means that he might to speak with the queen, but it would not be.

Now speak we of the fair maiden of Astolat, that made such sorrow day and night, that she never slept, eat, nor drank ; and ever she made her complaint unto Sir Launcelot. So when she had thus endured a ten days, that she feebled so that she must needs pass out of this world, then she shrived her clean, and received her Creator. And ever she complained still upon Sir Launcelot. Then her ghostly father bade her leave such thoughts. Then she said, Why should I leave such thoughts? am I not an earthly woman? and all the while the breath is in my body I may complain me, for my belief is I do none offence though I love an earthly man, and I take God to my record I never loved none but Sir Launcelot du Lake, nor never shall; and a pure maiden I am for him and for all other. And since it is the sufferance of God that I shall die for the love of so noble a knight, I beseech the High Father of heaven to have mercy upon my soul, and upon mine innumerable pains that I suffered may be allegiance of part of my sins. For sweet Lord Jesu, said the fair maiden, I take thee to record, on thee I was never great offender against thy laws, but that I loved this noble knight Sir Launcelot out of measure, and of myself, good Lord, I might not withstand the fervent love wherefore I have my death. And then she called her father Sir Bernard, and her brother Sir Tirre, and heartily she prayed her father that her brother might write a letter like as she did endite it; and so her father granted her. And when the letter was written word by word like as she devised, then she prayed her father that she might be watched until she were dead, — And while my body is hot, let this letter be put in my right hand, and my hand bound fast with the letter until that I be cold, and let me be put in a fair bed, with all the richest clothes that I have about me, and so let my bed, and all my richest clothes, be laid with me in a chariot unto the next place where Thames is, and there let me be put within a barget, and but one man with me, such as ye trust to steer me thither, and that my barget be covered with black samite, over and over. Thus, father, I beseech you, let it be done. So her father granted it her faithfully, all things should be done like as she had devised. Then her father and her brother made great dole, for, when this was done, anon she died. And so when she was dead, the corpse, and the bed, all was led the next way unto Thames, and there a man, and the corpse, and all, were put into Thames, and so the man steered the barget unto Westminster, and there he rowed a great while to and fro or any espied it.

CHAP. XX.

How the corpse of the maid of Astolat arrived tofore king Arthur, and of the burying, and how Sir Launcelot offered the mass-penny.

So by fortune king Arthur and the queen Guenever were speaking together at a window; and so as they looked into Thames, they espied this black barget, and had marvel what it meant. Then the king called Sir Kay, and shewed it him. Sir, said Sir Kay, wit you well there is some new tidings. Go thither, said the king to Sir Kay, and take with you Sir Brandiles and Agravaine, and bring me ready word what is there. Then these three knights departed, and came to the barget, and went in; and there they found the fairest corpse lying in a rich bed, and a poor man sitting in the barget's end, and no word would he speak. So these three knights returned unto the king again, and told him what they found. That fair corpse will I see, said the king. And so then the king took the queen by the hand and went thither. Then the king made the barget to be holden fast; and then the king and the queen entered, with certain knights with them. And there he saw the fairest woman lie in a rich bed, covered unto her middle with many rich clothes, and all was of cloth of gold, and she lay as though she had smiled. Then the queen espied a letter in her right hand, and told it to the king. Then the king took it, and said, Now I am sure this letter will tell what she was, and why she is come hither. Then the king and the queen went out of the barget, and so commanded a certain man to wait upon the barget. And so when the king was come within his chamber, he called many knights about him, and said that he would wit openly what was written within that letter. Then the king brake it, and made a clerk to read it; and this was the intent of the letter:—Most noble knight, Sir Launcelot, now hath death made us two at debate for your love; I was your lover, that men called the fair maiden of Astolat; therefore unto all ladies I make my moan; yet pray for my soul, and bury me at the least, and offer ye my mass-penny. This is my last request. And a clean maiden I died, I take God to witness. Pray for my soul, Sir Launcelot, as thou art peerless.—This was all the substance in the letter. And when it was read, the king, the queen, and all the knights wept for pity of the doleful complaints. Then was Sir Launcelot sent for. And when he was come, king Arthur made the letter to be read to him; and when Sir Launcelot heard it word by word, he said, My lord Arthur, wit ye well I am right heavy of the death of this fair damsel. God knoweth I was never causer of her death by my willing, and that will I report me to her own brother; here he is, Sir Lavaine. I will not say nay, said Sir Launcelot, but that she was both fair and good, and much I was beholden unto her, but she loved me out of measure. Ye might have shewed her, said the queen, some bounty and gentleness, that might have preserved her life. Madam, said Sir Launcelot, she would none other way be answered, but that she would be my wife, or else my love, and of these two I would not grant her; but I proffered her, for her good love that she shewed me, a thousand pound yearly to her and to her heirs, and to wed any manner knight that she could find best to love in her heart. For, madam, said Sir Launcelot, I love not to be constrained to love; for love must arise of the heart, and not by no constraint. That is truth, said the king, and many knights: love is free in himself, and never will be bounden; for where he is bounden he loseth himself. Then said the king unto Sir Launcelot, It will be your worship that ye oversee that she be interred worshipfully. Sir, said Sir

Launcelot, that shall be done as I can best devise. And so many knights went thither to behold that fair maiden. And so upon the morn she was interred richly, and Sir Launcelot offered her mass-penny, and all the knights of the Table Round that were there at that time offered with Sir Launcelot. And then the poor man went again with the barget. Then the queen sent for Sir Launcelot, and prayed him of mercy, for why she had been wroth with him causeless. This is not the first time, said Sir Launcelot, that ye have been displeased with me causeless; but, madam, ever I must suffer you, but what sorrow I endure I take no force. So this passed on all that winter, with all manner of hunting and hawking, and justs and tourneys were many betwixt many great lords; and ever in all places Sir Lavaine gat great worship, so that he was nobly renowned among many knights of the Table Round.

CHAP. XXI.

Of great justs done all a Christmas, and of a great justs and tourney ordained by king Arthur, and of Sir Launcelot.

THUS it passed on till Christmas, and every day there was justs made for a diamond, who that justed best should have a diamond. But Sir Launcelot would not just, but if it were at a great justs cried. But Sir Lavaine justed there all that Christmas passing well, and best was praised; for there were but few that did so well. Wherefore all manner of knights deemed that Sir Lavaine should be made knight of the Round Table at the next feast of Pentecost. So at after Christmas king Arthur let call unto him many knights, and there they advised together to make a party and a great tournament and justs. And the king of Northgalis said to Arthur he would have on his party king Anguish of Ireland, and the king with the hundred knights, and the king of Northumberland, and Sir Galahalt the haut prince; and so these four kings and this mighty duke took party against king Arthur and the knights of the Table Round. And the cry was made that the day of the justs should be beside Westminster on Candlemas day, whereof many knights were glad, and made them ready to be at that justs in the freshest manner. Then queen Guenever sent for Sir Launcelot, and said thus: I warn you that ye ride no more in no justs nor tournaments, but that your kinsmen may know you. And at these justs that shall be, ye shall have of me a sleeve of gold; and I pray you, for my sake, enforce yourself there that men may speak of you worship. But I charge you as ye will have my love, that ye warn your kinsmen that ye will bear that day the sleeve of gold upon your helmet. Madam, said Sir Launcelot, it shall be done. And so either made great joy of other. And when Sir Launcelot saw his time, he told Sir Bors that he would depart, and have no more with him but Sir Lavaine, unto the good hermit that dwelled in the forest of Windsor, his name was Sir Brastias, and there he thought to repose him, and to take all the rest that he might, because he would be fresh at that day of justs. So Sir Launcelot and Sir Lavaine departed, that no creature wist where he was become, but the noble men of his blood. And when he was come to the hermitage, wit you well he had good cheer. And so daily Sir Launcelot would go to a well fast by the hermitage, and there he would lie down, and see the well spring and bubble, and sometime he slept there. So at that time there was a lady dwelled in that forest, and she was a great huntress, and daily she used to hunt, and always she bare her bow with her; and no men went never with her, but always women, and they were shooters, and could well kill a deer, both at the stalk and at the trest; and they daily bare bows and arrows, horns and wood-knives, and many good dogs they had, both for the string and for a bait. So it happed that this lady, the huntress, had baited her dogs for the bow at a barren hind, and so this barren

hind took her flight over heaths and woods, and ever this lady and part of her gentlewomen coasted the hind, and checked it by the noise of the hounds, to have met with the hind at some water. And so it happed the hind came to the well whereas Sir Launcelot was sleeping and slumbering. And so when the hind came to the well, for heat she went to soil, and there she lay a great while; and the dogs came fast after, and umbecast about, for she had lost the very perfect track of the hind. Right so, there came that lady the huntress, that knew by the dog that she had that the hind was at the soil in that well. And there she came stiffly, and found the hind, and she put a broad arrow in her bow, and shot at the hind, and overshot the hind, and so, by misfortune, the arrow smote Sir Launcelot in the thick of the thigh, over the barbs. When Sir Launcelot felt himself so hurt, he hurled up woodly, and saw the lady that had smitten him. And when he saw she was a woman, he said thus, Lady, or damsel, what that thou be, in an evil time bare ye a bow, the devil made you a shooter.

CHAP. XXII.

How Launcelot after that he was hurt of a gentlewoman came to an hermit, and of other matters.

Now mercy, fair sir, said the lady, I am a gentlewoman that useth here in this forest hunting, and truly I saw you not, but as here was a barren hind at the soil in this well, and I wend to have done well, but my hand swerved. Alas, said Sir Launcelot, ye have mischieved me. And so the lady departed, and Sir Launcelot, as well as he might, pulled out the arrow, and the head abode still in his thigh; and so he went weakly to the hermitage, evermore bleeding as he went. And when Sir Lavaine and the hermit espied that Sir Launcelot was hurt, wit you well they were passing heavy: but Sir Lavaine nor the hermit wist not how he was hurt, nor by whom. And then they were wroth out of measure. Then with great pain the hermit gat out the arrow's head out of Sir Launcelot's thigh, and much of his blood he shed, and the wound was passing sore, and unhappily smitten; for it was in such a place that he might not sit in no saddle. Ah, mercy, said Sir Launcelot, I call myself the most unhappiest man that liveth; for ever when I would fainest have worship, there befalleth me ever some unhappy thing. Now, so heaven me help, I shall be in the field upon Candlemas day at the justs, whatsoever fall of it. So all that might be gotten to heal Sir Launcelot was had. So when the day was come, Sir Launcelot let devise that he was arrayed, and Sir Lavaine, and their horses, as though they had been Saracens. And so they departed, and came nigh to the field. The king of Northgalis with an hundred knights with him, and the king of Northumberland brought with him an hundred good knights, and king Anguish of Ireland brought with him an hundred good knights ready to just, and Sir Galahalt the haut prince brought with him an hundred good knights, and the king with the hundred knights brought with him as many; and all these were proved good knights. Then came in king Arthur's party, and there came in the king of Scots with an hundred knights, and king Uriens of Gore brought with him an hundred good knights, and king Howel of Britanny brought with him an hundred knights. And Chalance of Clarance brought with him an hundred knights, and king Arthur himself came into the field with two hundred knights, and the most part were knights of the Table Round that were proved noble knights. And there were old knights set in scaffolds, for to judge with the queen who did best.

CHAP. XXIII.

How Sir Launcelot behaved him at the justs, and other men also.

THEN they blew to the field, and there the king of Northgalis encountered with the king of Scots, and there the king of

Scots had a fall, and the king of Ireland smote down king Uriens, and the king of Northumberland smote down king Howel of Britanny, and Sir Galahalt, the haut prince, smote down Chalance of Clarance. And then king Arthur was wood wroth, and ran to the king with the hundred knights, and there king Arthur smote him down, and after with that same spear king Arthur smote down three other knights. And then when his spear was broken king Arthur did passing well. And so therewithal came in Sir Gawaine, and Sir Gaheris, Sir Agravaine, and Sir Mordred, and there every each of them smote down a knight, and Sir Gawaine smote down four knights. And then there began a strong meddle, for then there came in the knights of Launcelot's blood, and Sir Gareth and Sir Palamides with them, and many knights of the Table Round, and they began to hold the four kings and the mighty duke so hard that they were discomfit, but this duke Galahalt the haut prince was a noble knight, and by his mighty prowess of arms he held the knights of the Table Round straight enough. All this doing saw Sir Launcelot, and then he came into the field with Sir Lavaine, as it had been thunder. And then anon Sir Bors and the knights of his blood espied Sir Launcelot, and said to them all, I warn you beware of him with the sleeve of gold upon his head, for he is himself Sir Launcelot du Lake. And for great goodness Sir Bors warned Sir Gareth. I am well apayed, said Sir Gareth, that I may know him. But who is he, said they all, that rideth with him in the same array? That is the good and gentle knight Sir Lavaine, said Sir Bors. So Sir Launcelot encountered with Sir Gawaine, and there by force Sir Launcelot smote down Sir Gawaine and his horse to the earth, and so he smote down Sir Agravaine and Sir Gaheris, and also he smote down Sir Mordred, and all this was with one spear. Then Sir Lavaine met with Sir Palamides, and either met other so hard and so fiercely that both their horses fell to the earth. And then were they horsed again, and then met Sir Launcelot with Sir Palamides, and there Sir Palamides had a fall. And so Sir Launcelot, or ever he stint, as fast as he might get spears, he smote down thirty knights, and the most part of them were knights of the Table Round. And ever the knights of his blood withdrew them, and made them ado in other places where Sir Launcelot came not; and then king Arthur was wroth when he saw Sir Launcelot do such deeds, and then the king called unto him Sir Gawaine, Sir Mordred, Sir Kay, Sir Griflet, Sir Lucan the butler, Sir Bedivere, Sir Palamides, and Safere his brother; and so the king with these nine knights made them ready to set upon Sir Launcelot and upon Sir Lavaine. All this espied Sir Bors and Sir Gareth. Now I dread me sore, said Sir Bors, that my lord Sir Launcelot will be hard matched. By my head, said Sir Gareth, I will ride unto my lord Sir Launcelot for to help him, fall of him what may, for he is the same man that made me knight. Ye shall not so, said Sir Bors, by my counsel, unless that ye were disguised. Ye shall see me disguised, said Sir Gareth; and therewithal he espied a Welsh knight where he was to repose himself, and he was sore hurt afore by Sir Gawaine, and to him Sir Gareth rode, and prayed him of his knighthood to lend him his shield for his. I will well, said the Welsh knight. And when Sir Gareth had his shield, the book saith, it was green, with a maiden that seemed in it. Then Sir Gareth came driving to Sir Launcelot all that he might, and said, Knight, keep thyself, for yonder cometh king Arthur with nine noble knights with him to put you to a rebuke, and so I am come to bear you fellowship for old love ye have shewed me. Gramercy, said Sir Launcelot. Sir, said Sir Gareth, encounter ye with Sir Gawaine, and I shall encounter with Sir Palamides, and let Sir Lavaine match with the noble king Arthur. And when we have delivered them, let us three hold us sadly together. Then came king Arthur with his nine knights with him, and Sir Laun-

celot encountered with Sir Gawaine, and gave him such a buffet that the bow of his saddle brast, and Sir Gawaine fell to the earth. Then Sir Gareth encountered with the good knight Sir Palamides, and he gave him such a buffet that both his horse and he dashed to the earth. Then encountered king Arthur with Sir Lavaine, and there either of them smote other to the earth, horse and all, that they lay a great while. Then Sir Launcelot smote down Sir Agravaine, and Sir Gaheris, and Sir Mordred. And Sir Gareth smote down Sir Kay, Sir Safere, and Sir Griflet. And then Sir Lavaine was horsed again, and he smote down Sir Lucan the butler, and Sir Bedivere, and then there began great throng of good knights. Then Sir Launcelot hurtled here and there, and rased and pulled off helms, so that at that time there might none sit him a buffet with spear nor with sword. And Sir Gareth did such deeds of arms that all men wondered what knight he was with the green shield; for he smote down that day and pulled down more than thirty knights. And, as the French book saith, Sir Launcelot marvelled, when he beheld Sir Gareth do such deeds, what knight he might be: and Sir Lavaine pulled down and smote down twenty knights. Also Sir Launcelot knew not Sir Gareth, for, and Sir Tristram de Liones or Sir Lamorak de Galis had been alive, Sir Launcelot would have deemed he had been one of them twain. So ever as Sir Launcelot, Sir Gareth, Sir Lavaine, fought, and on the one side Sir Bors, Sir Ector de Maris, Sir Lionel, Sir Lamorak de Galis, Sir Bleoberis, Sir Galihud, Sir Galihodin, Sir Pelleas, and with more other of king Ban's blood, fought upon another party, and held the king with the hundred knights, and also the king of Northumberland, right straight.

CHAP. XXIV.

How king Arthur marvelled much of the justing in the field, and how he rode and found Sir Launcelot.

So this tournament and this justs

dured long, till it was near night, for the knights of the Round Table relieved ever unto king Arthur; for the king was wroth out of measure that he and his knights might not prevail that day. Then Sir Gawaine said to the king, I marvel where all this day Sir Bors de Ganis and his fellowship of Sir Launcelot's blood be. I marvel all this day they be not about you. It is for some cause, said Sir Gawaine. By my head, said Sir Kay, Sir Bors is yonder all this day upon the right hand of this field, and there he and his blood done more worshipfully than we do. It may well be, said Sir Gawaine, but I dread me ever of guile, for on pain of my life, said Sir Gawaine, this knight with the red sleeve of gold is himself Sir Launcelot, I see well by his riding and by his great strokes, and the other knight in the same colour is the good young knight Sir Lavaine. Also that knight with the green shield is my brother Sir Gareth, and yet he hath disguised himself, for no man shall never make him be against Sir Launcelot, because he made him knight. By my head, said Arthur, nephew, I believe you, therefore tell me now what is your best counsel? Sir, said Sir Gawaine, ye shall have my counsel. Let blow unto lodging, for, and he be Sir Launcelot du Lake, and my brother Sir Gareth with him, with the help of that good young knight Sir Lavaine, trust me truly it will be no boot to strive with them, but if we should fall ten or twelve upon one knight, and that were no worship, but shame. Ye say truth, said the king, and for to say sooth, said the king, it were shame to us, so many as we be, to set upon them any more. For wit ye well, said the king, they be three good knights, and namely that knight with the sleeve of gold. So then they blew unto lodging; but forthwithal king Arthur let send unto the four kings, and to the mighty duke, and prayed them that the knight with the sleeve of gold depart not from them, but that the king may speak with him. Then forthwithal king Arthur alight, and unarmed

him, and took a little hackney, and rode after Sir Launcelot, for ever he had a spy upon him; and so he found him among the four kings and the duke, and there the king prayed them all unto supper. And they said they would with good will. And so when they were unarmed, then king Arthur knew Sir Launcelot, Sir Lavaine, and Sir Gareth. Ah Sir Launcelot, said king Arthur, this day ye have heated me and my knights. So they went unto Arthur's lodging all together, and there was a great feast and great revel, and the prize was given unto Sir Launcelot, and by heralds they named him that he had smitten down fifty knights, and Sir Gareth five and thirty, and Sir Lavaine four and twenty knights. Then Sir Launcelot told the king and the queen how the lady huntress shot him in the forest of Windsor in the thigh with a broad arrow, and how the wound thereof was that time six inches deep, and in like long. Also Arthur blamed Sir Gareth, because he left his fellowship and held with Sir Launcelot. My lord, said Sir Gareth, he made me a knight, and when I saw him so hard bestad, me thought it was my worship to help him, for I saw him do so much, and so many noble knights against him. And when I understood that he was Sir Launcelot du Lake I shamed to see so many knights against him alone. Truly, said king Arthur unto Sir Gareth, ye say well, and worshipfully have ye done, and to yourself great worship, and all the days of my life, said king Arthur unto Sir Gareth, wit you well I shall love you and trust you the more better. For ever, said Arthur, it is a worshipful knight's deed to help another worshipful knight when he seeth him in a great danger, for ever a worshipful man will be loth to see a worshipful shamed, and he that is of no worship, and fareth with cowardice, never shall he shew gentleness, nor no manner of goodness, where he seeth a man in any danger, for then ever will a coward shew no mercy, and always a good man will do ever to another man as he would be done to himself. So then there were great feasts unto kings and dukes; and revel, game, and play, and all manner of nobleness was used; and he that was courteous, true, and faithful to his friend, was that time cherished.

CHAP. XXV.

How true love is likened to summer.

AND thus it passed on from Candlemas until after Easter, that the month of May was come, when every lusty heart beginneth to blossom and to bring forth fruit; for like as herbs and trees bring forth fruit and flourish in May, in likewise every lusty heart, that is in any manner a lover, springeth and flourisheth in lusty deeds. For it giveth unto all lovers courage, that lusty month of May, in some thing to constrain him to some manner of thing, more in that month than in any other month, for divers causes. For then all herbs and trees renew a man and woman, and in likewise lovers call again to their mind old gentleness and old service, and many kind deeds that were forgotten by negligence. For like as winter rasure doth always arase and deface green summer, so fareth it by unstable love in man and woman. For in many persons there is no stability, for we may see all day, for a little blast of winter's rasure, anon we shall deface and lay apart true love for little or nought, that cost much thing. This is no wisdom nor stability, but it is feeble-ness of nature and great disworship whosoever useth this. Therefore, like as May month flowereth and flourisheth in many gardens, so in likewise let every man of worship flourish his heart in this world, first unto God, and next unto the joy of them that he promised his faith unto, for there was never worshipful man nor worshipful woman, but they loved one better than another: and worship in arms may never be foiled, but first reserve the honour to God, and secondly the quarrel must come of thy lady: and such love I call virtuous love. But now-a-days men cannot love seven night but they must have all their desires, that love may not endure by reason; for where they be soon accorded, and hasty heat, soon it cooleth. Right so fareth love now-a-days; soon hot, soon cold. This is no stability, but the old love was not so. Men and women could love together seven years, and no wanton lusts were between them, and then was love truth and faithfulness. And lo in likewise was used love in king Arthur's days. Wherefore I liken love now-a-days unto summer and winter. For like as the one is hot and the other cold, so fareth love now-a-days. Therefore all ye that be lovers call unto your remembrance the month of May, like as did queen Guenever. For whom I make here a little mention, that while she lived she was a true lover, and therefore she had a good end.

𝕰𝖝𝖕𝖑𝖎𝖈𝖎𝖙 𝖑𝖎𝖇𝖊𝖗 𝕺𝖈𝖙𝖔𝖉𝖊𝖈𝖎𝖒𝖚𝖘.   𝕬𝖓𝖉 𝖍𝖊𝖗𝖊 𝖋𝖔𝖑𝖔𝖜𝖊𝖙𝖍 𝖑𝖎𝖇𝖊𝖗 𝖝𝖎𝖝.

𝕿𝖍𝖊 𝕹𝖎𝖓𝖊𝖙𝖊𝖊𝖓𝖙𝖍 𝕭𝖔𝖔𝖐.

CHAP. I.

How queen Guenever rode on Maying with certain knights of the Round Table and clad all in green.

So it befell in the month of May, queen Guenever called unto her knights of the Table Round, and she gave them warning that early upon the morrow she would ride on maying into woods and fields beside Westminster.— And I warn you that there be none of you but that he be well horsed, and that ye all be clothed in green, either in silk, either in cloth, and I shall bring with me ten ladies, and every knight shall have a lady behind him, and every knight shall have a squire and two yeomen, and I will that ye all be well horsed. So they made them ready in the freshest manner, and these were the names of the knights: Sir Kay the seneschal, Sir Agravaine, Sir Brandiles, Sir Sagramor le Desirous, Sir Dodinas le Savage, Sir Ozanna le Cure Hardy, Sir Ladinas of the Forest Savage, Sir Persant of Inde, Sir Ironside that was called the knight of the red lawns, and Sir Pelleas the lover, and these ten knights made them ready in the freshest manner to ride with the queen. And so upon the morn they took their horses, with the queen, and rode on maying in woods and meadows, as it pleased them, in great joy and delights: for the queen had cast to have been again with king Arthur at the furthest by ten of the clock, and so was that time her purpose. Then there was a knight, that hight Meliagrance, and he was son unto king Bagdemagus, and this knight had at that time a castle, of the gift of king Arthur, within seven mile of Westminster; and this knight Sir Meliagrance loved passing well queen Guenever, and so had he done long and many years. And the book saith he had lain in a wait for to steal away the queen, but evermore he forbare for because of Sir Launcelot, for in no wise he would meddle with the queen, and Sir Launcelot were in her company, or else and he were near hand her. And that time was such a custom the queen rode never without a great fellowship of men of arms about her; and they were many good knights, and the most part were young men that would have worship, and they were called the queen's knights, and never in no battle, tournament, nor justs, they bare none of them no manner of knowledging of their own arms, but plain white shields, and thereby they were called the queen's knights. And then when it happed any of them to be of great worship by his noble deeds,

then at the next feast of Pentecost, if there were any slain or dead, as there was no year that there failed but some were dead, then was there chosen in his stead that was dead the most men of worship that were called the queen's knights. And thus they came up all first, or they were renowned men of worship, both Sir Launcelot and all the remnant of them. But this knight, Sir Meliagrance, had espied the queen well and her purpose, and how Sir Launcelot was not with her, and how she had no men of arms with her but the ten noble knights all arrayed in green for maying. Then he provided him a twenty men of arms and an hundred archers, for to destroy the queen and her knights, for he thought that time was the best season to take the queen.

CHAP. II.

How Sir Meliagraunce took the queen and all her knights, which were sore hurt in fighting.

So as the queen had mayed and all her knights, all were bedashed with herbs, mosses, and flowers, in the best manner and freshest. Right so came out of a wood Sir Meliagrance with an eight score men well harnessed, as they should fight in a battle of arrest, and bad the queen and her knights abide, for maugre their heads they should abide. Traitor knight, said queen Guenever, what castest thou for to do? Wilt thou shame thyself? Bethink thee how thou art a king's son, and knight of the Table Round, and thou to be about to dishonour the noble king that made thee knight: thou shamest all knighthood and thyself, and me, I let thee wit, shalt thou never shame, for I had lever cut my throat in twain than thou shouldest dishonour me. As for all this language, said Sir Meliagrance, be it as it may, for wit you well, madam, I have loved you many a year, and never or now could I get you at such an advantage as I do now, and therefore I will take you as I find you. Then spake all the ten noble knights at once, and said, Sir Meliagrance, wit thou well ye are about to jeopard your worship to dishonour, and also ye cast to jeopard our persons; howbeit we be unarmed, ye have us at a great avail, for it seemeth by you that ye have laid watch upon us, but rather then ye should put the queen to shame, and us all, we had as lief to depart from our lives, for and if we other ways did we were shamed for ever. Then Sir Meliagrance said, Dress you as well as ye can, and keep the queen. Then the ten knights of the Table Round drew their swords, and the other let run at them with their spears, and the ten knights manly abode them, and smote away their spears, that no spear did them none harm. Then they lashed together with swords, and anon Sir Kay, Sir Sagramor, Sir Agravaine, Sir Dodinas, Sir Ladinas, and Sir Ozanna, were smitten to the earth with grimly wounds. Then Sir Brandiles, and Sir Persant, Sir Ironside, Sir Pelleas, fought long, and they were sore wounded: for these ten knights, or ever they were laid to the ground, slew forty men of the boldest and the best of them. So when the queen saw her knights thus dolefully wounded, and needs must be slain at the last, then for pity and sorrow she cried, Sir Meliagrance, slay not my noble knights, and I will go with thee upon this covenant, that thou save them, and suffer them not to be no more hurt, with this, that they be led with me wheresoever thou leadest me; for I will rather slay myself than I will go with thee, unless that these my noble knights may be in my presence. Madam, said Meliagrance, for your sake they shall be led with you into mine own castle, with that ye will be ruled and ride with me. Then the queen prayed the four knights to leave their fighting, and she and they would not part. Madam, said Sir Pelleas, we will do as ye do, for as for me I take no force of my life nor death. For, as the French book saith, Sir Pelleas gave such buffets there that none armour might hold him.

CHAP. III.

How Sir Launcelot had word how the queen was taken, and how Sir Meliagraunce laid a bushment for Launcelot.

THEN by the queen's commandment they left battle, and dressed the wounded knights on horseback, some sitting, some overthwart their horses, that it was pity to behold them. And then Sir Meliagrance charged the queen and all her knights that none of all her fellowship should depart from her; for full sore he drad Sir Launcelot du Lake, lest he should have any knowledging. All this espied the queen, and privily she called unto her a child of her chamber, that was swiftly horsed, to whom she said, Go thou, when thou seest thy time, and bear this ring unto Sir Launcelot du Lake, and pray him as he loveth me, that he will see me, and rescue me if ever he will have joy of me; and spare thou not thy horse, said the queen, neither for water, neither for land. So the child espied his time, and lightly he took his horse with the spurs, and departed as fast as he might. And when Sir Meliagrance saw him so flee, he understood that it was by the queen's commandment for to warn Sir Launcelot. Then they that were best horsed chased him, and shot at him, but from them all the child went suddenly; and then Sir Meliagrance said unto the queen, Madam, ye are about to betray me, but I shall ordain for Sir Launcelot that he shall not come lightly at you. And then he rode with her and they all to his castle in all the haste that he might. And by the way Sir Meliagrance laid in an enbushment the best archers that he might get in his country, to the number of a thirty, to await upon Sir Launcelot, charging them that if they saw such a manner of knight come by the way upon a white horse, that in any wise they slay his horse, but in no manner of wise have not ado with him bodily, for he is over hard to be overcome. So this was done, and they were come to his castle, but in no wise the queen would never let none of the ten knights and her ladies out of her sight, but always they were in her presence, for the book saith Sir Meliagrance durst make no masteries for dread of Sir Launcelot, in so much he deemed that he had warning. So when the child was departed from the fellowship of Sir Meliagrance, within awhile he came to Westminster. And anon he found Sir Launcelot. And when he had told his message, and delivered him the queen's ring, Alas, said Sir Launcelot, now am I shamed for ever, unless that I may rescue that noble lady from dishonour. Then eagerly he asked his armour, and ever the child told Sir Launcelot how the ten knights fought marvellously, and how Sir Pelleas, and Sir Ironside, and Sir Brandiles, and Sir Persant of Inde, fought strongly, but namely Sir Pelleas, there might none withstand him, and how they all fought till at the last they were laid to the earth, and then the queen made appointment for to save their lives, and go with Sir Meliagrance. Alas, said Sir Launcelot, that most noble lady, that she should be so destroyed! I had lever, said Sir Launcelot, than all France that I had been there well armed. So when Sir Launcelot was armed and upon his horse, he prayed the child of the queen's chamber to warn Sir Lavaine how suddenly he was departed, and for what cause,—And pray him, as he loveth me, that he will hie him after me, and that he stint not until he come to the castle where Sir Meliagrance abideth or dwelleth, for there, said Sir Launcelot, shall he hear of me and I am a man living, and rescue the queen and the ten knights the which he traitorously hath taken, and that shall I prove upon his head, and all them that hold with him.

CHAP. IV.

How Sir Launcelot's horse was slain, and how Sir Launcelot rode in a cart for to rescue the queen.

THEN Sir Launcelot rode as fast as he might, and the book saith he took the water at Westminster bridge, and made his horse to swim over Thames to Lambeth. And then within a while he came to the place there as the ten knights had fought with Sir Meliagrance, and then Sir Launcelot followed that track until that he came to a wood, and there was a strait way, and there the thirty archers bad Sir Launcelot turn again, and follow no longer that track. What commandment have ye thereto, said Sir Launcelot, to cause me, that am a knight of the Round Table, to leave my right way? This way shalt thou leave, or else thou shalt go it on thy foot, for wit thou well thy horse shall be slain. That is little mastery, said Sir Launcelot, to slay my horse, but as for myself, when my horse is slain, I give right nought for you, not and ye were five hundred more. So then they shot Sir Launcelot's horse, and smote him with many arrows. And then Sir Launcelot avoided his horse, and went on foot: but there were so many ditches and hedges betwixt them and him, that he might not meddle with none of them. Alas, for shame, said Launcelot, that ever one knight should betray another knight, but it is an old saw, A good man is never in danger but when he is in the danger of a coward. Then Sir Launcelot went a while, and then he was foul cumbered of his armour, his shield, and his spear, and all that longed unto him. Wit ye well he was full sore annoyed, and full loth he was to leave any thing that longed unto him, for he drad sore the treason of Sir Meliagrance. And then by fortune there came by a chariot, that came thither for to fetch wood. Say me, carter, said Sir Launcelot, what shall I give thee for to suffer me to leap into thy chariot, and that thou bring me unto a castle within this two mile? Thou shalt not come within my chariot, said the carter, for I am sent for to fetch wood for my lord Sir Meliagrance. — With him would I speak.—Thou shalt not go with me, said the carter. Then Sir Launcelot lept to him, and gave him such a buffet that he fell to the earth stark dead.

Then the other carter his fellow was afeard, and wend to have gone the same way, and then he cried, Fair lord, save my life, and I shall bring you where you will. Then I charge thee, said Sir Launcelot, that thou drive me and this chariot, even unto Sir Meliagrance's gate. Leap up into the chariot, said the carter, and ye shall be there anon. So the carter drove on a great wallop, and Sir Launcelot's horse followed the chariot, with more than a forty arrows broad and rough in him: and more than an hour and an half dame Guenever was in a bay window with her ladies, and espied an armed knight standing in a chariot. See madam, said a lady, where rideth in a chariot a goodly armed knight, I suppose he rideth unto hanging. Where? said the queen. Then she espied by his shield that he was there himself Sir Launcelot du Lake. And then she was ware where came his horse ever after that chariot, and ever he trod his entrails and his paunch under his feet. Alas, said the queen, now I see well and prove that well is him that hath a trusty friend. Ha, a, most noble knight, I see well thou art hard bestad when thou ridest in a chariot. Then she rebuked that lady that likened Sir Launcelot to ride in a chariot to hanging. It was foul mouthed, said the queen, and evil likened, so for to liken the most noble knight of the world unto such a shameful death. O Jesu defend him and keep him, said the queen, from all mischievous end! By this was Sir Launcelot come to the gates of that castle, and there he descended down, and cried, that all the castle rang of it, Where art thou, false traitor Sir Meliagrance, and knight of the Table Round? Now come forth here thou traitor knight, thou and thy fellowship with thee: for here I am, Sir Launcelot du Lake, that shall fight with you. And therewithal he bare the gate wide open upon the porter, and smote him under his ear with his gauntlet that his neck brast in sunder.

CHAP. V.

How Sir Meliagraunce required forgiveness of the queen, and how she appeased Sir Launcelot, and other matters.

WHEN Sir Meliagrance heard that Sir Launcelot was there, he ran unto queen Guenever, and fell upon his knee, and said, Mercy, madam, now I put me wholly into your grace. What aileth you now? said queen Guenever. Forsooth I might well wit some good knight would revenge me, though my lord Arthur wist not of this your work. Madam, said Sir Meliagrance, all this that is amiss on my part shall be amended right as yourself will devise, and wholly I put me in your grace. What would ye that I did? said the queen. I would no more, said Meliagrance, but that ye would take all in your own hands, and that ye will rule my lord Sir Launcelot, and such cheer as may be made him in this poor castle ye and he shall have until to-morn, and then may ye and all they return unto Westminster, and my body and all that I have I shall put in your rule. Ye say well, said the queen, and better is peace than ever war, and the less noise the more is my worship. Then the queen and her ladies went down unto the knight Sir Launcelot, that stood wroth out of measure in the inner court, to abide battle; and ever he bade—Thou traitor knight, come forth! Then the queen came to him and said, Sir Launcelot, why be ye so moved? Ha, madam, said Sir Launcelot, why ask ye me that question? me seemeth, said Sir Launcelot, ye ought to be more wroth than I am, for ye have the hurt and the dishonour. For wit ye well, madam, my hurt is but little, for the killing of a mare's son; but the despite grieveth me much more than all my hurt. Truly, said the queen, ye say truth, but heartily I thank you, said the queen, but ye must come in with me peaceably, for all thing is put in my hand, and all that is evil shall be for the best, for the knight full sore repenteth him of the misadventure that is befallen him. Madam, said Sir

Launcelot, sith it is so that ye are accorded with him, as for me I may not be against it, howbeit Sir Meliagrance hath done full shamefully to me, and cowardly. Ah, madam, and I had wist ye would have been so soon accorded with him, I would not have made such haste unto you. Why say ye so? said the queen, do ye forthink yourself of your good deeds? Wit you well, said the queen, I accorded never unto him for favour nor love that I had unto him, but for to lay down every shameful noise. Madam, said Sir Launcelot, ye understand full well I was never willing nor glad of shameful slander, nor noise; and there is neither king, queen, nor knight, that beareth the life, except my lord king Arthur, and you, madam, that should let me, but I should make Sir Meliagrance's heart full cold or ever I departed from hence. That I wot well, said the queen, but what will ye more? ye shall have all thing ruled as ye list to have it. Madam, said Sir Launcelot, so ye be pleased I care not, as for my part ye shall soon please. Right so the queen took Sir Launcelot by the bare hand, for he had put off his gauntlet, and so she went with him till her chamber; and then she commanded him to be unarmed, and then Sir Launcelot asked where the ten knights were that were wounded sore. So she shewed them unto Sir Launcelot, and there they made great joy of the coming of him, and Sir Launcelot made great dole of their hurts, and bewailed them greatly; and there Sir Launcelot told them how cowardly and traitorly Meliagrance set archers to slay his horse, and how he was fain to put himself in a chariot. Thus they complained every each to other, and full fain they would have been revenged, but they peaced themself because of the queen. Then, as the French book saith, Sir Launcelot was called many a day after, Le Chevaler du Chariot, and did many deeds, and great adventures he had. And so leave we of this tale, Le Chevaler du Chariot, and turn we to this tale..

So Sir Launcelot had great cheer with the queen, and then Sir Launcelot made a promise with the queen, that the same night Sir Launcelot should come to a window outward toward a garden, and that window was y-barred with iron; and there Sir Launcelot promised to meet her when all folks were on sleep. So then came Sir Lavaine, driving to the gates, crying, Where is my lord Sir Launcelot du Lake? Then was he sent for, and when Sir Lavaine saw Sir Launcelot, he said: My lord, I found well how ye were hard bestad, for I have found your horse, that was slain with arrows. As for that, said Sir Launcelot, I pray you Sir Lavaine speak ye of other matters, and let ye this pass, and we shall right it another time, when we best may.

CHAP. VI.

How Sir Launcelot came in the night to the queen, and how Sir Meliagraunce appeached the queen of treason.

THEN the knights that were hurt were searched, and soft salves were laid to their wounds, and so it passed on till supper time; and all the cheer that might be made them there was done unto the queen and all her knights. Then when season was they went unto their chambers. But in no wise the queen would not suffer the wounded knights to be from her, but that they were laid within draughts by her chamber, upon beds and pillows, that she herself might see to them, that they wanted nothing. So when Launcelot was in his chamber that was assigned unto him, he called unto Sir Lavaine, and told him that he must go speak with his lady, dame Guenever. Sir, said Sir Lavaine, let me go with you, and it please you, for I dread me sore of the treason of Sir Meliagrance. Nay, said Sir Launcelot, I thank you, but I will have nobody with me. Then Sir Launcelot took his sword in his hand, and privily went unto a place whereas he had espied a ladder toforehand, and that he took under his arm and bare it through the garden, and set it up to the window. And there anon the queen was ready to meet him. And then they made either to other their complaints of many divers things. And then Sir Launcelot wished that he might have come in to her. Wit ye well, said the queen, I would as fain as ye that ye might come in to me. Would ye, madam, said Sir Launcelot, with your heart that I were with you? Yea truly, said the queen. Now shall I prove my might, said Sir Launcelot, for your love. And then he set his hands upon the bars of iron, and pulled at them with such a might that he brast them clean out of the stone walls. And therewithal one of the bars of iron cut the brawn of his hands throughout to the bone, and then he lept into the chamber to the queen. Make ye no noise, said the queen, for my wounded knights lie here fast by me. And when he saw his time that he might tarry no longer, he took his leave and departed at the window, and put it together as well as he might again, and so departed unto his own chamber; and there he told Sir Lavaine how he was hurt; then Sir Lavaine dressed his hand, and staunched it, and put upon it a glove, that it should not be espied. And so the queen lay long in her bed, until it was nine of the clock. Then Sir Meliagrance went to the queen's chamber, and found her ladies there ready clothed. Mercy, said Sir Meliagrance, what aileth you, madam, that ye sleep thus long? And then was he ware of the blood of Sir Launcelot's hurt hand. And when Sir Meliagrance espied that blood, then he deemed in himself that she was false unto the king, and that it was the blood of some of the wounded knights. Ah, madam, said Sir Meliagrance, now I have founden you a false traitress unto my lord Arthur; for now I prove well it was not for nought that ye laid these wounded knights within the bounds of your chamber: therefore I will call you of treason before my lord king Arthur, and now I have proved you, madam, with a shameful deed, and that they be all false, or some of them, I will

make good, for a wounded knight hath been here. That is false, said the queen, and that I will report me to them all. Then when the ten knights heard Sir Meliagrance's words, they spake all in one voice and said unto Sir Meliagrance, Thou sayest falsely, and wrongfully puttest upon us such a deed, and that we will make good any of us, choose which thou list of us, when we are whole of our wounds. Ye shall not, said Sir Meliagrance, away with your proud language, for here ye may all see that a wounded knight hath been here. Then were they all ashamed when they saw that blood, and wit you well Sir Meliagrance was passing glad that he had the queen at such an advantage, for he deemed by that to hide his treason. So with this rumour came in Sir Launcelot, and found them all at a great array.

CHAP. VII.

How Sir Launcelot answered for the queen, and waged battle against Sir Meliagraunce. And how Sir Launcelot was taken in a trap.

WHAT array is this? said Sir Launcelot. Then Sir Meliagrance told him what he had found, and shewed him the blood. Truly, said Sir Launcelot, ye did not your part nor knightly toward the queen, and therefore have ye done unworshipfully and shamefully to yourself. I wot not what ye mean, said Sir Meliagrance, but well I am sure there hath been one of her wounded knights here, and therefore I will prove with my hands that she is a traitress unto my lord Arthur. Beware what ye do, said Sir Launcelot, for and ye say so, and that ye will prove it, it will be taken at your hands. My lord Sir Launcelot, said Sir Meliagrance, I rede you beware what ye do, for though ye are never so good a knight, as ye wot well that ye are renowned the best knight of the world, yet should ye be advised to do battle in a wrong quarrel, for God will have a stroke in every battle. As for that, said Sir Launcelot, God is to be dread. But as to that

I say nay plainly, that this night none of these ten wounded knights was here with my lady queen Guenever, and that will I prove with my hands, that ye say untruly in that now. Hold, said Sir Meliagrance, here is my glove, that she is traitress unto my lord king Arthur, and that one of the wounded knights was here. And I receive your glove, said Sir Launcelot. And so they were sealed with their signets, and delivered unto the ten knights. At what day shall we do battle together? said Sir Launcelot. This day eight days, said Sir Meliagrance, in the field beside Westminster. I am agreed, said Sir Launcelot. But now, said Sir Meliagrance, sithen it is that we must fight together, I beseech you, as ye are a noble knight, await me with no treason, nor none villainy the meanwhile, nor none for you. So God me help, said Sir Launcelot, ye shall right well wit I was never of no such conditions, for I report me to all knights that ever have known me, I fared never with no treason, nor I loved never the fellowship of no man that fared with treason. Then let us go to dinner, said Meliagrance, and after dinner ye and the queen and ye may ride all to Westminster. I will well, said Sir Launcelot. And Sir Meliagrance said to Sir Launcelot, Pleaseth it you to see the eftures of this castle? With a good will, said Sir Launcelot. And then they went together from chamber to chamber, for Sir Launcelot dread no perils. For ever a man of worship and of prowess dreadeth least always perils: for they ween every man be as they be. But ever he that fareth with treason putteth oft a man in great danger. So it befell upon Sir Launcelot that no peril dread. As he went with Sir Meliagrance, he trod on a trap, and the board rolled, and therewith Sir Launcelot fell down more than ten fathom into a cave full of straw. And then Sir Meliagrance departed, and made no fare as that he nist where he was. And when Sir Launcelot was thus missed, they marvelled where he was become. And

then queen Guenever and many of them deemed that he was departed as he was wont to do, suddenly. For Sir Meliagrance made suddenly to put away on side Sir Lavaine's horse, that they might all understand that Sir Launcelot was departed suddenly. So it past on till after dinner, and then Sir Lavaine would not stint until that he ordained litters for the wounded knights, that they might be laid in them, and so with the queen and them all, both ladies and gentlewomen and other, went unto Westminster, and there the knights told king Arthur how Meliagrance had appealed the queen of high treason, and how Sir Launcelot had received the glove of him, and this day eight days they shall do battle afore you. By my head, said king Arthur, I am afeard Sir Meliagrance hath taken upon him a great charge. But where is Sir Launcelot? said the king. Sir, said they all, we wot not where he is, but we deem he is ridden to some adventures, as he is ofttimes wont to do, for he hath Sir Lavaine's horse. Let him be, said the king, he will be founden, but if he be trapped with some treason.

CHAP. VIII.

How Sir Launcelot was delivered out of prison by a lady, and took a white courser, and came for to keep his day.

So leave we Sir Launcelot, lying within that cave in great pain, and every day there came a lady and brought him his meat and his drink, and wooed him to love her. And ever the noble knight Sir Launcelot said her nay. Sir Launcelot, said she, ye are not wise, for ye may never out of this prison but if ye have my help, and also your lady queen Guenever shall be burnt in your default, unless that ye be there at the day of battle. God defend, said Sir Launcelot, that she should be burnt in my default: and if it be so, said Sir Launcelot, that I may not be there, it shall be well understood both at the king and at the queen, and with all men of worship, that I am dead, sick, or in prison. For all men that know me will say for me that I am in some evil case, and I be not there that day, and well I wot there is some good knight, either of my blood, or some other that loveth me, that will take my quarrel in hand : and, therefore, said Sir Launcelot, wit ye well ye shall not fear me. And if there were no more women in all this land but you, I would not say otherwise. Then art thou shamed, said the lady, and destroyed for ever. As for world's shame, Jesu defend me; and as for my distress, it is welcome, whatsoever it be that God sendeth me. So she came to him the same day that the battle should be, and said, Sir Launcelot, me thinketh ye are too hardhearted, but wouldest thou but kiss me once I should deliver thee and thine armour, and the best horse that is within Sir Meliagrance's stable. As for to kiss you, said Sir Launcelot, I may do that, and lose no worship, and wit ye well, and I understood there were any disworship for to kiss you, I would not do it. Then he kissed her, and then she gat him and brought him to his armour. And when he was armed, she brought him to a stable, where stood twelve good coursers, and bad him choose the best. Then Sir Launcelot looked upon a white courser, the which liked him best, and anon he commanded the keepers fast to saddle him with the best saddle of war that there was, and so it was done as he bade. Then gat he his spear in his hand, and his sword by his side, and commanded the lady unto God, and said, Lady, for this good deed I shall do you service if ever it be in my power.

CHAP. IX.

How Sir Launcelot came the same time that Sir Meliagraunce abode him in the field, and dressed him to battle.

Now leave we Sir Launcelot gallop all that he might, and speak we of queen Guenever that was brought to a fire to be burnt, for Sir Meliagrance was sure, him thought, that Sir Laun-

celot should not be at that battle, therefore he ever cried upon king Arthur to do him justice, or else bring forth Sir Launcelot du Lake. Then was the king and all the court full sore abashed and shamed that the queen should be burnt in the default of Sir Launcelot. My lord Arthur, said Sir Lavaine, ye may understand that it is not well with my lord Sir Launcelot, for and he were on live, so that he be not sick or in prison, wit ye well he would be here, for never heard ye that ever he failed his part for whom he should do battle for. And therefore, said Sir Lavaine, my lord king Arthur, I beseech you give me licence to do battle here this day for my lord and master, and for to save my lady the queen. Gramercy, gentle knight, Sir Lavaine, said king Arthur, for I dare say all that Sir Meliagrance putteth upon my lady the queen is wrong, for I have spoken with all the ten wounded knights, and there is not one of them, and he were whole and able to do battle, but he would prove upon Sir Meliagrance's body that it is false that he putteth upon my queen. So shall I, said Sir Lavaine, in the defence of my lord Sir Launcelot, and ye will give me leave. Now I give you leave, said king Arthur, and do your best, for I dare well say there is some treason done to Sir Launcelot. Then was Sir Lavaine horsed, and suddenly at the list's end he rode to perform this battle. And right as the heralds should cry Lesses les aler, right so came in Sir Launcelot driving with all the force of his horse. And then Arthur cried, Ho! and Abide! Then was Sir Launcelot called on horseback tofore king Arthur, and there he told openly tofore the king and all, how Sir Meliagrance had served him first and last. And when the king and the queen and all the lords knew of the treason of Sir Meliagrance, they were all ashamed on his behalf. Then was queen Guenever sent for, and set by the king in great trust of her champion. And then there was no more else to say, but Sir Launcelot and Sir Meliagrance dressed them unto battle, and took their spears, and so they came together as thunder, and there Sir Launcelot bare him down quite over his horse croup. And then Sir Launcelot alight, and dressed his shield on his shoulder with his sword in his hand, and Sir Meliagrance in the same wise dressed him unto him, and there they smote many great strokes together, and at the last Sir Launcelot smote him such a buffet upon the helmet, that he fell on the one side to the earth, and then he cried upon him aloud, Most noble knight, Sir Launcelot du Lake, save my life, for I yield me unto you, and I beseech you, as ye be a knight and fellow of the Table Round, slay me not, for I yield me as overcomen, and whether I shall live or die I put me in the king's hands and yours. Then Sir Launcelot wist not what to do, for he had lever than all the good of the world he might have been revenged upon Sir Meliagrance; and Sir Launcelot looked toward queen Guenever if he might espy by any sign or countenance what she would have done. And then the queen wagged her head upon Sir Launcelot, as though she would say slay him. Full well knew Sir Launcelot by the wagging of her head that she would have had him dead: then Sir Launcelot bad him rise for shame, and perform that battle to the utterance. Nay, said Sir Meliagrance, I will never arise until ye take me as yielden and recreant. I shall proffer you large proffers, said Sir Launcelot, that is to say, I shall unarm my head and my left quarter of my body, all that may be unarmed, and let bind my left hand behind me, so that it shall not help me, and right so I shall do battle with you. Then Sir Meliagrance start up upon his legs, and said on high, My lord Arthur, take heed to this proffer, for I will take it, and let him be disarmed and bounden according to his proffer. What say ye, said king Arthur unto Sir Launcelot, will ye abide by your proffer? Yea, my lord, said Sir Launcelot, I will never go from that I have once said. Then the knights

parters of the field disarmed Sir Launcelot, first his head, and sithen his left arm and his left side, and they bound his left arm behind his back, without shield or anything, and then they were put together. Wit you well there was many a lady and knight marvelled that Sir Launcelot would jeopardy himself in such wise. Then Sir Meliagrance came with his sword all on high, and Sir Launcelot shewed him openly his bare head and the bare left side. And when he wend to have smitten him upon the bare head, then lightly he avoided the left leg and the left side, and put his right hand and his sword to that stroke, and so put it on side with great sleight, and then with great force Sir Launcelot smote him on the helmet such a buffet that the stroke carved the head in two parts. Then there was no more to do but he was drawn out of the field. And at the great instance of the knights of the Table Round the king suffered him to be interred, and the mention made upon him who slew him, and for what cause he was slain. And then the king and the queen made more of Sir Launcelot, and more he was cherished, than ever he was aforehand.

CHAP. X.

How Sir Urre came into Arthur's court for to be healed of his wounds, and how king Arthur would begin to handle him.

THEN, as the French book maketh mention, there was a good knight in the land of Hungary, his name was Sir Urre, and he was an adventurous knight, and in all places where he might hear of any deeds of worship, there would he be. So it happened in Spain there was an earl's son, his name was Alphegus, and at a great tournament in Spain this Sir Urre, knight of Hungary, and Sir Alphegus of Spain, encountered together for very envy, and so either undertook other to the utterance, and by fortune Sir Urre slew Sir Alphegus, the earl's son of Spain. But this knight that was slain had given Sir Urre, or ever he was slain, seven great wounds, three on the head, and four on his body and upon his left hand. And this Sir Alphegus had a mother, the which was a great sorceress, and she, for the despite of her son's death, wrought by her subtile crafts that Sir Urre should never be whole, but ever his wounds should one time fester and another time bleed, so that he should never be whole, until the best knight of the world had searched his wounds, and thus she made her avaunt, where through it was known that Sir Urre should never be whole. Then his mother let make an horse-litter, and put him therein under two palfreys, and then she took Sir Urre's sister with him, a full fair damsel, whose name was Felelolie, and then she took a page with him to keep their horses, and so they led Sir Urre through many countries. For, as the French book saith, she led him so seven year through all lands christened, and never she could find no knight that might ease her son. So she came into Scotland, and into the lands of England, and by fortune she came nigh the feast of Pentecost until Arthur's court, that at that time was holden at Carlisle. And when she came there, then she made it openly to be known how that she was come into that land for to heal her son.

Then king Arthur let call the lady, and asked her the cause why she brought that hurt knight into that land. My most noble king, said that lady, wit you well I brought him hither for to be healed of his wounds, that of all this seven year he might not be whole. And then she told the king where he was wounded, and of whom, and how his mother had discovered in her pride how she had wrought that by enchantment, so that he should never be whole until the best knight of the world had searched his wounds :—And so I have passed through all the lands christened to have him healed, except this land : and if I fail to heal him here in this land, I will never take more pain upon me, and that is pity, for he was a good knight, and of great noble-

ness. What is his name? said Arthur. My good and gracious lord, she said, his name is Sir Urre of the Mount. In good time, said the king, and sith ye are come into this land ye are right welcome. And wit you well here shall your son be healed, and ever any christian man may heal him. And for to give all other men of worship courage I myself will assay to handle your son, and so shall all the kings, dukes, and earls that be here present with me at this time; thereto will I command them, and well I wot they shall obey and do after my commandment. And wit you well, said king Arthur unto Urre's sister, I shall begin to handle him and search unto my power, not presuming upon me that I am so worthy to heal your son by my deeds, but I will encourage other men of worship to do as I will do. And then the king commanded all the kings, dukes, and earls, and all noble knights of the Round Table that were there that time present, to come into the meadow of Carlisle. And so at that time there were but an hundred and ten of the Round Table, for forty knights were that time away. And so here we must begin at king Arthur, as is kindly to begin at him that was the most man of worship that was christened at that time.

CHAP. XI.

How king Arthur handled Sir Urre, and after him many other knights of the Round Table.

THEN king Arthur looked upon Sir Urre, and the king thought he was a full likely man when he was whole. And king Arthur made him to be taken down off the litter, and laid him upon the earth, and there was laid a cushion of gold that he should kneel upon. And then Arthur said, Noble fair knight, me repenteth of thy hurt, and for to courage all other noble knights I will pray thee softly to suffer me to handle your wounds. Most noble christened king, said Urre, do as ye list, for I am at the mercy of God, and at your commandment. So then Arthur softly handled him, and then some of his wounds renewed upon bleeding. Then the king Clariance of Northumberland searched, and it would not be. And then Sir Barant le Apres, that was called the king with the hundred knights, he assayed, and failed; and so did king Urience, of the land of Gore. So did king Anguissance of Ireland; so did king Nentres of Garloth; so did king Carados of Scotland; so did the duke Galahalt, the haut prince; so did Constantine, that was Sir Carados's son, of Cornwall; so did duke Chalance of Clarance; so did the earl Ulbause; so did the earl Lambaile; so did the earl Aristause. Then came in Sir Gawaine, with his three sons, Sir Gingalin, Sir Florence, and Sir Lovel; these two were begotten upon Sir Brandiles's sister; and all they failed. Then came in Sir Agravaine, Sir Gaheris, Sir Mordred, and the good knight Sir Gareth, which was of very knighthood worth all the brethren. So came knights of Launcelot's kin, but Sir Launcelot was not that time in the court, for he was that time upon his adventures. Then Sir Lionel, Sir Ector de Maris, Sir Bors de Ganis, Sir Blamor de Ganis, Sir Bleoberis de Ganis, Sir Gahalantine, Sir Galihodin, Sir Menadeuke, Sir Villiars the valiant, Sir Hebes le Renoumes. All these were of Sir Launcelot's kin, and all they failed. Then came in Sir Sagramor le Desirous, Sir Dodinas le Savage, Sir Dinadan, Sir Bruin le Noire, that Sir Kay named la Cote Male Taile, and Sir Kay the seneschal, Sir Kay de Stranges, Sir Meliot de Logris, Sir Petipase of Winchelsea, Sir Galleron of Galway, Sir Melion of the mountain, Sir Cardok, Sir Uwaine les Avoutres, and Sir Ozanna le Cure Hardy. Then came in Sir Astamore, and Sir Gromere, Grummor's son, Sir Crosselme, Sir Servause le Breuse, that was called a passing strong knight. For, as the book saith, the chief Lady of the lake feasted this Sir Launcelot, and Sir Servause le Breuse, and when she had feasted them both at sundry

times, she prayed them to give her a boon, and they granted it her, and then she prayed Sir Servause that he would promise her never to do battle against Sir Launcelot du Lake; and in the same wise she prayed Sir Launcelot never to do battle against Sir Servause; and so either promised her. For the French book saith that Sir Servause had never courage nor lust to do battle against no man, but if it were against giants, and against dragons, and wild beasts. So we pass unto them that, at the king's request, made them all that were there at that high feast, as of the knights of the Table Round, for to search Sir Urre: to that intent the king did it, to wit which was the noblest knight among them.

Then there came Sir Aglovale, Sir Durnore, Sir Tor, and king Pellinore begat them all, first, Sir Tor, Sir Aglovale, Sir Durnore, Sir Lamorak, the most noblest knight, one that ever was in Arthur's days as for a worldly knight, and Sir Percivale that was peerless, except Sir Galahad, in holy deeds, but they died in the quest of the Sancgreal. Then came Sir Griflet le Fise de Dieu, Sir Luca the botteler, Sir Bedivere his brother, Sir Brandiles, Sir Constantine, Sir Cador's son of Cornwall, that was king after Arthur's days, and Sir Clegis, Sir Sadok, Sir Dinas le seneschal of Cornwall, Sir Fergus, Sir Driant, Sir Lambegus, Sir Clarrus of Cleremont, Sir Cloddrus, Sir Hectimere, Sir Edward of Carnarvan, Sir Dinas, Sir Priamus, that was christened by Sir Tristram the the noble knight, and these three were brethren; Sir Hellaine le Blank, that was son unto Sir Bors and king Brandegoris's daughter, and Sir Brian de Listinoise; Sir Gautere, Sir Reynold, Sir Gillemere, were three brethren that Sir Launcelot won upon a bridge in Sir Kay's arms. Sir Guiart le Petite, Sir Bellangere le Beuse, that was son to the good knight Sir Alisander le Orphelin, that was slain by the treason of king Mark. Also that traitor king slew the noble knight Sir Tristram, as he sat harping afore his lady La Beale

Isoud, with a trenchant glaive, for whose death was much bewailing of every knight that ever were in Arthur's days: there were never none so bewailed as was Sir Tristram and Sir Lamorak, for they were traitorously slain, Sir Tristram by king Mark, and Sir Lamorak by Sir Gawaine and his brethren. And this Sir Bellangere revenged the death of his father Alisander, and Sir Tristram, slew king Mark, and La Beale Isoud died, swooning upon the cross of Sir Tristram, whereof was great pity. And all that were with king Mark, that were consenting to the death of Sir Tristram, were slain, as Sir Andred, and many other. Then came Sir Hebes, Sir Morganore, Sir Sentraile, Sir Suppinabiles, Sir Bellangere le Orgulous, that the good knight Sir Lamorak wan in plain battle; Sir Nerovens, and Sir Plenorius, two good knights that Sir Launcelot wan; Sir Darras, Sir Harry le Fise Lake, Sir Erminide, brother to king Hermance for whom Sir Palamides fought at the red city with two brethren; and Sir Selises of the dolorous tower, Sir Edward of Orkney, and Sir Ironside, that was called the noble knight of the red lawns, that Sir Gareth wan for the love of dame Liones; Sir Arrok de Grevant, Sir Degrane Sance Vilany, that fought with the giant of the black lowe; Sir Epinogris, that was the king's son of Northumberland; Sir Pelleas, that loved the lady Ettard, and he had died for her love, had not been one of the ladies of the lake, her name was dame Nimue, and she wedded Sir Pelleas, and she saved him that he was never slain, and he was a full noble knight; and Sir Lamiel of Cardiff, that was a great lover; Sir Plaine de Force, Sir Meleaus de Lile, Sir Bobart le Cure Hardy, that was king Arthur's son, Sir Mador de la Porte, Sir Colgrevance, Sir Hervise de la Forest Savage, Sir Marrok, the good knight that was betrayed with his wife, for she made him seven year a werwolf; Sir Persant, Sir Pertilope his brother, that was called the green knight, and

Sir Perimones, brother to them both, that was called the red knight, that Sir Gareth wan when he was called Beaumains. All these hundred knights and ten searched Sir Urre's wounds, by the commandment of king Arthur.

CHAP. XII.

How Sir Launcelot was commanded by Arthur to handle his wounds, and anon he was all whole, and how they thanked God.

MERCY, said king Arthur, where is Sir Launcelot du Lake, that he is not here at this time? Thus as they stood and spake of many things, there was espied Sir Launcelot, that came riding toward them, and told the king. Peace, said the king, let no manner thing be said until he be come to us. So when Sir Launcelot espied king Arthur he descended from his horse, and came to the king, and saluted him, and them all. Anon as the maid, Sir Urre's sister, saw Sir Launcelot, she ran to her brother there as he lay in his litter, and said, Brother, here is come a knight that my heart giveth greatly unto. Fair sister, said Sir Urre, so doth my heart light against him, and certainly I hope now to be healed, for my heart giveth unto him more than to all these that have searched me. Then said king Arthur unto Sir Launcelot, Ye must do as we have done; and told Sir Launcelot what they had done, and shewed him them all that had searched him. Heaven defend me, said Sir Launcelot, when so many kings and knights have assayed and failed, that I should presume upon me to achieve that all ye my lords might not achieve. Ye shall not choose, said king Arthur, for I will command you for to do as we all have done. My most renowned lord, said Sir Launcelot, ye know well I dare not nor may not disobey your commandment, but and I might or durst, wit you well I would not take upon me to touch that wounded knight, to that intent that I should pass all other knights; heaven defend me from that shame. Ye take it wrong, said king Arthur, ye shall not do it for no presumption, but for to bear us fellowship, insomuch ye be a fellow of the Table Round, and wit you well, said king Arthur, and ye prevail not and heal him, I dare say there is no knight in this land may heal him, and therefore I pray you do as we have done. And then all the kings and knights for the most part prayed Sir Launcelot to search him, and then the wounded knight Sir Urre set him up weakly, and prayed Sir Launcelot heartily, saying, Courteous knight, I require thee for God's sake heal my wounds, for me thinketh, ever sithen ye came here my wounds grieve me not. Ah my fair lord, said Sir Launcelot, Jesu would that I might help you, I shame me sore that I should be thus rebuked, for never was I able in worthiness to do so high a thing. Then Sir Launcelot kneeled down by the wounded knight, saying, My lord Arthur, I must do your commandment, the which is sore against my heart. And then he held up his hands, and looked into the east, saying secretly unto himself, Thou blessed Father, Son, and Holy Ghost, I beseech thee of thy mercy, that my simple worship and honesty be saved, and thou, blessed Trinity, thou mayest give power to heal this sick knight, by thy great virtue and grace of thee, but, good Lord, never of myself. And then Sir Launcelot prayed Sir Urre to let him see his head; and then, devoutly kneeling, he ransacked the three wounds, that they bled a little, and forthwith all the wounds fair healed, and seemed as they had been whole a seven year. And in likewise he searched his body of other three wounds, and they healed in likewise. And then the last of all he searched the which was in his hand, and, anon, it healed fair. Then king Arthur, and all the kings and knights, kneeled down, and gave thanks and lovings unto God, and to his blessed mother, and ever Sir Launcelot wept as he had been a child that had been beaten. Then king Arthur let array priests and clerks in the most devoutest manner, to bring in Sir Urre within Carlisle, with singing and loving to God. And when this was done, the king let clothe him in the richest manner that could be thought; and then were but few better made knights in all the court, for he was passingly well made and bigly : and Arthur asked Sir Urre how he felt himself. My good lord, he said, I felt myself never so lusty. Will ye just, and do deeds of arms? said king Arthur. Sir, said Sir Urre, and I had all that longed unto justs, I would soon be ready.

CHAP. XIII.

How there was a party made of an hundred knights against an hundred knights, and of other matters.

THEN king Arthur made a party of hundred knights to be against an hundred knights. And so, upon the morn, they justed for a diamond ; but there justed none of the dangerous knights ; and so, for to shorten this tale, Sir Urre and Sir Lavaine justed best that day, for there was none of them but he overthrew and pulled down thirty knights ; and then, by the assent of all the kings and lords, Sir Urre and Sir Lavaine were made knights of the Table Round. And Sir Lavaine cast his love to dame Felelolie, Sir Urre's sister, and then they were wedded together with great joy, and king Arthur gave to every each of them a barony of lands. And this Sir Urre would never go from Sir Launcelot, but he, and Sir Lavaine, awaited evermore upon him ; and they were in all the court accounted for good knights, and full desirous in arms ; and many noble deeds they did, for they would have no rest, but ever sought adventures. Thus they lived in the court, with great nobleness and joy, long time. But every night and day Sir Agravaine, Sir Gawaine's brother, awaited queen Guenever and Sir Launcelot du Lake, to put them to a rebuke and shame. And so leave I here of this tale, and overskip great books of Sir Launcelot du Lake, what great adventures he did when he was called Le Chevaler du Chariot. For, as the French book saith, because of despite that knights and ladies called him the knight that rode in the chariot, as he were judged to the gallows; therefore, in despite of all them that named him so, he was carried in a chariot a twelve month, for but little after that he had slain Sir Meliagrance in the queen's quarrel, he never in a twelve month came on horseback. And, as the French book saith, he did that twelve month more than forty battles. And because I have lost the very matter of Le Chevaler du Chariot, I depart from the tale of Sir Launcelot, and here I go unto the Morte of king Arthur, and that caused Sir Agravaine.

Explicit liber xix.

And here after soloweth the moost pytous history of the morte of kynge Arthur, the whiche is the xx. book.

The Twentieth Book.

CHAP. I.

How Sir Agravaine and Sir Mordred were busy upon Sir Gawaine for to disclose the love between Sir Launcelot and queen Guenever.

In May, when every lusty heart flourisheth and burgeneth; for as the season is lusty to behold and comfortable, so man and woman rejoice and gladden of summer coming with his fresh flowers: for winter, with his rough winds and blasts, causeth a lusty man and woman to cower and sit fast by the fire. So in this season, as in the month of May, it befell a great anger and unhap that stinted not till the flower of chivalry of all the world was destroyed and slain: and all was long upon two unhappy knights, the which were named Sir Agravaine and Sir Mordred that were brethren unto Sir Gawaine. For this Sir Agravaine and Sir Mordred had ever a privy hate unto the queen dame Guenever, and to Sir Launcelot, and daily and nightly they ever watched upon Sir Launcelot. So it mis-happed Sir Gawaine and all his brethren were in king Arthur's chamber, and then Sir Agravaine said thus openly, and not in no counsel, that many knights might hear it, I marvel that we all be not ashamed both to see and to know how Sir Laun-

celot goeth with the queen, and all we know it so, and it is shamefully suffered of us all, that we all should suffer so noble a king as king Arthur is so to be shamed. Then spake Sir Gawaine, and said, Brother, Sir Agravaine, I pray you, and charge you, move no such matters no more afore me; for wit ye well, said Sir Gawaine, I will not be of your counsel. Truly, said Sir Gaheris and Sir Gareth, we will not be knowing, brother Agravaine, of your deeds. Then will I, said Sir Mordred. I believe well that, said Sir Gawaine, for ever, unto all unhappiness, brother Sir Mordred, thereto will ye grant, and I would that ye left all this, and made you not so busy, for I know, said Sir Gawaine, what will fall of it. Fall of it what fall may, said Sir Agravaine, I will disclose it to the king. Not by my counsel, said Sir Gawaine, for and there rise war and wrake betwixt Sir Launcelot and us, wit you well, brother, there will many kings and great lords hold with Sir Launcelot. Also, brother Sir Agravaine, said Sir Gawaine, ye must remember how ofttimes Sir Launcelot hath rescued the king and the queen, and the best of us all had been full cold at the heart-root, had not Sir Launcelot been better than we; and that hath he proved himself full oft. And as for my part, said Sir Gawaine, I will never be against Sir Launcelot, for one day's deed, when he rescued me from king Carados of the dolorous tower, and slew him, and saved my life. Also, brother Sir Agravaine, and Sir Mordred, in likewise Sir Launcelot rescued you both, and three-score and two, from Sir Turquin. Me thinketh, brother, such kind deeds and kindness should be remembered. Do as ye list, said Sir Agravaine, for I will hide it no longer. With these words came to them king Arthur. Now, brother, stint your noise, said Sir Gawaine. We will not, said Sir Agravaine and Sir Mordred. Will ye so? said Sir Gawaine, then God speed you, for I will not hear your tales, nor be of your counsel. No more will I, said Sir Gareth and Sir Gaheris, for we will never say evil by that man : for because, said Sir Gareth, Sir Launcelot made me knight, by no manner ought I to say ill of him. And therewithal they three departed, making great dole. Alas, said Sir Gawaine and Sir Gareth, now is this realm wholly mischieved, and the noble fellowship of the Round Table shall be dispersed. So they departed.

CHAP. II.

How Sir Agravaine disclosed their love to king Arthur, and how king Arthur gave them licence to take him.

AND then Sir Arthur asked them what noise they made. My lord, said Agravaine, I shall tell you that I may keep no longer. Here is I and my brother, Sir Mordred, brake unto my brother Sir Gawaine, Sir Gaheris, and to Sir Gareth, how this we know all, that Sir Launcelot holdeth your queen, and hath done long, and we be your sister's sons, and we may suffer it no longer ; and all we wot that ye should be above Sir Launcelot, and ye are the king that made him knight, and, therefore, we will prove it that he is a traitor to your person. If it be so, said Sir Arthur, wit you well he is none other, but I would be loth to begin such a thing, but I might have proofs upon it; for Sir Launcelot is an hardy knight, and all ye know he is the best knight among us all, and, but if he be taken with the deed, he will fight with him that bringeth up the noise, and I know no knight that is able to match him. Therefore, and it be sooth as ye say, I would he were taken with the deed. For, as the French book saith, the king was full loth thereto, that any noise should be upon Sir Launcelot and his queen ; for the king had a deeming, but he would not hear of it, for Sir Launcelot had done so much for him and for the queen so many times, that, wit ye well, the king loved him passingly well. My lord, said Sir Agravaine, ye shall ride to-morrow on hunting, and doubt ye not, Sir Launcelot will not go with you. Then when it draweth toward night, ye may send the queen word that ye will lie out all that night, and so may ye send for your cooks; and then, upon pain of death, we shall take him with the queen, and either we shall bring him to you dead or quick. I will well, said the king, then I counsel you, said the king, take with you sure fellowship. Sir, said Agravaine, my brother, Sir Mordred, and I will take with us twelve knights of the Round Table. Beware, said king Arthur, for I warn you ye shall find him wight. Let us deal, said Sir Agravaine and Sir Mordred. So on the morn, king Arthur rode on hunting, and sent word to the queen that he would be out all that night. Then Sir Agravaine and Sir Mordred gat to them twelve knights, and did themselves in a chamber, in the castle of Carlisle, and these were their names : Sir Colgrevance, Sir Mador de la Porte, Sir Gingaline, Sir Meliot de Logris, Sir Petipase of Winchelsea, Sir Galleron of Galway, Sir Melion of the mountain, Sir Astamore, Sir Gromore Somir Joure, Sir Curselaine, Sir Florence, Sir Lovel. So these twelve knights were with Sir Mordred and Sir Agravaine. And all they were of Scotland, either of Sir Gawaine's kin, either well willers to his brethren. So when the night came, Sir Launcelot told Sir Bors how he would go that night, and speak with the queen. Sir, said Sir Bors, ye shall not go this night, by my counsel. Why? said Sir Launcelot. Sir, said Sir Bors, I dread me ever of Sir Agravaine, that waiteth you daily, to do you shame, and us all, and never gave my heart against no going that ever ye went to the queen, so much as now, for I mistrust that the king is out this night from the queen, because, peradventure, he hath lain some watch for you and the queen, and therefore I dread me sore of treason. Have ye no dread, said Sir Launcelot, for I shall go, and come again, and make no tarrying. Sir, said Sir Bors, that me sore repenteth, for I dread me sore that your going out this night shall wrath us all. Fair nephew, said Sir Launcelot, I marvel me much why ye say thus, sithen the queen hath sent for me, and wit ye well that I will not be so much a coward, but she shall understand I will see her good grace. God speed you well, said Sir Bors, and send you sound and safe again.

CHAP. III.

How Sir Launcelot was espied in the queen's chamber, and how Sir Agravaine and Sir Mordred came with twelve knights to slay him.

So Sir Launcelot departed, and took his sword under his arm, and so in his mantle that noble knight put himself in great jeopardy, and so he passed till he came to the queen's chamber. And then, as the French book saith, there came Sir Agravaine, and Sir Mordred, with twelve knights with them of the Round Table, and they said with crying voice, Traitor knight, Sir Launcelot du Lake, now art thou taken. And thus they cried with a loud voice that all the court might hear it: and they all fourteen were armed at all points as they should fight in a battle. Alas, said queen Guenever, now are we mischieved both. Madam, said Sir Launcelot, is there here any armour within your chamber that I might cover my poor body withal, and if there be any, give it me, and I shall soon stint their malice. Truly, said

the queen, I have none armour, shield, sword, nor spear, wherefore I dread me sore our long love is come to a mischievous end; for, I hear by their noise, there be many noble knights, and well I wot they be surely armed, against them ye may make no resistance; wherefore ye are likely to be slain, and then shall I be burnt. For, and ye might escape them, said the queen, I would not doubt but that ye would rescue me in what danger that ever I stood in. Alas, said Sir Launcelot, in all my life was I never bested that I should be thus shamefully slain for lack of mine armour. But ever in one Sir Agravaine and Sir Mordred cried, Traitor knight, come out of the queen's chamber, for wit thou well thou art so beset that thou shalt not escape. Oh mercy, said Sir Launcelot, this shameful cry and noise I may not suffer, for better were death at once, than thus to endure this pain. Then he took the queen in his arms, and kissed her, and said, Most noble christian queen, I beseech you, as ye have ever been my special good lady, and I at all times your true poor knight unto my power, and as I never failed you in right nor in wrong, since the first day that king Arthur made me knight, that ye will pray for my soul if that I here be slain. For well I am well assured that Sir Bors my nephew and all the remnant of my kin, with Sir Lavaine and Sir Urre, that they will not fail you to rescue you from the fire, and therefore, mine own lady, recomfort yourself whatsoever come of me, that ye go with Sir Bors my nephew, and Sir Urre, and they all will do you all the pleasure that they can or may, that ye shall live like a queen upon my lands. Nay, Launcelot, said the queen, wit thou well I will never live after thy days, but, and thou be slain, I will take my death as meekly for Jesu Christ's sake, as ever did any Christian queen. Well, madam, said Launcelot, sith it is so that the day is come that our love must depart, wit you well I shall sell my life as dear as I may, and a thousand fold, said Sir Launcelot, I am more heavier for you than for myself. And now I had lever than to be lord of all Christendom, that I had sure armour upon me, that men might speak of my deeds or ever I were slain. Truly, said the queen, I would and it might please God that they would take me and slay me, and suffer you to escape. That shall never be, said Sir Launcelot. God defend me from such a shame, but Jesu be thou my shield and mine armour.

CHAP. IV.

How Sir Launcelot slew Sir Colgrevance, and armed him in his harness, and after slew Sir Agravaine and twelve of his fellows.

AND therewith Sir Launcelot wrapped his mantle about his arm well and surely; and by then they had gotten a great form out of the hall, and therewithal they rashed at the door. Fair lords, said Sir Launcelot, leave your noise and your rashing, and I shall set open this door, and then may ye do with me what it liketh you. Come off then, said they all, and do it, for it availeth thee not to strive against us all, and therefore let us into this chamber, and we shall save thy life until thou come to king Arthur. Then Launcelot unbarred the door, and with his left hand he held it open a little so that but one man might come in at once. And so anon, there came striding a good knight, a much man and large, and his name was Colgrevance of Gore, and he with a sword strake at Sir Launcelot mightily, and he put aside the stroke, and gave him such a buffet upon the helmet that he fell groveling dead within the chamber door, and then Sir Launcelot with great might drew that dead knight within the chamber door; and then Sir Launcelot with the help of the queen and her ladies was lightly armed in Sir Colgrevance's armour. And ever stood Sir Agravaine and Sir Mordred, crying, Traitor knight, come out of the queen's chamber. Leave your noise, said Sir Launcelot unto Sir Agravaine, for wit ye well, Sir Agravaine, ye shall not prison me this night, and therefore and ye do by my counsel, go ye all from this chamber door, and make not such crying and such manner of slander as ye do, for I promise you by my knighthood, and ye will depart and make no more noise, I shall as to-morn appear before you all, before the king, and then let it be seen which of you all, and either else ye all, will accuse me of treason, and there I shall answer you as a knight should, that hither I came to the queen for no manner of malengine, and that will I prove and make it good upon you with mine hands. Fie on thee traitor, said Sir Agravaine and Sir Mordred, we will have thee, maugre thy head, and slay thee if we list, for we let thee wit, we have the choice of king Arthur, to save thee or to slay thee. Ah sirs, said Sir Launcelot, is there none other grace with you? then keep yourself. So then Sir Launcelot set all open the chamber door, and mightily and knightly he strode in amongst them, and anon at the first buffet he slew Sir Agravaine, and twelve of his fellows within a little while after he laid them cold to the earth, for there was none of the twelve that might stand Sir Launcelot one buffet. Also Sir Launcelot wounded Sir Mordred, and he fled with all his might. And then Sir Launcelot returned again unto the queen, and said, Madam, now wit you well all our true love is brought to an end, for now will king Arthur ever be my foe, and therefore, madam, and it like you that I may have you with me, I shall save you from all manner adventures dangerous. That is not best, said the queen, me seemeth now ye have done so much harm, it will be best ye hold you still with this. And if ye see that as to-morn they will put me unto the death, then may ye rescue me as ye think best. I will well, said Sir Launcelot, for have ye no doubt while I am living I shall rescue you. And then he kissed her, and either gave other a ring, and so there he left the queen and went until his lodging.

CHAP. V.

How Sir Launcelot came to Sir Bors and told him how he had sped, and in what adventure he had been, and how he escaped.

WHEN Sir Bors saw Sir Launcelot, he was never so glad of his home coming as he was then. Mercy, said Sir Launcelot, why be ye all armed? What meaneth this? Sir, said Sir Bors, after that ye were departed from us, we all that be of your blood, and your well willers, were so troubled, that some of us lept out of our beds naked, and some in their dreams caught naked swords in their hands, therefore, said Sir Bors, we deem there is some great strife at hand; and then we all deemed that ye were betrapped with some treason, and therefore we made us thus ready, what need that ever ye were in. My fair nephew, said Sir Launcelot unto Sir Bors, now shall ye wit all, that this night I was more harder bested than ever I was in my life, and yet I escaped. And so he told them all how, and in what manner, as ye have heard tofore. And therefore my fellows, said Sir Launcelot, I pray you all that ye will be of good heart in what need soever I stand, for now is war come to us all. Sir, said Sir Bors, all is welcome that God sendeth us, and we have had much weal with you and much worship, and therefore we will take the woe with you as we have taken the weal. And therefore they said all, there were many good knights, Look ye take no discomfort, for there nis no band of knights under heaven but that we shall be able to grieve them as much as they may us. And therefore discomfort not yourself by no manner, and ye shall gather together that we love, and that loveth us, and what that ye will have done shall be done. And therefore, Sir Launcelot, said they, we will take the woe with the weal. Gramercy, said Sir Launcelot, of your good comfort, for in my great distress, my fair nephew, ye comfort me greatly, and much I am beholden unto you. But this, my fair nephew, I would that ye

did in all haste that ye may, or it be forth-days, that ye will look in their lodging that been lodged here nigh about the king, which will hold with me, and which will not, for now I would know which were my friends from my foes. Sir, said Sir Bors, I shall do my pain, and, or it be seven of the clock, I shall wit of such as ye have said before, who will hold with you.

Then Sir Bors called unto him Sir Lionel, Sir Ector de Maris, Sir Blamor de Ganis, Sir Bleoberis de Ganis, Sir Gahalantine, Sir Galihodin, Sir Galihud, Sir Menadeuke, with Sir Villiers the Valiant, Sir Hebes le Renoumes, Sir Lavaine, Sir Urre of Hungary, Sir Nerouneus, Sir Plenorius: these two knights Sir Launcelot made, and the one he wan upon a bridge, and therefore they would never be against him. And Sir Harry le Fise du Lake and Sir Selises of the dolorous tower, and Sir Melias de Lile, and Sir Bellangere le Beuse, which was Sir Alisaunder's le Orphelin's son, because his mother, dame Alis le Beale Pilgrim, and she was kin unto Sir Launcelot, and he held with him. So there came Sir Palamides, and Sir Safere his brother, to hold with Sir Launcelot, and Sir Clegis of Sadok, and Sir Dinas, Sir Clarius of Cleremont. So these two and twenty knights drew them together; and by then they were armed on horseback, and promised Sir Launcelot to do what he would. Then there fell to them, what of Northgalis and of Cornwall, for Sir Lamorak's sake and for Sir Tristram's sake, to the number of a fourscore knights.

My lords, said Sir Launcelot, wit you well I have been, ever since I came into this country, well willed unto my lord king Arthur, and unto my lady queen Guenever, unto my power, and this night, because my lady the queen sent for me to speak with her, I suppose it was made by treason, howbeit I dare largely excuse her person, notwithstanding I was there by a forecast nigh slain, but, as God provided me, I escaped all their malice and treason. And then that noble knight, Sir Launcelot, told them all how he was hard bested in the queen's chamber, and how and in what manner he escaped from them. And therefore, said Sir Launcelot, wit you well, my fair lords, I am sure there nis but war unto me and mine. And for because I have slain this night these knights, I wot well as is Sir Agravaine Sir Gawaine's brother, and at the least twelve of his fellows, for this cause now I am sure of mortal war, for these knights were sent and ordained by king Arthur to betray me, and therefore the king will in this heat and malice judge the queen to the fire, and that may I not suffer, that she should be burnt for my sake. For, and I may be heard and suffered, and so taken, I will fight for the queen, that she is a true lady unto her lord. But the king in his heat I dread me will not take me as I ought to be taken.

CHAP. VI.

Of the counsel and advice which was taken by Sir Launcelot and by his friends for to save the queen.

My lord Sir Launcelot, said Sir Bors, by mine advice ye shall take the woe with the weal, and take it in patience, and thank God of it. And sithen it is fallen as it is, I counsel you keep yourself, for, and ye will yourself, there is no fellowship of knights christened that shall do you wrong. Also I will counsel you, my lord Sir Launcelot, that and my lady queen Guenever be in distress, insomuch as she is in pain for your sake, that ye knightly rescue her: and ye did other ways, all the world will speak of you shame to the world's end, insomuch as ye were taken with her, whether ye did right or wrong. It is now your part to hold with the queen, that she be not slain and put to a mischievous death, for, and she so die, the shame shall be yours. Jesu defend me from shame, said Sir Launcelot, and keep and save my lady the queen from villainy and shameful death, and that she never be destroyed in my default: wherefore, my fair lords, my kin and my friends, what will ye do? Then

they said all, We will do as ye will do. I put this to you, said Sir Launcelot, that if my lord Arthur by evil counsel will to-morn in his heat put my lady the queen to the fire, there to be burnt, —now, I pray you, counsel me what is best to do? Then they said all at once with one voice, Sir, us thinketh best, that ye knightly rescue the queen; insomuch as she shall be burnt, it is for your sake, and it is to suppose, and ye might be handled, ye should have the same death, or a more shamefuller death; and, sir, we say all, that ye have many times rescued her from death for other men's quarrels, us seemeth it is more your worship that ye rescue the queen from this peril, insomuch she hath it for your sake.

Then Sir Launcelot stood still, and said, My fair lords, wit you well, I would be loth to do that thing that should dishonour you or my blood, and wit you well, I would be loth that my lady the queen should die a shameful death, but and it be so that ye will counsel me to rescue her, I must do much harm or I rescue her, and peradventure I shall there destroy some of my best friends, that should much repent me: and peradventure there be some, and they could well bring it about, or disobey my lord king Arthur, they would soon come to me, the which I were loth to hurt: and if so be that I rescue her, where shall I keep her? That shall be the least care of us all, said Sir Bors: how did the noble knight Sir Tristram by your good will? Kept not he with him La Beale Isoud near three year in Joyous Gard, the which was done by your elders' device, and that same place is your own, and in likewise may ye do, and ye list, and take the queen lightly away, if it so be the king will judge her to be burnt, and in Joyous Gard ye may keep her long enough, until the heat of the king be past. And then shall ye bring again the queen to the king with great worship, and then, peradventure, ye shall have thank for her bringing home, and love and thank where other shall have maugre. That is hard to do, said Sir Launcelot, for by Sir Tristram I may have a warning. For when by means of treaties Sir Tristram brought again La Beale Isoud unto king Mark from Joyous Gard, look what befell on the end, how shamefully that false traitor king Mark slew him as he sat harping afore his lady La Beale Isoud, with a grounden glaive he thrust him in behind to the heart. It grieveth me, said Sir Launcelot, to speak of his death, for all the world may not find such a knight. All this is truth, said Sir Bors, but there is one thing shall courage you and us all : ye know well that king Arthur and king Mark were never like of conditions, for there was never yet man that could prove king Arthur untrue of his promise. So, to make short tale, they were all consented that for better or for worse, if so were that the queen were on that morn brought to the fire, shortly they all would rescue her. And so by the advice of Sir Launcelot they put them all in an enbushment in a wood as nigh Carlisle as they might. And there they abode still to wit what the king would do.

CHAP. VII.

How Sir Mordred rode hastily to the king to tell him of the affray and death of Sir Agravaine and the other knights.

Now turn we again unto Sir Mordred, that when he was escaped from the noble knight Sir Launcelot, he anon gat his horse and mounted upon him, and rode unto king Arthur, sore wounded and smitten, and all for-bled. And there he told the king all how it was, and how they were all slain save himself all only. Mercy, how may this be, said the king; took ye him in the queen's chamber? Yea, truly, said Sir Mordred, there we found him unarmed, and there he slew Colgrevance, and armed him in his armour. And all this he told the king, from the beginning to the ending. Ah, mercy, said the king, he is a marvellous knight of prowess. Alas, me sore repenteth, said the king, that ever Sir Launcelot should be against me. Now I am sure the noble fellowship of the Round Table is broken for ever, for with him will many a noble knight hold : and now it is fallen so, said the king, that I may not with my worship but the queen must suffer the death. So then there was made great ordinance in this heat, that the queen must be judged to the death. And the law was such in those days, that whatsoever they were, of what estate or degree, if they were found guilty of treason, there should be none other remedy but death, and either the men or the taking with the deed should be causer of their hasty judgment. And right so was it ordained for queen Guenever, because Sir Mordred was escaped sore wounded, and the death of thirteen knights of the Round Table :—these proofs and experiences caused king Arthur to command the queen to the fire, there to be burnt. Then spake Sir Gawaine and said : My lord Arthur, I would counsel you not to be over hasty, but that ye would put it in respite, this judgment of my lady the queen, for many causes. One it is, though it were so that Sir Launcelot were found in the queen's chamber, yet it might be that he came thither for none evil, for ye know, my lord, said Sir Gawaine, that the queen is much beholden unto Sir Launcelot, more than unto any other knight, for oft-times he hath saved her life, and done battle for her when all the court refused the queen, and, peradventure, she sent for him for goodness and for none evil, to reward him for his good deeds that he had done to her in time past. And, peradventure, my lady the queen sent for him to that intent that Sir Launcelot should come to her good grace privily and secretly, weening to her that it was best so to do, in eschewing and dreading of slander. For oft-times we do many things that we ween it be for the best, and yet, peradventure, it turneth to the worst. For I dare say, said Sir Gawaine, that my lady your queen is to you both good and true. And as for Sir Launcelot, said Sir

Gawaine, I dare say he will make it good upon any knight living that will put upon himself villainy or shame, and in likewise he will make good for my lady dame Guenever. That I believe well, said king Arthur, but I will not that way with Sir Launcelot, for he trusteth so much upon his hands and his might that he doubteth no man, and therefore for my queen he shall never fight more, for she shall have the law. And if I may get Sir Launcelot, wit ye well he shall have a shameful death. Jesu defend, said Sir Gawaine, that I may never see it. Why say ye so? said king Arthur, for sooth ye have no cause to love Sir Launcelot, for this night last past he slew your brother Sir Agravaine, a full good knight, and also almost he had slain your other brother Sir Mordred; and also there he slew thirteen noble knights; and also, Sir Gawaine, remember ye he slew two sons of yours, Sir Florence and Sir Lovel. My lord, said Sir Gawaine, of all this I have knowledge, of whose deaths I repent me sore, but insomuch I gave them warning, and told my brethren and my sons aforehand, what would fall in the end, insomuch they would not do by my counsel I will not meddle me thereof, nor revenge me nothing of their deaths, for I told them it was no bote to strive with Sir Launcelot; howbeit I am sorry of the death of my brethren and of my sons, for they are the causers of their own death. For oft-times I warned my brother Sir Agravaine, and I told him the perils the which be now fallen.

CHAP. VIII.

How Sir Launcelot and his kinsmen rescued the queen from the fire, and how he slew many knights.

Then said the noble king Arthur to Sir Gawaine, Dear nephew, I pray you make you ready in your best armour, with your brethren Sir Gaheris and Sir Gareth, to bring my queen to the fire, there to have her judgment, and receive the death. Nay, my most noble lord, said Sir Gawaine, that will I never do,

for, wit you well, I will never be in that place where so noble a queen as is my lady dame Guenever shall take a shameful end. For wit you well, said Sir Gawaine, my heart will never serve me to see her die, and it shall never be said that even I was of your counsel of her death. Then, said the king to Sir Gawaine, suffer your brothers Sir Gaheris and Sir Gareth to be there. My lord, said Sir Gawaine, wit you well they will be loth to be there present, because of many adventures the which be like there to fall, but they are young and full unable to say you nay. Then spake Sir Gaheris and the good knight Sir Gareth unto Sir Arthur, Sir, ye may well command us to be there, but wit you well it shall be sore against our will; but and we be there by your strait commandment, ye shall plainly hold us there excused, we will be there in peaceable wise, and bear none harness of war upon us. In the name of God, said the king, then make you ready, for she shall soon have her judgment anon. Alas, said Sir Gawaine, that ever I should endure to see this woefull day. So Sir Gawaine turned him, and wept heartily, and so he went into his chamber, and then the queen was led forth without Carlisle, and there she was despoiled into her smock. And so then her ghostly father was brought to her, to be shriven of her misdeeds. Then was there weeping, and wailing, and wringing of hands, of many lords and ladies. But there were but few in comparison that would bear any armour for to strength the death of the queen. Then was there one that Sir Launcelot had sent unto that place for to espy what time the queen should go unto her death. And anon, as he saw the queen despoiled into her smock, and so shriven, then he gave Sir Launcelot warning. Then was there but spurring and plucking up of horses, and right so they came to the fire, and who that stood against them, there they were slain, there might none withstand Sir Launcelot, so all that bare arms and withstood them, there were they slain—full many a noble knight. For there was slain Sir Belias le Orgulous, Sir Segwarides, Sir Griflet, Sir Brandiles, Sir Aglovale, Sir Tor, Sir Gauter, Sir Gillimer, Sir Reynold's three brethren, Sir Damas, Sir Priamus, Sir Kay the stranger, Sir Driant, Sir Lambegus, Sir Herminde, Sir Pertilope, Sir Perimones, two brethren, that were called the green knight and the red knight. And so in this rashing and hurling as Sir Launcelot thrang here and there, it mishapped him to slay Gaheris and Sir Gareth, the noble knight, for they were unarmed and unaware, for, as the French book saith, Sir Launcelot smote Sir Gareth and Sir Gaheris upon the brain pans, where through they were slain in the field, howbeit in very truth Sir Launcelot saw them not, and so were they found dead among the thickest of the press. Then when Sir Launcelot had thus done and slain, and put to flight all that would withstand him, then he rode straight unto dame Guenever, and made a kirtle and a gown to be cast upon her, and then he made her to be set behind him, and prayed her to be of good cheer. Wit you well the queen was glad that she was escaped from the death, and then she thanked God and Sir Launcelot. And so he rode his way with the queen, as the French book saith, unto Joyous Gard, and there he kept her as a noble knight should do, and many great lords and some kings sent Sir Launcelot many good knights, and many noble knights drew unto Sir Launcelot. When this was known openly, that king Arthur and Sir Launcelot were at debate, and many were full heavy of their debate.

CHAP. IX.

Of the sorrow and lamentation of king Arthur for the death of his nephews and other good knights, and also for the queen his wife.

So turn we again unto king Arthur, that when it was told him how, and in what manner of wise the queen was taken away from the fire, and when he heard of the death of his noble knights,

and in especial for Sir Gaheris' and Sir Gareth's death, then the king swooned for pure sorrow. And when he awoke of his swoon, then he said, Alas that ever I bare crown upon my head, for now have I lost the fairest fellowship of noble knights that ever held christian king together. Alas, my good knights be slain away from me, now within these two days I have lost forty knights, and also the noble fellowship of Sir Launcelot and his blood, for now I may never hold them together no more with my worship. Alas, that ever this war began. Now, fair fellows, said the king, I charge you that no man tell Sir Gawaine of the death of his two brethren, for I am sure, said the king, when Sir Gawaine heareth tell that Sir Gareth is dead, he will go nigh out of his mind. Mercy, said the king, why slew he Sir Gareth and Sir Gaheris! for I dare say as for Sir Gareth he loved Sir Launcelot above all men earthly. That is truth, said some knights, but they were slain in the hurtling, as Sir Launcelot thrang in the thick of the press, and as they were unarmed he smote them, and wist not whom that he smote, and so unhappily they were slain. The death of them, said Arthur, will cause the greatest mortal war that ever was. I am sure, wist Sir Gawaine that Sir Gareth were slain, I should never have rest of him till I had destroyed Sir Launcelot's kin and himself both, or else he to destroy me; and therefore, said the king, wit you well my heart was never so heavy as it is now, and much more I am sorrier for my good knights' loss, than for the loss of my fair queen, for queens I might have enow, but such a fellowship of good knights shall never be together in no company; and now I dare say, said king Arthur, that there was never christian king held such a fellowship together, and alas that ever Sir Launcelot and I should be at debate. Ah, Agravaine, Agravaine, said the king, Jesu forgive it thy soul, for thine evil will, that thou and thy brother Sir Mordred haddest unto Sir Launcelot, hath caused all this sorrow. And ever among these complaints the king wept and swooned.

Then there came one unto Sir Gawaine, and told him how the queen was led away with Sir Launcelot, and nigh a twentyfour knights slain. O Jesu defend my brethren, said Sir Gawaine, for full well wist I that Sir Launcelot would rescue her, or else he would die in that field; and to say the truth he had not been a man of worship, had he not rescued the queen that day, in so much she should have been burnt for his sake: and as in that, said Sir Gawaine, he hath done but knightly, and as I would have done myself, and I had stood in like case. But where are my brethren? said Sir Gawaine, I marvel I hear not of them. Truly, said that man, Sir Gareth and Sir Gaheris be slain. Jesu defend, said Sir Gawaine, for all the world I would not that they were slain, and in especial my good brother Sir Gareth. Sir, said the man, he is slain, and that is great pity. Who slew him? said Sir Gawaine. Sir, said the man, Launcelot slew them both. That may I not believe, said Sir Gawaine, that he slew my brother Sir Gareth, for I dare say my brother Gareth loved him better than me and all his brethren, and the king both. Also I dare say, and Sir Launcelot had desired my brother Sir Gareth with him, he would have been with him against the king and us all, and therefore I may never believe that Sir Launcelot slew my brother. Sir, said this man, it is noised that he slew him.

CHAP. X.

How king Arthur at the request of Sir Gawaine concluded to make war against Sir Launcelot, and laid siege to his castle called Joyous Gard.

ALAS, said Sir Gawaine, now is my joy gone. And then he fell down and swooned, and long he lay there as he had been dead. And then when he arose of his swoon, he cried out sorrowfully and said, Alas! And right so Sir Gawaine ran to the king crying and weeping, O king Arthur, mine uncle, my good brother Sir Gareth is slain, and so is my brother Sir Gaheris, the which were two noble knights. Then the king wept and he both, and so they fell on swooning. And when they were revived, then spake Sir Gawaine, Sir, I will go see my brother Sir Gareth. Ye may not see him, said the king, for I caused him to be interred, and Sir Gaheris both; for I well understood that ye would make over much sorrow, and the sight of Sir Gareth should have caused your double sorrow. Alas, my lord, said Sir Gawaine, how slew he my brother Sir Gareth? mine own good lord, I pray you tell me. Truly, said the king, I shall tell you as it is told me, Sir Launcelot slew him and Sir Gaheris both. Alas, said Sir Gawaine, they bare none arms against him, neither of them both. I wot not how it was, said the king, but, as it is said, Sir Launcelot slew them both in the thickest of the press, and knew them not; and therefore let us shape a remedy for to revenge their deaths. My king, my lord, and mine uncle, said Sir Gawaine, wit you well, now I shall make you a promise that I shall hold by my knighthood, that from this day I shall never fail Sir Launcelot, until the one of us have slain the other: and therefore I require you, my lord and king, dress you to the war, for wit you well I will be revenged upon Sir Launcelot, and therefore, as ye will have my service and my love, now haste you thereto, and assay your friends. For I promise unto God, said Sir Gawaine, for the death of my brother Sir Gareth I shall seek Sir Launcelot throughout seven kings' realms but I shall slay him, or else he shall slay me. Ye shall not need to seek him so far, said the king, for, as I hear say, Sir Launcelot will abide me and you in the Joyous Gard, and much people draweth unto him as I hear say. That may I believe, said Sir Gawaine, but my lord, he said, assay your friends, and I will assay mine. It shall be done, said the king, and, as I suppose, I shall be big enough to draw him out of the biggest tower of his castle. So then the king sent letters and writs throughout all England, both in the length and the breadth, for to assummon all his knights. And so unto Arthur drew many knights, dukes, and earls, so that he had a great host. And when they were assembled, the king informed them all how Sir Launcelot had bereft him his queen. Then the king and all his host made them ready to lay siege about Sir Launcelot, where he lay within Joyous Gard. Thereof heard Sir Launcelot, and purveyed him of many good knights, for with him held many knights, and some for his own sake, and some for the queen's sake. Thus they were on both parties well furnished and garnished of all manner of things that longed to the war. But king Arthur's host was so big that Sir Launcelot would not abide him in the field, for he was full loth to do battle against the king; but Sir Launcelot drew him to his strong castle with all manner of victual, and as many noble men as he might suffice within the town and the castle. Then came king Arthur with Sir Gawaine, with an huge host, and laid a siege all about Joyous Gard, both at the town and at the castle, and there they made strong war on both parties. But in no wise Sir Launcelot would ride·out nor go out of his castle of long time, neither he would none of his good knights to issue out, neither none of the town nor of the castle, until fifteen weeks were past.

CHAP. XI.

Of the communication between king Arthur and Sir Launcelot, and how king Arthur reproved him.

THEN it befell upon a day in harvest time, Sir Launcelot looked over the walls, and spake on high unto king Arthur and Sir Gawaine, My lords both, wit ye well all is in vain that ye make at this siege, for here win ye no worship, but maugre and dishonour, for and it list me to come myself out, and my good knights, I should full soon make an end of this war. Come forth, said Arthur unto Launcelot, and thou darest,

and I promise thee I shall meet thee in midst of the field. God defend me, said Sir Launcelot, that ever I should encounter with the most noble king that made me knight. Fie upon thy fair language, said the king, for wit you well, and trust it, I am thy mortal foe, and ever will to my death day, for thou hast slain my good knights and full noble men of my blood, that I shall never recover again: also thou hast dishonoured my queen, and holden her many winters, and sithen like a traitor taken her from me by force. My most noble lord and king, said Sir Launcelot, ye may say what ye will, for ye wot well with yourself I will not strive, but there as ye say I have slain your good knights, I wot well that I have done so, and that me sore repenteth, but I was enforced to do battle with them, in saving of my life, or else I must have suffered them to have slain me. And as for my lady queen Guenever, except your person of your highness, and my lord Sir Gawaine, there is no knight under heaven that dare make it good upon me, that ever I was traitor unto your person. And where it pleaseth you to say that I have holden my lady your queen years and winters, unto that I shall make a large answer, and prove it upon any knight that beareth the life, except your person and Sir Gawaine, that my lady queen Guenever is a true lady unto your person, as any is living unto her lord, and that will I make good with my hands; howbeit, it hath liked her good grace to have me in charity, and to cherish me more than any other knight, and unto my power I again have deserved her love, for oft-times, my lord, ye have consented that she should be burnt and destroyed in your heat, and then it fortuned me to do battle for her, and or I departed from her adversary they confessed their untruth, and she full worshipfully excused. And at such times, my lord Arthur, said Sir Launcelot, ye loved me, and thanked me when I saved your queen from the fire, and then ye promised me for ever to be my good lord, and now me thinketh ye reward me full ill for my good service; and, my good lord, me seemeth I had lost a great part of my worship in my knighthood, and I had suffered my lady your queen to have been burnt, and insomuch she should have been burnt for my sake. For sithen I have done battles for your queen in other quarrels than in mine own, me seemeth now I had more right to do battle for her in right quarrel, and therefore my good and gracious lord, said Sir Launcelot, take your queen unto your good grace, for she is both fair, true, and good. Fie on thee, false recreant knight, said Sir Gawaine, I let thee wit my lord mine uncle king Arthur shall have his queen and thee, maugre thy visage, and slay you both whether it please him. It may well be, said Sir Launcelot, but wit ye well, my lord Sir Gawaine, and me list to come out of this castle, ye should win me and the queen more harder than ever ye wan a strong battle. Fie on thy proud words, said Sir Gawaine; as for my lady the queen, I will never say of her shame, but thou false and recreant knight, said Sir Gawaine, what cause hadst thou to slay my good brother Sir Gareth, that loved thee more than all my kin? Alas, thou madest him knight with thine own hands; why slewest thou him that loved thee so well? For to excuse me, said Sir Launcelot, it helpeth me not, but by the faith that I owe to the high order of knighthood, I should with as good will have slain my nephew Sir Bors de Ganis at that time: but alas, that ever I was so unhappy, said Launcelot, that I had not seen Sir Gareth and Sir Gaheris. Thou liest, recreant knight, said Sir Gawaine, thou slewest him in despite of me: and therefore wit thou well I shall make war to thee, and all the while that I may live. That me repenteth, said Sir Launcelot, for well I understand it helpeth me not to seek none accordment, while ye Sir Gawaine are so mischievously set. And if ye were not, I would not doubt to have the good grace of my lord Arthur. I believe it well, false recreant knight, said Sir Gawaine, for thou hast many long days overled me, and us all, and destroyed

many of our good knights. Ye say as it pleaseth you, said Sir Launcelot, and yet may it never be said on me and openly proved, that ever I before cast of treason, slew no good knight, as, my lord Sir Gawaine, ye have done. And so did I never, but in my defence, that I was driven thereto, in saving of my life. Ah, false knight, said Sir Gawaine, that thou meanest by Sir Lamorak: wit thou well I slew him. Ye slew him not yourself, said Sir Launcelot, it had been over much on hand for you to have slain him, for he was one of the best knights christened of his age, and it was great pity of his death.

CHAP. XII.

How the cousins and kinsmen of Sir Launcelot excited him to go out to battle, and how they made them ready.

WELL, well, said Sir Gawaine to Sir Launcelot, sithen thou upbraidest me of Sir Lamorak, wit thou well I shall never leave thee till I have thee at such avail that thou shalt not escape my hands. I trust you well enough, said Sir Launcelot, and ye may get me I shall get but little mercy. But, as the French book saith, the noble king Arthur would have taken his queen again, and have been accorded with Sir Launcelot, but Sir Gawaine would not suffer him by no manner of mean. And then Sir Gawaine made many men to blow upon Sir Launcelot, and all at once they called him False recreant knight! Then when Sir Bors de Ganis, Sir Ector de Maris, and Sir Lionel heard this outcry, they called to them Sir Palamides, Sir Safere's brother, and Sir Lavaine, with many more of their blood, and all they went unto Sir Launcelot, and said thus, My lord Sir Launcelot, wit ye well we have great scorn of the great rebukes that we heard Gawaine say to you; wherefore we pray you and charge you, as ye will have our service, keep us no longer within these walls, for wit you well, plainly, we will ride into the field, and do battle with them. For ye fare as a man that were afeard, and for all your fair speech it will not avail you. For wit you well, Sir Gawaine will not suffer you to be accorded with king Arthur; and therefore fight for your life, and your right, and ye dare. Alas, said Sir Launcelot, for to ride out of this castle and to do battle, I am full loth. Then Sir Launcelot spake on high unto Sir Arthur and Sir Gawaine, My lords, I require you and beseech you, sithen that I am thus required and conjured to ride into the field, that neither you my lord king Arthur, nor you Sir Gawaine, come not into the field. What shall we do then? said Sir Gawaine, is this the king's quarrel with thee to fight? and it is my quarrel to fight with thee Sir Launcelot, because of the death of my brother Sir Gareth. Then must I needs unto battle, said Sir Launcelot; now wit you well, my lord Arthur, and Sir Gawaine, ye will repent it whensoever I do battle with you. And so then they departed either from other, and then either party made them ready on the morn for to do battle, and great purveyance was made on both sides. And Sir Gawaine let purvey many knights for to wait upon Sir Launcelot for to overset him, and to slay him. And on the morn at undorne Sir Arthur was ready in the field with three great hosts, and then Sir Launcelot's fellowship came out at three gates, in a full good array. And Sir Lionel came in the foremost battle, and Sir Launcelot came in the middle, and Sir Bors came out at the third gate. Thus they came in order and rule as full noble knights. And always Sir Launcelot charged all his knights in any wise to save king Arthur and Sir Gawaine.

CHAP. XIII.

How Sir Gawaine justed and smote down Sir Lionel, and how Sir Launcelot horsed king Arthur.

THEN came forth Sir Gawaine from the king's host, and he came before and proffered to just. and Sir Lionel was a fierce knight, and lightly he encountered with Sir Gawaine, and there Sir Gawaine smote Sir Lionel throughout the body,

that he dashed to the earth like as he had been dead. And then Sir Ector de Maris and other more bare him into the castle. Then began a great stoure, and much people was slain, and ever Sir Launcelot did what he might to save the people on king Arthur's party. For Sir Palamides, and Sir Bors, and Sir Safere overthrew many knights, for they were deadly knights, and Sir Blamor de Ganis, and Sir Bleoberis de Ganis, with Sir Bellangere le Beuse, these six knights did much harm. And ever king Arthur was nigh about Sir Launcelot to have slain him, and Sir Launcelot suffered him, and would not strike again. So Sir Bors encountered with king Arthur, and there with a spear Sir Bors smote him down; and so he alight and drew his sword, and said to Sir Launcelot, Shall I make an end of this war? and that he meant to have slain king Arthur. Not so hardy, said Sir Launcelot, upon pain of thy head, that thou touch him no more: for I will never see that most noble king, that made me knight, neither slain ne shamed. And therewithal Sir Launcelot alight off his horse, and took up the king, and horsed him again, and said thus, My lord Arthur, for God's love stint this strife, for ye get here no worship and I would do mine utterance, but always I forbear you, and ye, nor none of yours, forbeareth me: my lord remember what I have done in many places, and now I am evil rewarded.

Then when king Arthur was on horseback, he looked upon Sir Launcelot, and then the tears brast out of his eyes, thinking on the great courtesy that was in Sir Launcelot, more than in any other man. And therewith the king rode his way, and might no longer behold him, and said, Alas, that ever this war began! And then either parties of the battles withdrew them to repose them, and buried the dead, and to the wounded men they laid soft salves, and thus they endured that night till on the morn, and on the morn by undorne they made them ready to do battle. And then Sir Bors led the forward. So upon the morn there came Sir Gawaine as brim as any boar, with a great spear in his hand, and when Sir Bors saw him, he thought to revenge his brother Sir Lionel of the despite that Sir Gawaine did him the other day. And so they that knew either other feutered their spears, and with all their mights of their horses and themselves they met together so felonously that either bare other through, and so they fell both to the earth; and then the battles joined, and there was much slaughter on both parties. Then Sir Launcelot rescued Sir Bors, and sent him into the castle. But neither Sir Gawaine nor Sir Bors died not of their wounds; for they were all holpen. Then Sir Lavaine and Sir Urre prayed Sir Launcelot to do his pain, and fight as they had done:—For we see ye forbear and spare, and that doth much harm, therefore we pray you spare not your enemies no more than they do you. Alas, said Sir Launcelot, I have no heart to fight against my lord Arthur, for ever me seemeth I do not as I ought to do. My lord, said Sir Palamides, though ye spare them all this day they will never give you thank; and if they may get you at avail ye are but dead. So then Sir Launcelot understood that they said him truth, and then he strained himself more than he did aforehand, and because his nephew Sir Bors was sore wounded. And then within a little while, by even-song time, Sir Launcelot and his party better stood, for their horses went in blood past the fetlocks, there was so much people slain. And then, for pity, Sir Launcelot withheld his knights, and suffered king Arthur's party for to withdraw them on side. And then Sir Launcelot's party withdrew them into his castle, and either party buried the dead bodies and put salve unto the wounded men. So when Sir Gawaine was hurt, they on king Arthur's party were not so orgulous as they were toforehand to do battle. Of this war was noised through all Christendom, and at the last it was noised afore the Pope; and he considering the great goodness of king Arthur

and of Sir Launcelot, that was called the most noblest knights of the world, wherefore the Pope called unto him a noble clerk, that at that time was there present,—the French book saith it was the bishop of Rochester—and the Pope gave him bulls under lead unto king Arthur of England, charging him upon pain of interdicting of all England, that he take his queen dame Guenever unto him again, and accord with Sir Launcelot.

CHAP. XIV.

How the pope sent down his bulls to make peace, and how Sir Launcelot brought the queen to king Arthur.

So when this bishop was come to Carlisle he shewed the king these bulls. And when the king understood these bulls, he nist what to do: full fain he would have been accorded with Sir Launcelot, but Sir Gawaine would not suffer him; but as for to have the queen, thereto he agreed. But in no wise Sir Gawaine would not suffer the king to accord with Sir Launcelot, but as for the queen he consented. And then the bishop had of the king his great seal, and his assurance, as he was a true anointed king, that Sir Launcelot should come safe and go safe, and that the queen should not be spoken unto, of the king, nor of none other, for no thing done afore time past. And of all these appointments the bishop brought with him sure assurance and writing, to shew Sir Launcelot. So when the bishop was come to Joyous Gard, there he shewed Sir Launcelot how the Pope had written to Arthur and unto him, and there he told him the perils if he withheld the queen from the king. It was never in my thought, said Launcelot, to withhold the queen from my lord Arthur; but in so much she should have been dead for my sake, me seemeth it was my part to save her life, and put her from that danger till better recover might come. And now I thank God, said Sir Launcelot, that the Pope hath made her peace; for God knoweth, said Sir Launcelot, I will be a thousand fold more gladder to bring her again than ever I was of her taking away,— with this, I may be sure to come safe and go safe, and that the queen shall have her liberty as she had before, and never for no thing that hath been surmised afore this time, she never from this day stand in no peril; for else, said Sir Launcelot, I dare adventure me to keep her from an harder shower than ever I kept her. It shall not need you, said the bishop, to dread so much: for wit you well the Pope must be obeyed; and it were not the Pope's worship nor my poor honesty to wit you distressed, neither the queen, neither in peril nor shamed. And then he shewed Sir Launcelot all his writing, both from the Pope and from king Arthur. This is sure enough, said Sir Launcelot, for full well I dare trust my lord's own writing and his seal, for he was never shamed of his promise.

Therefore, said Sir Launcelot unto the bishop, ye shall ride unto the king afore, and recommand me unto his good grace, and let him have knowledging that this same day eight days, by the grace of God, I myself shall bring my lady queen Guenever unto him. And then say ye unto my most redoubted king, that I will say largely for the queen, that I shall none except for dread, nor fear, but the king himself, and my lord Sir Gawaine, and that is more for the king's love than for himself. So the bishop departed, and came to the king at Carlisle, and told him all how Sir Launcelot answered him: and then the tears brast out of the king's eyes. Then Sir Launcelot purveyed him an hundred knights, and all were clothed in green velvet, and their horses trapped to their heels, and every knight held a branch of olive in his hand in tokening of peace, and the queen had four and twenty gentlewomen following her in the same wise, and Sir Launcelot had twelve coursers following him, and on every courser sat a young gentleman, and all they were arrayed in green velvet, with sarpis of gold about their quarters, and the horse trapped in the

same wise down to the heels with many ouches, set with stones and pearls in gold, to the number of a thousand; and she and Sir Launcelot were clothed in white cloth of gold tissue, and right so as ye have heard, as the French book maketh mention, he rode with the queen from Joyous Gard to Carlisle, and so Sir Launcelot rode throughout Carlisle, and so in the castle, that all men might behold and wit you well there was many a weeping eye. And then Sir Launcelot himself alight, and avoided his horse, and took the queen, and so led her where king Arthur was in his seat, and Sir Gawaine sat afore him, and many other great lords. So when Sir Launcelot saw the king and Sir Gawaine, then he led the queen by the arm, and then he kneeled down, and the queen both. Wit you well, then was there many bold knights there with king Arthur that wept as tenderly as though they had seen all their kin afore them. So the king sat still, and said no word. And when Sir Launcelot saw his countenance, he arose and pulled up the queen with him, and thus he spake full knightly:—

CHAP. XV.

Of the deliverance of the queen to the king by Sir Launcelot, and what language Sir Gawaine had to Sir Launcelot.

My most redoubted king, ye shall understand, by the Pope's commandment, and yours, I have brought to you my lady the queen, as right requireth; and if there be any knight, of whatsoever degree that he be, except your person, that will say or dare say but that she is true to you, I here myself, Sir Launcelot du Lake, will make it good upon his body that she is a true lady unto you: but liars ye have listened, and that has caused debate betwixt you and me. For time hath been, my lord Arthur, that ye have been greatly pleased with me, when I did battle for my lady your queen; and full well ye know my most noble king, that she hath been put to great wrong or this time, and sithen it pleased you at many times that I should fight for her, me seemeth, my good lord, I had more cause to rescue her from the fire, insomuch she should have been burnt for my sake. For they that told you those tales were liars, and so it fell upon them. For, by likelihood, had not the might of God been with me, I might never have endured fourteen knights, and they armed and afore purposed, and I unarmed and not purposed; for I was sent for unto my lady your queen, I wot not for what cause, but I was not so soon within the chamber door, but anon Sir Agravaine and Sir Mordred called me traitor and recreant knight. They called thee right, said Sir Gawaine. My lord Sir Gawaine, said Sir Launcelot, in their quarrel they proved themselves not in the right. Well, well, Sir Launcelot, said king Arthur, I have given thee no cause to do to me as thou hast done, for I have worshipped thee and thine more than any of all my knights. My good lord, said Sir Launcelot, so ye be not displeased, ye shall understand I and mine have done you oft better service than any other knights have done in many divers places; and where ye have been full hard bested divers times, I have myself rescued you from many dangers, and ever unto my power I was glad to please you, and my lord Sir Gawaine both, in justs and tournaments, and in battles set, both on horseback and on foot, I have often rescued you, and my lord Sir Gawaine, and many more of your knights in many divers places. For now I will make avaunt, said Sir Launcelot, I will that ye all wit that yet I found never no manner of knight, but that I was over-hard for him, and I had done my utterance, thanked be God; howbeit I have been matched with good knights, as Sir Tristram and Sir Lamorak, but ever I had a favour unto them, and a deeming what they were; and I take God to record, said Sir Launcelot, I never was wroth nor greatly heavy with no good knight, and I saw him busy about to win worship: and full glad I was ever when I found any knight that might endure me

on horseback and on foot. Howbeit, Sir Carados of the dolorous tower was a full noble knight, and a passing strong man, and that wot ye, my lord Sir Gawaine; for he might well be called a noble knight, when he by fine force pulled you out of your saddle, and bound you overthwart afore him to his saddle bow; and there, my lord Sir Gawaine, I rescued you, and slew him afore your sight. Also I found his brother, Sir Turquin, in like wise leading Sir Gaheris your brother bounden afore him, and there I rescued your brother, and slew that Sir Turquin, and delivered threescore and four of my lord Arthur's knights out of his prison. And now I dare say, said Sir Launcelot, I met never with so strong knights, nor so well fighting, as was Sir Carados and Sir Turquin, for I fought with them to the uttermost; and therefore, said Sir Launcelot unto Sir Gawaine, me seemeth ye ought of right for to remember this: for and I might have your good will, I would trust to God to have my lord Arthur's good grace.

CHAP. XVI.

Of the communication between Sir Gawaine and Sir Launcelot, with much other language.

THE king may do as he will, said Sir Gawaine, but wit thou well, Sir Launcelot, thou and I shall never be accorded while we live, for thou hast slain three of my brethren, and twain of them ye slew traitorly and piteously, for they bare none harness against thee, nor none would bear. God would they had been armed, said Sir Launcelot, for then had they been on live. And wit ye well, Sir Gawaine, as for Sir Gareth, I love none of my kinsmen so much as I did him, and ever while I live, said Sir Launcelot, I will bewail Sir Gareth's death, not all only for the great fear that I have of you, but many causes causen me to be sorrowful. One is, for I made him knight; another is, I wot well he loved me above all other knights; and the third is, he was passing noble, true, courteous, and gentle, and well conditioned; the fourth is, I wist well, anon as I heard that Sir Gareth was dead, I should never after have your love, but everlasting war betwixt us; and also I wist well that ye would cause my noble lord Arthur for ever to be my mortal foe, and as Jesu be my help, said Sir Launcelot, I slew never Sir Gareth nor Sir Gaheris by my will, but alas, that ever they were unarmed that unhappy day. But thus much I shall offer me, said Sir Launcelot, if it may please the king's good grace, and you, my lord Sir Gawaine: I shall first begin at Sandwich, and there I shall go in my shirt, barefoot, and at every ten miles end I will found, and cause to make an house of religion, of what order that ye will assign me, with an whole convent to sing and read day and night in especial for Sir Gareth's sake and Sir Gaheris. And this shall I perform from Sandwich unto Carlisle; and every house shall have sufficient livelihood, and this shall I perform while I have any livelihood in Christendom, and there is none of all these religious places, but they shall be performed, furnished and garnished in all things as an holy place ought to be, I promise you faithfully. And this, Sir Gawaine, me thinketh were more fairer, holier, and more better to their souls, than ye my most noble king, and you, Sir Gawaine, to war upon me, for thereby shall ye get none avail. Then all knights and ladies that were there wept as they were mad, and the tears fell on king Arthur's cheeks. Sir Launcelot, said Sir Gawaine, I have right well heard thy speech, and thy great proffers, but wit thou well, let the king do as it pleaseth him, I will never forgive my brothers' death, and in especial the death of my brother Sir Gareth: and if mine uncle, king Arthur, will accord with thee, he shall lose my service: for wit thou well, thou art both false to the king and to me. Sir, said Sir Launcelot, he beareth not the life that may make that good, and if that ye, Sir Gawaine, will charge me with so high a thing, ye must pardon me, for

then needs must I answer you. Nay, said Sir Gawaine, we are past that at this time, and that caused the Pope, for he hath charged mine uncle the king, that he shall take his queen again, and to accord with thee, Sir Launcelot, as for this season, and therefore thou shalt go safe, as thou camest. But in this land thou shalt not abide past fifteen days, such summons I give you;—so the king and we were consented and accorded, or thou camest hither; and else, said Sir Gawaine, wit thou well, that thou shouldest not have come here, but if it were maugre thy head. And if it were not for the Pope's commandment, said Sir Gawaine, I should do battle with mine own body against my body, and prove it upon thee that thou hast been both false unto mine uncle king Arthur, and to me both, and that shall I prove upon thy body when thou art departed from hence, wheresoever I find thee.

CHAP. XVII.

How Sir Launcelot departed from the king and from Joyous Gard over seaward, and what knights went with him.

THEN Sir Launcelot sighed, and therewith the tears fell on his cheeks, and then he said thus: Alas, most noble christian realm, whom I have loved above all other realms, and in thee have I gotten a great part of my worship, and now I shall depart in this wise. Truly me repenteth that ever I came in this realm that should be thus shamefully banished, undeserved and causeless. But fortune is so variant, and the wheel so movable, there is no constant abiding, and that may be proved by many old chronicles of noble Hector, and Troilus, and Alisander the mighty conqueror, and many other more. When they were most in their royalty, they alight lowest; and so fareth by me, said Sir Launcelot, for in this realm I had worship, and by me and mine all the whole Round Table hath been increased more in worship by me and my blood than by any other. And therefore wit thou well, Sir Gawaine, I may live upon my lands as well as any knight that here is. And if ye, most redoubted king, will come upon my lands with Sir Gawaine, to war upon me, I must endure you as well as I may. But as to you, Sir Gawaine, if that ye come there, I pray you charge me not with treason nor felony, for, and ye do, I must answer you. Do thou thy best, said Sir Gawaine, therefore hie thee fast that thou were gone, and wit thou well we shall soon come after, and break the strongest castle that thou hast upon thy head. That shall not need, said Sir Launcelot, for and I were as orgulous set as ye are, wit ye well I should meet with you in midst of the field. Make thou no more language, said Sir Gawaine, but deliver the queen from thee, and pike thee lightly out of this court. Well, said Sir Launcelot, and I had wist of this short coming, I would have advised me twice or that I had come hither; for and the queen had been so dear to me as ye noise her, I durst have kept her from the fellowship of the best knights under heaven. And then Sir Launcelot said unto Guenever, in hearing of the king and them all, Madam, now I must depart from you and this noble fellowship for ever; and sithen it is so, I beseech you to pray for me, and say me well, and if ye be hard bestad by any false tongues, lightly, my lady, let send me word, and if any knight's hands may deliver you by battle, I shall deliver you. And therewithal Sir Launcelot kissed the queen, and then he said all openly, Now let see what he be in this place, that dare say the queen is not true unto my lord Arthur: let see who will speak, and he dare speak. And therewith he brought the queen to the king, and then Sir Launcelot took his leave and departed; and there was neither king, duke ne earl, baron ne knight, lady nor gentlewoman, but all they wept as people out of their mind, except Sir Gawaine; and when the noble Sir Launcelot took his horse, to ride out of Carlisle, there was sobbing and weeping for pure dole of his departing; and so he took his way unto Joyous Gard,

and then ever after he called it the Dolorous Gard. And thus departed Sir Launcelot from the court for ever. And so when he came to Joyous Gard, he called his fellowship unto him, and asked them what they would do. Then they answered all wholly together with one voice, they would as he would do. My fair fellows, said Sir Launcelot, I must depart out of this most noble realm, and now I shall depart it grieveth me sore, for I shall depart with no worship. For a banished man departed never out of no realm with no worship, and that is my heaviness, for ever I fear after my days that they shall chronicle upon me that I was banished out of this land; and else, my fair lords, be ye sure, and I had not dread shame, my lady queen Guenever and I should never have departed. Then spake many noble knights, as Sir Palamides, Sir Safir his brother, and Sir Bellangere le Beuse, and Sir Urre with Sir Lavaine, with many other, Sir, and ye be so disposed to abide in this country, we will never fail you; and if ye list not to abide in this land, there is none of the good knights that here be will fail you, for many causes. One is, all we that be not of your blood shall never be welcome to the court. And sithen it liked us to take a part with you in your distress and heaviness in this realm, wit you well it shall like us as well to go in other countries with you, and there to take such part as ye do. My fair lords, said Sir Launcelot, I well understand you, and, as I can, thank you: and ye shall understand such livelihood as I am born unto I shall depart with you, in this manner of wise, that is for to say, I shall depart all my livelihood and all my lands freely among you, and I myself will have as little as any of you, for have I sufficient that may long to my person, I will ask none other rich array; and I trust to God to maintain you on my lands as well as ever were maintained any knights. Then spake all the knights at once, He have shame that will leave you; for we all understand in this realm will be now no quiet, but ever strife and debate, now the fellowship of the Round Table is broken; for by the noble fellowship of the Round Table was king Arthur upborne, and by their nobleness the king and all his realm was in quiet and in rest. And a great part, they said all, was because of your nobleness.

CHAP. XVIII.

How Sir Launcelot passed over the sea, and how he made great lords of the knights that went with him.

TRULY, said Sir Launcelot, I thank you all of your good saying, howbeit, I wot well, in me was not all the stability of this realm. But in that I might I did my devoir, and well, I am sure, I knew many rebellions in my days that by me were appeased; and I trow we all shall hear of them in short space, and that me sore repenteth. For ever I dread me, said Sir Launcelot, that Sir Mordred will make trouble, for he is passing envious, and applieth him to trouble. So they were accorded to go with Sir Launcelot to his lands. And to make short tale, they trussed, and paid all that would ask them. And wholly an hundred knights departed with Sir Launcelot at once, and made their avows they would never leave him for weal nor for woe; and so they shipped at Cardiff, and sailed unto Benwick: some men call it Bayonne, and some men call it Beaume, where the wine of Beaume is. But to say the sooth, Sir Launcelot and his nephews were lords of all France, and of all the lands that longed unto France, he and his kindred rejoiced it all through Sir Launcelot's noble prowess. And then Sir Launcelot stuffed and furnished and garnished all his noble towns and castles. Then all the people of those lands came unto Sir Launcelot on foot and hands. And so when he had established all these countries, he shortly called a parliament; and there he crowned Sir Lionel king of France; and Sir Bors he crowned him king of all king Claudas' lands; and Sir Ector de Maris, that

was Sir Launcelot's youngest brother, he crowned him king of Benwick, and also king of all Guienne, that was Sir Launcelot's own land. And he made Sir Ector prince of them all, and thus he departed. Then Sir Launcelot advanced all his noble knights, and first he advanced them of his blood; that was Sir Blamor he made him duke of Limosin in Guienne, and Sir Bleoberis he made him duke of Poictiers, and Sir Gahalantin he made him duke of Querne, and Sir Galihodin he made him duke of Sentonge, and Sir Galihud he made him earl of Perigot, and Sir Menadeuke he made him earl of Roerge, and Sir Villiers the valiant he made him earl of Bearn, and Sir Hebes le Renoumes he made him earl of Comange, and Sir Lavaine he made him earl of Arminak, and Sir Urre he made him earl of Estrake, and Sir Neroneus he made him earl of Pardiak, and Sir Plenorius he made him earl of Foise, and Sir Selises of the dolorous tower he made him earl of Masauke, and Sir Melias de Lile he made him earl of Tursauk, and Sir Bellangere le Bewse he made him earl of the Landes, and Sir Palamides he made him duke of the Provence, and Sir Safir he made him duke of Langedok, and Sir Clegis he gave him the earldom of Agente, and Sir Sadok he gave him the earldom of Surlat, and Sir Dinas le seneschal he made him duke of Anjou, and Sir Clarrus he made him duke of Normandy. Thus Sir Launcelot rewarded his noble knights, and many more, that me seemeth it were too long to rehearse.

CHAP. XIX.

How king Arthur and Sir Gawaine made a great host ready to go over sea to make war on Sir Launcelot.

So leave we Sir Launcelot in his lands, and his noble knights with him, and return we again unto king Arthur and to Sir Gawaine, that made a great host ready, to the number of threescore thousand, and all thing was made ready for their shipping to pass over the sea;

and so they shipped at Cardiff. And there king Arthur made Sir Mordred chief ruler of all England, and also he put queen Guenever under his governance; because Sir Mordred was king Arthur's son, he gave him the rule of his land, and of his wife, and so king Arthur passed over the sea and landed upon Sir Launcelot's lands, and there he burnt and wasted, through the vengeance of Sir Gawaine, all that they might overrun. When this word came to Sir Launcelot, that king Arthur and Sir Gawaine were landed upon his lands, and made a full destruction and waste, then spake Sir Bors and said, My lord Sir Launcelot, it is shame that we suffer them thus to ride over our lands, for wit you well, suffer ye them as long as ye will, they will do you no favour, and they may handle you. Then said Sir Lionel, that was ware and wise, My lord Sir Launcelot, I will give you this counsel, let us keep our strong walled towns until they have hunger and cold, and blow on their nails, and then let us freshly set upon them, and shred them down as sheep in a field, that aliens may take ensample for ever how they land upon our lands. Then spake king Bagdemagus to Sir Launcelot, Sir, your courtesy will shend us all, and thy courtesy hath waked all this sorrow: for, and they thus over our lands ride, they shall by process bring us all to nought, whilst we thus in holes us hide. Then said Sir Galihud unto Sir Launcelot, Sir, here be knights come of kings' blood that will not long droop, and they are within these walls, therefore give us leave, like as we be knights, to meet them in the field, and we shall slay them, that they shall curse the time that ever they came into this country. Then spake seven brethren of North Wales, and they were seven noble knights, a man might seek in seven lands or he might find such seven knights: then they all said at once, Sir Launcelot, let us out ride with Sir Galihud, for we be never wont to cower in castles nor in noble towns. Then spake Sir Launcelot, that was master

and governor of them all, My fair lords, wit you well I am full loth to ride out with my knights, for shedding of christian blood; and yet my lands I understand be full bare to sustain any host a while, for the mighty wars that whilom made king Claudus upon this country, upon my father king Ban, and on mine uncle king Bors; howbeit we will as at this time keep our strong walls, and I shall send a messager unto my lord Arthur, a treaty for to take, for better is peace than always war. So Sir Launcelot sent forth a damsel, and a dwarf with her, requiring king Arthur to leave his warring upon his lands, and so she start upon a palfrey, and the dwarf ran by her side. And when she came to the pavilion of king Arthur, there she alight, and there met her a gentle knight Sir Lucan the butler, and said, Fair damsel, come ye from Sir Launcelot du Lake? Yea, sir, she said, therefore I come hither to speak with my lord the king. Alas, said Sir Lucan, my lord Arthur would love Launcelot, but Sir Gawaine will not suffer him. And then he said, I pray to God, damsel, ye may speed well, for all we that be about the king would that Sir Launcelot did best of any knight living. And so with this Lucan led the damsel unto the king, where he sat with Sir Gawaine for to hear what she would say. So when she had told her tale, the water ran out of the king's eyes, and all the lords were full glad for to advise the king as to be accorded with Sir Launcelot, save all only Sir Gawaine, and he said, My lord, mine uncle, what will ye do? will ye now turn again, now ye are past thus far upon this journey? all the world will speak of you villainy. Nay, said Arthur, wit thou well, Sir Gawaine, I will do as ye will advise me; and yet me seemeth, said Arthur, his fair proffers were not good to be refused: but sithen I am comen so far upon this journey, I will that ye give the damsel her answer, for I may not speak to her for pity, for her proffers be so large.

CHAP. XX.

What message Sir Gawaine sent to Sir Launcelot, and king Arthur laid siege to Benwick, and other matters.

THEN Sir Gawaine said to the damsel thus: Damsel, say ye to Sir Launcelot, that it is waste labour, now to sue to mine uncle. For tell him, and he would have made any labour for peace, he should have made it or this time: for tell him now it is too late. And say, that I, Sir Gawaine, so send him word, that I promise him, by the faith I owe unto God, and to knighthood, I shall never leave him till he have slain me, or I him. So the damsel wept and departed, and there were many weeping eyes: and so Sir Lucan brought the damsel to her palfrey, and so she came to Sir Launcelot, where he was among all his knights; and when Sir Launcelot had heard this answer, then the tears ran down by his cheeks. And then his noble knights strode about him, and said, Sir Launcelot, wherefore make ye such cheer: think what ye are, and what men we are, and let us noble knights match them in midst of the field. That may be lightly done, said Sir Launcelot, but I was never so loth to do battle, and therefore, I pray you, fair sirs, as ye love me, be ruled as I will have you, for I will always flee that noble king that made me knight. And when I may no farther, I must needs defend me, and that will be more worship for me, and us all, than to compare with that noble king whom we have all served. Then they held their language, and as that night they took their rest. And upon the morn, early, in the dawning of the day, as knights looked out, they saw the city of Benwick besieged round about, and fast they began to set up ladders. And then they defied them out of the town, and beat them from the walls mightily. Then came forth Sir Gawaine, well armed, upon a stiff steed, and he came before the chief gate with his spear in his hand, crying, Sir Launcelot, where art thou, is there none of you proud knights dare break a spear with me? Then Sir Bors made him ready, and came forth out of the town, and there Sir Gawaine encountered with Sir Bors; and at that time he smote Sir Bors down from his horse, and almost he had slain him, and so Sir Bors was rescued, and borne into the town. Then came forth Sir Lionel, brother to Sir Bors, and thought to revenge him, and either feutred their spears, and ran together, and there they met spitefully, but Sir Gawaine had such grace that he smote Sir Lionel down, and wounded him there passing sore, and then Sir Lionel was rescued, and borne into the town. And this Sir Gawaine came every day, and he failed not, but that he smote down one knight or other. So thus they endured half a year, and much slaughter was of people on both parties. Then it befell upon a day, Sir Gawaine came before the gates armed at all pieces, on a noble horse, with a great spear in his hand, and then he cried with a loud voice, Where art thou now, thou false traitor, Sir Launcelot? Why hidest thou thyself within holes and walls like a coward? Look out now, thou false traitor knight, and here I shall revenge upon thy body the death of my three brethren. All this language heard Sir Launcelot every deal, and his kin and his knights drew about him, and all they said at once to Sir Launcelot, Sir Launcelot, now must ye defend you like a knight, or else ye be shamed for ever: for now ye be called upon treason, it is time for you to stir, for ye have slept over long, and suffered over much. So God me help, said Sir Launcelot, I am right heavy of Sir Gawaine's words, for now he charged me with a great charge; and therefore I wot it as well as ye, that I must defend me, or else to be recreant. Then Sir Launcelot bade saddle his strongest horse, and bad let fetch his arms, and bring all unto the gate of the tower. And then Sir Launcelot spake on high unto king Arthur, and said, My lord Arthur, and noble king that made me knight, wit you well I am right heavy for your sake, that ye thus sue upon me, and

always I forbear you, for, and I would
have been vengeable, I might have met
you in midst of the field, and there to
have made your boldest knights full
tame: and now I have forborne half a
year, and suffered you and Sir Gawaine
to do what ye would do, and now I
may endure it no longer, now must I
needs defend myself, insomuch Sir Gawaine hath appealed me of treason,—
the which is greatly against my will,
that ever I should fight against any of
your blood; but now I may not forsake
it, I am driven thereto as a beast till a
bay. Then Sir Gawaine said, Sir Launcelot, and thou darest do battle, leave
thy babbling and come off, and let us
ease our hearts. Then Sir Launcelot
armed him lightly, and mounted upon
his horse. And either of the knights
gat great spears in their hands, and the
host without stood still all apart, and
the noble knights came out of the city
by a great number, insomuch that when
Arthur saw the number of men and
knights he marvelled, and said to himself, Alas, that ever Sir Launcelot was
against me, for now I see he hath forborne me. And so the covenant was
made, there should no man nigh them,
nor deal with them, till the one were
dead or yielden.

CHAP. XXI.

*How Sir Gawaine and Sir Launcelot did
battle together, and how Sir Gawaine
was overthrown and hurt.*

THEN Sir Gawaine and Sir Launcelot
departed a great way in sunder, and
then they came together with all their
horses' might as they might run, and
either smote other in midst of their
shields, but the knights were so strong,
and their spears so big, that their horses
might not endure their buffets, and so the
horses fell to the earth. And then they
avoided their horses, and dressed their
shields afore them. Then they stood
together, and gave many sad strokes
on divers places of their bodies, that the
blood brast out on many sides and places.
Then had Sir Gawaine such a grace and

gift that an holy man had given to him,
that every day in the year, from underne
till high noon, his might increased those
three hours, as much as thrice his
strength, and that caused Sir Gawaine
to win great honour. And for his sake
king Arthur made an ordinance that all
manner of battles for any quarrels that
should be done before king Arthur,
should begin at underne, and all was
done for Sir Gawaine's love, that by
likelihood if that Sir Gawaine were on
the one part he should have the better
in battle, while his strength endured
three hours, but there were but few
knights that time living that knew this
advantage that Sir Gawaine had, but
king Arthur all only. Thus Sir Launcelot fought with Sir Gawaine, and
when Sir Launcelot felt his might evermore increase, Sir Launcelot wondered,
and dread him sore to be shamed.
For, as the French book saith, Sir
Launcelot wend, when he felt Sir Gawaine double his strength, that he had
been a fiend and no earthly man, wherefore Sir Launcelot traced and traversed,
and covered himself with his shield, and
kept his might and his braid during
three hours: and that while Sir Gawaine
gave him many sad brunts and many
sad strokes, that all the knights that
beheld Sir Launcelot marvelled how he
might endure him, but full little understood they that travail that Sir Launcelot
had for to endure him. And then when
it was past noon, Sir Gawaine had no
more but his own might. Then Sir
Launcelot felt him so come down; then
he stretched him up, and stood near Sir
Gawaine, and said thus, My lord Sir
Gawaine, now I feel ye have done, now
my lord Sir Gawaine I must do my
part, for many great and grievous
strokes I have endured you this day
with great pain. Then Sir Launcelot
doubled his strokes, and gave Sir Gawaine such a buffet on the helmet, that
he fell down on his side, and Sir Launcelot withdrew him from him. Why
withdrawest thou thee? said Sir Gawaine; now turn again, false traitor
knight, and slay me; for and thou

leave me thus, when I am whole I shall do battle with thee again.—I shall endure you, sir, by God's grace, but wit thou well, Sir Gawaine, I will never smite a felled knight. And so Sir Launcelot went into the city, and Sir Gawaine was borne into one of king Arthur's pavilions, and leeches were brought to him, and searched and salved with soft ointments. And then Sir Launcelot said, Now have good day, my lord the king, for, wit you well, ye win no worship at these walls; and if I would my knights out bring, there should many a man die. Therefore, my lord Arthur, remember you of old kindness, and however I fare Jesu be your guide in all places.

CHAP. XXII.

Of the sorrow that king Arthur made for the war, and of another battle where also Sir Gawaine had the worse.

ALAS, said the king, that ever this unhappy war was begun, for ever Sir Launcelot forbeareth me in all places, and in likewise my kin, and that is seen well this day by my nephew Sir Gawaine. Then king Arthur fell sick for sorrow of Sir Gawaine, that he was sore hurt, and because of the war betwixt him and Sir Launcelot. So then they on king Arthur's party kept the siege with little war withoutforth, and they withinforth kept their walls, and defended them when need was. Thus Sir Gawaine lay sick about three weeks in his tents, with all manner of leech-craft that might be had: and as soon as Sir Gawaine might go and ride, he armed him at all points, and start upon a courser, and gat a spear in his hand, and so he came riding afore the chief gate of Benwick, and there he cried on high, Where art thou, Sir Launcelot? come forth thou false traitor knight, and recreant, for I am here, Sir Gawaine, will prove this that I say on thee. All this language Sir Launcelot heard, and then he said thus, Sir Gawaine, me repenteth of your foul saying, that ye will not cease of your language, for you

wot well, Sir Gawaine, I know your might, and all that ye may do, and well ye wot, Sir Gawaine, ye may not greatly hurt me. Come down, traitor knight, said he, and make it good the contrary with thy hands: for it mishapped me the last battle to be hurt of thy hands, therefore, wit thou well, that I am come this day to make amends, for I ween this day to lay thee as low as thou laidest me. Defend me, said Sir Launcelot, that ever I be so far in your danger as ye have been in mine, for then my days were done. But Sir Gawaine, said Sir Launcelot, ye shall not think that I tarry long, but sithen that ye so unknightly call me of treason, ye shall have both your hands full of me. And then Sir Launcelot armed him at all points, and mounted upon his horse, and gat a great spear in his hand, and rode out at the gate. And both the hosts were assembled, of them without, and of them within, and stood in array full manly. And both parties were charged to hold them still, to see and behold the battle of these two noble knights. And then they laid their spears in their rests, and they came together as thunder. And Sir Gawaine brake his spear upon Sir Launcelot in an hundred pieces unto his hand, and Sir Launcelot smote him with a greater might, that Sir Gawaine's horse feet raised, and so the horse and he fell to the earth. Then Sir Gawaine deliverly avoided his horse, and put his shield afore him, and eagerly drew his sword, and bad Sir Launcelot, Alight, traitor knight, for if this mare's son hath failed me, wit thou well a king's son and a queen's son shall not fail thee.

Then Sir Launcelot avoided his horse, and dressed his shield afore him, and drew his sword, and so stood they together, and gave many sad strokes, that all men on both parties had thereof passing great wonder. But when Sir Launcelot felt Sir Gawaine's might so marvellously increase, he then withheld his courage and his wind, and kept himself wonder covert of his might, and under his shield he traced and traversed here and there, to break

Sir Gawaine's strokes and his courage; and Sir Gawaine enforced himself with all his might and power to destroy Sir Launcelot, for, as the French book saith, ever as Sir Gawaine's might increased, right so increased his wind and his evil will. Thus Sir Gawaine did great pain unto Sir Launcelot three hours, that he had great pain for to defend him. And when the three hours were passed, that Sir Launcelot felt that Sir Gawaine was come to his own proper strength, then Sir Launcelot said unto Sir Gawaine, Now have I proved you twice, that ye are a full dangerous knight, and a wonderful man of your might, and many wonderful deeds have you done in your days: for by your might increasing you have deceived many a full noble and valiant knight; and now I feel that ye have done your mighty deeds. Now wit you well I must do my deeds. And then Sir Launcelot stood near Sir Gawaine, and then Sir Launcelot doubled his strokes, and Sir Gawaine defended him mightily. But nevertheless Sir Launcelot smote such a stroke upon Sir Gawaine's helm, and upon the old wound, that Sir Gawaine sinked down upon his one side in a swoon. And anon as he did awake, he waved and foined at Sir Launcelot as he lay, and said, Traitor knight, wit thou well I am not yet slain: come thou near me, and perform this battle unto the uttermost. I will no more do than I have done, said Sir Launcelot; for when I see you on foot I will do battle upon you all the while I see you stand on your feet; but for to smite a wounded man, that may not stand, God defend me from such a shame. And then he turned him and went his way toward the city, and Sir Gawaine evermore calling him traitor knight, and said, Wit thou well, Sir Launcelot, when I am whole, I shall do battle with thee again; for I shall never leave thee till that one of us be slain. Thus as this siege endured, and as Sir Gawaine lay sick near a month, and when he was well recovered, and ready within three days to do battle again with Sir Launcelot, right so came tidings unto Arthur from England, that made king Arthur and all his host to remove.

Here foloweth the xxi book.

The Twenty-first Book.

CHAP. I.

How Sir Mordred presumed and took on him to be king of England, and would have married the queen, his uncle's wife.

As Sir Mordred was ruler of all England, he did do make letters as though that they came from beyond the sea, and the letters specified that king Arthur was slain in batule with Sir Launcelot. Wherefore Sir Mordred made a Parliament, and called the lords together, and there he made them to choose him king, and so was he crowned at Canterbury, and held a feast there fifteen days, and afterward he drew him unto Winchester, and there he took the queen Guenever, and said plainly, that he would wed her which was his uncle's wife, and his father's wife. And so he made ready for the feast, and a day prefixed that they should be wedded; wherefore queen Guenever was passing heavy. But she durst not discover her heart, but spake fair, and agreed to Sir Mordred's will. Then she desired of Sir Mordred for to go to London, to buy all manner of things that longed unto the wedding. And because of her fair speech Sir Mordred trusted her well enough, and gave her leave to go. And so when she came to London, she took the tower of London, and suddenly, in all haste possible, she stuffed it with all manner of victual, and well garnished it with men, and so kept it.

Then when Sir Mordred wist and understood how he was beguiled, he was passing wroth out of measure. And a short tale for to make, he went and laid a mighty siege about the tower of London, and made many great assaults thereat, and threw many great engines unto them, and shot great guns. But all might not prevail Sir Mordred, for queen Guenever would never, for fair speech nor for foul, would never trust to come in his hands again. And then came the bishop of Canterbury, the which was a noble clerk and an holy man, and thus he said to Sir Mordred: Sir, what will ye do, will ye first displease God, and sithen shame yourself and all knighthood? Is not king Arthur your uncle, no further but your mother's brother, and are ye not his son, therefore how may ye wed your father's wife? Sir, said the noble clerk, leave this opinion, or else I shall curse you with book, and bell, and candle. Do thou thy worst, said Sir Mordred, wit thou well I shall defy thee. Sir, said the bishop, and wit you well I shall not fear me to do that me ought to do. Also where ye noise where my lord Arthur is slain, and that is not so, and therefore ye will make a foul work in this land. Peace, thou false priest, said Sir Mordred, for, and thou chafe me any more, I shall make strike off thy head. So the bishop departed, and did the curse in the most orgulous wise that might be done. And then Sir Mordred sought the bishop of Canterbury for to have slain him. Then the bishop fled, and took part of his goods with him, and went nigh unto Glastonbury, and there he was as priest hermit in a chapel, and lived in poverty and in holy prayers: for well he understood that mischievous war was at hand. Then Sir Mordred sought on queen Guenever by letters and sondes, and by fair means and foul means, for to have her to come out of the tower of London, but all this availed not, for she answered him shortly, openly and privily, that she had lever slay herself than to be married with him. Then came word to Sir Mordred that king Arthur had raised the siege from Sir Launcelot, and he was coming homeward with a great host, to be avenged upon Sir Mordred. Wherefore Sir Mordred made write writs to all the barony of this land, and much people drew to him. For then was the common voice among them, that with Arthur was none other life but war and strife, and with Sir Mordred was great joy and bliss. Thus was Sir Arthur depraved and evil said of. And many there were that king Arthur had made up of nought, and given them lands, might not then say of him a good word.

Lo ye, all Englishmen, see ye not what a mischief here was, for he that was the most king and knight of the world, and most loved the fellowship of noble knights, and by him they were all upholden. Now might not these Englishmen hold us content with him. Lo, thus was the old custom and usage of this land. And also men say, that we of this land have not yet lost nor forgotten that custom and usage. Alas, this is a great default of all Englishmen, for there may no thing please us no term. And so fared the people at that time; they were better pleased with Sir Mordred than they were with king Arthur, and much people drew unto Sir Mordred, and said they would abide with him for better and for worse. And so Sir Mordred drew with a great host to Dover, for there he heard say that Sir Arthur would arrive, and so he thought to beat his own father from his lands. And the most party of all England held with Sir Mordred, the people were so new fangle.

CHAP. II.

How after that king Arthur had tidings he returned and came to Dover, where Sir Mordred met him to let his landing, and of the death of Sir Gawaine.

AND so as Sir Mordred was at Dover with his host, there came king Arthur with a great navy of ships, galleys, and carracks. And there was Sir Mordred ready awaiting upon his landage, to let his own father to land upon the land that he was king over. Then there was launching of great boats and small, and full of noble men of arms, and there was much slaughter of gentle knights, and many a full bold baron was laid full low on both parties. But king Arthur was so courageous, that there might no manner of knights let him to land, and his knights fiercely followed him. And so they landed, maugre Sir Mordred and all his power, and put Sir Mordred aback, that he fled and all his people. So when this battle was done, king Arthur let bury his people that were dead, and then was the noble knight Sir Gawaine found in a great boat lying more than half dead. When Sir Arthur wist that Sir Gawaine was laid so low, he went unto him, and there the king made sorrow out of measure, and took Sir Gawaine in his arms, and thrice he there swooned. And when he awaked he said, Alas, Sir Gawaine, my sister's son, here now thou liest, the man in the world that I loved most, and now is my joy gone: for now, my nephew Sir Gawaine, I will discover me unto your person; in Sir Launcelot and you I most had my joy, and mine affiance, and now have I lost my joy of you both, wherefore all mine earthly joy is gone from me. Mine uncle king Arthur, said Sir Gawaine, wit you well, my death day is come, and all is through mine own hastiness and wilfulness, for I am smitten upon the old wound the which Sir Launcelot gave me, on the which I feel well I must die, and had Sir Launcelot been with you as he was, this unhappy war had never begun, and of all this am I causer, for Sir Launcelot and his blood through their prowess held all your cankered enemies in subjection and danger: and now, said Sir Gawaine, ye shall miss Sir Launcelot. But, alas, I would not accord with him, and therefore, said Sir Gawaine, I pray you, fair uncle, that I may have paper, pen, and ink, that I may write to Sir Launcelot a schedule with mine own hands. And then when paper and ink was brought, then Gawaine was set up

weakly by king Arthur, for he was shriven a little tofore, and then he wrote thus, as the French book maketh mention,—Unto Sir Launcelot, flower of all noble knights that ever I heard of, or saw by my days, I Sir Gawaine, king Lot's son, of Orkney, sister's son unto the noble king Arthur, send thee greeting, and let thee have knowledge, that the tenth day of May I was smitten upon the old wound that thou gavest me afore the city of Benwick, and through the same wound that thou gavest me I am come to my death-day. And I will that all the world wit that I, Sir Gawaine, knight of the Table Round, sought my death, and not through thy deserving, but it was mine own seeking, wherefore I beseech thee, Sir Launcelot, to return again unto this realm, and see my tomb, and pray some prayer, more or less, for my soul. And this same day that I wrote this schedule, I was hurt to the death in the same wound, the which I had of thy hand, Sir Launcelot. For of a more nobler man might I not be slain. Also, Sir Launcelot, for all the love that ever was betwixt us, make no tarrying, but come over the sea in all haste, that thou mayest with thy noble knights rescue that noble king that made thee knight, that is my lord Arthur, for he is full straitly bestad with a false traitor, that is my half brother Sir Mordred, and he hath let crown him king, and would have wedded my lady queen Guenever, and so had he done, had she not put herself in the tower of London. And so the tenth day of May last past, my lord Arthur and we all landed upon them at Dover, and there we put that false traitor Sir Mordred to flight, and there it misfortuned me to be stricken upon thy stroke, and at the date of this letter was written but two hours and an half afore my death, written with mine own hand, and so subscribed with part of my heart's blood. And I require thee, most famous knight of the world, that thou wilt see my tomb.—And then Sir Gawaine wept, and king Arthur wept, and then they swooned both. And when they awaked both, the king made Sir Gawaine to receive his Saviour. And then Sir Gawaine prayed the king to send for Sir Launcelot, and to cherish him above all other knights. And so at the hour of noon, Sir Gawaine yielded up the spirit. And then the king let inter him in a chapel within Dover castle; and there yet all men may see the skull of him, and the same wound is seen that Sir Launcelot gave him in battle. Then was it told king Arthur that Sir Mordred had pitched a new field upon Barham Down. And upon the morn the king rode thither to him, and there was a great battle betwixt them, and much people were slain on both parties. But at the last Sir Arthur's party stood best, and Sir Mordred and his party fled unto Canterbury.

CHAP. III.

How after Sir Gawaine's ghost appeared to king Arthur, and warned him that he should not fight that day.

AND then the king let search all the towns for his knights that were slain, and interred them; and salved them with soft salves that so sore were wounded. Then much people drew unto king Arthur. And then they said that Sir Mordred warred upon king Arthur with wrong. And then king Arthur drew him with his host down by the sea side, westward toward Salisbury, and there was a day assigned between king Arthur and Sir Mordred, and they should meet upon a down beside Salisbury, and not far from the sea side, and this day was assigned on a Monday after Trinity Sunday, whereof king Arthur was passing glad, that he might be avenged upon Sir Mordred. Then Sir Mordred araised much people about London, for they of Kent, Southsex, and Surrey, Estsex, and Southfolk, and of Northfolk, held the most party with Sir Mordred, and many a full noble knight drew unto Sir Mordred and to the king; but they that loved Sir Launcelot drew unto Sir Mordred. So upon Trinity Sunday at night king Arthur dreamed a wonderful dream, and that was this, that him seemed he sat upon a chaflet in a chair, and the chair was fast to a wheel, and thereupon sat king Arthur in the richest cloth of gold that might be made : and the king thought there was under him, far from him, an hideous deep black water, and therein were all manner of serpents, and worms, and wild beasts, foul and horrible : and suddenly the king thought the wheel turned up so down, and he fell among the serpents, and every beast took him by a limb. And then the king cried as he lay in his bed and slept, Help! And then knights, squires, and yeomen awaked the king; and then he was so amazed that he wist not where he was. And then he fell on slumbering again, not sleeping nor thoroughly waking. So the king seemed verily that there came Sir Gawaine unto him with a number of fair ladies with him. And when king Arthur saw him, then he said, Welcome, my sister's son, I wend thou hadst been dead, and now I see thee on live, much am I beholding unto Almighty Jesu. Oh, fair nephew, and my sister's son, what be these ladies that hither be come with you? Sir, said Sir Gawaine, all these be ladies for whom I have foughten when I was man living : and all these are those that I did battle for in righteous quarrel. And God hath given them that grace at their great prayer, because I did battle for them, that they should bring me hither unto you, thus much had God given me leave, for to warn you of your death; for and ye fight as to-morn with Sir Mordred, as ye both have assigned, doubt ye not ye must be slain, and the most part of your people on both parties. And for the great grace and goodness that Almighty Jesu hath unto you, and for pity of you and many more other good men there shall be slain, God hath sent me to you, of his special grace, to give you warning, that in no wise ye do battle as to-morn, but that ye take a treaty for a month day; and proffer you largely, so as to-morn to be put in a delay. For within a month shall come Sir Launcelot, with all his noble knights, and rescue you worshipfully, and slay Sir Mordred and all that ever will hold with him. Then Sir Gawaine and all the ladies vanished. And anon the king called upon his knights, squires, and yeomen, and charged them wightly to fetch his noble lords and wise bishops unto him. And when they were come, the king told them his vision, what Sir Gawaine had told him, and warned him that if he fought on the morn he should be slain. Then the king commanded Sir Lucan de butlere, and his brother Sir Bedivere, with two bishops with them, and charged them in any wise and they might take a treaty for a month day with Sir Mordred ;—And spare not, proffer him lands and goods, as much as ye think best. So then they departed, and came to Sir Mordred, where he had a grim host of an hundred thousand men. And there they intreated Sir Mordred long time, and at the last Sir Mordred was ⸜agreed for to have Cornwall and Kent, by king Arthur's days :—after, all England, after the days of king Arthur.

CHAP. IV.

How by misadventure of an adder the battle began, where Mordred was slain, and Arthur burt to the death.

THEN were they condescended that king Arthur and Sir Mordred should meet betwixt both their hosts, and every each of them should bring fourteen persons. And they came with this word unto king Arthur. Then said he, I am glad that this is done. And so he went into the field. And when Arthur should depart, he warned all his host that and they see any sword drawn, Look ye come on fiercely, and slay that traitor Sir Mordred, for I in no wise trust him. In like wise Sir Mordred warned his host that, — And ye see any sword drawn, look that ye come on fiercely, and so slay all that ever before you standeth : for in no wise I will not trust for this treaty : for I know well my father will be avenged upon me. And so they met as their pointment was, and so they were agreed and accorded thoroughly : and wine was fetched, and

they drank. Right so came an adder out of a little heath bush, and it stung a knight on the foot. And when the knight felt him stungen, he looked down and saw the adder, and then he drew his sword to slay the adder, and thought of none other harm. And when the host on both parties saw that sword drawn, then they blew beames, trumpets, and horns, and shouted grimly. And so both hosts dressed them together. And king Arthur took his horse, and said, Alas this unhappy day, and so rode to his party : and Sir Mordred in likewise. And never was there seen a more dolefuller battle in no christian land. For there was but rushing and riding, foining and striking, and many a grim word was there spoken either to other, and many a deadly stroke. But ever king Arthur rode throughout the battle of Sir Mordred many times, and did full nobly as a noble king should ; and at all times he fainted never. And Sir Mordred that day put him in devoir, and in great peril. And thus they fought all the long day, and never stinted, till the noble knights were laid to the cold ground, and ever they fought still, till it was near night, and by that time was there an hundred thousand laid dead upon the down. Then was Arthur wroth out of measure, when he saw his people so slain from him. Then the king looked about him, and then was he ware of all his host, and of all his good knights, were left no more on live but two knights, that was Sir Lucan de butlere, and his brother Sir Bedivere : and they full were sore wounded. Jesu mercy, said the king, where are all my noble knights becomen. Alas that ever I should see this doleful day. For now, said Arthur, I am come to mine end. But would to God that I wist where were that traitor Sir Mordred, that hath caused all this mischief. Then was king Arthur ware where Sir Mordred leaned upon his sword among a great heap of dead men. Now give me my spear, said Arthur unto Sir Lucan, for yonder I have espied the traitor that all this woe hath wrought. Sir, let him be, said Sir Lucan, for he is unhappy: and if ye pass this unhappy day, ye shall be right well revenged upon him. Good lord, remember ye of your night's dream, and what the spirit of Sir Gawaine told you this night, yet God of his great goodness hath preserved you hitherto. Therefore, for God's sake, my lord, leave off by this. For blessed be God ye have won the field: for here we be three on live, and with Sir Mordred is none on live. And if ye leave off now, this wicked day of destiny is past. Tide me death, betide me life, saith the king, now I see him yonder alone, he shall never escape mine hands, for at a better avail shall I never have him. God speed you well, said Sir Bedivere. Then the king gat his spear in both his hands, and ran toward Sir Mordred, crying, Traitor, now is thy death day come. And when Sir Mordred heard Sir Arthur, he ran until him with his sword drawn in his hand. And then king Arthur smote Sir Mordred under the shield, with a foin of his spear through-out the body more than a fathom. And when Sir Mordred felt that he had his death's wound, he thrust himself, with the might that he had, up to the bur of king Arthur's spear. And right so he smote his father Arthur with his sword holden in both his hands, on the side of the head, that the sword pierced the helmet and the brain-pan, and there-withal Sir Mordred fell stark dead to the earth. And the noble Arthur fell in a swoon to the earth, and there he swooned oft-times. And Sir Lucan de butlere and Sir Bedivere oft-times heaved him up, and so weakly they led him betwixt them both to a little chapel not far from the sea side. And when the king was there, he thought him well eased. Then heard they people cry in the field. Now go thou, Sir Lucan, said the king, and do me to wit what betokens that noise in the field. So Sir Lucan departed, for he was griev-ously wounded in many places. And so as he went, he saw and hearkened by the moon-light, how the pillers and rob-bers were come into the field to pill and

to rob many a full noble knight of broaches and beads, of many a good ring, and of many a rich jewel; and who that were not dead all out, there they slew them for their harness and their riches. When Sir Lucan under-stood this work, he came to the king as soon as he might, and told him all what he had heard and seen. Therefore by mine advice, said Sir Lucan, it is best that we bring you to some town. I would it were so, said the king,—

CHAP. V.

How king Arthur commanded to cast his sword Excalibur into the water, and how he was delivered to ladies in a barge.

BUT I may not stand, my head works so. Ah, Sir Launcelot, said king Ar-thur, this day have I sore missed thee. Alas, that ever I was against thee, for now have I my death, whereof Sir Gawaine me warned in my dream. Then Sir Lucan took up the king the one part, and Sir Bedivere the other part, and in the lifting, the king swooned, and Sir Lucan fell in a swoon with the lift, that the part of his bowels fell out of his body, and therewith the noble knight's heart brast. And when king Arthur came to himself again, he beheld Sir Lucan how he lay foaming at the mouth, and part of his bowels lay at his feet. Alas, said the king, this is unto me a full heavy sight to see this noble duke so die for my sake, for he would have holpen me that had more need of help than I. Alas, he would not complain him, his heart was so set to help me. Now Jesu have mercy upon his soul. Then Sir Bedivere wept for the death of his brother. Leave this mourning and weeping, said the king, for all this will not avail me: for, wit thou well, and I might live myself the death of Sir Lucan would grieve me evermore; but my time hieth fast, said the king. Therefore, said Arthur, take thou Excalibur, my good sword, and go with it to yonder water side, and when thou comest there, I charge thee throw my sword in that water, and come again, and tell me what thou there seest. My lord, said Bedivere, your commandment shall be done, and lightly bring you word again. So Sir Bedivere departed, and by the way he beheld that noble sword, that the pommel and haft were all of precious stones, and then he said to himself, If I throw this rich sword in the water, thereof shall never come good, but harm and loss. And then Sir Bedivere hid Excalibur under a tree. And as soon as he might he came again unto the king, and said he had been at the water, and had thrown the sword into the water. What sawest thou there? said the king. Sir, he said, I saw nothing but waves and winds. That is untruly said of thee, said the king; therefore go thou lightly again, and do my command as thou art to me lief and dear, spare not, but throw it in. Then Sir Bedivere returned again, and took the sword in his hand; and then him thought sin and shame to throw away that noble sword; and so eft he hid the sword, and returned again, and told to the king that he had been at the water, and done his commandment. What saw thou there? said the king. Sir, he said, I saw nothing but the waters wap and the waves wan. Ah, traitor, untrue, said king Arthur, now hast thou betrayed me twice. Who would have wend that thou that hast been to me so lief and dear, and thou art named a noble knight, and would betray me for the riches of the sword. But now go again lightly, for thy long tarrying putteth me in great jeopardy of my life, for I have taken cold. And but if thou do now as I bid thee, if ever I may see thee, I shall slay thee with mine own hands, for thou wouldest for my rich sword see me dead. Then Sir Bedivere departed, and went to the sword, and lightly took it up, and went to the water side, and there he bound the girdle about the hilts, and then he threw the sword as far into the water as he might, and there came an arm and an hand above the water, and met it, and caught it, and so shook it thrice and brandished, and then vanished away the hand with the sword in the water.

So Sir Bedivere came again to the king, and told him what he saw. Alas, said the king, help me hence, for I dread me I have tarried over long. Then Sir Bedivere took the king upon his back, and so went with him to that water side. And when they were at the water side, even fast by the bank hoved a little barge, with many fair ladies in it, and among them all was a queen, and all they had black hoods, and all they wept and shrieked when they saw king Arthur. Now put me into the barge, said the king: and so he did softly. And there received him three queens with great mourning, and so they set him down, and in one of their laps king Arthur laid his head, and then that queen said, Ah, dear brother, why have ye tarried so long from me? Alas, this wound on your head hath caught over much cold. And so then they rowed from the land; and Sir Bedivere beheld all those ladies go from him. Then Sir Bedivere cried, Ah, my lord Arthur, what shall become of me now ye go from me, and leave me here alone among mine enemies. Comfort thyself, said the king, and do as well as thou mayest, for in me is no trust for to trust in. For I will into the vale of Avilion, to heal me of my grievous wound. And if thou hear never more of me, pray for my soul. But ever the queens and the ladies wept and shrieked, that it was pity to hear. And as soon as Sir Bedivere had lost the sight of the barge, he wept and wailed, and so took the forest, and so he went all that night, and in the morning he was ware betwixt two holts hoar of a chapel and an hermitage.

CHAP. VI.

How Sir Bedivere found him on the morrow dead in an hermitage, and how he abode there with the hermit.

THEN was Sir Bedivere glad, and thither he went; and when he came into the chapel, he saw where lay an hermit groveling on all four, there fast by a tomb was new graven. When the hermit saw Sir Bedivere, he knew him well, for he was but a little before bishop of Canterbury, that Sir Mordred banished. Sir, said Sir Bedivere, what man is there interred that ye pray so fast for? Fair son, said the hermit, I wot not verily, but by deeming. But this night, at midnight, here came a number of ladies, and brought hither a dead corpse, and prayed me to bury him; and here they offered an hundred tapers, and gave me an hundred besants. Alas, said Sir Bedivere, that was my lord king Arthur, that here lieth buried in this chapel! Then Sir Bedivere swooned, and when he awoke he prayed the hermit he might abide with him still there, to live with fasting and prayers. For from hence will I never go, said Sir Bedivere, by my will, but all the days of my life here to pray for my lord Arthur. Ye are welcome to me, said the hermit, for I know you better than ye ween that I do. Ye are the bold Bedivere, and the full noble duke Sir Lucan de butlere was your brother. Then Sir Bedivere told the hermit all as ye have heard tofore. So there bode Sir Bedivere with the hermit, that was tofore bishop of Canterbury, and there Sir Bedivere put upon him poor clothes, and served the hermit full lowly in fasting and in prayers.

Thus of Arthur I find never more written in books that be authorized, nor more of the certainty of his death heard I never tell, but thus was he led away in a ship wherein were three queens; that one was king Arthur's sister queen Morgan le Fay; the other was the queen of Northgalis; the third was the queen of the Waste Lands. Also there was Nimue, the chief Lady of the lake, that had wedded Pelleas the good knight; and this lady had done much for king Arthur; for she would never suffer Sir Pelleas to be in no place where he should be in danger of his life, and so he lived to the uttermost of his days with her in great rest. More of the death of king Arthur could I never find, but that ladies brought him to his burials; and such one was buried there, that the hermit bare witness that some time was bishop of Canterbury, but yet the hermit knew not in certain that he was verily the body of king Arthur;— for this tale Sir Bedivere, knight of the Round Table, made it to be written.

CHAP. VII.

Of the opinion of some men of the death of king Arthur; and how queen Guenever made her a nun in Almesbury.

YET some men yet say in many parts of England that king Arthur is not dead, but had by the will of our Lord Jesu in another place. And men say that he shall come again, and he shall win the holy cross. I will not say it shall be so, but rather I will say, here in this world he changed his life. But many men say that there is written upon his tomb this verse,

Hic iacet Arthurus Rex quondam Rex que futurus.

Thus leave I here Sir Bedivere with the hermit, that dwelled that time in a chapel beside Glastonbury, and there was his hermitage. And so they lived in their prayers and fastings and great abstinence. And when queen Guenever understood that king Arthur was slain, and all the noble knights, Sir Mordred and all the remnant, then the queen stole away, and five ladies with her, and so she went to Almesbury, and there she let make herself a nun, and wore white clothes and black, and great penance she took, as ever did sinful lady in this land, and never creature could make her merry, but lived in fasting, prayers, and alms-deeds, that all manner of people marvelled how virtuously she was changed. Now leave we queen Guenever in Almesbury a nun in white clothes and black, and there she was abbess and ruler, as reason would; and turn we from her, and speak we of Sir Launcelot du Lake.

CHAP. VIII.

How when Sir Launcelot heard of the death of king Arthur, and of Sir Ga-waine, and other matters, he came into England.

AND when he heard in his country that Sir Mordred was crowned king in

England, and made war against king Arthur his own father, and would let him to land in his own land; also it was told Sir Launcelot how that Sir Mordred had laid siege about the tower of London, because the queen would not wed him; then was Sir Launcelot wroth out of measure, and said to his kinsmen, Alas, that double traitor Sir Mordred, now me repenteth that ever he escaped my hands, for much shame hath he done unto my lord Arthur. For all I feel by the doleful letter that my lord Gawaine sent me, on whose soul Jesu have mercy, that my lord Arthur is right hard bested. Alas, said Sir Launcelot, that ever I should live to hear that most noble king, that made me knight, thus to be overset with his subject in his own realm. And this doleful letter that my lord Sir Gawaine hath sent me afore his death, praying me to see his tomb, wit you well his doleful words shall never go from mine heart. For he was a full noble knight as ever was born, and in an unhappy hour was I born, that ever I should have that unhap to slay first Sir Gawaine, Sir Gaheris the good knight, and mine own friend Sir Gareth, that full noble knight. Alas, I may say I am unhappy, said Sir Launcelot, that ever I should do thus unhappily; and, alas, yet might I never have hap to slay that traitor Sir Mordred. Leave your complaints, said Sir Bors, and first revenge you of the death of Sir Gawaine, and it will be well done that ye see Sir Gawaine's tomb, and secondly that ye revenge my lord Arthur and my lady queen Guenever. I thank you, said Sir Launcelot, for ever ye will my worship. Then they made them ready in all the haste that might be, with ships and galleys with Sir Launcelot and his host, to pass into England. And so he passed over the sea till he came to Dover: and there he landed with seven kings, and the number was hideous to behold. Then Sir Launcelot enquired of men of Dover where was king Arthur become? Then the people told him how that he was slain, and Sir Mordred and an hundred thousand died on

a day, and how Sir Mordred gave king Arthur there the first battle at his landing, and there was good Sir Gawaine slain, and on the morn Sir Mordred fought with the king upon Barham Down, and there the king put Sir Mordred to the worse. Alas, said Sir Launcelot, this is the heaviest tidings that ever came to me. Now, fair sirs, said Sir Launcelot, shew me the tomb of Sir Gawaine. And then certain people of the town brought him into the castle of Dover, and showed him the tomb. Then Sir Launcelot kneeled down and wept and prayed heartily for his soul. And that night he made a dole, and all they that would come had as much flesh, fish, wine, and ale, and every man and woman had twelve pence, come who would. Thus with his own hand dealt he his money in a mourning gown; and ever he wept, and prayed them to pray for the soul of Sir Gawaine. And on the morn all the priests and clerks that might be gotten in the country were there, and sung mass of Requiem. And there offered first Sir Launcelot, and he offered an hundred pound, and then the seven kings offered forty pound a piece, and also there was a thousand knights, and each of them offered a pound, and the offering dured from morn till night. And Sir Launcelot lay two nights on his tomb in prayers and in weeping. Then on the third day Sir Launcelot called the kings, dukes, earls, barons and knights, and said thus: My fair lords, I thank you all of your coming into this country with me; but we come too late, and that shall repent me while I live, but against death may no man rebel. But sithen it is so, said Sir Launcelot, I will myself ride and seek my lady queen Guenever, for as I hear say, she hath great pain and much disease, and I heard say that she is fled into the west country, therefore ye all that abide me here, and but if I come again within fifteen days, then take your ships, and your fellowship, and depart into your country. For I will do as I say to you.

CHAP. IX.

How Sir Launcelot departed to seek the queen Guenever, and how he found her at Almesbury.

THEN came Sir Bors de Ganis, and said, My lord Sir Launcelot, what think ye for to do, now to ride in this realm? wit thou well ye shall find few friends. Be as be may, said Sir Launcelot, keep you still here, for I will forth on my journey, and no man nor child shall go with me. So it was no boot to strive, but he departed and rode westerly, and there he sought a seven or eight days, and at the last he came to a nunnery, and then was queen Guenever ware of Sir Launcelot as he walked in the cloister, and when she saw him there she swooned thrice, that all the ladies and gentlewomen had work enough to hold the queen up. So when she might speak, she called ladies and gentlewomen to her, and said, Ye marvel, fair ladies, why I make this fare. Truly, she said, it is for the sight of yonder knight that yonder standeth : wherefore, I pray you all, call him to me. When Sir Launcelot was brought to her, then she said to all the ladies, Through this man and me hath all this war been wrought, and the death of the most noblest knights of the world; for through our love that we have loved together is my most noble lord slain. Therefore, Sir Launcelot, wit thou well I am set in such a plight to get my soul's health; and yet I trust, through God's grace, that after my death to have a sight of the blessed face of Christ, and at doomsday to sit on his right side, for as sinful as ever I was are saints in heaven. Therefore, Sir Launcelot, I require thee and beseech thee heartily, for all the love that ever was betwixt us, that thou never see me more in the visage; and I command thee on God's behalf, that thou forsake my company, and to thy kingdom thou turn again and keep well thy realm from war and wrack. For as well as I have loved thee, mine heart will not serve me to see thee; for through thee and me is the flower of kings and knights destroyed. Therefore, Sir Launcelot, go to thy realm, and there take thee a wife, and live with her with joy and bliss, and I pray thee heartily pray for me to our Lord, that I may amend my mis-living. Now, sweet madam, said Sir Launcelot, would ye that I should return again unto my country, and there to wed a lady? Nay, madam, wit you well that shall I never do : for I shall never be so false to you of that I have promised, but the same destiny that ye have taken you to, I will take me unto, for to please Jesu, and ever for you I cast me specially to pray. If thou wilt do so, said the queen, hold thy promise ; but I may never believe but that thou wilt turn to the world again. Well, madam, said he, ye say as pleaseth you, yet wist you me never false of my promise, and God defend but I should forsake the world as ye have done. For in the quest of the Sancgreal I had forsaken the vanities of the world, had not your lord been. And if I had done so at that time with my heart, will, and thought, I had passed all the knights that were in the Sancgreal, except Sir Galahad my son. And therefore, lady, sithen ye have taken you to perfection, I must needs take me to perfection of right. For I take record of God, in you I have had mine earthly joy. And if I had found you now so disposed, I had cast me to have had you into mine own realm.

CHAP. X.

How Sir Launcelot came to the hermitage where the archbishop of Canterbury was, and how he took the habit on him.

BUT sithen I find you thus disposed, I insure you faithfully I will ever take me to penance, and pray while my life lasteth, if that I may find any hermit either grey or white that will receive me. Wherefore, madam, I pray you kiss me, and never no more. Nay, said the queen, that shall I never do, but abstain you from such works. And they departed. But there was never so hard an hearted man, but he would have wept to see the dolour that they made. For there was lamentation as they had been stung with spears, and many times they swooned. And the ladies bare the queen to her chamber, and Sir Launcelot awoke, and went and took his horse, and rode all that day and all that night in a forest, weeping. And at the last he was ware of an hermitage and a chapel stood betwixt two cliffs, and then he heard a little bell ring to mass, and thither he rode and alight, and tied his horse to the gate, and heard mass. And he that sang mass was the bishop of Canterbury. Both the bishop and Sir Bedivere knew Sir Launcelot, and they spake together after mass. But when Sir Bedivere had told his tale all whole, Sir Launcelot's heart almost brast for sorrow, and Sir Launcelot threw his arms abroad, and said, Alas, who may trust this world! And then he kneeled down on his knees, and prayed the bishop to shrive him and assoil him. And then he besought the bishop that he might be his brother. Then the bishop said, I will gladly : and there he put an habit upon Sir Launcelot, and there he served God day and night with prayers and fastings.

Thus the great host abode at Dover. And then Sir Lionel took fifteen lords with him, and rode to London to seek Sir Launcelot. And there Sir Lionel was slain and many of his lords. Then Sir Bors de Ganis made the great host for to go home again. And Sir Bors, Sir Ector de Maris, Sir Blamor, Sir Bleoberis, with more other of Sir Launcelot's kin, took on them to ride all England overthwart and endlong, to seek Sir Launcelot. So Sir Bors by fortune rode so long till he came to the same chapel where Sir Launcelot was. And so Sir Bors heard a little bell knell that rang to mass, and there he alight, and heard mass. And when mass was done, the bishop, Sir Launcelot, and Sir Bedivere came to Sir Bors. And when Sir Bors saw Sir Launcelot in that manner clothing, then he prayed the bishop that he might be in the same suit. And so there was an habit put upon him, and there he lived in prayers and fasting.

And within half a year there was come Sir Galihud, Sir Galihodin, Sir Blamor, Sir Bleoberis, Sir Williars, Sir Clarrus, and Sir Gahalantine. So all these seven noble knights there abode still. And when they saw Sir Launcelot had taken him unto such perfection, they had no list to depart, but took such an habit as he had. Thus they endured in great penance six year, and then Sir Launcelot took the habit of priesthood, and a twelvemonth he sang mass. And there was none of these other knights but they read in books, and holp to sing mass, and rang bells, and did bodily all manner of service. And so their horses went where they would, for they took no regard of no worldly riches. For when they saw Sir Launcelot endure such penance, in prayers and fasting, they took no force what pain they endured, for to see the noblest knight of the world take such abstinence, that he waxed full lean. And thus upon a night there came a vision to Sir Launcelot, and charged him, in remission of his sins, to haste him unto Almesbury,— And by then thou come there, thou shalt find queen Guenever dead : and therefore take thy fellows with thee, and purvey them of an horse bier, and fetch thou the corpse of her, and bury her by her husband the noble king Arthur. So this vision came to Launcelot thrice in one night.

CHAP. XI.

How Sir Launcelot went with his seven fellows to Almesbury, and found there queen Guenever dead, whom they brought to Glastonbury.

THEN Sir Launcelot rose up or day, and told the hermit. It were well done, said the hermit, that ye made you ready, and that ye disobey not the vision. Then Sir Launcelot took his seven fellows with him, and on foot they went from Glastonbury to Almesbury, the which is little more than thirty miles. And thither they came within two days, for they were weak and feeble to go. And when Sir Launcelot was come to Almesbury, within the nunnery, queen

Guenever died but half an hour before. And the ladies told Sir Launcelot that queen Guenever told them all, or she passed, that Sir Launcelot had been priest near a twelvemonth,—And hither he cometh as fast as he may to fetch my corpse: and beside my lord king Arthur he shall bury me. Wherefore the queen said in hearing of them all, I beseech Almighty God that I may never have power to see Sir Launcelot with my worldly eyes. And thus, said all the ladies, was ever her prayer these two days, till she was dead. Then Sir Launcelot saw her visage, but he wept not greatly, but sighed. And so he did all the observance of the service himself, both the Dirige, and on the morn he sang mass. And there was ordained an horse bier; and so with an hundred torches ever burning about the corpse of the queen, and ever Sir Launcelot with his eight fellows went about the horse bier singing and reading many an holy orison, and frankincense upon the corpse incensed. Thus Sir Launcelot and his eight fellows went on foot from Almesbury unto Glastonbury; and when they were come to the chapel and the hermitage, there she had a Dirige with great devotion. And on the morn the hermit, that sometime was bishop of Canterbury, sang the mass of Requiem with great devotion: and Sir Launcelot was the first that offered, and then all his eight fellows. And then she was wrapped in cered cloth of Raines, from the top to the toe in thirty fold, and after she was put in a web of lead, and then in a coffin of marble. And when she was put in the earth, Sir Launcelot swooned, and lay long still, while the hermit came out and awaked him, and said, Ye be to blame, for ye displease God with such manner of sorrow making. Truly, said Sir Launcelot, I trust I do not displease God, for He knoweth mine intent, for my sorrow was not, nor is not, for any rejoicing of sin, but my sorrow may never have end. For when I remember of her beauty, and of her noblesse, that was both with her king

and with her; so when I saw his corpse and her corpse so lie together, truly mine heart would not serve to sustain my careful body. Also when I remember me, how by my default, mine orgule, and my pride, that they were both laid full low, that were peerless that ever was living of christian people, wit you well, said Sir Launcelot, this remembered, of their kindness and mine unkindness, sank so to my heart, that I might not sustain myself. So the French book maketh mention.

CHAP. XII.

How Sir Launcelot began to sicken, and after died, whose body was borne to Joyous Gard for to be buried.

THEN Sir Launcelot never after eat but little meat, nor drank, till he was dead; for then he sickened more and more, and dried and dwined away; for the bishop nor none of his fellows might not make him to eat, and little he drank, that he was waxen by a cubit shorter than he was, that the people could not know him; for evermore day and night he prayed, but sometime he slumbered a broken sleep, and ever he was lying groveling on the tomb of king Arthur and queen Guenever. And there was no comfort that the bishop, nor Sir Bors, nor none of his fellows could make him, it availed not. So within six weeks after, Sir Launcelot fell sick, and lay in his bed; and then he sent for the bishop that there was hermit, and all his true fellows. Then Sir Launcelot said with dreary voice, Sir bishop, I pray you give to me all my rights that longeth to a christian man. It shall not need you, said the hermit and all his fellows, it is but heaviness of your blood: ye shall be well amended by the grace of God to-morn. My fair lords, said Sir Launcelot, wit you well, my careful body will into the earth, I have warning more then now I will say, therefore give me my rights. So when he was houseled and eneled, and had all that a christian man ought to have, he prayed the bishop that his fellows might bear his body to Joyous Gard. Some men say it was Anwick, and some men say it was Bamborow. Howbeit, said Sir Launcelot, me repenteth sore, but I made mine avow sometime that in Joyous Gard I would be buried, and because of breaking of mine avow, I pray you all lead me thither. Then there was weeping and wringing of hands among his fellows. So at a season of the night they went all to their beds, for they all lay in one chamber. And so after midnight, against day, the bishop that was hermit, as he lay in his bed asleep, he fell upon a great laughter; and therewith all the fellowship awoke, and came unto the bishop, and asked him what he ailed. Alas, said the bishop, why did ye awake me, I was never in all my life so merry and so well at ease. Wherefore? said Sir Bors. Truly, said the bishop, here was Sir Launcelot with me, with more angels than ever I saw men upon one day; and I saw the angels heave Sir Launcelot unto heaven, and the gates of heaven opened against him. It is but the vexing of dreams, said Sir Bors, for I doubt not Sir Launcelot aileth nothing but good. It may well be, said the bishop, go ye to his bed, and then shall ye prove the sooth. So when Sir Bors and his fellows came to his bed they found him stark dead, and he lay as he had smiled, and the sweetest savour about him that ever they felt. Then was there weeping and wringing of hands, and the greatest dole they made that ever made men. And on the morn the bishop did his mass of Requiem; and after the bishop and all the nine knights put Sir Launcelot in the same horse bier that queen Guenever was laid in tofore that she was buried: and so the bishop and they altogether went with the corpse of Sir Launcelot daily, till they came to Joyous Gard, and ever they had an hundred torches burning about him; and so within fifteen days they came to Joyous Gard. And there they laid his corpse in the body of the quire, and sang and read many psalters and prayers over him and about him;

and ever his visage was laid open and naked, that all folk might behold him; for such was the custom in those days, that all men of worship should so lie with open visage till that they were buried. And right thus as they were at their service, there came Sir Ector de Maris, that had seven year sought all England, Scotland, and Wales, seeking his brother Sir Launcelot.

CHAP. XIII.

How Sir Ector found Sir Launcelot his brother dead. And how Constantine reigned next after Arthur, and of the end of this book.

AND when Sir Ector heard such noise and light in the quire of Joyous Gard, he alight and put his horse from him, and came into the quire, and there he saw men sing and weep. And all they knew Sir Ector, but he knew not them. Then went Sir Bors unto Sir Ector, and told him how there lay his brother Sir Launcelot dead. And then Sir Ector threw his shield, sword, and helm from him; and when he beheld Sir Launcelot's visage he fell down in a swoon. And when he awaked it were hard any tongue to tell the doleful complaints that he made for his brother. Ah, Launcelot, he said, thou were head of all christian knights; and now I dare say, said Sir Ector, thou Sir Launcelot, there thou liest, that thou were never matched of earthly knight's hand; and thou were the courtiest knight that ever bare shield; and thou were the truest friend to thy lover that ever bestrode horse; and thou were the truest lover of a sinful man that ever loved woman; and thou were the kindest man that ever strake with sword; and thou were the goodliest person ever came among press of knights; and thou was the meekest man and the gentlest that ever ate in hall among ladies; and thou were the sternest knight to thy mortal foe that ever put spear in the rest.

Then there was weeping and dolour out of measure. Thus they kept Sir

Launcelot's corpse on loft fifteen days, and then they buried it with great devotion. And then at leisure they went all with the bishop of Canterbury to his hermitage, and there they were together more than a month. Then Sir Constantine, that was Sir Cador's son, of Cornwall, was chosen king of England; and he was a full noble knight, and worshipfully he ruled this realm. And then this king Constantine sent for the bishop of Canterbury, for he heard say where he was; and so he was restored unto his bishopric, and left that hermitage; and Sir Bedivere was there ever still hermit to his life's end. Then Sir Bors de Ganis, Sir Ector de Maris, Sir Gahalantine, Sir Galihud, Sir Galihodin, Sir Blamor, Sir Bleoberis, Sir Williars le Valiant, Sir Clarrus of Cleremont; all these knights drew them to their countries. Howbeit king Constantine would have had them with him, but they would not abide in this realm; and there they lived in their countries as holy men. And some English books make mention that they went never out of England after the death of Sir Launcelot, but that was but favour of makers. For the French book maketh mention, and is authorised, that Sir Bors, Sir Ector, Sir Blamor, and Sir Bleoberis, went into the holy land, there as Jesu Christ was quick and dead, and anon as they had stablished their lands; for the book saith so Sir Launcelot commanded them for to do, or ever he passed out of this wo:ld. And these four knights did many battles upon the miscreants or Turks. And there they died upon a Good Friday, for God's sake.

Here is the end of the whole book of king Arthur, and of his noble knights of the Round Table, that when they were whole together there was ever an hundred and forty. And here is the end of the Death of Arthur. I pray you all gentlemen and gentlewomen that read this book of Arthur and his knights from the beginning to the ending, pray for me while I am on live that God send me good deliverance, and when I am dead, I pray you all pray for my soul; for this book was ended the ninth year of the reign of king Edward the Fourth by Sir Thomas Maleore, knight, as Jesu help him for his great might, as he is the servant of Jesu both day and night.

❡ Thus endeth thys noble and Joyous book entytled le morte Darthur / Notwithstondyng it treateth of the byrth / lyf / and actes of the sayd kynge Arthur / of his noble knyghtes of the rounde table / theyr meruayllous enquestes and aduentures / thachyeuyng of the sangreal / & in thende the dolourous deth & departyng out of thys world of them al / Whiche book was reduced in to englysshe by syr Thomas Malory knyght as afore is sayd / and by me deuyded in to xxi bookes chapytred and enprynted / and fynysshed in thabbey westmestre the last day of Iuyl the yere of our lord M / CCCC / lxxx / V /

❡ Caxton me fieri fecit.

NOTE A.

See Introduction, page xiv. *note* 3.

'OH ye mighty and pompous lords, shining in the glory transitory of this unstable life, as in reigning over realms great, and mighty countries, fortified with strong castles and towers, edified with many a rich city. Ye also, ye fierce and mighty chivalers, so valiant in adventurous deeds of arms, behold, behold, see how this mighty conqueror Arthur, whom in his human life all the world doubted—ye also, the noble queen Guenever, that sometime sat in her chair adorned with gold, pearls, and precious stones, now lie full low in obscure foss or pit covered with clods of earth and clay. Behold also this mighty champion Launcelot, peerless of knighthood, see now how he lieth groveling on the cold mould, now being so feeble and faint that sometime was so terrible, how and in what manner ought ye to be so desirous of the mundane honour so dangerous. Therefore me thinketh this present book called La Morte Darthur is right necessary often to be read, for in it shall ye find the gracious, knightly, and virtuous war of most noble knights of the world, whereby they gat praising continual. Also me seemeth by the oft reading thereof ye shall greatly desire to accustom yourself in following of those gracious knightly deeds, that is to say, to dread God, and to love rightwiseness, faithfully and courageously to serve your sovereign prince. And the more that God hath given you the triumphal honour the meeker ye ought to be, ever fearing the unstableness of this deceivable world. And so I pass over, and turn again to my matter.'

NOTE B.

See Introduction, page xvii. *note* 3.

For those who may care to see more of the manner in which the text of the interpolated passages has been formed, I give the following specimens in detail.

The first is from the beginning of the 11th Chapter of Book XXI.

CAXTON.

'Than syr Launcelot rose vp or day/& tolde the heremyte/It were wel done sayd the heremyte that ye made you redy/& that ye dyshobeye not the auysyon/ Than syr Launcelot toke his vii felowes with hym/& on fote they yede from glastynburye to almysburye the whyche is lytel more than xxx myle/& thyder they came within two dayes for they were wayke and feble to goo/& whan syr Launcelot was come to almysburye within the Nunerye quene gweneuer deyed but halfe an oure afore/and the ladyes tolde syr Launcelot that quene Gueneuer tolde hem al or she passyd/that syr Launcelot had been preest nere a twelue monthe/& hyder he cometh as faste as he may to fetch my cors/& besyde my lord kyng Arthur he shal berye me/'

WYNKYN DE WORDE, 1498.

' Thenne syre Launcelot rose vp or day. And tolde the heremyte. It were well doon sayd the heremyte / that ye made ye redy / and that ye dysobeye not the aduysyon. Thenē syr Launcelot toke his .vij. felowes wᵗ hym/& on fote they yede from Glastynbury to Almesbury. the whyche is lytyl more than .xxx. myle. And thyder they came wythin two dayes for they were weyke & feble to go. And whan syr Launcelot was come to Almesbury wythin the Nunnery / quene Gweneuer deyed but halfe an houre afore / And the ladyes tolde syr Launcelot / that quene Gweneuer tolde them all or she passyd / that syr Launcelot had be preest nere a twelue month and hither he cometh as fast as he may / to fetche my corps. And besyde my lorde kyng Arthur / he shal bury me.'

UPCOTT.

' Than syr Launcelot rose vp or it was day, and tolde the heremyte therof. It were well done sayd the heremyte that ye made you redy, and that ye dysobeye not thys aduysyon. Thene syr Launcelot toke his .vii. felawes with hym, & on foote they yede from Glastynbury to Almesbury, the whyche is lytyl more than xxx myle. And thyder they came wythin two dayes for they were weyke and feble to go. And whan syr Launcelot was come to Almesbury wythin the Nonnery, quene Gweneuer deyed but halfe an houre afore. And the ladyes tolde syre Launcelot that quene Gueneuer tolde them all or she passyd, that syr Launcelot had been preest nere a twelue moneth, and hither he cometh as faste as he may for to fetche my corps. And besyde my lorde kynge Arthur he shal burye me.'

The last lines of the same Chapter are as follows :—

CAXTON.

' For whan I remembre of hir beaulte and of hir noblesse that was bothe with hyr king & with hyr / So whan I sawe his corps and hir corps so lye togyders / truly myn herte wold not serue to susteyne my careful body / Also whan I remēbre me how by my defaut & myn orgule and my pryde / that they were bothe layed ful lowe that were pereles that euer was lyuyng of cristen people, wyt you wel sayd syr Launcelot / this remembred of there kyndnes and myn vnkyndnes sanke so to myn herte that I miȝt not susteyne myself so the frensshe book maketh mencyon.'

UPCOTT,

(Who follows Wynkyn de Worde exactly, except in the spelling, and in the insertion of ' me' after ' wold not serue.')

' For whan I remembre *& calle to mynde* her beaute, *bountee &* noblesse, that was *as wel* wyth her kyng *my lord Arthur* as wyth her. *And also* whanne I saw *the corses of that noble kinge & noble quene* so lye to gyder *in that colde graue made of erthe, that somtyme were so hyghly sette in moost honourable places,* truly myn herte wolde not serue *me* to susteyne my *wretchyd &* carefull body. Also whan I remembre me how by my defawte myn orgulyte and my pride, that they were both layed full lowe whyche were pereles that euer were lyuenge of crysten peple, wyte yow wel sayd syr Launcelot, this remembred, of ther kyndnesse & *of* myn vnkyndnesse, sanke *and enprest* soo *in* to my herte that *all my natural strengthe fayled me, so that* I myghte not susteyne my selfe. Soo the frensshe boke makyth mencyon.'

The several colophons are as follows:—

CAXTON.

· 'Thus endeth thys noble and Ioyous book entytled le morte Darthur/Notwith-standyng it treateth of the byrth/lyf/and actes of the sayd kynge Arthur/of his noble knyghtes of the rounde table/theyr meruayllous enquestes and aduentures/ thachyeuyng of the sangreal/& in thende the dolourous deth & departyng out of thys world of them al/Whiche book was reduced in to englysshe by syr Thomas Malory knyght as afore is sayd/and by me deuyded in to xxi bookes chapytred and enprynted/and fynysshed in thabbey westmestre the last day of Iuyl the yere of our lord M/CCCC/lxxx/V/   Caxton me fieri fecit.'/

WYNKYN DE WORDE, 1498.

'Thus endyth this noble and Ioyous boke entytled Le morte dathur. Notwyth-standyng it treateth of the byrth lyf & actes of the sayd kynge Arthur of his noble knyghtes of the rounde table. theyr merueyllous enquestes & aduentures. thachyeu-ynge of the Sancgreall. And in the ende the dolorous deth. & depaytynge out of this worlde of them al. Whyche boke was reduced in to Englysshe by the well dysposyd knyghte afore namyd. And deuyde[d] into .xxi. bokes chapitred. & en-prynt[ed] fyrst by Wylliam Caxton/on who[se] soule god haue mercy. And newel[ye] prynfed. and chapitres of the sam[e ru-]brisshed at Westmestre, by Wynk[yn de] Worde ye yere of our lord. M.C[CCC].lxxxxviij. and ended the .xxv [daye of] Marche. the same yere.'

AMES.

'Thus endeth this noble and joyous boke, entytled La morte d'Arthur. Not-withstondyng it treateth of the byrth, lyf, and actes of the sayd Kynge Arthur, of his noble knyghts of the rounde table, theyr merueylous enquestes and aduentures, thacheuynge of the Sancgreal, and in the ende the dolourous deth and depaytynge out of this worlde of them al; whyche boke was reduced into Englysshe by syr Thomas Malory, Knight, as afore is sayd, and by me devyded into xxi. bookes, chapitred and enprynted, and fynisshed in thabbey, Westmestre, the last day of Juyl, the yere of our Lord MCCCCLXXXV.   Caxton me fieri fecit.'

HARLEIAN CATALOGUE.

'The Byrth, Lyf, and Actes of Kyng Arthur; of his noble Knyghtes of the Rounde Table, theyr marvayllous Enquestes and Adventures; the Achyeviyng of the Sang real; and in the end le Morte d'Arthur, with the dolourous Deth and Departyng out of thys world of them Al. Whiche Book was reduced to the Englysshe, by Syr Thomas Malory Knyght, and by me (*W. Caxton*) devyded into 21 bookes, chaptyred and emprynted, and fynyshed in th' Abbey Westmestre, the last day of July, the yere of our Lord 1485.'

UPCOTT.

'Thus endeth this noble & joyous booke entytled *La* Mort *dathur.* Notwyth-standing it treateth of the byrth, lyf & actes of the sayd Kynge Arthur, *&* of his noble knyghtes of the Rounde Table, theyr marueyllous Enquestes & aduentures, thacheyuyng of the *Sang real,* and in the ende *le Morte darthur with* the dolourous deth and departyng out of thys worlde of them al. Whiche booke was reduced in to Englysshe by Syr Thomas Malory knyght *as afore is sayd,* and by me deuyded in to xxi bookes chaptyred and emprynted and fynysshed in thabbey Westmestre the last day of July the yere of our lord MCCCCLXXXV. *Caxton me fieri fecit.'*

On a comparison of these colophons we see that the article *La* is only in Ames: the spelling of *dathur* is peculiar to Wynkyn de Worde, who has it also in another passage; the words *le Morte darthur with* are in the Harleian Catalogue only: *as afore is said* is in neither of these, but it is in Ames: the peculiar mode of writing *Sang real*[1], and the spelling of *chaptyred, emprynted, July,* are those of the Harleian Catalogue: the *&* introduced after *Arthur* in the second line is only in Upcott. *Caxton me fieri fecit* is in Ames, but not in the Harleian Catalogue.

When I say in Ames or the Harleian Catalogue only, it will be understood that I include with the colophon of the former its modernised copy in Dibdin; and with that of the latter its copies in Herbert and the Biographia Britannica; the references to all which I have given in the passage of the Introduction to which this is a Note. The first words of the colophon are omitted in the Harleian Catalogue, which gives it as the title of the book, as do the Biographia Britannica and Herbert. The framer of the Catalogue probably quotes directly, though inaccu-rately, from the Harleian (now the Osterley) Morte Darthur: and Ames must have made his extract independently from the same volume. Dibdin attributes both the Harleian Catalogue and the article in the Biographia Britannica to Oldys.

[1] The division of the word indicates that the writer adopts the plausible notion that Sangreal means Real (or Royal) Blood; and no doubt in ancient as well as mo-dern times the spelling and sound would suggest this meaning : but Roquefort shows clearly that the other is the proper expla-nation, both in etymology and (so to speak) historically. And Helinand, a monk of Fromont (A.D. 717), gives the Latin *Gra-dale,* which supplies the link between *Graal* and *Crater* from which Roquefort derives the former. Helinand's words are,—' Hoc tempore, in Britannia, cuidam eremitae monstrata est mirabilis quaedam visio per angelum de sancto Josepho decurione nobili qui corpus Domini deposuit de cruce, et de catino illo vel paropside in quo Dominus coenavit cum discipulis suis; de quâ ab eodem eremita descripta est historia quae dicitur *de Gradal. Gradalis* autem vel *Gradale* dicitur Gallicè scutella lata et aliquantulum profunda in qua pretiosae dapes, cum suo jure, divitibus solent apponi, et dicitur nomine *Graal.* ... Hanc historiam latine scriptam invenire non potui, sed tantum Gallicè scripta habetur a quibusdam proceribus, nec facile ut aiunt tota inveniri potest.' Helinandi Historia, quoted in L'Essai Historique et Literaire sur l'Abbaye de Fécamp par Leroux de Lincy, Rouen, 1840.

INDEX.

Battles, armies, battalions, 105, 265.

Baudwin of Britain, Sir, 30, 31, 101; is a surgeon, 423; 428.

Bayonne, 469.

Beale Isould, 101.

Beale-Valet, castle of, 262.

Beame, trumpet, 478.

Bearn, earl of, 469.

Beaumains (Fair-hands), 129; is called a kitchen-boy, 135; 140; beats the red knight of the red lawns, 143; 148.

Beaume (Bayonne), 469.

Bedegraine, forest of, 34; castle of, 35; 41; battle of, 42.

Bedivere, Sir, 102, 103, 152, 421, 434, 448, 478; throws Excalibur into the water, 480; finds where Arthur is buried, 481; meets with Sir Launcelot, 484; is an hermit, 487.

Bee, ring, bracelet, or other ornament, 159.

Behest, promise, 209.

Behight, promise, 411.

Behote, promise, 168.

Belias le Orgulous, Sir, is slain, 459.

Belinus, king of Britain, 99.

Bellangere (a constable), 268.

Bellangere le Orgulous, Sir, 449.

Bellaus, 40.

Bellengerus le Beuse, 274, 421, 448, 455, 468.

Belleus, Sir, 115; wounded by Launcelot, 115; 128.

Belliance le Orgulous, Sir, 198.

Bellias of Flanders, 37.

Bendelaine, Sir, 157.

Benoye, country of, 274, 343.

Benwick, city of, 33; 34, 41; land of, 75; some call it Bayonne, 469; 471.

Berel, Sir, 104.

Berluse, Sir, 247.

Bernard of Astolat, Sir, 419, 420, 429.

Berrant le Apres, king, 295.

Bersules, Sir, 245, 251.

Bertelot, Sir, 338.

Bery, apparently meant for Bere, bier, or bear, 385.

Besaunt, a gold coin first coined at Byzantium, 95, 481.

Beseen, adorned, clothed, 51.

Bestad, Bested, beset, 476.

Betaught, recommended, 359.

Betid, happened, was; or, beat, 141, 332.

Bishop, the first, 407.

Black, all, 133.

Blamore de Ganis, Sir, 139, 173, 176, 179, 224, 230, 277, 413, 421, 448; made a duke, 469; 484.

Bleise, 41.

Bleoberis de Ganis, Sir, 38, 139, 154, 173, 175, 177, 179, 199, 208, 223, 231, 275, 278, 287, 317, 413, 421, 435, 448; made a duke, 469; 484.

Bliant, Sir, 338; castle of, 341.

Bloias de la Flandres, 37.

Blois de la Case, 40.

Board, deck, 370.

Bobart le Cure Hardy, Sir, Arthur's son, 449.

Bole, trunk of a tree, 126.

Book, swear upon a, 230, 259.

Boot, help, 162.

Borre, 41.

Bors de Ganis, Sir, 89, 103, 105, 139, 152, 154, 218, 230, 328; sees a dragon, 330; 333, 343, 381; joins in the quest, 383; 387, 390, 392, 397, 401, 407; has his adventures chronicled, 411; 413, 421; finds Sir Launcelot ill, 427; 435, 448; is crowned, 469; 482.

Bors of Gaul, king, 32, 38, 41.

Boudwin, Sir, 267.

Brabant, 107.

Brachet, a small scenting dog, 66, 70, 79, 123, 165, 215.

Bragwaine, dame, 181, 185, 191, 205, 215, 220, 225, 230.

Braid, hastiness, 472.

Brain-pan, 167, 184.

Brandegore, king, 343.

Brandegoris of Stranggore, king, 35, 36.

Brandel, Sir, 118.

Brandiles, Sir, 152, 205, 209, 248, 250, 256, 413, 421, 431, 438, 448; is slain, 459.

Brasias, Sir, 413; a hermit, 415.

Brast, brake, 117.

Brastias, Sir, 26, 27, 28, 30, 33, 36, 433.

Brawn, muscular part of the hand, palm, 443.

Brenius, king of Britain, 99.

Breunor, Sir, 181.

Clarrus of Cleremont, Sir, 448, 455, 469, 484, 487.

Claudas, king, 32, 34, 41, 75, 100, 330, 470.

Claudine, 409.

Clegis, Sir, 107, 448.

Clegis of Sadok, Sir, 455, 469.

Cleped, called, 409.

Cleremond, Sir, 107.

Cloddrus, Sir, 448.

Cloth of gold, 33.

Coasted, kept at the side, in a parallel course, 433.

Cogge, cock, i e. cock-boat, 101.

Cognisance, badge, mark of distinction, 241, 302.

Colgrevance, Sir, 218, 389, 449, 452.

Colgrevaunce de Gorre, Sir, 40.

Collibe, sea of, 392.

Cologne, 100.

Colombe, 54, 243.

Comange, earl of, 469.

Commonalty, 228.

Commons, 30, 81; children of, 102.

Constantine, son of queen Heleine, 99; country of, 102.

Constantine, Sir (Sir Cador's son). Arthur wishes him to be his heir, 101, 448; was chosen king after Arthur, 487.

Corbin, bridge of, 326; 330; city of, 340.

Corneus, duke, 33.

Cornwall, 25, 49, 75, 96, 151, 161, 163, 165, 174, 177, 181, 193, 205, 232, 249, 259, 262, 266, 268, 286, 478.

Coronation, 30.

Corsabrin, Sir, 279.

Courtelage, court-yard, or garden, 94, 121, 379.

Covin, deceit, plot, 360.

Cradelmas, king, 35, 37.

Cradelment of North Wales, king, 37.

Croft, vault, 406.

Crosselme, Sir, 448.

Curselaine, Sir, 452.

Cyprus, 100.

Daffish, foolish, 236.

Dagonet, Sir (Arthur's fool), 199, 212, 249, 256.

Dalan, 261.

Damas, Sir, 79, 81, 459.

Damaske, country of, 100.

Damiete, 100.

Daname, Sir, 230.

Darras, Sir, 229, 230, 449.

David, 395.

Debate, strife, 459.

Debonair, courteous, 394.

Defoil, trample under foot, overcome, 200.

Degrane, Sance Vilany, Sir, 449.

Delectable Isle, 297.

Deliverly, actively, 473.

Denmark, king of, 76, 357.

Depart, part, 483.

De Vance, lady, 55.

Devise, look carefully at, 402.

Devoir, knightly duty, 149, 469.

Diamond, justed for daily, 432.

Dight, dressed, 79

Dinadan, Sir, 129, 152, 216, 227, 246, 253, 257, 261, 276, 280; forced into woman's garment, 282; best jester, 290; 317, 448.

Dinant, Sir, 214.

Dinas, Sir, 153, 167, 188, 215, 232, 263, 268; rises against king Mark, 284; 448, 455, 469.

Disworship, disgrace, 67.

Dodinas le Savage, Sir, 96, 154, 169, 175, 228, 241, 302, 421, 438, 448.

Dole, grief, 45.

Dolphine, 108.

Dornar, Sir, 259.

Dornard, Sir, 281.

Dover, 34, 110, 475; castle, 477, 482, 484.

Dragon (description of), 101; spitting fire, 326.

Draughts, apparently recesses parted off from the main room, 442.

Dress, turn towards, address, 402.

Driant, Sir, 188, 218, 448; is slain, 459.

Dromon, a vessel of war, 101.

Duresse, bondage, 357.

Durnore, Sir, 448.

Dutchmen, duke of, 109.

Dwarf, attendant, 53, 69, 80, 90.

Dwine, dwindle, 485.

Easter, 30.

Eastland, queen of, 113.

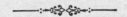